DISCARD

NEW
DIRECTIONS
IN
GROUP
COMMUNICATION

Editor

LAWRENCE R. FREY
The University of Memphis

Sage Publications
International Educational and Professional Publisher
Thousand Oaks ▪ London ▪ New Delhi

For information:

Sage Publications, Inc.
2455 Teller Road
Thousand Oaks, California 91320
E-mail: order@sagepub.com

Sage Publications Ltd.
6 Bonhill Street
London EC2A 4PU
United Kingdom

Sage Publications India Pvt. Ltd.
M-32 Market
Greater Kailash I
New Delhi 110 048 India

Printed in the United States of America

Library of Congress Cataloging-in-Publication Data

New directions in group communication / edited by Lawrence R. Frey.
    p. cm.
    Includes bibliographical references and index.
    ISBN 0-7619-1280-0 (cloth : alk. paper)
    ISBN 0-7619-1281-9 (pbk. : alk. paper)
    1. Communication in small groups.
    2. Interpersonal communication. I. Frey, Lawrence R.
    HM736 .N48 2002
    302.3'4—dc21   2001005424

This book is printed on acid-free paper.

02 03 04 05 06 7 6 5 4 3 2 1

Acquisition Editor:	Margaret H. Seawell
Editorial Assistant:	Alicia Carter
Production Editor:	Sanford Robinson
Copy Editor:	Linda Gray
Proofreader:	Jamie Robinson
Editorial Assistant:	Ester Marcelino
Typesetter:	Marion Warren
Indexer:	Molly Hall
Cover Designer:	Jane Quaney

Contents

PART I: Theoretical Perspectives

PART II: Methodological Procedures

Introduction

New Directions in Group Communication

LAWRENCE R. FREY
The University of Memphis

The field of group communication, depending on where one draws historical lines in the proverbial sands of time, is more than a half-century old. Over the course of those years, group communication theory, research, pedagogy, and other practices have waxed and waned. From the early years of primarily pedagogical scholarship (circa 1920-1945) to the grand old days where group research flourished (1950-1970) to the decade of discontent (the 1970s) that called into question virtually everything that had been done before to a time of prolific theory development (1980-1990) to a period of critical reflection, reconstruction, and research (the 1990s), the field of group communication has scaled many heights and crossed many valleys (see Frey, 1996; Gouran, 1999).

The study of group communication is currently in one of its healthiest stages yet. Indications of this health are all around; two such indicators are the recent creation of the National Communication Association's (NCA) Group Communication Division (see the division's

Web site at http://communication.wcupa.edu/groupdiv/), which required a minimum of 300 members, and the recently published text *The Handbook of Group Communication Theory & Research* (Frey, Gouran, & Poole, 1999), which summarized the wealth of scholarship in this field. Perhaps the best signs of the vitality of the field are the extent to which other areas of the communication discipline (e.g., organizational, family, and health communication) are interested in and have become infused by the study of group communication (see Propp & Kreps, 1994) and the presence that the study of group communication has established within the general field of group studies (see Gouran, 1999). The field is so healthy that I can no longer joke, as I did in convention presentations just a little while ago, clearly in jest but also with a hint of truth to it, that there were barely enough group communication scholars to form a small group. Today, we have a vibrant group of such scholars and the future looks even brighter; as the (slightly revised) lyrics from a recent popular song go, "The future's so bright, group communication scholars have got to wear shades."

The breadth and depth of group communication scholarship was documented, to a large extent, in Frey et al.'s (1999) handbook, which received the 2000 Ernest Bormann Research Award from NCA's Group Communication Division. The sections in that text examined (a) theoretical developments (Poole, 1999; Mabry, 1999), including a history of the emergence and evolution of the group communication field (Gouran, 1999) and methodological issues and considerations that inform its study (Poole, Keyton, & Frey, 1999); (b) individuals and group communication (specifically, individual differences, Haslett & Ruebush, 1999, and socialization processes, Anderson, Riddle, & Martin, 1999); (c) task (Hirokawa & Salazar, 1999) and relational (Keyton, 1999) group communication; (d) five key group communication processes (collective information processes, Propp, 1999; nonverbal group communication, Ketrow, 1999; influence processes, Meyers & Brashers, 1999; leadership, Pavitt, 1999; and group communication and creativity, Jarboe, 1999); (e) group facilitation practices (Schultz, 1999; Sunwolf & Seibold, 1999), including recent technological innovations (Scott, 1999); and (f) the application of group communication to four important contexts (family units, Socha, 1999; the formal educational context, Allen & Plax, 1999; social support groups, Cline, 1999; and organizational work groups, Greenbaum & Query, 1999). Each chapter reviewed and organized relevant literature about the group communication topic or area being examined in original, coherent, and pedagogically sound ways (e.g., through typologies and models) and suggested agendas for future theory, research, and practice.

The chapters in that handbook, however, concentrated on summarizing what is currently known about, and setting agendas for, relatively developed topics and areas of the field rather than exploring new and innovative directions for which there might not yet be a wealth of literature available. That was a conscious choice I made in consultation with the associate editors. In response to the open call for proposals for chapters in that handbook, I received a substantial number of proposals that articulated exciting new directions for group communication theory, research, and practice. One way to include those new directions would have been to select some and place them together in a separate section of the text. There were, however, too many good proposals from which to choose; selecting only a few would not have documented very well the many new and diverse directions being pursued by scholars in the field.

I called Margaret Seawell, executive editor at Sage Publications, and proposed to her a separate edited text that featured new directions in group communication theory, research, and practice. She immediately saw the benefits of publishing such a text. On behalf of all of the authors in this text and the many other authors in the group communication texts she publishes, I want to thank Margaret for being such a valuable friend and advocate for the field of group communication; out of her support was born this text. I also want to thank all the contributors to this text, not only for their excellent work and receptivity to my seemingly unending editing but also for their patience with me in bringing this text to publication; becoming a chairperson during the making of this text, with all the new responsibilities that position entails, definitely took a toll on the publication timeline I had originally planned. I also thank Linda Gray for her outstanding work as Sage's copy editor for this text; I have worked with many copy editors, and Linda is one of the very best. Most of all, I dedicate this text with love to Janellen Hill for sacrificing many dyadic interactions with me so I could work on this and my other group projects.

OVERVIEW OF THE TEXT

The purpose of this text is to showcase new, innovative, cutting-edge directions for—as well as substantive extensions of current—

group communication theory, research methods, research topics, pedagogy, facilitation, and other applications and practices. The text takes as its fundamental mission the setting of agendas for future group communication theory, research, and practice.

The text is divided into six sections: (a) theoretical perspectives, (b) methodological procedures, (c) antecedent factors affecting group communication, (d) group communication processes, (e) group communication facilitation and educational practices, and (f) group communication contexts. Each of these sections and the chapters in them are explained next.

Part I:
Theoretical Perspectives

The 1930s movie detective Charlie Chan, once said, "Theories are like the mist on one's eyeglasses: They tend to obscure one's vision." If that is the case, group communication scholars must quickly be going blind; ever since the 1980s, the field has witnessed a rapid growth in the development of theoretical frameworks and perspectives (see Poole, 1999). These theoretical frameworks and perspectives include (a) general theories of group communication (e.g., functional theory, Gouran & Hirokawa, 1996; structuration theory, Poole, Seibold, & McPhee, 1996; and symbolic convergence theory, Bormann, 1996); (b) focused theories emerging from the study of particular group communication phenomena (e.g., theories of group leadership, Pavitt, 1999, and group communication and creativity processes, Jarboe, 1999); and (c) relatively new agenda-setting perspectives (e.g., the bona fide group perspective, Putnam & Stohl, 1996, and the naturalistic paradigm as applied to the study of groups, Frey, 1994). The three chapters in this section focus on the general theories of group communication mentioned (as well as the application of a general theory from another domain to the group context) and on some of these agenda-setting perspectives.

Jennifer H. Waldeck, Carolyn A. Shepard, Jeremy Teitelbaum, W. Jeffrey Farrar, and David R. Seibold begin the examination of theoretical perspectives in Chapter 1 by providing a review and critique of the three major theoretical bases that have, since the mid-1980s, dominated the group communication landscape—functional theory, symbolic convergence theory, and structuration theory—as well as the relatively new theory—the bona fide group perspective—that has attracted much interest. They note how these theories of group communication have prospered both in quantity and in the depth of their explanatory power. Simultaneously, they offer three recommendations for increasing the depth and precision of each theory: (a) the formalization of each perspective, especially the bona fide group perspective, the newest one; (b) the need for researchers working from long-standing perspectives (e.g., structuration theory) to investigate more thoroughly process-product linkages; and (c) a demand for better, more precise construct explication for theories in which ambiguities have been noted throughout the literature (e.g., functional theory and the bona fide group perspective). Finally, Waldeck et al. suggest new constructs, advance propositions, and propose empirical studies to address the concerns highlighted in their review and analysis of the literature on these group communication theories.

In Chapter 2, Scott D. Johnson and Lynette M. Long apply dialectical theory to the study of group communication. As they point out, although scholars of interpersonal communication over the past two decades have applied dialectical theory to the study of dyadic relationships, few group communication scholars have followed suit. Johnson and Long provide a rationale for applying dialectical theory in group communication research, address relevant issues in applying the theory, and suggest some guidelines for how to begin applying the theory to the group context. They argue that, in pursuing this application, group communication scholars must be willing to expand their thinking and look in new ways at what has become familiar and taken for granted. To illustrate this goal, they (a) show how a dialectical frame can be used to redefine the concept of "groups," (b) reconsider familiar group processes such as norms and roles, and (c) take a below-the-surface look at the tensions that inspire and impede people's communicative behavior in groups. They conclude the chapter by discussing the need for methodological eclecticism and offering some words of caution regarding the hazards inherent in using a dialectical approach in group communication research.

Chapter 3, by Nancy Wyatt, concludes this section of the text with a foregrounding of feminist theory in group communication research. Building on some of her earlier scholarship (e.g., Wyatt, 1993) and that of others (e.g., Meyers & Brashers, 1994), she identifies new areas for group communication research from three feminist perspectives: liberal, radical, and standpoint feminism. She briefly describes the philosophical and theoretical assumptions that underlie each of these perspectives, reviews extant research drawn from these perspectives, and speculates on new research directions that might develop from the application of a variety of feminist perspectives to the study of group communication.

Part II:
Methodological Procedures

In speaking about new, cutting-edge theories of social behavior and the essays and reports based on them, Turner (1978) once said, "New theoretical wine demands new presentational bottles." I would extend that metaphor by adding, "and new ways of pressing grapes," for innovative theoretical developments in group communication must be accompanied by corresponding methodological developments. The chapters in this section explore two new methodological ways of pressing group communication grapes—one at the macro level that illustrates the value of using ethnographic practices for the study of group communication and the other at the micro level that advances a new methodological instrument that should be of interest to qualitative and quantitative group communication researchers alike.

In Chapter 4, Natalie J. Dollar and Gerianne M. Merrigan examine potential contributions that ethnographic practices can make to the study of group communication. Specifically, they illustrate how ethnographic practices can be used to (a) validate and extend group communication research conducted in laboratory settings; (b) generate group communication theory; (c) generate research questions that have been unasked or inadequately answered by other research methods; and (d) investigate the assumption of shared meaning in groups by verifying, or at least qualifying, the concept of "sharedness" in ethnographic research and by recognizing shared meaning as a *means* to something rather than an *end* in itself. In explicating these contributions, Dollar and Merrigan provide examples and exemplars of ethnographic group communication research.

Randall S. Peterson, in Chapter 5, unveils a new research methodology for the study of group communication: the Group Dynamics Q-Sort (GDQ). The GDQ is a 100-item instrument designed to study group interaction across many different situations and using a variety of data sources. It combines the richness of addressing a diverse array of qualitative questions about group dynamics with the rigor of a quantitative approach. The method is particularly well suited to studying bona fide groups (see the essays in Frey, in press; Putnam & Stohl, 1990, 1996; Stohl & Putnam, 1994; Stohl & Walker, this volume; Waldeck et al., this volume) because it assesses group boundaries and the contexts in which groups are embedded. Peterson introduces the GDQ in three sections that explicate (a) its development, (b) the mechanics of employing it, and (c) its use in group communication research compared with other methods commonly used (specifically, experiments, case studies, and Bales's, 1950, interaction process analysis). The result is a new and useful method to add to group communication researchers' methodological toolbox.

Part III:
Antecedent Factors Affecting Group Communication

A famous defense attorney, who shall remain nameless but who wins virtually all his trials, once stated in a public speech that by the time he picked the jury, the case was already won or lost. He went on to explain that it didn't really matter what evidence he presented (within reason); the verdict was already predetermined by the backgrounds of the jurors—that is, by characteristics such as jurors' sex, race, and socioeconomic status. This line of reasoning is frightening to those who study group communication, for we would like to think that what people say in groups makes a difference, although Hewes (1986, 1996), in his socio-egocentric model, has argued that communication may not, and has not been unambiguously shown to, have much effect on group outcomes.

Although both the attorney and Hewes (see Poole, 1999) may be overstating the case, their points are well-taken: Important factors precede and help to explain group processes (including communication) and outcomes. This section of the text explores the effects of two antecedent factors on group communication and group outcomes: group members' traits and the influence of culture.

In Chapter 6, Joann Keyton and Lawrence R. Frey explore how traits and predispositions affect members' behavior in groups and group processes and outcomes. They begin, after defining and explaining views of the central construct of trait, by reviewing the state of trait research, summarizing the literature on personality traits in the group context, and focusing in some detail on *communication traits*—those traits related to message behavior. Their review reveals that scholars have not paid sufficient attention to the role that personality and communication traits play in the group context. They subsequently advance an agenda for future research that involves identifying people's predispositions toward groups and studying traits at the group level, and they examine some important

methodological considerations that need to be taken into account to accomplish those goals.

Chapter 7, by John G. Oetzel, examines the effects of culture and cultural diversity on group communication. After explaining the significant demographic changes that have and will continue to result in people working in culturally diverse groups, Oetzel explores two competing theoretical perspectives used to investigate communication in multicultural groups: (a) vertical differences—status differences that exist in a group because of various factors, including ethnicity, nationality, sex, tenure, knowledge, and position in an organizational hierarchy—and (b) cultural differences—general patterns of cultural values, attitudes, and communicative behaviors associated with specific sets of individuals. Oetzel synthesizes the research that employs either a vertical- or cultural-difference perspective to explain the effects of culture and cultural diversity on communication in work groups and notes the importance of considering the relationship between vertical and cultural differences. He outlines a research agenda that identifies the types of investigation needed to advance understanding of how both types of differences affect communication in culturally diverse work groups. He concludes the chapter by advancing suggestions for testing a model that focuses on how vertical and cultural differences influence group members' "face" needs (self or other) and subsequently affect group communication processes; these communication processes influence both task (e.g., decision making and problem solving) and relational (e.g., group cohesion and member satisfaction) outcomes and, in turn, reinforce and/or change vertical and cultural differences and individuals' face needs.

Part IV:
Group Communication Processes

There is a popular adage, "It's not what you say, it's what you do that counts." Although people's statements sometimes do contradict their actions, communication itself is an important action that also "counts," and this is particularly true in the group context; as Sigmund Freud once said, "A group is subject to the truly magical power of words" (cited in Shilling & Fuller, 1997, p. 100). Ultimately, what differentiates a communication approach to understanding groups from other approaches (e.g., psychological or sociological) is a focus on the messages exchanged between group members. The chapters in this section of the text examine two important group communication processes—argument and dialogue—as well as how communication processes affect group creativity.

In Chapter 8, Renée A. Meyers and Dale E. Brashers rethink some traditional conceptions about group argument by first examining four fundamental underlying principles of the traditional view of argument: argument as rational, convergence seeking, decorous, and verbal. They then introduce four argumentative strategies (slogans and chants, vilification of opponents, expression of anger, and visual persuasion) used by the activist group AIDS Coalition to Unleash Power (ACT UP) that do not fit neatly into the traditional model of argument. They illustrate how such nonnormative argument forms serve as the impetus for rethinking traditional assumptions about argument and conclude the chapter by discussing both the theoretical and pedagogical implications of their analysis.

J. Kevin Barge, in Chapter 9, examines the benefits of viewing group communication as dialogue rather than discussion. He argues that group communication scholars have long been interested in the relationship between group discourse and democracy but that, historically, this relationship has privileged the language of debate and discussion as the primary linguistic forms for promoting democracy. He explains how recent theoretical moves emphasizing more appreciative and dialogic forms of discourse have emerged as a counterpoint to the traditional discourses of debate and discussion. Barge takes the position that the language associated with group discourse needs to be enlarged to include appreciative inquiry and dialogue as well as discussion and debate. He offers a case study to (a) illustrate how these appreciative and dialogic forms of discourse may be created in groups and (b) highlight the implications for our understanding of group communication when these forms are adopted.

In Chapter 10, Abran J. Salazar explores the relationship between communication and creativity in groups. He argues that previous research on group creativity has largely neglected the role of communication in the production of novel ideas, responses, processes, and products; he seeks to fill this gap by examining the role of communication in promoting and hindering group creativity. This examination is grounded in complex adaptive systems and self-organizing systems perspectives; from these perspectives, group creativity is viewed as an emergent phenomenon of group communication. The key postulate that Salazar advances is that truly creative activity in a group is possible only when a group has changed or has achieved a state of complexity, such that it is able to adapt its structures to fit the moment—that is, able to adapt to a changing environment. Accordingly, he investigates how communication may be involved in the creation and maintenance of complex group states. He concludes the chapter by suggesting future directions for research on communication and group creativity that emerge from the complex adaptive systems and self-organizing systems perspectives.

Part V:
Group Communication Facilitation and Educational Practices

There is so much complaining about the inefficiency of groups and group meetings that it has become the basis for an entire genre of jokes (see, e.g., Frey, 1995; Seibold & Krikorian, 1997): "A committee is a group of the unfit, appointed by the unwilling, that meets to do the unnecessary." "A group meeting is a cul-de-sac down which promising young ideas are lured and quietly strangled."

"To kill time, a group meeting is the perfect weapon." These jokes may be funny, but the consequences of inefficiency in groups are quite serious; as an example, Mosvick and Nelson (1987) reported that inefficient group meetings cost one international corporation $71 million each year for several years.

To avoid the pitfalls and capitalize on the advantages associated with group work (see, e.g., Davis, 1969; Hoffman, 1965; Maier, 1970; Poole, 1991; Seibold & Krikorian, 1997; Shaw, 1981; Zander, 1994), groups often need *facilitation*—"any meeting technique, procedure, or practice that makes it easier for groups to interact and/or accomplish their goals" (Frey, 1995, p. 4; see also Poole, 1991; Schultz, 1999; Seibold & Krikorian, 1997; Sunwolf & Seibold, 1999)—and group members often need education. The chapters in this section of the text examine facilitation practices for promoting group creativity and educational practices for learning about relationships from participating in group communication.

In Chapter 11, Sunwolf continues the examination of the intriguing concept of creativity explored in Chapter 10, this time directed toward its facilitation. She starts by explaining that creativity has too often been associated with idea generation by individuals, which is unfortunate given that task groups are increasingly being challenged to provide a continuous supply of innovative ideas to novel problems. She then reviews prior research on creative group problem-solving methods, including 36 techniques that have received scant research attention, and offers new directions in understanding and facilitating creative group processes that can enrich research agendas and enhance educational practices. Seven agenda-setting questions are set forth and six paradoxes of the creative problem-solving phenomenon are offered to provoke future research and pedagogy.

In Chapter 12, Terre H. Allen and Timothy G. Plax explore the consequences of group communication in the classroom, specifically with regard to understanding its role in learn-ing about relationships. As they show, although scholars have examined the interpersonal/relational aspects of groups, limited attention has been paid to the classroom context. Moreover, although well-documented lines of research continue to explicate the role of group interaction in cognitive and affective learning outcomes, little is known about what effects participation in classroom groups has on how students learn about relationships. Allen and Plax detail what is known about relational communication in groups and what that can teach us about the relational aspects of group communication in the classroom; they, thus, examine what goes on in classroom groups from a different vantage point than what has been the traditional focus—learning outcomes. Their central concern is exploring what knowledge individuals derive about relationships from their participation in instructional groups. They propose a new direction for inquiry into classroom groups by providing a metatheoretical perspective for understanding group communication processes and by identifying and defining relational learning as a critical consequence of group communication in the classroom. They conclude the chapter by establishing an agenda for future research regarding communication processes and relational learning in classroom groups.

Part VI:
Group Communication Contexts

Group communication does not occur in a vacuum: It always takes place in some context, be that a geographical location (e.g., in the United States vs. in Japan), a particular site (e.g., in a laboratory vs. in an organization), via a specific medium (e.g., face-to-face vs. mediated), or some other context. The context within which groups are embedded, of course, makes a tremendous difference in terms of group inputs, processes (including communication), and outcomes; indeed, using the vernacular of the 1990 presidential campaign slogan, "It's the context, stupid."

The chapters in this section of the text explore four important contexts for group communication. The first two chapters focus on group communication contexts at the micro level with respect to two particular types of groups: collaborating groups and top management teams. The last two chapters examine contexts at the macro level with respect to how group communication is influenced by nation-state and technology.

In Chapter 13, Cynthia Stohl and Kasey Walker explore the nature of collaborating groups. As they explain, in today's complex and competitive global environment, collaborative arrangements provide organizations with the alliances and resources necessary to address increasing development and production costs, decreasing research-to-market times, and escalating problem and product complexity. At the center of these collaborative efforts are work groups composed of employees from different organizations, who stay together only for the duration of a special project and often meet face-to-face only sporadically. Stohl and Walker expand the conception of "group" to take into account the interorganizational and dynamic nature of these collaborating groups and explicate how these dynamics necessitate a radical shift in models for understanding group action. They then propose and explain a bona fide group collaboration model that identifies these unique features and reconceptualizes traditional group constructs.

Chapter 14, by Theodore E. Zorn and George H. Tompson, focuses on the communicative practices of top management teams (TMTs), groups, rather than individuals, relied on by organizations to provide leadership. As they show, research in the discipline of business policy and strategy (BPS) has focused extensively on TMT composition and processes as predictors of organizational success; what has been underemphasized in existing BPS research, despite their critical role in the effectiveness of such groups, are the communicative practices of TMTs. Zorn and Tompson review relevant group communication literature and BPS research to examine what is currently known or hypothesized about TMT communication. On the basis of their review, they suggest new directions for research and practice.

In Chapter 15, Robert Shuter reviews and analyzes available cross-national research that was identified after examining over 25,000 studies of groups conducted since 1955. He finds that although group research has flourished in the communication field since the 1960s, communication scholars have conducted few cross-national investigations of groups. The cross-national research that does exist focuses on six classical group processes: conformity, leadership, risky shift, cooperation and competition, social loafing, and communication networks. Shuter concludes the chapter by offering a research agenda for the 21st century that would position cross-national studies in a central place in group communication scholarship.

Chapter 16, by Edward A. Mabry, concludes both this section and the text with an examination of group communication and technology. Mabry's central premise is that group tasks and technologies group members must use for task operations and communicating with each other coproduce a group's goal-related interaction and performance outcomes. He starts by framing group work in relation to the ways in which members communicate, distinguishing between concepts such as modality and channel and explaining various types and characteristics of communication modalities. He then explores the interdependencies of tasks, technologies, and communication, focusing on (a) the way in which communication technologies are transformed from playing only an instrumental role in a group to holding a social role that supports the technology as part of the group's social context and (b) the communicative utility of communication technologies that proscribes their sense of purpose in the formation of a group's task representations and ensuing productive consequences. He subsequently synthesizes these issues into a heuristic perspective that views groups themselves as communication modalities.

CONCLUSION

The field of group communication has never been healthier: There is a developed body of knowledge about group communication theories, methods, and practices that reflects the maturity of the field, and as the chapters in this text show, there is no shortage of new and exciting ideas. The maturity of the field is, thus, accompanied by a vitality that is producing a wealth of new and diverse views of group communication.

There is an old saying that "everything old is new again." In part, this means that good ideas stand the test of time and that they help to generate new perspectives and ideas. Whether the chapters in this text will stand the test of time—that is, become old and then new again—is, of course, a story yet to be written. I am very hopeful that they will.

REFERENCES

Allen, T. H., & Plax, T. G. (1999). Group communication in the formal educational context. In L. R. Frey (Ed.), D. S. Gouran, & M. S. Poole (Assoc. Eds.), *The handbook of group communication theory & research* (pp. 493-515). Thousand Oaks, CA: Sage.

Anderson, C. M., Riddle, B. L., & Martin, M. M. (1999). Socialization processes in groups. In L. R. Frey (Ed.), D. S. Gouran, & M. S. Poole (Assoc. Eds.), *The handbook of group communication theory & research* (pp. 139-163). Thousand Oaks, CA: Sage.

Bales, R. F. (1950). *Interaction process analysis: A method for the study of small groups.* Reading, MA: Addison-Wesley.

Bormann, E. G. (1996). Symbolic convergence theory and communication in group decision making. In R. Y. Hirokawa & M. S. Poole (Eds.), *Communication and group decision making* (2nd ed., pp. 81-113). Thousand Oaks, CA: Sage.

Cline, R. J. W. (1999). Communication in social support groups. In L. R. Frey (Ed.), D. S. Gouran, & M. S. Poole (Assoc. Eds.), *The handbook of group communication theory & research* (pp. 516-538). Thousand Oaks, CA: Sage.

Davis, J. H. (1969). *Group performance.* Reading, MA: Addison-Wesley.

Frey, L. R. (1994). The naturalistic paradigm: Studying small groups in the postmodern era. *Small Group Research, 25,* 551-577.

Frey, L. R. (1995). Introduction: Applied communication research on group facilitation in natural settings. In L. R. Frey (Ed.), *Innovations in group facilitation: Applications in natural settings* (pp. 1-23). Cresskill, NJ: Hampton Press.

Frey, L. R. (1996). Remembering and "re-membering": A history of theory and research on communication and group decision making. In R. Y. Hirokawa & M. S. Poole (Eds.), *Communication and group decision making* (2nd ed., pp. 19-51). Thousand Oaks, CA: Sage.

Frey, L. R. (Ed.). (in press). *Group communication in context: Studies of bona fide groups* (2nd ed.). Mahwah, NJ: Lawrence Erlbaum.

Frey, L. R. (Ed.), Gouran, D. S., & Poole, M. S. (Assoc. Eds.). (1999). *The handbook of group communication theory & research.* Thousand Oaks, CA: Sage.

Gouran, D. S. (1999). Communication in groups: The emergence and evolution of a field of study. In L. R. Frey (Ed.), D. S. Gouran, & M. S. Poole (Assoc. Eds.), *The handbook of group communication theory & research* (pp. 3-36). Thousand Oaks, CA: Sage.

Gouran, D. S., & Hirokawa, R. Y. (1996). Functional theory and communication in decision-making and problem-solving groups: An expanded view. In R. Y. Hirokawa & M. S. Poole (Eds.), *Communication and group decision making* (2nd ed., pp. 55-80). Thousand Oaks, CA: Sage.

Greenbaum, H. H., & Query, J. L., Jr. (1999). Communication in organizational work groups: A review and analysis of natural work group studies. In L. R. Frey (Ed.), D. S. Gouran, & M. S. Poole (Assoc. Eds.), *The handbook of group communication theory & research* (pp. 539-564). Thousand Oaks, CA: Sage.

Haslett, B. R., & Ruebush, J. (1999). What differences do individual differences in groups make? The effects of individuals, culture, and group composition. In L. R. Frey (Ed.), D. S. Gouran, & M. S. Poole (Assoc. Eds.), *The handbook of group communication theory & research* (pp. 115-138). Thousand Oaks, CA: Sage.

Hewes, D. F. (1986). A socio-egocentric model of group decision-making. In R. Y. Hirokawa & M. S. Poole (Eds.), *Communication and group decision-making* (pp. 265-312). Beverly Hills, CA: Sage.

Hewes, D. F. (1996). Small group communication may not influence decision making: An amplification of socio-egocentric theory. In R. Y. Hirokawa & M. S. Poole (Eds.), *Communication and group decision making* (2nd ed., pp. 179-213). Thousand Oaks, CA: Sage.

Hirokawa, R. Y., & Salazar, A. J. (1999). Task-group communication and decision-making performance. In L. R. Frey (Ed.), D. S. Gouran, & M. S. Poole (Assoc. Eds.), *The handbook of group communication theory & research* (pp. 167-191). Thousand Oaks, CA: Sage.

Hoffman, L. R. (1965). Group problem solving. In L. Berkowitz (Ed.), *Advances in experimental social psychology* (Vol. 2, pp. 99-132). New York: Academic Press.

Jarboe, S. (1999). Group communication and creativity processes. In L. R. Frey (Ed.), D. S. Gouran, & M. S. Poole (Assoc. Eds.), *The handbook of group communication theory & research* (pp. 335-368). Thousand Oaks, CA: Sage.

Ketrow, S. M. (1999). Nonverbal aspects of group communication. In L. R. Frey (Ed.), D. S. Gouran, & M. S.

Poole (Assoc. Eds.), *The handbook of group communication theory & research* (pp. 251-287). Thousand Oaks, CA: Sage.

Keyton, J. (1999). Relational communication in groups. In L. R. Frey (Ed.), D. S. Gouran, & M. S. Poole (Assoc. Eds.), *The handbook of group communication theory & research* (pp. 192-222). Thousand Oaks, CA: Sage.

Mabry, E. A. (1999). The systems metaphor in group communication. In L. R. Frey (Ed.), D. S. Gouran, & M. S. Poole (Assoc. Eds.), *The handbook of group communication theory & research* (pp. 71-91). Thousand Oaks, CA: Sage.

Maier, N. R. F. (1970). *Problem solving and creativity in individuals and groups.* Belmont, CA: Brooks-Cole.

Meyers, R. A., & Brashers, D. E. (1994). Expanding the boundaries of small group communication research: Exploring a feminist perspective. *Communication Studies, 45,* 68-85.

Meyers, R. A., & Brashers, D. E. (1999). Influence processes in group interaction. In L. R. Frey (Ed.), D. S. Gouran, & M. S. Poole (Assoc. Eds.), *The handbook of group communication theory & research* (pp. 288-312). Thousand Oaks, CA: Sage.

Mosvick, R. K., & Nelson, R. B. (1987). *We've got to start meeting like this: A guide to successful business meeting management.* Glenview, IL: Scott, Foresman.

Pavitt, C. (1999). Theorizing about the group communication-leadership relationship: Input-process-output and functional models. In L. R. Frey (Ed.), D. S. Gouran, & M. S. Poole (Assoc. Eds.), *The handbook of group communication theory & research* (pp. 313-334). Thousand Oaks, CA: Sage.

Poole, M. S. (1991). Procedures for managing meetings: Social and technological innovation. In R. A. Swanson & B. O. Knapp (Eds.), *Innovative meeting management* (pp. 53-100). Austin, TX: 3M Meeting Management Institute.

Poole, M. S. (1999). Group communication theory. In L. R. Frey (Ed.), D. S. Gouran, & M. S. Poole (Assoc. Eds.), *The handbook of group communication theory & research* (pp. 37-70). Thousand Oaks, CA: Sage.

Poole, M. S., Keyton, J., & Frey, L. R. (1999). Group communication methodology: Issues and considerations. In L. R. Frey (Ed.), D. S. Gouran, & M. S. Poole (Assoc. Eds.), *The handbook of group communication theory & research* (pp. 92-112). Thousand Oaks, CA: Sage.

Poole, M. S., Seibold, D. R., & McPhee, R. D. (1996). The structuration of group decisions. In R. Y. Hirokawa & M. S. Poole (Eds.), *Communication and group decision making* (2nd ed., pp. 114-146). Thousand Oaks, CA: Sage.

Propp, K. M. (1999). Collective information processing in groups. In L. R. Frey (Ed.), D. S. Gouran, & M. S. Poole (Assoc. Eds.), *The handbook of group communication theory & research* (pp. 225-250). Thousand Oaks, CA: Sage.

Propp, K. M., & Kreps, G. L. (1994). A rose by any other name: The vitality of group communication research. *Communication Studies, 45,* 7-19.

Putnam, L. L., & Stohl, C. (1990). Bona fide groups: A reconceptualization of groups in context. *Communication Studies, 41,* 284-265.

Putnam, L. L., & Stohl, C. (1996). Bona fide groups: An alternative perspective for communication and small group decision making. In R. Y. Hirokawa & M. S. Poole (Eds.), *Communication and group decision making* (2nd ed., pp. 147-178). Thousand Oaks, CA: Sage.

Schultz, B. G. (1999). Improving group communication performance: An overview of diagnosis and intervention. In L. R. Frey (Ed), D. S. Gouran, & M. S. Poole (Assoc. Eds.), *The handbook of group communication theory & research* (pp. 371-394). Thousand Oaks, CA: Sage.

Scott, C. R. (1999). Communication technology and group communication. In L. R. Frey (Ed.), D. S. Gouran, & M. S. Poole (Assoc. Eds.), *The handbook of group communication theory & research* (pp. 432-472). Thousand Oaks, CA: Sage.

Seibold, D. R., & Krikorian, D. H. (1997). Planning and facilitating group meetings. In L. R. Frey & J. K. Barge (Eds.), *Managing group life: Communicating in decision-making groups* (pp. 270-305). Boston: Houghton Mifflin.

Shaw, M. E. (1981). *Group dynamics: The psychology of group behavior* (3rd ed.). New York: McGraw-Hill.

Shilling, L. M., & Fuller, L. K. (1997). *Dictionary of quotations in communications.* Westport, CT: Greenwood Press.

Socha, T. J. (1999). Communication in family units: Studying the first "group." In L. R. Frey (Ed.), D. S. Gouran, & M. S. Poole (Assoc. Eds.), *The handbook of group communication theory & research* (pp. 475-492). Thousand Oaks, CA: Sage.

Stohl, C., & Putnam, L. L. (1994). Group communication in context: Implications for the study of bona fide groups. In L. R. Frey (Ed.), *Group communication in context: Studies of natural groups* (pp. 284-292). Hillsdale, NJ: Lawrence Erlbaum.

Sunwolf, & Seibold, D. R. (1999). The impact of formal procedures on group processes, members, and task outcomes. In L. R. Frey (Ed.), D. S. Gouran, & M. S. Poole (Assoc. Eds.), *The handbook of group communication theory & research* (pp. 395-431). Thousand Oaks, CA: Sage.

Turner, V. (1978). Foreword. In B. Meyeroff, *Number our days* (pp. xii-xvii). New York: Touchstone.

Wyatt, N. (1993). Organizing and relating: Feminist critique of small group communication. In S. P. Bowen & N. Wyatt (Eds.), *Transforming visions: Feminist critiques in communication studies* (pp. 51-86). Cresskill, NJ: Hampton Press.

Zander, A. (1994). *Making groups effective* (2nd ed.). San Francisco: Jossey-Bass.

PART I

Theoretical Perspectives

1

New Directions for Functional, Symbolic Convergence, Structuration, and Bona Fide Group Perspectives of Group Communication

JENNIFER H. WALDECK
University of Kansas

CAROLYN A. SHEPARD
JEREMY TEITELBAUM
W. JEFFREY FARRAR
DAVID R. SEIBOLD
University of California, Santa Barbara

The study of group processes has enjoyed a long and vital role in the social sciences in general and in communication in particular (see Seibold, 1994). Not coincidentally, the importance of *communication* has become increasingly evident. As Frey (1994) observed, "Communication is the lifeblood that flows through the veins of groups" (p. x). Cragan and Wright (1990) noted that 64 of 114 studies published about small groups within the communication discipline between 1980 and 1990 "clearly worked toward providing a communication explanation of group processes" (p. 212).

Concomitant with the centrality of group communication studies has been the emergence of four theoretical approaches to understanding and explaining communication in groups: (a) functional theory (Gouran, Hirokawa, Julian, & Leatham, 1993), (b) symbolic convergence theory (Bormann, 1983b), (c) group structuration theory (Poole, Seibold, & McPhee, 1985), and (d) the bona fide group perspective (Putnam & Stohl, 1990). So prominent have these theoretical positions become that Cragan and Wright (1990) opined that "it's difficult to believe that small group research was so theory-barren in the 1970s when one considers how theory-rich it has become" (p. 226). However, these perspectives have evolved relatively autonomously and, with few exceptions (see, e.g., Frey, 1996; Stohl & Holmes, 1993; Wyatt, 1993), free of critique (see Poole, 1999, for a thorough review of these four theories).

In this essay, we offer new directions for these four prominent theoretical approaches to group communication. Toward that end, we briefly explicate each theory, offer relevant critique, and provide directions for future research.

FUNCTIONAL THEORY

The foundations of functional theory can be found in the early 1980s (for a comprehensive review of the theory, see Gouran & Hirokawa, 1996). During the last two decades, scholars have explicated the theory (Gouran & Hirokawa, 1996; Hirokawa, 1980a, 1980b, 1983), found empirical support for many of its predictions (Hirokawa, 1980a, 1980b, 1985, 1988), and offered both conceptual and methodological enhancements of it (Gouran & Hirokawa, 1996; Gouran et al., 1993; Propp & Nelson, 1996).

Overview

Conceptual framework. The basic premise of functional theory is that group performance depends on how well communication functions within the context of a group to satisfy requisite conditions for successful group problem solving and decision making. Functional theorists propose that communication is the means by which the following critical *requirements* of a task are satisfied by group members (Gouran et al., 1993; Hirokawa, 1988). Specifically, members must do the following:

1. Show correct understanding of the issues to be resolved
2. Determine the minimal characteristics that any alternative, to be acceptable, must possess
3. Identify a relevant and realistic set of alternatives
4. Examine carefully the alternatives in relationship to each previously agreed-upon characteristic of an acceptable choice
5. Select the alternative that analysis reveals to be the most likely to have desired characteristics (Gouran et al., 1993, p. 580)

More recently, Gouran and Hirokawa (1996) proposed that communication not only functions to meet these five functional task requirements but is instrumental in minimizing various contextual constraints that limit the ability of group members to accomplish their tasks. Thus, communication also functions to enable group members in these ways:

1. To make clear their interest in arriving at the best possible decision
2. To identify the resources necessary for making such a decision
3. To recognize possible obstacles to be confronted
4. To specify the procedures to be followed
5. To establish ground rules for interaction
6. To employ appropriate interventions for overcoming cognitive, affiliative, and egocentric constraints that are interfering with the satisfaction of fundamental task requirements
7. To review the process by which the group comes to a decision and, if indicated, reconsider judgments rendered (even to the point of starting over) (Gouran & Hirokawa, 1996, p. 76)

Functional theory is based on the following set of primary *assumptions* that has been modified as the theory has evolved (see Gouran & Hirokawa, 1996):

1. The members of a decision-making or problem-solving group are motivated to make an appropriate choice.
2. The choice confronted is nonobvious.
3. The collective resources of the group in respect to the particular task exceed those of individual members.
4. The requisites of the task are specifiable.
5. Relevant information is available to the members or can be acquired.

6. The task is within the intellectual capabilities of the members to perform.
7. One or more of the members of the group must be capable of recognizing and interpreting the signs of unwanted cognitive, affiliative, and egocentric constraints.
8. Communication is instrumental.
9. Members are aware at any given time of how well interaction is serving to satisfy fundamental task requirements.
10. Members will take steps to minimize and counteract sources of influence that limit prospects for adequately fulfilling fundamental task requirements.

Critique and Directions for Research

The need to study natural groups. One of the primary criticisms of functional theory involves the methods and contexts used to test the perspective. Critics claim that the procedures typically used in such research lack relevance to real-world groups and their problems (Cragan & Wright, 1990; Poole, 1990; Sykes, 1990). More specifically, they argue that (a) zero-history groups, such as those formed for research purposes and relied on in this research, are rare in "natural" group decision-making contexts, and (b) the tasks presented to research participants in laboratory studies—the typical type of study conducted in testing functional theory—lack real-world significance. These methodological shortcomings, critics suggest, lead to findings that lack ecological validity.

Some scholars have sought to address these methodological problems. Propp and Nelson (1996), for example, selected work teams active in a manufacturing firm in which members had prior experience working with one another and expected to work together after the conclusion of the group project analyzed in this study. To analyze these "real" groups as they performed their tasks "in action," the researchers used an updated and parsimonious

version of the Function-Oriented Coding Scheme (FOICS; Hirokawa, 1988; Hirokawa & Rost, 1992). As a result, coders were able to quickly classify the teams' communication into one of seven categories. Anticipating coders' difficulty in classifying interactions on a "live" basis, the researchers conducted several training sessions in which the coding scheme was explained and trainees were given the opportunity to code transcribed group discussions. This practice continued until the percentage of unit-by-unit agreement between coder trainees and the lead researcher reached 90%. Coders then attended numerous group meetings in the organization under study to practice coding live conversations before actually collecting usable data. Propp and Nelson's study, thus, meaningfully redressed some of the important concerns about the research methods used to test functional theory.

We recommend that researchers employing functional theory continue the practice initiated by Propp and Nelson (1996) of studying natural groups. To substantiate the theory's utility and generalizability, realize the benefits to the theory of studying bona fide groups (Stohl & Holmes, 1993), and lessen the degree to which group and organizational studies are bifurcated (Seibold, 1998), more studies are needed that demonstrate the relationship between meeting functional requisites and outcomes in groups working on various types of tasks across various types of organizations.

Solve the problem of ambiguous use of terminology. Critiques of functional theory note the lack of precision with which key terms are defined and used. For instance, Jarboe (1996) pointed out that the literature on groups in general, and functional theory specifically, references decision-making procedures in various and confusing ways, including "discussion, method, agenda, format, system, pattern, process, scheme, approach, strategy, technique, and model, among other labels" (p. 346). Moreover, these terms are *defined* in varied ways. In addition, Stohl and

Holmes (1993) observed that functional theory is limited by the ambiguous use of the term "function:"

> The potential confusion of function as a noun (task component, a special purpose, or an action contributing to a larger action) and function as a verb (task accomplishment; to serve, to act, to work) may underlie the alarming imprecision with which functions are conceptualized throughout the literature. (p. 602)

We add that not only is the term "function" conceptualized in a confusing way throughout the literature but so are the functional requisites themselves, thus rendering the precise operationalizations contained within the function-oriented coding scheme problematic. Simply put, terms are used interchangeably without justification. For instance, Hirokawa (1985) referred to the functional requisite of "accurate understanding of the problem," but this requisite previously had been labeled "analysis of the problem" (Hirokawa, 1983). Analysis may, but need not necessarily, result in "accurate understanding." Consequently, other researchers are left to wonder whether a thorough analysis or an accurate understanding of the problem is the more salient predictor of group decision-making effectiveness.

Elsewhere, Hirokawa (1985) identified two additional functional requisites: "accurate assessment of the (a) positive and (b) negative qualities of alternatives." These functional requisites would seem to imply that groups must consider the positive and negative aspects of various decision alternatives. However, Propp and Nelson (1996) referred to those same requisites as "evaluation positive" and "evaluation negative." These terms could imply that group members evaluate their decisions, rather than the alternatives under question, either positively or negatively. Absent conceptual precision and consistency, operational and interpretive inconsistency may follow. In that sense, Chaffee's (1991) recommendation is relevant: "One long-run goal of concept explication is to use that term consistently to refer to that concept, and not to conflate it with related concepts or alternative usages of the term" (p. 40).

Clarify the concept of performance effectiveness. Numerous theorists have suggested that the notion of group effectiveness or performance be revisited (Gouran, 1988; Hirokawa, Erbert, & Hurst, 1996; Janis & Mann, 1977; Poole, 1990; Stohl & Holmes, 1993). Stohl and Holmes (1993) argued that effectiveness is neither defined nor explained by functional theory; rather, measures of effectiveness are inherent in the tasks used to test functional theory. They called for the acknowledgment of multiple perspectives in conceptualizing decision quality and argued that quality may be a socially constructed function of a group rather than of the task or some authority outside the group. Gouran (1988) described how typical tests of effectiveness delineated within functional theory (correctness, quality, and utility of decision) are unverifiable, reliant on subjective perceptions of either members or judges, or imperceptible.

We propose that the matter is not as problematic for the vitality of functional theory as critics suggest. Criteria for good decisions remain a function of the task in addition to members' and experts' perceptions of what constitutes a high-quality decision. In real-world organizational groups, outcomes are as effective or ineffective as stakeholders affected by those outcomes perceive them to be. Given this position, functional theory treats decision evaluation appropriately, and the methods employed by functional theorists for evaluating group decision quality are rigorous.

However, functional theory would benefit from more careful analyses of the processes that lead groups to effective or ineffective decisions. Although employing sound methods for determining criteria for outcome effectiveness, functional theorists have neglected the dynamics of how groups arrive at effective or ineffective decisions. More detailed research focus on processes, in addition to inputs (emphasized by the bona fide group perspective; see discussion later in this chapter) and outputs (emphasized by functional theory) is necessary. Further content analyses of interaction data already obtained may reveal more subtle nuances of the communication that leads groups to either effective or ineffective decisions. For instance, Gouran (1994) has proposed that functional theory researchers

> might begin looking for occurrences in interaction that account for differences in the same level of conformity to the sequences of activity implied by the task requirements. A potentially critical factor may be the sorts of interventions that occur in response to digressions, process disruptions, and inadequacies in task performance. (p. 36)

Moreover, certain group member demographic variables, such as cultural background and gender, may influence particular communication styles enacted within groups and, consequently, the resulting decisions (see Kearney & Plax, 1999, for an overview of the literature on cultural styles of communicating). For instance, Oetzel (1995) pointed out that group members from an individualistic culture are more likely to be task oriented and to expect confrontation from others in groups than those from a collectivistic culture (see also Oetzel, this volume). Moreover, despite research that demonstrates that both men and women can be effective leaders (Chemers & Murphy, 1995; Eagly & Johnson, 1990), reviews of literature indicate that stereotypes about sex/gender and its effects on group processes persist (Eagly, Karau, & Makhijani, 1995)—specifically, the belief that women function more effectively in roles that demand a "relational" versus a "task" focus (Eagly & Karau, 1991). Consequently, to better understand process-outcome linkages predicted by functional theory, researchers should analyze group interaction for differences on certain member demographic variables, such as sex/gender and cultural background, to determine whether they are salient predictors of communication and of decision quality. In these ways, the data indicating that "group de-

cision-making performance is . . . affected by the extent to which [communicative behaviors] allow group members to perform important decision-making functions" (Gouran & Hirokawa, 1983, p. 170) might be better understood in an applied and meaningful fashion.

Relevant information may be unavailable or misunderstood. Jarboe (1996) contended that the rational/functional assumption that group members systematically "collect data" and assess the problem before generating a solution may be misleading. Researchers cannot assume that members have access to relevant and accurate information or that they will interpret the information they bring to the group correctly (Janis & Mann, 1977; Propp, 1999). Similarly, Stohl and Holmes's (1993) suggestion that functional theory is "appropriate only when groups know or can find out what constitutes relevant information" (p. 605) needs to be further examined. Researchers need to examine the processes by which individual group members obtain information from outside their group and convey it to the group. Studies employing observational, self-report, and diary methods may indicate the answers to a number of pressing questions: (a) What channels do people use to acquire information in groups? (b) Are group members, in general, able to correctly and objectively evaluate the information they obtain in terms of its relevance? (c) Do group members typically convey information accurately? (d) Do individuals apply arbitrary criteria in judging the worthiness of information and neglect to share information that may indeed be relevant and accurate? In sum, researchers studying the functional nature of group problem solving and decision making should not presume that in all cases groups base their decisions on relevant and/or accurate data.

Additional functions that need to be incorporated. Stohl and Holmes (1993) proposed the addition of two sets of functions: (a) *historical functions* that "accomplish the embedding of a decision in ongoing group life"

(p. 610) and (b) *institutional functions* that "accomplish the embedding of a decision in a permeable context" (p. 610). Such functions certainly would be useful to extending functional theory. Group decisions may indeed be well-informed by prior decisions and activities of the group or organization in which the groups are embedded, and groups are influenced by the broad, as well as specific, implications of their decisions (Janis, 1989). With this in mind, a more concrete delineation of historical and institutional functions is in order—specifically, how organizational groups satisfy these functional requisites, the processes by which groups learn the history of their organizations, and the degree to which the satisfaction of historical and institutional functions predicts quality of group outcomes. Ultimately, empirical validation of these functions and their relationship to group outcomes is necessary. Importantly, researchers should focus on specific communication strategies that groups employ to determine (a) prior decision-making habits and outcomes of groups that preceded them within the organization and (b) the implications of their decisions on the life of the group, specifically, and the organization, more generally.

Uncovering cognitive, affiliative, and egocentric constraints. In addressing the functional requisites added most recently, Gouran (1998) noted,

> Most problematic with the perspective [functional theory] at this point is . . . that groups are most likely to make appropriate choices when their members' interaction serves to help them employ appropriate interventions for overcoming cognitive, affiliation, and egocentric constraints that are interfering with the satisfaction of [other] fundamental task requirements. (p. 98)

More specifically, *cognitive constraints* occur when little information is available to solve a problem or make a decision, time is limited, and/or the issue is more complex than one with which the group typically deals. *Affiliative constraints* arise when relationships are an important concern for group members, particularly when relationships are deteriorating. Finally, *egocentric constraints* oppress groups when at least one member has a "highly pronounced need for control or is otherwise driven by personal motivations" (Gouran & Hirokawa, 1996, p. 61). We concur with Gouran (1998) that researchers should uncover the operational signs of these constraints within the context of problem-solving and decision-making interactions. Gouran has posited manifestations of these constraints (e.g., members might ask during group interaction, "How can they expect us to have something on this by next week?" to suggest a cognitive constraint posed by time pressures), and researchers should work to verify these empirically.

Overall, functional theory has been developed and tested in a methodologically rigorous way. After a review of the theory and its empirical tests, we urge researchers to (a) continue to study natural groups, (b) work to precisely define constructs central to the theory and use those definitions consistently, and (c) examine further how specific communication processes and communicator characteristics might predict the effectiveness of group decision making and problem solving. Finally, research attention should focus on any additional communication functions relevant to group tasks that may exist and the various constraints that might operate within groups. As a result of these continued paradigmatic developments, functional theory should remain a viable framework for understanding group communication.

SYMBOLIC CONVERGENCE THEORY

Symbolic convergence theory (SCT) was developed by Ernest Bormann (1972, 1973, 1975), with roots in the group communication work of Robert Freed Bales (1970). Over nearly three decades, communication scholars have developed the theory (e.g., Bormann, Cragan, & Shields, 1996; Chesebro, Cragan, & McCullough, 1973; Cragan & Shields, 1981; Shields, 1981b), applied it to diverse areas of the field of communication (e.g., Bormann, 1973, 1982a, 1982b, 1983a, 1985a, 1990, 1996; Bormann, Bormann, & Harty, 1995; Bormann, Koester, & Bennett, 1978; Bormann, Pratt, & Putnam, 1978; Chesebro et al., 1973; Cragan, 1981; Cragan & Shields, 1977, 1992; Cragan, Shields, Pairitz, & Jackson, 1981; Lesch, 1994; Putnam, Van Hoeven, & Bullis, 1991; Shields, 1981a, 1981b, 1981c; Shields & Cragan, 1981), and conceptually refined and methodologically extended SCT in response to several critiques of the theory (e.g., Bormann, 1982c; Bormann, Cragan, & Shields, 1994, 1996). In the sections that follow, we first explicate symbolic convergence theory by outlining the basic propositions and definitions important to the theory, then review and address recent critiques, and propose directions for future research.

Overview

The basic assumption of SCT is that *humans, by nature, interpret and give meaning to the signs, objects, and people they encounter.* SCT scholars argue that when groups of people share and interpret human symbols, or messages, they create a common consciousness, or shared reality. That is, through interaction, two or more "symbolic worlds" move close to one another or even overlap (Bormann, 1982a, 1982c, 1996). When several people develop overlapping portions of their symbolic worlds, they develop shared meanings and have the basis to "create community, [to] discuss their common experiences, and to achieve mutual understanding" (Bormann, 1982c, p. 51). Thus, through the process of symbolic convergence, Bormann and colleagues argue that groups begin to interpret and assign meaning to their environment in much the same way that individuals do, insofar as groups begin to understand events in a similar way.

The cornerstone of SCT is the *fantasy,* a "creative and imaginative shared interpreta-

tion of events that fulfills a group psychological or rhetorical need" (Bormann et al., 1995, p. 201). A fantasy does not refer to the "here and now" but to another time or place outside the direct deliberations of a group. Shared group stories, or fantasies, are expressed in the form of a *dramatizing message* that catches a group's attention and results in *fantasy chaining,* a process in which group members contribute to the fantasy (or story), resulting in excitement and group involvement around the message. Dramatizing messages that trigger fantasy chaining contain a *fantasy theme,* or main idea—an observable record of the nature and content of the shared group consciousness (Cragan & Shields, 1992). Once a group converges around a fantasy theme, members begin to display *inside cues,* or communicative acts in which a speaker uses a nonverbal or verbal signal to allude to a previously shared fantasy. In turn, this sparks a response similar in mood and tone to the original response when group members first created the consciousness associated with the fantasy (Bormann, 1983a).

Through fantasy chaining, fantasy themes develop into *fantasy types,* or stock scenarios, repeated again and again by the same or similar characters (Bormann, 1996). Fantasy involves sharing the same story with different characters and slightly different events, or repeated stories with a "common narrative spine" (Bormann, 1983b, p. 74). Integration of several fantasies and fantasy types creates a *rhetorical vision,* or a composite drama that draws people into a common symbolic reality (Bormann, 1983a; Bormann et al., 1994; Cragan & Shields, 1992). Three primary master analogues drive rhetorical visions: *righteous analogues* ("right and wrong, proper and improper, superior and inferior, moral and immoral, and just and unjust," Cragan & Shields, 1992, p. 202), *social analogues* (containing relational factors, such as "friendship, trust, caring, comradeship, compatibility, family ties, brotherhood, sisterhood, and humaneness," Cragan & Shields, 1992, p. 202), or *pragmatic analogues* (stressing "expediency, utility, efficiency, parsimony, simplicity, practicality, cost effectiveness, and minimal emotional involvement," Cragan & Shields, 1992, p. 202).

Those who participate in a rhetorical vision are considered a *rhetorical community* that shares symbolic ground and responds to messages in tune with their rhetorical vision. In addition, the motives, or needs, of a rhetorical community can be understood by the master analogue that drives their rhetorical vision. Of particular importance for group communication is Bormann's (Bormann et al., 1996) emerging theory of group consciousness, a perspective that looks at the life span of a rhetorical vision of a group, or even a large rhetorical community, by examining the stages of group consciousness creation, raising, maintenance, and decline. In this explication, Bormann further delineates the larger context of influences on, and outcomes of, group activity.

Critique

Group communication researchers have strengthened the general theory of symbolic convergence outlined above by providing some empirical support through systematic research. Excerpts from transcripts of group interaction have been used as evidence of different stages in the convergence process in conceptual essays (Bormann, 1972, 1975, 1980, 1983a, 1983b, 1985b, 1990). Over the past 20 years, SCT has been reviewed and critiqued in light of such investigations; Bormann et al. (1994) reviewed four indictments against SCT and responded to each; the reader should refer to the original article for a full discussion of all the indictments. Our purpose here is to review only those arguments and SCT proponents' responses relevant to our discussion; in addition, we suggest an overarching concern regarding SCT's utility. Finally, we offer suggestions for future research that may serve to enhance the vitality of SCT.

Need to increase the generalizability of SCT findings. Mohrmann (1982a) argued that the basic presuppositions of SCT have not been explained clearly within the existing literature. Bormann et al. (1994) rejoined by adding the following four propositions. First, SCT is a grounded approach to theory building; thus, clear definitions of terms will be outcomes of research, not theory-building efforts. Second, observational studies using an SCT framework provide a "viable account of the rhetorical relationship between the rational and the irrational" (p. 264) components of group interaction. Third, research participants are an important part of any analysis using SCT (i.e., the individuals experiencing group life are the focus of SCT-grounded studies of group communication). Fourth, as a result of SCT analyses, researchers can make generalizations to other types of groups.

Although case studies and other observations appear to support the first three claims, we take issue with the fourth proposition. Specifically, Bormann et al. (1994) suggested that, given the importance of context for symbolic convergence (e.g., group history, rhetorical skills of participants, and individuals' varying levels of group identification), the only finding generalizable across groups is the ability to identify the creation and formation of group fantasies. What utility is this finding to small groups? Given the correct participant rhetorical skill and group dynamic, groups will chain on certain fantasies and develop rhetorical visions, but how do these fantasies help or hurt groups in general, what are the consequences of these fantasies, and are they necessary for effective group interplay? In particular, because case studies of single groups and convenience samples of multiple groups have been the norm in SCT investigations, SCT researchers' inattention to ensuring the representativeness of groups sampled for study, in turn, raises questions about the generalizability of SCT claims—foundational to the fourth proposition.

For SCT to be a more useful theory of small groups, researchers need to document the existence of fantasies less often and begin to examine how this inevitable group process relates to other group outcomes. In fact, some researchers argue that the field of group communication, in general, is in need of theories that lend themselves to predicting specific process-product linkages (Hewes, 1986, 1996). Although SCT studies generate rich descriptions of the process of fantasy chaining and development of rhetorical visions, they have offered far less in terms of explanation and prediction of how these rhetorical visions affect group outcomes and group environment. Thus, operational propositions that contribute to a process-outcome model of the relationship between group communication and group decision making are needed.

Intersubjectivity of SCT. A final indictment to which Bormann et al. (1994) responded is the argument that "SCT's insights are researcher-dependent and not theory-dependent" (p. 275). A number of scholars (cf. Ivie, 1987; Mohrmann, 1982b; Osborn, 1986; Poole, 1990) have suggested that the "insights flowing from SCT studies and fantasy theme analysis might be due to the researcher's perspicacity and not to the application of SCT and its attended methods" (Bormann et al., 1994, p. 275). However, SCT proponents argue that the theory does provide a reliable framework for classifying messages that contribute to fantasy, rhetorical vision, and ultimately, symbolic convergence. For example, Bormann et al. (1994) noted that SCT does not stress "a unique reading of myth, metaphor, narrative, or story but provides a clear technical vocabulary for the general analysis of imaginative [group] language" (p. 276). In sum, SCT scholars believe that the presence of fantasies, fantasy types, and ultimately, rhetorical visions across several divergent areas of research demonstrates the existence of symbolic convergence as a phenomenon and group process. As such, SCT provides the "technical vocabulary . . . for analysis . . . and provides a way to make a coherent analysis of a community's otherwise abstract public consciousness" (Bormann et al., 1994, p. 276).

Although we agree with Bormann and colleagues' response to the previous criticism, we also believe that they must continue to pursue this issue. Consistent, precise conceptualizations are a starting ground for observation that leads to predictive power, explanatory power, or both; however, a reliable coding and observational scheme for analyzing group fantasies and symbolic convergence that eliminates researcher bias and dependency on contextualization is needed. Although SCT researchers have been ameliorating this situation recently by using quantitative statistical procedures, such as Q-sort analyses, QUANAL factor analyses, and content analyses, these studies are primarily case studies driven by the method used to identify and verify the existence of fantasy themes rather than attempts to test propositions derived from theory. Thus, SCT researchers should work toward a systematic procedure for organizing and classifying antecedent conditions and group behaviors that lead to communication dynamics associated with symbolic convergence *across* group contexts.

Nonetheless, we commend SCT researchers' attempts at making abstract "fantasies" identifiable. Bormann et al. (1994) argued that SCT is developed at a more superior, abstract level of analysis than specific theories that guide practice. However, after 20 years of establishing the existence of symbolic convergence, we suggest that it is time to forward the application of the theory in group communication research to more utilitarian modes. Although this was not the original intent of SCT theorists, moving research in this direction could vitalize the utility of the perspective in contemporary group communication research. Perhaps SCT theorists could borrow functional theorists' methods of identifying specific "functions" necessary for symbolic convergence to occur or functions that specific master analogues fulfill within groups and organizations. In addition, the presence of certain master analogues in a group could be linked empirically to specific group outcomes.

It may be useful to those working to understand how groups perform different functions for SCT scholars to forward specific propositions that link group (a) composition characteristics, (b) messages, (c) visions, and (d) fantasies to group outcomes. In other words, on the basis of significant descriptions of group interaction that stem from researchers' employment of SCT, researchers should work toward improving the *predictive* power of the theory. For instance, member characteristics, specific group needs, or both may influence the enactment of specific message/vision/fantasy classifications. These features of interaction, then, may predict certain group outcomes.

In addition to this method of developing a theory of groups and organizations in general, or decision making specifically, Bormann (1996) indirectly outlined some possible propositions for SCT as applied to decision making in small groups. We extend them as follows:

Proposition 1: Symbolic convergence, as evidenced by identification of a collective self, is predictive of higher degrees of the following group aspects than in groups with no identification of a collective self:

(a) group norms, (b) role definition, (c) group "culture," (d) commitment to the group, (e) satisfaction with the group, (f) efficient decision making, (g) ritualistic behaviors

Proposition 2: Higher degrees of symbolic convergence predict the following:

(a) more agreement between group members about appropriate information-processing techniques, (b) more agreement between group members about what constitutes good evidence, (c) more agreement between group members about acceptable decision-making procedures

Proposition 3: Groups making decisions on the basis of achievement (or pragmatic) analogues will make more efficient decisions than groups that use righteous or social analogues.

Conclusion

SCT research to date has served principally to validate the processes through which fantasy themes build into fantasy types and, eventually, into rhetorical visions. Thus, the outcome of SCT research has been development and refinement of the theory itself. Although theory building is a necessary and important component of scholarship, SCT research may also be useful as a predictive and explanatory tool to explain small group processes and outcomes. Unfortunately, at this stage, SCT research does not possess such explanatory and predictive power. For example, Bormann (1996) pointed out that SCT can describe the processes through which groups achieve a shared consciousness, but it cannot predict the trajectory of group fantasizing. Although SCT research is beginning to expand beyond the identification of group rhetorical visions (e.g., Bormann, Knutson, & Musolf, 1997), future research may profit from generating more domain-specific theories of SCT rather than continuing only to validate the general process of fantasy theme creation and building. Although Bormann et al. (1994) contended that identification of symbolic convergence processes across many contexts is evidence of a higher level of philosophical theorizing, it is time to take this knowledge claim one step further by applying SCT more specifically to group processes, in particular, seeking to reveal how knowledge of convergence or SCT principles may be used to inform and help understand group processes. By forwarding the preceding theoretical propositions and conceptual linkages, we hope that SCT research will move in new and profitable directions.

STRUCTURATION THEORY

Historically, group communication researchers have struggled to conceptually integrate individual-level symbolic activity and macro-level structural factors. There is, of course, a recursivity between structure and action. Furthermore, group researchers have struggled with a second tension: Aspects of groups are commonly conceptualized as either stable or as emergent. As applied to group decision making, structuration theory addresses these tensions. Poole, Seibold, and McPhee (1996) proposed that a structurational approach

> provides a unified theory of individual and systemic processes in groups, an account of how institutions figure in group processes, and an integrated explanation of structural stability and change. It provides a theory of group interaction commensurate with the complexities of the phenomenon. (p. 116)

The main concepts of structuration theory are presented below (for a complete treatment of the theory, see Poole et al., 1985, 1986, 1996). Thereafter, we offer a critique of structuration research and directions for future investigations.

Overview

Structuration theory, articulated by Giddens (1976) as a sociological explanation of societal-level phenomena has as its crux the recursive relationship between collective action and social institutions. As Poole et al. (1996) observed, "Action and structure both enable and constrain each other in the continuous flow of intentionality" (p. 118). Action originates from (a) group members (*actors*), who operate with knowledge of the *system* that is the result of their actions, and (b) *structures,* defined as rules and resources that produce and reproduce the system (Poole et al., 1985, 1986, 1996). *Structuration,* the recursive process of action and structuring, is self-correcting and continuous; it exists within a group at present, engages what has gone before and what is occurring outside the group, and is possible only in the interactions between people (Poole et al., 1985).

Action and structure have dual natures; they both enable and constrain each other in

interaction. Structure shapes interaction while simultaneously being reproduced through that interaction (Poole et al., 1985, 1986, 1996). Interaction and structure are linked in three modalities (Poole et al., 1985, 1986):

1. *Interpretive schemes* link communication (interaction) and signification (structure).
2. *Norms* link morality (interaction) and legitimation (structure).
3. *Facilities* link power (interaction) and domination (structure).

It is useful to think of these modalities of action as intersections between action and structure (Poole et al., 1986) and to realize that these modalities are the key to the dual nature of action and structure.

Structuration theory is most useful (and most used) for *explaining* the processes that occur when people come together in collective, organized action rather than for *predicting* specific outcomes. Structurational analysis offers a theoretical base from which to situate groups in context. Indeed, structuration theory has been applied not only to group decision making but also to theorizing about organizations and using technology (e.g., Barley, 1986; Orlikowski & Robey, 1991).

Review and Critique of Structuration Research on Group Decision Making

Although structuration theory is directly applicable to studies of group decision making, evidenced by the program of research involving group argumentation (Canary, Brossman, & Seibold, 1987; Meyers, 1989a, 1989b; Meyers & Seibold, 1990; see, also, Meyers & Brashers, 1999), the recursive process of structure constraining interaction is missing from these analyses. Furthermore, as the theory has been presented, it is difficult to predict behavioral outcomes. And although the theory does have a great deal of explanatory power, it needs to include more predictive propositions. Although structuration theory has been influential and useful, some research suggests the need for refinement of the theory.

Prominent in all the research on structuration in group decision making is a focus on decision rules (e.g., Meyers & Seibold, 1990; Meyers, Seibold, & Brashers, 1991; Poole, McPhee, & Seibold, 1982). A *decision rule* can best be thought of as the structure supporting a method or mode of decision making, and it is potentially observable in the pattern of group interaction. Small groups in these studies have consequently been examined with attention to these patterns. Absent from analyses of this type, however, is a concern for the content of the arguments in relation to the context of the problem about which a decision is being sought (for an exception, see Meyers & Brashers, 1998). Instead, group arguments in this line of research have been studied by examining structural features of the discourse and positive or negative reactions to arguments rather than how well the content of the argument and pattern of argumentation relate to the decision a group is trying to make. That is, examination of the structuration process has not included an analysis of the mediating or contradictory nature of argument structures or of their interpenetration with other decision-making structures, areas that Poole et al. (1986) long ago proposed that structuration research should address.

Poole et al. (1985) proposed that structuration subsumes a traditional input-throughput-output model for theorizing about group processes. Although theoretically recognizing the inseparable nature of these dimensions of group dynamics, structuration research has been limited to studies of how interaction is affected by various structural elements, with attention given to the input each member gives in discussion, such as in persuasive arguments theory (PAT; Meyers & Seibold, 1990). Separate research has focused on the link between throughputs and outputs (Meyers & Brashers, 1998). To truly meet the challenge of examining the relationships between distinct input, throughput, and out-come variables, however, structuration research needs to simultaneously examine these facets of group decision dynamics.

Elsewhere, in a critique of structuration theory, Gouran (1990) indicated that the predictive potential of the theory was not being exploited. Gouran proposed that structuration research has been limited to post hoc explanations of how a group decision is made. He forwarded three propositions that predict outcomes mostly from frequencies of arguments advanced during group discussion and one that predicts outcomes depending on how well arguments are substantiated. Although Meyers and Brashers (1998) responded to this critique with a study and discussion of the strength of persuasive arguments as a factor, neither their work nor Gouran's goes far enough in accounting for structural production or constraints, which is crucial to an effective structuration theory of group decision making.

Directions for Future Research

Structuration research would benefit, in particular, from analyses of the action-producing and reproducing structures, the effects of those structures on action, and the interplay of structures, all of which are conspicuously absent from group decision-making research, especially given that it was advocated by Poole et al. (1986) some time ago. Concomitant with that wider analytic lens, a focus on communicative interacts (such as in Meyers et al., 1991)—with particular attention to the content, as well as the form, of the argument—would make this theory more explicitly communicative and more theoretically powerful.

Structuration researchers must also empirically demonstrate the recursivity of action and structure. As Poole (1990) lamented, proponents

blandly throw out the notion that social structures are produced and reproduced by actors... [while] detailed analysis of their long-term implications is largely omitted. What determines, for example, whether a process replicates itself, changes in regular cycles over time, gradually decays, or follows some other interesting trajectory? (p. 24)

Contractor and Seibold (1993) used self-organizing systems theory to dynamically specify how groups' initial conditions may influence the likelihood of appropriating a specific set of norms, a tenet of structuration theory, and challenged structuration researchers to empirically demonstrate the same. Certainly, the concept of structuration is rich with possibilities for new and exciting research about group processes, but significant empirical spadework remains. Indeed, two of the most important strides remaining for structuration researchers are to (a) undertake dynamic analyses of how group structures stabilize and change over time and (b) develop ways to assay transitional periods that "connect" action and structure (cf. Archer, 1982).

Functional theory may help to illuminate structuration theory. If one views structuration theory as a process model and functional theory as an input-output model, there is a complementarity. A study that integrates analysis of interaction from a structurational point of view with an analysis of group requisite functions as structures that are produced and reproduced in interaction would probably benefit both theories.

A related line of study is adaptive structuration theory (AST; Poole & DeSanctis, 1990), which has been concerned with the interpenetration of groups and technology. Although research into the structuration of new group technologies and argumentation patterns has evolved from the same theory, little integration exists between the two. In particular, AST research has illuminated how groups appropriate structures into the group. PAT research has indicated that patterns of communication among group members is crucial to decision-making processes. Although the AST line of research focuses on group decision support systems (GDSSs, a specific technology), the explication of the appropriation process would be useful to group decision-making researchers

and would bring argumentation research alongside studies of GDSSs (see Poole et al., 1996). These two bodies of literature would, thus, benefit from cross-pollination.

Conclusion

As Orlikowski and Robey (1991) stated, the study of structuration "provides a metatheory" (p. 165) rather than a lower level, proposition-based theory. Research on group structuration and AST has resulted in "situated" theories of structuration (Poole, 1999), although even these have focused on processes rather than on process-outcome relationships. Although structuration theory as applied to group decision making is arguably closer to a predictive model than implied by evaluations limiting structuration to metatheory (Orlikowski & Robey, 1991) or post hoc description (Gouran, 1990), endeavors such as those we have proposed above will aid in linking its metatheoretical character to situated dynamics and in generating predictions concerning input-process-output relationships.

BONA FIDE GROUP PERSPECTIVE

The newest member to the family of group communication theory is the bona fide group perspective (BFGP); indeed, BFGP is so nascent that Poole (1999) treated it as one of several evolving "agenda-setting perspectives." Among the most important contributions of this perspective (see Putnam, 1988, 1989, Putnam & Stohl, 1990, 1996; Stohl & Holmes, 1993; Stohl & Putnam, 1994) is the recognition of the embeddedness of small groups in larger organizational systems and, hence, the inclusion of embeddedness as a proposition central to the perspective and to the study of small groups. This inclusion has come in the light of criticism of group research for neglecting the relationship between groups and their larger social systems (see, e.g., Ancona, 1987; Frey, 1994; Putnam, 1989; Putnam & Stohl, 1990, 1996; Poole et al., 1996; Seibold, 1994). Researchers studying groups in context have acknowledged and demonstrated that the borders of groups and the environments in which they are embedded change, a notion central to the theory of embedded intergroup relations (see Alderfer 1977, 1986; Ancona, 1990; Berteotti & Seibold, 1994; Cragan & Wright, 1990; Geist & Chandler, 1994; Gersick, 1988, 1989; Jablin & Susman, 1983; McGrath, 1986; Poole, 1990; Poole & Roth, 1989). In response to this research, the core ideas of the BFGP are encapsulated by two general propositions: (a) Groups have permeable and fluid boundaries, and (b) groups are interdependent with the contexts in which they exist. Although there is a third proposition of "unstable and ambiguous borders," which is a valuable contribution to the perspective, concerns surrounding the more well-established foci encourage this more narrow treatment. We first provide an overview of the BFGP and then offer new directions for research.

Overview

Permeable and fluid boundaries. Group members bring to any group interaction ongoing memberships in multiple groups, varying past experiences in groups, and numerous expectations about how to make decisions and behave in group life. Fundamental to embedded intergroup relations theory (Alderfer, 1977, 1986), this experience of individuals suggests that their cognitions, emotions, and behaviors are shaped through multiple group memberships and multiple group representative roles. The BFGP explicitly identifies these permeable and fluid group boundaries in four ways: (a) Group members maintain multiple group memberships, and their involvement in those many groups often results in conflicting group identity (Ancona & Caldwell, 1988; Berteotti & Seibold, 1994; Gersick, 1988, 1989; Gladstein & Caldwell, 1988; Olsen, 1976); (b) group members play representative roles, in which they serve implicitly as boundary spanners who communicate with individuals outside the group (Ancona & Caldwell,

1988; Tushman, 1977; Tushman & Scanlan, 1981); (c) new members shift role functions and patterns of interaction in groups that lead to fluctuations in membership (Bormann, 1975; Putnam & Stohl, 1996); and (d) the degree to which members enact a sense of belongingness, loyalty, or commitment to groups leads to group identity formation (Berteotti & Seibold, 1994; Donnellon, 1994; Geist & Chandler, 1984).

Interdependence with context. The second major proposition undergirding the BFGP asserts that there is a relationship between a group and its environments. Early theorizing (Putnam, 1989) described this relationship in four ways: (a) Individuals communicate with people across groups, which leads to intergroup communication (Brett & Rognes, 1986; Gladstein, 1984); (b) groups within organizations often must coordinate actions, which results in those groups being interlocked (Berteotti & Seibold, 1994; Brett & Rognes, 1986); (c) group members often must negotiate jurisdiction and autonomy within the organizations in which they are embedded (Ancona & Caldwell, 1988; Geist & Chandler, 1984; Gladstein & Caldwell, 1985); and (d) because groups are composed of members with overlapping group membership and are embedded in larger organizational systems, group members will have to construct interpretations for making sense of existing intergroup relationships (Ancona & Caldwell, 1988; Berteotti & Seibold, 1994; Brett & Rognes, 1986; Donnellon, 1994; Geist & Chandler, 1984; Sabourin & Geist, 1990).

Directions for Research

The strengths of the BFGP lie in the recognition of the fluid boundaries and embeddedness of groups in larger organizational and social systems. However, the drawbacks to the perspective are twofold. First, the major propositions of this perspective are currently not conducive to empirical testing due to a lack of operationalization of key terms. Second, the explanatory power of this perspective is limited. The theory tends to be *descriptive* in nature because it does not *explain* how groups are related to their larger organizational systems, nor does it *predict* outcomes of this complex relationship between groups and organizations. We recommend three potential improvements for the BFGP and highlight preliminary research by scholars working to extend this perspective.

In their study of surgical teams, Lammers and Krikorian (1997) operationally defined the construct of "permeable and fluid boundaries" in terms of *stability, permeability, connectivity, overlapping membership, relations among members in other contexts,* and *fluctuations in membership;* they defined the construct of "interdependence with context" as *multiple levels of operation, tight or loose coupling, task jurisdiction, temporal control, resource dependency, competing internal and external authority systems,* and *border ambiguity and negotiation.* They also extended the perspective by adding the constructs of age of a group, task duration, a group's pool characteristics, and its institutional history.

Although these scholars have made a significant contribution to the perspective by better explicating and operationalizing BFGP constructs, only limited improvements have been offered in moving the perspective beyond description, our second concern. Of benefit to group researchers would be some predictions about how larger organizational social systems and fluid group boundaries influence group behaviors and group outcomes (e.g., decision making, task completion, and group effectiveness). Group researchers have incorporated elements of social networks as a means of understanding how group members belong to multiple groups (Ancona & Caldwell, 1988; Gladstein & Caldwell, 1985), act as boundary spanners across groups (Ancona & Caldwell, 1988), and shift roles and patterns of interaction (Berteotti & Seibold, 1994; Bormann, 1975; Putnam & Stohl, 1996). However, the BFGP is ripe for using stronger network-analytic procedures as a means for providing some predictability about how communication networks and network structures influence groups (Stohl, 1986). For example, a structural property such as centrality (either actor centrality or group centrality) is likely to mean that a group or group member will be an important channel of information (Wasserman & Faust, 1994). Ancona and Caldwell (1988) and Thornton (1978) found that isolated groups were less effective; other things being equal, centralized groups were likely to have greater access to resources and decisions makers and should, therefore, be more effective. In addition, Mayer (1998) found that decision making in groups was more effective when there was full participation of group members. This may indicate that in addition to improved decision making by groups with multiple ties outside the boundaries, groups with multiple ties within group boundaries (e.g., the strength of ties; Granovetter, 1973) positively affect group decision making.

Extending notions of the duality of affiliation relationships (Breiger, 1974) beyond examining the overlapping relationship between individuals and groups, Galois or concept lattices (Duquenne 1987, 1991; Freeman & White, 1993; Wille, 1995) can illustrate mutual dual subsets of any associated elements. Researchers using these techniques have been able to show relationships not only between individuals and groups but between actors and events as well. Recent extensions of these methods are advancing them from bipartite arrays to tripartite arrays and further (Mische & Pattison, 2000). This type of analysis will be useful in showing how the relationships of groups to larger organizational systems influence one another, for these methods shed some light on the influence of overlapping network relationships between individuals, groups, or organizations and affiliation with particular events. Researchers interested in, for example, the effects of group participation in multifunctional, interdisciplinary work groups across multiple divisions should find these methods illuminating.

Last, the BFGP could be enlightened by a better understanding of the influence that organizations have on groups and group processes (above and beyond overlapping networks). Lammers and Teitelbaum (1997) outlined a path model of the relationships between organizational behaviors, group behaviors, and group outcomes. In analyzing 168 multiple-quality improvement teams at each of 30 hospital sites, they proposed that group effectiveness is influenced by organizational processes (e.g., organization-wide training) and that groups do not function independently of the organizations to which they belong. They found support for a hierarchical structural model of influence. Specifically, several activities coordinated by organizations were found to correlate with activities used by groups, and both were correlated with group effectiveness. Future work in this area should continue to investigate what specific constraints and functions at the organizational level directly and indirectly influence group behaviors and group outcomes. These specific functions could then guide development of general models that examine the relationships between variables such as (a) organizational structure, including traditional bureaucracies versus network, market, and virtual organizational forms (Ahuja & Carley, 1998; Davidow & Malone, 1992; Monge, 1995; Mowshowitz, 1994; Nohria & Berkley, 1994; Powell, 1990); (b) teamwork (DeSanctis & Poole, 1997); and (c) virtual teams (Jarvenpaa & Leidner, 1998).

Conclusion

The bona fide group perspective has advanced group communication theory with the inclusion of the notion of groups being embedded in larger organizational systems. Although we recognize the limitations of this perspective, we also believe the advantages of incorporating the foregoing suggestions within the BFGP are twofold. First, work from this framework provides an opportunity to link groups to organizations empirically. Second, such research will better position the study of groups to accommodate recent trends that include greater use of communica-

tion technology (see Fulk & Steinfield, 1990) and the increased tendency for dispersed group members who work remotely (DeSanctis & Poole, 1997).

CHAPTER SUMMARY

In our review and critique of the theoretical bases of group communication study, we noted that they have prospered—both in quantity and in the depth of their explanatory power. Simultaneously, we made specific recommendations for increasing the depth and precision of each perspective. Generally, we suggested (a) the formalization of extant perspectives, particularly the bona fide group perspective, the newest one; (b) that researchers working from long-standing perspectives (e.g., structuration) should more thoroughly investigate process-product linkages; and (c) the need for better, more precise construct explication in theories in which ambiguities have been noted throughout the literature (e.g., functional theory and bona fide group perspectives). Toward those ends, we advanced propositions, proposed empirical studies, and suggested new constructs that should address the concerns highlighted in our review and analysis of the literature on group communication theory. As the use of groups and teams in organizations becomes more commonplace and as individuals seek to connect with groups as a way of building their communities, communication scholars' focus on groups is becoming increasingly critical. Thoughtful consideration of our recommendations should provide a basis for their work and further position the study of group communication centrally within the communication discipline.

REFERENCES

Ahuja, M. K., & Carley, K. M. (1998). Network structure in virtual organizations. *Journal of Computer Mediated Communication, 3*(4). Retrieved May 1, 2001, from the World Wide Web: www.ascusc.org/jcmc/vol3/issue4/ahuja.html

Alderfer, C. P. (1977). Group and intergroup relations. In J. Hackman & J. Suttle (Eds.), *Improving life at work* (pp. 227-296). Santa Monica, CA: Goodyear.

Alderfer, C. P. (1986). An intergroup perspective on group dynamics. In J. Lorsch (Ed.), *Handbook of organizational behavior* (pp. 190-222). Englewood Cliffs, NJ: Prentice Hall.

Ancona, D. G. (1987). Groups in organizations: Extending laboratory models. In C. Henrick (Ed.), *Annual review of personality and social psychology: Group and intergroup processes* (pp. 207-231). Newbury Park, CA: Sage.

Ancona, D. G. (1990). Outward bound: Strategies for team survival in an organization. *Academy of Management Journal, 33,* 334-365.

Ancona, D. G., & Caldwell, D. F. (1988). Beyond task and maintenance: Defining external functions in groups. *Group and Organization Studies, 13,* 468-494.

Archer, M. (1982). Morphogenesis versus structuration: On connecting structure and action. *British Journal of Sociology, 23,* 634-665.

Bales, R. F. (1970). *Personality and interpersonal behavior.* New York: Holt, Rinehart & Winston.

Barley, S. (1986). Technology as an occasion for structuring: Evidence from observation of CT scanners and the social order of radiology departments. *Administrative Science Quarterly, 31,* 78-108.

Berteotti, C. R., & Seibold, D. R. (1994). Coordination and role-definition problems in health care teams: A hospice case study. In L. R. Frey (Ed.), *Group communication in context: Studies of natural groups* (pp. 107-131). Hillsdale, NJ: Lawrence Erlbaum.

Bormann, E. G. (1972). Fantasy and rhetorical vision: The rhetorical criticism of social reality. *Quarterly Journal of Speech, 58,* 396-407.

Bormann, E. G. (1973). The Eagleton affair: A fantasy theme analysis. *Quarterly Journal of Speech, 59,* 143-159.

Bormann, E. G. (1975). *Discussion and group methods: Theory and practice* (2nd ed.). New York: Harper & Row.

Bormann, E. G. (1980). *Communication theory.* New York: Holt, Rinehart & Winston.

Bormann, E. G. (1982a). Fantasy and rhetorical vision: Ten years later. *Quarterly Journal of Speech, 68,* 288-305.

Bormann, E. G. (1982b). A fantasy theme analysis of the television coverage of the hostage release and the Reagan inaugural. *Quarterly Journal of Speech, 68,* 133-145.

Bormann, E. G. (1982c). The symbolic convergence theory of communication: Applications and implications for teachers and consultants. *Journal of Applied Communication Research, 10,* 50-61.

Bormann, E. G. (1983a). Symbolic convergence: Organizational communication and culture. In L. Putnam & M. E. Pacanowsky (Eds.), *Communication and organizations: An interpretive approach* (pp. 99-122). Beverly Hills, CA: Sage.

Bormann, E. G. (1983b). The symbolic convergence theory of communication and the creation, raising, and sustaining of public consciousness. In J. I. Sisco (Ed.), *The Jensen lectures: Contemporary communication studies* (pp. 71-90). Tampa: University of South Florida, Department of Communication.

Bormann, E. G. (1985a). *The force of fantasy: Restoring the American dream.* Carbondale: Southern Illinois University Press.

Bormann, E. G. (1985b). Symbolic convergence theory: A communication formulation based on *homo narrans. Journal of Communication, 35*(4), 128-139.

Bormann, E. G. (1990). *Small group communication: Theory and practice* (3rd ed.). New York: HarperCollins.

Bormann, E. G. (1996). Symbolic convergence theory and communication in group decision making. In R. Y. Hirokawa & M. S. Poole (Eds.), *Communication and group decision making* (2nd ed., pp. 81-113). Thousand Oaks, CA: Sage.

Bormann, E. G., Bormann, E., & Harty, K. C. (1995). Using symbolic convergence theory and focus group interviews to develop communication designed to stop teenage use of tobacco. In L. R. Frey (Ed.), *Innovations in group facilitation: Applications in natural settings* (pp. 200-232). Cresskill, NJ: Hampton Press.

Bormann, E. G., Cragan, J. F., & Shields, D. C. (1994). In defense of symbolic convergence theory: A look at the theory and its criticism after two decades. *Communication Theory, 44,* 259-294.

Bormann, E. G., Cragan, J. F., & Shields, D. C. (1996). An expansion of the rhetorical vision component of the symbolic convergence theory: The cold war paradigm case. *Communication Monographs, 63,* 1-28.

Bormann, E. G., Knutson, R. L., & Musolf, K. (1997). Why do people share fantasies? An empirical investigation of a basic tenet of the symbolic convergence communication theory. *Communication Studies, 48,* 254-276.

Bormann, E. G., Koester, J., & Bennett, J. (1978). Political cartoons and salient rhetorical fantasies: An empirical analysis of the '76 presidential campaign. *Communication Monographs, 45,* 317-329.

Bormann, E. G., Pratt, J., & Putnam, L. (1978). Power authority, and sex: Male response to female leadership. *Communication Monographs, 45,* 119-155.

Breiger, R. (1974). The duality of persons and groups. *Social Forces, 53,* 181-190.

Brett, J. M., & Rognes, J. K. (1986). Intergroup relations in organizations: A negotiations perspective. In P. S. Goodman (Ed.), *Designing effective work groups* (pp. 202-236). San Francisco: Jossey-Bass.

Canary, D. J., Brossman, B. G., & Seibold, D. R. (1987). Argument structures in decision-making groups. *Southern Speech Communication Journal, 53,* 18-37.

Chaffee, S. H. (1991). *Explication.* Newbury Park, CA: Sage.

Chemers, M. M., & Murphy, S. E. (1995). Leadership and diversity in groups in organizations. In M. M. Chemers, S. Oskamp, & M. A. Costanzo (Eds.), *Di-*

versity in organizations: New perspectives for a changing workplace (pp. 157-188). Thousand Oaks, CA: Sage.

Chesebro, J. W., Cragan, J. F., & McCullough, P. W. (1973). The small group techniques of the radical revolutionary: A synthetic study of consciousness raising. *Communication Monographs, 40,* 136-146.

Contractor, N. S., & Seibold, D. R. (1993). Theoretical frameworks for the study of structuring processes in group decision support systems: Adaptive structuration theory and self-organizing systems theory. *Human Communication Research, 19,* 528-563.

Cragan, J. F. (1981). The origins and nature of the Cold War rhetorical vision, 1946-1972. In J. F. Cragan & D. C. Shields (Eds.), *Applied communication research: A dramatistic approach* (pp. 47-66). Prospect Heights, IL: Waveland Press.

Cragan, J. F., & Shields, D. C. (1977). Foreign policy communication dramas: How mediated rhetoric played in Peoria in Campaign '76. *Quarterly Journal of Speech, 63,* 274-289.

Cragan, J. F., & Shields, D. C. (1981). *Applied communication research: A dramatistic approach.* Prospect Heights, IL: Waveland Press.

Cragan, J. F., & Shields, D. C. (1992). The use of symbolic convergence theory in corporate strategic planning: A case study. *Journal of Applied Communication Research, 20,* 199-218.

Cragan, J. F., Shields, D. C., Pairitz, L. A., & Jackson, L. H. (1981). The identifying characteristics of public fire safety educators: An empirical analysis. In J. F. Cragan & D. C. Shields (Eds.), *Applied communication research: A dramatistic approach* (pp. 219-234). Prospect Heights, IL: Waveland Press.

Cragan, J. F., & Wright, D. W. (1990). Small group communication research of the 1980s: A synthesis and critique. *Communication Studies, 41,* 212-236.

Davidow, W. H., & Malone, M. S. (1992). *The virtual corporation.* New York: Harper Collins.

DeSanctis, G., & Poole, M. S. (1997). Transitions in teamwork in new organizational forms. *Advances in Group Processes, 14,* 157-176.

Donnellon, A. (1994). Team work: Linguistic models of negotiating differences. In R. J. Lewicki, B. H. Sheppard, & R. Bies (Eds.), *Research on negotiation in organizations* (Vol. 4, pp. 71-123). Greenwich, CT: JAI Press.

Duquenne, V. (1987). Contextual implications between attributes and some representation principles for finite lattices. In B. Ganter, R. Wille, & K. E. Wolf (Eds.), *Beitraege zur begriffsanalyse* [Contributions to the analysis of ideas] (pp. 213-239). Mannheim, Germany: Wissenschaftsverlag.

Duquenne, V. (1991). On the core of finite lattices. *Discrete Mathematics, 88,* 133-147.

Eagly, A. H., & Johnson, B. T. (1990). Gender and leadership style: A meta-analysis. *Psychological Bulletin, 108,* 233-256.

Eagly, A. H., & Karau, S. J. (1991). Gender and the emergence of leaders: A meta-analysis. *Journal of Personality and Social Psychology, 60,* 685-710.

Eagly, A. H., Karau, S. J., & Makhijani, M. G. (1995). Gender and effectiveness of leaders: A meta-analysis. *Psychological Bulletin, 117,* 125-145.

Freeman, L. C., & White, D. R. (1993). Using Galois lattices to represent network data. In P. V. Marsden (Ed.), *Sociological methodology* (Vol. 23, pp. 127-145). Oxford, UK: Basil Blackwell.

Frey, L. R. (1994). The call of the field: Studying communication in natural groups. In L. R. Frey (Ed.), *Group communication in context: Studies of natural groups* (pp. ix-xiv). Hillsdale, NJ: Lawrence Erlbaum.

Frey, L. R. (1996). Remembering and "re-membering": A history of theory and research on communication and group decision making. In R. Y. Hirokawa & M. S. Poole (Eds.), *Communication and group decision making* (2nd ed., pp. 19-51). Newbury Park, CA: Sage.

Fulk, J., & Steinfield, C. (Eds.). (1990). *Organizations and communication technology.* Newbury Park, CA: Sage.

Geist, P., & Chandler, T. (1984). Account analysis of influence in group decision-making. *Communication Monographs, 51,* 67-78.

Gersick, C. J. G. (1988). Time and transition in work teams: Toward a new model of group development. *Academy of Management Journal, 31,* 9-41.

Gersick, C. J. G. (1989). Marking time: Predictable transitions in work groups. *Academy of Management, 32,* 274-309.

Giddens, A. (1976). *New rules of sociological method.* New York: Basic Books.

Gladstein, D. L., & Caldwell, D. (1985). Boundary management in new product teams. In *Academy of Management Proceedings* (pp. 161-165). San Diego: Academy of Management Association.

Gouran, D. S. (1988). Group decision making: An approach to integrative research. In C. H. Tardy (Ed.), *A handbook for the study of human communication* (pp. 247-267). Norwood, NJ: Ablex.

Gouran, D. S. (1990). Exploiting the predictive potential of structuration theory. In J. A. Anderson (Ed.), *Communication yearbook* (Vol. 13, pp. 313-322). Thousand Oaks, CA: Sage.

Gouran, D. S. (1994). The future of small group communication research: Revitalization or continued good health? *Communication Studies, 45,* 29-39.

Gouran, D. S. (1998). The signs of cognitive, affiliative, and egocentric constraints in patterns of interaction in decision-making and problem-solving groups and their potential effects on outcomes. In J. S. Trent (Ed.), *Communication: Views from the helm for the twenty-first century* (pp. 98-102). Needham Heights, MA: Allyn & Bacon.

Gouran, D. S., & Hirokawa, R. Y. (1983). The role of communication in decision-making groups: A functional perspective. In M. S. Mander (Ed.), *Communications in transition: Issues and debates in current research* (pp. 168-185). New York: Praeger.

Gouran, D. S., & Hirokawa, R. Y. (1996). Functional theory and communication in decision-making and problem-solving groups: An expanded view. In R. Y.

Hirokawa & M. S. Poole (Eds.), *Communication and group decision making* (2nd ed., pp. 55-80). Thousand Oaks, CA: Sage.

Gouran, D. S., Hirokawa, R. Y., Julian, K. M., & Leatham, G. B. (1993). The evolution and current status of the functional perspective on communication in decision-making and problem solving groups. In S. A. Deetz (Ed.), *Communication yearbook* (Vol. 16, pp. 573-600). Newbury Park, CA: Sage.

Granovetter, M. S. (1973). The strength of weak ties. *American Journal of Sociology, 81,* 1287-1303.

Hewes, D. E. (1986). A socio-egocentric model of group decision-making. In R. Y. Hirokawa & M. S. Poole (Eds.), *Comunication and group decision-making* (pp. 265-312). Beverly Hills, CA: Sage.

Hewes, D. E. (1996). Small group communication may not influence decision making: An amplification of socio-egocentric theory. In R. Y. Hirokawa & M. S. Poole (Eds.), *Communication and group decision-making* (2nd ed., pp. 179-213). Thousand Oaks, CA: Sage.

Hirokawa, R. Y. (1980a). A comparative analysis of communication patterns within effective and ineffective decision-making groups. *Communication Monographs, 47,* 313-321.

Hirokawa, R. Y. (1980b). *A function-oriented analysis of small group interaction within effective and ineffective decision-making groups: An exploratory investigation.* Unpublished doctoral dissertation, University of Washington, Seattle.

Hirokawa, R. Y. (1983). Communication and problem-solving effectiveness II: An exploratory investigation of procedural functions. *Western Journal of Speech Communication, 47,* 59-74.

Hirokawa, R. Y. (1985). Discussion procedures and decision-making performance: A test of a functional perspective. *Human Communication Research, 12,* 203-224.

Hirokawa, R. Y. (1988). Group communication and decision-making performance: A continued test of the functional perspective. *Human Communication Research, 18,* 487-515.

Hirokawa, R. Y., Erbert, L., & Hurst, A. (1996). Communication and group decision-making effectiveness. In R. Y. Hirokawa & M. S. Poole (Eds.), *Communication and group decision making* (2nd ed., pp. 269-300). Thousand Oaks, CA: Sage.

Hirokawa, R. Y., & Rost, K. M. (1992). Effective group decision making in organizations: Field test of the vigilant interaction theory. *Management Communication Quarterly, 5,* 267-288.

Ivie, R. L. (1987). The complete criticism of political rhetoric. *Quarterly Journal of Speech, 73,* 98-107.

Jablin, F., & Susman, L. (1983). Organizational group communication: A review of the literature and model of the process. In H. Greenbaum, R. Falcione, & S. Hellweg (Eds.), *Organizational communication: Abstracts, analysis, and overview* (Vol. 8, pp. 11-50). Beverly Hills, CA: Sage.

Janis, I. L. (1989). *Crucial decisions: Leadership in policy making and crisis management.* New York: Free Press.

Janis, I. L., & Mann, L. (1977). *Decision making: A psychological analysis of conflict, choice, and commitment.* New York: Free Press.

Jarboe, S. (1996). Procedures for enhancing group decision making. In R. Y. Hirokawa & M. S. Poole (Eds.), *Communication and group decision making* (2nd ed., pp. 345-383). Thousand Oaks, CA: Sage.

Jarvenpaa, S. L., & Leidner, D. E. (1998). Communication and trust in global virtual teams. *Journal of Computer-Mediated Communication, 3*(4). Retrieved May 1, 2001, from the World Wide Web: www.ascusc.org/jcmc/vol3/issue4/jarvenpaa.html

Kearney, P., & Plax, T. G. (1999). *Public speaking in a diverse society* (2nd ed.). Mountain View, CA: Mayfield.

Lammers, J. C., & Krikorian, D. (1997). Theoretical extension and operationalization of the bona fide group construct with an application to surgical teams. *Journal of Applied Communication, 25,* 17-38.

Lammers, J. C., & Teitelbaum, J. B. (1997, November). *Confronting the team-organization gap: Causal links between organizational and team activities in quality improvement.* Paper presented at the meeting of the National Communication Association, Chicago.

Lesch, C. L. (1994). Observing theory in practice: Sustaining consciousness in a coven. In L. R. Frey (Ed.), *Group communication in context: Studies of natural groups* (pp. 57-82). Hillsdale, NJ: Lawrence Erlbaum.

Mayer, M. E. (1998). Behaviors leading to more effective decisions in small groups embedded in organizations. *Communication Reports, 11,* 123-132.

McGrath, J. E. (1986). Studying groups at work: Ten critical needs for theory and practice. In P. S. Goodman (Ed.), *Designing effective work groups* (pp. 362-391). San Francisco: Jossey-Bass.

Meyers, R. A. (1989a). Persuasive arguments theory: A test of assumptions. *Human Communication Research, 15,* 357-381.

Meyers, R. A. (1989b). Testing persuasive argument theory's predictor model: Alternative interactional accounts of group argument and influence. *Communication Monographs, 56,* 112-132.

Meyers, R. A., & Brashers, D. E. (1998). Argument in group decision making: Explicating a process model and investigating the argument-outcome link. *Communication Monographs, 65,* 261-281.

Meyers, R. A., & Brashers, D. (1999). Influence processes in group interaction. In L. R. Frey (Ed.), D. S. Gouran, & M. S. Poole (Assoc. Eds.), *The handbook of group communication theory & research* (pp. 288-312). Thousand Oaks, CA: Sage.

Meyers, R. A., & Seibold, D. R. (1990). Perspectives on group argument: A critical review of persuasive arguments theory and an alternative structurational view. In J. A. Anderson (Ed.), *Communication yearbook 13* (pp. 268-302). Newbury Park, CA: Sage.

Meyers, R. A., Seibold, D. R., & Brashers, D. (1991). Argument in initial group decision-making discussions: Refinement of a coding scheme and a descriptive quantitative analysis. *Western Journal of Speech Communication, 55,* 47-68.

Mische, A., & Pattison, P. (2000). Composing a civic arena: Publics, projects, and social settings. *Poetics, 27,* 163-194.

Monge, P. R. (1995). Global network organizations. In R. Cesaria & P. Shockley-Zalabak (Eds.), *Organization means communication: Making the organizational communication concept relevant to practice* (pp. 135-151). Rome, Italy: Sipi Editore.

Mohrmann, G. P. (1982a). An essay on fantasy theme criticism. *Quarterly Journal of Speech, 68,* 109-132.

Mohrmann, G. P. (1982b). Fantasy theme criticism: A peroration. *Quarterly Journal of Speech, 68,* 306-313.

Mowshowitz, A. (1994). Virtual organization: A vision of management in the information age. *The Information Society, 10,* 267-288.

Nohria, N., & Berkley, J. D. (1994). The virtual organization: Bureaucracy, technology, and the implosion of control. In C. Heckscher & A. Donnellon (Eds.), *The post-bureaucratic organization: New perspectives on organizational change* (pp. 108-128). Thousand Oaks, CA: Sage.

Oetzel, J. G. (1995). Intercultural small groups: An effective decision-making theory. In R. L. Wiseman (Ed.), *Intercultural communication theories* (pp. 247-270). Newbury Park, CA: Sage.

Olsen, J. P. (1976). Choice in an organized anarchy. In J. G. March & J. P. Olsen (Eds.), *Ambiguity and choice in organizations* (pp. 82-139). Bergen, Norway: Universitetsforlaget.

Orlikowski, W. J., & Robey, D. (1991). Information technology and the structuring of organizations. *Information Systems Research, 2,* 143-169.

Osborn, M. (1986). [Review of the book *The force of fantasy: Restoring the American dream*]. *Communication Education, 35,* 204-205.

Poole, M. S. (1990). Do we have any theories of group communication? *Communication Studies, 41,* 45-55.

Poole, M. S. (1999). Group communication theory. In L. R. Frey (Ed.), D. S. Gouran & M. S. Poole (Assoc. Eds.), *The handbook of group communication theory & research* (pp. 37-70). Thousand Oaks, CA: Sage.

Poole, M. S., & DeSanctis, G. (1990). Understanding the use of group decision support systems: The theory of adaptive structuration. In J. Fulk & C. Steinfield (Eds.), *Organizations and communication technology* (pp. 175-195). Newbury Park, CA: Sage.

Poole, M. S., McPhee, R. D., & Seibold, D. R. (1982). A comparison of normative and interactional explanations of group decision-making: Social decision schemes versus valence distributions. *Communication Monographs, 49,* 1-19.

Poole, M. S., & Roth, J. (1989). Decision development in small groups IV: A typology of group decision paths. *Human Communication Research, 15,* 323-356.

Poole, M. S., Seibold, D. R., & McPhee, R. D. (1985). Group decision making as a structurational process. *Quarterly Journal of Speech, 71,* 74-102.

Poole, M. S., Seibold, D. R., & McPhee, R. D. (1986). A structurational approach to theory-building in group decision-making research. In R. Y. Hirokawa & M. S. Poole (Eds.), *Communication and group decision-making* (pp. 237-264). Beverly Hills, CA: Sage.

Poole, M. S., Seibold, D. R., & McPhee, R. D. (1996). The structuration of group decisions. In R. Y. Hirokawa & M. S. Poole (Eds.), *Communication and group decision making* (2nd ed., pp. 114-146). Thousand Oaks, CA: Sage.

Powell, W. W. (1990). Neither market nor hierarchy: Network forms of organization. *Research in Organizational Behavior, 12,* 295-336.

Propp, K. M. (1999). Collective information processing in groups. In L. R. Frey (Ed.), D. S. Gouran & M. S. Poole (Assoc. Eds.), *The handbook of group communication theory & research* (pp. 225-250). Thousand Oaks, CA: Sage.

Propp, K. M., & Nelson, D. (1996). Problem-solving performance in naturalistic groups: The ecological validity of the functional perspective. *Communication Studies, 47,* 127-139.

Putnam, L. L. (1989). Perspectives for research on group embeddedness in organizations. In S. S. King (Ed.), *Human communication as a field of study* (pp. 163-181). Albany: State University of New York Press.

Putnam, L. L., & Stohl, C. (1990). Bona fide groups: A reconceptualization of groups in context. *Communication Studies, 41,* 248-265.

Putnam, L. L., & Stohl, C. (1996). Bona fide groups: An alternative perspective for communication and small group decision making. In R. Y. Hirokawa & M. S. Poole (Eds.), *Communication and group decision making* (2nd ed., pp. 147-178). Thousand Oaks, CA: Sage.

Putnam, L. L., Van Hoeven, S. A., & Bullis, C. A. (1991). The role of rituals and fantasy themes in teachers' bargaining. *Western Journal of Speech Communication, 55,* 85-103.

Sabourin, T. C., & Geist, P. (1990). Collaborative production of proposals in group decision making. *Small Group Research, 21,* 404-427.

Seibold, D. R. (1994). More reflection or more research? To (re)vitalize small group communication research, let's "just do it." *Communication Studies, 45,* 103-110.

Seibold, D. R. (1998). Groups and organizations: Premises and perspectives. In J. S. Trent (Ed.), *Communication: Views from the helm for the twenty-first century* (pp. 162-168). Needham Heights, MA: Allyn & Bacon.

Shields, D. C. (1981a). A dramatistic approach to applied communication research. In J. F. Cragan & D. C. Shields (Eds.), *Applied communication research: A dramatistic approach* (pp. 5-13). Prospect Heights, IL: Waveland Press.

Shields, D. C. (1981b). Malcolm X's Black unity addresses: Espousing middle-class fantasy themes as American as apple pie. In J. F. Cragan & D. C. Shields (Eds.), *Applied communication research: A dramatistic approach* (pp. 79-91). Prospect Heights, IL: Waveland Press.

Shields, D. C. (1981c). The St. Paul fire fighters' *dramatis personae:* Concurrent and construct validity for the theory of rhetorical vision. In J. F. Cragan & D. C. Shields (Eds.), *Applied communication research: A dramatistic approach* (pp. 235-270). Prospect Heights, IL: Waveland Press.

Shields, D. C., & Cragan, J. F. (1981). A communication-based political campaign: A rhetorical and methodological perspective. In J. F. Cragan & D. C. Shields (Eds.), *Applied communication research: A dramatistic approach* (pp. 177-196). Prospect Heights, IL: Waveland Press.

Stohl, C. (1986). Quality circles and changing patterns of communication. In M. L. McLaughlin (Ed.), *Communication yearbook* (vol. 9, pp. 511-531). Beverly Hills, CA: Sage.

Stohl, C., & Holmes, M. E. (1993). A functional perspective for bona fide groups. In S. A. Deetz (Ed.), *Communication yearbook* (vol. 16, pp. 601-614). Newbury Park, CA: Sage.

Stohl, C., & Putnam, L. L. (1994). Group communication in context: Implications for the study of bona fide groups. In L. R. Frey (Ed.), *Group communication in context: Studies of natural groups* (pp. 285-292). Hillsdale, NJ: Lawrence Erlbaum.

Sykes, R. E. (1990). Imagining what we might study if we really studied small groups from a speech perspective. *Communication Studies, 41,* 200-211.

Thornton, B. C. (1978). Health care teams and multimethodological research. In B. D. Ruben (Ed.), *Communication yearbook* (vol. 2, pp. 539-553). New Brunswick, NJ: Transaction Books.

Wasserman, S., & Faust, K. (1994). *Social network analysis: Methods and applications.* Cambridge, UK: Cambridge University Press.

Wille, R. (1995). The basic theorem of triadic concept analysis. *Order, 12,* 149-158.

Wyatt, N. (1993). Organizing and relating: Feminist critique of small group communication. In S. P. Brown & N. Wyatt (Eds.), *Transforming visions: Feminist critiques of communication studies* (pp. 51-86). Cresskill, NJ: Hampton Press.

2

"Being a Part and Being Apart"

Dialectics and
Group Communication

SCOTT D. JOHNSON
University of Richmond

LYNETTE M. LONG
James Madison University

In recent years, interpersonal communication scholars have begun studying and theorizing about personal relationships through the lens of dialectical theory. This metatheoretical perspective highlights the mutually defining and processual nature of dialectical tensions that exist within, and form the context of, interpersonal relations. The application of dialectical theory to the study of interpersonal communication has engendered innovative scholarship that has recast theoretical assumptions, proposed alternative means for understanding and assessing relationships, and encouraged methodological eclecticism. To date, however, little systematic effort has been made to apply a dialectical perspective to the study of group communication. The purpose of this essay is to extend the metatheoretical insights of scholarship on dialectics to the concerns of group communication scholars, practitioners, and group members. In the sections that follow, we (a) provide a description of dialectics (from our view), (b) examine some specific ways this perspective can help expand our understanding of group communication, and (c) offer some important considerations for using this approach in group communication research. In so doing, it is our hope that this chapter inspires the reader to see and study group communication in new ways.

DIALECTICAL THEORY IN COMMUNICATION RESEARCH

Before we begin a discussion of the dialectical dimensions of group communication, the word "dialectic," which has an expansive

AUTHORS' NOTE: The authors would like to thank W. Andrew Atwood, Lee Beville, Erin Fox, Theresa Higgs, M. Scott Luchetti, and A. Townsend Tucker for their assistance in shaping the ideas in this essay.

history and carries varied connotative meanings, needs to be clarified. Dialectical theory has a rich history; here, we provide only a brief orientation to the literature, not an exhaustive review (for such a review, see Baxter & Montgomery, 1996).

Discussions of dialectic in the Western academy date back to ancient Greece. The word "dialectic" comes from a Greek word usually translated as "the art of debate." Plato privileged dialectic (i.e., debate) over rhetoric (i.e., persuasive monologue) as *the* means for reaching well-reasoned conclusions for action in civic and personal affairs. With its emphasis on reasoning and the use of contradiction and opposing positions to pursue the discovery of "Truth," dialectic was perceived by Plato to be in some sense superior to rhetoric. Aristotle, however, considered dialectic to be the counterpart to rhetoric and conceded that the general public did not have the time, patience, or education to participate in the sort of technical and tedious discourse that constituted dialectic; hence, he directed attention toward the art of speaking persuasively to public audiences on matters (preferably) decided through prior dialectic (debate). Aristotle recommended dialectic as the preferred method for debating propositions but encouraged ethical uses of rhetoric to deliver these conclusions to the public.

The ancient idea of dialectic as debate, particularly in the Aristotelian tradition, is largely epistemological; that is, it is a means for gaining insight and knowledge that, with few exceptions, remained the special province of philosophers until the 19th and 20th centuries when it was revived as a means of viewing human social processes. Most particularly, through the original and extended works of Hegel (1812-1816/1929, 1807/1931), Marx (1867/1906), Mead (1934), Burke (1962), Beauvoir (1968), and Bakhtin (1981, 1986), among others, dialectic was gradually transformed from a method of epistemic inquiry into an ontological framework and axiomatic, pragmatic social consideration. The view of dialectic as a method of reasoning has, thus,

shifted to include new views—ones suggesting that dialectic is inherent to all social phenomena. Although these new conceptualizations of dialectic have branched off from traditional thinking of dialectic as debate, they have retained an explicit emphasis on inherent elements of debate (particularly opposition and interaction) in human communication. Contemporary uses of dialectic in communication, then, include both the traditional form of epistemic inquiry (dialectic as debate) and more recent forms that examine ontological and practical relational exigencies that are present and pressing in all human communication (dialectic as "dialogue"). As we discuss in greater detail shortly, the "dialectic as dialogue" view considers social phenomena to be derived from and literally constituted within what are variously termed dialectical tensions, oppositions, or contradictions. These tensions (e.g., the tension between autonomy and connection—between remaining an individual and blending with another/others) are thought to be inherent to all relationships and serve to inspire our communicative behavior.

Recent use of dialectic in communication theory is prevalent in contemporary discussions of qualitative methods, particularly those inspired by feminist approaches to inquiry. Indeed, the second wave of feminism, inspired, in part, in the 20th century by Beauvior's (1968) work, can be viewed in one sense as the study of the dialectical tensions (i.e., inherent contradictions) and relational exigencies existing for women within modern patriarchal social systems that divide and hierarchize the sexes. Indeed, much feminist work has investigated the contradictions of women's lives, particularly as women struggle to find their "voice" and a self in relation to others while not being bound to oppressive notions of femininity and domination (see, e.g., Bartky, 1990; Belenky, Clinchy, Goldberger, & Tarule, 1986; Gilligan, 1982). Growing out of a heritage of public persuasion and interpersonal consciousness-raising for women's liberation, some contemporary feminist inquiry is inherently and characteristically dialectical in that it seeks to understand, through dialogue, the fundamental tensions that exist in women's lives and how women negotiate them (Westkott, 1979). In meeting others and generating knowledge, in finding one's "voice" and yet remaining connected to others, this feminist sense of dialectic is grounded in communication (Lorde, 1984). Through the work of feminist theorists (and many other social theorists), dialectical theory is being shaped and transformed to describe the everyday pragmatics of interpersonal interactions within contexts of human difference.

One of the most significant influences on the transformation of dialectical theory toward a notion of dialogue is the work of Russian intellectual and literary critic Mikhail Bakhtin (1981, 1986). Bakhtin's dialogic view has only recently become the focus of scholars studying relational communication, but it provides an approach that promotes relational equity and the potential for tensions to be conceived of and managed as ongoing, omnipresent social forces rather than as recurrent problems needing resolution. The use of a dialectical/dialogical frame to study the pragmatics of interpersonal relationships has been significantly deepened in recent years through the systematic work of interpersonal communication scholars, such as Baxter (1988, 1990, 1993), Goldsmith (1990), Montgomery (1993), and Rawlins (1983, 1989, 1992). For example, Rawlins (1983) examined 10 intensive case studies and found that dialectical tensions were inherent to the strategic maintenance of close friendships. As he explained,

> Many decisions to reveal or conceal are situational or topic-centered and involve accumulated knowledge of the other person, relational precedents, and tacit agreements regarding discretion. . . . Appropriately managing the persisting dilemmas of candor versus restraint engenders a mode of mutual interaction simultaneously expressive and protective that permits the ongoing exchange of personal ideas and emotions between two people. (p. 13)

As Rawlins's work showed, dialectical tensions such as candor/restraint are at the core of ongoing friendships, and awareness of these tensions is crucial to the successful negotiation and maintenance of these relationships.

Baxter's (1988, 1991, 1993) early investigations of dialectical tensions in romantic relationships have progressed from a more dualistic approach toward a dialogic stance (cf., Baxter 1988, 1994; Baxter & Montgomery, 1996). In her early studies, Baxter demonstrated that romantic relations (and, presumably, other relations as well) manifest a number of dialectical tensions, including autonomy/connection, openness/closedness, and novelty/predictability. She also found that couples manage these tensions in different ways, with some management processes said to be more effective than others at maintaining the relationship. Later work demonstrated how relationships themselves are constituted in talk inspired by negotiations of relevant relational dialectics (see Goldsmith & Baxter, 1996).

Recently, Baxter and Montgomery (1996) developed a thorough and compelling explication of dialectical theory for the study of interpersonal communication. Here, we draw on their work, relying on the four central tenets of contradiction, change, praxis, and totality, to lay the basic foundation of a dialectical perspective useful for the study of group communication.

Contradiction

In dialectical thinking, contradiction (also termed "opposition" or "tension") is the driving force underlying all social interaction. Baxter and Montgomery (1996) described social interaction as "the dynamic interplay between unified oppositions" (p. 8), and they indicated that attributes of sociality gain their meaning and significance to interactants through their interpreted relationship to other attributes. For example, the notion of "relational connection" of one partner to another has meaning because of its relationship to "autonomy"—disconnection from others. Similarly, "certainty" has meaning because of its relationship to "uncertainty," and "openness" has meaning because of its relationship to "closedness." However, these relational attributes are not clearly defined and concrete ("A/Not A"); each might best be viewed as a "fuzzy set" of concepts intricately related to other fuzzy sets ("A/B-Z . . . "). For example, the complex idea of certainty might be opposed by unpredictability, novelty, mystery, excitement, uncertainty, and so forth, in ways that generate unique but pragmatic meanings (Baxter & Montgomery, 1996). These tensions do not function in a dualistic way, with choices made between mutually exclusive polar opposites, but as ongoing "pulls," with each tension exerting continual pressure in opposing directions on relational partners and creating exigencies that must be negotiated through communicative action. Thus, there is a simultaneous draw toward seemingly contradictory forces such as certainty and mystery, autonomy and connection, predictability and novelty. These forces aren't simply polar opposites; rather, they are inextricably related, with an "inseparable interconnection and struggle of the opposite(s)" (Cornforth, 1971, p. 69) that suggests each force gains its significance from the other in an inherent, ongoing relationship. These relational tensions, or dialectics, create a complex web of forces, intertwined so that adjustments to one have an impact on others. One might picture a set of strings meeting centrally (a "hub" or a "knot," as Cornforth, 1971, p. 111, suggested) and stretching out in all directions. Should the hub be adjusted (via a specific communicative behavior chosen in response to a dialectical tension) toward one end or another of one of the strings (e.g., toward greater connection and away from personal autonomy), the other strings are affected, and thus, new adjustment is required. This process of adjustment continues with

each shift, regardless of size or intent, creating the need for additional adjustments. For dialectical theorists, then, relationships are literally constituted by the communicative responses to these various tensions, and each behavioral choice represents an adjustment that "plucks the strings" and, thereby, creates a cacophony of relational tensions, exigencies, and adjustments.

To illustrate this "dynamic interplay of tensions," consider the case of a romantic couple (familiar to one of the authors) who dated nearly a year. One partner, a devout Catholic, envisions a future raising children within the Catholic faith, whereas the other partner, devoutly Jewish, envisions raising children within the Jewish faith. In their day-to-day efforts to manage tensions related to openness/closedness (choosing at times to/not to discuss their conflicting views of faith, visions of the future, etc.), they inevitably experience in varying intensity tensions related to autonomy/connection (i.e., "Should we stay together despite our differences or separate because of them?"). Their ultimate decision to break off the relationship (a life-changing response to the autonomy/connection tension), despite their sincere desire to remain together "out of love," might well have come in response to their choices regarding openness/closedness (and, of course, other tensions, such as "ideal/real"). The female partner stated, "I just couldn't lie to him or me anymore. I had to tell him how I felt, and it meant we couldn't be together. We hate it, but we know that's what it means." Thus, the tensions experienced, and the behaviors chosen in response to them, created a complex web of opposition and adjustment, managed moment to moment by these partners throughout the course of their relationship.

Change

To remain intellectually honest, a dialectical theorist cannot simply say, "Relationships continually change." Change must be viewed as existing dialectically with stability. As Baxter and Montgomery (1996) explained,

"Stability punctuates change, providing the 'baseline' moments by which change is discerned. Put simply, dialectical change is the interplay of stability and flux" (p. 10). Although some relational conceptualizations view "positive" changes as those that are made toward greater relational connection or openness and "negative" changes as those that are made away from connection or openness (e.g., Altman & Taylor's, 1973, social penetration theory), a dialectical perspective is not similarly teleological in nature. There is no ideal end-state toward which a relationship progresses; instead, dialectical tensions always exist, and relationships are crafted within and through them. Hence, the goal is not stability or even little change; rather, the goal is understanding and working flexibly and effectively within a fluid, changing web of human tensions and responses.

Praxis

How do relational partners manage various dialectical tensions? As Baxter and Montgomery (1996) explained,

[Dialectical theorists] emphasize communication as a symbolic resource through which meanings are produced and reproduced. Through their jointly enacted communication choices, relationship parties respond to dialectical exigencies that have been produced from their past interactional history together. At the same time, the communicative choices of the moment alter the dialectical circumstances that the pair will face in future interactions together. (p. 14)

Dialectical tensions in social relationships, thus, produce exigencies to which members must respond if the relationship is to continue (given, again, that relationships are constituted within these tensions and responses). Communicative behaviors (varying in mindfulness and intention) are chosen in response to the dialectical tensions at work in the relationship within the relevant contexts. Over time, patterns of behavior emerge from the communicative choices partners make as they

attempt to return to those communicative behaviors that have successfully served to manage tensions in the past. However, the nature of the given situation, the present influence of new or recurring struggles and tensions, and the continuing creation of narrative relational culture may serve to make such communication patterns more or less effective over time, producing the need for ongoing behavioral adjustments. The notion of praxis refers to the (mindful or mindless) efforts of relational parties to respond to dialectical exigencies and, thereby, play out the "dynamic interplay of oppositions" in lived experience. As the relationship continues, ritualized responses to relational tensions come to constitute the relations themselves—that is, they become part of the relational culture (Wood, 1982).

In the example given previously of the interfaith romantic couple, the partners engaged in various avoidance behaviors during the early part of their relationship regarding issues of religious faith. These behaviors became ritualized and facilitated the continuance of the relationship, but at a later point in their relationship, in response to new exigencies created by pressing changes in employment and locale, their behaviors changed, as evidenced by the woman saying, "I just couldn't lie to him or me anymore." The changes in the ways they attempted to manage the tensions—what Baxter and Montgomery (1996) called "praxis patterns"—thus, came in response to changes in context.

Totality

In dialectical theory, *totality* suggests a way of viewing the world that does not seek generalizations of behavior or the search for predictable and certain variables. Instead, the social world is understood as a world in process—one that is fleeting and shifting, with phenomena understood only in relationship to other phenomena. Communication (not merely cognition) is the foundation of reality and relationships, and interpreted meanings and subsequent actions are critical components in evaluating situational communication competence. Behavioral choices, relational partners, and social forces all must be viewed in context (within a given time and place), because context influences the tensions that are present and pressing, and it shapes the communicative resources members can bring to bear in responding to those exigencies. The time and space of the interactions—or "chronotope" (Bakhtin, 1981)—become crucial considerations in how interactional partners interpret and respond to dialectical exigencies.

A dialectical perspective is, thus, fundamentally rooted in the dynamic interplay of ubiquitous tensions and relational exigencies grounded in the constitutive functions of communication. Dialectical tensions and exigencies are inherent to social interaction and inspire communicative adjustments by interactants to the choices they make moment by moment, day by day, to define their relationship. To understand "the relationship," we must consider the partners, their behaviors, and the dialectical tensions all together, within a given context of time, place, and history (i.e., chronotope). In contrast to the totality of a dialectical approach, traditional atomistic approaches provide a comparatively limited view of communication. In a dialectical perspective, however, totality suggests that the synergistic whole (partners, tensions, responses, and context) must be considered to gain an adequate view of situated social interaction.

THE TANGLED WEBS OF GROUP INTERACTION

The question of what is a small group has been answered variously by scholars, with definitions focusing on elements of members' commonality, goals, fate, structure, or interaction (see Shaw, 1976). Adopting a dialectical perspective offers new opportunities for defining groups and provides additional ways to address some of the essential "why" and "how" questions asked about group commu-

nication. Specifically, the dialectical perspective proposed here provides a view of the small group as being born from contradiction and change and founded on mutual and ongoing member influence. The primary foci are on the tensions and exigencies inherent in group interaction and on members' communicative behaviors (including their interpretations of their own and others' communication) as responses to them.

An essential starting point for applying dialectical theory to the small group is with the theory's conceptual "messiness." This is not a theory that lends itself to simple models of group interaction or platitudinous statements that provide "keys" to successful group membership. Rather, dialectical perspectives thrive in abstractness and deliberately break with the traditions of social-scientific research to make group communication processes (processes that are, themselves, messy, ambiguous, and in flux) understandable in new ways. As Murphy (1971) suggested, dialectical theory is "destructive of neat systems and ordered structures, and compatible with the notion of a social universe that has neither fixity or solid boundaries" (p. 90). Groups and their communication processes are constituted within the inherent tensions—and efforts to respond to those tensions—present in human interaction. Such tensions are not limited to dyadic relationships, as studied in current interpersonal communication scholarship, but extend to all social interaction, including that which occurs in groups.

Extant group communication scholarship has, with few exceptions (see Adelman & Frey, 1994; Frey, 1994; Poole, Seibold, & McPhee, 1985), employed approaches that are either monologic (unidimensional, unidirectional, with singular variables) or dualistic (bidirectional, involving static polar opposites—such as Bales, 1950). Monologic approaches are well illustrated in group communication pedagogy. Students of group communication learn about, for example, members who adopt roles, behave according to norms, follow leaders, and use various decision-making methods to solve problems. They hear about cohesiveness (with more cohesive groups said to be more effective), group maturity, and the development of group culture as progressing through stages in a fairly linear manner (e.g., Fisher, 1970; Tuckman, 1965). Dualistic approaches are also well illustrated in research that studies group concepts paired with their polar opposites. For example, Bales's (1950, 1970) classic interaction process analysis for studying group communication is based on dichotomies such as "seems friendly/seems unfriendly" and "agrees/disagrees." Such views are appropriate and useful, but the picture they paint of groups is hardly complete. Our desire here is to move from monologic and dualistic conceptualizations of the group toward a dialectical conceptualization—one that values the pragmatic adjustments members make through their communicative responses to the dialectical tensions and exigencies of group life.

From a dialectical perspective, a group might be conceived as follows: *A group is constituted in the dynamic interplay of dialectical tensions, exigencies, and communicative responses among members of an assembly within its relevant contexts.* The emphasis in this description is on the tensions—the dialectics themselves—and on the communication that constitutes and manages these tensions. People begin responding to these dialectics immediately upon entering a group through their communicative behavior and, thereby, create other dialectical tensions and exigencies; thus, the sum of the tensions and members' responses, within the group's relevant contexts, literally *is* "the group." The tensions may vary from group to group (and even from context to context within the same group), and members' efforts to manage these tensions are diverse and vary in magnitude of influence, but the focus on these elements is the heart of a dialectical perspective.

Consider, for instance, the first moments of a "leaderless, zero-history, task-oriented group." It is axiomatic that the initial minutes of such a group are typically uncomfortable for members, involve tentative communication, and are formative in shaping future group practices. But why is this so? Dialectical theory approaches these moments with a focus on the tensions that characterize social interaction and examines how the group members begin to manage them through communicative behavior. By maintaining the focus on tensions, responses, and contexts, dialectical scholars can follow a group's history from its first moments and observe how and why the group becomes what it becomes and does what it does.

Group Norms as Communicative Responses to Dialectical Exigencies

As one way to further envision what a dialectical approach "looks and sounds like," we begin with an examination of the familiar notion of group norms, as informed by the tenets of contradiction, change, praxis, and totality. *Norms* are commonly characterized as implicit or explicit guidelines that establish limitations for group members' behavior. Bormann's (1990) concise definition of norms as "shared expectation of right action" (p. 180) alludes to the expectation of conformity by group members to what is perceived as "correct" behavior. Conformity to group expectations has remained a prominent theme across the decades in group scholarship, with research often focusing on the development of norms and their enforcement with violators (e.g., Festinger, Schachter, & Back, 1968; Katz, 1982; Moscovici, 1985; Sherif, 1936). Such definitions and corresponding research, however, obscure the dialectical nature of norms and their development within groups. They suggest that norms are developed and followed by group members in a fairly clean, linear manner, with some behaviors on the "right" side of a line and some behaviors on the "wrong" side. But what makes some behaviors right and others wrong within a group, and why does that change? In fact, why do groups establish norms at all, and why do members adhere to them? Such questions are usually addressed via general, rather than specific, assertions (e.g., "The human animal apparently has a strong desire to follow the herd," Ellis & Fisher, 1996, p. 128). A dialectical perspective, in contrast, reframes entirely the notion of group norms and, thereby, offers opportunities to explore such questions in new and fruitful ways.

Norms are perhaps the clearest evidence of the influence of dialectical tensions on group members' behavior. At their very essence, norms represent group efforts to respond to contradictions; that is, norms are developed as members experience dialectical tensions and attempt to manage them through their communication. These ongoing tension management attempts result in patterns of communicative behavior; if these patterns prove effective at managing tensions at any given time, they may well be repeated. The tensions, of course, are not eliminated at this point. As a group's history continues, the patterns of behaviors are either repeated or not, depending on their perceived effectiveness, as responses to the ongoing presence of tensions within a changing context. Hence, adopting a dialectical perspective allows an initial answer to the question of why groups create norms: Quite simply, groups create norms (patterns of communicative behavior) as responses to ongoing dialectical tensions and exigencies.

Viewing norms from a dialectical perspective means moving away from the idea of shared, self-governing behaviors on either side of a "line of correctness" to behaviors created in response to a web of tensions and relational exigencies. A norm isn't a tangible "thing" (i.e., an implicit code that differs from an explicit rule only because it has not been written or otherwise formalized) to which one does or does not adhere; rather, it is the result of the dynamic interplay of tensions created by and constituting a group. This complex set of tensions is not easily reduced to simple oppositions (e.g., norms/chaos), but rather, at each end of each dialectic is a somewhat fuzzy set of pressures, all intricately intertwined with the others, that serve to guide group members' behaviors through conformity is-

sues. Hence, following a norm isn't akin to choosing whether to step over a specific line; rather, a single norm involves members in complex processes of negotiation and choice making within dialectical exigencies. As members choose their communicative behaviors, the various relational and contextual influences create further tensions to which they must adjust. In addition, the range of possible communicative behaviors is indeterminate, and any given behavior might serve to violate a norm in one instance and adhere to it in another, further complicating members' choices. To violate a norm is to respond in a manner that creates new tensions that must then be managed, that increases the awareness (and, therefore, influence) of already prominent tensions, or both. Because tensions can be quite strong and may create significant discomfort as they are experienced by group members, it seems likely that members typically enact those behaviors that seem to manage the tensions most effectively (i.e., reducing the discomfort) at any given time.

One can identify particularly potent dialectical tensions and exigencies by examining the norms most readily apparent at a given time. Consider a brief example:

> One member of a stoic, highly task-oriented business group begins to cry and blurts out that he has received a preliminary diagnosis that suggests he has a life-threatening illness. This group has never before discussed personal issues in meetings, and the members are initially baffled about how to respond; they sit there for several moments in stunned, uncomfortable silence.

This member's startling openness not only serves to reemphasize previously experienced tensions, thus far managed through the use of low levels of self-disclosure, but it may also serve to establish the significance of new tensions—for example, warmth/coldness, caring/disinterest, or approach/avoidance. Thus, norms are not only a way to define group behavior ("a shared expectation of right action"); they can also be viewed as manifestations of group members' efforts to manage the many tensions within which their interaction is created. Norms become obvious in their repetition (or absence) as patterns of communicative behavior and, thereby, make relevant dialectics more readily apparent.

To make this more clear, while simultaneously highlighting its complexity, here is another specific extended example drawn from a set of observations and student journal entries collected by one of the authors:

> Upon assembly, one undergraduate student group in a small group communication course created norms of minimal social interaction, strong task focus, and high productivity. They worked longer, faster, and were awarded higher grades on assignments during the first half of the course than any other group. A few of the other class members ridiculed the group members because of their behavior, calling them "brownnosers." Although most members of this particular group did not find these external pressures compelling, two did. Their performance within the group subsequently diminished, and the group itself became much less productive and the members became much less satisfied overall.

According to students' journal entries, the initial norms seem to have been derived from strong tensions related to esteem (from how one is perceived by fellow group members), with several members viewing themselves as top students in competition with one another. The other students in the group responded by raising their own levels of performance as well. (One student wrote, "This group has really helped me work hard . . . harder than I do for most classes. . . . I mean, it's not like I want them to think I'm stupid.") The dynamic interplay of tensions such as apathy/investment or inclusion/exclusion (among many others), and member management of these tensions as initiated by the higher achievers and adopted by the lower achievers (possibly in response to other face-related tensions), created expectations for group members to work hard and achieve their goals. However, when pressures

from outside the group increased (as other students teased members of this group), the lower achieving members adjusted their behavior, and ultimately, the group norms changed. These students experienced tensions from both within and outside the group that inspired their behavioral adjustments; these adjustments, in turn, created new tensions in the group that, of course, again required management. (The same student quoted previously later wrote, in reference to other group members, "I don't care what they think of me.")

Several important insights about dialectical tensions and their management can be gained from this example. First, as we have mentioned, the idea of contradiction includes the assumption that each dialectical tension is composed not of clear, distinct poles but of interconnected, opposing pressures. To conform to a group norm is not usually as simple as choosing between two specific behaviors. Conformity in the preceding case might include tensions such as remain/leave, investment/apathy, and comply/defy all at the same time, each a slightly different manifestation of similar tensions. The presence of apathy (which is fuzzy in the sense that it could involve issues such as punctuality, time commitment, and disinterest) gives significance to the conformity pressure for investment (similarly fuzzy), and this interconnectedness creates the ongoing nature of group member communication. These group members didn't simply resolve the tension by conforming to the group's initial task norms and then moving on. Rather, the tensions that inspired the initial norms continued throughout the group's life and created the need for ongoing choice making. That is, the members didn't solve this tension by putting in high-level effort throughout the course of the group's life; at each moment, members chose the amount of effort they would put forth, choosing again and again, meeting to meeting and task to task.

Hence, a dialectical view of norms examines more than simply conforming/not conforming in regard to any specific behavior. A dialectical perspective sees norms as patterns of communicative behavior established and continued (or not) as responses to ongoing tensions. When a member violates a norm, new tensions are created and adjustments are required. Sometimes the behavior is quickly extinguished—by self-reflection or sanction from others—because the discomfort the tension creates is too much for the group members to manage. Other times, the behavior is initially disruptive but then quickly embraced, and members adapt to the tensions by adjusting expectations and creating new patterns of communicative behavior (e.g., as one student wrote, "We never teased each other before, but after Bob ripped on Eric that way and everyone, even Eric, laughed, teasing became normal"). Overall, members make complex, sometimes difficult choices as they manage conformity tensions that are, at their essence, group-established attempts to manage dialectics.

The complex web of dialectical tensions and responses that constitute group communication is intricate and likely obscured by static evaluations of groups. The previous example focused on just one set of behaviors within a particular group. We could have chosen to expand our consideration to include the group members' sense of humor, the roles played by specific members, or the final task products of this group, and considered the web of tensions and its influence on each, or all, of these (or other) elements. Moreover, each individual members' communicative behavior might also be examined as a response to tensions, or certain types of communication behaviors (e.g., those related to decision making or leadership) might be considered. Overall, though, the notions of change and totality suggest that applying a dialectical viewpoint requires more than a simple identification of two or three relevant tensions that seemingly explain an aspect of group life. Instead, this perspective involves scholars, educators, practitioners, and group members in a holistic, in-depth study of tensions and responses across several levels of a group's experience and within its relevant contests.

The Multidimensional Nature of Dialectics in Groups

As suggested in the previous example, dialectics function simultaneously at different levels for members of groups. This multidimensionality means that dialectics in groups are not readily ascertained by using static models of explanation or formulas. In addition to dialectics within the group, dialectics exist between a group and those outside of it. Moreover, interpersonal-level dialectics are intertwined with group-level dialectics. Dialectics are also present in group discussion as members find the very content of their work fraught with conflict and collective decision-making dialectics. Hence, doing a dialectical analysis means creating a fluid, multidimensional image of a group that accounts for tensions across a variety of levels and in a manner that facilitates ongoing study. It also necessitates viewing the locus of the tensions as based in relationships rather than in the individuals. Dialectical tensions are jointly shared by interactants, regardless of whether that relationship is at the interpersonal, multipersonal (group), intergroup, or societal level. Although it is possible, even typical, that members' experiences of the same dialectics are dissimilar, the tensions themselves are "owned" by the relationships created via the formation of a group (see Baxter & Montgomery, 1996). Members behave in response to these tensions, sometimes in harmony with the choices of other members and sometimes in ways that are "out of sync" with those of others. In this way, tensions are both created and managed in the group members' ongoing interaction.

One of the central differences in applying a dialectical approach to groups as opposed to interpersonal relationships (as has primarily been the case thus far in communication scholarship) is the complexity created by the multidimensionality of a group; hence, the importance of developing a multidimensional view to study groups needs to be highlighted even further when using a dialectical approach. Here, we assert that dialectics operate on at least three internal levels (within a group), and on at least one external level (i.e., between a group and those outside it). Considering each of these levels, and their interrelationships, is an essential part of applying a dialectical perspective to the study of groups.

Internal dialectics. On at least three levels, dialectics exist within a group and influence members' behavior. First, as discussed earlier, there are interpersonal dialectics (see, e.g., Altman, 1993; Altman, Vinsel, & Brown, 1981; Baxter & Montgomery, 1996; Rawlins, 1992). Group members frequently engage in interpersonal dialogues, sometimes even talking about the group itself with another member. The dialectical tensions that create and are created by interpersonal relationships do not disappear when relational partners join a group; rather, they remain and influence (and are influenced by) group interaction. For example, two people who have worked together for an extended period of time and who have over the years become close friends might find their willingness to disagree with one another openly in a work group meeting either reduced or enhanced by their close relationship. In turn, other members who perceive the familiarity between these two friends might sense their communicative choices (going easier on or being tougher on one another than they are on other group members) and attempt to compensate for the friends' closeness by adjusting their own communicative behavior. Either way, the interpersonal dialectics are influenced by the group context and have influenced the larger group dynamics.

Second, there are dialectics between individual members and a kind of "generalized-group-other" audience (see Mead's, 1934, "generalized other" or Bakhtin's, 1986, "superaddressee"). When someone begins a meeting by saying, "Okay, let's get started. Is there any new business we should consider?" these comments are likely influenced by a sense of the group members as a whole, as though addressing a composite or "average" group member. The person's communicative choices may be directed by a sense of what he or she believes "they" expect or how "they" might react. When members speak up, they sometimes direct their comments to other individuals (and, thus, are influenced by interpersonal dialectics), but they also maintain a sense of what the larger group thinks as it (the generalized-group-other) observes. This relationship between the one and the combined many creates a set of dialectics to which members must respond and that might be perceived as both interpersonal and group level in nature. This also creates an abstract level of tensions for members, because individual communicative behaviors are now often chosen (somewhat self-reflexively) in relationship to a generalized "them." Evidence for the existence of this level as distinct from other levels exists in roles and role-specific norms. Scholars suggest that individual group members begin to exhibit unique behavioral patterns that serve various functions within the group, with these patterns typically called *roles* (e.g., Benne & Sheats, 1948; Hare, 1994). Associated with most roles are individualized expectations of each member by the larger group; hence, individual members relate to the group differently, and the group relates to each individual differently. Various tensions are more or less potent for each individual, and behavioral choices (and responses to these choices) are made with this unique relationship in mind. As individual members create patterns of behavior that vary from the overall patterns acceptable for the group in general, the group's communicative behaviors serve to encourage or discourage these patterns based on the tensions they create. When these unique individual patterns are accepted (and even rewarded), despite their variance from the larger group's more accepted patterns, the group and its members have responded to tensions operating on distinct (although intertwined) levels.

Third, there are group-level dialectics that influence and are influenced by all the members of a group and that are related most closely to norms (as previously discussed). The unique, synergistic nature of groups and the patterns of communication developed within each individual group provide evidence of dialectics at this level. As Ellis and Fisher (1996) suggested, "A group almost has a 'mind' of its own—a way of thinking and a pattern of emotions quite separate from those of the individual members" (p. 6). Groups manage tensions that relate to their social interaction, their members' willingness to express ideas, and their members' personal involvement in the group goals, among countless others. It is likely that numerous dialectics of varying degrees of significance potentially influence members' behavior in any given group at any given moment in the group's life.

External dialectics. The complexity of dialectics is not limited to multiple levels within a group; tensions are also created by the group's relationship with outsiders. The existence of these dialectics, which might be termed "external" dialectics (see Baxter & Montgomery, 1996, p. 16), finds support in the work of scholars who adopt the bona fide group perspective, with their assertions of permeable group boundaries and the interdependence of a group with its context (see Putnam & Stohl, 1990, 1996; Stohl & Putnam, 1994). External dialectics can exist between a group and its parent organization, a community, or the society in which it is embedded. For example, members of a university committee respond not only to tensions present between the committee members themselves, but the committee's permeable boundaries mean that the members also consider the views of the larger faculty, administrators, various communities within which the university resides, and perhaps the larger professional societal groups to which members belong. At each level, dialectics are present and influence members' communicative choices. One example might be found in a committee established to hire a new university president. Such committees are typically composed of members of the board of trustees (or other ad-

ministrators), faculty, staff, and students. As the committee meets, it works within the internal dialectics discussed earlier. However, the committee (or individual members of it) may also interact with the current university president; receive feedback from other board members, administrators, faculty, staff, or students; and hear comments from community members about the kind of person who should be hired. These various voices (internal and external) create a kind of chorus of tensions within which this group must operate and from which the group is derived. Literally, the group both is and becomes its responses to the dialectics at every level. Group members choose communicative behaviors in response to this chorus of tensions, and these behaviors, in turn, define the group.

The example given previously of students pressured by other students in class shows another illustration of the presence and influence of external tensions. In this case, the intertwined set of tensions pulled continually on the group members. They had to choose their behaviors from within these competing claims and manage the tensions in the group as they simultaneously managed tensions from outside. Some students in this group clearly found the influence of these external dialectics more and more compelling and eventually changed their initial patterns to manage within the group both the internal and external tensions. This decision, of course, created new tensions within the group, and the ongoing process of adjustment continued.

All of this complexity may lead one to wonder why, with so many levels and such conceptual fuzziness, a dialectical approach to the study of groups would be advocated. Is such an approach even possible on a practical level? We believe it is both possible and valuable for furthering our understanding of group communication. Ultimately, what we (and a few others, such as Barge & Frey, 1997; Frey, 1999; Smith & Berg, 1987, whose work on paradoxes in groups led to the notion of individuals' desire to be both a part of a group and apart from it, which we adopted for the chapter title) are advocating is a means of viewing group communication using (instead of ignoring) the paradoxical nature of social phenomena. A dialectical view looks at members' communicative behaviors, but it does not see them apart from the tensions that inspire them. It provides a different means of seeing below the surface of the traditional linear view into the nature and effect of group communication itself. Yet the question of how one might conduct a dialectical analysis of group communication remains. How might this perspective be enacted in research to develop greater insights into the communicative processes of groups? We now turn our attention to answering this question and drawing together our considerations of the multilevel nature of dialectics in groups.

Methodological Eclecticism

Applying a dialectical approach to the study of groups is undoubtedly a complex endeavor. However, the rewards go beyond identifying a specific aspect of relevant group communication or creating a model to help groups make decisions more effectively. A dialectical analysis involves the researcher in a comprehensive study of group communication and members' motivations for enacting selected communicative behaviors. It takes the researcher beneath the surface and into the foundation of a group.

One of the most tempting first steps in taking a dialectical approach is to attempt to assemble a list of *the* primary dialectics that characterize all groups. It seems, at first glance, as if identifying fundamental dialectics that groups experience would be the best initial course of action, with other elements (such as identifying methods of tension management) following later. Applying Baxter and Montgomery's (1996) assertions about interpersonal research to the study of groups, we suggest that the development of such a taxonomy should be a later, rather than an earlier, course of study. It may be that, after extensive time researching various groups, some

consistent primary dialectics will emerge. However, it is possible that there are countless dialectics, with each group a unique assembly of tensions and responses. That is, what might be a core dialectic in one group may be a minor dialectic in another. In addition, dialectical theory is not a static theory; it is grounded in the continual tension between stability and change. Hence, what may be a primary dialectic for a group today may become a tertiary dialectic for it tomorrow.

What is most needed at this early stage of dialectical research on groups is the pursuit of the *processes* by which dialectics are created and managed. Although identifying relevant dialectics for a specific group can be illuminating and useful, more useful is understanding how a group creates and manages those tensions—that is, how members create and recreate their group day to day within the tensions they experience. As one example, Adelman and Frey (1994, 1997), in their work on communication and community building at Bonaventure House, a residential facility for people with AIDS, have both identified relevant dialectics and examined the processes by which they are created and managed. Adelman and Frey identified important tensions, such as attachment/detachment, but the main contribution of their research is the focus in greater depth on how members of this particular group respond to those tensions using collective communicative practices and, thereby, maintain their group despite constantly changing membership. Such insights are useful to scholars, practitioners, and group members, as well as to members of other groups as they consider their own group processes.

Researching groups from a dialectical perspective places several demands on the researcher. First, it is essential that those who research dialectics be methodologically flexible. Because of its inherent complexity, dialectical analysis demands an eclectic approach that uses multiple methods to explore a group and its communication. The utility of diverse methods is highlighted by Montgomery and Baxter's (1998) edited work on using dialectical approaches in researching personal relationships. Their text contains essays on using ethnographic, narrative, and even quantitative approaches, among others, to study social phenomena using a dialectical frame. The diversity of methods in that text indicates both the complexity and opportunity of adopting a dialectical approach.

In addition to methodological flexibility, several elements seem essential to studying a group using a dialectical approach. First, whenever possible, a researcher should study a group from within as a participant-observer or should at least have a confederate who understands the project and can serve as both group member and observer. Observing a group in action, viewing patterns of behavior firsthand, seeing the intricacies of context, and even experiencing the dialectics personally when possible add vital depth to the research.

Obtaining the comments and interpretive insights of group members is also essential, even when the researcher or a confederate is a member of a group. Other members may see issues differently, experience tensions uniquely, and possess hidden motivations, and a researcher may discover such insights through interviews or possibly even questionnaires. A thorough dialectical analysis, therefore, will explore the communicative behaviors, motivations, perceptions, and feelings of group members. Furthermore, because participating personally in a group can potentially produce a myopic view, a researcher should pursue the members' perspectives to expand personal understanding. Group members can provide insights into what they intended by a specific comment or behavior, how they were feeling at a given time, or why they responded in a certain way to the comments of another.

A dialectical analysis should also seek to explore the complexity hidden within the various levels of internal and external tensions. For example, to understand a specific group (and its relevant tensions) within an organization, one might need to be familiar with that organization, its rules, and its history, as well as the roles of that specific group within the organization. If, for instance, one were not aware of an organization's history of firing whole employee groups that are unproductive, one could easily miss an important set of intense tensions during an analysis of a particular task group within that organization. A researcher should also examine the interpersonal dynamics and history among group members (prior to group membership if potentially relevant), because any such relationships will likely contribute to the group's dialectics. Overall, the researcher should consider as many levels of dialectics as possible and, thereby, demonstrate an expansive breadth in the research.

Ultimately, the goal of a dialectical analysis should involve more than a singular theoretical discovery or confirmation of a specific hypothesis; it should explicate the pragmatic processes by which group members create and manage tensions. Moreover, it should consider relevant dialectics throughout a group's history (or throughout as much of that group's history as possible). The relevant dialectics would likely change as the group changes, with new tensions resulting from ongoing adjustments in members' behavior. In the end, a substantive dialectical analysis will have theoretical value, pedagogical value, value to members of the group studied, and value to other such groups. Through its depth and breadth, it will explore beneath the surface to reveal the tensions and the processes they engender in a group. Such processes may be discussed in relation to group outcomes, such as effectiveness or satisfaction, but care should be taken in doing so to avoid conducting an analysis dialectically and then presenting results in a linear manner (e.g., "An effective group is one in which members use X communication practices to manage dialectic Y").

RESEARCH CONSIDERATIONS

A dialectical analysis involves in-depth exploration of group members' behaviors, perceptions, and motivations. Researchers who adopt this approach confront issues of confidentiality and potential personal harm to group members, because having a researcher examine members' views of one another, their individual and collective views of an organization (or supervisor), or their personal motivations is clearly a loaded enterprise. As a result, research itself becomes a dialectical endeavor. A researcher's relationship with group members potentially creates many tensions, as does the researcher's relationship with other scholars (e.g., tensions related to integrity, productivity, identity, privacy, and openness). Care must be taken, in the management of these tensions, to reduce the potential of harm to those studied.

A dialectical analysis of a group also requires several other important considerations. First, as discussed, the multiple levels on which dialectics occur among group members need to be examined. Although the preceding discussion highlights internal and external dialectics, the prominence of differing levels of dialectics will be unique from group to group. For example, a committee of officials assembled to review policies or procedures that could affect tax revenues for a geographical area would likely find external dialectics to be more prominent than, say, a group of college students engaged in an evening of movie watching. Such emphases do not mean the other levels aren't important to consider; rather, certain levels of dialectics are likely to be more influential than others at given times in a group's history.

This consideration leads naturally to another: A group is a work in process—an ongoing creation and re-creation that occurs through social interaction. This understanding places a researcher within a dialectic of sorts between the present and the future, between stability and change. The researcher must, of course, study a group within the moment of its present context (or chronotope), yet the researcher must also be aware that the group will continue to change. Specific levels and processes of dialectics are likely to be more prominent than others at any given point in a group's history, and they change as the group changes over time. The researcher, therefore, has no choice but to create findings in a here and now that changes continually.

A third consideration involves methodological rigor. If a group is changing continually, what does that suggest about making reliable and valid observations? That is, how can one replicate findings and/or be certain one is measuring what one purports to measure within a theory that holds change as a central tenet? Questions of reliability and validity in interpretive research have been adequately addressed by numerous scholars of qualitative methods (see, e.g., the essays in Denzin & Lincoln, 2000; also see Lincoln & Guba, 1985) who suggest that researchers can examine ongoing social processes in an appropriately rigorous manner despite an inability to stop or fully capture them. With dialectical analyses, as with any good research, methodological rigor is achieved through thorough, careful, and in-depth study. Although a group changes continually, evidence can certainly be gathered in support of conclusions drawn at any given time. In addition, the group members themselves can provide useful resources for examining conclusions. Given that members' motives, thoughts, and feelings are an integral part of a dialectical analysis, asking them to review conclusions (making "member checks") can often increase the validity of the research. For example, Adelman and Frey's (1994, 1997) research at Bonaventure House (cited previously) was a cooperative venture in which house members' responses to initial written drafts of research reports were incorporated into the final version. Indeed, the contract they worked out with house administrators mandated that such a review of participant perceptions occur. This *in situ* study is exemplary in nature and shows both some means and significance of applying a dialectical frame in group communication research.

CONCLUSION

A dialectical perspective is not new, nor are we the first to propose its application to social interaction. However, this perspective has not been applied sufficiently to group communication, and that is unfortunate, for it has much to offer this field. Recent attempts by scholars to inspire creative group communication research have met with some success, but we still have much to learn about group communication. Although group communication researchers have observed how leaders and decisions emerge, constructed lengthy lists of member roles, developed prescriptions for effective decision making, and espoused theories about social influence, they have too seldom gone beneath the surface in groups to study the interpretive, adaptive, and ongoing social processes that constitute and maintain them. Dialectical theory provides communication scholars, in particular, with an important means to study what and how a group becomes and remains a group. Examining dialectical tensions, and members' communicative responses to those tensions, provides group communication researchers with a new way to observe how communication constitutes groups rather than simply studying what groups do with communication.

REFERENCES

Adelman, M. B., & Frey, L. R. (1994). The pilgrim must embark: Creating and sustaining community in a residential facility for people with AIDS. In L. R. Frey (Ed.), *Group communication in context: Studies of natural groups* (pp. 3-21). Hillsdale, NJ: Lawrence Erlbaum.

Adelman, M. B., & Frey, L. R. (1997). *The fragile community: Living together with AIDS.* Mahwah, NJ: Lawrence Erlbaum.

Altman, I. (1993). Dialectics, physical environments, and personal relationships. *Communication Monographs, 60,* 26-34.

Altman, I., & Taylor, D. (1973). *Social penetration: The development of interpersonal relationships.* New York: Holt, Rinehart & Winston.

Altman, I., Vinsel, A., & Brown, B. B. (1981). Dialectical conceptions in social psychology: An application to social penetration and privacy regulation. In L. Berkowitz (Ed.), *Advances in experimental social psychology* (Vol. 14, pp. 257-273). New York: John Wiley.

Bakhtin, M. M. (1981). *The dialogic imagination: Four essays by M. M. Bakhtin* (M. Holquist, Ed.; C. Emerson & M. Holquist, Trans.). Austin: University of Texas Press.

Bakhtin, M. M. (1986). *Speech genres and other late essays* (C. Emerson & M. Holquist, Eds.; V. McGee, Trans.). Austin: University of Texas Press.

Bales, R. F. (1950). *Interaction process analysis: A method for the study of small groups.* Cambridge, MA: Addison-Wesley.

Bales, R. F. (1970). *Personality and interpersonal behavior.* New York: Rinehart & Winston.

Barge, J. K., & Frey, L. R. (1997). Life in a task group. In L. R. Frey & J. K. Barge (Eds.), *Managing group life: Communicating in decision-making groups* (pp. 29-51). Boston: Houghton Mifflin.

Bartky, S. L. (1990). *Femininity and domination: Studies in the phenomenology of oppression.* New York: Routledge.

Baxter, L. A. (1988). A dialectical perspective on communication strategies in relationship development. In S. Duck (Ed.), *Handbook of personal relationships: Theory research, and interventions* (pp. 257-273). Chichester, UK: Wiley.

Baxter, L. A. (1990). Dialectical contradictions in relational development. *Journal of Social and Personal Relationships, 7,* 69-88.

Baxter, L. A. (1991, November). *Bakhtin's ghost: Dialectical communication in relationships.* Paper presented at the meeting of the Speech Communication Association, Atlanta, GA.

Baxter, L. A. (1993). The social side of personal relationships: A dialectical perspective. In S. Duck (Ed.), *Social context and relationships: Understanding relationship processes* (Vol. 3, pp. 139-165). Newbury Park, CA: Sage.

Baxter, L. A. (1994). A dialogic approach to relationship maintenance. In D. J. Canary & L. Stafford (Eds.), *Communication and relational maintenance* (pp. 233-254). San Diego, CA: Academic Press.

Baxter, L. A., & Montgomery, B. M. (1996). *Relating: Dialogues and dialectics.* New York: Guilford Press.

Beauvoir, S. de (1968). *The second sex* (H. M. Parshley Ed. and Trans.). New York: Random House. (Original work published 1949)

Belenky, M. F., Clinchy, B. M., Goldberger, N. R., & Tarule, J. M. (1986). *Women's ways of knowing: The development of self, voice, and mind.* New York: Basic Books.

Benne, K. D., & Sheats, P. (1948). Functional roles of group members. *Human Relations, 9,* 41-49.

Bormann, E. G. (1990). *Small group communication: Theory and practice* (3rd ed.). New York: Harper & Row.

Burke, K. (1962). *A grammar of motives.* Berkeley: University of California Press. (Original work published 1945)

Cornforth, M. (1971). *Materialism and the dialectical method.* New York: International.

Denzin, N. K., & Lincoln, Y. S. (Eds.). (2000). *Handbook of qualitative research* (2nd ed.). Thousand Oaks, CA: Sage.

Ellis, D. G., & Fisher, B. A. (1996). *Small group decision making: Communication and the group process* (4th ed.). New York: McGraw-Hill

Festinger, L., Schachter, S., & Back, K. (1968). Operation of group standards. In D. Cartwright & A. Zander (Eds.), *Group dynamics: Research and theory* (3rd ed., pp. 152-164). New York: Harper & Row.

Fisher, B. A. (1970). Decision emergence: Phases in group decision making. *Speech Monographs, 37,* 53-66.

Frey, L. R. (1994). The naturalistic paradigm: Studying small groups in the postmodern era. *Small Group Research, 25,* 53-66.

Frey, L. R. (1999). Teaching small group communication. In A. L. Vangelisti, J. A. Daly, & G. W. Friedrich (Eds.), *Teaching communication: Theory, research, and methods* (2nd ed., pp. 99-113). Mahwah, NJ: Lawrence Erlbaum.

Gilligan, C. (1982). *In a different voice: Psychological theory and women's development.* Cambridge, MA: Harvard University Press.

Goldsmith, D. (1990). A dialectical perspective on the expression of autonomy and connection in romantic relationships. *Western Journal of Speech, 54,* 537-556.

Goldsmith, D., & Baxter, L. A. (1996). Constituting relationships in talk: A taxonomy of speech events in social and personal relationships. *Human Communication Research, 23,* 87-114.

Hare, A. P. (1994). Types of roles in small groups: A bit of history and a current perspective. *Small Group Research, 25,* 433-448.

Hegel, G. W. F. (1929). *The science of logic* (W. H. Johnston & L. G. Struthers, Trans.). New York: Macmillan. (Original work published 1812-1816)

Hegel, G. W. F. (1931). *The phenomenology of mind* (2nd ed., J. B. Ballie, Trans.). New York: Macmillan. (Original work published 1807)

Katz, G. M. (1982). Previous conformity, status, and the rejection of the deviant. *Small Group Behavior, 13,* 403-413.

Lincoln, Y. S., & Guba, E. G. (1985). *Naturalistic inquiry.* Beverly Hills, CA: Sage.

Lorde, A. (1984). *Sister outsider: Essays and speeches.* Trumansburg, NY: Crossing Press.

Marx, K. (1906). *Capital* (Vol. 1, S. Moore & E. Aveling, Trans.). Chicago: Charles H. Kerr. (Original work published in 1867)

Mead, G. H. (1934). *Mind, self, and society.* Chicago: University of Chicago Press.

Montgomery, B. M. (1993). Relationship maintenance versus relationship change: A dialectical dilemma. *Journal of Social and Personal Relationships, 10,* 205-224.

Montgomery, B. M., & Baxter, L. A. (Eds.). (1998). *Dialectical approaches to studying personal relationships.* Mahwah, NJ: Lawrence Erlbaum.

Moscovici, S. (1985). Social influence and conformity. In G. Lindzey & E. Aronson (Eds.), *The handbook of social psychology* (3rd ed., Vol. 2, pp. 347-412). New York: Random House.

Murphy, R. F. (1971). *The dialectics of social life: Alarms and excursions in anthropological theory.* New York: Basic Books.

Poole, M. S., Seibold, D. R., & McPhee, R. (1985). Group decision-making as a structurational process. *Quarterly Journal of Speech, 71,* 74-102.

Putnam, L. L., & Stohl, C. (1990). Bona fide groups: A reconceptualization of groups in context. *Communication Studies, 41,* 248-265.

Putnam, L. L., & Stohl, C. (1996). Bona fide groups: An alternative perspective for communication and small group decision making. In R. Y. Hirokawa & M. S. Poole (Eds.), *Communication and group decision making* (2nd ed., pp. 147-178). Thousand Oaks, CA: Sage.

Rawlins, W. K. (1983). Openness as problematic in ongoing friendships: Two conversational dilemmas. *Communication Monographs, 50,* 1-13.

Rawlins, W. K. (1989). A dialectical analysis of the tensions, functions, and strategic challenges of communication in young adult friendships. In J. A. Anderson (Ed.), *Communication yearbook* (Vol. 12, pp. 157-189). Newbury Park, CA: Sage.

Rawlins, W. K. (1992). *Friendship matters: Communication, dialectics, and the life course.* New York: Aldine de Gruyter.

Shaw, M. E. (1976). *Group dynamics: The psychology of small group behavior* (2nd ed.). New York: McGraw-Hill.

Sherif, M. (1936). *The psychology of social norms.* New York: Harper.

Smith, K. K., & Berg, D. N. (1987). *Paradoxes of group life: Understanding conflict, paralysis, and movement in group dynamics.* San Francisco: Jossey-Bass.

Stohl, C., & Putnam, L. L. (1994). Group communication in context: Implications of the study of bona fide groups. In L. R. Frey (Ed.), *Group communication in context: Studies of natural groups* (pp. 284-292). Hillsdale, NJ: Lawrence Erlbaum.

Tuckman, B. W. (1965). Developmental sequence in small groups. *Psychological Bulletin, 63,* 384-399.

Westkott, M. (1979). Feminist criticism of the social sciences. *Harvard Educational Review, 49,* 422-430.

Wood, J. T. (1982). Communication and relational culture: Bases for the study of human relationships. *Communication Quarterly, 30,* 75-84.

3

Foregrounding Feminist Theory in Group Communication Research

NANCY WYATT
Penn State University Delaware County

Previous feminist critiques have rendered problematic many aspects of traditional group communication scholarship, called for more attention to women's groups, and identified cooperation and collaboration as group processes that should inform research (see, e.g., Meyers & Brashers, 1994; Wyatt, 1994). Those efforts critiqued extant small group communication scholarship from a feminist perspective. In this chapter, I extend the feminist critique of group communication scholarship, beginning with feminist theory as the foundation of the essay to see what group communication scholars may have missed from this perspective.

Feminist theory differs from traditional scholarship mainly in centering attention on women's experiences and in dealing explicitly with issues of privilege and power. However, feminism is multivocal; there are many feminisms. Feminist scholars may identify themselves or be identified by others as liberal, radical, socialist, Marxist, postmodern, psychoanalytic, or standpoint feminists, among other labels. African American feminist scholars often call themselves "womanist" to distinguish their perspective from that of

mainly White mainstream feminism. All feminists, however, resist oppressive social practices toward women and other disenfranchised groups (see Bullis & Bach, 1996; S. K. Foss, 1997). Hence, feminist perspectives can offer valuable new directions for group communication scholarship. For this essay, I selected liberal, radical, and standpoint feminisms as perspectives from which to reconceptualize group communication research. Liberal feminism has already brought new perspectives to group communication scholarship, and radical feminism has had some limited influence as well. Standpoint feminism, however, has not yet been applied to the study of group communication.

Throughout this discussion, I use the term "feminism" instead of referring to "feminists" to emphasize that my analysis focuses on philosophical grounding and social practices, not on the work of individual scholars who may or may not identify with particular labels. In the following three sections, I describe each theoretical framework, explain its influence on group communication theory, and suggest new directions for group communication research that emerge from each perspective.

LIBERAL FEMINISM

Liberal feminism developed in the 19th century in the United States in response to women's lack of participation in the political sphere. For example, women in the United States were first allowed to vote in national elections in 1920 with the ratification of the 19th Amendment to the Constitution. In the 19th century and continuing into the 20th century, arguments against women's participation in the public sphere were grounded partly in a Western dualism that separated reason from emotion and assigned reason to men and emotion to women. Men were assumed to act in reasoned self-interest, whereas women were categorized with children and slaves as incapable of exercising responsible citizenship. Legal and social sanctions prevented all but the most courageous women from access to or participation in higher education, public speaking, political office, and most professions.

Early liberal feminists argued that women were equally as rational as men and at least as capable as men to participate in public affairs. Assuming that legal and political equality would end discrimination against women, liberal feminists did not question the basic liberal assumption that reasoned self-interest exercised on the level of the individual citizen is the basis of civil society. Liberal feminism today retains its concern for women's equal participation in the public sphere. Cirksena and Cuklanz (1992) identified Betty Friedan, Ellen Goodman, Barbara Jordan, Patricia Schroeder, Gloria Steinem, Faye Wattleton, and Molly Yard as well-known modern liberal feminists.

Liberal feminism made its way into group communication scholarship mainly through the study of gender differences as they relate to leadership. Studies have compared male and female leadership and perceptions of such leadership (for reviews, see Baird, 1976; Cragan & Wright, 1990; Duerst-Lahti & Kelly, 1995; Pearson, 1985; Shimanoff & Jenkins, 1996). Conclusions have been contradictory, partly because researchers made different assumptions about what constitutes leadership, used different methods to study leadership, and studied leadership in a wide variety of contexts. Few of these studies replicated previous studies; many of these studies confounded biological sex and gender roles.

In addition, most scholars reviewing studies of gender and leadership have failed to heed Korzybski's (1958) injunction to index their knowledge to reflect the fact that attitudes and social practices change over time. In their reviews of previous scholarship, many scholars have not distinguished between studies done in the 1950s and studies done in the 1980s. Hence, their reviews fail to acknowledge the impact of important social changes such as the advent of nonsexist language, affirmative action, and changing public perceptions of and attitudes toward women in leadership positions. Therefore, trends over time have not emerged clearly in the literature, although they may exist in reality.

Research questions concerning gender difference and leadership have been successful, however, in calling public attention to gender inequities in position, power, and authority and in the perception of women in leadership positions. Nevertheless, inequities remain, and hence, the liberal feminist goal of equal participation of women in the public sphere remains both desirable and elusive. Rather than speculating about whether women and men lead differently, are simply perceived to lead differently, or even whether putative differences are significant, other avenues of research from a liberal feminist perspective hold much promise for group communication scholarship.

Group communication scholarship can learn from the contributions that liberal feminism has made to rhetorical studies that reveal past achievements of women orators (e.g., Campbell, 1989, 1993), develop new feminist definitions of rhetoric (e.g., K. A. Foss & S. K. Foss, 1991; S. K. Foss, 1997), and focus attention on previously ignored rhetoric of marginalized women's groups (e.g., Wertheimer, 1997). Given that rhetoric always takes place within a group context, the attention of group scholars to feminist rhetorical studies of women's leadership would serve also to inform group communication theory. For example, a rhetor requires an audience. We need studies of the group processes that gathered audiences to listen to early female rhetors to supplement studies of their rhetoric. We need studies of the groups that sustained these women and their efforts in the face of sometimes extreme hostility from powerful antagonists.

A critical/historical approach to the study of male leadership led to the conceptualization of "groupthink" (Hart, 1994; Janis, 1982); critical/historical analyses of women's organizing and leadership might lead to similarly heuristic concepts. Sources and topics for such research are easily available. In 1917, for instance, the National American Women Suffrage Association (NAWSA), headed by Carrie Chapman Catt, had 2 million members and organized lobbying efforts from the national to the local level. NAWSA maintained a publishing house, a speakers' bureau, and a publicity service ("Suffragists' Machine," 1917). Critical/historical studies of women's leadership in this and other contexts, such as the women's club movement, can help rectify the false impression that women have historically not been leaders and, possibly, broaden our understanding of leadership.

Liberal feminism can also provide a useful framework for looking at previously undervalued or ignored group processes. Social activism, in which small groups work for the empowerment of minorities, is one such process. *Facts on File Encyclopedia of Black Women in America: Social Activism* (Hine, 1997) listed 64 women and 17 organizations whose social activism merits study. The same source noted that recent historical reassessments of the civil rights movement reveal that women's organizing efforts behind the scenes were much more influential than previously recognized. For example, Nasstrom (1999) documented extensive but unacknowledged work by women's groups in registering Black people to vote in Atlanta that preceded the growth of publicly recognized male leadership in that city. She also explained the process by which the press contributed to the invisibility of women's activities.

Although the male leadership of the National Association for the Advancement of Colored People (NAACP) and the Southern Christian Leadership Conference (SCLC) spoke out publicly against segregation laws, organizers such as Ella Baker, Septima Clark, Virginia Durr, and Fanny Lou Hamer raised money and recruited members for a variety of groups active in the civil rights movement in communities throughout the South. Citizenship schools developed at Highlander Folk School in Monteagle, Tennessee, and later run throughout the South by the SCLC taught African Americans how to read and how to register to vote. Voter registration drives coordinated by many groups, including the Student Nonviolent Coordinating Committee (SNCC), assisted African Americans to register to vote in the face of violent opposition by Whites. These are only a few examples of group efforts that have been undervalued in our understanding of the civil rights movement.

Group-centered leadership, a strategy articulated by Ella Baker (described in Payne, 1989) to integrate ordinary Black citizens into the civil rights movement, deserves more scholarly attention. Baker asserted that only mass participation of Black citizens who were allowed to set their own goals and develop their own organizational strategies for empowerment could sustain the civil rights movement over time. Baker argued against exclusive reliance on charismatic leaders such as Martin Luther King, Jr. Baker's ideas about group leadership influenced student leaders who organized the SNCC. Louis's (1997) eloquent description of grassroots organizing among "movement people" should inspire scholars to pay closer attention to social movements as an important site for theorizing about group communication in organizing and leadership.

Any exploration of the U.S. civil rights movement will inevitably lead to the Highlander Folk School mentioned earlier. This institution, founded by Myles Horton in 1930, facilitated the growth of union organizing in the South in the 1930s and 1940s and the civil rights movement in late 1950s and 1960s. Among other strategies, Highlander Folk School used drama and music as group processes to empower poor rural people to develop practical goals and confidence in their own ability to work for social change. Several accounts of the use of drama and music to empower oppressed people (Belenky, Bond, & Weinstock, 1997; Elias, 1993; Kaltoft, 1990; Petty, 1979) point to the importance of these activities in organizing for social change. Apparently, drama and music are instrumental in enabling oppressed people to create a vision of a new social order for which to strive. This vision, in turn, is instrumental in creating group solidarity that can inspire the personal courage necessary to resist the inevitable physical and psychological violence directed by authority against serious attempts at fundamental, structural social change. The relationships between music, drama, and empowerment of oppressed people deserve more scholarly attention from group communication scholars. Highlander Folk School is one good starting point for such investigations.

Studies of organizing and leadership in abolition, suffrage, prohibition, civil rights, feminist, and antiwar movements can add to our understanding of group communication. Studies of such successful organizing efforts can also demonstrate to scholars and the public at large that women have always been influential leaders. Accounts of traditions of women's leadership that have not been included in malestream history are beginning to appear (see, e.g., Belenky et al., 1997; Nasstrom, 1999). From such historical studies, communication scholars can develop new definitions, concepts, and accounts of group organizing and leadership to balance the male-centered, White, corporate models that currently dominate discourse about these concepts. In addition to mining historical sources from the United States, scholars should also broaden their vision to include accounts of women's organizing worldwide. Studies of women organizing for social change in Third World countries are rapidly expanding (e.g., Basu, 1992, 1995; Calman, 1992; Hust, 1998; Jeffrey & Basu, 1998; Momsen, 1991, 1993; Momsen & Kinnaird, 1993; Papa, 1995; Radcliffe & Westwood, 1993; Shefner-Rogers, 1998) and should be better represented in group communication scholarship.

In summary, liberal feminism argues for inclusion and equal valuation of women's participation and leadership in the political sphere. Within group communication scholarship, liberal feminism has focused primarily on understanding gender differences in group communication processes, mainly with respect to leadership. I have suggested that continued comparisons of women's and men's leadership behaviors offer limited value for scholars. Instead, historical and contemporary studies of social transformation efforts, such as the abolition, prohibition, labor organizing, antiwar, feminist, civil rights, and gay rights movements in the United States, as well as empowerment movements worldwide, offer fertile opportunities for expansion of group communication scholarship. Such studies may also lead to the development, elaboration, and refinement of group communication concepts and processes.

RADICAL FEMINISM

Liberal feminism has based its social action strategies on the twin assumptions that human nature is essentially rational and that rational critique of social inequities will eventually dismantle oppressive social structures. These assumptions, unfortunately, have not been borne out in the academy or the workplace. Acknowledging that social behavior is seldom rational, radical feminism has generally eschewed rational critique and chosen instead either to organize for social change or to create new venues for nontraditional research. This perspective has much to suggest for the study of group communication.

Summarizing radical feminism is difficult because it is extremely diverse, addressing a wide variety of social, political, and economic issues. In addition, radical feminism is more likely to be found in the activist community than in the academy; hence, such theory does not appear in forums familiar to most academic scholars who are not based in or conversant with feminist theory. Moreover, many accounts of radical feminism are written from the perspective of critics, not proponents; hence, these accounts are often hostile to the perspective. Still, some basic assumptions and positions of the perspective can be identified.

Cirksena and Cuklanz (1992) characterized radical feminism as concerned with the Western dualism of nature and civilization. Western philosophy has traditionally cast men as civilized, apart from and superior to nature, and women as close to nature and intrinsically uncivilized, like natural forces needing to be "tamed." The result of this dualism is a philosophical subordination of all things female and natural to all things male and civilized; social practices based on these philosophical premises lead to political structures that create and sustain male hegemony. Radical feminism envisions this power differential between women and men as primary and irrational and does not, therefore, expect rational argument to equalize the existing power structure. Consequently, radical feminism is usually activist in nature, often directly confronting the dominant power structure but occasionally withdrawing completely into separate women's communities.

The most common theme among radical feminist scholars is male violence against women and against nature (Cirksena & Cuklanz, 1992). Analysis of and suggestions for countering male violence against both women and nature has taken many forms, including the study of the misogynist nature of many languages, the development of ecofeminism, proposals for separate lesbian communities, and development of a separate women's spirituality. Mary Daly, Andrea Dworkin, Susan Griffin, and Catherine MacKinnon are well-known modern radical feminists. Drawing from Marxist theory, these and other radical feminist scholars define the "group" as essentially a site of struggle. This radical feminist perspective contrasts vividly with traditional malestream and liberal feminist scholarship, which assume that social structures result from cooperation among individuals and view conflict as deviant and dangerous. Radical feminism assumes struggle over power to be a basic social process; thus, conflict is both natural and inescapable.

Radical feminism has influenced communication scholarship mainly by drawing attention to the sexist nature of language, which serves to disempower women by casting them as "other" (Bullis & Bach, 1996) or reducing them to primarily sexual beings. Such attention has been largely successful; misogynist tendencies in language are now widely acknowledged and sexist language is no longer widely acceptable. At its inception, however, the critique of language as a carrier of misogynist messages was an extremely radical and controversial idea. Many years of scholarship and activism were required to establish, promote, and institutionalize nonsexist language guidelines. Rearguard actions against nonsexist language guidelines continue to be fought in popular and commercial venues.

Connections between language usage and groups are complex but profound. Language facilitates the creation and maintenance of groups by providing the labels and the shared terms that define group boundaries. Groups provide the context in which use of racist and sexist language and ideas flourish. Aryan Nation and the Klan, for example, provide havens for racism, expressed through language as well as action. Philipsen's (1975) study of the sexist use of language in Teamsterville documented connections between language and group identity. Sanday (1990) argued that verbalized hostility in fraternity houses and military units toward women and gays encourages violent behavior toward women and gays. Several studies (Kalof, 1993; Kalof & Cargill, 1991; Martin & Hummer, 1989) have reported that fraternity members are more likely than independent students to believe that it is legitimate for a man to use force to have sex with a woman. College athletes are more likely than other college men to use force to coerce women to have sex with them (Boeringer, 1996).

Currently, scholars are extending the critique of language to document linguistic bias against minorities, as evidenced, for example, in the connotations in English of "dark" and "black" as evil and "white" and "light" as good. Linguistic and cultural analyses of the concept of "Whiteness" are expanding scholarly understanding of the relationships between language and social structures and processes (see, e.g., Babb, 1998; Berbrier, 1998; Hill, 1997; Jackson, 1999; Nakayama & Martin, 1999). For example, language elements can function to separate people into privileged and oppressed groups. Clearly, more work remains to uncover verbal and linguistic elements in the encoding and enactment of privilege and oppression that characterize the drawing of group boundaries. Scholars have an important opportunity to study and redress the stratification of social groups through linguistic processes.

The connection between language and violence is another area deserving of scholarly attention. Work in this area has already begun, although it has thus far typically not been incorporated into group communication scholarship. For example, Elgin (1980, 1987) documented many patterns in English usage that create privilege and contribute to verbal and physical violence against subordinated groups. Elgin focused on medicine (Elgin, 1990a) and law enforcement (Elgin, 1990b) as two important sites of violence against women.

Elgin (1980) claimed that all physical violence is preceded by verbal violence; she developed "verbal self-defense" as a means to stop verbal violence. Verbal self-defense has four principles: (a) recognizing verbal violence, (b) recognizing the kind of verbal attack, (c) knowing how to fit the defense to the attack, and (d) knowing how to follow through with a specific linguistic defense. Re-

garding the first principle, Elgin explained that verbal attacks are recognizable by paralinguistic elements of the message, which she called "tunes." With regard to the second and third principles, Elgin worked out several common types of attack and responses for different contexts and situations. For example, the statement "I cannot understand how nurses can make such mistakes" may be a request for understanding or a verbal attack. Elgin (1990a) advised nurses to attend to intonation patterns to distinguish between the two different meanings and to respond appropriately. Nurses should respond to a request for information with relevant information: "One reason nurses make such mistakes is the difficulty of reading some physicians' handwriting." Nurses should respond to a verbal attack with a verbal defense: "Really, doctor? That doesn't speak very well for your understanding, does it?" The fourth principle, following through, identifies ways of preventing verbal violence. For example, the nurse in the previous example might suggest that the health care team analyze the situation surrounding the alleged mistake to make sure that no such mistakes happen in the future. Elgin's work deserves more attention from group communication scholars, because most verbal violence and harassment have a basis in group norms, through at least tacit social approval, if not through conscious support of the harassment.

One specific instance of verbal violence created and sustained through group communication processes is sexual harassment, a concern that has been extended from the workplace to the schoolyard. In *Davis v. Monroe County Board of Education* (Legal Information Institute, 1998), the U.S. Supreme Court recently held that school administrators are responsible for preventing peer-to-peer sexual harassment in their schools. In an exemplary study, Smith (1998) described ways in which gossip and graffiti in high school stigmatize homosexuality and create a hostile environment for homosexual students. Many girls suffer similar verbal violence as a normal part of their school experience. One common response to sexual harassment among school children, usually phrased as "boys will be boys," points to connections between group norms, language, and harassment. Hence, although it might appear to be the case, sexual harassment is not merely a situation involving a problem individual; rather, the climate of a group or organization supports abusive behavior toward women, homosexuals, and other stigmatized minorities. Thus, sexual harassment is a group-based phenomenon. Group communication scholars, however, have not yet systematically explored the connections between sexual and other forms of harassment, language, and group processes.

Hartman's (1987) study of housework as the locus of gender, class, and political struggle within the family draws from a Marxist perspective to provide another model for theorizing group process. Comparing family structures under capitalism with those in a subsistence economy, Hartman pointed out that the family is not only a kinship structure but also a location where production and distribution of goods and services take place.

To this point, I have suggested new directions for group communication research based on the radical feminist strategy of confronting male violence against women. A different radical feminist response to male power and violence has been to withdraw from patriarchal social structures to create separate communities of women or nonhierarchical social structures for both women and men. Some analysis of communication within women's groups has appeared in our field (Bate & Taylor, 1988); however, most of the groups studied were not radical, and many were not even feminist. Lont's (1988) study of the lesbian feminist folksinger Holly Near's efforts to create an egalitarian community of women within the context of commercial record production comes closest to a pattern for the type of research I am suggesting. A central question is the extent to which the irrational conflict and violence that characterize much group behavior derive from hierarchical social structures or from biological sources. Studies of communities of

women or communities organized in nonhierarchical structures may shed light on that basic question.

Scholars who take a historical or critical approach will find abundant opportunities to study communication within groups that have disengaged from dominant social structures, given that many utopian or religious groups have established communities outside mainstream dominant patriarchy. For example, in 1857 Rebecca Cox Jackson established an all-Black Shaker community that existed until the 1900s (Hine, 1997); this was only one of many all-Black settlements established in the 19th century. The study of such groups, informed with a radical feminist sensitivity to issues of power within the community and between the community and the outside world, should expand our understanding of the processes of discrimination, oppression, and liberation as manifested in communicative practices.

Belenky et al. (1997) recount organizing within several different women's groups in Germany, in Mississippi, on Long Island, and in the Bronx. These groups shared a style of organizing and type of leadership that Belenky and her colleagues called "developmental leadership," because the process aims to develop the capacity of all members of the group to work for social change. The organizing described by Belenky et al. was similar to the type of organizing encouraged at Highlander Folk School (Wyatt, 1998), especially with regard to its emphasis on the use of art, music, and drama to empower a vision of new possibilities. Leaders engaged in dialogue with community members and concentrated on listening instead of speaking. The goal of the process was to develop community members' communication competence and confidence so that action to change the existing social structure came from community members themselves, not from an outside agent.

In summary, radical feminism assumes that human nature is irrational and that conflict is intrinsic to group process. Radical feminism suggests to group communication scholarship a focus on the relationships between language, groups, and violence against women. I have suggested that group communication scholars look more closely at the intersections of group communication and the processes of oppression and privilege. I have also suggested that sexual harassment is better characterized as a dysfunctional group process than as an individual phenomenon. Radical feminism suggests the study of collaborative or developmental leadership, as well as the study of alternative groups and communities as important sites for group communication research.

STANDPOINT FEMINISM

In contrast to the grounding of liberal and radical feminisms in individualism and ontology, standpoint theory begins from a social perspective and from epistemology. That is, standpoint feminism begins from a different place with a different set of questions. Specifically, standpoint feminism begins from the perspective of the social structure and looks at individuals as positioned within and, hence, at least partly created by their location within that social structure. For standpoint theory, then, a "group" is defined as a collection of individuals similarly positioned within a larger social structure; hence, to a very large extent, the group creates the individual.

Standpoint theory, which emerged from Marxist analysis of material conditions of living, observes that groups of people occupy different positions within hierarchically organized social structures:

> The notion of standpoint refers to groups having shared histories based on their shared location in relations of power—standpoints arise neither from crowds of individuals nor from groups analytically created by scholars or bureaucrats. . . . [Standpoint] is a common location within hierarchical power relations that creates groups, not the results of collective decision making of the individuals within the groups. Race, gender, social class, ethnicity, age, and sexuality . . . emerge as fundamental devices that foster inequality resulting in groups. (Collins, 1997, p. 376)

Standpoint theory begins with epistemology, asking how knowledge is created and validated. Specifically, standpoint theory contests the assumption of any common framework for understanding or participating in an interaction by emphasizing the inescapable positionality of epistemology (Hekman, 1997; Longino, 1993). Hence, for standpoint theory, there are not just multiple perspectives but multiple knowledges. Standpoint feminism focuses on the production of knowledge about and by women from their own unique standpoint in a social hierarchy.

Specifically, standpoint feminism calls to our attention the twin issues of privilege and power. Standpoint theory notes that some social positions are privileged, whereas others are marginalized. Social position, consequently, facilitates and constrains both ways of knowing and relative power within social structures. Standpoint theory holds that knowledge is not the product of an individual intellect or a particular research program but instead inheres in the standpoint from which the knower views the social scene. Hence, multiple knowledges are not equally valued within the larger social structure. Because women as a group occupy a relatively lower position in the social hierarchy than men, women's knowledge has been marginalized and devalued.

Moreover, standpoint theorists argue, individuals within a standpoint may not even be aware of their positionality or of the limited vision their positionality affords them. For example, slave owners, as a ruling class, controlled the production of knowledge in their societies; slaves' knowledge was never formally recognized nor validated within those societies. Standpoint theory argues that slaves had important particular and intimate knowledge of slavery as a social system that should have been recognized and validated. Similarly, standpoint feminism focuses on the subordination of women and argues that women's knowledge has not been recognized or validated by men, who have largely controlled the production of knowledge through their privileged position in the social structure. Standpoint feminism is, therefore, intrinsically activist in nature, arguing for development and validation of knowledge from women's subordinated position within hierarchical social structures.

Because the definition of group that emerges from this perspective is a radical change from the definition traditionally used in our field, one might ask how to connect standpoint feminism with group communication scholarship. A case study in medical decision making illustrates some ways in which standpoint feminism might produce new insights into group process. Anspach (1987) studied how decisions were made to terminate life support for infants in neonatal intensive care units. She conceptualized the hospital as a hierarchically organized social structure that allocates different knowledge to persons occupying different strata within that social structure—that is, nurses, residents, and attending physicians. Anspach described considerable dispute among nurses, residents, and attending physicians regarding the prognosis for individual babies. Attending physicians and residents used a combination of technological cues (results of various tests and procedures) and perceptual cues from physical examinations to derive a prognosis for each infant. Nurses, however, used interactive cues and their own emotional responses to the infants as sources of knowledge to derive prognoses for the infants. Physicians devalued the nurses' knowledge, citing its basis in feelings; when opinions differed, the physicians' opinions won out. Anspach concluded, "The status of the various forms of knowledge closely parallels the stratification of the various occupational groups" (p. 227).

Anspach considered but rejected an argument that gender played a part in the devaluation of the nurses' information, because female physicians relied on the same technological cues as male physicians. Standpoint feminism, however, argues that gender is not exclusively an aspect of the individual but is associated with hierarchical positions within organizations (Keller, 1985). Traditionally, physicians have been male and nurses female;

hence, their bases of knowledge are similarly gendered. Because women have traditionally been responsible for maintenance and support functions best served by attending to interactive cues, both the maintenance roles and the forms of knowledge associated with those roles have also become "gendered" as female. These maintenance roles and the knowledge derived from relationships have subsequently been devalued, whether women or men serve those functions. Therefore, female physicians have adopted traditionally "male" roles and ways of knowing, and male nurses must adopt traditionally "female" roles and ways of knowing. Gender does, indeed, play an important role in determining which standpoint is valued more highly, but standpoints as well as persons may be gendered.

A second example in a different context demonstrates the power of standpoint feminism to provide new directions in group communication scholarship. Louis's (1997) account of "Bagel Babies," young Jewish women in the North who supported the civil rights movement financially and morally, reveals the way in which a position within a social hierarchy can influence the development of values, communication choices, and strategies for action. The Bagel Babies were encouraged by their liberal parents to improve race relations through analysis and discussion in youth groups. Louis explains that the ideological conflicts between these young women, who drew parallels between the Nazi treatment of Jews and southern treatment of Blacks, and their parents, who didn't understand why Black Americans could not improve their lot just as immigrant Jews from Hitler's Germany had improved their lot, derived from their differing standpoints. Louis's explanation demonstrated as well the development of another standpoint for Jewish boys, whose parents strongly encouraged them to develop professional careers to support families. Consequently, young Jewish men who made a commitment to civil rights had to make a complete break with their parents and were much more likely to become full-time movement personnel than were young women, whose commitment could be demonstrated by fund-raising and discussion within their own social circles.

The implications for group communication scholarship of standpoint feminism are complex. However, in this chapter, I have chosen to develop two: the process of consciousness-raising and the design of research studies. The relationship between standpoint feminism and consciousness-raising draws on two tenets of standpoint theory: the definition of standpoint and the observation that persons occupying a standpoint may not be aware of their own positionality. Members of a standpoint group share a common history and common experiences and knowledge, but they may never have met or interacted with one another. Only by meeting and talking with one another can the individual members who occupy a common position become aware not only of their positionality but also of their unique and valuable knowledge. We can trace the growth and development of consciousness-raising through a variety of social movements: the temperance movement, the abolition movement, the feminist movement, the civil rights movement, and more recently, lesbian and gay rights movements. The process by which individuals become aware that their situations, including oppression from which they suffer, result not from their own failings but from social power structures that systematically oppress them is called *consciousness-raising*. This process consists mainly in sharing and analyzing common experiences through group storytelling and discussion (Chesebro, Cragan, & McCullough, 1973).

Consciousness-raising ignited the second wave of feminism in the United States, but the process has also been used in many lesser known contexts. For example, Highlander Folk School used such a process to empower labor and civil rights organizers in the South from 1930 through 1970 (Horton, 1997) and is currently using the process with environmental groups in the South. Belenky et al. (1997) described several women's groups that used consciousness-raising to achieve political

and social goals. Freire (1970) and his colleagues in Latin and South America used community education grounded in consciousness-raising to empower the poor to political activism. Bell (1996) studied consciousness-raising to empower girls in an inner-city elementary school. Jane Sapp (reported in Elias, 1993) used consciousness-raising among Black people in the Mississippi Delta. Consciousness-raising, thus, offers fertile ground for group communication scholarship in a variety of contexts.

The connections between knowledge and the methods of generating knowledge are the focus of the second point in this discussion of standpoint feminism. Standpoint feminism requires reconfiguring the research process to foreground status and power differences between researchers and those with whom they work, because an important goal of standpoint theory is to validate knowledge from previously marginalized standpoints. Standpoint feminism also requires that an account of the process of negotiating those differences be included in reports of research, because the process of generating knowledge is as important as the knowledge itself. Feminist standpoint scholars are, thus, challenged to design truly collaborative studies.

Standpoint feminism presents significant challenges for academic researchers, who, in general, occupy social positions that mediate, if not actively support, governing structures that authorize and fund social research: universities, corporations, and government agencies. Universities, as well as sponsoring agencies or corporations, are centers of social power with opportunities, means, and, often, motives to stifle dissent. Warren's (1982) appendix to *The Court of Last Resort*, for instance, described an account of the influences exerted on her research reports by her relationships with influential persons in the courts in which she conducted her research, as well as by funding sources and other gatekeepers in the publishing process. The paradox facing a communication scholar who wants to work from standpoint feminism is not only to understand the world from the perspective of the marginalized group with which she is working but also to negotiate with funding sources to conduct the research project in a way that will respect the values, goals, and perspectives of her collaborators.

Applied anthropology, although not the only discipline to struggle with these issues, has considerable experience with "collaborative" or "participatory" research, which can serve to demonstrate some of the methodological approaches that have been developed. Since the 1960s, many applied anthropologists have been concerned with helping marginalized groups that have relatively little access to social, political, and economic resources. Over the years, they have developed three approaches to such research (Stull & Schensul, 1987). Some applied anthropologists have chosen to build the capability of marginalized groups to design their own research studies and to advocate on their own behalf with external agencies and institutions. Other applied anthropologists represent the perspective of marginalized groups in institutionally supported academic research programs. Still other applied anthropologists build connections between marginalized groups and external research or social service agencies, brokering the process of research. Each of these approaches has advantages and drawbacks, but they all would achieve the goals of standpoint feminism to foreground issues of privilege and power in the research process and to represent the perspectives of marginalized or oppressed groups in the creation of knowledge.

Standpoint feminism offers group communication scholars opportunities to collaborate with marginalized women whose knowledge has not been represented in our theories and to validate their knowledge. Because much of this knowledge is very likely to be carried in shared stories or in activities such as mothering, group communication researchers will find research methods pioneered by applied anthropologists and ethnographers most useful for working with such groups.

In summary, standpoint feminism begins with epistemology, defining a group's standpoint as a common position within a hierarchical social structure characterized by members' common experiences and history. Privileged standpoints have controlled the creation of knowledge, whereas knowledge generated from oppressed or subordinated standpoints has generally not been recognized or validated by the ruling classes. Standpoint feminism calls for increased attention to the standpoints of women and to the intersection of their standpoints with other standpoints, such as race and class. Consciousness-raising, a process by which members of a standpoint come to recognize their common oppression, is one promising site of research on group communication suggested by this perspective. Scholars working from standpoint feminism foreground power differences between themselves and their collaborators, negotiate with collaborators the choice of research goals and methods, and present findings from the varied perspectives of all parties to the research project.

CONCLUSION

Feminism provides a broad range of theoretical, philosophical, and methodological possibilities for enriching and expanding our understanding of group communication and the role of groups in creating and sustaining larger social structures, as well as influencing individual behavior. I have described three feminisms and indicated actual and potential contributions of these perspectives for group communication scholarship. Liberal feminism calls attention to women's historical role in the development of social structure and to the history of women's leadership that has not been adequately recognized or validated. Radical feminism emphasizes connections between language and violence and between oppression and subordination. Standpoint theory encourages new understanding of the political processes that influence the creation of knowledge and also encourages self-reflective research practices that deal explicitly with issues of power and privilege.

Liberal feminism is concerned with women's participation in political decision making and suggests for research historical and critical analyses of that participation. Studies of women's organizing in the temperance, abolition, suffrage, union organizing, prohibition, feminist, and civil rights movements will create a better-balanced account of women's participation and leadership in the public sphere. Analysis of women's organizing in social activism, as well as the traditions of women's leadership worldwide, may lead to the development of new perspectives on group communication. The use of music, art, and drama in creating and sustaining community in social activism provides valuable opportunities for group scholars.

A radical feminist perspective suggests some of the same themes, as well as additional opportunities. Radical feminism focuses mainly on male violence against women and nature and promotes analysis of the connections between language, privilege, power, and violence in a variety of contexts. Sexual harassment is one such context, but verbal violence unrelated to sex also calls out for our attention. The assumption that conflict is a basic social process can lead to new ways of analyzing primary groups such as the family. The application of Marxist analysis of economic and political influences on groups also suggests new foci for research. In particular, radical feminism suggests historical as well as sociological attention to groups and communities outside the mainstream that attempt to create nonhierarchical and egalitarian forms of organization.

Standpoint feminism offers a primarily epistemological basis for theorizing about group process. The twin assumptions that knowledge is inherently situated in material conditions of living and that all standpoints have value for society suggest consciousness-raising as an important focus for group communication scholarship. Standpoint feminism promotes collaboration in designing participatory research programs and the reporting and validating of all participants' perspectives and knowledge. Standpoint feminism, thus, encourages scholars to imagine and work toward the creation of more egalitarian social structures.

Feminist theories are still relatively new within group communication scholarship. Adopting the feminist perspectives that I have advocated in this chapter presents both opportunities and challenges to communication scholars. Perhaps the most important opportunity that emerges is a focus on community organizing and social activism. Women have been acknowledged leaders in many social movements, such as the temperance, abolition, and, of course, feminist movement. Recent scholarship, however, demonstrates that much of the civil rights movement also rested on women's community organizing and fundraising to a far greater extent than previously recognized. Group communication scholars, thus, have the opportunity to expand their understanding of the dynamics of groups working for social change.

Another major theme that unites the three feminist perspectives is increased collaboration between scholars from many different disciplines who are working on issues of privilege and power in group contexts. Other than those in communication, I have cited the work of historians, anthropologists, and independent feminist scholars, but the themes explored in this chapter also suggest collaboration with scholars in economics, political science, art, music, and literature, as well as applied fields such as social work.

Feminist perspectives offer a variety of new and very promising directions for group communication research. Attention to women's organizing and participation in social activism, especially to their own perspectives on those experiences, and attention to the topics of power, privilege, subordination, and liberation hold great promise for new directions in group communication research that should occupy scholars well into this new millennium.

REFERENCES

Anspach, R. R. (1987). Prognostic conflict in life-and-death decisions: The organization as an ecology of knowledge. *Journal of Health and Social Behavior, 28,* 215-231.

Babb, V. M. (1998). *Whiteness visible: The meaning of Whiteness in American literature and culture.* New York: New York University Press.

Baird, J. E., Jr. (1976). Sex differences in group communication: A review of relevant research. *Quarterly Journal of Speech, 62,* 179-192.

Basu, A. (1992). *Two faces of protest: Contrasting modes of women's activism in India.* Berkeley: University of California Press.

Basu, A. (Ed.). (1995). *The challenge of local feminisms: Women's movements in global perspective.* Boulder, CO: Westview.

Bate, B., & Taylor, A. (Eds.). (1988). *Women communicating: Studies of women's talk.* Norwood, NJ: Ablex.

Belenky, M. F., Bond, L. A., & Weinstock, J. S. (1997). *A tradition that has no name: Nurturing the development of people, families, and communities.* New York: Basic Books.

Bell, L. A. (1996). In danger of winning: Consciousness-raising strategies for empowering girls in the United States. *Women's Studies International Forum, 19,* 419-427.

Berbrier, M. (1998). White supremacists and the (pan-)ethnic imperative: On "European-Americans" and "White Student Unions." *Sociological Inquiry, 68,* 498-516.

Boeringer, S. B. (1996). Influences of fraternity membership, athletics, and male living arrangements on sexual aggression. *Violence Against Women, 2,* 134-147.

Bullis, C., & Bach, B. W. (1996). Feminism and the disenfranchised: Listening beyond the "other." In E. B. Ray (Ed.), *Communication and disenfranchisement: Social health issues and implications* (pp. 3-28). Mahwah, NJ: Lawrence Erlbaum.

Calman, L. J. (1992). *Toward empowerment: Women and movement politics in India.* Boulder, CO: Westview.

Campbell, K. K. (1989). *Man cannot speak for her.* New York: Greenwood Press.

Campbell, K. K. (Ed.). (1993). *Women public speakers in the United States, 1800-1925: A bio-critical sourcebook.* Westport, CT: Greenwood Press.

Chesebro, J. W., Cragan, J. F., & McCullough, P. (1973). The small group technique of the radical revolutionary: A synthetic study of consciousness raising. *Communication Monographs, 40,* 136-146.

Cirksena, K., & Cuklanz, L. (1992). Male is to female as ____ is to ____: A guided tour of five feminist frameworks for communication studies. In L. R. Rakow (Ed.), *Women making meaning: New feminist directions in communication* (pp. 18-44). New York: Routledge.

Collins, P. H. (1997). Comments on Hekman's "Truth and method: Feminist standpoint theory revisited": Where's the power? *Signs: Journal of Women in Culture and Society, 22,* 375-381.

Cragan, J. F., & Wright, D. W. (1990). Small group communication research of the 1980s: A synthesis and critique. *Communication Studies, 41,* 212-236.

Duerst-Lahti, G., & Kelly, R. M. (Eds.). (1995). *Gender, power, leadership, and governance.* Ann Arbor: University of Michigan Press.

Elgin, S. H. (1980). *The gentle art of verbal self-defense.* New York: Dorset.

Elgin, S. H. (1987). *The last word on the gentle art of verbal self-defense.* New York: Prentice Hall.

Elgin, S. H. (1990a). *Language in emergency medicine: A gentle art of verbal self-defense handbook.* Huntsville, AR: Ozark Center for Language Studies Press.

Elgin, S. H. (1990b). *Language in law enforcement: A gentle art of verbal self-defense handbook.* Huntsville, AR: Ozark Center for Language Studies Press.

Elias, D. G. (1993). *Educating leaders for social transformation.* Unpublished doctoral dissertation, Teachers College, Columbia University, New York.

Foss, K. A., & Foss, S. K. (1991). *Women speak: The eloquence of women's lives.* Prospect Heights, IL: Waveland Press.

Foss, S. K. (1997). Transforming rhetoric through feminist reconstruction: A response to the gender diversity perspective. *Women's Studies in Communication, 20,* 117-135.

Freire, P. (1970). *Pedagogy of the oppressed* (M. B. Ramos, trans.). New York: Herder & Herder.

Hart, Paul 't. (1994). *Groupthink in government: A study of small groups and policy failure.* Baltimore: Johns Hopkins University Press.

Hartman, H. I. (1987). The family as the locus of gender, class, and political struggle: The example of housework. In S. Harding (Ed.), *Feminism and methodology: Social science issues* (pp. 104-134). Bloomington: Indiana University Press.

Hekman, S. (1997). Truth and method: Feminist standpoint theory revisited. *Signs: Journal of Women in Culture and Society, 22,* 341-365.

Hill, M. (Ed.). (1997). *Whiteness: A critical reader.* New York: New York University Press.

Hine, D. C. (Ed.). (1997). *Facts on file encyclopedia of Black women in America: Social activism.* New York: Facts on File.

Horton, M. (1997). *The long haul: An autobiography.* New York: Columbia University Press.

Hust, E. (1998). The empowerment of women in India: Grassroots women's networks and the state. *Contemporary South Asia, 7,* 373-375.

Jackson, R. L. (1999). White space, White privilege: Mapping discursive inquiry into the self. *Quarterly Journal of Speech, 85,* 38-54.

Janis, I. L. (1982). *Groupthink: Psychological studies of policy decisions and fiascoes* (2nd ed.). Boston: Houghton Mifflin.

Jeffrey, P., & Basu, A. (Eds.). (1998). *Appropriating gender: Women's activism and politicized religion in South Asia.* New York: Routledge.

Kalof, L. (1993). Rape-supportive attitudes and sexual victimization experiences of sorority and nonsorority women. *Sex Roles, 29,* 1-14.

Kalof, L., & Cargill, T. (1991). Fraternity and sorority membership and gender dominance attitudes. *Sex Roles, 25,* 419-425.

Kaltoft, G. (1990). *Music and emancipatory learning in three community education programs.* Unpublished doctoral dissertation, Teachers College, Columbia University, New York.

Keller, E. F. (1985). *Reflections on gender and science.* New Haven, CT: Yale University Press.

Korzybski, A. (1958). *Science and sanity: An introduction to non-Aristotelian systems and general semantics* (4th ed.). Lakeville, CT: International Non-Aristotelian Library.

Legal Information Institute. (1998). *Supreme Court collection.* Retrieved May 1, 2000 from the World Wide Web: http://supct.law.cornell.edu/supct/htm/97-843.ZS.html

Longino, H. E. (1993). Feminist standpoint theory and the problems of knowledge. *Signs: Journal of Women in Culture and Society, 19,* 210-212.

Lont, C. (1988). Redwood Records: Principles and profits in women's music. In B. Bate & A. Taylor (Eds.). *Women communicating: Studies of women's talk* (pp. 234-250). Norwood, NJ: Ablex.

Louis, D. (1997). *And we are not saved: A history of the movement as people.* Columbia, MD: Press at Water's Edge.

Martin, P. Y., & Hummer, R. A. (1989). Fraternities and rape on campus. *Gender & Society, 3,* 457-473.

Meyers, R. A., & Brashers, D. E. (1994). Expanding the boundaries of small group communication research: Exploring a feminist perspective. *Communication Studies, 45,* 68-85.

Momsen, J. H. (1991). *Women and development in the third world.* London: Routledge.

Momsen, J. H. (Ed.). (1993). *Women and change in the Caribbean: A Pan-Caribbean perspective.* Bloomington: Indiana University Press.

Momsen, J. H., & Kinnaird, V. (Eds.). (1993). *Different places, different voices: Gender and development in Africa, Asia, and Latin America.* London: Routledge.

Nakayama, T. K., & Martin, J. N. (Eds.). (1999). *Whiteness: The communication of social identity.* Thousand Oaks, CA: Sage.

Nasstrom, K. (1999). Down to now: Memory, narrative, and women's leadership in the civil rights movement in Atlanta, Georgia. *Gender & History, 11,* 113-144.

Papa, M. J. (1995). Dialectic of control and emancipation in organizing for social change: A multitheoretic study of the Grameen Bank in Bangladesh. *Communication Theory, 5,* 189-223.

Payne, C. (1989). Ella Baker and models of social change. *Signs: Journal of Women in Culture and Society, 14,* 885-899.

Pearson, J. C. (1985). *Gender and communication.* Dubuque, IA: William C. Brown.

Petty, A. W. (1979). *Dramatic activities and workers' education at Highlander Folk School 1932-1942.* Unpublished doctoral dissertation. Bowling Green State University, Bowling Green, OH.

Philipsen, G. (1975). Speaking "like a man" in Teamsterville: Culture patterns of role enactment in an urban neighborhood. *Quarterly Journal of Speech, 61,* 13-22.

Radcliffe, S. A., & Westwood, S. (Eds.). (1993). *"Viva": Women and popular protest in Latin America.* London: Routledge.

Sanday, P. R. (1990). *Sex, brotherhood, and privilege on campus.* New York: New York University Press.

Shefner-Rogers, C. L. (1998). The empowerment of women dairy farmers in India. *Journal of Applied Communication Research, 26,* 319-337.

Shimanoff, S. B., & Jenkins, M. M. (1996). Leadership and gender: Challenging assumptions and recognizing resources. In R. S. Cathcart, L. A. Samovar, & L. D. Henman (Eds.), *Small group communication: Theory and practice* (7th ed., pp. 327-344). Madison, WI: Brown & Benchmark.

Smith, G. W. (1998). The ideology of "fag": The school experience of gay students. *Sociological Quarterly, 39,* 309-335.

Stull, D. D., & Schensul, J. J. (Eds.). (1987). *Collaborative research and social change: Applied anthropology in action.* Boulder, CO: Westview.

"Suffragists' machine perfected in all states under Mrs. Catt's rule." (1917, April 29). *New York Times,* p. 8.

Warren, C. A. B. (1982). *The court of last resort: Mental illness and the law.* Chicago: University of Chicago Press.

Wertheimer, M. M. (Ed.). (1997). *Listening to their voices: The rhetorical activities of historical women.* Columbia: South Carolina University Press.

Wyatt, N. (1994). Organizing and relating: Small group communication from a feminist perspective. In S. P. Bowen & N. Wyatt (Eds.), *Transforming visions: Feminist critiques in speech communication* (pp. 51-86). Cresskill, NJ: Hampton Press.

Wyatt, N. (1998, July). *Using group process to facilitate social and political change: Lessons from the Highlander Folk School.* Paper presented at the XVI International Colloquium on Communication, Eotvos Lorand University, Budapest, Hungary.

PART II

Methodological Procedures

4

Ethnographic Practices in Group Communication Research

NATALIE J. DOLLAR
Oregon State University

GERIANNE M. MERRIGAN
San Francisco State University

Over the past few decades, a number of scholars have criticized group communication research for its reliance on the study of groups, primarily student groups, in the laboratory (Bormann, 1970; Cragan & Wright, 1980, 1990; Frey, 1994c; Putnam & Stohl, 1990; Sykes, 1990). More recently, communication scholars have turned their attention toward the study of natural groups (see, e.g., the collection of essays in Frey, 1994b, 1995, in press). These studies, many of which are case studies, offer scholars, students, and practitioners new insights into group communication processes and practices. Case studies, for example, have advanced our understanding of antecedent influences on group problem-solving and decision-making communication, as well as of the role of environmental influences on group communication (see Gouran, 1994).

The focus on natural groups, as opposed to zero-history, laboratory groups, poses significant methodological considerations (see Frey, 1994a, 1994c). In response to these consider-

ations, a number of scholars have embraced the naturalistic paradigm—and more specifically, ethnography—to study group communication. The goal of this chapter is to show how this conceptualization and methodological pursuit can yield important insights into group communication. Although it is not our intent to provide a full explication of ethnography and its benefits as applied to the study of group communication, it is important to characterize what we treat as ethnography to provide readers with a sense of the types of studies covered in this review. We begin with a succinct overview of the naturalistic paradigm and move quickly to a discussion of ethnography as both a theory and method that can profitably guide group communication research.

ETHNOGRAPHY AND THE STUDY OF GROUP COMMUNICATION

As noted earlier, ethnography arises from the naturalistic paradigm, an approach to studying human behavior that is different from, yet compatible with, traditional social-scientific research. According to Lincoln and Guba (1985), assumptions of this paradigm include the acknowledgment of (a) multiple constructed realities; (b) the researchers' inherent bias or value position, both in the research design and analysis of data; and (c) the situatedness of human behavior, in a particular context, at a particular time, never to be repeated. Frey (1994c) used these assumptions as starting points from which to lay out his call for group communication research using the naturalistic paradigm. Some of the methodological consequences for naturalistic group communication research that Frey discussed included, but are not limited to, making observations in situ, in the groups' natural contexts; concentrating on group communication processes other than group decision making, such as relational communication; studying groups other than classroom, laboratory, and business-type groups, such as family, peer, and social support groups; and using qualitative methods, such as participant observation, in-depth interviewing, and textual analysis. It is the intent of naturalistic researchers to use these and other naturalistic methods to produce "thick descriptions" (Geertz, 1973) that do justice to the complexity of natural human behavior—natural group communication processes in this case.

Ethnography is but one type of communication research emerging from the naturalistic paradigm; others include, but are not limited to, performance studies, discourse analysis, and conversation analysis. Ethnography is a term used to reference both methods and theories; however, the term "ethnographic methods" does not imply the use of ethnographic theory, and the term "ethnographic theories" does not imply the use of ethnographic methods. Although some group communication scholars pursue research considered ethnographic theory, which we discuss later in this section, other communication scholars have combined ethnographic methods with nonethnographic macro-level

theoretical perspectives. Lesch (1994), for instance, used ethnographic methods to collect data and symbolic convergence theory rather than ethnography of communication, for example, to inform her data analysis. Although all research reviewed in this chapter employed ethnographic methods, only some can be considered ethnographic theory.

Ethnographic methods are intended to provide researchers with means for collecting data that can be used to construct a descriptive account of the phenomena being investigated. Ethnographers seek to provide an explanation of sorts, an account that takes seriously the participants' perspective by foregrounding it. Ethnographic methods, such as participant observation, allow researchers to know and understand by doing and participating, albeit at different levels of participation depending on the study and the researcher. As a naturalistic approach, ethnographic methods assume that all behavior, including group communication, is situated in a context. By spending extended periods of time with a group, ethnographers become familiar with the group and its communication environment, which allows them to recognize significant group communication processes taking place within their natural situations. Dollar and Zimmers (1998), for instance, noticed the significance of street youths' references to themselves as "houseless" instead of "homeless." A researcher with little experience in this cultural world likely would hear these two terms to be variants of the same self-referent. However, having spent more than 5 years working as a street youth outreach worker, Zimmers recognized the use of "houseless" to be meaningful—that is, as a choice made by street youths to manage their social identity. Without the perspective afforded through intense, prolonged fieldwork, in which the researcher participates as a member to some degree, such insight is not reasonable to expect.

In addition to participant observation, ethnographers rely on interviews, communication artifacts (such as documents and other textual data), and participants' own observational notes (such as communication diaries to inform the complexity of their ethnographic account). Ethnographic interviews range from spontaneous, in-the-field interviews to loosely structured, planned interviews that rely on a guide rather than a standardized interview questionnaire, as is often used in survey research. Interviews across participants may be similar or not, because interviewees are selected purposefully within ethnographic studies rather than randomly as in survey and, sometimes, experimental research. Ethnographic interviews tend to be inductive and rely mostly on open questions. Survey interviews, in contrast, tend to be deductive and use relatively closed questions. In addition, ethnographers treat the interview as a specific communicative context, an analytical consideration ignored in other forms of research (see Briggs, 1986).

Ethnographers also often collect documents produced in the specific context being studied, including those that establish the social, political, and historical contexts of the communication being investigated. Examples include memos, e-mail messages, group charters and/or bylaws, and stories written by the participants. These and other textual data provide ethnographers a means of triangulating their observations and interviews and of locating relevant and appropriate communication data. Details recorded in participants' diaries, for instance, could direct an ethnographer to a communication process not yet observed by the researcher.

Ethnographers, thus, use a variety of methods, only a sample of which is described above. They seek to produce multilayered, descriptive accounts and are, therefore, interested in a variety of data that enable them to consider the complexity of the phenomenon of interest in its natural environment. Each ethnographic study, of course, places different demands on this process.

As noted in the introduction, many group communication researchers employ ethnographic methods but not ethnographic theory. Most of the studies reviewed in this essay fall into this category. However, some studies do adhere to particular ethnographic theories—namely, ethnography of communication, critical ethnography, and autoethnography. We briefly consider these theoretical perspectives before discussing the contributions ethnographic studies make to group communication research.

Ethnography of communication refers to a specific theoretical and methodological approach that focuses on speech communities—groups of persons who share rules for both using and interpreting a linguistic code, speech, and other forms of community-specific communication (Hymes, 1972). Examples of speech communities represented in published research include street youth (Dollar & Zimmers, 1998), members of a charismatic church (Sequeira, 1993), members of a regional symphony (Rudd, 1995), organizational groups in a television station (Carbaugh, 1988b), and a group of Vietnam veterans (C. Braithwaite, 1997b). Focusing attention on context, form, and meaning, these studies have contributed to understanding issues such as symbols and forms for communicating (e.g., Carbaugh, 1988b; Fitch, 1990/ 1991; Sequeira, 1993), rules and norms for communicating (e. g. Dollar, 1999; Philipsen, 1992), and the relationship between communication and group identity (e.g., C. Braithwaite, 1997b; Dollar & Zimmers, 1998; Rudd, 1995).

Critical ethnography seeks to illuminate the role of power within groups and organizations (see Conquergood, 1991, 1995; Cushman, 1989/1990; Thomas, 1993). Critical ethnographers aim to provide social commentary or social critique as a means of exposing the unequal distribution and use of power within human interactions. Huspek (1986), for example, explored linguistic variability within some U.S. North American workers' speech from the viewpoint that "variant selections are not two different ways of 'saying the same thing,' but rather that they may say quite different things about the speaker's values, his [or her] identity, and his [or her] attitudes toward self and others inside and outside the speech community" (p. 159). Huspek concluded that workers chose the "low prestige variant" not only as a means of unifying with other members but also to express "the workers' lot" (pp. 158-159), a communicative move, he argued, that reproduced their lot as well.

Many critical ethnographers attempt to take action against the social inequalities exposed in their research, action aimed at challenging the status quo and calling for a rebalancing of power. Conquergood (1994), for example, used his ethnographic research with the Latin Kings, a Chicago Latino gang, to present an alternative voice, a compassionate voice, to the demonization of gangs by media. His social action approach involved raising money for gang members' bail, testifying in court on behalf of gang members, and teaching gang members to read and write. One particular outcome of his efforts was the production of a documentary about gang communication that emphasized gang members' voices and involved them as coparticipants in its production (Conquergood & Siegel, 1990).

Autoethnography offers yet another theoretical perspective for framing ethnographic studies of group communication. Crawford (1996) used this perspective in "(re)present[ing]" (p. 167) the accounts of one group of Peace Corp volunteers' group communication. Autoethnography, Crawford explained, seeks to "(re)position the researcher as an object of inquiry who depicts a site of interest in terms of personal awareness and experience" (p. 167). In other words, group communication is viewed through the perspective of the ethnographer, who is most likely a member of the group being studied. This personal research perspective, however, is treated not as a coherent, organized perspective but as a fragmented, changing, and locally grounded view. Similar to critical ethnography, autoethnography emphasizes the inherently subjective, dynamic nature of ethnographic research. It differs, however, in the phenomenon of interest; autoethnography focuses on the researcher's personal depiction and experience of the communication phenomenon, whereas critical ethnography is not limited to the researcher as source of insight.

In this chapter, we use the term *ethnography* to refer to the epistemological positions discussed earlier that necessarily entail using ethnographic methods. "Ethnography of communication," "critical ethnography," and "autoethnography" are used when referencing the particular theoretical approach employed.

Before moving to a discussion of ethnographic group communication research, we want to highlight the parameters of this review. Although we cannot and do not consider every study that employed ethnographic methods, we did attempt to locate a diverse range of such studies. We employed several techniques to locate relevant scholarship. The search included several computer databases, such as Educational Resource Information Clearinghouse (ERIC), *Communication Abstracts* from the Communication Institute for Online Scholarship (CIOS), and FirstSearch. These searches were conducted using various combinations of the following keywords: group, communication, ethnography, and ethnographic methods. Finally, we looked for more recent studies in communication and ethnographic-oriented journals not covered by those sources.

The purpose of this chapter is to foreground the contributions that ethnographic practice can make to the study of group communication, *not* to review the group communication research literature per se. Accordingly, we see four potential contributions of ethnographic practices (the order of these does not indicate their potential worth or relative value): (a) They may be used to validate and extend group communication research conducted in laboratory settings; (b) they can themselves be used to generate group communication theory; (c) they can generate research questions that have been unasked or are inadequately answered by other research methods, through consideration of contextual factors that have been insufficiently addressed by traditional group communication research (e.g., relational history of group members and degree of group membership); and (d) they can investigate in two ways the assumption of "shared meaning" that underlies studies of "groupness" by verifying, or at least qualifying, the concept of shared meaning in ethnographic research and by recognizing shared meaning as a *means* to something rather than an *end* in itself. It is important to note that these four contributions are not mutually exclusive. In the following sections, we discuss specific studies relevant to each of the four areas.

VALIDATING AND EXTENDING GROUP COMMUNICATION RESEARCH

Ethnographic studies can contribute to the study of group communication by validating and extending research conducted using other methods. Typically, laboratory groups have been studied using research designs in which group composition, member roles, and tasks are manipulated, or at least established, by the researcher. Cragan and Wright (1990) reported that only 12 of the 96 group communication studies published in the 1980s that they reviewed gathered data from natural groups. So the first way that ethnographic research can contribute to the study of group communication is to ecologically validate group communication processes that have been studied primarily in the laboratory setting (see Smith, 1988). Two such studies of group decision making, and one study of an HIV support group, are examined below to illustrate this role. Second, ethnographic observations can contribute to a form of triangulation by providing context-rich "thick descriptions" (Geertz, 1973) of group communicative behaviors that also have been measured by quantitative methods. Third, by instantiating cases that fit a particular communication theory and by elucidating the effects, over time, of group members' interactions on relevant group outcomes (see, Howard & Geist, 1995), ethnographic practices contribute to knowledge of the scope

and boundary conditions of group and other communication theories. Fourth, ethnographic observations can provide a rough form of triangulation (Carbaugh, 1988b) to ensure the reliability and validity of observations about group communication.

Ecologically Validating Group Processes

A recent study by Weitzel and Geist (1998) illustrates the contextual contributions of studying group decision making by using ethnographic methods. These researchers conducted a multiphase study of parliamentary procedure in community groups. The purpose of this study was to extend vigilant interaction theory (Hirokawa & Rost, 1992), which "examines the ways group interaction affects critical thinking" (Weitzel & Geist, 1998, p. 246). At each phase of the study, the authors narrowed their field of decision-making groups: They first interviewed by telephone members of 15 for-profit and nonprofit organizations to determine if, and how, parliamentary procedure was used in those organizations. They then attended 15 different community-planning committees as observers and took field notes. After those meetings, they interviewed (by phone or in person) more than 70 members of the planning committee members. Finally, they observed two meetings and analyzed transcripts of a third meeting of a nonprofit, citizen planning council. Weitzel and Geist's study extended prior research on parliamentary procedure and group decision making by showing "that there is considerable variation in the correct use of parliamentary procedure in community groups" and that "effective group communication is not necessarily prohibited by the lack of technical adeptness" (p. 255). In this case, vigilant interactions about the legality of their actions rather than correct technical use of the parliamentary procedures accounted for the members' ability to make effective community-planning decisions. As the authors concluded,

Parliamentary procedure involves the use of good judgment in lieu of mechanical rules, and it should be used for carrying out the good will of the group. This probably should be the prevailing view when teaching parliamentary procedure within communication departments. (p. 257)

The extensive field observations and interviews conducted by Weitzel and Geist, and the breadth of the organizations sampled in their research, help to establish the ecological validity of their conclusions about the citizen planning council they observed.

Eisenberg, Murphy, and Andrews's (1998) study of openness and decision making in a university's search for a new provost explored the organizational cultural aspects of group decision making and problem solving, processes that have frequently been studied in laboratory settings but less frequently examined in their naturally occurring contexts. The researchers attended all four meetings of the search committee and the interviews with the five finalists for the position. Members of the research team later interviewed most of the 25 members of the search committee, as well as other university employees suggested by these members, to discover how this group conducted itself in the process of "pure organizing," or sense making within a limited time frame. Thus, this study examined decision making by bona fide group members—that is, groups that have permeable boundaries, shifting borders, and are interdependent with their contexts (regarding the bona fide group perspective, see Putnam & Stohl, 1990; Stohl & Putnam, 1994)—on actual tasks, in real time. Search committee meetings were shown to be sites where meanings were created, but not all group members agreed on the meanings. Three "vying narratives" coexisted both during and after the search, and the researchers acknowledged that plural interpretations were embraced and pursued by the research team, as well as by the search committee members. As Eisenberg et al. (1998) explained, the recognition of this diversity in meanings "problematizes notions of organizational boundaries and uniqueness," and "this expanded view transcends all three narratives" (p. 17). The authors presented the three narratives as reflecting the various intersections of participants' institutional, group, and individual lives and showed how the participants used these narratives as rhetorical resources for performing arguments with different audiences.

In an ethnographic study that related group interaction to health and well-being, Cawyer and Smith-Dupré (1995) engaged in observations of a support group to extend prior research on social support message types and their functions to the HIV and AIDS communities. Cawyer attended weekly support group meetings over a 3-month period, as both an observer and a group member, because she was a "caretaker and loved one of an AIDS patient" (p. 247). Her field notes contained verbatim quotes from group members' talk, as well as her own observations made during and after the meetings. Cawyer and Smith-Dupré individually categorized these field notes into supportive episodes, compared their results, and resolved differences as needed.

Although the context-general functions of supportive messages are well documented, Cawyer and Smith-Dupré's study validated four functions used specifically in the HIV and AIDS communities: "communication as a healing agent, as a preparatory mechanism for living with HIV/AIDS, as an outlet for expressing emotions, and as a means of changing society" (p. 243). The researchers concluded that a primary contribution of their study was "its extension of our understanding of the relationship between communication and social support" (p. 255), by demonstrating the communicative overlap between "giving" and "taking" support and by illustrating ways in which some supportive messages can have mixed or negative results. This study and those discussed previously illuminate the situatedness of all group behavior and describe the particular contextual influences salient to group processes such as decision making and social support. Such contributions extend previous research by demonstrating the ecological validity of prior laboratory studies of group communication behaviors and processes.

Context-Rich Thick Descriptions of Group Communicative Behaviors

Crawford's (1996) article, titled "Personal Ethnography," began with the author's first-person recounting of a swimming game he participated in with four other Peace Corps volunteers in Africa. At the start of that game, the volunteers had just met, and the story (which ended tragically in the death of one volunteer who was eaten by a crocodile in the river in which they were all swimming), showed graphically how quickly these five strangers developed a sense of "we-ness" during this activity. Quoting Victor Turner (1986), Crawford (1996) wrote that what happened "converted mere experience into an experience" and, in part, was responsible for his "taking the ethnographic turn" (p. 161). The process of group members coming to see themselves as a "we," a unified group that represents more than just a collection of individuals, is one of the fundamental precepts of group communication theory and research, and Crawford's context-specific description showed how it can be demonstrated using, in this case, autoethnography.

Schely-Newman's (1997) study of locale narratives among members of an Israeli *moshav* (or settlement) provides context-rich illustrations of the concept of *code switching*. As the author explained,

> Members of the older generation speak Arabic, French, and Hebrew with varying degrees of fluency, and code-switching is an unmarked choice in the community. However, as the formality of the event and heterogeneity of the participants increases, the mixing of languages occurs less often. (p. 405)

It is unlikely that any participant-observer who was not a full-fledged member of the cultural group being studied, as Schely-Newman was, would gain the access needed to make this observation. Her analysis also requires a group member's interpretive competence to recognize the interaction of situation and group composition variables as they affect rules for language use. Providing such context-rich description is important for its own sake, but it also helps to reveal the scope and boundary conditions of group communication theories by showing how group members' narratives not only document shared meanings but also serve to create their community, by placing the group in the context of its larger society.

Illuminating Scope and Boundary Conditions of Communication Theories

C. Braithwaite's (1997a) observational case study of interactions at a community blood donation center provides a context-rich description of interaction management and suggests that previous formulations of this theory were inadequate in their scope. Braithwaite asked, "How do interactants adapt when the conversational rules identified as essential for successful interaction are repeatedly and consistently violated?" (p. 63). As a participant-observer, he donated blood plasma 16 times over a 2-month period. He wrote field notes during his visits and analyzed the ways in which conversations were managed between technicians and donors by applying Wiemann's (1977) five conversational rules. Braithwaite's (1997a) analysis of the conversational rule violations showed how group members in the blood bank context "normalized the violations by their failure to repair the violations unless called to account" (p. 70). His analysis extended the boundaries of Pearce and Conklin's (1979) rules hierarchy, by showing that "what counts as a violation under one set of rules can become coherent and unproblematic under a 'higher' set of rules" (C. Braithwaite, 1997a, p. 70).

Cawyer and Smith-Dupré's (1995) study of communication in a social support group, discussed previously, pointed out a boundary issue for another area of communication theory, this time in the area of interpersonal communication: Taylor and Altman's (1987) traditional wisdom on the progressive, incrementally increasing nature of appropriate self-disclosure. Cawyer and Smith-Dupré (1995) found that "in the confines of the support group, initial exchanges appear to occur at the most intimate level" (p. 256), thereby offering an example of a context within which appropriate disclosure seemed to defy the traditional U.S. cultural norms. This study shows that communicative behavior, such as appropriate self-disclosure levels, can be gauged only within a culture and, even more specifically, within a particular situational context.

Finders (1996) conducted an elaborate critical ethnographic study of literacy and peer allegiance in junior high school girls' small group interactions, by following four early adolescent girls through completion of their 7th-grade year at school. Finders used participant observation and individual and group interviews with the girls, their mothers, teachers, and friends to document the ways that literate practices marked social boundaries. Finders pointed out several myths within educators' discourse about student-centered pedagogy, including the myths of inclusion, the safe haven, comfort, and free choice. For example, many educators believe that students learn best in the presence of their slightly more advanced peers and that students responding directly to one another's writing will lead to greater empowerment for all students. In Finders's study, however, one student's attempt to respond to her classmate's writing actually marked her as an outsider in the area being written about (sports) and set her up for ridicule by her peers. The situated knowledge required to make this observation is most likely held by "insiders" and can potentially be richly revealed by ethnographic methods, such as in-depth interviews and sustained observation. Such details are unlikely to emerge in survey data collection (see Allen & Plax, 1999, for a review of group communication in educational contexts).

Ethnographic research conducted on bona fide groups, therefore, can contribute to locating the scope and boundaries of group communication theory in two ways. First, as Crawford (1996) and Schely-Newman (1997) showed, ethnographic methods can uncover rich, contextual instances of group communicative behaviors, which, when such studies are viewed comparatively, can display the scope of the behavior in praxis. Second, as Cawyer and Smith-Dupré's (1995) study of the boundaries of self-disclosure norms in a social support group and C. Braithwaite's (1997a) study of rule violations at a blood bank demonstrated, ethnographic data can reveal the boundary conditions of particular theories.

Providing Triangulation for Reliable and Valid Group Observations

In addition to ecologically validating group communication processes and extending explorations of the nature and effects of group interaction, ethnographic methods can be used to ensure reliable and valid observations about group communicative behaviors. Carbaugh (1988b) described a rough form of triangulation that involved using a combination of interviews, participant observation, and archival documents collected over a 9-month period to investigate the cultural terms used by employees at a television station. Carbaugh interviewed station workers, observed production of several shows, and volunteered during a 10-day telethon fundraiser. He scanned all these data for themes and then checked his reading of the television station workers' discourse by using a pattern he had inferred while talking with the workers: He called this a *performance test*. He then solicited feedback from the workers, both verbally and nonverbally, which confirmed or disconfirmed his interpretations. Carbaugh used these performance tests during interviews and during informal discourse with workers; thus, the triangulation of observation, interviews, and discursive performance tests provided evidence about both the reliability and validity of the themes he had identified from the discourse of these group members. This was especially important because Carbaugh was not a member of the group (i.e., he was not employed at the television station) and, therefore, did not have firsthand knowledge of the objects and events referred to in those themes.

GENERATING THEORY

Scholars using ethnographic theory and/or methods have generated group communication theory in at least four areas: (a) organizational group theory; (b) theories of codes for communicating, both localized, particular codes and speech code theory more generally (Philipsen, 1997); (c) managing the individual/collective tension experienced by group members; and (d) the creation, maintenance, and sustenance of community. Studies conducted often contribute to more than one line of theory generation. Adelman and Frey's (1994, 1997) studies of group communication within a residential facility for persons with AIDS, for instance, contributes to generating theory about a localized code of communicating; managing the individual/collective tension; and the creation, maintenance, and sustenance of community. Given space limitations, we are not able to discuss how specific studies contribute to more than one line; instead, we discuss the studies that most clearly illustrate the four theoretical lines emerging from ethnographic group communication research. All case studies, however, contribute at least to the localized theory line and, more often than not, to at least one of the other three lines.

Organizational Group Theory

Carbaugh (1985, 1986) formulated a theoretical approach for studying cultural communication within organizational groups. This approach points researchers toward the discovery and elucidation of group members' communication systems for rending their organizational world meaningful. These systems are part of an *organizational culture,* the code shared by members of an organizational community. Within an organization, Carbaugh's theoretical approach aims to discover the communicative system members rely on to "enact and reveal" shared meaning and "to create and regulate a sense of community," or what he refers to as *cultural communication* (Carbaugh, 1986, p. 89). He set forth a descriptive framework, arising from the ethnography of communication (Hymes, 1972), to guide research to this end. The framework directs researchers in studying context, shared meanings and cultural codes, and other communicative forms. Of particular value for group communication researchers and practitioners, including educators, is Carbaugh's emphasis on speech and other forms of communication, instead of psychological and sociological group variables.

An additional advantage of Carbaugh's approach is its inductive analysis of group members' communication rather than the use of preformulated coding schemes. This is not to say this approach is not compatible with the more traditional group communication research approach of using a priori coding schemes. For example, Carbaugh's (1988b) analysis of television employees' communication revealed important insight into the construction and maintenance of status and structure in groups within that organization. Using three primary terms referenced by employees in their talk ("types of people," "building situation," and "the communication problem"), Carbaugh illustrated symbolic tensions as they were created, negotiated, and maintained in employees' daily communication. Howard and Geist's (1995) ethnography of organizational employees' ideological positioning during a proposed merger used a similar approach, with different categories to illustrate the dialectic of control—the tension between autonomy and dependence—enacted in organizational discourse. The end result in both studies was an analysis that combined context, form, and meaning to formulate a way of speaking used by a particular group of communicators in a particular context where status and structure are enacted in communicative processes, as well as in outcomes (see also Rudd, 1995).

Localized Group Communication Theories

Scholars adopting an ethnographic approach have significantly advanced the understanding of particular, localized group communication theories—that is, theories informed by group members working with researchers. These formulations have been advanced from a variety of theoretical perspectives, including emergent literacy theory (Kliewer, 1998), symbolic convergence theory (Lesch, 1994), cultural theory (Conquergood, 1994), ethnography of communication (Dollar, 1993), and dialectical theory (Adelman & Frey, 1994, 1997). Although theoretically diverse, these studies have embraced ethnographic methods to investigate and articulate group members' communication theories. These researchers, thus, use ethnographic methods to formulate theories about group members' communication and to help articulate members' own theories about their communication. Together, these studies offer communication theories grounded in naturally occurring group interaction. Although generalizations may often be drawn from these studies, their strength lies in the construction of localized theories.

Conquergood's (1994) study of communication within a Chicago gang provides a good example of a localized group communication theory by offering an empirical account of members' construction of a "sheltering world of mutual support and well-being, a hood, through complex and creative communication" (p. 52). Conquergood spent 20 months living in Big Red, a tenement building in Chicago's "Little Beirut," the heart of the Latin Kings' territory. After 3 years of participant observation, during which time he became trusted enough by gang members to read their underground manifestos and charters, Conquergood advanced a theoretical claim for *intracommunal communication*, a concept that puts the collective rather than the "individual as the locus of personhood"

(p. 24). He then situated the members' communication theory in "macrocontexts of communication" that surround the "gang problem." Conquergood discussed the larger contexts that influenced the group or gang context—more specifically, the communication within these contexts. He argued, for example, that viewing gang members as deviants is a rhetorical construction that emerges from the communication tactics of individuals living in more affluent, mainstream contexts outside the gang context. He argued for the need to understand gang communication within the contexts of deindustrialization, economic polarization, residential segregation, and other outside, macrocontextual factors.

A more traditional study that imposed a preformulated theory or method for treating gang members' communication would not have allowed the localized communication theory to emerge from the members' communication. Conquergood's emic approach helps scholars, students, and practitioners understand, given the contexts and characteristics of this group, how and why these gang members communicate as they do, toward what intended ends, and with what particular outcomes.

With regard to localized theory, Philipsen (1997) advanced a theoretical and methodological approach to explain how members of groups "thematize, constitute or reconstitute, and manage" connections between and among people (p. 119), or what he referred to as *speech codes*. One advance emerging from this work is the recognition of diversity as an essential component of a group's code for communicating. Embracing the notion of diversity has allowed researchers to begin discovering and describing the complex communication processes encountered in natural groups. Dollar (1993), for instance, illustrated sorority members' diverse, yet systematic use of their code of membership. After describing the common code to which group members oriented in their talk with one another, and its four most salient symbols ("sisterhood," "commitment," "involvement," and "class"), Dollar described how members use these symbols in systematically variant ways and thereby render the enactment of several sets of dichotomous identities—namely, "old school" versus "new school," "pledges" versus "actives," "townies" versus "live-ins," and "chapter" versus "national." Work oriented toward investigating diversity helps researchers investigate not only the shared aspects of group communication codes but the contested aspects as well. We return to a discussion of this research focus in the "shared meaning" section below.

Managing the Individual/ Collective Tension

A third theoretical line to emerge from ethnographic group communication research concerns the struggle members encounter between individuality and collectivity. Some, but not all, of this research has been conducted by ethnographers of communication. Philipsen (1987) issued a call for studies of *cultural communication,* the creation, affirmation, and negotiation of shared identity, part of which concerns how members of groups communicatively manage the inevitable tension between individuality and collectivity. Specifically, he advocated the analysis of group rituals, myths, social dramas, and other communicative forms, to study members' response to this tension. A growing body of scholarship supports Philipsen's theory of cultural communication and offers rich descriptions of the communicative forms members of different groups call on to manage their struggle for individuality while simultaneously maintaining a sense of collectivity (see, e.g., C. Braithwaite, 1997b; Carbaugh, 1988b; Dollar, 1999).

Ethnographic studies by Adelman and Frey (1994, 1997) also explore this communicative tension, albeit from a theoretical perspective other than ethnography of communication. Although their studies focused specifically on creating and sustaining community, they are reviewed here because of the significant contributions they make to understanding the in-dividual/collective dialectic. Combining dialectical theory with 8 years of participant observation; in-depth interviews with residents, staff, and volunteers; textual analysis of documents; and questionnaires completed by residents four times across 2 years, Adelman and Frey explored this membership struggle within a residential facility for people with AIDS. They described the staff-imposed communicative responses to the individual/collective tension (e.g., team interviews with prospective members and weekly house meetings), as well as the informal, resident-generated ones (e.g., a balloon ceremony and parting ritual enacted when a resident dies). By including the responses of residents and staff, Adelman and Frey offered a holistic view of the group that afforded insight into a number of issues relevant to group communication research, such as the relationship between group interactional patterns and group outcomes (e.g., residents complaining to staff and the creation of rules in response to complaints). Moreover, these processes and outcomes were considered within the dialectical contexts deemed relevant by members. The consideration of these contexts produces the rich ethnographic interpretations that do justice to the complexity of natural groups and, more specifically, to participants' communicative responses to the inevitable dialectical tension of the individual and the collective.

Creating, Maintaining, and Sustaining Community

The fourth theoretical line represented in ethnographic group communication research seeks to understand the communicative construction, negotiation, and maintenance of community. Ethnographic studies suggest that groups vary in their views of community and ways of creating and sustaining it. Given that community cannot be constructed in the laboratory, researchers must turn to the study of natural groups, and ethnographic methods provide scholars with productive means for studying the communication processes associated with community development. The studies reviewed show that community is a situated accomplishment, often contested, and is a communicative symbol used in differing ways toward various ends. Two studies in particular illustrate these points.

Schely-Newman (1993) relied on participant observation and in-depth interviewing to study the function of *communal narrative* within her hometown community. More specifically, Schely-Newman investigated the situated telling of a historical communal narrative as a means of understanding community building. The story of a woman breaking community morals that resulted in her accidental shooting, Schely-Newman noticed, was being retold with considerable frequency in modern times. Her analysis revealed that each telling mixed present concerns with the traditionally expected female morality, a move she interpreted as reiterating the community members' commitment to traditional morals even in the face of modern challenges. By telling the story today, in the context of young community members who often desire to move away from traditional roles and values to those articulated in more contemporary societies, members of the community exercised some "social control and the keeping of moral values" (p. 300). Not every telling of the narrative was exactly the same, but all maintained consistency in terms of the moral and community values emphasized. As such, this historical, communal narrative was used by members both to instruct other members and to reemphasize to themselves the traditional gender roles within this community for the purposes of maintaining and sustaining their community.

A second study that advances understanding of the maintenance and sustenance of community is Lesch's (1994) study of a small witches' coven. Using symbolic convergence theory (Bormann, 1983, 1990), Lesch studied "consciousness-sustaining communication"— that is, members' use of narratives to sustain and maintain the in-group consciousness, the community's shared symbolic views. Lesch was able to study this process specifically because she began her observations when the group had lost a member and was seeking to replace her. Lesch's data collection methods consisted of observing three monthly meetings; collecting journals kept by coven members, as well as pamphlets on witches; interviewing members; and soliciting the witches' responses to the final report. She analyzed these data using fantasy theme analysis to study the use of narrative in maintaining and sustaining community consciousness. She found that members called on both structural and symbolic communicative practices. More specifically, members relied on consensus decision making, turn-taking speaking rounds, and shared planning activities to prevent the emergence of a hierarchical structure; in articulating group identity, they relied on significant symbols, such as welcoming rituals.

As evidenced in these two studies, ethnographers study community both as a communication process and as an outcome. These studies also demonstrate that community is a dynamic, not a static, concept. Finally, each of these studies articulates a localized group communication theory—specifically, a theory for communicatively creating, maintaining, and sustaining community.

UNASKED AND INADEQUATELY ANSWERED QUESTIONS ABOUT GROUP COMMUNICATION

Ethnographic practices can potentially answer research questions about group communication that have been overlooked or inadequately answered by other research methods, precisely because ethnographic practices require consideration of context factors (e.g., relational history of members and degree of group membership) that are insufficiently addressed by traditional methods. What has been overlooked in group communication research are the ways in which meanings are constructed in interaction among group members, including process-oriented questions about labeling, language use, the role of questions asked, and nonverbal regulation. In addition, the roles of multiple meanings and multiple-goal interactions have been insufficiently addressed in group research. Furthermore, the study of non-task-related groups has been virtually absent in this research.

Frey (1994a, 1994c) outlined some challenges of studying communication in natural groups, including gaining access and establishing relations with participants; forging agreements between participants and researchers about copyright, control, and confidentiality; designing longitudinal studies of sufficient time and considering the impact of the time spent in the field on the researcher and the participants; and treating research participants as coresearchers or providing other benefits for the group members studied. As Frey (1994c) concluded, "Researchers have traded real-world significance for perceived methodological rigor—a false dichotomy if ever one existed. The result is research that often is internally sound, but empty of life" (p. 573). The challenges listed here suggest why few researchers engage in naturalistic studies of group communication. Nonetheless, some researchers have conducted ethnographic studies that either asked questions ignored by other methodologies or answered questions more satisfactorily than was possible using other methods.

Asking New Questions

Ethnographic methods foreground participants' views, which, in some areas of communication research, have not been sought using other research techniques. Smythe's (1995) ethnography of a discourse community composed of regular members of a women's fitness facility called Bodyworks provides one example of research aimed at showing "how the experiences of a community were construed among women members" (p. 259). Smythe conducted covert observations at Bodyworks over 7 months, as a long-term member of that facility. She used field notes from talk that occurred naturally during fitness classes and from "guided conversations," to categorize the content, participants, and duration of interactions. She then revealed her researcher role and conducted in-depth

interviews with eight long-term members to gauge their feelings about the activities in which they participated. Smythe showed how women who "fit in" could "talk the talk" of bodywork, including physiology, diagnosing injuries, and sharing war stories of pain and injury (p. 250). The themes she identified of performance, power, and affirmation showed how these women constructed a shared vision of empowerment through fitness, a vision that involved either "embracing the cultural norms for feminine beauty and attractiveness" or "recasting the fitness vision in such a way that the dominant cultural discourse on feminine beauty was transformed" (p. 258).

In addition to focusing on participants' views, ethnographic research can address questions about types of groups and communication processes that have been ignored by traditional research. Group communication research typically has focused on task-oriented groups, particularly with respect to group meetings as a site for information-sharing and decision-making processes. Frey (1994c) reported that "all but 4.3% of the group communication research [that he reviewed in 1988] focused on decision-making activity, as if this were the only thing that groups do" (p. 557). Frey argued that "other types of groups and important processes that characterize them deserve attention" (p. 557). Two of these processes include the dynamics of group living situations (see Adelman & Frey, 1994, 1997), and "dealing with" rather than necessarily resolving the inherent dialectical tensions of group life, such as conflicting individual and collective needs.

D. Braithwaite's (1995) study of ritualized embarrassment at coed wedding and baby showers addressed one such group type and process: The author challenged the "implicit assumption that embarrassment has a negative impact on interaction, if not on entire relationships" (p. 145). Braithwaite participated in and observed 12 showers over a 20-month period and interviewed 20 participants. She found that embarrassment was not seen as negative by participants if it was deemed appropriate in that context, by that situation, and concluded that "context is essential in understanding how embarrassment functions" (p. 154). Within the context of showers, a "formerly gender specific activity" (p. 146), embarrassment may help to socialize males and to maintain solidarity between men and women. Indeed, more than one group process that has been studied in the laboratory or by survey methods looks quite different when examined in context, using ethnographic methods.

Bastien and Hostager (1992) used ethnographic observation and in-depth interviewing of a key informant to examine how one zero-history group accomplished a cooperative social activity—performing a jazz concert. Although traditional communication research has often addressed task performance in zero-history groups, these authors' use of videotaped observation and "instant-by-instant interpretations and explanations by one of the participants" (p. 97) who watched the videotaped performance showed how the group members combined task knowledge about jazz music with knowledge of the social conventions of professional musicians to allow "cooperative action among strangers" (p. 101). The synchronization of actions, based on the individual members' performance histories, allowed the jazz group members to be productive despite their lack of shared relational history. Bastien and Hostager suggested that their method and conclusions hold promise for the study of group productivity in organizations. Scholars seeking to understand other group outcomes and contexts also would benefit from adding participant observations and contexted descriptions to their existing research lines.

Questions Inadequately Answered by Other Methods

One common area of group research that has received substantial attention has focused on the outcomes of group interaction, especially cohesion, satisfaction of members, and group productivity on tasks. Several recent studies of group communication processes

and outcomes show how more satisfying answers can be arrived at by using ethnographic methods than those achieved in prior research. For example, Lesch's (1994) study of the ways coven members sustained their consciousness helped to answer Bormann's (1983) question, "What keeps members interested and engaged in the ongoing group?" (p. 84). Lesch's participant observation and in-depth interviews over a 3-month period, coupled with her analysis of group members' metacommunication in their written journals, provided a more valid and grounded base for explication of themes than did the traditional method of rhetorical criticism of extant texts.

Ethnographic immersion in a group setting and observations of natural communicative behaviors also allow researchers to tease out the role that communication plays in "creating and sustaining group life" (Frey, 1994c, p. 571). Over time, observational data could show the relational dimensions of task-group communication in ways that a priori, one-shot coding of relational communication demonstrated in meeting transcripts cannot illuminate. Longitudinal data collection and some type of partnership between the researcher(s) and participants is required to adequately elucidate the dynamic group process of community building (Frey, 1994a) and to reduce participant and researcher apprehension. Reduced apprehension should increase the likelihood of observing the natural behavior of group members and of members giving authentic responses during in-depth interviews. Furthermore, Lofland and Lofland (1984) suggested that "group interviews may be most productive on topics that are reasonably public and are not matters of any particular embarrassment" (p. 14). Group interviews, in which more than one member is present, provide synergy in recall process and an interchange between contrasting perspectives that contribute to the effectiveness of these interviews in studying group communication processes. Thus, for example, group interviews may give more satisfying answers than individual interviews for questions about the factors that increase or decrease group cohesion, whereas participant observation (contrasted with participants' self-reports) could elucidate the observable indices of group cohesion.

Two ethnographic studies of group members' storytelling are examined next that illustrate the strategic functions stories play in promoting group cohesion and building community, questions that are inadequately answered by research methods other than participant observation and interviews. Peterson (1987) analyzed the way stories of pregnancy function to generate and reproduce small group cultures as those stories are developed, stored, retrieved, and transmitted over several generations. On the basis of pregnancy stories collected from popular accounts and reflections, interview data, diaries, and nursing textbooks, Peterson showed how the repetition of pregnancy stories from one generation to the next transformed a "romantic couple" into a "family," with the "birth of a child" (p. 41). He analyzed the content of pregnancy stories along two themes, the scientific and romantic, as that content was organized for effective cross-generational transmission by its structure, generality, and timing. As Peterson concluded,

> Continued unreflective acceptance of a "normative family" as a site for communication research and practice only participates in patriarchal strategies that ignore variability and deny "marginal"—women and minorities—experiences. Instead, a strategic model offers possibilities for growth, nurturance, and transformation of small group cultures. (p. 46)

In another ethnographic study of the group functions of storytelling, Hollihan and Riley (1987) showed how a "Toughlove" parent support group "completely absolved parents of their guilt and relieved their sense of failure" (p. 23) for their children's' delinquent social conduct. Hollihan and Riley observed four consecutive meetings of the Los Angeles-area support group and, following those observations, interviewed randomly selected group members. Analyzing messages collected through both field notes and interview transcripts, the authors observed that the "Toughlove" story, which is based on old-fashioned discipline and rejects the "modern approach" to child rearing, including the role of child care professionals, was "powerful, compelling, and cohesive" (p. 17) for the parents. But the story also was dangerous because parents were encouraged to eject their child from the house if she or he did not meet the "bottom line" rules for behavior, even if that child was unprepared to face life alone and might become a threat to society. As Hollihan and Riley concluded,

> The truth or falsity of the Toughlove story is not really at issue in this study. What is important, is that through an analysis we can come to understand the appeal of stories and perhaps even learn how to avoid the creation of stories which might precipitate harmful consequences. (p. 24)

The extent to which members of a group or culture share meanings is one of the key questions ethnography can potentially illuminate better than other methods. Rudd's (1995) study of oppositional terms in the discourse of regional symphony members showed how group identity was achieved, not in a unified, shared form but in coexisting, contested forms among members of this organization. Rudd's study can be linked to much of the previous work on group and organizational identification; research that typically has been conducted using quantitative survey methodology and has failed to reveal the phenomena of opposing, role-based identifications among organizational members. Rudd's finding might explain why prior organizational identification hypotheses, such as the prediction of positive correlations of organizational identification with outcomes such as productivity and member satisfaction, were not supported, because statistical analyses of identification levels, which are based on "average scores," attenuate the differences in identification levels among opposing, role-based subgroup members.

Baxter and Goldsmith's (1990) ethnography of cultural terms for communication events among U.S. high school adolescents also contributes to answering the question of how group members come to share meanings. The authors conducted in-depth interviews, engaged in participant observation, and used cluster analysis to understand the terms adolescents used for settings, participants, speech acts, and purposes in everyday life. Comparing their results with Moffatt's (1989) study of adolescents at Rutgers University, which found that similarities in interactions of adolescents were based on their coming of age, Baxter and Goldsmith concluded: "Adolescents do not constitute a homogeneous cultural group but rather consist of distinctive groups that share common cultural elements. The communication codes of these two adolescent groups are like dialects of a broader American cultural code" (p. 392). The issue of solidarity, or how group members share meanings, is the focus of the next section.

SHARED MEANING/SHAREDNESS

The final area of contribution we have identified that ethnography can make to the study of group communication concerns the notion of "sharedness" among group communicators. First, some ethnographers would argue that reconceptualizing groupness is necessary to better understand sharedness as a quality of group communication. More specifically, these ethnographers problematize group communication researchers' assumption of solidarity as an essential component of groupness (see, e.g., Bales & Strodtbeck, 1951; Poole, 1983), an assumption explored later. The studies reviewed here suggest that solidarity is a dynamic concept within groups; it is sometimes a desired end and other times a means to an end, both relevant topics for group communication research. Ethnographic studies allow researchers to study the dynamic nature of solidarity, because as discussed earlier, ethnographers are well suited to discover the nuances of group communication, including its changes over time and the ability to view it from the mem-

bers' perspective; the researchers' extended time in the field provides a more holistic frame for analysis than does reliance on a single type of data, as is characteristic of most survey studies (i.e., questionnaires or preformulated interviews). Second, the studies reviewed here problematize the notion of sharedness within group communication research; specifically, they reveal that sharedness does not imply agreement per se. Ethnographies are helpful for understanding the nature of sharedness because of researchers' orientation toward building grounded, localized theory. By allowing the data to guide theoretical understanding, ethnographers do not assume a priori that sharedness implies agreement.

Qualifying Groupness

Many scholars have called for research that takes seriously the notion of "groupness" (e.g., Bales & Strodtbeck, 1951; Bormann, 1970; Cragan & Wright, 1980, 1990). Groupness includes "incentives for members to maintain solidarity" and "pressure to finish the task" (Poole, 1983, p. 333). It is our belief, as it is many of the aforementioned critics' belief, that groupness can rarely be manufactured in a zero-history laboratory group. As such, attention needs to be focused on understanding groupness in natural groups. This methodological move raises the question of whether incentive to maintain solidarity and pressure to complete the task are necessary and sufficient characteristics to define groupness. Furthermore, these characteristics may or may not cover the various types of groups subsumed more recently under the realm of group communication research, such as gang members and witches covens (see, e.g., Propp & Kreps, 1994). Of particular interest is the emphasis that Poole and others place on *solidarity* as a defining feature of group life.

Our review of the ethnographic literature suggests that groups vary in the emphasis that members put on maintaining solidarity. At some times, solidarity is a desired outcome, but at other times, it is not even expected. Lesch's (1994) study of the witches' coven provides insight into the fluctuation between members' performance of group versus individual communication strategies. At times, bonding and stabilizing, both of which emphasize solidarity, were desired outcomes of this group. On other occasions, the long-term goal of group survival necessitated communication that was oriented toward individuals and their various perspectives, and emphasized difference rather than solidarity. Other ethnographic studies suggest that solidarity may emerge as more important to members within particular subgroups (see, e.g., Rudd, 1995). Our point is not to argue against solidarity as an important constituent of groupness but to call for a more careful consideration of solidarity and for analyses that consider the dynamic aspect of solidarity as a group characteristic. Ethnographers accomplish this by searching for local communication theories and acknowledging that solidarity may or may not be part of the local theory. When solidarity is considered salient, ethnographers must work with the members to understand how it is part of their local communication theory. Resisting a priori coding schemes, therefore, is necessary in fulfilling these methodological, interpretive tasks.

Qualifying Sharedness

Much group research is concerned with sharedness—shared meaning, shared ways of communicating, and shared ways of interpreting communication. Two aspects of sharedness appear to have gone without comment in much of the extant group communication research. First, what do researchers mean when they say that group members share goals, a communication system, or a role system? Do they mean that members agree on a system and the meanings rendered while using that system? Most research appears to suggest this agreement, whether intentional or not. Sharedness, however, does not necessitate

agreement. Drawing on the work of a number of scholars, we take sharedness to mean that group members find their communication system, for instance, commonly intelligible, not that they agree on all aspects of it or the ways in which it is to be used (see Carbaugh, 1988a; Hymes, 1972; Schneider, 1976). Sharedness, thus, implies a range of acceptability within which there is organized diversity. Sharedness does not exclude difference, and we take this to be a critical point that is missing in traditional group communication research.

Carbaugh (1988b) was among the first to take seriously the notion of diversity within culture—that is, within the code of symbols, meanings, rules, and premises shared by groups of communicators. He showed that the spoken symbol system, although intelligible to the workers he studied, was not a single, agreed-on meaning set but, rather, that the code was characterized by its tensional nature, thereby demonstrating the contested nature of cultural codes. Della-Piana and Anderson (1995) recognized this contested aspect in their study of how "community" is used by members of a student-oriented community service group both to produce shared meaning and to manage diversity in membership. The result was the production of divergent lines of talk within the group. Although the members of the group recognized boundaries that distinguished their sense of community from that of other groups, there was also an acceptable range of difference within the group members' use of this symbol. Each of these studies illustrates the diversity within communities' systems of discourse, a diversity that is often overlooked by scholars who assume that sharing meaning implies agreement among members.

Second, the role of sharedness within group communication ought to be problematized. Specifically, sharedness can be a means to an end in addition to the intended ends. Furthermore, members' understandings of the nuances of their group's shared code come into play when considering member communication competence as a group variable. That is, competent group members recognize this diversity and are able to manage it to desired ends (see Chien, 1996, for an example of how members use code switching differently to express group solidarity and social distance, depending on their communicative intent).

Eisenberg et al.'s (1998) research on decision making by a university selection committee clearly illustrates how group members may use sharedness as a means to varied and multiple ends. As noted earlier, these researchers located three competing narratives that emerged in the group process of selecting a university provost. Members of this search committee, when interviewed, reported using all three narratives, depending on the audience and their personal "communication demands" (p. 21). In other words, members shifted their perspective as a rhetorical strategy that exercised sharedness as a means to an end; the speakers' sense of sharedness (what perspective is shared and with whom, for example) varied depending on the situation. For these communicators, differing levels of sharedness were achieved and evoked throughout the group decision-making process. In the end, however, sharedness in this study was not an end state but a means of answering to different audiences, including the university administration, the larger community, and peers in committee members' academic departments.

Group communication researchers, thus, benefit from an ethnographic perspective that considers in some ways issues of groupness and sharedness . The ethnographic studies reviewed illustrate that sharedness may be as much a communicative resource for group members as it is a desired end state and that sharedness does not equal agreement.

CONCLUSION

In this chapter, we have argued that ethnography can be used to validate and extend group communication research by ecologically validating group processes, providing context-rich instantiations of group commu-

nicative behavior, and illuminating scope and boundary conditions for group communication theory. One of the reasons these outcomes occur is that ethnographers often triangulate data collected from participant observation, in-depth interviews, and textual analysis to ensure valid and reliable observations of group behavior. In this way, ethnographic research can also generate new theories about types of groups and communicative processes that have been ignored by more traditional methodologies. In particular, the investigation of how meanings and group outcomes are socially constructed in interaction among members is a promising avenue for ethnographic research on group communication. Critical analyses of these processes and outcomes also should contribute to the application value of this research for practitioners and group participants, as well as for researchers.

In closing, we would like to stress the need for group communication researchers to continue using ethnographic theory and methods. As demonstrated in this chapter, ethnographic approaches to group communication research allow researchers to study groups in their natural environments as they engage in natural group processes, albeit within the constraints of a given situation. Not all ethnographic studies attend to these natural qualities, but the ethnographic studies we call for most certainly do. In the final analysis, studying groups in situ can advance our understanding of localized group communication practices and processes, as well as extant group communication theory.

REFERENCES

Adelman, M. B., & Frey, L. R. (1994). The pilgrim must embark: Creating and sustaining community in a residential facility for people with AIDS. In L. R. Frey (Ed.), *Group communication in context: Studies of natural groups* (pp. 3-22). Hillsdale, NJ: Lawrence Erlbaum.

Adelman, M. B., & Frey, L. R. (1997). *The fragile community: Living together with AIDS*. Mahwah, NJ: Lawrence Erlbaum.

Allen, T. H., & Plax, T. G. (1999). Group communication in the formal educational context. In L. R. Frey (Ed.),

D. S. Gouran, & M. S. Poole (Assoc. Eds.), *Handbook of group communication theory & research* (pp. 493-515). Thousand Oaks, CA: Sage.

Bales, R. F., & Strodtbeck, F. L. (1951). Phases in groups. *Journal of Abnormal and Social Psychology, 46,* 485-495.

Bastien, D. T., & Hostager, T. J. (1992). Cooperation as communicative accomplishment: A symbolic interaction analysis of an improvised jazz concert. *Communication Studies, 43,* 92-104.

Baxter, L. A., & Goldsmith, D. (1990). Cultural terms for communication events among some American high school adolescents. *Western Journal of Speech Communication, 54,* 377-394.

Bormann, E. G. (1970). The paradox and promise of small group research. *Communication Monographs, 37,* 211-217.

Bormann, E. G. (1983). The symbolic convergence theory of communication and the creation, raising, and sustaining of public consciousness. In J. I. Sisco (Ed.), *The Jensen lectures: Contemporary communication studies* (pp. 71-90). Tampa: University of South Florida, Department of Communication.

Bormann, E. G. (1990). *Small group communication: Theory and practice* (3rd ed.). New York: Harper & Row.

Braithwaite, C. (1997a). Blood money: The routine violation of conversational rules. *Communication Reports, 10,* 63-73.

Braithwaite, C. (1997b). Were you there? A ritual of legitimacy among Vietnam veterans. *Western Journal of Communication, 61,* 423-447.

Braithwaite, D. (1995). Ritualized embarrassment at "coed" wedding and baby showers. *Communication Reports, 8,* 145-157.

Briggs, C. L. (1986). *Learning how to ask: A sociolinguistic appraisal of the role of the interview in social science research.* Cambridge, UK: Cambridge University Press.

Carbaugh, D. (1985). Cultural communication and organizing. In W. B. Gudykunst, L. P. Stewart, & S. Ting-Toomey (Eds.), *Communication, culture and organizational processes* (pp. 31-47). Beverly Hills, CA: Sage.

Carbaugh, D. (1986). Some thoughts on organizing as cultural communication. In L. Thayer (Ed.), *Organizational communication: Emerging perspectives* (pp. 85-101). Norwood, NJ: Ablex.

Carbaugh, D. (1988a). Comments on "culture" in communication inquiry. *Communication Reports, 1,* 38-41.

Carbaugh, D. (1988b). Cultural terms and tensions in the speech at a television station. *Western Journal of Speech Communication, 52,* 216-237.

Cawyer, C. S., & Smith-Dupré, A. (1995). Communicating social support: Identifying supportive episodes in an HIV/AIDS support group. *Communication Quarterly, 43,* 243-258.

Chien, S. C. (1996). Code-switching as a verbal strategy among Chinese in a campus setting in Taiwan. *World Englishes, 15,* 267-280.

Conquergood, D. (1991). Rethinking ethnography: Towards a critical cultural politics. *Communication Monographs, 58,* 179-194.

Conquergood, D. (1994). Homeboys and hoods: Gang communication and cultural space. In L. R. Frey (Ed.), *Group communication in context: Studies of natural groups* (pp. 23-55). Hillsdale, NJ: Lawrence Erlbaum.

Conquergood, D. (1995). Between rigor and relevance: Rethinking applied communication. In K. N. Cissna (Ed.), *Applied communication in the 21st century* (pp. 79-96). Mahwah, NJ: Lawrence Erlbaum.

Conquergood, D. (Producer), & Siegel, T. (Producer & Director). (1990). *The heart broken in half* [Videotape]. New York: Filmmakers Library.

Cragan, J. F., & Wright, D. W. (1980). Small group communication research of the 1970s: A synthesis and critique. *Central States Speech Journal, 31,* 197-213.

Cragan, J. F., & Wright, D. W. (1990). Small group communication research of the 1980s: A synthesis and critique. *Communication Studies, 41,* 212-236.

Crawford, L. (1996). Personal ethnography. *Communication Monographs, 63,* 158-170.

Cushman, D. (1989/1990). The role of critique in the ethnographic study of human communication practices. *Research on Language and Social Interaction, 23,* 243-250.

Della-Piana, C. K., & Anderson, J. A. (1995). Performing community: Community service as cultural conversation. *Communication Studies, 46,* 187-200.

Dollar, N. J. (1993). *Communicating like an Aiko Aiko: An ethnographic analysis of a code of membership.* Unpublished doctoral dissertation, University of Washington, Seattle.

Dollar, N. J. (1999). "Show talk" and communal identity: An analysis of Deadheads' ways of speaking. *Journal of the Northwestern Communication Association, 27,* 101-120.

Dollar, N. J., & Zimmers, B. G. (1998). Social identity and communicative boundaries: An analysis of youth and young adult street speakers in a U.S. American community. *Communication Research, 25,* 596-617.

Eisenberg, E., Murphy, A., & Andrews, L. (1998). Openness and decision-making in the search of a university provost. *Communication Monographs, 65,* 1-23.

Finders, M. J. (1996). Just girls: Literature and allegiance in junior high school females. *Written Communication, 13,* 93-129.

Fitch, K. L. (1990/1991). A ritual for attempting leave-taking in Columbia. *Research on Language and Social Interaction, 24,* 209-224.

Frey, L. R. (1994a). Call and response: The challenge of conducting research on natural group communication. In L. R. Frey (Ed.), *Group communication in context: Studies of natural groups* (pp. 293-304). Hillsdale, NJ: Lawrence Erlbaum.

Frey, L. R. (Ed.). (1994b). *Group communication in context. Studies of natural groups.* Hillsdale, NJ: Lawrence Erlbaum.

Frey, L. R. (1994c), The naturalistic paradigm: Studying small groups in the postmodern era. *Small Group Research, 25,* 551-577.

Frey, L. R. (Ed.). (1995). *Innovations in group facilitation: Applications in natural settings.* Cresskill, NJ: Hampton Press.

Frey, L. R. (in press). *Group communication in context: Studies of bona fide groups* (2nd ed.). Mahwah, NJ: Lawrence Erlbaum.

Geertz, C. (1973). *The interpretation of cultures: Selected essays.* New York: Basic Books.

Gouran, D. S. (1994). On the value of case studies of decision-making and problem-solving groups. In L. R. Frey (Ed.), *Group communication in context: Studies of natural groups* (pp. 305-315). Hillsdale, NJ: Lawrence Erlbaum.

Hirokawa, R. Y., & Rost, K. M. (1992). Effective group decision making in organizations: Field test of the vigilant interaction theory. *Management Communication Quarterly, 5,* 267-288.

Hollihan, T. A., & Riley, P. (1987). The rhetorical power of a compelling story: A critique of a "Toughlove" parental support group. *Communication Quarterly, 35,* 13-25.

Howard, L. A., & Geist, P. (1995). Ideological positioning in organizational change: The dialectic of control in a merging organization. *Communication Monographs, 62,* 110-131.

Huspek, M. R. (1986). Linguistic variation, context, and meaning: A case of -*ing/in* variation in North American workers' speech. *Language in Society, 15,* 149-164.

Hymes, D. (1972). Models of the interaction of language and social life. In J. J. Gumperz & D. Hymes (Eds.), *Directions in sociolinguistics* (pp. 35-71). New York: Holt, Rinehart & Winston.

Kliewer, C. (1998). Citizenship in the literate community: An ethnography of children with Down syndrome and the written word. *Exceptional Children, 64,* 167-180.

Lesch, C. L. (1994). Observing theory in practice: Sustaining consciousness in a coven. In L. R. Frey (Ed.), *Group communication in context: Studies of natural groups* (pp. 57-84). Hillsdale, NJ: Lawrence Erlbaum.

Lincoln, Y. S., & Guba, E. G. (1985). *Naturalistic inquiry.* Beverly Hills, CA: Sage.

Lofland, J., & Lofland, L. H. (1984). *Analyzing social settings: A guide to qualitative observation and analysis* (2nd ed.). Belmont, CA: Wadsworth.

Moffat, M. (1989). *Coming of age in New Jersey: College and American culture.* New Brunswick, NJ: Rutgers University Press.

Pearce, W. B., & Conklin, F. (1979). A model of hierarchical meanings in coherent conversation and a study of "indirect response." *Communication Monographs, 46,* 75-87.

Peterson, E. E. (1987). The stories of pregnancy: On interpretation of small-group cultures. *Communication Quarterly, 35,* 39-47.

Philipsen, G. (1987). The prospect for cultural communication. In D. Kincaid (Ed.), *Communication theory from Eastern and Western perspectives* (pp. 245-254). New York: Academic Press.

Philipsen, G. (1992). *Speaking culturally: Explorations in social communication.* Albany: State University of New York Press.

Philipsen, G. (1997). A theory of speech codes. In G. Philipsen & T. Albrecht (Eds.), *Developing communication theories* (pp. 119-156). Albany: State University of New York Press.

Poole, M. S. (1983). Decision development in small groups: III. A multiple sequence model of group decision development. *Communication Monographs, 50,* 321-341.

Propp, K. M., & Kreps, G. L. (1994). A rose by any other name: The vitality of group communication research. *Communication Studies, 45,* 7-19.

Putnam, L. L., & Stohl, C. (1990). Bona fide groups: A reconceptualization of groups in context. *Communication Studies, 41,* 248-265.

Rudd, G. (1995). The symbolic construction of organizational identities and community in a regional symphony. *Communication Studies, 46,* 201-222.

Schely-Newman, E. (1993). The woman who was shot: A communal tale. *Journal of American Folklore, 106,* 285-303.

Schely-Newman, E. (1997). Finding one's place: Locale narratives in an Israeli Moshav. *Quarterly Journal of Speech, 83,* 401-415.

Schneider, D. (1976). Notes toward a theory of culture. In K. Basso & H. Selby (Eds.), *Meaning in anthropology* (pp. 197-220). Albuquerque: University of New Mexico Press.

Sequeira, D. L. (1993). Personal address as negotiated meaning in an American church community. *Research on Language and Social Interaction, 26,* 259-285.

Smith, M. J. (1988). *Contemporary communication research methods.* Belmont, CA: Wadsworth.

Smythe, M. J. (1995). Talking bodies: Body talk at Bodyworks. *Communication Studies, 46,* 245-260.

Stohl, C., & Putnam, L. L. (1994). Group communication in context: Implications for the study of bona fide groups. In L. R. Frey (Ed.), *Group communication in context: Studies of natural groups* (pp. 285-292). Hillsdale, NJ: Lawrence Erlbaum.

Sykes, R. E. (1990). Imagining what we might study if we really studied small groups from a speech perspective. *Communication Studies, 41,* 200-211.

Taylor, D. A., & Altman, I. (1987). Communication in interpersonal relationships: Social penetration theory. In M. E. Roloff & G. R. Miller (Eds.), *Interpersonal processes: New directions in communication research* (pp. 252-277). Newbury Park, CA: Sage.

Thomas, J. (1993). *Doing critical ethnography.* Newbury Park, CA: Sage.

Weitzel, A., & Geist, P. (1998). Parliamentary procedure in a community group: Communication and vigilant decision making. *Communication Monographs, 65,* 245-259.

Wiemann, J. (1977). Explication and a test of a model of communicative competence. *Human Communication Research, 3,* 195-213.

5

The Group Dynamics Q-Sort in Group Communication Research

RANDALL S. PETERSON
London Business School

A number of communication scholars have openly questioned the validity of group communication research, in part because a large majority of it has been conducted in the laboratory with zero-history, short-term (e.g., 1-hour) student groups solving artificial tasks created by researchers. These scholars have made increasingly impassioned pleas for the study of natural or "real-world" groups (see Cragan & Wright, 1990; Frey, 1994; Poole, 1990; Putnam & Stohl, 1990, 1996; Sykes, 1990). More specifically, Putnam and Stohl (1990, 1996) argued that group communication researchers should study bona fide groups that (a) have stable yet permeable boundaries, (b) demonstrate shifting borders, and (c) are interdependent with their contexts. Although the critics include some of our most accomplished and respected scholars, the research strategy of relying on laboratory groups does not appear to have changed a great deal in response (see Frey, 1996).

One change that has occurred in response to the call for more ecologically valid research is the number of researchers who have turned to using qualitative research methods (see Frey, 1994, for some examples). One key reason for this shift is the descriptive richness captured by these methods. The detailed and nuanced storytelling that characterizes these methods is appealing from both an intuitive and a persuasive standpoint. Compared with much quantitative research, the "thick" descriptions of group process afforded by qualitative case studies allow for a more thorough understanding of the contexts in which a group is imbedded, have greater external validity, and are more likely to be longitudinal in nature (see Dollar & Merrigan, this volume).

The classic problem with the case study approach from a social-scientific perspective, of course, is its lack of rigor. The specific language and emphasis of each researcher that leads to unique insights into group functioning is also

AUTHOR'S NOTE: I thank Michael Roloff, Pamela Owens, Scott Alberts, and Ed Mabry for thoughtful reviews of earlier versions of this essay.

the very cause of difficulty in assessing agreement between researchers. It is often exceedingly difficult to assess the level of agreement between two experts who study the same group (e.g., the many descriptions of the group processes that led to the *Challenger* space shuttle disaster). One scholar may emphasize a group's problems with processing of information about technical issues, whereas another might emphasize the external social and political pressures placed on the group. The reader might well be left with the impression that these two scholars disagree about the dynamics of the group when, in fact, they are in fundamental agreement about a complex reality. But even as difficult as it is to understand differences between researchers' descriptions of the same group, compounding this with different researchers studying different groups makes the job of generalizing all but impossible. There is, in short, no good systematic way of adding many case studies together to come to reliable conclusions (Verba, 1967). Without a clear understanding of where there is underlying agreement, it is impossible to build a cumulative knowledge of group communication.

My purpose in this chapter is to propose an additional way of addressing the concern for ecologically valid group communication research that attempts to blend some of the richness of a qualitative approach with the rigor of a quantitative approach—the Group Dynamics Q-Sort (GDQ). The GDQ advances the study of group communication by addressing the concerns of scholars who want greater external validity but who also do not want to forgo the rigor of using quantitative methods. The GDQ is, in brief, a 100-item instrument that requires the user to place each item on a 1 to 9 Likert-type scale. Each item has two polar-opposite statements (e.g., group members devote enormous attention to detail vs. group members are oblivious to detail). Raters are asked to identify the extent to which one or the other of the extreme statements characterizes the group in question. The GDQ addresses the concern about increasing the external validity of group communication scholarship by considering a wide variety of items, including appraisals of group boundaries, the contexts in which a group is located, and a detailed assessment of the interactions of group members, which makes this instrument sympathetic to the qualitative strategy. The GDQ also addresses concern for increased external validity by being compatible with longitudinal research of groups and drawing on a variety of data sources that historically have been available to qualitative researchers and of limited use for quantitative study (e.g., academic historical case studies, popular press accounts of group dynamics, and participant observation). The q-sort method, therefore, addresses some of the weakness of both qualitative and quantitative (e.g., experimental) methods. It allows for theory testing and detailed group description across numerous (bona fide) groups with a standardized data language.

This chapter explains this new method and how can it be used. First, a brief history is presented of the q-sort method and its recent adaptation for groups. This is followed by a discussion of the technical aspects of how the GDQ works (instructions, scales, etc.). Finally, potential applications of the GDQ to the study of group communication are discussed and compared with other methods currently available to researchers (e.g., case study, interaction process analysis, and experiments).

THE DEVELOPMENT OF THE GROUP DYNAMICS Q-SORT

Although only recently introduced to the literature on groups, the q-sort method is actually not new. The method was developed in the 1940s and 1950s by Stephenson (1953) and refined by Block (1978), primarily as a method for assessing personality. The idea behind a q-sort is that the instrument should ask a comprehensive variety of questions within a specified domain. Hence, to assess personality, the items ask about a comprehensive set of attributes of an individual's personality (e.g., extroversion, openness to new experiences, agreeableness, emotional stability, and conscientiousness). For a group, the items cover a comprehensive set of attributes about a group's functioning (e.g., cohesion, norms, leadership, tolerance for dissent, situational stress, and boundary management). The set of items should be comprehensive enough to give a rich sense of the subject being studied rather than being a focused set of questions about one particular hypothesis or theory. The number of items in the q-sort should be sufficient to give depth and breadth of understanding about the person or group being assessed. There is no set number of items, but the most common number is 100.

Q-sorts are also ipsative in the sense that the number of items to be placed in each category is specified. When raters are forced to use the same distribution of items, this has two beneficial effects on the quality of the data. First, it encourages raters to think more carefully about each item and, thereby, reduces random error variance. Second, the forced distribution eliminates one form of interrater disagreement about groups altogether (really pseudodisagreement) that comes from individual tendencies of the raters to place items in the middle or extreme positions of the scale (Block, 1978). This procedure, thus, decreases the total amount of error in the data, resulting in a reduced need for research participants (often a significant problem for those who study groups). The one drawback of using restricted categories is that there is not complete independence of item placement. That is, the 100th item is determined once the first 99 have been placed. Strictly speaking, this requirement violates the independence assumption of most statistical models. With 100 items, however, the data-analytic effects are minimal (see Block, 1978).

One important property of a q-sort is that it requires idiographic assessments; that is, topical experts (personality observers or group researchers) must make decisions about which items are more descriptive than others (i.e., whether Category 9 items are more descriptive than Category 8 items). Thus, because items are rank-ordered relative to one another, the data are ordinal in nature. The advantage of this property is that q-sort items and scales can legitimately be compared to highlight key areas of similarity and dissimilarity between groups. For example, Tetlock, Peterson, McGuire, Chang, and Feld (1992) used a q-sort technique to confirm Janis's (1982) hypothesis that groups that experience groupthink show greater rigidity and conformity than do vigilant decision-making groups.

Each of the items in a q-sort also requires raters to assess messo-level impressions of the group or individual being assessed. This is distinct from micro-level behavioral coding (e.g., Bales, 1950, 1958), which builds group-level constructs statistically from behaviors observed at the individual level. It is also distinct from molar or macro-level impressions designed to assess overall process impressions (e.g., group cohesion or leader strength). Rather, raters are asked to make specified impressions on the basis of discrete sets of behaviors. For example, Item 3 in the GDQ asks raters to assess the extent to which "group members are blocking the efforts of the leader" rather than asking them to count behaviors related to that or asking about overall "leader strength."[1]

Another important feature of the q-sort methodology is the ability to create a priori theoretically derived "ideal types" and compare them directly with the actual groups or individuals being studied (for a discussion of template matching, see Bem & Funder, 1978; Block, 1978). More specifically, a theory can be translated into an ideal type by categorizing the q-sort items according to that theory. For example, groupthink theory can be translated into an ideal type by asking the question, How would Janis (1982) have placed the items for groups that demonstrate groupthink? Real groups in the study can then be statistically compared to assess the overall degree of fit between the theory and their actual behavior. Tetlock et al. (1992), for example, compared Janis's (1972, 1982) groupthink theory with each of the individual cases Janis used as examples of the theory and found that the Nixon White House case was the strongest match to the theoretical ideal of groupthink.

The Group Dynamics Q-Sort

The q-sort was first adapted for use in studying groups by Tetlock et al. (1992), who investigated elite political decision-making teams (e.g., presidents and their cabinets). That version of the q-sort was designed explicitly to assess the dynamics of political leadership groups. It was developed by asking experts in political science, history, leadership, and group decision making to assess a number of groups, using over 300 potential GDQ items. The number of items was reduced to 100 through empirical testing and advice from the experts, who suggested that items that could be combined or eliminated. The study itself used the GDQ to explore the theoretical and empirical foundations of groupthink theory. This was done by using the instrument to assess the group dynamics of the 10 decision episodes that Janis (1982) studied. Each of Janis's portrayals was also compared with at least three other historical sources on the group dynamics of the cases. The results suggested general agreement between Janis (1982) and the historical sources, but they also revealed some underlying problems with the theoretical constructs in the groupthink model.

Peterson (1997) later created a general version of the GDQ (the one presented here) by rewriting the items in the political version of the instrument to eliminate specific reference to the elite political environment. This was done to compare directly a much wider variety of groups (e.g., political, community, business, and laboratory created). The resulting instrument is not as well suited to the elite political decision-making environment as the political GDQ. However, the general version of the GDQ presented here still assesses a great deal of information about a group's context and boundaries. For example, Item 31 asks whether the group perceives a serious external threat, and Item 26 asks how long the group has been organized in its current form.

This version of the GDQ was successfully used, in fact, to study leader directiveness in city councils in the San Francisco Bay area in addition to laboratory-created groups (Peterson, 1997). Top management teams of *Fortune 500* corporations have also been studied using another, somewhat modified form of the GDQ—the organizational GDQ (Peterson, Owens, Tetlock, Fan, & Martorana, 1998)[2] In sum, bona fide groups have been successfully studied with the GDQ. Moreover, these studies have employed a variety of data sources not typically used by quantitative researchers in studying group communication (e.g., academic historical case studies, videotapes of meetings, and popular press accounts of group dynamics).

The 100 items of the GDQ (see the appendix on p. 87) are grouped into eight process indicator scales to provide an easy way to summarize the large number of individual items. The eight scales are (a) intellectual rigidity-flexibility, with higher scores indicating a greater likelihood of seeing problems in multidimensional ways and changing the group's mind in response to new evidence; (b) sense of control-crisis, with higher scores indicating a sense of urgency or emergency; (c) optimism-pessimism, with higher scores indicating that the group is pessimistic about achieving its goals; (d) leader weakness-strength, with higher scores indicating greater leader control over the group and a more directive approach by the leader toward other group members; (e) factionalism-cohesion, with higher scores indicating a group in which the members get along with one another and work together as a mutually supportive team; (f) legalism-corruption, with higher scores indicating a group run by backroom deals, nepotism, and self-serving interests; (g) decentralization-centralization of power, with higher scores indicating a group more centrally controlled by a strong leader or a small subgroup; and (h) risk aversion-risk taking, with higher scores indicating a group willing to take calculated risks. These eight scales represent broad process dynamics in groups. Any number of other, more detailed scales could be developed from the 100 items to test specific constructs or theories. For example, Peterson (1997) created scales for (i) leader process directiveness—the degree to which the leader regulates the process by which the group reaches a decision; (j) leader outcome directiveness—the degree to which the leader advocates a favored solution; and (k) process quality—the degree to which the group considers all available evidence before coming to a decision. In sum, the 100 items of the GDQ can be used to test a broad spectrum of group communication theory because the items explore a diverse array of group dynamic concerns.

THE MECHANICS OF EMPLOYING THE GROUP DYNAMICS Q-SORT

The GDQ is a 100-item set of questions designed to permit the portrayal of virtually any kind of group. The 100 items ask a variety of questions about group functioning. Each item has two polar-opposite statements that the rater must place in one of nine categories from "the top statement is extremely characteristic" of the group in question (Category 1) to "the bottom statement is extremely characteristic" (Category 9). The middle category (5) is for items for which there is conflicting evidence or no information is available. For example, Item 31 reads as follows:

The group perceives a serious external threat to its continued existence.

vs.

The group confronts a placid, relatively benign external environment (i.e., the environment may even be supportive).

The number of items that can be placed in each category is also restricted to produce a quasi-normal distribution of items (i.e., more items in the middle, see Table 5.1). This forces raters to make fine-tuned distinctions between items and eliminates individual tenden-

TABLE 5.1 Q-Sorting Distribution Constraints

Category	Label	No. of Cards
	Upper Statement	
1	Extremely characteristic	5
2	Highly characteristic	8
3	Quite characteristic	12
4	Slightly characteristic	16
	Middle Category	
5	Neither upper nor lower statement is characteristic	18
	Lower Statement	
6	Slightly characteristic	16
7	Quite characteristic	12
8	Highly characteristic	8
9	Extremely characteristic	5

cies to place items at the extremes or in the middle (a significant source of variability). Data sources for q-sorting can be individual experiences (e.g., a member of the group sorts on the basis of personal impressions of group functioning), observations of a group (e.g., personal impressions made by a nongroup member about group functioning), videotapes of group interaction, a written text, and so forth. Once a dataset has been established and reviewed, a trained rater can complete the q-sort in 20 to 30 minutes.

The item texts are usually printed on cards and issued with these instructions.

INSTRUCTIONS FOR THE GROUP DYNAMICS Q-SORT

The purpose of the 100 items in the Group Dynamics Q-Sort is to describe group experiences. The items are designed to permit the portrayal of virtually any kind of group, including top management teams, inner cabinets of governments, social groups, and laboratory-created groups. There should, for all practical purposes, be no limit to the range of group dynamics that can be described by the q-sort.

The q-sorting procedure is simple but somewhat time-consuming. With the group to be assessed in mind, look through the deck of 100 cards. You will note that each card has an upper statement and a lower statement that are opposites. First, sort the cards into three stacks in a column. Place in the upper stack all those cards for which the upper statement is characteristic of the group. Place in the lower stack all of those cards for which the lower statement is characteristic of the group. Place in the middle the remaining cards where there is conflicting evidence or a lack of evidence. No attention need be paid to the number of cards in each grouping at this time.

When the three stacks have been established, they must be further divided into a column of nine categories, each with an exact number of cards in it—5, 8, 12, 16, 18, 16, 12, 8, and 5. For example, you should place the five most characteristic statements in each of the two end rows (as shown in Table 5.1). You may feel frustrated by the constraints of the sorting procedure. In justification, it should be noted that specifying the number of cards to be assigned to each category has proven to be a more valuable procedure than the freer situation in which a rater can assign any number of cards to a category. Past research indicates that we underestimate the degree of interrater agreement when there are no constraints on sorting. The reason is simple. When we compare two free-form q-sorts, there are three causes of disagreement at work: real differences in point of view, random error variance (mood, carelessness, etc.), and differences in how raters use the rating scale (we know that some people make extreme judgments, whereas others are fence-sitters). When we compare two forced-distribution q-sorts, we eliminate this third source of interjudge disagreement (really pseudodisagreement) by standardizing how everyone uses the rating scale. This forced-distribution q-sort also has another related advantage. Because the q-sort technique limits the number of items per scale category, the forced-distribution q-sort puts pressure on judges to make frequent comparisons of the rel-

ative descriptive appropriateness of items. It is possible to highlight only so many items in the "extremely characteristic" categories. One must ask oneself the following: Given that I can highlight only a handful of statements as extremely characteristic, which ones are particularly worthy of being singled out? Making compromises of this sort is not easy, but it does increase both the interrater reliability and predictive value of q-sorts.

Scales and Ideal Types

The eight scales of items described earlier were created by clustering theoretically related and empirically correlated items together. Each scale is calculated by taking the mean score across all of the items in the scale so that the scale scores are nicely comparable and on the same metric as individual items (i.e., 1 to 9 scoring). This also means that each scale is bipolar. The scale items include the following:

a. *Intellectual rigidity-flexibility:* Items 19, 37, 40, 58 reversed, 66 reversed, 68, 71, 74 reversed, 81, 82 reversed, 88, 98 reversed
b. *Sense of control-crisis:* Items 21 reversed, 27, 31 reversed, 38 reversed, 54, 56 reversed, 93 reversed
c. *Optimism-pessimism:* Items 17, 22, 55, 64 reversed, 76 reversed
d. *Leader strength-weakness:* Items 6 reversed, 32, 39, 44, 60, 63, 83, 97
e. *Factionalism-cohesion:* Items 1 reversed, 3, 7, 9, 11, 23 reversed, 41, 46 reversed, 47, 51, 70 reversed, 72 reversed, 73 reversed, 78, 86 reversed, 99
f. *Legalism-corruption:* Items 10, 16, 18, 43 reversed, 67 reversed, 79 reversed, 89 reversed, 95
g. *Decentralization-centralization of power:* Items 4, 5, 12, 13 reversed, 14, 24, 53 reversed
h. *Risk aversion-risk taking* Items 25 reversed, 29 reversed, 50 reversed, 62 reversed, 84, 87 reversed

It is possible to create scales to test most theories in the group communication literature, given the breadth of items in the GDQ.

Two theoretical ideal types were created by Randall Peterson and Pamela Owens (average initial $r = .76$). These ideal types represent Janis's (1982) groupthink and vigilant decision-making models. The groupthink ideal type includes the following:

a. *Category 1:* Items 1, 36, 40, 73, 88
b. *Category 2:* Items 15, 38, 55, 56, 68, 70, 72, 97
c. *Category 3:* Items 19, 22, 23, 32, 37, 39, 53, 63, 81, 83, 89, 96
d. *Category 4:* Items 8, 9, 16, 17, 29, 31, 35, 45, 46, 59, 60, 65, 71, 76, 77, 86
e. *Category 5:* Items 6, 13, 21, 25, 33, 43, 48, 50, 51, 54, 57, 75, 80, 85, 87, 92, 94, 100
f. *Category 6:* Items 2, 5, 10, 14, 18, 20, 26, 27, 28, 42, 44, 52, 82, 84, 91, 95
g. *Category 7:* Items 4, 7, 24, 41, 47, 61, 62, 78, 79, 90, 93, 99
h. *Category 8:* Items 3, 11, 30, 34, 64, 67, 69, 74
i. *Category 9:* Items 12, 49, 58, 66, 98

The vigilant decision-making ideal type includes the following:

a. *Category 1:* Items 4, 14, 18, 35, 98
b. *Category 2:* Items 10, 12, 16, 46, 66, 74, 82, 92
c. *Category 3:* Items 17, 24, 29, 30, 49, 51, 52, 54, 58, 67, 84, 94
d. *Category 4:* Items 5, 13, 20, 22, 27, 42, 44, 45, 47, 55, 57, 59, 72, 80, 83, 87
e. *Category 5:* Items 3, 6, 23, 25, 26, 28, 31, 38, 39, 50, 60, 62, 63, 70, 75, 76, 90, 100
f. *Category 6:* Items 8, 9, 15, 32, 33, 34, 41, 43, 48, 56, 64, 65, 78, 85, 93, 96
g. *Category 7:* Items 7, 19, 37, 61, 69, 73, 81, 86, 88, 89, 91, 97
h. *Category 8:* Items 1, 2, 11, 21, 36, 53, 77, 79
i. *Category 9:* Items 40, 68, 71, 95, 99

These ideal types can be used to gauge the resemblance of actual groups sorted to groupthink and vigilant decision making. This comparison is best made by calculating a simple Pearson correlation coefficient (by transposing the data and correlating across the 100 items; see Block, 1978). Again, it is possible to use the GDQ to create templates for a variety of group communication theories or variables (e.g., quality of group decision process, according to Gouran & Hirokawa's, 1996, functional theory).

THE GROUP DYNAMICS Q-SORT AND GROUP COMMUNICATION RESEARCH

The GDQ is an advance in the study of group communication because it addresses the two key components of the call for a bona fide group perspective. The first component is the need to study groups with stable yet permeable boundaries. The GDQ does this because it requires an identifiable group; to place the items accurately, the expert rater must know who is and who is not in the group. Concurrently, a number of items tap how a group manages its membership boundaries, including whether (a) the group requires strict conformity for a person to be included as a member (Item 15); (b) the leader or someone else determines membership (Item 32); and (c) the group members represent outside interests, divisions, and so forth (Item 51). Thus, group boundary issues are a central feature of any GDQ assessment. In fact, the GDQ is better suited to the study of bona fide groups than to laboratory-created groups because quite a number of the items ask explicitly about external-boundary management issues. In other words, there are a number of q-sort items without clear answers, and hence, these are automatically placed in the middle category for a q-sort when assessing laboratory groups compared with bona fide groups.

The GDQ also addresses the second key issue of the interdependence of a group with its contexts. The items of the GDQ ask about a wide range of contextual issues, including (a) any external threat to a group's existence (Item 31), (b) whether external observers are holding a group responsible for its performance (Items 28, 85), (c) pressure created by workload (Item 38), (d) group reputation (Item 45), (e) protection of a group by powerful outsiders (Item 91), and (f) an external assessment of group legitimacy (Item 93). Group contexts are, thus, central to the GDQ assessment. As an example, Peterson, Owens, and Martorana (1999a) provided evidence to suggest that top management team dynamics are both the cause of (the usual argument) and caused by organizational performance.

The GDQ is also ideal for studying changes in bona fide groups over time. Each q-sort is a "snapshot" picture of a group at one point in time. The snapshots can be linked together to obtain a longitudinal and dynamic representation of a group or particular members, much like individual photos taken in rapid succession form a film. Tetlock et al. (1992), for example, described how multiple q-sorts of the Soviet Politburo were created from the early years of Joseph Stalin through the later years of Mikhail Gorbachev. The Politburo was, thus, tracked over a 60-year time span with multiple turnovers of leadership and membership. Similarly, Peterson, Owens, and Martorana (1999b) tracked the increasing pessimism, risk aversion, and sense of crisis in Lee Iacocca's administration of Chrysler between 1984 and 1990. The GDQ is, in short, quite well suited to the longitudinal study of bona fide groups.

Comparing the GDQ With Existing Research Methods

Although no method for developing and testing propositions derived from group communication theory is perfect, there are distinct advantages of the GDQ for studying bona fide groups over more traditional research methods. With case studies, for example, it is exceedingly difficult to make systematic comparisons across analysts' assessments of the same group, across assessments of the same group at different times, and across assessments of different groups. Case studies can be rigorously researched and compellingly written, but they do not easily "add up" (Verba, 1967). The GDQ addresses this problem by (a) providing a common descriptive language for capturing experts' assessments of group processes and (b) creating a standardized metric for interrater and intergroup comparisons. Although researchers do lose some descriptive richness by accepting the common language of the GDQ, that loss is limited by the comprehensiveness of the set of 100 items available. In exchange for some loss of descriptive richness, researchers gain the ability to make systematic and quantitative comparisons across groups, researchers, and time. This seems a more acceptable trade-off for scholars interested in the hypothetico-deductive study of group communication when compared with the virtually complete loss of systematic comparison involved with case studies.[3]

The trade-offs of using the GDQ instead of experiments, on the other hand, are almost a mirror image. Experimentation allows for making strong causal inferences, but this comes at the cost of loss of virtually all information about how groups manage their boundaries and respond to their contexts (i.e., a bona fide group perspective). The great strength of the experimental method also defines its very real weakness—control of external influences. Experiments are useful for clarifying a relatively narrow causal link, but they do not assess as wide a range of attributes of group functioning, nor do they describe group functioning in as idiographically sensitive a way as case studies or the GDQ. For group communication scholars interested in understanding how groups manage their boundaries and how they are interdependent with their contexts, experimentation appears limited in its potential value (cf., Cragan & Wright, 1990; Putnam & Stohl, 1996, 1990; Sykes, 1990). Moreover, the ability to track groups over time allows for the testing of causal hypotheses using the GDQ.

Finally, interaction analysis (e.g., Bales, 1950) has proven useful for making quantitative assessments of group communication across observers, time, and groups. It allows for exploration of groups embedded in context and across time (i.e., bona fide groups). This benefit, however, comes at the cost of a virtually complete loss of ability to investigate context and boundary management directly. This loss happens because behavioral process coding infers group-level processes from individual-level observations. Contextual variables, such as group reputation or external accountability pressures, can never be directly assessed. Process coding, in short, is generally one step removed from making molar group judgments, whereas the GDQ is not. In other words, process coding infers group-level phenomenon from individual-level data, but the GDQ does not. As a result, interaction analysis is of limited use for group communication scholars interested in understanding how groups manage their boundaries and interact with their contexts.

CONCLUSION

The GDQ represents an important methodological advance in group communication research. It gives researchers an additional tool for studying groups and the processes that characterize them. This tool is potentially significant because it is well suited to the study of bona fide groups—groups that have stable but permeable boundaries, are interdependent with their contexts, and exist over extended periods of time. The GDQ is, thus, in a position to help scholars address many of the questions that critics of group communication theory and research have asked: Will our theories stand the ecological validity test? What are the key contextual variables that explain group behavior? And will the study of groups over time reveal new insights into group functioning? Answers to these questions promise to advance group communication research, pedagogy, and practice. The ability to provide answers to such questions is the *real* test of the GDQ's contribution to the study of group communication.

APPENDIX A

Item Listing for the
Group Dynamics Q-Sort

1. The group members are primarily concerned with how well they get along with one another (i.e., group solidarity, loyalty, and consensus are everything).
   vs.
   Group solidarity and loyalty are unimportant.

2. Group members believe that leadership requires special knowledge of that group (the knowledge can be historical, procedural, technical, etc.).
   vs.
   Leadership in the group is based on leadership skill rather than expertise.

3. Group members are effectively blocking the efforts of the leader.
   vs.
   Group members generally follow the leader, even when they disagree with the decisions made by the leader.

4. The group always includes the widest possible range of people in its decisions.
   vs.
   The group keeps important decisions in the hands of a few key players.

5. Power in the group is personal, not positional (i.e., power depends on the individual, not on her or his formal position in the group).
   vs.
   Power in the group is positional (i.e., one gets power in the group by getting a position).

6. There is open rebellion against the leader among group members.

   vs.

   Group members are fiercely loyal to the leader.

7. Group members are contentious, are prone to divisive attacks on one another, and often make assertions of self-interest.

   vs.

   Group members are deferential, believe in self-sacrifice, and are willing to subordinate their interests to the collective good.

8. The group has an orderly and hierarchical structure (i.e., everyone knows who is in charge and who reports to whom).

   vs.

   All group members have completely equal authority in the group; no one outranks anyone else.

9. Group meetings are highly formal (i.e., rules are followed to the letter).

   vs.

   Group meetings are very informal affairs, with few rules or norms to be followed.
   (*Note.* Code as neutral if the meetings are orderly but relaxed.)

10. Rules are applied in a consistent, legalistic way to all members.

    vs.

    Rules are applied selectively, depending on "who one is" or "whom one knows."

11. Group members see their own success as tied to the failure of other group members.

    vs.

    Group members perceive a "common fate"—we all succeed or fail together.

12. The group prefers to seek a great deal of information before making any decision, even when that may compromise secrecy or require a deadline to be missed.

    vs.

    Group members prefer to make decisions based on what they already know, even if that restricts the level of information available to the group.

13. The group likes to work out every detail of its decisions as a whole group.

    vs.

    The group makes general decisions, leaving the details to individual members, committees, or subgroups.

14. Information flows freely among group members (i.e., full disclosure is the norm).

    vs.

    Information is often withheld from some of the members of the group.

15. To be a member in good standing in the group, one needs to conform to strict codes of dress and conduct.

    vs.

    The group tolerates a very wide range of lifestyles among its members.

16. Group members are governed by rules of fair play beyond the written rules (i.e., personal agendas are secondary).

    vs.

    Group members are governed by a desire to achieve their personal goals (i.e., there is a feeling that anything is fair as long as it isn't expressly forbidden by the group).

17. The group is optimistic about its ability to accomplish its goals.

    vs.

    Pessimism and cynicism pervade group discussions.

18. Group members are remarkably honest, open, and candid in their dealings with one another.

vs.

False appearances and deception are so common as to be a way of life (i.e., nothing can be taken at face value).

19. The group holds resolutely to its decisions (i.e., it is unable to see how its own actions are responsible for current problems).

vs.

The group recognizes shortcomings in its decisions and makes midcourse changes.

20. The group is widely recognized as creative and inventive.

vs.

The group has a reputation for following old solutions to new problems.

21. The group is unable to make decisions unless there is a crisis.

vs.

The group is capable of decisive action before problems deteriorate into crises (i.e., implies a capacity both to anticipate events and to mobilize resources to shape those events).

22. The group is confident in its legitimacy (i.e., the group members believe there is widespread acceptance of their right to make decisions).

vs.

The group is very unsure and self-conscious of its legitimacy.
(*Note.* This item refers to the group's own view; the outsider's view is to be rated in Item 93.)

23. Relations among group members are warm and friendly.

vs.

Relations among group members are charged with hostility and rivalry.

(*Note.* Code as neutral if relations between group members tend to be affectively neutral and businesslike.)

24. The group consists of a number of equally dominant people.

vs.

One member dominates the group, and other members work to achieve the favor of this leader.

25. The group tends to make risky decisions.

vs.

The group tends to make risk-averse, "safe" decisions.

26. The group is in an early power consolidation phase.

vs.

The group has been organized for a long time, and power has stabilized.

27. The group is in complete control of its destiny.

vs.

The group is fighting desperately for survival (i.e., external forces are threatening the group).

28. The group is accountable to another group or individual.

vs.

The group is completely free to make whatever decisions it wants (i.e., it is beholden to no one).

29. The group is driven by deeply held values (e.g., a group of true believers who are determined to achieve their vision of a better world).

vs.

The group is driven by the desire to succeed (e.g., group members are pragmatic and willing to compromise their values to get what they want).

30. The group is diverse along ethnic, religious, or ideological lines.

vs.

The group is remarkable homogeneous.

31. The group perceives a serious external threat to its continued existence.

    vs.

    The group confronts a placid, relatively benign external environment (e.g., the environment may even be supportive).

32. The leader has complete control over who is admitted to the group.

    vs.

    Group members do not owe their positions to the leader; the leader does not control who becomes a member of the group.

33. Peculiar, even pathological, conduct by the leader is tolerated.

    vs.

    Peculiar or pathological behavior by the leader is not tolerated.

34. Interaction among group members is confined to official meetings and group-related gatherings.

    vs.

    Group members know one another well and socialize together.

35. There is a no-nonsense, task-oriented feeling to the group—a genuine common commitment to solving problems.

    vs.

    Group members are more interested in achieving their individual goals than solving group problems.

36. The group leader makes no secret of his or her preferences for group decisions.

    vs.

    Group members are often in doubt as to exactly where the group leader stands on important issues.

37. There is a great deal of xenophobia or suspiciousness toward outsiders within the group.

    vs.

    The group is open to a wide range of cultural and intellectual influences.

38. The group is under enormous pressure or stress to solve looming problems (i.e., challenges far exceed capabilities).

    vs.

    The group does not feel pressured by existing problems and challenges.

39. The group leader is an extremely forceful and ambitious person.

    vs.

    The group leader is passive and withdrawn.

40. Dissent is not acceptable within meetings; the group ostracizes dissenters and/or punishes dissenters.

    vs.

    Dissent within group meetings is not only acceptable, it is actively encouraged as a way of improving group decisions.

41. There is a serious rift in the group between the forces of change and the forces supporting the ways and understandings of the past.

    vs.

    The group is united in the pace of change.

42. The group leader is highly task oriented and insensitive to the impact that group decisions have on others.

    vs.

    The group leader is highly concerned with not upsetting traditional arrangements to the point of avoiding badly needed changes.

43. Resource decisions in the group are made according to political criteria (e.g., whom one knows or political skills).

    vs.

    Resource decisions in the group are made according to reasoned criteria (e.g., equity, equality, or need).

44. The group leader has a laissez-faire style (i.e., pays no attention to how other group members accomplish their assignments).
    vs.
    The leader closely monitors the work of other group members.

45. The group has a reputation for accomplishing a great many things.
    vs.
    The group is not widely recognized for its accomplishments.

46. Group members feel completely included in group decisions.
    vs.
    Some group members feel excluded from group decisions (e.g., the group leader or a small subgroup makes all the important decisions).

47. Authority within the group is highly fragmented (i.e., different individuals in the group have distinct responsibilities and authority).
    vs.
    Authority within the group is highly centralized (i.e., one individual or a small subset of the group has virtually total control).

48. Group members have the freedom to act individually; they are not responsible to others outside the group.
    vs.
    Group members have constituencies they must represent and follow closely.

49. Group members can challenge collective decisions in public without direct penalty.
    vs.
    Once the group makes a decision, other members of the group are expected to publicly support the decision (i.e., the appearance of unanimity to the outside world is important).

50. Different issues activate different coalition patterns within the group.
    vs.
    There is a stable and predictable division of opinion within the group.

51. The group consists of individuals who represent certain outside groups or constituencies.
    vs.
    The group consists of "generalists" without particular constituencies.

52. There are effective mechanisms for resolving conflicts within the group (i.e., short of resignations).
    vs.
    There are no effective mechanisms for resolving conflicts within the group.

53. Power is concentrated within a small subset of the group.
    vs.
    Power is dispersed across the group members.

54. The group is capable of acting quickly in an emergency.
    vs.
    Even in emergencies, the group is unable to act in a cohesive or unified way.

55. The group shows strong esprit de corps and group solidarity.
    vs.
    The group is badly demoralized.

56. The group is between a rock and a hard place; the group faces an impossible task of meeting conflicting demands placed on it.
    vs.
    The group has no difficulty meeting the demands placed on it by others.

57. The group has an orderly procedure for leadership succession.
    vs.
    The group has failed to deal with the leadership succession problem.

58. Group members are highly attuned to major changes occurring around them.

    vs.

    Group members are extremely slow to recognize major changes occurring around them.

59. Group rules are informal and unwritten.

    vs.

    Group rules are formally adopted and recorded.

60. The group displays automatic and unquestioning obedience toward the leader.

    vs.

    The leader is often ignored or even overruled by the group.
    (*Note.* Code as neutral if the leader generally expects deference but does not have the right to rule arbitrarily.)

61. The group leader behaves in an unpredictable, even mercurial, manner.

    vs.

    The group leader behaves in a stable, predictable manner.

62. The group pursues initiatives unexpectedly (i.e., predicting group decisions is never easy).

    vs.

    Group decisions are predictable (i.e., the group sticks with things that have worked in the past).

63. Group members are convinced that the leader possesses special skills that are critical for achieving group goals.

    vs.

    Group members harbor serious doubts about the leader's effectiveness.

64. The group suffers from an inferiority complex.

    vs.

The group displays enormous confidence in itself.

65. Explicit norms and procedures regulate competition for power within the group.

    vs.

    There are no normative constraints on political maneuvering within the group.

66. The group places much more emphasis on consultation and soliciting expert advice than it does on preserving absolute control over decisions.

    vs.

    The group places much more importance on preserving absolute control over making decisions than on consultation and soliciting expert advice (i.e., the group prefers to draw on the expertise of its members).

67. The group respects basic civil liberties and rights of nongroup members.

    vs.

    The group has an elitist attitude toward nongroup members; members believe they are morally or intellectually superior to nongroup members.

68. The group leader is insulated from criticism.

    vs.

    The group leader is exposed to a wide range of views and arguments (e.g., the leader may even encourage criticism).

69. The group is beholden to a subgroup with extreme views (i.e., subgroup members will delay action until their demands are met).

    vs.

    The group can act without the approval of an extreme subgroup.
    (*Note.* Code as neutral if no extreme subgroup exists.)

70. The group leader demonstrates intense loyalty to close supporters and advisors.
    vs.
    The group leader shows no loyalty to close supporters and advisors.

71. Group members are defensive, insecure people who do not respond well to criticism.
    vs.
    Group members are open, confident people who are willing to consider that they might be wrong.

72. The group never acts unless unanimity or consensus has been achieved.
    vs.
    The group frequently undertakes decisions that a substantial faction of the group opposes.

73. A state of emergency has created intense pressure to forge a common front.
    vs.
    There is little external pressure to forge a common front.

74. The group believes that painful and divisive choices cannot be avoided.
    vs.
    The group believes that trade-offs can be avoided.

75. Disputes among members are resolved through formal procedures.
    vs.
    Member disputes are handled informally as needed in the group.

76. The group is suffering from serious setbacks or injuries to its collective self-esteem.
    vs.
    The group is "riding high" as a result of successes.

77. The group acts impulsively (i.e., it responds emotionally and rarely makes contingency plans).
    vs.

The group acts carefully and deliberately.

78. Some members are dissatisfied with the division of resources in the group (e.g., money and prestige).
    vs.
    All members are satisfied with the division of resources in the group.

79. There is a pervasive lack of accountability within the group (i.e., members are not held responsible for doing what they said they would do).
    vs.
    Group members feel strictly accountable for their responsibilities (i.e., members accept responsibility when they make a mistake or do not complete an assigned task).

80. A new generation of leadership has recently come to power.
    vs.
    The existing generation of leadership is systematically excluding a new cohort of leaders.

81. The group leader is insensitive, even oblivious, to other points of view within the group.
    vs.
    The group leader is a good listener who pays careful attention to what others say and is good at understanding divergent viewpoints.

82. The group leader has a versatile, multidimensional mind.
    vs.
    The group leader is narrow-minded and dogmatic.

83. No member of the group comes even close to matching the skills and stature of the leader.
    vs.
    The group leader is overshadowed or eclipsed by other group members.

84. The group leader's opinions are in the middle of the continuum of opinion within the group.
    vs.
    The group leader is identified with an extreme subgroup.

85. The group can plausibly blame others for current woes (i.e., even outside observers agree that responsibility lies elsewhere).
    vs.
    The group must accept responsibility for current woes (i.e., the group is being held accountable for its problems).

86. The leader ensures that the group maintains order (e.g., without the leader, factions within the group would collide).
    vs.
    The disappearance of the leader would not alter the balance of power in the group (i.e., the group would continue to function pretty much as it does now).

87. There is a radical flavor to the rhetoric and/or objectives of the group (e.g., the group rethinks old approaches, adopts new strategies, etc.).
    vs.
    There is a conservative flavor to the rhetoric and/or objectives of the group (e.g., "if it ain't broke, don't fix it").

88. The group members see the world as dichotomous (e.g., good versus bad, in-group versus out-group, etc.).
    vs.
    The group members believe that reasonable people can disagree over important issues (i.e., see the world in "shades of gray").

89. The group plays on popular prejudices (e.g., racial or religious) as a source of power.
    vs.
    The group makes extraordinary efforts to display its impartiality (e.g., with respect to ethnicity, race, religion, etc.).

90. The most influential members of the group are poorly educated (i.e., have little formal education or narrow technical training).
    vs.
    The most influential members of the group are extremely well educated (i.e., have advanced degrees from major universities).

91. The group is confident that, even if its current plans fail, it will be "bailed out" by powerful protectors (e.g., protection could come from large cash reserves, government action, strong reputation, administrators higher in the organization, etc.).
    vs.
    The group realizes it is on its own (i.e., success or failure depends on its own efforts).

92. The leader respects the concerns and feelings of other group members.
    vs.
    The leader shows contempt for the concerns and feelings of other group members.

93. The group's legitimate authority has not been earned or has been utterly discredited.
    vs.
    The group's legitimacy is widely accepted within the community.
    (*Note.* This item refers to outsider's view of the group; the group's own view is to be rated in Item 22.)

94. The relationship between the group leader and other members of the group is remarkably easygoing and relaxed (e.g., people feel free to speak their minds and even to joke occasionally).

vs.

The relationship between the group leader and other members is formal and tense (e.g., no spontaneity or humor).

95. Group members are opportunists guided only by self-interest and a desire to accomplish personal goals.

vs.

Group members are guided by a collective identity (e.g., they want to do the "right thing" for the "right reasons").

96. The group tends toward overcontrol (i.e., wanting to control everything it can).

vs.

The group tends toward undercontrol (i.e., not wanting to control anything more than it must).

97. The group leader makes major efforts to persuade others to redefine their goals and priorities.

vs.

The group leader places little emphasis on persuading others to redefine their goals and priorities (i.e., works within the constraints of current opinion).

98. The group believes that most decisions require a fluid process, weighing competing values and making subtle trade-off judgments (i.e., decisions are made in many ways depending on the circumstances).

vs.

The group believes there are clear right and wrong, good and bad ways of making decisions (i.e., the process by which decisions are made is rigid).

99. There is an atmosphere of suspicion and fear within the group.

vs.

There is an atmosphere of trust and mutual support among group members.

100. Virtually all that is known about the group's functioning is based on highly speculative reconstruction of fragmentary evidence.

vs.

There is a great deal of highly reliable evidence about the internal functioning of the group.

NOTES

1. Most q-sorts are designed for topical experts. However, there are self-rated q-sorts (called s-sorts) for research on both personality (Stephenson, 1953) and groups (Alberts, 1999).

2. There is also a third version of the GDQ designed to assess group dynamics specifically within the organizational context (for details on the method, see Peterson, Owens, & Martorana, 1999b; for an application of the method, see Peterson et al. 1998).

3. It is important to note that using case studies as the data source for the GDQ assessments generates some of the same concerns that have been articulated about case studies in general. Specifically, skeptics can question the accuracy of the research conclusions derived from cases that are not well researched. In other words, the method can produce reliable assessments of the group dynamics that are not valid (i.e., garbage in leads to garbage out). Hence, GDQ data derived from case studies require an additional burden of proof that q-sort data generated from observation or participation do not.

REFERENCES

Alberts, K. S. (1999). *Diagnosing decision making groups: Testing the general group dynamics self-administered q-sorts (GDS) using faculty and administrative groups from Oberlin College.* Unpublished doctoral dissertation, Northwestern University, Evanston, IL.

Bales, R. F. (1950). *Interaction process analysis: A method for the study of small groups.* Cambridge, MA: Addison-Wesley.

Bales, R. F. (1958). Task roles and social roles in problem solving groups. In E. E. Maccoby, T. M. Newcomb, & E. L. Hartley (Eds.), *Readings in social psychology* (pp. 437-446). New York: Holt, Rinehart & Winston.

Bem, D. J., & Funder, D. C. (1978). Predicting more of the people more of the time: Assessing the personality of the situations. *Psychological Review, 85,* 485-501.

Block, J. (1978). *The q-sort method in personality assessment and psychiatric research* (2nd ed.). Palo Alto, CA: Consulting Psychologists Press.

Cragan, J. F., & Wright, D. W. (1990). Small group communication research of the 1980s: A synthesis and critique. *Communication Studies, 41,* 212-236.

Frey, L. R. (1994). The naturalistic paradigm: Studying small groups in the postmodern era. *Small Group Research, 25,* 551-577.

Frey, L. R. (1996). Remembering and "re-remembering": A history of theory and research on communication and group decision making. In R. Y. Hirokawa & M. S. Poole (Eds.), *Communication and group decision making* (2nd ed., pp. 19-51). Thousand Oaks, CA: Sage.

Gouran, D. S., & Hirokawa, R. Y. (1996). Functional theory and communication in decision-making and problem-solving groups: An expanded view. In R. Y. Hirokawa & M. S. Poole (Eds.), *Communication and group decision making* (2nd ed., pp. 55-80). Thousand Oaks, CA: Sage.

Janis, I. L. (1972). *Victims of groupthink: A psychological study of foreign-policy decisions and fiascoes.* Boston: Houghton Mifflin.

Janis, I. L. (1982). *Groupthink: Psychological studies of policies and fiascoes* (2nd ed.). Boston: Houghton Mifflin.

Peterson, R. S. (1997). A directive leadership style in group decision making is both virtue and vice: Evidence from elite and experimental groups. *Journal of Personality and Social Psychology, 72,* 1107-1121.

Peterson, R. S., Owens, P. D., & Martorana, P. V. (1999a). Cause or effect? An investigation of the relationship between top management team dynamics and organizational performance. In M. A. Neale, E. A. Mannix, & R. Wageman (Eds.), *Research on managing groups and teams: Vol. 2. Context* (pp. 49-69). Greenwich, CT: JAI Press.

Peterson, R. S., Owens, P. D., & Martorana, P. V. (1999b). The group dynamics q-sort in organizational research: A new method for studying familiar problem. *Organizational Research Methods, 2,* 107-136.

Peterson, R. S., Owens, P. D., Tetlock, P. E., Fan, E., & Martorana, P. (1998). Group dynamics in top management teams: Groupthink, vigilance and alternative models of organizational failure and success. *Organizational Behavior and Human Decision Processes, 73,* 272-305.

Poole, M. S. (1990). Do we have any theories of group communication? *Communication Studies, 41,* 237-248.

Putnam, L. L., & Stohl, C. (1990). Bona fide groups: A reconceptualization of groups in context. *Communication Studies, 41,* 248-265.

Putnam, L. L., & Stohl, C. (1996). Bona fide groups: An alternative perspective for communication and small group decision making. In R. Hirokawa & M. S. Poole (Eds.), *Communication and group decision making* (2nd ed., pp. 147-178). Thousand Oaks, CA: Sage.

Stephenson, W. (1953). *The study of behavior: Q-technique and its methodology.* Chicago: University of Chicago Press.

Sykes, R. E. (1990). Imagining what we might study if we really studied small groups from a speech perspective. *Communication Studies, 41,* 200-211.

Tetlock, P. E., Peterson, R. S., McGuire, C., Chang, S., & Feld, P. (1992). Assessing political group dynamics: A test of the groupthink model. *Journal of Personality and Social Psychology, 63,* 403-425.

Verba, S. (1967). Some dilemmas in comparative research. *World Politics, 20,* 111-127.

PART III

Antecedent Factors Affecting Group Communication

6

The State of Traits

Predispositions and Group Communication

JOANN KEYTON
LAWRENCE R. FREY
The University of Memphis

In a provocative article titled "Humans Would Do Better Without Groups," Buys (1978) argued that because of the many problems that groups cause, people would be better off without groups. In response, L. R. Anderson (1978) penned an essay titled "Groups Would Do Better Without Humans," in which he asserted that the problem was not groups per se but the people who composed them, in that "humans seldom work at maximum ability levels, seldom communicate with any degree of accuracy or logic and are constantly in need of social-emotional satisfaction for their simpering insecurities about affection, esteem, love, etc." (p. 557). Although written tongue-in-cheek, Anderson has a point: Groups often are only as good as the members that make them up.

The individual member is, thus, an important starting point for understanding the nature of groups. This initial boundary condition is apparent even in the genesis of the term *member,* as Arrow and McGrath (1993) explained:

Small groups operate within a physical, technological, temporal, and social environment. The boundary of a small group forms a "membrane" across which resources and products move in and out of the group. And the most fundamental resource of any group is the people who form the groups—its *members.* The word *member* comes from the same Latin root—*membrum*—as membrane and referred at first chiefly to the various parts of a body (members) that are enclosed within the boundary of the skin, the *membrana* (*Webster's Ninth,* 1985). Extending the concept to the group level, *members* came to mean the distinguishable parts—the people—within the group's boundaries. (p. 337)

Group members, therefore, are an important antecedent variable that needs to be foregrounded when studying group communication. Gouran (1994), in setting the agenda for group communication scholarship, claimed that

we must begin to pay more attention to antecedents that predispose members of groups, or otherwise incline them, to perform particular acts by acquiring specific information about them. . . . [This will] require that we learn a good deal more about the group members

99

whose discussions we study than scholars typically have been accustomed to learning. (p. 31)

There are, of course, many characteristics of group members that could be studied, ranging from social characteristics (biological and physical traits, such as sex and age, as well as traits society uses to assign status, such as seniority and wealth) to abilities (both general abilities, such as intelligence, and specific abilities relevant to a particular group situation, such as previous experience with the task) to personality characteristics, or what are called "traits" or "predispositions."[1] We have chosen to focus on traits/predispositions and the role that they play in explaining group communication (for reviews of social characteristics and abilities, and/or traits, in the group context, see, e.g., Davies, 1994; Frey, 1997; Haslett & Ruebush, 1999; Mann, 1959; Shaw, 1981; Stogdill, 1948). We first define traits and discuss reasons for studying them. We then review some of the extant research on those traits that have been shown to be relevant to the group (communication) context. On the basis of that review, we propose an agenda for promoting such research.

THE NATURE OF TRAITS

With over 20,000 terms available to describe various traits, the attribution of traits to individuals is a common occurrence (Andersen, 1987); indeed, it is one of the main ways in which people are differentiated from one another. In fact, according to Guilford (1959), a *trait* means "any distinguishable, relatively enduring way in which one individual differs from others" (p. 6). Focusing only on differences, however, obscures the way in which the attribution of traits links people together into a group. For example, scholars and practitioners are concerned about helping the group of people who suffer from shyness. Traits, thus, create a group boundary for a set of people that simultaneously links them together and distinguishes them from other groups of people.

Traits, of course, are attributions that people assign to themselves and others on the basis of perceived, relatively enduring ways of behaving, thinking, and/or feeling. Traits, therefore, are socially constructed constructs rather than objective referents or attributes. Hence, for example, a "paranoid person" does not walk down the street; a person displaying behaviors that people commonly associate with paranoia (e.g., constantly looking over one's shoulder) walks down the street.

There is much debate about the difference between traits, enduring ways of being (e.g., being paranoid across many different situations and, thereby, possessing such a trait), and *states,* the enactment of particular behaviors, thoughts, and/or feelings in specific situations (e.g., repeatedly looking over one's shoulder when being stalked). However, as Daly and Bippus (1998) suggested, "The differences between trait and state are, in actuality, primarily differences of emphasis" (p. 2). They argued that the distinction between these constructs has become blurred in recent years and that scholars now see traits and states as complementary (see also Chaplin, John, & Goldberg, 1988). For instance, Revelle (1995) explained that traits are

summary statements describing likelihood of and rates of change in behavior in response to particular situational cues. In addition to their relationship to the probability and latency of response, stable predispositions may be conceptualized in terms of differential sensitivities to situations and differential response biases. Intervening between traits, situations, and responses are momentary affective and cognitive states. (p. 315)

Traits, however conceived in relation to states, are, therefore, an attribution that references a generative mechanism that predisposes people to behave, think, and/or feel in particular ways (Beatty, 1998). These predispositions, of course, include not only how people perceive, think, or feel, traditionally the province of personality traits, but also people's behaviors, thoughts, and feelings regarding communication; hence, when a trait is attributed to a person, he or she may be predisposed toward communicating with others in certain ways in terms of message production and/or reception. As Daly and Diesel (1992) explained, personality traits are "directly relevant to communication insofar as each is related to how people communicate or how they come to understand others' messages" (p. 405). In that sense, "Trait approaches to communication place the locus of action in the predispositions of individuals to initiate action or to react to behavior" (Hewes & Planalp, 1987, p. 149). McCroskey, Daly, Martin, and Beatty (1998) even went so far as to conclude that "individuals' patterns of communication behavior are largely a manifestation of their individual traits" (p. vii).

There is, however, a mutually generative relationship between personality traits and communicative behavior. As Daly and Bippus (1998) explained,

> Traits are correlated with communication-related variables in meaningful ways. They account for significant variation in communication behavior as well as communication-based perceptions. At the same time, communication plays an important role in the development and maintenance of dispositional tendencies. (p. 22)

Weaver's (1998) review of the literature led him to conclude, "The essence of one's personality (i.e., self-conception) emerges from and is refined through communicative interactions with others in society" (p. 96). Perhaps Daly (1987) summed up this reciprocal relationship best: "Personality and communication are inherently intertwined" (p. 29).

THE STATE OF TRAIT RESEARCH

The literature on traits is enormous, reaching far beyond the confines of the psychology and communication literatures and dating back to ancient Greece (see Weaver, 1998). The study of personality traits in groups, however, is only about 50 years old. Hare (1976) described the major dimensions of

personality in a group context as predispositions toward being dominant (or submissive), positive (or negative), serious (or expressive), and conforming (or nonconforming). More recently, psychologists have advanced the "big five" approach to personality: extroversion or sociability, agreeableness, conscientiousness, neuroticism, and openness to experience (Digman, 1990). Still other scholars have reduced these five attributes to three (see, e.g., Eysenck, 1986, 1991; Zuckerman, 1995): (a) psychoticism-emotional control (P) to include hostility and aggression, (b) extraversion-introversion (E) to include cooperativeness and sociability, and (c) neuroticism-emotional stability (N) to include fearful avoidance. Table 6.1 summarizes the effects of these and related personality traits on group behavior.

Given the focus of this text on group communication, we examine here in some detail *communication traits*—those traits that "account for enduring consistencies and differences in individuals' message-sending and message-receiving behaviors" (Infante, Rancer, & Womack, 1997, p. 104). More specifically, we focus on the following four communication traits that have been shown to be relevant to the group context: aggressive communication, communication apprehension, communicator style, and interaction involvement.

Aggressive Communication

Communication, according to Infante et al. (1997), is *aggressive* "when a person tries to 'force' another person to believe something or to behave in a particular way" (p. 126). Aggressive communication consists of four traits, with the first two being potentially constructive and the latter two usually being destructive (Infante et al., 1997): (a) *assertiveness*—a "person's general tendency to be interpersonally dominant, ascendant, and forceful" (p. 127); (b) *argumentativeness*—"a personality trait in which individuals present and defend positions on controversial issues while attempting to refute the positions of other people" (p. 129); (c) *hostility*—"symbolic

(Text continued on page 105)

TABLE 6.1 Research Findings on the Effects of Personality Traits on Group Behavior

Approach-Avoidance Tendencies

People who like, respect, or trust other people (approach tendency) enhanced social interaction, cohesiveness, and morale in groups and suppressed competitiveness, whereas those who dislike and distrust other people (avoidance tendency) suppressed friendliness and cohesiveness (Haythorn, 1953).

Ascendant Tendencies

Assertive/dominant people, in comparison with those who were timid/submissive, communicated more (Bass, Wurster, Doll, & Clair, 1953; Watson, 1971), engaged in more individual-prominence communicative acts and were more effective group discussants (Scheidel, Crowell, & Shepherd, 1958), chose more "forcing" modes of conflict resolution (Aries, Gold, & Weigel, 1983), conformed less to group norms (McDavid & Sistrunk, 1964; Williams & Warchal, 1981), promoted more group cohesiveness (Haythorn, 1953), attempted more leadership and emerged more as leaders (Bass, Wurster, et al., 1953; Borg, 1960; Cattell & Stice, 1960; Lord, DeVader, & Alliger, 1986; Scioli, Dyson, & Fleitas, 1974; Smith & Cook, 1973), and had more influence on group decisions (Shaw, 1959; Shaw & Harkey, 1976).

Authoritarianism/Dogmatism

Authoritarianism (high needs for power and authority) was positively associated with conformity to group norms (Beloff, 1958; Crutchfield, 1955; Nadler, 1959); authoritarian jurors were more likely to convict defendants (Bray & Noble, 1978; Werner, Kagehiro, & Strube, 1982) and awarded more severe punishments (Bray & Noble, 1978; Friend & Vinson, 1974) than nonauthoritarians; high authoritarians showed more pre- to postdiscussion verdict changes than low authoritarians (Bray & Noble, 1978) and were more influenced by extralegal factors, such as the defendant's sex (Siegel & Mitchell, 1979); and groups composed of high-dogmatic members (showing rigidity in thinking and intolerance for cognitive and message inconsistency) demonstrated less risky shift than groups composed of low-dogmatic members (Rosenfeld & Plax, 1976).

Cognitive Complexity

Group members who held majority opinions exhibited greater integrative complexity (tendency to exhibit conceptual differentiation and integration) than members of groups who held minority or unanimous opinions, regardless of whether the reasoning was given in public or described privately (Gruenfeld, Thomas-Hunt, & Kim, 1998).

Cognitive Style

Mutlitemperament groups (groups balanced on the four dimensions of the Myers-Briggs Type Inventory of introversion-extraversion, sensing-intuition, thinking-feeling, and judging-perceiving) developed and used explicit governing objectives (discussions and decisions on objectives) in formulating the problem, whereas single-temperament groups (composed of all sensing-judging individuals) did not, and outperformed single-temperament groups (Volkema & Gorman, 1998); intuitive individuals and homogeneous intuitive teams initiated more social-emotional acts and engaged in more task-oriented behaviors than analytic individuals and homogeneous analytic teams, and teams tended to select intuitive individuals as leaders (Armstrong & Priola, 2001).

Dependability

Dependable people tended more often to emerge as leaders and were more successful in helping groups to effectively accomplish the task (Stogdill, 1948); undependability was associated with less group productivity (Haythorn, 1953).

Dependence

Presence of dependent personality disorder characteristics, compared with their absence, was associated with higher levels of work in a small psychodynamic group as rated by both therapists and other group members but not by the person being judged, and the effect was enhanced for those participants diagnosed with this disorder who demonstrated psychological mindfulness (McCallum & Piper, 1999).

Depression

Depressed group members talked less, were perceived to contribute less, and were selected as leaders less often than nondepressed members (Petzel, Johnson, Homer, & Kowalski, 1981).

Emotional Stability/Psychological Adjustment

Emotional stability/psychological adjustment was positively associated with helping groups to develop cohesion and morale (Haythorn, 1953), effective decision making (Greer, 1955), and leadership emergence (Bass, Wurster, et al., 1953; Stogdill, 1948); emotional instability/psychological maladjustment was associated with less communication efficiency (Bixenstine & Douglas, 1967), lower aspirations for the group (Beckwith, Iverson, & Render, 1965), more conformity (Meunier & Rule, 1967), more performance variability (Ryan & Lakie, 1965), risky group shifts (Kogan & Wallach, 1967), and more satisfaction with the group (Zander & Wulff, 1966).

Extraversion

Extroverts (those who are outgoing) scored lower on both small group and meeting communication apprehension than neurotics and psychotics (Weaver, 1998); extraversion was perceived by other group members as the key personality trait, increasing the proportion of high-extraversion group members did not decrease task focus (as hypothesized), and there was an inverted-curvilinear relationship between proportion of group members high in extraversion and quality of group performance, such that groups having 20% to 40% high-extraversion members outperformed groups with fewer or more such members (Barry & Stewart, 1997); and extraversion played a significant role in the group decision-making process only when the stimulus was of low (versus high) ambiguity and when information was relatively plentiful (versus rare) (Bonner, 2000).

Locus of Control

Internals (those who attribute responsibility for others' behavior to internal forces such as personality) and externals (those who attribute responsibility to external forces such as fate) forwarded arguments in attribution-of-responsibility judgment groups in line with their predisposition (Alderton, 1980, 1982; Alderton & Frey, 1983); locus of control was associated with leadership emergence, influence, and power in groups (Lord, Phillips, & Rush, 1980); and people low in desire for control were more likely to agree with confederate group members than those high in desire (Burger, 1987).

Machiavellianism

Machiavellians (those who are able to control social situations for their own purposes; Machs) tended to contribute more to a group discussion and favored certain styles of communication (e.g., asking for information, making suggestions for action, and greater use of negative socioemotional interaction) than did other members (Hacker & Gaitz, 1970), and they also participated more often, offered more specific task information, and influenced the group more than other members did at critical phases (Bochner, di Salvo, & Jonas, 1975); low Machs helped more than high Machs in an emergency, especially when group members could communicate with one another (compared with noncommunicating groups or acting alone) (Gleason, Seaman, & Hollander, 1978); high Machs felt less influential and less accepted in the group than did low Machs (Bochner & Bochner, 1972) but had greater influence on other members and usually were identified as task leaders (Geis, 1964; Geis, Krupat, & Berger, 1965; Oskenberg, 1968; Rim, 1966), although medium Machs were rated more as leaders than high or low Machs, particularly for unstructured tasks (Wolfson, 1981); as low-Mach group membership increased, task activity increased (Bochner & Bochner, 1972); and high-Mach groups were more successful than low-Mach groups because of establishing better operating decisions (Jones & White, 1983).

Neuroticism

Neurotics (those with high anxiety and emotionality and a negative self-image) scored highest on both small group and meeting communication apprehension compared with extraverts and psychotics (Weaver, 1998).

Paranoia

Presence of paranoid personality disorder characteristics, compared with their absence, was associated with higher levels of self-rated work in a small psychodynamic group, but these ratings were not corroborated by therapists or by other patients (McCallum & Piper, 1999).

Psychological Gender/Sex-Type Orientation

Psychological gender orientation—masculine, feminine, or androgynous (equal identification with masculine and feminine psychological traits)—predicted task-oriented group activity, such that individuals with high masculine scores were perceived to have talked more in group discussions and to have had good ideas (Jose & McCarthy, 1988) and demonstrated higher levels of initiation and dominance behavior in groups compared with those with high feminine scores, who demonstrated higher levels of consideration and greater degrees of submissive behavior (Seibert

(Continued)

TABLE 6.1 Continued

& Gruenfeld, 1992); traditional males and androgynous females, in contrast to traditional females and androgynous males, tended to be more vigilant in group decision making with respect to offering alternatives and supporting ideas with information, but no differences were found for suggesting goals of alternatives and reviewing tentative decisions (Dilberto, 1992); members of masculine and feminine groups communicated according to their type, whereas groups with androgynous members did not (D. G. Ellis & McCallister, 1980); and masculine and androgynous groups demonstrated higher expectancies for performance, better performance, and greater perceived success than feminine groups (Alagna, 1982).

Psychoticism
Psychotics (those who display a high level of social deviance, impulsivity, and a lack of restraint) scored in the middle on both small group and meeting communication apprehension compared with extraverts and psychotics (Weaver, 1998).

Self-Esteem
People with low self-esteem, compared with those with high self-esteem, were more susceptible to the influence of others and social cues (Brockner, O'Malley, Hite, & Davies, 1987; Weiss, 1977), took greater risks when performing alone than in front of a group of people (Cohen & Sheposh, 1977), and rated both in-group and out-group less favorably (Crocker & Schwartz, 1985); and high self-esteem people felt that their failed solutions to problems were influenced by other group members but not their successful solutions, whereas low self-esteem people were equally influenced in both conditions (Schlenker, Soraci, & McCarthy, 1976).

Self-Monitoring
High self-monitors (those who pay attention to and adapt their verbal and nonverbal behaviors to the requirements of social situations) were more likely than low self-monitors to be influenced by group members who argued for positions different from their own (Andrews, 1985); and high self-monitors emerged more frequently as leaders in group situations (R. J. Ellis, Adamson, Deszca, & Cawsey, 1988), but this relationship was mediated by (a) members' sex (effects held for males but not females in mixed-sex groups, R. J. Ellis, 1988; R. J. Ellis & Cronshaw, 1992, and for those in female brainstorming groups, Garland & Beard, 1979), (b) social cues indicating the appropriateness of a structuring style of leadership (high self-monitors receiving such a cue emerged more frequently as leaders of problem-solving groups than high self-monitors without the social cue or low self-monitors with or without the social cue), and (c) favorable attitudes toward leadership (low self-monitors with unfavorable attitudes emerged less frequently as leaders than low self-monitors with favorable attitudes or high self-monitors with favorable or unfavorable attitudes, Cronshaw & Ellis, 1991).

Sociability
Group members high in affiliation (the need to build and maintain attachment to others) engaged in more group sociability communicative acts than those low in affiliation, although ineffective group discussants were higher on affiliation than effective discussants (Scheidel et al., 1958); group members high in agreeableness (the motive to maintain positive social relations) were less competitive and more cooperative than those low on this trait, although members high in agreeableness when partnered with more competitive partners could be persuaded to engage in competitive behavior (Graziano, Hair, & Finch, 1997); friendliness was positively related to group members' use of integrative or cooperative conflict management strategies (Wall & Galanes, 1986); lonely people, compared with nonlonely persons, were more inhibited in group interactions, speaking less (Sloan & Solano, 1984) and being less confident in their opinions and less willing to advance their opinions publicly (Hansson & Jones, 1981), and demonstrated less group satisfaction (C. M. Anderson & Martin, 1995); lonely males conformed less to a social consensus, whereas lonely females conformed more and were more influenced by such consensus (Hansson & Jones, 1981); and approval-oriented group members performed faster in groups than in individual competition (Sorrentino & Sheppard, 1978).

Social Sensitivity
Social sensitivity (the degree to which an individual perceives and responds to the needs of others, sometimes labeled empathy) was positively correlated with amount of participation (Bass, McGehee, Hawkins, Young, & Gebel, 1953; Cattell & Stice, 1960), leadership attempts and success (Bell & Hall, 1954; Meyer, 1951; Stogdill, 1948), acceptance by other group members (Cattell & Stice, 1960), and group effectiveness (Bouchard, 1969), whereas independence and resoluteness (opposites of social sensitivity) were negatively related with social interaction (Haythorn, 1953).

expression of irritability, negativism, resentment, and suspicion" (p. 132); and (d) *verbal aggressiveness*—"attacking the self-concept of people instead of, or in addition to, their positions" (p. 133).

Most research on aggressive communication has focused on the interpersonal context (for reviews, see Infante, 1987; Infante & Rancer, 1996; Rancer, 1998; Wigley, 1998), but a few studies demonstrate the relevance of this communication trait to the group context. In her studies of group leadership, Schultz (1974, 1978, 1980, 1982) found that group members who were highly or extremely argumentative were nominated more often as the leader than those who were moderately or mildly argumentative; in addition, highly argumentative individuals were rated by fellow group members as most influential, and extremely argumentative individuals, although downgraded in group ratings of their influence, actually had a disproportionate influence on the group's decision. One reason argumentative members may have a positive effect on group decision making is that they produce more statements disputing other members' ideas (Kazoleas & Kay, 1994), which potentially helps a group to critically address issues, problems, and solutions and avoid pitfalls such as "groupthink" (see Janis, 1982).

With respect to other outcomes, C. M. Anderson and Martin (1999) surveyed members of ongoing task groups and found that argumentativeness was not significantly correlated with group members' communication satisfaction or their perceptions of their group's cohesion and consensus; however, verbal aggressiveness was negatively related to satisfaction and consensus. The findings also showed that members who were moderately high on argumentativeness and very low on verbal aggressiveness were highly satisfied with their communication and perceived their group as reaching consensus and, to a lesser extent, to be cohesive; the reverse was true for those high in verbal aggressiveness and low in argumentativeness. These findings provide support for Kraus's (1997) argument that

scholars and practitioners typically view aggressive behavior in groups, at least in the form of the destructive trait of verbal aggressiveness, as "unwanted, undesirable, and unproductive" (p. 123).

Communication Apprehension

One of the most frequently studied and best-known communication traits is *communication apprehension* (CA), "an individual's level of fear or anxiety associated with either real or anticipated communication with another person or persons" (McCroskey, 1977, p. 78; for a review of this concept and corresponding literature, see McCroskey & Beatty, 1998; Richmond & McCroskey, 1985). Although CA is probably the most common term used, Patterson and Ritts (1997) pointed to the similarity of other constructs referencing anxiety in social settings: shyness, reticence, evaluation anxiety, social-communicative anxiety, and interpersonal anxiousness; receiver apprehension (Wheeless, 1975) and willingness/unwillingness to communicate (Burgoon, 1976; McCroskey & Richmond, 1987, 1998) can also be added to this list.

Although scholars have vigorously debated whether CA is a trait or a state, it can be viewed in at least four ways: (a) traitlike CA, a personality orientation that reflects a stable degree of anxiety across communication contexts and over time; (b) context-based CA, varying across situations; (c) audience-based CA, experienced with particular types of people regardless of context or time, and (d) situational CA, experienced with a particular person or group in a particular situation (see Infante et al., 1997). Of these, traitlike CA has received the most attention from scholars.

The instrument typically used to measure CA, the Personal Report of Communication Apprehension (PRCA-24; McCroskey, 1970), assesses CA in four contexts: group discussions, meetings, interpersonal conversations, and public speaking. The majority of the CA research has focused on the interpersonal context (for a review, see Patterson & Ritts, 1997), and the physiological, cognitive, behavioral, and relational effects of CA in that context have been well documented. The public speaking component (the one on which most people score highest) has also proven valuable from a pedagogical perspective for identifying those who suffer from such anxiety and designing interventions to help them cope with it.

In research specific to the group setting, CA has been found to affect members' behaviors and feelings. Research has consistently shown, for instance, that apprehensive people participate less frequently in groups than those who are not apprehensive (Burgoon, 1977; Daly, 1974; Heston, 1974; McCroskey & Richmond, 1992). In interacting brainstorming groups, members with low CA contributed significantly more ideas than did those with high CA (Comadena, 1984; Jablin, Seibold, & Sorensen, 1977; Jablin & Sussman, 1978), although that difference did not occur in nominal brainstorming groups, in which people work individually on a problem and then are assigned to be members of imaginary groups that never actually meet (Jablin, 1981). These findings may help to explain why people with high CA were more dissatisfied with their group's communication and performance, and perceived more status differentiation to exist in the group, than did those with low CA (C. M. Anderson & Martin, 1994; Jablin, 1981; Rubin & Rubin, 1989), although G. Sorensen and McCroskey (1977) did find, for both zero-history and intact groups, that CA had an inverse relationship with the amount of tension people exhibited in groups.

CA has also been shown to affect the way in which group members are perceived by others. For instance, apprehensive members, in contrast to their nonapprehensive counterparts, were perceived to be less credible, effective, and liked, and their contributions were judged to be less relevant (McCroskey, Hamilton, & Weiner, 1974; McCroskey & Richmond, 1976; McKinney, 1982; Wells & Lashbrook, 1970). Perhaps that is why those who scored higher on CA were rated lower— by themselves and by others—on both social and task attraction and on leadership emergence (Hawkins & Stewart, 1991), although Frey (1989) found no significant relationship between CA and group leadership ratings.

Finally, CA potentially affects the processes and outcomes at the group level. Avtgis (1999), examining the construct of unwillingness to communicate within the family context, found that those who approached interaction favorably reported (a) higher levels of conversation orientation, (b) encouragement by parents of conversation and the free flow of information and ideas, and (c) lower levels of conformity orientation, or the use of parental power to force children to conform; in contrast, communication avoidance was significantly related to lower conversation orientation, although it was not related to conformity orientation.

These findings demonstrate the significance of CA to the group context, leading McCroskey and Richmond (1992) to conclude, "In no communication situation is CA more important than in the small group context. It is not an exaggeration to suggest that CA may be the single most important factor in predicting communication behavior in a small group" (p. 368).

Communicator Style

Communicator style is "the way one verbally, nonverbally, and paraverbally interacts to signal how literal meaning should be taken, interpreted, filtered, or understood" (Norton, 1978, p. 99; see also Norton, 1983). Communication style is composed of 10 factors: animated, attentive, contentious/argumentative, dominant, dramatic, friendly, impression leaving, precise, open, and relaxed.

Despite the intuitive appeal of communicator style as a potential explanatory predictor of group communication and outcomes, almost no research on communicator style has been conducted in the group context. Research from the organizational context, however, shows that superiors and subordinates differ on their communicator style, with superiors scoring higher on dominant, impression leaving, and relaxed and lower on contentious/argumentative and dramatic (Infante & Gordon, 1981). Baker and Ganster (1985) also found that subordinates perceived leaders as being high on open, friendly, relaxed, and attentive communicator styles. Seeking to extend these findings to the group context, Frey (1989) investigated whether there were meaningful relationships between communicator style, member argumentation, and leadership emergence over the course of policy discussion groups meeting for 6 weeks. The results showed that the communicator styles of contentious/argumentative and friendly were correlated positively with four aspects of group argumentation and that attentive, open, and relaxed correlated positively with three aspects. As examples, the contentious/argumentative style was positively associated with forwarding data-based arguments, the attentive style with forwarding procedural arguments and those that summarized the discussion, and the friendly style with offering positive reactions to others' arguments. Only one significant difference between communicator styles with respect to leadership was discovered, with leaders being significantly friendlier than nonleaders.

Interaction Involvement

Interaction involvement is the "extent to which an individual partakes in a social environment" (Cegala, 1981, p. 112), representing an individual's tendency and willingness to become involved in interaction with others. Interaction involvement was originally designed to measure Goffman's (1963, 1967) concepts of *perceptiveness*—being aware of message meanings—and *attentiveness*—hearing and observing interaction; a third dimension, *responsiveness*—a person's certainty about how to respond to others during a conversation (Cegala, Savage, Brunner & Conrad, 1982)—was also added.

In the one study to date that has applied interaction involvement to the group context, Cegala, Wall, and Rippey (1987) found that high- and low-involved group members saw themselves very differently in terms of how they communicated in their pursuit of task-oriented goals. High-involved members saw themselves as exerting control and influence during the group meeting by engaging in frequent, purposeful, positive, dominant, controlling, and powerful communication; by seeking input from others; and by not feeling threatened by conflict. In contrast, low-involved members saw themselves as ineffective in pursuing their goals (and resented others for pursuing goals), passive and obedient, threatened by disagreement and conflict, and lacking the ability to influence others and affect group decision making; even when they were able to pursue their goals, they saw their communication as unfriendly, uncooperative, and generally inappropriate.

SETTING THE AGENDA FOR GROUP COMMUNICATION TRAIT RESEARCH

Our review of the literature on traits as applied to the group setting leads to two conclusions. First, scholars have paid limited attention to the role of traits, and this is especially true with respect to how traits affect group communication processes. This conclusion supports Hoyle and Crawford's (1994) assertion that "surprisingly few studies have examined the relation between personality and group life" (p. 473). Second, most of the studies conducted are quite old; there are relatively few recent studies and no research programs of which to speak. Given the current state of this research, it is difficult to know whether traits provide important explanations for group (communication) processes and outcomes. In this section, we propose two important tasks confronting group communication scholars who would engage the study of traits—identifying individuals' predispositions toward groups and studying traits at the group level—and discuss some methodological considerations that must be taken into account to accomplish these tasks.

Identifying Individuals' Predispositions Toward Groups

The limited research available has focused on how personality and communication traits that are not endemic to the group context per se (such as self-esteem and communicator style) are related to people's behavior in groups. Although this work is important and should continue, what is most needed at this stage is some understanding of people's *predispositions toward groups.*

Only a few scholars have focused on such predispositions; one of the earliest approaches was the work done by Bion (1961). Working from the classic distinction between task and socioemotional aspects of groups, Bion argued that group members sometimes acted as if the socioemotional activities were the actual task of the group and that this occurred as a result of underlying assumptions shared by group members. He identified three types of "basic assumption groups" that produced nonwork activity: (a) *dependency assumption group,* in which group members avoid work by relying on other members, especially the group leader, to provide direction and make decisions; (b) *fight-flight assumption group,* in which group members avoid work by engaging in conflict with one another (fight) or by physically or psychologically leaving the situation (flight); and (c) *pairing assumption group,* in which group members avoid work by forming dyadic alliances (see Lion & Gruenfeld, 1993; Pfeiffer & Jones, 1974). On the basis of Bion's belief that individuals have a tendency to adopt certain modes of behavior in groups as a result of characteristic behavioral dispositions (see Lion & Gruenfeld, 1993), Stock and Thelen (1958) developed a sentence-completion test, later called the "Reactions to Group Situations Test" (RGST; Pfeiffer & Jones, 1974), to measure individuals' preferences for the five

modes of work, dependency, fight, flight, and pairing. Evidence of the reliability and validity of this instrument was provided by Thelen, Hawkes, and Strattner (1969).

Lion and Gruenfeld (1993) appear to have conducted the only study that employed the RGST (in modified form) in their investigation of the relationship between people's work and basic assumption group styles and their behavior (assessed by retrospective ratings made by members at the end of the group interactions and by descriptions generated by observers who watched the interactions from behind a two-way mirror) in four academic self-study groups. The results showed that those who employed the work mode were dominant, friendly, task oriented, and emotionally controlled. In contrast, those who adopted the dependency or flight modes were submissive, friendly, and emotionally expressive; those who adopted the fight mode were dominant and unfriendly; and those who adopted the pairing mode were friendly. This study, thus, demonstrated that individuals talk and act differently when operating in these modes.

Another attempt to understand people's predispositions toward groups was Putnam's (1979) creation and validation of an instrument to measure *preference for procedural order* (PPO), the degree to which people prefer systematic order in the procedural behaviors that occur in task groups. As Putnam explained, "Preference for procedural order as a communicative-based construct refers to a predisposition for group work norms characterized by two sets of procedural message patterns: high procedural order and low procedural order" (p. 216). High PPO is characterized by a preference to use planned, sequential patterns for organizing work activities; a concern for time management; an emphasis on regular, predictable procedures; and an emphasis on clarifying group procedures and reminding members to adhere to the task. In contrast, low PPO is characterized by a preference for a cyclical procedural pattern (e.g., jumping back and forth between group discussion and the use of a facilitation technique such as brainstorming); flexibility in establishing and changing plans; obliviousness to time constraints; and a tendency to vacillate between task and socioemotional aspects of the group. The Group Procedural Order Questionnaire (GPOQ) that Putnam developed and tested demonstrated excellent reliability and validity in differentiating those with high and low PPO, especially with respect to the communicative acts they forwarded during task group interaction.

Although the PPO predisposition is firmly grounded in the task group context, the only study to date that appears to have employed it is one by Hirokawa, Ice, and Cook (1988) that investigated the relationship between discussion procedures and decision performance as mediated by PPO. They found, as predicted, that (a) groups composed of high-PPO members produced higher quality decisions when using a high-structure versus a low-structure procedure and (b) low-PPO groups produced higher quality decisions than high-PPO groups when using a low-structure procedure. They also found that groups composed of low-PPO members produced decisions of equal quality whether they used a low-structure or high-structure procedure. Whereas high-PPO groups worked best with a high-structured discussion format, low-PPO groups worked best with either discussion structure, suggesting that the GPOQ tapped into flexibility or adaptability. These results suggest that PPO is a potentially important predisposition that may affect group processes and outcomes.

A more recent conceptualization of individuals' predispositions toward groups is Keyton, Harmon, and Frey's (1996) operationalization of S. Sorensen's (1981) concept of *grouphate*, the negative feelings and attitudes that cause group members to detest, loathe, or abhor working in groups. A number of scholars (e.g., Frey, 1995; Poole, 1994) have discussed people's general dislike for working in groups and the need to change that attitude, especially given its detrimental effects; Freeman (1996), for instance, found

that students' negative attitude toward working in groups was associated with less success in the academic context (e.g., grades), whereas the opposite was the case for those students who held a positive attitude.

Keyton et al. (1996) developed and tested a grouphate scale composed of the following six items: (a) I like working in groups; (b) I would rather work alone; (c) Group work is fun; (d) Groups are terrible; (e) I would prefer to work in an organization in which teams are used; and (f) My ideal job is where I can be interdependent with others. Items (a), (c), (e), and (f) were reversed scored and added to the other two items, such that higher scores indicated a more negative feeling or attitude about working in task groups or teams. The researchers also constructed a group attribute scale, composed of a positive group attribute (PGA) subscale and a negative group attribute (NGA) subscale, to identify what characteristics about task group interaction people liked and disliked. These scales were tested with 223 individuals who regularly worked in teams or groups in their work environment. The researchers also asked participants to complete the group and meeting subscales of the CA instrument (PRCA-24) and to answer questions about their experiences in groups.

Keyton et al. (1996) found, as predicted, a significant negative correlation between participants' PGA and grouphate scores; hence, as participants' identification of positive group attributes increased, their negative feelings about group work decreased. There was, however, no significant correlation between participants' NGA and grouphate scores. Examination of the portion of the sample that reported (a) both low NGA and PGA scores (apathetic members), (b) both high NGA and PGA scores (highly involved members), (c) high NGA and low PGA scores (those who disliked groups intensely), and (d) high PGA and low NGA scores (those who liked groups intensely) showed the ability of these groupings to predict grouphate, with PGA scores accounting for most of the variance. The findings also showed that the gender composition of work teams affected participants' perceptions of positive and negative group attributes, with all-female groups having significantly higher PGA scores and lower NGA scores than all-male or mixed-sex groups. Gender composition also affected grouphate, such that all-female groups demonstrated lower grouphate than mixed-sex groups, which demonstrated lower grouphate than all-male groups, although, interestingly, mixed-sex groups had lower group apprehension scores than all-female and all-male groups. Finally, the amount of group experience participants had did not affect grouphate, although the more experience they had, the lower their group apprehension.

The conceptualization of, and the development, testing, and use of, instruments designed to measure, individuals' predispositions toward groups is important for both research and application purposes. From a research standpoint, determining these predispositions will make it possible to answer some important questions. One question concerns how these predispositions come to be, such as whether people are born with them (as might be suggested by the communibiological perspective; see, e.g., Beatty & McCroskey, 1998; Beatty, McCroskey, & Heisel, 1998; Valencic, Beatty, Rudd, Dobos, & Heisel, 1998) or develop them on the basis of their experiences. Another question is how various combinations of these predispositions interact. D. G. Ellis (1977), for instance, found that people's use of one-up and one-down relational control styles in group interaction could be predicted from specific trait profiles of CA; interpersonal communication inventory, a general measure of interpersonal skills; intolerance for ambiguity; anomie; inclusion, control, and affection needs; approach-avoidance tendencies; concern for status; and least preferred coworker, which measures interpersonal versus task orientation toward others. Barrick, Stewart, Neubert, and Mount (1998) also found that combinations of personality measures (e.g., extraversion and emotional stability) had an indirect relationship to teams' abilities to maintain themselves over time. And, of course, an important question is how these personality traits influence individuals' (communicative) behavior in groups and group (communication) processes and outcomes. Hare (1976), for instance, proposed that particular personality traits were more suitable for (and perhaps more effective in) specific group roles (e.g., members high in argumentativeness might more naturally play the role of devil's advocate). Communication scholars, however, should focus not only on how people's predispositions toward groups influence their communicative behavior but also on assessing people's *predispositions toward communicative behavior in groups*. To date, only the CA instrument (PRCA-24) and, to a lesser extent, the GPOQ attempt to assess such predispositions.

From an application standpoint, understanding individuals' predispositions toward groups and group communication may help to structure educational environments in which people can learn how to participate more effectively in groups. As mentioned previously, communication educators have been very effective, for instance, in identifying those who suffer from extreme CA about presenting public speeches and designing intervention programs to help them manage that apprehension. Similar interventions could potentially be developed in the group context; for instance, diagnostic evaluations could be conducted using the grouphate instrument, appropriate exercises (e.g., simulations and role plays) could be designed, and analytical debriefings could be provided after the exercises to help those who suffer from grouphate. Jarboe (1992) noted that one of the initial challenges in the group communication classroom is that "students come with their own group experiences that have shaped their attitudes and created their assumptions about groups" (p. 16). Understanding and assessing these attitudes and assumptions is an important step in creating the most meaningful educational environments in which to learn about group communication and become a better group communicator.

Studying Traits at the Group Level

In addition to identifying individuals' predispositions toward groups, scholars also need to study traits at the group level. Three ways in which traits can be conceptualized at the group level are by (a) the composition of groups vis-à-vis individual members' traits, (b) the effects of the group situation on members' traits, and (c) the unique group personality that can form.

First, most research conducted in the group context has been concerned with the way in which traits affect the behavior of individual group members; substantially less attention has focused on the effects associated with the composition of groups with respect to members' traits. As Moreland, Levine, and Wingert (1996) were forced to conclude, "Few researchers study group composition and no general theory guides their work" (p. 1). This is unfortunate, for as Shaw (1981) pointed out,

> It is not the particular characteristics of an individual group member that are of interest, but rather the relative characteristics of the various persons who compose the group.... Individuals contribute differently to the group product, depending upon the particular other individuals with whom they are grouped. (pp. 211, 213)

Some scholars have studied the trait composition of groups, such as Hirokawa et al.'s (1988) research on groups composed either of members with high or low PPO, but not enough of these studies have been conducted, and, hence, our knowledge of trait compositional effects in groups is limited. One unanswered question concerns the critical mass of people that makes a difference with respect to the influence or offsetting of particular personality predispositions, such as the threshold number of people with grouphate in a given-sized task group that potentially makes a difference in the way the group communicates and makes decisions. Another unanswered question concerns the group-level effects of diversity in members' traits (see Moreland

et al., 1996). Although diversity has been studied with regard to numerous demographic variables (see, e.g., Clark, Anand, & Robertson, 2000; Haslett & Ruebush, 1999), no attention appears to have been paid to diversity in terms of members' personality and communication traits. A related question concerns the effects of group compatibility and incompatibility with respect to members' traits. Schutz (1966) proposed that group members with compatible needs (specifically, inclusion, control, and affection needs) would be more likely to achieve their goals and be more mutually satisfied and cohesive; the same prediction could be made about groups in which members demonstrate compatible traits. Studies using Schutz's conceptualizations of compatibility, however, have found mixed results (Shaw et al., 1979; Shaw & Webb, 1982); most recently, Keyton (1992) found that interchange compatibility between group members—when all group members mutually express the same need—predicted group member cohesiveness but not member satisfaction or group outcome effectiveness. Additional research is clearly needed to answer the many questions regarding group trait composition.

Second, researchers should examine how particular group situations affect the relevance and influence of members' traits. Traits have been studied almost exclusively as an input variable that affects group processes and outcomes, but one could also examine how group processes and outcomes affect predispositional behavior in groups, such as how that behavior is decreased, maintained, or elevated on the basis of particular group processes and outcomes. Bond and Shiu (1997), for instance, investigated the relationship between eight personality traits and two dimensions of group process—(a) performance focus, a group's unity and effectiveness in achieving its assigned goals, and (b) shared exchange, a group's ability to create egalitarian participation and an open, responsive meeting environment to accomplish the performance focus—across two time periods of group interaction (5 weeks into a semester and at the end of the course). Assertiveness was the only personality trait that predicted performance focus across both time periods, with helpfulness a significant predictor at the second time period; openness to experience was a significant (negative) predictor of shared exchange across both time periods, with application being a significant predictor at the first time period and emotional stability and assertiveness significant (negative) predictors at the second time period. These results suggest that particular dimensions and stages of group life influence the relative value of members' traits (and corresponding behavior). Moreover, as some communication trait research has suggested, the interactive environment of communicators can alter people's predispositions (Conrad, 1991).

Third, groups themselves can demonstrate personality and communication traits. Cattell (1948) was one of the first scholars to argue that groups possess personality traits that are analogous to individual personality traits and that can be inferred from group behavior; he proposed the concept of *group syntality* to reference the personality of a group. Bion (1961) later claimed that group personality traits develop, in part, from members' predispositions but even more important, from the patterns of interpersonal dynamics that occur in groups. Unfortunately, scholars have not investigated group traits (notable exceptions include van de Wetering's, 1996, articulation of authoritarianism as a group-level adaptation and Kraus's, 1997, theory of group aggression), principally because of "the domination of research models that use the individual as the primary investigative unit of analysis" (Kraus, 1997, p. 127). Durkheim (1938) warned long ago that "if, then, we begin with the individual we shall be able to understand nothing of what takes place in the group" (p. 104). Although Durkheim overstated the case, his point is well taken in that scholars who study traits (and other topics) in groups need to pay attention not only to the individual members but to the collective group as well.

Methodological Considerations for Trait Research

The agenda we have called for to identify individuals' predispositions toward groups and to study traits at the group level must be accompanied by careful consideration of the methodological procedures best used to accomplish these goals. Poole, Keyton, and Frey (1999) addressed in substantive detail important issues and methodological practices confronting group communication scholars; here, we briefly highlight some of those issues and practices for the study of traits in the group context.

With respect to the identification of individuals' predispositions toward groups, researchers have tended to rely on self-reports as the predominant methodology for assessing individuals' traits (Daly & Bippus, 1998), a methodology well-known for its limitations. Perhaps that reliance explains, in part, why the effects of group members' traits are typically not large and are often moderated by other factors (Bonito & Hollingshead, 1997). Observer (or other group members') ratings can be used as an alternative to self-reports, but this technique is also potentially problematic for reasons that have been well documented elsewhere. Perhaps the best procedure, according to Daly and Bippus (1998), is to use both self-reports and observer ratings. Bond and Shiu (1997), in fact, used four types of self-reports and observer ratings: (a) total self-ratings, (b) total other-member ratings, (c) variance of self-ratings, and (d) variance of other-member ratings. They found that self-ratings generated significant, positive correlations with group task and relational measures, whereas variance of self- and other-member ratings were negatively correlated with group relational measures, demonstrating that the particular method used to measure traits affects the research outcomes.

One interesting methodological procedure for assessing traits at the individual level is the coding of written descriptions provided by research participants, such as the descriptions of family disagreement that Infante, Myers, and Buerkel (1994) employed to measure their research participants' argumentativeness and verbal aggressiveness. Another promising technique is the derivation of scales measuring psychological traits (e.g., anxiety and hostility) from the content analysis of verbal behavior (Gottschalk, 1997).

With respect to the study of traits at the group level, researchers have too frequently relied on measures of central tendency that "assess the proportion of group members who possess a characteristic or the mean level of that characteristic within the group" (Moreland et al., 1996, p. 11). An alternative is to use the total level of a personality trait in a group, as George (1990) did in her study of positive and negative affectivity in groups, the total levels of which were related to the positive and negative tones of the groups studied and to the degree of absenteeism (negatively) and prosocial behavior (negatively) demonstrated by group members. Both approaches, however, assume that each member increases the collective pool of the characteristic being assessed; such aggregation can mask important information when individual characteristics do not combine additively to form a collective resource pool (Barrick et al., 1998).

Using variance scores, as Bond and Shiu (1997) did (see also Wall & Galanes, 1986), can provide information about the fit among team members and is appropriate for examining group-level relationships (Barrick et al., 1998). A more extreme approach is to use the highest or lowest individual scores for the group, a technique that assumes that a single member can significantly affect a group. Comparing these four operationalizations of team composition (central tendency, variance, highest score, and lowest score), Barrick et al. (1998) concluded that the method of constructing group composition scores must be congruent with the theoretical focus of the study.

Researchers have, thus, tended to employ an additive strategy to understand and operationalize group-level constructs, in which the "effects of individual members on a group are independent . . . [in] that a person will affect every group that he or she joins in about the same way," as opposed to an interactive strategy, which "implies that a person will affect every group that he or she joins differently, depending on who else belongs" (Moreland et al., 1996, p. 21). The presence of additive effects in the literature may also be due to the preponderance of research conducted on zero-history laboratory groups discussing for a limited amount of time rigidly structured, objectively correct, decision-making tasks. These groups promote additive effects and inhibit the likelihood of interactive effects, which seem to develop over time as documented in research on natural groups (see Moreland et al., 1996). Unfortunately, most research conducted on natural groups has ignored traits as a significant input variable in favor of a focus on processes and outcomes. What research does exist suggests that the research setting plays an important role; G. Sorensen and McCroskey (1977), for instance, found that completely different sets of personality traits predicted different combinations of interaction characteristics when zero-history groups were compared with intact groups.

One particularly relevant methodology used to study both natural and laboratory groups is the system for the multiple level observation of groups (SYMLOG), developed by Bales and Cohen (1979). This methodology is flexible in allowing group members or observers to capture the ways in which particular traits are communicated in groups at both the individual and group levels (see Keyton, 1995); dimensional predispositions can be retained at the individual level for analysis, and members' scores can be analyzed at the group level according to their congruence or dispersion (see Wall & Galanes, 1986).

As this brief analysis suggests, researchers studying traits in the group context face some important methodological issues and questions. As we engage in the process of conceptualizing such traits, we must continue refining the methods we use to study them.

CONCLUSION

The study of personality and communication traits in the group context is an important direction for scholars who wish to understand how antecedent factors affect group (communication) processes and outcomes. As Klein (1959) argued, "A group—whether small or large—consists of individuals in a relationship to one another; and therefore the understanding of personality [and communication traits] is the foundation for the understanding of social life" (p. 291).

There is, as we acknowledged previously, much debate about traits versus states, a debate that will probably never be resolved. Although we agree that the trait perspective by itself, and even in conjunction with a situational approach, is undoubtedly an incomplete explanation of group behavior, ultimately, we agree with Shaw (1981) that "one cannot hope to fully understand group behavior without knowing at least some of the ways the personal characteristics of group members affect group process [and outcomes]" (p. 167).

The small group offers an ideal context for understanding how members' traits affect and are affected by situations that confront group members. Unfortunately, the present state of trait research in the group context leaves many questions unanswered. We hope that the agenda we articulated in this chapter will help to predispose group communication scholars to change the fate of trait research.

NOTE

1. Some scholars make a distinction between traits and predispositions. Horvath (1998), for instance, claimed that a trait describes an individual's entire personality, whereas a "predisposition is limited to a set of behaviors" (p. 89); he, thus, referred to predispositions as a "close relative" of personality traits. From our perspective, a trait tends to predispose people to act in particular ways; consequently, we use the terms trait and predispositions interchangeably.

REFERENCES

Alagna, S. W. (1982). Sex role identity, peer evaluation of competition, and the responses of women and men in a competitive situation. *Journal of Personality and Social Psychology, 43,* 546-554.

Alderton, S. M. (1980). Attributions of responsibility for socially deviant behavior in decision-making discussions as a function of situation and locus of control. *Central States Speech Journal, 31,* 117-127.

Alderton, S. M. (1982). Locus of control-based argumentation as a predictor of group polarization. *Communication Quarterly, 30,* 381-387.

Alderton, S. M., & Frey, L. R. (1983). Effects of reactions to arguments on group outcome: The case of group polarization. *Central States Speech Journal, 34,* 88-95.

Andersen, P. A. (1987). The trait debate: A critical examination of the individual differences paradigm in interpersonal communication. In B. Dervin & M. J. Voigt (Eds.), *Progress in communication* (Vol. 8, pp. 47-82). Norwood, NJ: Ablex.

Anderson, C. M., & Martin, M. M. (1994, November). *How argumentativeness, verbal aggressiveness, and communication apprehension affect members' perceptions of cohesion, consensus, and satisfaction in small groups.* Paper presented at the meeting of the Speech Communication Association, New Orleans, LA.

Anderson, C. M., & Martin, M. M. (1995). The effects of communication motives, interaction involvement, and loneliness on satisfaction: A model of small groups. *Small Group Research, 26,* 118-137.

Anderson, C. M., & Martin, M. M. (1999). The relationship of argumentativeness and verbal aggressiveness to cohesion, consensus, and satisfaction in small groups. *Communication Reports, 12,* 21-31.

Anderson, L. R. (1978). Groups would do better without humans. *Personality and Social Psychology Bulletin, 4,* 557-558.

Andrews, P. H. (1985). Ego-involvement, self-monitoring, and conformity in small groups: A communicative analysis. *Central States Speech Journal, 36,* 51-61.

Aries, E. J., Gold, C., & Weigel, R. H. (1983). Dispositional and situational influences on dominance behavior in small groups. *Journal of Personality and Social Psychology, 44,* 779-786.

Armstrong, S. J., & Priola, V. (2001). Individual differences in cognitive style and their effects on task and social orientations of self-managed work teams. *Small Group Research, 32,* 283-312.

Arrow, H., & McGrath, J. E. (1993). Membership matters: How member change and continuity affect small group structure, process and performance. *Small Group Research, 24,* 334-361.

Avtgis, T. A. (1999). The relationship between unwillingness to communicate and family communication patterns. *Communication Research Reports, 16,* 333-338.

Baker, D. D., & Ganster, D. C. (1985). Leader communication styles: A test of average versus vertical dyad linkage models. *Group & Organization Studies, 10,* 242-259.

Bales, R. F., & Cohen, S. P. (1979). *SYMLOG: A system for the multiple level observation of groups.* New York: Free Press.

Barrick, M. R., Stewart, G. L., Neubert, M. J., & Mount, M. K. (1998). Relating member ability and personality to work-team processes and team effectiveness. *Journal of Applied Psychology, 83,* 377-391.

Barry, B., & Stewart, G. L. (1997). Composition, process, and performance in self-managed groups: The role of personality. *Journal of Applied Psychology, 82,* 62-78.

Bass, B. M., McGehee, C. R., Hawkins, W. C., Young, P. C., & Gebel, A. S. (1953). Personality variables related to leaderless group discussion. *Journal of Abnormal and Social Psychology, 48,* 120-128.

Bass, B. M., Wurster, C. R., Doll, P. A., & Clair, D. J. (1953). Situational and personality factors in leadership among sorority women. *Psychological Monographs, 67*(16, Series No. 366).

Beatty, M. J. (1998). Future directions in communication trait theory and research. In J. C. McCroskey, J. A. Daly, M. M. Martin, & M. J. Beatty (Eds.), *Communication and personality: Trait perspectives* (pp. 309-319). Cresskill, NJ: Hampton Press.

Beatty, M. J., & McCroskey, J. C. (1998). Interpersonal communication as temperamental expression: A communibiological paradigm. In J. C. McCroskey, J. A. Daly, M. M. Martin, & M. J. Beatty (Eds.), *Communication and personality: Trait perspectives* (pp. 41-67). Cresskill, NJ: Hampton Press.

Beatty, M. J., McCroskey, J. C., & Heisel, A. D. (1998). Communication apprehension as temperamental expression: A communibiological paradigm. *Communication Monographs, 65,* 197-219.

Beckwith, J., Iverson, M. A., & Render, M. E. (1965). Test anxiety, task relevance of group experience, and change in level of aspiration. *Journal of Personality and Social Psychology, 1,* 579-588.

Bell, G. B., & Hall, H. E., Jr. (1954). The relationship between leadership and empathy. *Journal of Abnormal Psychology, 47,* 156-157.

Beloff, H. (1958). Two forms of social conformity: Acquiescence and conventionality. *Journal of Abnormal and Social Psychology, 56,* 99-104.

Bion, W. R. (1961). *Experiences in groups, and other papers.* New York: Basic Books.

Bixenstine, V. E., & Douglas, J. (1967). Effects of psychopathology on group consensus and cooperative choice in a six-person game. *Journal of Personality and Social Psychology, 5,* 32-37.

Bochner, A. P., & Bochner, B. (1972). A multivariate investigation of Machiavellianism and task structure in four-man groups. *Speech Monographs, 39,* 277-285.

Bochner, A. P., di Salvo, V., & Jonas, T. (1975). A computer-analysis of small group process: An investigation of two Machiavellian groups. *Small Group Behavior, 6,* 187-203.

Bond, M. H., & Shiu, W. Y. (1997). The relationship between a group's personality resources and the two dimensions of its group process. *Small Group Research, 28,* 194-217.

Bonito, J. A., & Hollingshead, A. B. (1997). Participation in small groups. In B. R. Burleson (Ed.), *Communication yearbook* (Vol. 20, pp. 227-261). Thousand Oaks, CA: Sage.

Bonner, B. L. (2000). The effects of extraversion on influence in ambiguous group tasks. *Small Group Research, 31,* 225-244.

Borg, W. R. (1960). Prediction of small group role behavior from personality variables. *Journal of Abnormal and Social Psychology, 60,* 112-116.

Bouchard, T. J., Jr. (1969). Personality, problem-solving procedure, and performance in small groups. *Journal of Applied Psychology, 53,* 1-29.

Bray, R. M., & Noble, A. M. (1978). Authoritarianism and decisions of mock juries: Evidence of jury bias and group polarization. *Journal of Personality and Social Psychology, 36,* 1424-1430.

Brockner, J., O'Malley, M. N., Hite, T., & Davies, D. K. (1987). Reward allocation and self-esteem: The roles of modeling and equity restoration. *Journal of Personal and Social Psychology, 52,* 844-850.

Burger, J. M. (1987). Desire for control and conformity to a perceived norm. *Journal of Personality and Social Psychology, 53,* 335-360.

Burgoon, J. K. (1976). The unwillingness-to-communicate scale: Development and validation. *Communication Monographs, 43,* 60-69.

Burgoon, J. K. (1977). Unwillingness to communicate as a predictor of small group discussion behaviors and evaluations. *Central States Speech Journal, 28,* 122-133.

Buys, C. J. (1978). Humans would do better without groups. *Personality and Social Psychology Bulletin, 4,* 123-125.

Cattell, R. B. (1948). Concepts and methods in the measurement of group syntality. *Psychological Review, 55,* 48-63.

Cattell, R. B., & Stice, G. F. (1960). *The dimensions of groups and their relations to the behavior of members.* Champaign, IL: Institute for Personality and Ability Testing.

Cegala, D. J. (1981). Interaction involvement: A cognitive dimension of communicative competence. *Communication Education, 30,* 109-121.

Cegala, D. J., Savage, G. T., Brunner, C. C., & Conrad, A. B. (1982). An elaboration of the meaning of interaction involvement: Toward the development of a theoretical concept. *Communication Monographs, 49,* 229-248.

Cegala, D. J., Wall, V. D., & Rippey, G. (1987). An investigation of interaction involvement and the dimensions of SYMLOG: Perceived communication behaviors of persons in task-oriented groups. *Central States Speech Journal, 38,* 81-93.

Chaplin, W., John, O., & Goldberg, L. (1988). Conceptions of states and traits: Dimensional attributes with ideals as prototypes. *Journal of Personality and Social Psychology, 47,* 1074-1090.

Clark, M. A., Anand, V., & Robertson, L. (2000). Resolving meaning: Interpretation in diverse decision-making groups. *Group Dynamics: Theory, Research, and Practice, 4,* 211-221.

Cohen, P. A., & Sheposh, J. P. (1977). Audience and level of esteem as determinants of risk taking. *Personality and Social Psychology Bulletin, 3,* 119-122.

Comadena, M. E. (1984). Brainstorming groups: Ambiguity tolerance, communication apprehension, task attraction, and individual productivity. *Small Group Behavior, 15,* 241-264.

Conrad, C. (1991). Communication in conflict: Style-strategy relationships. *Communication Monographs, 58,* 135-155.

Crocker, J., & Schwartz, I. (1985). Prejudice and ingroup favoritism in a minimal intergroup situation: Effects of self-esteem. *Personality and Social Psychology Bulletin, 11,* 379-386.

Cronshaw, S. F., & Ellis, R. J. (1991). A process investigation of self-monitoring and leader emergence. *Small Group Research, 22,* 403-420.

Crutchfield, R. S. (1955). Conformity and character. *American Psychologist, 10,* 191-198.

Daly, J. A. (1974). *The effects of differential durations of time on interpersonal judgments based on vocal activity.* Unpublished master's thesis, West Virginia University, Morgantown.

Daly, J. A. (1987). Personality and interpersonal communication: Issues and directions. In J. C. McCroskey & J. A. Daly (Eds.), *Personality and interpersonal communication* (pp. 13-41). Newbury Park, CA: Sage.

Daly, J. A., & Bippus. A. M. (1998). Personality and interpersonal communication: Issues and directions. In J. C. McCroskey, J. A. Daly, M. M. Martin, & M. J. Beatty (Eds.), *Communication and personality: Trait perspectives* (pp. 1-40). Cresskill, NJ: Hampton Press.

Daly, J. A., & Diesel, C. A. (1992). Measures of communication-related personality variables. *Communication Education, 41,* 405-414.

Davies, M. F. (1994). Personality and social characteristics. In A. P. Hare, H. H. Blumberg, M. F. Davies, & M. V. Kent (Eds.), *Small group research: A handbook* (pp. 41-78). Norwood, NJ: Ablex.

Digman, J. M. (1990). Personality structure: Emergence of the five-factor model. *Annual Review of Psychology, 41* 447-440.

Dilberto, J-J. A. (1992). A communication study of possible relationships between psychological sex type and decision-making effectiveness. *Small Group Research, 23,* 379-407.

Durkheim, E. (1938). *The rules of sociological method.* New York: Free Press.

Ellis, D. G. (1977). Trait predictions of relational control. In B. D. Ruben (Ed.), *Communication yearbook* (Vol. 2, pp. 185-191). New Brunswick, NJ: Transaction Books.

Ellis, D. G., & McCallister, L. (1980). Relational control sequences in sex-typed and androgynous groups. *Western Journal of Speech Communication, 44,* 35-49.

Ellis, R. J. (1988). Self-monitoring and leadership emergence in groups. *Personality and Social Psychology Bulletin, 14,* 681-693.

Ellis, R. J., Adamson, R. S., Deszca, G., & Cawsey, T. F. (1988). Self-monitoring and leadership emergence. *Small Group Behavior, 19,* 312-324.

Ellis, R. J., & Cronshaw, S. F. (1992). Self-monitoring and leader emergence: A test of moderator effects. *Small Group Research, 23,* 113-129.

Eysenck, H. J. (1986). Can personality study ever be scientific? *Journal of Social Behavior and Personality, 1,* 309-314.

Eysenck, H. J. (1991). Biological dimensions of personality. In L. A. Pervin (Ed.), *Handbook of personality: Theory and research* (pp. 244-276). New York: Guilford Press.

Freeman, K. A. (1996). Attitudes toward work in project groups as predictors of group performance. *Small Group Research, 27,* 265-282.

Frey, L. R. (1989). Exploring the input-throughput-output relationship in small groups: Communicative predispositions, argumentation and leadership. *World Communication, 18*(2), 43-70.

Frey, L. R. (1995). Introduction: Applied communication research on group facilitation in natural settings. In L. R. Frey (Ed.), *Innovations in group facilitation: Applications in natural settings* (pp. 1-23). Cresskill, NJ: Hampton Press.

Frey, L. R. (1997). Individuals in groups. In L. R. Frey & J. K. Barge (Eds.), *Managing group life: Communicating in decision-making groups* (pp. 52-79). Boston: Houghton Mifflin.

Friend, R. M., & Vinson, M. (1974). Leaning over backwards: Jurors' responses to defendants' attractiveness. *Journal of Communication, 24,* 124-129.

Garland, H., & Beard, J. F. (1979). Relationship between self-monitoring and leader emergence across two task situations. *Journal of Applied Psychology, 64,* 77-81.

Geis, F. L. (1964). *Machiavellianism and success in a three-person game.* Unpublished doctoral dissertation, Columbia University, New York City.

Geis, F. L., Krupat, E., & Berger, D. (1965). *Taking over in group discussion.* Unpublished manuscript, New York University.

George, J. M. (1990). Personality, affect, and behavior in groups. *Journal of Applied Psychology, 75,* 107-116.

Gleason, J. M., Seaman, F. J., & Hollander, E. P. (1978). Emergent leadership processes as a function of task structure and Machiavellianism. *Social Behavior and Personality, 6,* 33-36.

Goffman, E. (1963). *Behavior in public places.* New York: Free Press.

Goffman, E. (1967). *Interaction ritual: Essays in face-to-face behavior.* Chicago: Aldine.

Gottschalk, L. A. (1997). The unobtrusive measurement of psychological states and traits. In C. W. Roberts (Ed.), *Text analysis for the social sciences: Methods for drawing statistical inferences from texts and transcripts* (pp. 117-129). Mahwah, NJ: Lawrence Erlbaum.

Gouran, D. S. (1994). The future of small group communication research: Revitalization or good health? *Communication Studies, 45,* 29-39.

Graziano, W. G., Hair, E. C., & Finch, J. F. (1997). Competitiveness mediates the link between personality and group performance. *Journal of Personality and Social Psychology, 73,* 1394-1408.

Greer, F. L. (1955). *Small group effectiveness* (Institute Report No. 6). Philadelphia: Institute for Research in Human Relations.

Gruenfeld, D. H., Thomas-Hunt, M. C., & Kim, P. H. (1998). Cognitive flexibility, communication strategy, and integrative complexity in groups: Public versus private reactions to majority and minority status. *Journal of Experimental Social Psychology, 34,* 202-226.

Guilford, J. P. (1959). *Personality.* New York: McGraw-Hill.

Hacker, S., & Gaitz, C. M. (1970). Interaction and performance correlates of Machiavellianism. *Sociological Quarterly, 2,* 94-102.

Hansson, R. O., & Jones, W. H. (1981). Loneliness, cooperation, and conformity among American undergraduates. *Journal of Social Psychology, 115,* 103-108.

Hare, A. P. (1976). *Handbook of small group research* (2nd ed.). New York: Free Press.

Haslett, B. B., & Ruebush, J. (1999). What differences do individual differences in groups make? The effects of individuals, culture, and group composition. In L. R. Frey (Ed.), D. S. Gouran, & M. S. Poole (Assoc. Eds.), *The handbook of group communication theory & research* (pp. 115-138). Thousand Oaks, CA: Sage.

Hawkins, K., & Stewart, R. A. (1991). Effects of communication apprehension on perceptions of leadership and intragroup attraction in small task-oriented groups. *Southern Communication Journal, 57,* 1-10.

Haythorn, W. (1953). The influence of individual members on the characteristics of small groups. *Journal of Abnormal and Social Psychology, 48,* 276-284.

Heston, J. K. (1974). *Unwillingness to communicate and conflict as predictors of information processing behaviors.* Unpublished doctoral dissertation, West Virginia University, Morgantown.

Hewes, D. E., & Planalp, S. (1987). The individual's place in communication science. In C. R. Berger & S. H. Chaffee (Eds.), *Handbook of communication science* (pp. 146-183). Newbury Park, CA: Sage.

Hirokawa, R. Y., Ice, R., & Cook, J. (1988). Preference for procedural order, discussion structure, and group decision performance. *Communication Quarterly, 36,* 217-226.

Horvath, C. W. (1998). Biological origins of communicator style. In J. C. McCroskey, J. A. Daly, M. M. Martin, & M. J. Beatty (Eds.), *Communication and personality: Trait perspectives* (pp. 69-94). Cresskill, NJ: Hampton Press.

Hoyle, R. H., & Crawford, A. M. (1994). Use of individual-level data to investigate group phenomena: Issues and strategies. *Small Group Research, 25,* 464-485.

Infante, D. A. (1987). Aggressiveness. In J. C. McCroskey & J. A. Daly (Eds.), *Personality and interpersonal communication* (pp. 157-192). Newbury Park, CA: Sage.

Infante, D. A., & Gordon, W. I. (1985). Superiors' argumentativeness and verbal aggressiveness as predictors of subordinates' satisfaction. *Human Communication Research, 12,* 117-125.

Infante, D. A., Myers, S. A., & Buerkel, R. A. (1994). Argument and verbal aggression in constructive and destructive family and organizational disagreements. *Western Journal of Communication, 58,* 73-84.

Infante, D. A., & Rancer, A. S. (1996). Argumentativeness and verbal aggressiveness: A review of recent theory and research. In B. R. Burleson (Ed.), *Communication yearbook* (Vol. 19, pp. 319-351). Thousand Oaks, CA: Sage.

Infante, D. A., Rancer, A. S., & Womack, D. F. (1997). *Building communication theory* (3rd ed.). Prospect Heights, IL: Waveland Press.

Jablin, F. M. (1981). Cultivating imagination: Factors that enhance and inhibit creativity in brainstorming groups. *Human Communication Research, 7,* 245-258.

Jablin, F. M., Seibold, D. R., & Sorensen, R. L. (1977) Potential inhibitory effects of group participation on brainstorming performance. *Central States Speech Journal, 18,* 113-121.

Jablin, F. M., & Sussman, L. (1978). An exploration of communication and productivity in real brainstorming groups. *Human Communication Research, 4,* 329-337.

Janis, I. (1982). *Groupthink: Psychological studies of policy decision and fiascoes* (2nd ed.). Boston: Houghton Mifflin.

Jarboe, S. (1992). What we know about individual performance in groups: Myths and realities. In G. M. Phillips (Ed.), *Teaching how to work in groups* (pp. 13-49). Norwood, NJ: Ablex.

Jones, R. E., & White, C. S. (1983). Relationships between Machiavellianism, task orientation, and team effectiveness. *Psychological Reports, 53,* 859-866.

Jose, P. E., & McCarthy, W. (1988). Perceived agentic and communal behavior in mixed-sex group interactions. *Personality and Social Psychology Bulletin, 14,* 57-67.

Kazoleas, D., & Kay, B. (1994, November). *Are argumentatives really more argumentative? The behavior of argumentatives in group deliberations over controversial issues.* Paper presented at the meeting of the Speech Communication Association, New Orleans, LA.

Keyton, J. (1992). Challenging interpersonal compatibility in groups. *Kansas Speech Journal, 52*(1), 1-18.

Keyton, J. (1995). Using SYMLOG as a self-analytical group facilitation technique. In L. R. Frey (Ed.), *Innovations in group facilitation: Applications in natural settings* (pp. 148-174). Cresskill, NJ: Hampton Press.

Keyton, J., Harmon, N., & Frey, L. R. (1996, November). *Grouphate: Its impact on teaching group communication.* Paper presented at the meeting of the Speech Communication Association, San Diego, CA.

Klein, M. (1959). Our adult world and its roots in infancy. *Human Relations, 12,* 291-303.

Kogan, N., & Wallach, M. A. (1967). Group risk taking as a function of members' anxiety and defensiveness. *Journal of Personality, 35,* 50-63.

Kraus, G. (1997). The psychodynamics of constructive aggression in small groups. *Small Group Research, 28,* 122-145.

Lion, C. L., & Gruenfeld, L. W. (1993). The behavior and personality of work group and basic assumption group members. *Small Group Research, 24,* 236-257.

Lord, R. G., DeVader, C. L., & Alliger, G. M. (1986). A meta-analysis of the relation between personality traits and leadership perceptions: An application of validity generalization procedures. *Journal of Applied Psychology, 71,* 402-410.

Lord, R. G., Phillips, J. S., & Rush, M. C. (1980). Effects of sex and personality on perceptions of emergent leadership, influence, and social power. *Journal of Applied Psychology, 65,* 176-182.

Mann, R. D. (1959). A review of the relationship between personality and performance in small groups. *Psychological Bulletin, 56,* 241-270.

McCallum, M., & Piper, W. E. (1999). Personality disorders and response to group-oriented evening treatment. *Group Dynamics: Theory, Research, and Practice, 3,* 3-14.

McCroskey, J. C. (1970). Measures of communication-based anxiety. *Communication Monographs, 52,* 92-101.

McCroskey, J. C. (1977). Oral communication apprehension: A summary of recent theory and research. *Human Communication Research, 1,* 78-96.

McCroskey, J. C., & Beatty, M. J. (1998). Communication apprehension. In J. C. McCroskey, J. A. Daly, M. M. Martin, & M. J. Beatty (Eds.), *Communication and personality: Trait perspectives* (pp. 215-231). Cresskill, NJ: Hampton Press.

McCroskey, J. C., Daly, J. A., Martin, M. M., & Beatty, M. J. (Eds.). (1998). *Communication and personality: Trait perspectives.* Cresskill, NJ: Hampton Press.

McCroskey, J. C., Hamilton, P. R., & Weiner, A. N. (1974). The effect of interaction behavior on source credibility, homophily, and interpersonal attraction. *Human Communication Research, 1,* 42-52.

McCroskey, J. C., & Richmond, V. P. (1976). The effects of communication apprehension on the perceptions of peers. *Western Speech Communication, 40,* 14-21.

McCroskey, J. C., & Richmond, V. P. (1987). Willingness to communicate. In J. C. McCroskey & J. A. Daly (Eds.), *Personality and interpersonal communication* (pp. 129-156). Newbury Park, CA: Sage.

McCroskey, J. C., & Richmond, V. P. (1992). Communication apprehension and small group communication. In R. S. Cathcart & L. A. Samovar (Eds.), *Small group communication: A reader* (6th ed., pp. 361-374). Dubuque, IA: William C. Brown.

McCroskey, J. C., & Richmond, V. P. (1998). Willingness to communicate. In J. C. McCroskey, J. A. Daly, M. M. Martin, & M. J. Beatty (Eds.), *Communication and personality: Trait perspectives* (pp. 119-131). Cresskill, NJ: Hampton Press.

McDavid, J. R., & Sistrunk, F. (1964). Personality correlates of two kinds of conforming behavior. *Journal of Personality, 32,* 420-435.

McKinney, B. C. (1982). The effects of reticence on group interaction. *Communication Quarterly, 30,* 124-128.

Meunier, C., & Rule, B. G. (1967). Anxiety, confidence, and conformity. *Journal of Personality, 35,* 498-504.

Meyer, H. H. (1951). Factors related to success in the human relations aspect of workgroup leadership. *Psychological Monographs, 65*(3, Serial No. 320).

Moreland, R. L., Levine, J. M., & Wingert, M. L. (1996). Creating the ideal group: Composition effects at work. In E. H. Witte & J. H. Davis (Eds.), *Understanding group behavior: Small group processes and interpersonal relation* (Vol. 2, pp. 11-35). Mahwah, NJ: Lawrence Erlbaum.

Nadler, E. B. (1959). Yielding, authoritarianism, and authoritarian ideology regarding groups. *Journal of Abnormal and Social Psychology, 58,* 408-410.

Norton, R. W. (1978). Foundation of a communicator style construct. *Human Communication Research, 4,* 99-112.

Norton, R. W. (1983). *Communicator style: Theory, applications, and measures.* Beverly Hills, CA: Sage.

Oskenberg, L. (1968). *Machiavellianism and organization in five-man task-oriented groups.* Unpublished doctoral dissertation, Columbia University, New York City.

Patterson, M. L., & Ritts, V. (1997). Social and communicative anxiety: A review and meta-analysis. In B. R. Burleson (Ed.), *Communication yearbook* (Vol. 20, pp. 263-303). Thousand Oaks, CA: Sage.

Petzel, T. P., Johnson, J. E., Homer, H., & Kowalski, J. (1981). Behavior of depressed subjects in problem solving groups. *Journal of Research in Personality, 15,* 389-398.

Pfeiffer, J. W., & Jones, J. E. (1974). *The 1974 handbook for group facilitators* La Jolla, CA: University Associates.

Poole, M. S. (1994). Breaking the isolation of small group communication studies. *Communication Studies, 41* 237-247.

Poole, M. S., Keyton, J., & Frey, L. R. (1999). Group communication methodology: Issues and considerations. In L. R. Frey (Ed.), D. S. Gouran, & M. S. Poole (Assoc. Eds.), *The handbook of group communication theory & research* (pp. 92-112). Thousand Oaks, CA: Sage.

Putnam, L. L. (1979). Preference for procedural order in task-oriented small groups. *Communication Monographs, 46,* 193-218.

Rancer, A. S. (1998). Argumentativeness. In J. C. McCroskey, J. A. Daly, M. M. Martin, & M. J. Beatty (Eds.), *Communication and personality: Trait perspectives* (pp. 149-171). Cresskill, NJ: Hampton Press.

Revelle, W. (1995). Personality processes. *Annual Review of Psychology, 46,* 295-328.

Richmond, V. P., & McCroskey, J. C. (1985). *Communication: Apprehension avoidance, and effectiveness.* Scottsdale, AZ: Gorsuch Scarisbrick.

Rim, Y. (1966). Machiavellianism and decision involving risks. *British Journal of Social and Clinical Psychology, 5,* 36-50.

Rosenfeld, L. B., & Plax, T. G. (1976). Personality discriminants of reticence. *Western Speech Communication, 40,* 14-21.

Rubin, R. B., & Rubin, A. M. (1989). Communication apprehension and satisfaction in interpersonal relationships. *Communication Research Reports, 6,* 13-20.

Ryan, E. D., & Lakie, W. L. (1965). Competitive and noncompetitive performance in relation to achievement motive and manifest anxiety. *Journal of Personality and Social Psychology, 1,* 342-345.

Scheidel, T. M., Crowell, L., & Shepherd, J. R. (1958). Personality and discussion behavior: A study of possible relationships. *Speech Monographs, 25,* 261-267.

Schultz, B. (1974). Characteristics of emergent leaders of continuing problem-solving groups. *Journal of Psychology, 88,* 167-173.

Schultz, B. (1978). Predicting emergent leaders: An exploratory study of the salience of communicative functions. *Small Group Research, 9,* 109-114.

Schultz, B. (1980). Communication correlates of perceived leaders. *Small Group Behavior, 11,* 175-191.

Schultz, B. (1982). Argumentativeness: Its effect in group decision-making and its role in leadership perception. *Communication Quarterly, 30,* 368-375.

Schutz, W. C. (1966). *The interpersonal underworld.* Palo Alto, CA: Science & Behavior Books.

Schlenker, B. R., Soraci, S., & McCarthy, B. (1976). Self-esteem and group performance as determinants of egocentric perceptions in cooperative groups. *Human Relations, 29,* 1163-1176.

Scioli, F. P., Jr., Dyson, J. W., & Fleitas, D. W. (1974). The relationship of personality and decisional structure to leadership. *Small Group Behavior, 5,* 3-22.

Seibert, S., & Gruenfeld, L. (1992). Masculinity, femininity, and behavior in groups. *Small Group Research, 23,* 95-112.

Shaw, M. E. (1959). Some effects of individually prominent behavior upon group effectiveness and member satisfaction. *Journal of Abnormal and Social Psychology, 59,* 382-386.

Shaw, M. E. (1981). *Group dynamics: The psychology of small group behavior* (3rd ed.). New York: McGraw-Hill.

Shaw, M. E., Ackerman, B., McCown, N. E. Worsham, A. P., Haugh, L. D., Gebhardt, B. M., & Small, P. A., Jr. (1979). Interaction patterns and facilitation of peer learning. *Small Group Behavior, 10,* 214-223.

Shaw, M. E., & Harkey, B. (1976). Some effects of congruency of member characteristics and group structure upon group behavior. *Journal of Personality and Social Psychology, 34,* 412-418.

Shaw, M. E., & Webb, J. N. (1982). When compatibility interferes with group effectiveness. *Small Group Behavior, 13,* 555-564.

Siegel, J. M., & Mitchell, H. E. (1979). The influence of expectancy violations, sex, and authoritarianism on simulated trial outcomes. *Representative Research in Social Psychology, 10,* 37-47.

Sloan, W. W., & Solano, C. H. (1984). The conversational styles of lonely males with strangers and roommates. *Personality and Social Psychology Bulletin, 10,* 293-301.

Smith, R. J., & Cook, P. E. (1973). Leadership in dyadic groups as a function of dominance and incentives. *Sociometry, 36,* 561-568.

Sorensen, G., & McCroskey, J. C. (1977). The prediction of interaction behavior in small groups: Zero history vs. intact groups. *Communication Monographs, 44* 73-80.

Sorensen, S. (1981, May). *Grouphate.* Paper presented at the meeting of the International Communication Association, Minneapolis, MN.

Sorrentino, R. M., & Sheppard, B. H. (1978). Effects of affiliation-related motives on swimmers in individual versus group competition: A field experiment. *Journal of Personality and Social Psychology, 36,* 704-714.

Stock, D., & Thelen, H. (1958). *Emotional dynamics and group culture.* New York: New York University Press.

Stogdill, R. M. (1948). Personal factors associated with leadership: A survey of the literature. *Journal of Psychology, 25,* 35-71.

Thelen, H. A., Hawkes, T. H., & Strattner, N. S. (1969). *Role perception and task performance of experimentally composed small groups.* Unpublished manuscript, University of Chicago.

Valencic, K. M., Beatty, M. J., Rudd, J. E., Dobos, J. A., & Heisel, A. D. (1998). An empirical test of a communibiological model of trait verbal aggressiveness. *Communication Quarterly, 46,* 327-341.

van de Wetering, S. (1996). Authoritarianism as a group-level adaptation in humans. *Behavioral and Brain Sciences, 19,* 780-781.

Volkema, R. J., & Gorman, R. H. (1998). The influence of cognitive-based group composition on decision-making process and outcome. *Journal of Management Studies, 35* 105-122.

Wall, V. D., Jr., & Galanes, G. J. (1986). The SYMLOG dimensions and small group conflict. *Central States Speech Journal, 37,* 61-78.

Watson, D. (1971). Reinforcement theory of personality and social system: Dominance and position in a group power structure. *Journal of Personality and Social Psychology, 20,* 180-185.

Weaver, J. B., III. (1998). Personality and self-perceptions about communication. In J. C. McCroskey, J. A. Daly, M. M. Martin, & M. J. Beatty (Eds.), *Communication and personality: Trait perspectives* (pp. 95-117). Cresskill, NJ: Hampton Press.

Weiss, H. M. (1977). Subordinate imitation of supervisory behavior: The role of modeling in organizational socialization. *Organizational Behavior and Human Performance, 19,* 89-105.

Wells, J. R., & Lashbrook, B. A. (1970, November). *A study of the effects of systematic desensitization of the communication anxiety of individuals in small groups.* Paper presented at the meeting of the Speech Communication Association, New Orleans, LA.

Werner, C. M., Kagehiro, D. K., & Strube, M. J. (1982). Conviction proneness and the authoritarian juror: Inability to disregard information or attitudinal bias? *Journal of Applied Psychology, 67,* 629-636.

Wheeless, L. R. (1975). An investigation of receiver apprehension and social context dimensions of communication apprehension. *Speech Teacher, 24,* 261-265.

Wigley, C. J., III. (1998). Verbal aggressiveness. In J. C. McCroskey, J. A. Daly, M. M. Martin, & M. J. Beatty (Eds.), *Communication and personality: Trait perspectives* (pp. 191-214). Cresskill, NJ: Hampton Press.

Williams, J. M., & Warchal, J. (1981). The relationship between assertiveness, internal-external locus of control, and overt conformity. *Journal of Psychology, 109,* 93-96.

Wolfson, S. L. (1981). Effects of Machiavellianism and communication on helping behavior during an emergency. *British Journal of Social Psychology, 20,* 189-195.

Zander, A., & Wulff, D. (1966). Members' test anxiety and competence: Determinants of a group's aspirations. *Journal of Personality, 34,* 55-70.

Zuckerman, M. (1995). Good and bad humors: Biochemical bases of personality and its disorders. *Psychological Science, 6,* 325-332.

7

The Effects of Culture and Cultural Diversity on Communication in Work Groups

Synthesizing Vertical and Cultural Differences With a Face-Negotiation Perspective

JOHN G. OETZEL
University of New Mexico

Demographic changes in the United States are changing the face of organizations. If current trends continue, the majority of the net new entrants into organizations in the United States by the year 2020 will be of Latin, Asian, or African decent (listed in descending order) (Judy & D'Amico, 1997). As a result, it is and increasingly will be common for people of different nationalities and ethnicities to work together on a daily basis. These demographic changes, and the resulting increase in interactions between culturally diverse people, have created an impetus for an increasing number of studies about the effects of culture and cultural diversity on communication in work groups. Many of these studies explore how cultural diversity in group member composition influences group processes and outcomes (e.g., McLeod, Lobel, & Cox, 1996; Watson, Kumar, & Michaelson, 1993).

Some of the major conclusions reached by this line of research include the following: (a) Culturally diverse groups have more group process difficulty (e.g., more tension and conflict) than do culturally homogeneous groups; (b) cultural diversity can benefit group performance because of the infusion of different ideas and approaches to solving problems; and (c) benefits occur only if diversity is managed properly.

Although researchers know that diversity affects group communication, it is not known exactly why this occurs (see Sessa & Jackson, 1995). Two predominant approaches in the extant literature explain why culture and cultural diversity make a difference with respect to communicative behavior: vertical differences and cultural differences. *Vertical differences* are status differences that exist in a group because of various factors, including

AUTHOR'S NOTE: The author would like to thank Robert Shuter and Everett Rogers for helpful feedback on earlier drafts of this essay.

ethnicity, nationality, sex, tenure, knowledge, and position in the organizational hierarchy (Sessa & Jackson, 1995). Vertical differences have been shown to explain a variety of behaviors, such as member participation and influence in decision-making groups (Sessa & Jackson, 1995), leadership behavior in culturally diverse groups (Chemers & Murphy, 1995), members' approaches to conflict management (Espinoza & Garza, 1985; Garza & Santos, 1991), and positive and negative work group interactions (Larkey, 1996).

Cultural differences are general patterns of cultural values, attitudes, and communicative behaviors associated with specific sets of individuals (Chemers & Murphy, 1995). Cultural differences have been shown to explain a variety of interpersonal communicative behaviors (for an overview, see Gudykunst & Ting-Toomey, 1988). In fact, researchers have used a variety of dimensions—especially individualism-collectivism, that is, social patterns in which people view themselves as loosely connected and unique or closely linked and members of one or more in-groups, respectively (Triandis, 1995)—to explain the influence of culture on group communication (see Earley, 1993, 1994; Oetzel, 1995, 1998a, 1998b; Wagner, 1995). These dimensions have been found to explain members' conflict styles, participation and turn taking, leadership, and decision-making styles in work groups.

There is a tendency to dichotomize vertical and cultural differences in group membership and to argue that one perspective is superior to the other (see Tannen, 1994). For example, some researchers, such as Chemers and Murphy (1995), have argued that vertical differences explain better than cultural differences why culture and cultural diversity affect communicative behavior in groups. This argument is problematic because there is undoubtedly a relationship between vertical and cultural differences (Tannen, 1994). Instead of arguing that one perspective is better than the other, it is important to identify research that increases our understanding of how both vertical and cultural differences together relate to communication in work groups.

The purpose of this essay is to (a) synthesize research that uses either a vertical-difference or cultural-difference perspective to explain the influence of culture and cultural diversity on communication in work groups, while noting the importance of considering the relationship between vertical and cultural differences, and (b) offer a research agenda (that results in a model) that identifies the types of investigation needed to advance understanding of how both vertical and cultural differences affect communication in culturally diverse work groups. Although the focus of the essay is on *work groups*, groups that perform primarily problem-solving and decision-making tasks, vertical and cultural differences are certainly relevant to other types of groups, such as social groups and social support groups. Space limitations, however, necessitate focusing on a particular type of group; future theory and research will need to determine the extent to which the points are applicable to other types of groups.

CULTURAL COMPOSITION AND GROUP PROCESS DIFFICULTY

Cultural diversity "means the representation, in one social system, of people with distinctly different group affiliations of cultural significance" (Cox, 1994, p. 6). Cultural diversity can be indexed by national culture, ethnicity, language, gender, job position, age, and disability, to name a few.

How does cultural diversity influence communication in work groups? Cultural diversity in group membership is believed to benefit the performance of work groups through increased potential for creativity. This "value-in-diversity" hypothesis has been supported anecdotally, as well as empirically (see Cox, 1994; McLeod et al., 1996). However, cultural diversity is not without its costs. Researchers have found that cultural heterogeneity in group composition is associated with lower group cohesion and higher turnover of members (Jackson et al., 1991; O'Reilly, Caldwell, & Barnett, 1989; Wiersema & Bird, 1993), low group performance on a problem-solving task during initial meetings (Watson et al., 1993), and low member satisfaction and identification with the group (Milliken & Martins, 1996). These negative outcomes are attributed to the increased process difficulty that culturally diverse groups experience in comparison with culturally homogeneous groups. *Process difficulty* (or loss) has to do with interactional patterns that are not effective for accomplishing group outcomes (Steiner, 1972). Process difficulty can include tension, competitive conflict, power struggles, misunderstandings, and inequality in turn taking among members and generally refers to communication processes that hurt the performance of a group (Watson et al., 1993).

Several studies have found increased process difficulties in culturally heterogeneous, compared with culturally homogeneous, groups. Kirchmeyer and Cohen (1992) found that ethnic minorities contributed considerably less to decision making than nonminorities did in a study of 45 student groups working on a decision-making task. Watson et al.'s (1993) study of ethnically homogeneous and heterogeneous groups of students working on a case study assignment for a class found that homogeneous groups had higher quality processes during initial meetings, including fewer power struggles, greater equality in participation, and higher levels of group cohesion. However, over a period of 12 weeks, the heterogeneous groups made adjustments and attained processes at the level of the homogeneous groups. Finally, Oetzel (1998a) found that culturally diverse decision-making groups composed of European American and Japanese students relied more on majority, as opposed to consensus, decision making and had greater inequality in member turn taking than did culturally homogeneous groups of either all-European American or all-Japanese students.

Although these findings may be useful for facilitators and members of culturally diverse groups, why cultural diversity produces process difficulty in work groups remains to be explained adequately. Vertical difference is one perspective that attempts to explain how cultural diversity has an impact on communication processes in work groups.

THE VERTICAL-DIFFERENCE PERSPECTIVE

Vertical differences serve as cues used to assign people to a position in a hierarchy within a group or organization (Sessa & Jackson, 1995). The study of vertical differences and their effects on group communication processes has been conducted in light of various theoretical perspectives, including status characteristics theory, social identity theory, and the tokenism hypothesis. Each of these perspectives is briefly reviewed, and a research exemplar showing effects on communication in work groups is discussed.

Status Characteristics Theory

Status characteristics theory (SCT; Berger, Cohen, & Zelditch, 1973; Berger, Wagner, & Zelditch, 1985) explains how the attribution of status affects the behavior of individual group members. Specifically, SCT "specifies the processes through which evaluations of, and beliefs about, the characteristics of team members become the basis of observable inequalities in face-to-face social interactions" (Sessa & Jackson, 1995, p. 144). *Status characteristics* are hierarchical factors that influence evaluations of self and others and include both task-specific and diffuse characteristics. *Task-specific characteristics* are factors that indicate a person's perceived level of expertise regarding the task at hand. These characteristics can be assigned by one's job title or derived through interaction (e.g., a person makes important and relevant comments that assist a group in completing a task). *Diffuse characteristics* are factors that focus on broad master statuses, such as physical attractiveness, sex, and ethnic or cultural group membership. Individuals in a group are assigned status on the basis of their task-specific and diffuse characteristics; in turn, status level influences members' communicative behavior.

For example, high-status individuals, in comparison with low-status individuals, tend to participate more in group discussions, challenge contradictory ideas, and have more influence on group outcomes.

Using the principles of SCT, Sessa and Jackson (1995) advanced an argument that vertical differences need to be considered when theorizing about the effects of cultural diversity on group communication. They reviewed a variety of studies and concluded that higher status members are more assertive, exert more influence, take more turns, and interrupt others more than do lower status members. Sessa and Jackson noted that vertical differentiation (unequal statuses) interferes with team performance because low-status members may not voice their opinions or may be assigned a stereotypical role (e.g., secretary or gopher). Thus, the result is that potentially important or creative ideas may be silenced.

Social Identity Theory

Identity is one's self-conception and consists of both personal and social identities (Turner, 1987). *Personal identity* consists of views of self that differentiate an individual from other members of an in-group, whereas *social identity* consists of views of self shared by other members of an in-group (Turner, 1987). Social identity is defined by in-groups such as people of the same sex, national culture, and ethnic culture. Social identity theory (SIT) focuses on how the social categorization of people into groupings affects interactions between people of different social identities (Tajfel, 1978). According to SIT, awareness of membership in a social group is the most important factor that influences intergroup behavior. Awareness of social group membership results in a process of comparing oneself (and one's group) with others for the purpose of establishing a positive social identity. The desire to achieve a positive social identity results in a positive bias favoring the in-group (Tajfel & Turner, 1986; Turner, 1987). Individuals tend to engage in social competition to preserve a positive social identity when interacting with members of out-groups (Turner, 1975). A number of factors influence whether people representing different social categories will compete rather than cooperate when working with one another in groups. These conditions include unequal status, competition for resources, and imbalance between in-group and out-group members.

Garza and colleagues (Espinoza & Garza, 1985; Garza & Santos, 1991) conducted two studies to test the effects of social identity on cooperation and competition in diverse work groups. In the first study, Espinoza and Garza (1985) randomly assigned Anglo Americans and Hispanics to one of two conditions that required them to make a choice in a Prisoner's Dilemma-type game: a 3:1 or 1:3 ratio of in-group to out-group composition (same sex). In the second study, Garza and Santos (1991) used similar research procedures and types of participants as in the previous study but employed ratios varying from 1:5 up to 6:0. In both studies, they found that Hispanics competed with the others when they were in the minority (i.e., high-ethnic salience) condition (1:5, 2:4, or 1:3) and cooperated when they were equal in number with the Anglo members, a majority, or in an exclusive group. In contrast, Anglos were minimally affected by changes in in-group/out-group balance.

The researchers explained the findings in terms of SIT. Specifically, they argued that ethnic majority groups (e.g., Anglo Americans in the United States) already have a number of socially valued dimensions along which they can positively differentiate themselves from others (e.g., education and occupation). As a result, they do not have to consider the ethnic minority group members as a relevant group for social comparison and do not feel the need to compete with them. In contrast, the researchers argued that ethnic minority members (e.g., Hispanics) lack a preexisting positive social identity and, therefore, perceive the majority group as a relevant social comparison. Consequently, to achieve a positive social identity, ethnic minority group members feel the need to compete when they are in a numerical minority in a group. In further support of the usefulness of SIT and a vertical-difference perspective, Espinoza and Garza (1985) noted that most research shows that Hispanic cultural values indicate that Hispanics would cooperate with others.

Tokenism Hypothesis

A third approach to examining the effects of vertical differences on communication in work groups is Kanter's (1977) *tokensism hypothesis,* which states that the relative proportion of social types (salient external statuses, such as ethnicity and sex) in an organization results in organizations that are *uniform* (100% of same social type), *skewed* (minority members are 1-15%), *tilted* (minority members are 16-34%) or *balanced* (minority members are 35-65%). In skewed organizations, minority members tend to be viewed as "tokens," and a variety of adverse effects occur for such members, including interactional isolation, lower levels of opportunity for power, and being forced into playing stereotypical roles. The tokenism hypothesis predicts that as minority and majority social types within a group reach numerical parity, interactional isolation between the members of the two groups diminishes (Kanter, 1977).

Larkey (1996) used the ideas of the tokenism hypothesis to explain how diversity in organizations can affect work group interaction. She explained that group members can engage in two types of information processing: category-based and difference-based processing. *Category-based processing* focuses on stereotyping or in-group/out-group differentiation, whereas *difference-based processing* focuses on interpreting differences on an individual basis, even if one considers cultural information as part of understanding. On the basis of these two types of information processing, Larkey offered three general arguments: (a) Members of work groups in organizations with token representation are likely to use category-based processing and, as a result, are likely to negatively evaluate and exclude ethnic minorities; (b) members of work groups in organizations with uneven representation of minorities use both category- and difference-based processing and, as a result, will have divergent cultural patterns in the group, ideation that conforms to the dominant management standards, and frequent misunderstandings; and (c) members of work groups in multicultural organizations (organizations that have ethnic majority and minority members integrated at all levels of the organization) will use difference-based processing and, as a result, will demonstrate positive evaluation of differences, inclusion of all members, adjustment to other members, understanding of one another, and varied ideation. In essence, Larkey argued that cultural balance in work groups results in positive interactions among members, whereas imbalance results in negative interactions.

THE CULTURAL-DIFFERENCE PERSPECTIVE

Although the vertical-difference perspective has generated a number of theoretical models and research studies, a limitation of that research is that cultural differences have not been considered. Tannen (1994) argued that a cultural-difference perspective is critical for identifying and explaining misunderstandings, conflicts, and other troubling aspects of interactions between women and men. She advanced several arguments for the necessity of a cultural-difference perspective in the study of gender; these arguments also apply to culturally diverse work groups. The arguments center on the complementary, rather than dichotomous, nature of cultural-difference and vertical-difference frameworks. First, cultural differences show how status and power are created in interaction. Group member roles are created through interaction, not given. Through joint production by the parties involved, group members create positions in a hierarchy. Hence, power and dominance are created and re-created through social interaction. Second, a focus on cultural differences does not preclude attention to vertical differences. Cultural differences work to the disadvantage of members of groups who do not have power and to the advantage of members who have power. A third argument is that vertical differences are cultural in that status and power are tied to the *power distance*—the extent to which less powerful members of institutions accept that power is distributed unequally (Hofstede, 1991)—that characterizes a culture. Specifically, members of high-power distance cultures emphasize status and power more so than do members of low-power distance cultures (Hofstede, 1991). Through interaction, some cultures create hierarchies that are deemed acceptable and necessary. In essence, vertical differences are created as a result of cultural values.

The following section is devoted to a brief review and synthesis of studies that have taken a cultural-difference approach to the study of communication in work groups. First, studies comparing work groups across two different cultures are summarized. Second, and more important given the focus of this essay, studies that have used cultural differences to explain culturally diverse work groups are discussed.

Cross-Cultural Applications of the Cultural-Difference Perspective

One focus of cross-cultural research identifies aspects on which cultures can be considered to be similar or different. These aspects are labeled as dimensions of cultural variability and can be measured relative to other cultures (Hofstede, 1991). A primary dimension on which cultures vary is individualism-collectivism (Hui & Triandis, 1986; Triandis, 1995). In *individualistic cultures,* people focus on personal goals that overlap slightly with collective goals, such as immediate family and work. When personal and collective goals conflict, members of individualistic cultures typically choose to pursue personal goals over collective goals. In contrast, members of *collectivistic cultures* consider it socially desirable to put group goals ahead of individual goals (Triandis, 1995). In sum, members of collectivistic cultures draw on a "we" identity, whereas members of individu-

alistic cultures draw on an "I" identity (Ting-Toomey, 1988).

A variety of studies illustrate the relative influence of individualism and collectivism on communication in work groups. Bond, Leung, and Wan (1982), for example, studied how U.S. Americans and Hong Kong Chinese allocated rewards in group situations. U.S. Americans tended to use an equity principle (rewards allocated given the amount and/or quality of work performed by a member), whereas Hong Kong Chinese used an egalitarian principle (equal rewards among all group members). Earley (1989) studied the effects of individualism and collectivism in the work styles of U.S. and Chinese managers in groups. Group interaction led to social loafing (i.e., not doing a fair share of the work) by U.S. participants but to social striving (i.e., doing more work than one would do individually) by Chinese participants. Wagner (1995) found that individualism-collectivism influenced the level of cooperation among group members; specifically, individualists cooperated for personal gain, whereas collectivists cooperated for the good of the group. Although these studies do not provide direct evidence of the importance of a cultural-difference perspective in the study of culturally diverse work groups, they do have important implications for such a perspective. Individualists are likely to take a competitive stance, use majority decision-making procedures, and be direct when communicating, whereas collectivists are likely to cooperate and maintain group harmony, emphasize group interests over self-interests, use consensual decision making, and communicate in an indirect manner. These communication patterns help to illustrate why process difficulty occurs in culturally diverse groups composed of members from individualistic and collectivistic cultures.

Intercultural Applications of the Cultural-Difference Perspective

Although cross-cultural differences certainly have important implications for scholars and group members alike, the question remains whether cultural differences are useful in explaining the interactional patterns (especially problems and misunderstandings) of culturally diverse work groups. Problems, misunderstandings, and conflicts likely occur in groups that demonstrate cultural diversity because individuals tend to view norms and practices of interaction from their own cultural perspective (Nadler, Keeshan-Nadler, & Broome, 1985). For example, during interactions in heterogeneous groups, members from one co-culture use communication styles that may not correspond to the styles of members of a different co-culture. In essence, differences in the cultural backgrounds of the members of heterogeneous groups lead to different, and potentially difficult, communication processes more than in homogeneous groups. These differences potentially create misunderstandings in communication, at least during the initial meetings of a work group.

A number of scholars have used dimensions of cultural variability to explain communication patterns in culturally diverse groups. Once again, one of the most popular approaches is to use the individualism-versus-collectivism distinction. Cox, Lobel, and McLeod (1991), for example, studied the effects of individualism-collectivism on people's cooperative and competitive choices made during a Prisoner's Dilemma game. They assigned research participants to either an all-Anglo group or to a culturally diverse group (four members, one each from Asian American, Hispanic American, African American, and Anglo American ethnic groups). They found that groups composed of members with a collectivistic cultural tradition (i.e., Asian American, Hispanic American, and African American) displayed more cooperative choices than groups composed of members with an individualistic cultural tradition. This study not only showed the importance of individualism-collectivism on group behavior but also illustrated the importance of establishing a group norm in culturally diverse groups that reflects the summative cultural values of the individual members.

Oetzel (1998a, 1998b) conducted a research study using individualism-collectivism, measured at the individual level. He compared the communication patterns of homogeneous European American groups (an individualistic culture), homogeneous Japanese groups (a collectivistic culture), and heterogeneous groups composed of two Japanese and two European Americans working on a decision-making task. Instead of relying on national or ethnic culture to operationalize individualism and collectivism (see Cox et al., 1991), he measured participants' self-construals. *Self-construal* is one's perception of self as either independent or interdependent; the *independent construal of self* involves the view that an individual is a separate entity with a unique repertoire of feelings and thoughts, whereas the *interdependent construal of self* involves an emphasis on a person feeling connected to those around her or him (Markus & Kitayama, 1991). Gudykunst et al. (1996) argued that independent self-construals predominate in individualistic cultures, whereas interdependent self-construals predominate in collectivistic cultures. Extending this work, self-construals are more direct measures of an individual's value orientation than static ethnicity or nationality (Gudykunst et al., 1996; Kim et al., 1996; Singelis & Brown, 1995).

Oetzel's studies found that (a) heterogeneous groups were more likely to have unequal distribution of turns and to use majority decision-making procedures than were homogeneous groups; (b) homogeneous Japanese groups had fewer conflicts and used more cooperative conflict tactics and fewer competitive conflict tactics than did homogeneous European American groups; (c) groups composed of members with high independent self-construals were more likely to use competitive tactics and less likely to use cooperative tactics than were groups composed of members with low independent self-construals; and (d) because of their cultural background and self-construals, European Americans took more turns, initiated more conflicts, and used more competitive conflict tactics than did Japanese in these groups. These findings are consistent with a cultural-difference framework. First, differences between the European American and Japanese groups are consistent with individualistic and collectivistic values. Second, the problems experienced in the heterogeneous groups are also attributable to differences in these values. Third, differences in turn taking were better accounted for by self-construals and individualism-collectivism than by English language competency, which, in this case, is a status feature because the group meetings took place within the United States where competency in English is valued. Fourth, the groups displayed patterns that are summative of the values (or self-construals) of their individual members. From a vertical-difference perspective, the values of one (dominant) culture (European Americans in this case, given the context of the study) would be expected to prevail. However, this study measured only one status feature and, therefore, the extent to which vertical differences affected communication could be only minimally determined.

RESEARCH AGENDA

The cultural-difference perspective provides a useful way to examine the influence of culture and cultural diversity on communication processes in work groups. However, those studies examining cultural differences do not simultaneously measure vertical aspects, so it is impossible to determine which factor influences behavior (or whether both do). As noted earlier, the latter criticism can be levied against the vertical-difference research as well because it has not measured cultural values.

It appears that *both* vertical and cultural differences have an impact on group communication, but it is not clear how these differences work together. Further contributing to the problem is that the previously reviewed research is scattered and lacks a unifying theoretical focus. For example, a variety of communication processes and outcomes have

been explored, including turn taking, decision-making styles, leadership styles, conflict behavior, and influence behaviors. All of these variables may or may not be critical to culturally diverse groups, but without a sound theoretical focus, it is difficult to determine which variables are important, as well as difficult to synthesize vertical and cultural differences. At this juncture, what is needed is a sound theoretical focus to guide the research agenda. More important, that agenda needs to provide a focus on, and a synthesis of, vertical and cultural differences. To that end, an existing theoretical model of communication in culturally diverse work groups is first presented. The model is then expanded by discussing the importance of face negotiation during intercultural encounters (see Ting-Toomey, 1988; Ting-Toomey & Kurogi, 1998). Face negotiation provides an explanation for communication processes that occur in culturally diverse work groups. Finally, a new theoretical model is described that will (I hope) set the agenda for future research directed toward synthesizing the impact of vertical and cultural differences on communication in these groups.

A Model of Culturally Diverse Work Groups

A group can be thought of as a social system that consists of a set of component parts that have interdependent relationships (Ellis & Fisher, 1994). The group system is composed of inputs, processes, and outcomes, with inputs influencing processes, which, in turn, influence outcomes. Oetzel (1995) used these basic characteristics to create a model of communication in culturally diverse groups and focused, in particular, on the importance of individualistic and collectivistic cultural values as an input that affects group processes and outcomes. Individualism-collectivism was chosen because it has been identified as the single most important distinguishing characteristic of cultures (Hui & Triandis, 1986; Triandis, 1995). Oetzel's (1995) model identified group inputs as including cultural and individual characteristics of group members as evidenced by individualism-collectivism, as well as characteristics of the whole group, such as its homogeneity or heterogeneity.

To identify the important processes of culturally diverse work groups, Oetzel (1995) argued that group outcomes should be considered first to determine which communication processes are relevant. It has long been recognized that work groups have two important, yet interrelated, dimensions: a task and a social (or relational) dimension (Bales, 1950). The *task dimension* refers to the work of the group and tends to be measured as an outcome in terms of productivity or quality (see Hirokawa & Salazar, 1999), whereas the *relational dimension* is indexed by the relationships between group members and tends to be measured as an outcome in terms of member satisfaction or group cohesion (see Keyton, 1999). Hofstede (1991) found, anecdotally, that people from individualistic cultures focus primarily on the task dimension with a secondary concern for the relational dimension, whereas those from collectivistic cultures privilege the relational dimension and consider the task dimension to be secondary. Oetzel (1995), however, argued that, to be culturally inclusive, any evaluation of a task group composed of members from both individualistic and collectivistic cultures should include both task and relational outcomes. This expectation was supported empirically in a study by Oetzel and Bolton-Oetzel (1997) of attitudes toward group outcomes. They found that independent self-construal (i.e., individualism) was associated positively with a preference for task outcomes, whereas interdependent self-construal (i.e., collectivism) was associated positively with a preference for relational outcomes. Finally, Oetzel (1995) argued that the communication processes studied in culturally diverse groups should relate positively with *both* task and relational outcomes. In a survey of the extant literature, he identified three communication processes that meet this criterion: (a) equal distribution of turns, (b) consensus decision-making style, and (c) cooperative conflict style.

Although this explanation is intuitively appealing and has led to some useful research findings regarding the effects of individualism-collectivism on group communication processes (Oetzel, 1998a, 1998b), it has some limitations, especially given the context of this chapter. First, the model does not consider vertical differences, such as situational or structural factors, that may influence communication processes in culturally diverse work groups. Second, the model does not provide a strong theoretical explanation linking group inputs and processes. Oetzel (1995) designed the model as a work in progress; at this point, it is important to develop this model to provide a more concrete research agenda that can synthesize vertical and cultural differences in culturally diverse groups. This development will be accomplished by examining the concept of face and face-negotiation theory.

A Face-Negotiation Model of Culturally Diverse Work Groups

Face refers to a claimed sense of favorable social self-worth and/or projected other-worth in a public situation (Ting-Toomey & Kurogi, 1998). Hence, face includes two elements: (a) *self-face,* or concern for one's own image, and (b) *other-face,* or concern for another's image. *Facework* refers to the communicative strategies that an individual uses to enact self-face and to support or challenge another person's face (Ting-Toomey, 1988). Face is especially important in vulnerable interpersonal situations (such as uncertain or conflict situations) in which the situated identities of the communicators are called into question (see Ting-Toomey & Kurogi, 1998). It is a key concern in a culturally diverse group because uncertainty is likely prevalent due to differences in cultural values and expectations. Furthermore, cultural differences can lead to initial misunderstandings that can escalate into intensive, polarized conflict.

People in all cultures try to maintain and negotiate face in communicative situations (Ting-Toomey, 1988; Ting-Toomey et al., 1991); however, the manner in which self-

and other-face are negotiated, threatened, and maintained varies across cultures. Two cultural variables integrated into the theory are individualism-collectivism and power distance. Individualists have been found to have a high self-face concern that tends to result in their employing dominating conflict strategies in general, cooperating conflict strategies during task interactions, and self-honoring face behavior during competitive situations. In contrast, collectivists have been found to have a high other-face concern that leads them to use avoiding or obliging conflict strategies in general, cooperating conflict strategies during relational interactions, and self-effacement or in-group enhancement face behavior (Ting-Toomey et al., 1991; Ting-Toomey & Kurogi, 1998). In low-power distance cultures (such as Great Britain), high-status members appear to be self-focused and are verbally direct and use threats with low-status members, whereas low-status members are equally self- and other-focused and are indirect in managing face, become self-effacing, and use self-criticism when interacting with high-status members. In high-power distance cultures (such as Mexico), high-status members tend to be primarily other-focused (with some self-focus) and are indirect and benevolent, whereas low-status members are other-focused and are expected to play their role and correctly interpret high-status members' behaviors (Ting-Toomey & Kurogi, 1998).

Face is an extremely important concept for collectivistic cultures because of the importance placed in those cultures on social harmony (Cohen, 1991; Ting-Toomey, 1988). However, is face a salient concept in individualistic cultures, such as the United States (especially in the context of culturally diverse work groups)? The answer appears to be in the affirmative. First, a number of studies advocate the use of face to explain communicative behavior in a variety of U.S. interactional contexts, such as friendships (Cupach & Messman, 1999), as well as to explain general behavior (Goffman, 1959). More important, face has been found to be a useful explanatory mechanism for communicative behavior (e.g.,

conflict communication styles) in culturally diverse groups (Earley & Randel, 1997; Oetzel, 1998a, 1998b).

Second, face has components associated with individualistic and collectivistic values. Face is a cluster of identity- and relational-based issues (Ting-Toomey & Kurogi, 1998). Identity issues include reputation, honor, respect, and credibility, all of which are relevant for individualistic group members concerned with personal achievement. Such members are concerned with maintaining their self-image by doing good work (individually and collectively) as determined by relevant internal and external judges, such as bosses, teachers, or high-status members. Relational issues include group cohesion and commitment, which are important for collectivistic group members.

Third, face is especially relevant in the context of vertical differences in culturally diverse groups. Culturally diverse groups in the United States exist in a context in which ethnic majority members' identities and behaviors (i.e., Anglo Americans) are privileged. Group members from ethnic minority groups can feel that they are being marginalized or evaluated more strictly than dominant group members and, consequently, feel the need to defend and compete to preserve a positive self-face (Tajfel & Turner, 1986). In addition, members of ethnic minority groups tend to have their roots in collectivistic cultures, whereas ethnic majority groups tend to be more individualistic (Cox et al., 1991). This difference tends to exacerbate communication differences between ethnic majority and minority groups in the United States. However, it is important to note that individualism-collectivism is not the only distinguishing feature between ethnic or national cultural groups. In fact, there may be other relevant distinctions between culturally diverse group members (see Shuter, this volume). The face-negotiation model considers individualism-collectivism, as well as other cultural and vertical factors, to be inclusive of relevant issues for communication in culturally diverse groups.

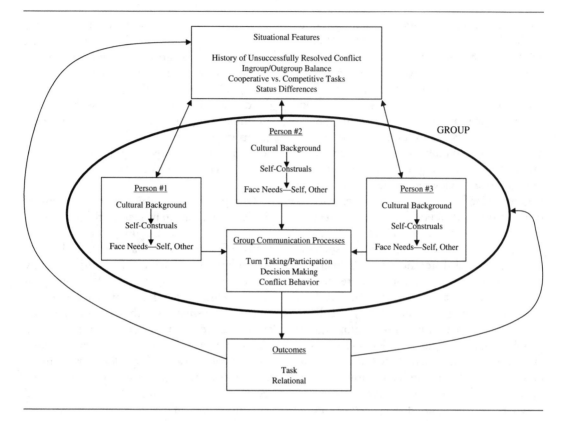

Figure 7.1. Face-Negotiation Model of Intercultural Work Group Communication

Ting-Toomey and Oetzel (2001) expanded face-negotiation theory to create a model that is useful for synthesizing vertical and cultural differences in work groups. Although the model focuses on intercultural conflict, other group processes that relate to face can also be considered. Furthermore, the face-negotiation model is consistent with Oetzel's (1995) model in that the face-negotiation model contains inputs, processes, and outputs. The face-negotiation model for a group of three members is displayed in Figure 7.1. The following sections briefly describe this model as it applies to communication in culturally diverse work groups (and vertical and cultural differences).

Group inputs. The face-negotiation model includes two broad inputs: situational factors and cultural and individual factors. Four situ-ational elements are considered: (a) a history of unsuccessfully resolved conflict between cultural/ethnic groups (e.g., the conflict between Israelis and Palestinians), (b) in-group/out-group balance—group composition, (c) cooperative versus competitive tasks, and (d) status differences between members (e.g., boss and employee). Each element can influence work group communication, although all four factors are generalizations that do not necessarily affect particular ethnic/cultural group members of particular work groups.

Situational factors appear to influence whether cultural or vertical differences are more important for explaining communication in culturally diverse work groups. Essentially, each of these four factors is a condition that helps or hinders the creation of a common in-group identity in a culturally diverse group (see Gaertner, Dovidio, & Bachman,

1996). The common in-group identity model is based on the *contact hypothesis* (Allport, 1954), which argues that certain conditions enable group members to create alliances and work toward common goals. A history of unsuccessfully resolved conflict, imbalance between in-group and out-group members, competitive tasks, and inequality of status among group members tends to result in members emphasizing differences between themselves and viewing those differences as negative (Gaertner et al., 1996). In such situations, group members focus on protecting their own (or the in-group's) face. These factors are vertical in nature and, thus, in such situations, vertical differences would likely be more important than cultural differences for explaining group communicative behavior. In contrast, a history of successfully resolving conflicts, balance between in-group/out-group membership, cooperative tasks, and equality among group members tends to result in members coming to share a common in-group identity in which cultural differences are respected. In such situations, group members focus on balancing self- and other-face needs. These factors are horizontal (or equal) in nature and, therefore, in such situations, cultural differences probably better explain group communication than do vertical differences.

The other input variables are the cultural and individual characteristics of the group members. These will not be discussed in detail, because these elements were introduced while describing face-negotiation theory. In short, cultural variables such as individualism-collectivism and power distance affect individual members' self-construals, which influence their face needs. Finally, the relationship between the situational features and the individual members' characteristics needs explanation. The double arrow between the situational features and each individual represents bidirectional influence. First, situational features affect individuals' face needs and behavior. Second, individuals' background partly influences which situational factors are perceived as relevant in a particular situation. For example, members of individualistic cultures do not make the strong distinction between in-group and out-group situations that members of collectivistic cultures make (Triandis, 1995). Thus, in general, a person from an individualistic culture would be less affected by an imbalance between in-group and out-group members than would be a person from a collectivistic culture (Espinoza & Garza, 1985; Garza & Santos, 1991).

Group processes. Another component of the face-negotiation model are the group processes/interactions. Group processes are directly influenced by the face needs of the individual members, which are influenced by vertical and cultural factors. Relevant processes include turn taking, influence, conflict, and decision-making behavior, all of which are influenced by face needs. For example, a person with a high self-face concern will likely take numerous turns to speak his or her mind and use dominating strategies to win conflicts, whereas a person with a high other-face need will most likely be concerned with sharing turns and use avoiding or obliging strategies.

Although the emphasis of face-negotiation theory is on how individuals behave, this does not preclude focusing on group behavior, such as how group members negotiate decisions. For example, understanding whether a group compromises to reach consensus or votes to reach a majority decision is likely reflective of members' individual and collective other- and self-face needs, respectively. Hence, a variety of processes can be considered under the unifying theme of negotiating face.

Group outcomes. The last factor of the face-negotiation model are group outcomes—the results of the interaction between group members. As in Oetzel's (1995) model, both task and relational outcomes are considered. Task outcomes are measured by criteria such as the effectiveness, quality, or productivity of the group's decision, whereas relational outcomes are measured by criteria such as member satisfaction and appropriate interaction between members. The face-negotiation model also includes a feedback loop; that is, the communication and outcomes of a group have the potential to affect both the situational factors and individual members. For example, if a group composed of members from two ethnic groups who have had a history of unsuccessfully resolving conflict is able to negotiate an outcome judged to be effective by the individual members (and relevant external judges), and if the group members are satisfied with the interaction, the perceived level of conflict (at least for these members) should be reduced. Another example is a group that reaches a poor-quality decision; the poor evaluation may result in an increased concern for self-face the next time these individuals interact in a group situation. These examples help to illustrate that group communication and outcomes can affect vertical and cultural aspects, as well as individuals' face needs, in a variety of group situations.

Overall, the face-negotiation model is dynamic and reflective of the complexity of interaction in culturally diverse work groups. Thus, it has potential for increasing our understanding of the relationship between vertical and cultural differences in culturally diverse groups. The model provides avenues for research to understand (a) the complex relationship between vertical and cultural differences; (b) how vertical and cultural differences, uniquely and conjointly, affect communication in culturally diverse work groups; and (c) how communication and outcomes in culturally diverse work groups affect vertical and cultural factors. In the next section, specific research procedures for investigating these issues are discussed.

Empirically Investigating the Face-Negotiation Model

A number of important questions need to be addressed to ascertain the usefulness of the face-negotiation model for culturally diverse work groups: (a) Is face important? (b) How can face be measured? (c) How can we determine the relationship between vertical and cultural differences? (d) What communicative behaviors affect group outcomes? To answer these questions, I advocate using multi-methodological (i.e., quantitative and qualitative) approaches (see Ting-Toomey, 1994) to study both researcher-created (e.g., laboratory experiments) and naturally occurring groups (e.g., management teams and student groups). The advantage of laboratory settings is that group composition can be manipulated and controlled, whereas the advantage of field settings is that group members are communicating in their natural environments and face may be a more salient factor because tangible rewards (e.g., performance evaluation) and long-term relationships are important issues. The use of both quantitative and qualitative methods helps to strengthen overall research because each has particular benefits (e.g., providing in-depth information and insider perspectives from qualitative methods and generalizability and control from quantitative methods). Regardless of the setting or procedure, it is also important to determine whether face is important in both initially formed and existing groups. Studying existing groups (or group development over time) is also important for understanding how communication and outcomes affect the vertical and cultural aspects of the group.

Quantitative procedures include the use of survey questionnaires and a priori observational techniques, such as interaction analysis (see Hirokawa, 1987). The first step is to be able to measure face. Ting-Toomey and Oetzel (2001) developed instruments to measure self-face, other-face, and facework behaviors. The instruments enable researchers to quantify the concern for self- and other-face and then statistically relate these concerns to communicative behaviors found (e.g., through self-report instruments) in culturally diverse groups. If the focus is on natural groups, vertical and cultural differences would need to be measured through self-report data. It is also possible to experimentally manipulate the composition of a group in a laboratory to represent various categories of vertical and cultural differences. Path model analysis and regression analysis can then be employed to determine whether face has explanatory value, which communicative behaviors are important, and which vertical and cultural variables (as well as how they interact to) influence face.

Qualitative inquiry is also useful for investigating face negotiation in culturally diverse groups. One approach is to interview members of naturally occurring, culturally diverse work groups about their face concerns and how they maintain their face and support others' face (see Ho, 1994; Tracy & Baratz, 1994). A second approach is to observe interaction in culturally diverse groups and infer face concerns via specific behaviors. Members can be made aware of these behaviors, and inquiries can be made as to their purpose. These procedures can then be used to develop a detailed construction of face and facework in a culturally diverse group in a particular setting. For instance, it is possible to investigate how individuals use communication to negotiate face, as well as how groups collectively negotiate face. The advantages of a qualitative approach are that it emphasizes the identification of specific face concerns as they are experienced by participants in a specific setting, and it provides a more thorough analysis of the "not-so-straightforward" functions of facework strategies (Tracy & Baratz, 1994). Furthermore, these approaches are likely to be very useful in understanding the relationship between vertical and cultural differences.

Although the face-negotiation model provides a general model for explaining communication in culturally diverse work groups, it does not identify specific communicative behaviors. As noted earlier, there are a number of face-related communicative behaviors, including turn taking, conflict, decision-making, and influence behaviors. However, these have not been specifically tested to determine their relevance for face issues or group outcomes. One strategy for determining useful communicative behaviors is to start with the face issues and finish with the outcomes. A wide variety of communicative behaviors should be considered initially, and these can

then be pared down if they are found not to be important (e.g., they do not explain unique variance or are not identified by members of diverse groups). If the behavior is relevant to face, then it can be determined if it is relevant to task and/or relational outcomes. An important communicative behavior should be influenced by face and affect outcomes. Oetzel (1995) argued that only communicative behaviors that relate to both task and relational outcomes should be considered. However, it may be that a different set of behaviors is associated with each of the outcomes (for a description of communicative behaviors associated with task outcomes and relational outcomes, respectively, see Hirokawa & Salazar, 1999; Keyton, 1999). This discrepancy can be addressed in future research as well.

Finally, although this chapter has focused on work groups, it is important to investigate other types of culturally diverse groups, such as support groups and friendship groups. Research on these groups will likely inform us (and perhaps even members of work groups) about various strategies to effectively manage face. For example, Conquergood's (1994) study of gangs explored communicative behaviors within (and among) culturally diverse gangs. These culturally diverse gangs were able to effectively manage face concerns and develop strong bonds of friendship within their gangs.

CONCLUSION

This chapter started by reviewing research that used vertical and cultural differences to explain the effects of culture and cultural diversity on group processes and outcomes. Both vertical and cultural differences are useful for explaining work group interaction, but presently, we do not yet know much about the relationship between vertical and cultural differences. A research agenda was offered to advance this goal. The agenda focused on explicating a face-negotiation model to guide future research and specified some procedures for investigating the usefulness of the model. The face-negotiation model focuses on why communicative behaviors occur in culturally diverse groups, as well as how communication shapes vertical and cultural conditions in these groups. This research is important for a culturally diverse society in which people from different cultural background with different statuses and power interact on a frequent basis. It is hoped that future research will help us to understand the effects of culture and cultural diversity on group communication processes so that it might be possible to facilitate and improve the interactions and outcomes derived from working in culturally diverse groups.

REFERENCES

Allport, G. W. (1954). *The nature of prejudice.* Cambridge, MA: Addison-Wesley.

Bales, R. F. (1950). *Interaction process analysis: A method for the study of small groups.* Reading, MA: Addison-Wesley.

Berger, J., Cohen, B. P., & Zelditch, M. (1973). Status characteristics and social interaction. In R. Ofshe (Ed.), *Interpersonal behavior in small groups* (pp. 194-216). Englewood Cliffs, NJ: Prentice Hall.

Berger, J., Wagner, D. G., & Zelditch, M. (1985). Introduction: Expectation states theory: Review and assessment. In J. Berger & M. Zelditch (Eds.), *Status, rewards, and influence* (pp. 1-72). San Francisco: Jossey-Bass.

Bond, M. H., Leung, K., & Wan, K. C. (1982). How does cultural collectivism operate? The impact of task and maintenance contributions on reward distribution. *Journal of Cross-Cultural Psychology, 13,* 186-200.

Chemers, M. M., & Murphy, S. E. (1995). Leadership and diversity in groups and organizations. In M. M. Chemers, S. Oskamp, & M. A. Costanzo (Eds.), *Diversity in organizations: New perspectives for a changing workplace* (pp. 157-188). Thousand Oaks, CA: Sage.

Cohen, R. (1991). *Negotiation across cultures: Communication obstacles in international diplomacy.* Washington, DC: U.S. Institute of Peace.

Conquergood, D. (1994). Homeboys and hoods: Gang communication and cultural space. In L. R. Frey (Ed.), *Group communication in context: Studies of natural groups* (pp. 23-55). Hillsdale, NJ: Lawrence Erlbaum.

Cox, T. H. (1994). *Cultural diversity in organizations: Theory, research, and practice.* San Francisco: Berrett-Koehler.

Cox, T. H., Lobel, S. A., & McLeod, P. L. (1991). Effects of ethnic group cultural differences on cooperative and competitive behavior on a group task. *Academy of Management Journal, 34,* 827-847.

Cupach, W. R., & Messman, S. J. (1999). Face predilections and friendship solidarity. *Communication Reports, 12,* 13-19.

Earley, P. C. (1989). Social loafing and collectivism. *Administrative Science Quarterly, 34,* 565-581.

Earley, P. C. (1993). East meets West meets Mideast: Further explorations of collectivistic and individualistic work groups. *Academy of Management Journal, 36,* 319-348.

Earley, P. C. (1994). Self or group? Cultural effects of training on self-efficacy and performance. *Administrative Science Quarterly, 39,* 89-117.

Earley, P. C., & Randel, A. E. (1997). Self and other: Face and work group dynamics. In C. S. Granrose & S. Oskamp (Eds.), *Cross-cultural work groups* (pp. 113-133). Thousand Oaks, CA: Sage.

Ellis, D. G., & Fisher, B. A. (1994). *Small group decision making: Communication and group processes* (4th ed.). New York: McGraw-Hill.

Espinoza, J. A., & Garza, R. T. (1985). Social group salience and intergroup cooperation. *Journal of Experimental Social Psychology, 21,* 380-392.

Gaertner, S. L., Dovidio, J. F., & Bachman, B. A. (1996). Revisiting the contact hypothesis: The induction of a common in-group identity. *International Journal of Intercultural Relations, 20,* 271-290.

Garza, R. T., & Santos, S. J. (1991). Ingroup/outgroup balance and interdependent interethnic behavior. *Journal of Experimental Social Psychology, 27,* 124-137.

Goffman, E. (1959). *The presentation of self in everyday life.* Garden City, NY: Doubleday.

Gudykunst, W. B., Matsumoto, Y., Ting-Toomey, S., Nishida, T., Kim, K. S., & Heyman, S. (1996). The influence of cultural individualism-collectivism, self construals, and individual values on communication styles across cultures. *Human Communication Research, 22,* 510-543.

Gudykunst, W. B., & Ting-Toomey, S. (with Chua, E.). (1988). *Culture and interpersonal communication.* Newbury Park, CA: Sage.

Hirokawa, R. Y. (1987). Group communication research: Considerations for the use of interaction analysis. In C. H. Tardy (Ed.), *A handbook for the study of human communication* (pp. 229-245). Norwood, NJ: Ablex.

Hirokawa, R. Y., & Salazar, A. J. (1999). Task-group communication and decision-making performance. In L. R. Frey (Ed.), D. S. Gouran, & M. S. Poole (Assoc. Eds.), *The handbook of group communication theory & research* (pp. 167-191). Thousand Oaks, CA: Sage.

Ho, D. Y. (1994). Face dynamics: From conceptualization to measurement. In S. Ting-Toomey (Ed.), *The challenge of facework: Cross-cultural and interpersonal issues* (pp. 269-286). Albany: State University of New York Press.

Hofstede, G. (1991). *Cultures and organizations: Software of the mind.* Maidenhead, UK: McGraw-Hill.

Hui, C., & Triandis, H. (1986). Individualism-collectivism: A study of cross-cultural researchers. *Journal of Cross-Cultural Psychology, 17,* 225-248.

Jackson, S. E., Brett, J. F., Sessa, V. I., Cooper, D. M., Julin, J. A., & Peyronnin, K. (1991). Some differences make a difference: Individual dissimilarity and group heterogeneity as correlates of recruitment, promotions, and turnover. *Journal of Applied Psychology, 76,* 675-689.

Judy, R. W., & D'Amico, C. (1997). *Workforce 2020: Work and workers for the 21st century.* Indianapolis, IN: Hudson Institute.

Kanter, R. M. (1977). *Men and women of the corporation.* New York: Basic Books.

Keyton, J. (1999). Relational communication in groups. In L. R. Frey (Ed.), D. S. Gouran, & M. S. Poole (Assoc. Eds.), *The handbook of group communication theory & research* (pp. 192-222). Thousand Oaks, CA: Sage.

Kim, M. S., Hunter, J. E., Miyahara, A., Horvath, A., Bresnahan, M., & Yoon, H. (1996). Individual- vs. cultural-level dimensions of individualism and collectivism: Effects on preferred conversational styles. *Communication Monographs, 63,* 28-49.

Kirchmeyer, C., & Cohen, A. (1992). Multicultural groups: Their performance and reactions with constructive conflict. *Group and Organization Management, 17,* 153-170.

Larkey, L. K. (1996). Toward a theory of communicative interactions in culturally diverse groups. *Academy of Management Review, 21,* 463-491.

Markus, H. R., & Kitayama, S. (1991). Culture and self: Implication for cognition, emotion, and motivation. *Psychological Review, 98,* 224-253.

McLeod, P. L., Lobel, S. A., & Cox, T. H. (1996). Ethnic diversity and creativity in small groups. *Small Group Research, 27,* 248-264.

Milliken, F. J., & Martins, L. L. (1996). Searching for common threads: Understanding the multiple effects of diversity in organizational groups. *Academy of Management Review, 21,* 402-433.

Nadler, L. B., Keeshan-Nadler, M., & Broome, B. J. (1985). Culture and the management of conflict situations. In W. Gudykunst, L. Stewart, & S. Ting-Toomey (Eds.), *Communication, culture, and organizational processes* (pp. 87-113). Beverly Hills, CA: Sage.

Oetzel, J. G. (1995). Intercultural small groups: An effective decision-making theory. In R. L. Wiseman (Ed.), *Intercultural communication theories* (pp. 247-270). Thousand Oaks, CA: Sage.

Oetzel, J. G. (1998a). Culturally homogeneous and heterogeneous groups: Explaining communication processes through individualism-collectivism and self-construal. *International Journal of Intercultural Relations, 22,* 135-161.

Oetzel, J. G. (1998b). Explaining individual communication processes in homogeneous and heterogeneous groups through individualism-collectivism and self-construal. *Human Communication Research, 25,* 202-224.

Oetzel, J. G., & Bolton-Oetzel, K. D. (1997). Exploring the relationship between self-construal and dimensions of group effectiveness. *Management Communication Quarterly, 10,* 289-315.

O'Reilly, C. A., Caldwell, D. F., & Barnett, W. P. (1989). Work group demography, social integration, and turnover. *Administrative Science Quarterly, 34,* 21-37.

Sessa, V. I., & Jackson, S. E. (1995). Diversity in decision-making teams: All differences are not created equal. In M. M. Chemers, S. Oskamp, & M. A. Costanzo (Eds.), *Diversity in organizations: New perspectives for a changing workplace* (pp. 133-156). Thousand Oaks, CA: Sage.

Singelis, T. M., & Brown, W. J. (1995). Culture, self, and collectivist communication: Linking culture to individual behavior. *Human Communication Research, 21,* 354-389.

Steiner, I. D. (1972). *Group process and productivity.* New York: Academic Press.

Tajfel, H. (1978). The achievement of group differentiation. In H. Tajfel (Ed.), *Differentiation between social groups: Studies in the social psychology of intergroup relations* (pp. 77-98). New York: Academic Press.

Tajfel, H., & Turner, J. C. (1986). The social identity theory of intergroup behavior. In S. Worchel & W. G. Austin (Eds.), *Pscyhology of intergroup relations* (2nd ed., pp. 7-24). Chicago: Nelson-Hall.

Tannen, D. (1994). *Gender and discourse.* New York: Oxford University Press.

Ting-Toomey, S. (1988). Intercultural conflict styles: A face negotiation theory. In Y. Y. Kim & W. B. Gudykunst (Eds.), *Theories in intercultural communication* (pp. 213-235). Newbury Park, CA: Sage.

Ting-Toomey, S. (Ed.). (1994). *The challenge of facework: Cross-cultural and interpersonal issues.* Albany: State University of New York Press.

Ting-Toomey, S., Gao, G., Trubinsky, P., Yang, Z., Kim, H. S., Lin, S. L., & Nishida, T. (1991). Culture, face maintenance, and styles of handling interpersonal conflict: A study in five cultures. *International Journal of Conflict Management, 2,* 275-296.

Ting-Toomey, S., & Kurogi, A. (1998). Facework competence in intercultural conflict: An updated face-negotiation theory. *International Journal of Intercultural Relations, 22,* 187-225.

Ting-Toomey, S., & Oetzel, J. G. (2001). *Managing intercultural conflicts effectively.* Thousand Oaks, CA: Sage.

Tracy, K., & Baratz, S. (1994). The case for case studies of facework. In S. Ting-Toomey (Ed.), *The challenge of facework: Cross-cultural and interpersonal issues* (pp. 287-305). Albany: State University of New York Press.

Triandis, H. C. (1995). *Individualism & collectivism.* Boulder, CO: Westview Press.

Turner, J. C. (1975). Social comparison and social identity: Some prospects for intergroup behaviour. *European Journal of Social Psychology, 5,* 5-34.

Turner, J. C. (1987). *Rediscovering the social group: A self-categorization theory.* Oxford, UK: Basil Blackwell.

Wagner, J. A. (1995). Studies of individualism-collectivism: Effects on cooperation in groups. *Academy of Management Journal, 38,* 152-172.

Watson, W. E., Kumar, K., & Michaelson, L. K. (1993). Cultural diversity's impact on interaction process and performance: Comparing homogeneous and diverse task groups. *Academy of Management Journal, 36,* 590-602.

Wiersema, M. F., & Bird, A. (1993). Organizational demography in Japanese firms: Group heterogeneity, individual dissimilarity, and top management team turnover. *Academy of Management Journal, 36,* 996-1025.

PART IV

Group Communication Processes

8

Rethinking Traditional Approaches to Argument in Groups

RENÉE A. MEYERS
University of Wisconsin—Milwaukee

DALE E. BRASHERS
University of Illinois—Urbana Champaign

On Sunday, December 10, 1989, parishioners at St. Patrick's Cathedral in New York City were joined by more than 4,500 AIDS and reproduction rights activists staging a "STOP THE CHURCH" protest. . . . Protesters held mock tombstones while hundreds of others lay down in the street, enacting one of ACT UP's (AIDS Coalition to Unleash Power) trademark "die-ins." . . . Throughout the crowd, signs declared: "Curb Your Dogma," "Papal Bull," and "Danger: Narrow Minded Church Ahead." . . . One activist yelled "Bigot" and "Stop the Murder" over Cardinal O'Connor's sermon, and other protesters soon joined in.

Christiansen and Hanson (1996, p. 157)

The form of protest described here, used by ACT UP (and other activist groups), violates many of the traditional conceptions of group argument as rational, convergence seeking, verbal, and decorous. Members intentionally disregard argumentative norms by flaunting sexuality, yelling profanities, and openly addressing taboo topics (see Brashers & Jackson, 1991; Fabj & Sobnosky, 1995). Participants demonstrate by "throwing condoms, necking in public places, speaking explicitly and positively about anal sex, 'camping it up' for the television cameras" (Gamson, 1989, p. 355). As Larry Kramer (1989), one of the founders of ACT UP, explained, "Surely ACT UP has taught everyone that you don't get anything by being nice, good little boys and girls. You do not get more with honey than with vinegar" (p. 290).

Recently, some scholars (mostly rhetoricians) have begun to recognize that factors beyond the scope of reason or traditional logic play an important role in argument production. They posit an "argument-in-use" model that often does not conform to traditional conceptions of argument as rational and logical. Some rhetoricians have suggested that arguments ought to be judged on validity (or soundness) rather than on logical form (see Farrell, 1977; Wenzel, 1977). Others have

141

proffered a situational or field-dependent definition of argument (Willard, 1983). Schuetz (1980) argued that rationality is not absolute but flexible and fluid:

> Rationality is not synonymous with the systematic reason of logical syllogisms or even the justifications found by applying Toulmin diagrams. Rationality does not always depend on the norms offered by capitalistic governments and Western thinking. Instead rationality is a somewhat fluid concept which depends on the social and economic circumstances and the intellectual, psychological, and moral predispositions of those who participate in reforms and revolutions. (pp. 87-88)

In this chapter, we rethink some traditional conceptions about group argument by first examining four fundamental underlying principles of traditional argument. Second, we introduce four argumentative strategies used by ACT UP (slogans and chants, vilification of opponents, expression of anger, and visual persuasion) that do not fit neatly into a traditional model of rational argument. Third, we illustrate how such non-normative argument forms serve as the impetus for rethinking traditional assumptions about argument. We conclude by discussing both the theoretical and pedagogical implications of our analysis.

TRADITIONAL APPROACHES TO GROUP ARGUMENT

The study of argument has played a central role in the intellectual development of the field of communication. In the past 15 years, the study of *group* argument has received increased research attention (see Alderton, 1982; Alderton & Frey, 1983, 1986; Brashers, Adkins, & Meyers, 1994; Canary, Brossmann, & Seibold, 1987; Ketrow, Meyers, & Schultz, 1997; Mayer, 1985, 1987; Meyers, 1989a, 1989b, 1997; Meyers & Brashers, 1995, 1998; Meyers, Brashers, Winston, & Grob, 1997; Meyers, Seibold, & Brashers, 1991; Schultz, 1983, 1989). Findings from this body of research have added to our knowledge about the structure and functions of argument as defined within a "normative" or "traditional" model. Such a model has its roots in logic, as well as in Toulmin's (1958) conception of the "ideal" argument (a set of ordered statements that includes claims, data, warrants, backing, qualifiers, and reservations), and is grounded in rationality, reasonableness, and a verbal syntax. The upshot of employing this type of model is that most scholars view this rational, ordered form of discourse as normative and as producing qualitatively "better" arguments than non-normative forms. In fact, so strong is this orientation, that much of the extant research and most of the discipline's textbooks still show a pronounced emphasis on the "rational" aspects of communication in argumentative contexts, while simultaneously excluding discussions of nonrational argument forms.

We posit that this traditional normative model of group argument is undergirded by four interrelated assumptions—argument as rational, convergence producing, decorous, and verbal. Each of these assumptions, and related research, is detailed below.

Argument as Rational

Communication researchers typically have defined argument as normative, structured, and rational. As Rowland (1995) stated in defending rational argument,

> A generation ago the idea of defending rational argument would have seemed ludicrous. Almost no one disputed the value of rationality or of argumentation as a means of attaining that end. . . . The conventional wisdom of the time might be stated quite simply: The most important characteristic defining what it means to be human is rationality and the most important means to attaining rationality is argument. (pp. 350-351)

Two exemplars of work within the group communication research domain that view argument as normative and rational are (a) research on conversational argument conducted within the structurational framework and (b) investigations of the personality characteristic of argumentativeness.

In their work on conversational argument in the group context, Seibold and Meyers (1986) weave traditional assumptions about argument into a structurational definition. They indicate that "as systems, arguments are observable patterns of interaction manifest *in discursive claiming and reason-giving*[italics added] during deliberations about simple or controversial matters of fact, value, or action" (p. 147). A coding system consonant with this definition has been constructed (see Canary, 1989; Canary et al., 1987; Canary, Ratledge, & Seibold, 1982; Gebhardt & Meyers, 1994; Meyers et al., 1991; Seibold, Canary, & Ratledge, 1983) and applied to group interactions (see Brashers, Haas, Klingle, & Neidig, 1997; Canary et al., 1982, 1987; Meyers & Brashers, 1995, 1998; Meyers et al., 1991, 1997; Seibold et al., 1983; Seibold, Poole, McPhee, Tanita, & Canary, 1981). The coding scheme is strongly influenced by Toulmin's (1958) model, although consonant with a structurational orientation, it also incorporates Perelman and Olbrechts-Tyteca's (1969) more global conception of argument processes and movement in discourse, as well as the conversational-analytic approach of Jackson and Jacobs (1980). Yet traditional, rational assumptions about group argument (e.g., Toulmin) are foundational to this scheme and to this general approach.

A second body of research that views argument as rational is investigation of argumentativeness as a personality characteristic (see Infante & Rancer, 1982; Infante, Trebing, Sheperd, & Seeds, 1984; Infante, Wall, Leap, & Danielson, 1984; see also Keyton & Frey, this volume). Although most of this research has been conducted in the individual cognitive domain, the findings have implications for understanding group members' argument behavior.

Argumentativeness typically is defined as "a personality trait which predisposes an individual to recognize controversial issues, to advocate positions on them, and to refute other

positions" (Infante et al., 1984, p. 68). A person who scores high on the Argumentativeness Scale (Infante & Rancer, 1982) likes defending a point of view and perceives argument as a reasonable and enjoyable form of communication. This type of person can be juxtaposed against an "aggressive" person who uses what are generally perceived to be more non-normative forms of discourse (e.g., yelling, physical gestures, and/or other emotional displays). Within this framework, the normatively defined argumentativeness characteristic is considered to be more desirable than the non-normative aggression characteristic.

A view of argument as normative and rational, as captured by these two recent research traditions, informs the general orientation of argumentation scholars today and is the cornerstone of theory and pedagogy on group argument. This view represents one of the most widely and deeply held assumptions about argument, in general, and group argument, more specifically.

Argument as Convergence Producing

In addition to viewing argument as rational, many scholars assume that argument moves differentiated group members toward convergence on a mutually acceptable proposal. For example, the structurational program of research identifies "convergence-seeking" as one of the distinguishing characteristics of group argument (see Brashers & Meyers, 1989; Canary, Brossmann, Brossmann, & Weger, 1995; Canary et al., 1982, 1987; Canary, Weger, & Stafford, 1991; Meyers, 1997; Meyers & Brashers, 1998; Meyers et al., 1997). As Canary et al. (1995) explained, "The notion of *convergence* is taken from Perelman and Olbrechts-Tyteca (1969) and is meant to imply two levels of discourse activity: (a) understanding and/or agreement on ideas and (b) movement toward agreement regarding a proposed course of action" (p. 185). Recent work in this area suggests that group members use agreement both to move subgroup members toward convergence and to direct the entire group toward a preferred solution (Brashers & Meyers, 1989; Meyers et al., 1991, 1997).

Much of the past research on group argument has, thus, assumed that the role of argument is to move groups toward consensus, and convergence production is certainly vital in groups that have to reach consensus (or near consensus). Such groups include juries and perhaps teams in organizations where strong commitment to the final solution is essential if it is to be implemented. However, as we shall argue later in the chapter, the assumption that all argument will, or should, lead to convergence may blind us to some of the advantages that accrue from prolonged, public, and contentious arguments that don't produce consensus.

Argument as Decorous

Not only have group communication scholars assumed that argument is rational and convergence producing, but they have conceived of it as decorous, civil, and refined. Translated into verbal syntax, argument is presumed to be primarily "claim-making and reason-giving" rather than emotional displays of hostility, yelling, and name-calling. As Fleming (1996) explained,

> The belief that an argument has two parts—"claim" and "support"—is a cornerstone of Western thought. The practice of bringing forth statements that explain, support, question, and comment on *other* statements was perhaps the most important contribution of Greek efforts of the 5th and 4th Centuries BCE, to systematize knowledge and edify public life. (p. 13)

This civilized notion of claim making is evident in modern definitions of argument as well. Thomas (1981) views argument as "a sentence or sequence of sentences containing statements some of which are set forth as supporting, making probable, or explaining, others" (p. 8). Toulmin (1958) indicates that, in all cases of argument, "we can challenge the assertion, and demand to have our attention drawn to the grounds (backing, data, facts, evidence, considerations, features) on which the merits of the assertion are to depend" (p. 11). Fleming (1996) suggests that argument is "an intentional human act in which support is offered on behalf of a debatable belief. It is characterized first and foremost by *reasonableness*" (p. 12).

Hence, argumentative discourse typically is viewed as a decorous, debate-style form of interaction in which claims are posited and evidence offered. This view permeates much of our teaching about argument and continues to frame most of our research efforts, including teaching and research about group argument.

Argument as Verbal

Traditionally, scholars have not only viewed argument as rational, convergence producing, and decorous but have also emphasized a verbal paradigm that views arguments as collections of words. As van Eemeren, Grootendorst, and Kruiger (1987) explained,

> Argumentation requires the use of language. A person engaged in argumentation makes an assertion or statement, assumes or doubts something, denies something, and so on. For the performance of all these activities he must utter words and sentences (whether spoken or written). . . . Argumentation without the use of language is impossible. (p. 3)

Birdsell and Groarke (1996) echoed these sentiments, indicating that "most scholars who study argumentation theory are, therefore, preoccupied with methods of analyzing arguments which emphasize verbal elements and show little or no recognition of other possibilities, or even the relationship between words and other symbolic forms" (p. 1). Indeed, Blair (1996) suggested that "the study of argument since Aristotle has assumed it to be paradigmatically verbal, if not essentially and exclusively so" (p. 23).

These four assumptions—argument as rational, convergence producing, decorous, and verbal—have underscored the study of argumentative discourse in groups for decades. However, these assumptions are increasingly being questioned as scholars examine argument in nontraditional contexts, unstructured interactions, and mediated forums. Argument occurs not only in traditional "debates" but also in the interpersonal (Brossmann & Canary, 1990; Canary & Sillars, 1992; Canary et al., 1991), small group, and organizational arenas (Brashers, 1991; Garrett & Meyers, 1991; Hollihan, Riley, & Freadhoff, 1986; Keough, 1987; Putnam, Wilson, Waltman, & Turner, 1986). This expansion of investigative efforts has created some consensus among scholars around an argument-in-use view (which will be discussed in more detail later)—a conception of argument as practical, plausible, and social rather than rational, logical, and solitary.

Many activist groups evidence this argument-in-use model today. The highly visible group ACT UP challenges most traditional assumptions about argument and persuasion and has had some success in doing so. ACT UP was formed in 1987 in New York City in response to the slow action by government agencies responsible for AIDS research (see Brashers et al., 1997; Brashers & Jackson, 1991). As Fabj and Sobnosky (1993) noted, "From its inception, ACT UP has attracted attention through its public demonstrations and the high level of visibility it maintains" (p. 93). As ACT UP's (ACT UP/New York, n.d.) new member information packet stated,

> ACT UP, the AIDS Coalition To Unleash Power, is a diverse, non-partisan group of individuals, united in anger and committed to direct action to end the AIDS crisis. We meet with government officials, we distribute the latest medical information, we protest and demonstrate. We are not silent.

ACT UP is noted for its direct action. According to Patton (1990), this activist movement started because "people with AIDS would not stay quiet for long. Their discourse shifted to a critique of the oppression of early

death and unnecessary infections resulting from treatments delayed and education denied" (p. 130). The group's motto "Silence = Death" reflects the members' view that inaction (e.g., failure to speak out against slow progress on treatments, discrimination against persons with HIV or AIDS, ineffective or nonexistent educational programs, lack of needle exchange for intravenous drug users, and failure to include women in trials of anti-HIV drugs) increases the likelihood that people will die from AIDS.

ACT UP has used civil disobedience and direct-action tactics to argue for changes in institutional practices in the United States as well as in other countries. In the next section, we identify four direct-action tactics that characterize ACT UP's argumentative practices: (a) slogans and chants, (b) vilification of opponents, (c) expressions of anger, and (d) visual persuasion. Each of these actions has important implications for challenging traditional assumptions about group argumentation, and together they serve as the impetus for a subsequent reevaluation of group argument.

ACT UP'S ARGUMENTATIVE PRACTICES

Chants and Slogans

At demonstrations, chants and slogans are common means of conveying activists' arguments. Chants such as "ACT UP, fight back, fight AIDS" and "We're here, we're queer, get used to it" are used to motivate protesters and send messages to those who pass by. ACT UP members chant "Greed kills: Access for all" to protest high drug prices. In response to President George Bush's attending a fund-raiser for North Carolina Senator Jesse Helms instead of the opening ceremonies of the Sixth International AIDS Conference in San Francisco, ACT UP members led conference attendees in a chant of "Three hundred thousand dead from AIDS: Where is George?" Activists confront drug company representatives over prices of anti-HIV drugs with chants of "Shame, shame, shame."

Signs at demonstrations also carry protesters' argumentative messages: "Pataki's Budget Kills Children" (in response to New York Governor George Pataki's proposed cuts to AIDS care funding); "Murder by Neglect: Bush = Death" (in response to President George Bush's inaction on AIDS treatment and education); and "AIDS Drugs: Your Money or Your Life" (in response to the high price of AIDS drugs). At a "Resist the List" demonstration to protest proposed legislation that would require reporting names of persons who are infected with HIV to the U.S. Health Department (current law requires only reporting of persons who have AIDS), a sign read, "Hitler Started With a List." Pharmaceutical companies targeted for protest have had signs posted on their property that read, "THIS FACILITY IS UNDER SURVEILLANCE BY THE AIDS COALITION TO UNLEASH POWER: ACT UP. AIDS IS GENOCIDE!!"

In short, the use of slogans and chants is central to the argumentative practices of ACT UP. These messages are at the core of many protests and are employed to simultaneously attract attention and deliver a persuasive appeal. Clearly, these strategies do not fit into a model of argument based on rational, logical, and decorous practices.

Vilification of Opponents

ACT UP opponents are commonly vilified by ACT UP members as "murderers," "AIDS profiteers," and "liars." As Vanderford (1989) noted, "Vilification is a rhetorical strategy that discredits adversaries by characterizing them as ungenuine and malevolent opponents" (p. 166). Vilification functions to (a) unify people within social movements by providing a clear target for action and by allowing activists to present themselves and their positions in opposition to their adversaries; (b) present an adversary as evil, which allows activists to present themselves as moral; (c) increase members' "commitment to the cause"

by creating a need for self-defense; and (d) provide "a reason for alarm and action" because it "magnifies the opponents' power" (pp. 166-167). For example, in a response to the "Stop the Church" action mentioned in the opening of this essay, ACT UP contended that

> John Cardinal O'Connor manipulates Catholic followers into believing his policies [on safe-sex education, condom use, homosexuality, and abortion] are the "word of god." What the Cardinal and the Archdiocese are doing is sinning. They kill, they lie, they intimidate and torture the people of New York City. (ACT UP/New York, 1990)

Similarly, identifying Health and Human Services Secretary Donna Shalala as an adversary, ACT UP documents described a press conference at the Eleventh International AIDS Conference in Vancouver, organized by ACT UP, along with Mexican and Canadian AIDS activists, that was canceled due to a lack of an agreement between the NAFTA countries, while "Donna Shalala, official hypocrite of the US Health and Human Services Administration, was reported to be enjoying the Vancouver sunshine" (ACT UP/New York, 1996).

Vilification of opponents has proved to be a controversial argumentative strategy for ACT UP activists. These messages are often rude, pointed, and in-your-face, but ACT UP leaders contend that such a strategy is necessary to draw attention to opponents' apathy, disinterest, and power. Clearly, such strategies do not lend themselves to quick, if any, convergence production, as traditional models of argument posit.

Expressions of Anger

Anger is a common theme in ACT UP's actions (e.g., Ariss, 1994; Brown, 1997; Cohen, 1998; Woolcock, 1998). Brown (1997) noted that "civil society (as a space) enabled ACT UP to vent publicly their enormous anger over the amount of death and government inaction vis-à-vis AIDS" (p. 68). ACT UP documents frequently mention anger as a motivating force:

- "ACT UP, the AIDS Coalition To Unleash Power, is a diverse, non-partisan group of individuals, united in anger and committed to direct action to end the AIDS crisis." (ACT UP/New York, n.d.-a)
- "Since the start, our anger has been positive—highly focused, disciplined, and directed. And the result has been enormous change in the treatment, perception, and understanding of AIDS at every level in our society." (ACT UP/New York, n.d.-b)
- "Anger is the origin of ACT UP." (ACT UP/Paris, n.d.-b)

Cohen (1998) labeled the expression of anger (and grief) in ACT UP members' actions as a "secondary symbolic effect" that is "part of the actual attractiveness of ACT UP demonstrations for participants" (p. 26).

Although ACT UP's actions are typically nonviolent, in one rare instance, Larry Kramer, an AIDS activist and one of the founders of ACT UP, called for members to display their anger by rioting at the Sixth International AIDS Conference. Activists were angry over the lack of progress on treatments and an immigration ban that prevented HIV-infected individuals who were not citizens from entering the United States to attend the conference in San Francisco. Kramer argued that the usual demonstrations would not be enough. Robert Wachter (1991), a physician, AIDS researcher, and one of the organizers of the conference, recalls that Kramer was widely criticized, even among coalitions within the activist and gay communities. In an "Open Letter to San Francisco" (published in the *Bay Area Reporter*), Kramer responded to the criticisms:

I'm sorry my recent call for riots at the Sixth Conference on AIDS has upset you. You are free not to riot and you are free to criticize my call to riot, and I am free not to comprehend your criti-

cism. And we are all free to die. (Wachter, 1991, p. 170)

Peter Staley, a member of ACT UP/New York, noted in his opening address at the conference, "My good friend Larry Kramer has been trying to talk me into being an AIDS terrorist. Is there any way we can avoid all this? I'm not sure anymore" (Wachter, 1991, p. 204). Although Kramer's call to arms did not result in riots, his action called attention to how continued frustration and unresolved anger might lead to escalation of ACT UP's activist tactics.

Portraying emotions, especially anger, is, thus, a trademark of ACT UP's activities. Members view the expression of anger as essential to delivering an urgent and persuasive argument. Given that the expression of emotion has typically been absent from traditional models of group argument, this strategy also does not fit neatly into normative conceptions of argument.

Use of Visual Elements

ACT UP's argumentative actions often are highly visual. "Kiss-ins" (in which same- and opposite-sex couples kiss) and "die-ins" (in which bodies are chalked on the pavement to represent victims murdered by inactivity on the part of the government) are common symbolic forms of protest (Cohen, 1998). Other times, members combine visual symbols with bottom-line slogans. One poster showed a picture of a rat in a laboratory and had the slogan "Mice are more likely to get experimental AIDS drugs than women." When ACT/UP London catapulted condoms and information sheets on safer needle use over the fence of a prison in response to government officials' refusal to provide inmates with these supplies, "visual reinforcement was provided by a giant pink catapult and condom" (ACT UP/London, 1990).

Highly visual, and very important to ACT UP's argumentative strategies, has been the human protest. The first documented ACT UP protest was in March 1987 and involved participants stopping traffic on Wall Street in New York City "to demand government and corporate action to end the AIDS crisis" (ACT UP/New York, 1999). The following day, *The New York Times* carried a picture of protesters lying in the street and being carried away by police, with the caption, "Homosexuals Arrested at AIDS Drug Protest" (Sotomayor, 1987). ACT UP used the "phone zap" to protest Northwest Airline's announcement that it would no longer allow persons with AIDS to fly on the airline: ACT UP members phoned Northwest's reservation lines constantly throughout the day and night to protest the policy and to make fake reservations, creating chaos at the airline. Northwest eventually reversed its policy (Nussbaum, 1990).

A 1989 protest on Wall Street to call attention to the high price of AZT (a product of the Burroughs Wellcome pharmaceutical company, which was the only approved drug at that time for HIV infection) stopped trading on the New York Stock Exchange for the first time in its history. ACT UP members posed as traders to gain entry to the New York Stock Exchange, then chained themselves to a balcony, blew horns, and unfurled a banner that read "Sell Wellcome." Burroughs Wellcome reduced the price of the drug 4 days later, although it claimed that the reduction was not due to ACT UP's pressure tactics (Burkett, 1995).

One form of protest that especially highlights the use of visual symbolism is the "political funeral." Typically private functions in which family and friends participate in the burial and remembrance of a loved one, funerals become a public forum for ACT UP activism. A number of these funerals have been held in Washington D.C. (e.g., funerals held in front of the White House) and New York City. In his statement "Bury Me Furiously," Mark Lowe Fisher anticipated dying and called for his funeral service to be held in public as a protest against inaction on the part of the government. He noted,

I have decided that when I die I want my fellow AIDS activists to execute my wishes for my po-

litical funeral. I suspect—I know—my funeral will shock people when it happens. We Americans are terrified of death. Death takes place behind closed doors and is removed from reality, from the living. I want to show the reality of my death, to display my body in public; I want the public to bear witness. We are not just spiraling statistics; we are people who have lives, who have purpose, who have lovers, friends and families. And we are dying of a disease maintained by a degree of criminal neglect so enormous that it amounts to genocide. I want my death to be as strong a statement as my life continues to be. I want my own funeral to be fierce and defiant, to make the public statement that my death from AIDS is a form of political assassination. (The full text of "Bury Me Furiously," pictures, and details of the protest and other political funerals are available at www.actupny. org.)

After his death, protestors in New York City marched in an open-coffin procession for Fisher more than 30 blocks up the Avenue of the Americas from the Village to Midtown and stopped in front of Republican Headquarters the day before the elections of November 2, 1992.

Among ACT UP protesters, the visual medium is viewed as necessary and effective. Sometimes paired with written or oral messages, sometimes standing alone, visual images send an argumentative message that is strongly persuasive. As explained previously, traditional models of group argument have consistently focused on the verbal domain, largely to the exclusion of the visual. Once again, ACT UP's strategies do not fit neatly into a normative vision of argumentation.

All four of these argumentative strategies appear largely incongruent with traditional assumptions about argument. The use of *slogans and chants* precludes the elaborated argument anticipated in rational models. Claims made through these means are used to simultaneously demand action and blame opposition, whereas evidence and reason giving are noticeably absent. The *vilification of oppo-*

nents violates assumptions about argument as convergence-producing discourse, in that this strategy is designed to create and sustain oppositional force. The *expression of anger* violates assumptions about civil and decorous argumentative interaction. ACT UP members contend that the expression of anger is necessary to motivate action on the part of those who would not otherwise be moved, yet within an "argument as rational discourse" paradigm, emotion is thought of as being in opposition to reason. Finally, the use of *visual images* contradicts assumptions that argument is primarily constituted of verbal discourse. For ACT UP, visuals are used to create images that may violate cultural and social norms and to both stand in place of and reinforce verbal messages. In the next section, we explore the fit between these four argumentative strategies and traditional assumptions held about argument. Specifically, we identify how non-normative forms of argument provide the impetus for a revised way of thinking and theorizing about group argument.

RETHINKING TRADITIONAL APPROACHES TO GROUP ARGUMENT

Rational Argument Versus Slogans and Chants

ACT UP's pervasive use of slogans and chants does not fit neatly into the traditional view of argument as a rational process of making claims and giving reasons for those claims. Slogans and chants preclude the elaborated argument anticipated in rational models and focus instead, on quick, short, eye-catching phrases that give the audience (e.g., passersby and the media) the bottom line. These messages are much more consistent with an argument-in-use view—that is, an informal, plausible, practical model of group argument.

Argumentation scholars are also slowly making a case for the validity of an argument-in-use view of group argument (see Billig,

1996; Canary et al., 1995; Leff & Hewes, 1981; Walton, 1992). These scholars conceive of argument as everyday, situation-specific reasoning rather than as traditional deductive logic—that is, as a type of informal reasoning that does not necessarily conform to definitions of argument as rational and normative (Canary et al., 1995; Meyers & Brashers, 1998).

Although consensus regarding a definition of "informal reasoning," "everyday reasoning," or "argument-in-use" is difficult to find, most scholars agree that, unlike formal reasoning, it is reasoning carried on outside the formal boundaries of mathematics and symbolic logic. Researchers view it as distinct from formal reasoning because instead of drawing logically necessary conclusions from premises, "the individual's task is to use his or her knowledge to identify premises relevant to a particular proposition and build plausible lines of argumentation" (Johnson & Blair, 1991, pp. 133-134). Willbrand and Rieke (1991) summarized this viewpoint by stating that "it is our position that the communicative act of people giving reasons should be examined without the preconceptions that come from our indoctrination in logic" (p. 415).

Some recent empirically based investigative work also lends support to an argument-in-use model, with findings showing that informal reasoning is the norm rather than the exception (see Perkins, 1985a, 1985b; Perkins, Farady, & Bushey, 1991). Relying on informal, non-normative modes of argument is not always in a group's best interest, however. In a collection of studies, Gouran and colleagues (Gouran, 1983, 1984, 1986, 1987, 1997; Gouran, Hirokawa, & Martz, 1986; Hirokawa & Pace, 1983) found that, rather than advancing claims and offering evidence, group members argued from fallacious inferences, which created poor-quality decision choices in real-life group situations. Their findings indicate that such inferences often go unchallenged and unheeded as a group adopts a non-normative, informal mode of argument. In several cases (e.g., Bay of Pigs, the

Challenger disaster, and Watergate), such "flawed" argument resulted in disastrous decision choices by groups.

In an examination of written accounts of international negotiation meetings, Axelrod (1977) found that the presentation of evidence in support of claims was infrequent (6% of all statements), reasoning from cause was practically nonexistent (1%-4% of all statements), and challenges or objections were all but lacking (2%-6% of all statements). Most statements were unsupported "truth" claims spoken so that the other side would know what the negotiator felt was important. Not surprisingly, Axelrod concluded that the traditional model of argument was not evident in these negotiation settings. Reviewing these findings, and others on informal reasoning, Voss (1991) suggested that, instead of following a traditional model, this argument process "likely involves individuals stressing points and stating positions, with the comparing and contrasting of differing positions essentially leading to a new, quite possibly acceptable solution, a more or less dialectical process" (p. 51).

Other work on group argument also raises questions about whether the traditional, normative model is followed. The "social" nature of groups, for example, appears to play a mediating role in the construction of argument. Leff and Hewes (1981) suggested that constraints in group decision-making interactions, such as pressure toward conformity, time, and status structures, push group members to rely on "implicit but identifiable social conditions and beliefs and thus on relatively abbreviated forms of argument" (p. 783). As they explained,

> Group discussion is a social activity. . . . An impeccably structured formal argument may fail to have any impact within the group's social world. And, likewise, a visceral reaction compelling to any one individual carries no necessary weight in a public forum. As a consequence, group members must rely on argumentative forms and beliefs that are accepted by convention. (p. 783)

In addition, results from the structurational program of research on conversational argument have revealed that group members often do not construct arguments in a traditional, rational manner. Instead, participants are most likely to produce simple arguments composed of assertions that are sometimes (but clearly not always) supported by evidence and that are seldom explicitly coupled with warrants or backing (see Canary et al., 1987; Meyers & Brashers, 1998; Meyers et al., 1991).

In sum, our analysis of ACT UP's use of slogans and chants as a central argumentative vehicle, and recent theorizing and research, supports an argument-in-use view wherein group argument is more often informal than formal, and more typically embodies practical reasoning than logical deduction. Walton's (1992) description of plausible argument closely fits this alternative conception of group argument:

> Plausible argumentation is based on a kind of reasoning that goes forward tentatively and provisionally in argumentation, subject to exceptions, qualifications, and rebuttals. Plausible argumentation is opinion-based—it is inherently subject to retraction as an argument continues and new evidence is brought into discussion. (p. 3)

Argument as Convergence Producing Versus Vilification of Opponents

ACT UP's vilification of its opponents does not fit neatly into the traditional model of argument as convergence-producing discourse, yet such discordant and negative messages are probably typical of many argumentative interactions. The past focus on a rational, convergence-producing model may have blinded us to the more tumultuous nature of group argument. In the past decade, however, some scholars have begun to identify argument as more divisive than convergent—that is, as more oppositional than cooperative. O'Keefe and Benoit (1982) asserted that "displays of overt opposition are part of every argument and that the relationship of opposition such displays create make other displays of opposition relevant" (p. 162). Moreover, Martin and Scheerhorn (1985) found that interactants often view arguments as "hostility-laden events" (p. 718), and Hicks (1991) discovered that participants typically perceive arguments as anger based and out of control. Arguments characterized by tumult, vilification of opponents, and discord may never reach convergence or may take paths to a final solution that do not resemble traditional conceptions of how arguers should converge. Although these arguments may beget negative results that do not conform to the convergence-producing effects that accompany traditional views of argumentative interaction, the developmental and protracted nature of these arguments can have positive impact on all parties involved.

Viewing argument as convergence producing may obscure the possibility that not all arguments can be, or should be, resolved. In many situations, the opportunities gained by continuation of argumentative interaction are ignored or devalued. Because many participants have an aversion to prolonged, unresolved arguments (see Martin & Scheerhorn, 1985; Walker, 1991), scholars have tended to overlook the communication insights that might be gleaned by examining more closely forms of extended argumentative interactions. For example, the "environment versus industry" controversy is continually enacted in new battles with no apparent convergence on the horizon. The extended nature of this argumentative interaction, however, has helped researchers, environmental practitioners, government officials, industry management, and the public to specify environmental standards, identify endangered species, reflect on our national values, raise awareness about environmental issues, and more carefully consider new solutions and compromises. The upshot of such an extended argument is that these issues remain current and at the forefront of our national decision-making agenda. Similarly, vilification has proved to be an important strategy in the abortion controversy—a case in which

there is little hope for convergence—for sustaining both sides of this value-laden issue (Vanderford, 1989). Although the positive outcomes of this argument are more difficult to catalogue, its sustained nature has forced both sides, and the public as a whole, to consider important questions about when life begins, women's rights, and what constitutes murder. In a similar manner, creating and maintaining oppositional force is important for sustaining a movement such as ACT UP, where there still appears little hope for convergence on many of the important issues but where maintaining the argument keeps those issues alive and in the public consciousness.

Argument as Decorous Versus Expression of Anger

As this analysis of ACT UP's actions shows, many contemporary group arguments involve communication tactics that are decidedly less refined, less decorous, and more emotional than current definitions prescribe. In fact, the recognition of emotion as integral to argumentative discourse is gaining acceptance. Gilbert (1995) defined an *emotional argument* as "one in which the words used are less important than the feelings being expressed" (p. 8). These arguments occur because there are times when the expression of feelings is more important to interactants than civil, decorous, reasoned discourse. As Gilbert suggested,

> Heightened emotion tends to occur more frequently when a) the arguers are familiar with each other, and b) the issue is a serially recurring one. When both these factors are taken into account it becomes even more clear that interpretations and transformations cannot be made in isolation of the feelings and personal history of the participants. (pp. 8-9)

McGee (1998) argued that Western philosophers have historically bracketed emotion in favor of reason in defining argument. Other scholars, however, have suggested that emotion is either a needed supplement to reason or is not analytically separable from reason. Jaggar (1989) argued that "emotions are neither more basic than observation, reason, or action in building theory, nor are they secondary to them" (p. 165). Wallace (1993) called for a form of argument that is "not exclusively identified with a narrow view of reason, that can account for how emotions and feelings function as judgments and can establish genuine parity for emotion in judicative processes" (p. 67-68). As Gilbert (1995) explained,

> Understanding emotional arguments means respecting the influence that emotion has on communication. If we do this, if we allow that even the simple comprehension of what is being said must take into account the emotional configuration of the arguers, then we can move forward to try to understand what is, for example, good and bad emotional argument. (p. 9)

Emotion, therefore, probably plays a significant role in many arguments. Although positive emotions such as joy and excitement can surface in argumentative interactions, it is more typically the negative emotions of anger, hate, fear, and disgust that accompany this form of discourse. The more committed group members are to a cause, the more familiar arguers are with one another, and the more the topic is recurrent, the more likely emotional arguments will surface. It clearly is time for argumentation scholars to take this form of interaction more seriously, by encouraging and pursuing the study of emotional argument.

Verbal Argument
Versus Visual Argument

Like many activist groups, some argumentation scholars are also expanding their views of argument beyond discursive forms to include presentational or visual modes. Although there is little consensus about whether visual forms truly constitute argument or whether differences exist between verbal and visual argument (see Birdsell & Groarke, 1996; Blair, 1996; Fleming, 1996; Pickering

& Lake, 1995), there is a growing interest of late in studying visual persuasion and argument (see Messaris, 1997). Some scholars claim that visual presentation merely accentuates or reinforces verbal argumentative text; in this sense, it serves as support for a linguistic claim, but by itself it is not an argument (Blair, 1996; Fleming, 1996). However, other scholars argue that we must "accept the possibility of visual meaning, we must make more of an effort to consider images in context, and we must recognize the argumentative aspects of representation and resemblance" (Birdsell & Groarke, 1996, p. 8).

In a recent book titled *Visual Persuasion: The Role of Images in Advertising,* Messaris (1997) suggested that because the visual does not contain propositional content, viewers may need to take a more active role in the construction of meaning than they do with verbal content, although "that fact should not blind us to the possibility that, in the hands of a skillful director, the conclusions at which the viewers arrive may be very substantially those that the director has invited them to draw" (p. 171). In addition, Messaris suggested that visual elements can function as stand-alone arguments when pictures are displayed as comparisons between two referents or candidates (e.g., two political candidates, such as juxtaposing pictures of Bill Clinton and John F. Kennedy in the 1992 presidential campaign) or when they serve as an analogy between a referent and some desirable quality or admirable object (e.g., showing a sports car and a tiger in the same advertisement). Pickering and Lake (1995) also suggested that visual images, although not propositional in nature, can be used to "refute" other images, which is at the heart of the argumentation process.

Although there is still much debate about whether visuals can function as true argument, there is growing evidence that groups (especially activist groups such as ACT UP) are increasingly employing the visual medium as a supplement for, or in place of, verbal arguments. Indeed, some groups, such as environmental groups, have used visual media for advocacy for more than a century (Messaris, 1997). Initially, activist groups used pictures of unblemished, environmentally pure landscapes. More recently, they have juxtaposed those pictures with images of tainted and depleted landscapes, sometimes using them in montage sequences or side by side in comparative ads (Messaris, 1997). Similarly, both sides of the abortion controversy have actively employed visual elements in their argumentative activities (Pickering & Lake, 1995). For example, pro-life advocates produced *Silent Scream*, a video documentary designed to "prove visually that the fetus is an unborn 'child' and that abortion is murder" (Pickering & Lake, 1995, p. 137). In a counterargument, Planned Parenthood produced a videotape called A *Planned Parenthood Response to "Silent Scream"* that used images of women, doctors, and experts to dissect, substitute for, and transform the claims originally posited by those pro-life advocates.

Visual argument and persuasion will undoubtedly continue to serve an important function in activist groups' rhetoric. Although different from verbal argumentation, Messaris (1997) argued that often the meanings of the visual and verbal are the same:

> Because picture-based communication does not have an explicit syntax for expressing causal claims, analogies, and other kinds of propositions, arguments made through sequences of images can be said, *in principle*, to be more open to the perceiver's own interpretation than are verbal arguments. In practice, of course, experienced creators of ads and other forms of visual persuasion are able to employ the tacit conventions of the medium in such a way as to elicit relatively uniform and consistent responses from their viewers. (p. 273)

IMPLICATIONS FOR GROUP COMMUNICATION SCHOLARSHIP AND PEDAGOGY

This analysis of ACT UP's argument-in-use practices has both theoretical and pedagogical implications for the study of group communication. Theoretically, this analysis suggests that argument-in-use strategies may differ from, but be complementary to, traditional argument forms. That is, to design a successful argumentative campaign, both normative and non-normative argument strategies are probably necessary. As we illustrate in more detail below, this is exactly what ACT UP has done. We contend further that, pedagogically, it is important to begin to teach students about the intersection of these forms rather than concentrating exclusively on the traditional, rational, and verbal model of argument.

By examining ACT UP's argumentative tactics and comparing them with traditional approaches to group argument, it becomes clear that activist groups employ both nontraditional (argument-in-use) tactics and more traditional argumentative actions (e.g., debate and negotiation). Many ACT UP groups identify this two-pronged argument strategy as central to their persuasive efforts. For example, ACT UP/Paris describes itself as an *activist group* (which "tries to attract media attention by staging 'zaps'—i.e., quick and very spectacular actions focused on particular issues"), a *lobby* (which expresses the point of view of people with AIDS to "political parties, members of parliament, pharmaceutical companies, research institutions, health care providers, and AIDS education authorities"), and a *militant organization* (which has "proved capable of organising massive demonstrations joined by several thousands of sympathisers") (ACT UP/Paris, n.d.-a). Many members believe that the "activist group" and "militant organization" (which use more nontraditional argument forms) enable the "lobby" (in the form of traditional, rational argument) to occur.

ACT UP's use of nontraditional argument strategies (i.e., demonstrations, slogans, chants, vilification of opponents, and visual images) to enable more traditional forms of argument (lobbying and negotiation) has, for the most part, been quite successful. As part of a participant-observation study, the second author (Brashers) joined ACT UP members in a number of protests. Although the ACT UP chapter was small (usually no more than 5 to 10 protesters), the group was very good at managing visual images so that television reports showed a large and disruptive protest. The result was that local health department officials perceived that they were "under siege" (and, perhaps more important, they believed that the public perceived them to be under siege) and became quite willing to meet and talk with the ACT UP group. As an ACT UP/Los Angeles (1991) fund-raising letter noted,

> Like the evolution of the AIDS epidemic, ACT UP/LA is changing too. Our militant tactics have opened doors and presented new challenges to activists. *ACT UP/LA has risen to those challenges.* While continuing to raise public awareness through nonviolent direct action tactics, members of ACT UP/LA are working hard to change within the system, making sure the voices of people affected by HIV are heard whenever and wherever the issues are discussed.

This two-pronged argument approach has been replicated in many other governmental and industrial organizations. Wachter (1991) argued that "the fuel that drives the activists is unbridled anger. This has made them unpredictable, but also exceptionally effective. . . . The anger works—it stimulates a stagnant system in ways that genteel dialogue never could" (p. 234). David Kessler, commissioner of the Food and Drug Administration (FDA), noted,

> What we have seen is a dramatic change in the last couple of years. Look where we started off. I mean, the activists were out there scaling this building, really, I mean, burning us in effigy. Now, they're sitting at the advisory committees, I mean knowing, bringing in an awful lot of expertise, scientific expertise. (quoted in ACT UP/New York, 1993)

Clearly, activist members see the advantages of using both normative and non-normative argumentative tactics. However, teachers of

argument tend to focus almost exclusively on the normative model of argument. In today's groups—where time is often of the essence, issues are emotionally charged, and members are less civil than in past decades—this model demands reevaluation. We certainly are not advocating the abandonment of instruction in traditional modes of arguing, but we think it important that argumentation scholars, teachers, and students identify, examine, and analyze these non-normative forms of argument as well. Perhaps we will find that the structure of an appropriate argument is situational or field dependent; that is, in some interactive situations, it would be considered completely appropriate to merely offer slogans and chants, whereas in other situations, it would be vitally important to provide detailed evidence, warrants, and backing (e.g., in debates with opponents). We might also find that groups generate their own unique forms of argument that differ significantly from interpersonal argument or traditional public forms of argument. We may also discover that the social nature of groups plays an important role in how argument unfolds and that, despite not adhering to the traditional model, non-normative group argument can produce high-quality discussion and decisions.

It is our contention that the traditional, rational model of argument serves us well in many situations and offers a wonderful baseline model from which to teach the "ideal" form of argument. Assuming that this model alone defines the "quality," "effectiveness," or "success" of an argument may be misleading, however. It is time to open our eyes to the possibility of varied forms, structures, and models of argument-in-use.

A second theoretical and pedagogical implication concerns current conceptions of argumentativeness and aggressiveness. As our analysis shows, despite the negative connotation typically attached to "aggressiveness," ACT UP members have been aggressive and believe that this trait is needed to strengthen their arguments. Because the issues they face are often matters of life and death, ACT UP chapters have justified actions that have, at times, been characterized as uncivil and offensive, but as Sobnosky and Hauser (1998) noted, "Issues receive attention and resources from the community to the extent they are recognized as public" (p. 27). ACT UP members have been successful because they combine strategies for gaining attention and public support (more aggressive tactics) with traditional argumentative strategies designed to intellectually challenge the status quo. This combination of argumentativeness and aggressiveness has proven very effective for ACT UP. Perhaps, both theoretically and pedagogically, these characteristics should be viewed not as separate but as elements of a single continuum. Groups may, thus, benefit most when members are able to identify both argumentative and aggressive tactics and to determine when each will be most effective.

CONCLUSION

Examining the argumentative practices of activist groups such as ACT UP provides opportunities to rethink the traditional assumptions that have guided group argument theory, research, and pedagogy. Activist groups often find it necessary to engage in argumentation that challenges traditional notions of argument as rational, convergence producing, decorous, and verbal. ACT UP (and other similar groups) shows how demonstrations marked by slogans, chants, vilification of opponents, expressions of emotion, and visual images, combined with more rational forms of argument, can produce important and needed changes. As we increasingly move toward an argument-in-use model in theory, research, and pedagogical practice in group communication, continued analysis of activist groups' argumentative practices is essential, as is the willingness of researchers and teachers to consider many alternative approaches to argument.

REFERENCES

ACT UP/London. (1990). *Action dateline*. London: Author.

ACT UP/Los Angeles. (1991). *ACT UP fundraising letter*. Los Angeles: Author.

ACT UP/New York. (n.d.-a). *New member information packet*. New York: Author. (Available at www.actupny.org)

ACT UP/New York. (n.d.-b). Untitled pamphlet. New York: Author.

ACT UP/New York. (1990). *Stop the church*. New York: Author.

ACT UP/New York. (1993). *Role of AIDS activists* (Damned Interfering Video Activists [DIVA] TV transcript). New York: Author. (Available at www.actupny.org/diva/divarole.html)

ACT UP/New York. (1996). *No immigration bans*. New York: Author. (Available at www.actupny.org)

ACT/New York. (1999). *The first ACT UP action*. New York: Author. (Available at www.actupny.org)

ACT UP/Paris. (n.d.-a). *ACT UP Paris information pamphlet*. Paris: Author.

ACT UP/Paris. (n.d.-b). *Fight back, fight AIDS*. Paris: Author.

Alderton, S. M. (1982). Locus of control-based argumentation as a predictor of group polarization. *Communication Quarterly, 30*, 381-387.

Alderton, S. M., & Frey, L. R. (1983). Effects of reactions to arguments on group outcomes: The case of group polarization. *Central States Speech Journal, 34*, 88-95.

Alderton, S. M., & Frey, L. R. (1986). Argumentation in small group decision-making. In R. Y. Hirokawa & M. S. Poole (Eds.), *Communication and group decision-making* (pp. 157-174). Beverly Hills, CA: Sage.

Ariss, P. (1994). Performing anger: Emotion in strategic responses to AIDS. *Australian Journal of Anthropology, 4*, 18-31.

Axelrod, R. (1977). Argumentation in foreign policy settings. *Journal of Conflict Resolution, 21*, 727-744.

Billig, M. (1996). *Arguing and thinking: A rhetorical approach to social psychology* (2nd ed.). Cambridge, UK: Cambridge University Press.

Birdsell, D. S., & Groarke, L. (1996). Toward a theory of visual argument. *Argumentation and Advocacy, 33*, 1-10.

Blair, J. A. (1996). The possibility and actuality of visual arguments. *Argumentation and Advocacy, 33*, 23-39.

Brashers, D. E. (1991). Consumer complaints as argument: Application of the structuration coding scheme. In D. W. Parson (Ed.), *Argument in controversy: Proceedings of the Seventh Speech Communication Association/American Forensics Association Conference on Argumentation* (pp. 147-153). Annandale, VA: Speech Communication Association.

Brashers, D. E., Adkins, M., & Meyers, R. A. (1994). Argumentation in computer-mediated decision making. In L. R. Frey (Ed.), *Group communication in context: Studies of natural groups* (pp. 262-283). Hillsdale, NJ: Lawrence Erlbaum.

Brashers, D. E., Haas, S. M., Klingle, R. S., & Neidig, J. L. (2000). Collective AIDS activism and individuals' perceived self-advocacy in physician-patient communication. *Human Communication Research, 26*, 372-402.

Brashers, D. E., & Jackson, S. (1991). "Politically-savvy sick people": Public penetration of the technical sphere. In D. W. Parson (Ed.), *Argument in controversy: Proceedings of the Seventh Speech Communication Association/American Forensics Association Conference on Argumentation* (pp. 284-288). Annandale, VA: Speech Communication Association.

Brashers, D. E., & Meyers, R. A. (1989). Tag-team argument and group decision-making: A preliminary investigation. In B. E. Gronbeck (Ed.), *Spheres of Argument: Proceedings of the Sixth Speech Communication Association/American Forensics Association Conference on Argumentation* (pp. 542-550). Annandale, VA: Speech Communication Association.

Brossmann, B. G., & Canary, D. J. (1990). An observational analysis of argument structures: The case of *Nightline. Argumentation, 4,* 199-212.

Brown, M. P. (1997). *Replacing citizenship: AIDS activism and radical democracy.* New York: Guilford Press.

Burkett, E. (1995). *The gravest show on earth: America in the age of AIDS.* New York: Houghton Mifflin.

Canary, D. J. (1989). *Manual for coding conversational argument.* Unpublished manuscript, Ohio University, Athens.

Canary, D. J., Brossmann, J. E., Brossmann, B. G., & Weger, H., Jr. (1995). Toward a theory of minimally rational argument: Analyses of episode-specific effects of argument structures. *Communication Monographs, 62,* 185-212.

Canary, D. J., Brossmann, B. G., & Seibold, D. R. (1987). Argument structures in decision-making groups. *Southern Speech Communication Journal, 53,* 18-37.

Canary, D. J., Ratledge, N. T., & Seibold, D. R. (1982, November). *Argument and group decision-making: Development of a coding scheme.* Paper presented at the meeting of the Speech Communication Association, Louisville, KY.

Canary, D. J., & Sillars, A. L. (1992). Argument in satisfied and dissatisfied married couples. In W. L. Benoit, D. Hample, & P. J. Benoit (Eds.), *Readings in argumentation* (pp. 737-764). New York: Foris.

Canary, D. J., Weger, H., Jr., & Stafford, L. (1991). Couples' argument sequences and their associations with relational characteristics. *Western Journal of Speech Communication, 55,* 159-179.

Christiansen, A. E., & Hanson, J. J. (1996). Comedy as cure for tragedy: ACT UP and the rhetoric of AIDS. *Quarterly Journal of Speech, 82,* 157-170.

Cohen, P. F. (1998). *Love and anger: Essays on AIDS, activism, and politics.* New York: Haworth.

Fabj, V., & Sobnosky, M. J. (1993). Responses from the street: ACT UP and the community organizing against AIDS. In S. C. Ratzan (Ed.), *AIDS: Effective health communication for the 90s* (pp. 91-109). Washington, DC: Taylor & Francis.

Fabj, V., & Sobnosky, M. J. (1995). AIDS activism and the rejuvenation of the public sphere. *Argumentation and Advocacy, 31,* 163-184.

Farrell, T. B. (1977). Validity and rationality: The rhetorical constituents of argumentative form. *Journal of the American Forensic Association, 13,* 142-149.

Fleming, D. (1996). Can pictures be arguments? *Argumentation and Advocacy, 33,* 11-22.

Gamson, J. (1989). Silence, death, and the invisible enemy: AIDS activism and social movement "newness." *Social Problems, 36,* 351-365.

Garrett, D. E., & Meyers, R. A. (1991). Interactive complaint communication: A reconceptualization of consumer complaint behavior. In D. W. Parson (Ed.), *Argument in controversy: Proceedings of the Seventh Speech Communication Association/American Forensics Association Conference on Argumentation* (pp. 159-166). Annandale, VA: Speech Communication Association.

Gebhardt, L. J., & Meyers, R. A. (1994). Subgroup influence in decision-making groups: Examining consistency from a communication perspective. *Small Group Research, 26,* 147-168.

Gilbert, M. A. (1995). What is an emotional argument or why do argument theorists quarrel with their mates? In F. H. van Eemeren, R. Grootendorst, J. A. Blair, & C. A. Willard (Eds.), *Analysis and evaluation: Proceedings of the Third International Conference on Argumentation* (Vol. 2, pp. 3-12). Amsterdam, The Netherlands: Sic Sat.

Gouran, D. S. (1983). Communicative influences on inferential judgments in decision-making groups: A descriptive analysis. In D. Zarefsky, M. O. Sillars, & J. Rhodes (Eds.), *Argument in transition: Proceedings of the Third Speech Communication Association/American Forensics Association Conference on Argumentation* (pp. 667-684). Annandale, VA: Speech Communication Association.

Gouran, D. S. (1984). Communicative influences related to the Watergate coverup: The failure of collective judgment. *Central States Speech Journal, 35,* 260-268.

Gouran, D. S. (1986). Inferential errors, interaction, and group decision-making. In R. Y. Hirokawa & M. S. Poole (Eds.), *Communication and group decision-making* (pp. 93-112). Beverly Hills, CA: Sage.

Gouran, D. S. (1987). The failure of argument in decisions leading to the *Challenger* disaster: A two-level analysis. In J. W. Wenzel (Ed.), *Argument and critical practices: Proceedings of the Fifth Speech Communication Association/American Forensics Association Conference on Argumentation* (pp. 439-448). Annandale, VA: Speech Communication Association.

Gouran, D. S. (1997). Effective versus ineffective decision making. In L. R. Frey & J. K. Barge (Eds.), *Managing group life: Communicating in decision-making groups* (pp. 133-155). Boston: Houghton Mifflin.

Gouran, D. S., Hirokawa, R. Y., & Martz, A. E. (1986). A critical analysis of factors related to decisional processes involved in the *Challenger* disaster. *Central States Speech Journal, 37,* 119-135.

Hicks, D. (1991). A descriptive account of interpersonal argument. In D. W. Parsons (Ed.), *Argument in controversy: Proceedings of the Seventh Speech Communication Association/American Forensics Association Conference on Argumentation* (pp. 167-174). Annandale, VA: Speech Communication Association.

Hirokawa, R. Y., & Pace, R. C. (1983). A descriptive investigation of the possible communication-based reasons for effective and ineffective group decision-making. *Communication Monographs, 50,* 363-379.

Hollihan, T. A., Riley, P., & Freadhoff, K. (1986). Arguing for justice: An analysis of arguing in small claims court. *Journal of the American Forensic Association, 22,* 187-195.

Infante, D. A., & Rancer, A. S. (1982). A conceptualization and measure of argumentativeness. *Journal of Personality Assessment, 46,* 72-80.

Infante, D. A., Trebing, J. D., Sheperd, P. E., & Seeds, D. E. (1984). The relationship of argumentativeness to verbal aggression. *Southern Speech Communication Journal, 50,* 67-77.

Infante, D. A., Wall, C. H., Leap, C. J., & Danielson, K. (1984). Verbal aggression as a function of the receiver's argumentativeness. *Communication Research Reports, 1,* 33-37.

Jackson, S., & Jacobs, S. (1980). Structure of conversational argument: Pragmatic cases for the enthymeme. *Quarterly Journal of Speech, 66,* 251-265.

Jaggar, A. M. (1989). Love and knowledge: Emotion in feminist epistemology. In A. M. Jaggar & S. R. Bordo (Eds.), *Gender/body/knowledge: Feminist reconstructions of being and knowing* (pp. 145-171). New Brunswick, NJ: Rutgers University Press.

Johnson, R. H., & Blair, J. A. (1991). Contexts of informal reasoning: Commentary. In J. F. Voss, D. N. Perkins, & J. W. Segal (Eds.), *Informal reasoning and education* (pp. 131-150). Hillsdale, NJ: Lawrence Erlbaum.

Keough, C. M. (1987). The nature and function of argument in organizational research. *Southern Speech Communication Journal, 53,* 1-17.

Ketrow, S. M., Meyers, R. A., & Schultz, B. (1997). Processes and outcomes related to nonrational argument in societal groups. In J. F. Klumpp (Ed.), *Argument in a time of change: Proceedings of the Tenth National Communication Association/ American Forensics Association Conference on Argumentation* (pp. 103-109). Annandale, VA: Speech Communication Association.

Kramer, L. (1989). *Reports from the holocaust: The making of an AIDS activist.* New York: St. Martin's Press.

Leff, M. G., & Hewes, D. E. (1981). Topical invention and group communication: Towards a sociology of inference. In G. Ziegelmueller & J. Rhodes (Eds.), *Dimensions of argument: Proceedings of the Second Speech Communication Association/American Forensics Association Conference on Argumentation* (pp. 770-789). Annandale, VA: Speech Communication Association.

Martin, R. W., & Scheerhorn, D. R. (1985). What are conversational arguments? Toward a natural language user's perspective. In J. R. Cox, M. O. Sillars, & G. B. Walker (Eds.), *Argument and social practice: Proceedings of the Fourth Speech Communication Association/American Forensics Association Conference on Argumentation* (pp. 705-722). Annandale, VA: Speech Communication Association.

Mayer, M. E. (1985). Explaining choice shift: An effects coded model. *Communication Monographs, 52,* 92-101.

Mayer, M. E. (1987). Explaining choice shifts: A comparison of competing effects-coded models. In M. L. McLaughlin (Ed.), *Communication yearbook* (Vol. 9, pp. 297-314). Beverly Hills, CA: Sage.

McGee, B. R. (1998). Rehabilitating emotion: The troublesome case of the Ku Klux Klan. *Argumentation and Advocacy, 34,* 173-188.

Messaris, P. (1997). *Visual persuasion: The role of images in advertising.* Thousand Oaks, CA: Sage.

Meyers, R. A. (1989a). Persuasive arguments theory: A test of assumptions. *Human Communication Research, 15,* 357-381.

Meyers, R. A. (1989b). Testing persuasive argument theory's predictor model: Alternative interactional accounts of group argument and influence. *Communication Monographs, 56,* 112-132.

Meyers, R. A. (1997). Social influence and argumentation. In L. R. Frey & J. K. Barge (Eds.), *Managing group life: Communicating in decision-making groups* (pp. 183-201). Boston: Houghton Mifflin.

Meyers, R. A., & Brashers, D. (1995). Multi-stage versus single-stage coding of small group argument: A preliminary comparative assessment. In S. Jackson (Ed.), *Argumentation and values: Proceedings of the Ninth Speech Communication Association/American Forensics Association Conference on Argumentation* (pp. 93-100). Annandale, VA: Speech Communication Association.

Meyers, R. A., & Brashers, D. E. (1998). Argument in group decision-making: Explicating a theoretical model and investigating the argument-outcome link. *Communication Monographs, 65,* 261-281.

Meyers, R. A., Brashers, D. E., Winston, L., & Grob, L. (1997). Sex differences and group argument: A theoretical framework and empirical investigation. *Communication Studies, 48,* 19-41.

Meyers, R. A., Seibold, D. R., & Brashers, D. (1991). Argument in initial group decision-making discussions: Refinement of a coding scheme and a descriptive quantitative analysis. *Western Journal of Speech Communication, 55,* 47-68.

Nussbaum, B. (1990). *Good intentions: How big business and the medical establishment are corrupting the fight against AIDS.* New York: Atlantic Monthly.

O'Keefe, B. J., & Benoit, P. J. (1982). Children's arguments. In J. R. Cox & C. A. Willard (Eds.), *Advances in argumentation theory and research* (pp. 154-183). Carbondale: Southern Illinois University Press.

Patton, C. (1990). *Inventing AIDS.* New York: Routledge.

Perelman, C., & Olbrechts-Tyteca, L. (1969). *The new rhetoric: A treatise on argumentation* (J. Wilkenson & P. Weaver, Trans.). Notre Dame, IN: University of Notre Dame Press.

Perkins, D. N. (1985a). Postprimary education has little impact on informal reasoning. *Journal of Educational Psychology, 77,* 562-571.

Perkins, D. N. (1985b). Reasoning as imagination. *Interchange, 16,* 14-26.

Perkins, D. N., Farady, M., & Bushey, B. (1991). Everyday reasoning and the roots of intelligence. In J. F. Voss, D. N. Perkins, & J. W. Segal (Eds.), *Informal reasoning and education* (pp. 83-105). Hillsdale, NJ: Lawrence Erlbaum.

Pickering, B. A., & Lake, R. A. (1995). Refutation in visual argument: An exploration. In F. H. van Eemeren, R. Grootendorst, J. A. Blair, & C. A. Willard (Eds.), *Reconstruction and application: Proceedings of the Third International Conference on Argumentation* (Vol. 3, pp. 134-143). Amsterdam, Netherlands: Sic Sat.

Putnam, L. L., Wilson, S. R., Waltman, M. S., & Turner, D. (1986). The evolution of case arguments in teachers' bargaining. *Journal of the American Forensic Association, 23,* 63-81.

Rowland, R. C. (1995). In defense of rational argument: A pragmatic justification of argumentation theory and response to the postmodern critique. *Philosophy and Rhetoric, 28,* 350-364.

Schuetz, J. (1980). Rationality and argumentation in reform and revolution. *Journal of the American Forensic Association, 17,* 85-101.

Schultz, B. (1983). Argumentativeness: Its role in leadership perception and group communication. In D. Zarefsky, M. O. Sillars, & J. Rhodes (Eds.), *Argument in transition: Proceedings of the Third Speech Communication Association/American Forensics Association Conference on Argumentation* (pp. 638-647). Annandale, VA: Speech Communication Association.

Schultz, B. (1989). The role of argumentativeness in the enhancement of the status of members of decision-making groups. In B. E. Gronbeck (Ed.), *Spheres of argument: Proceedings of the Sixth Speech Communication Association/American Forensics Association Conference on Argumentation* (pp. 558-562). Annandale, VA: Speech Communication Association.

Seibold, D. R., Canary, D. J., & Ratledge, N. T. (1983, November). *Argument and group decision-making: Interim report on a structurational research program.* Paper presented at the meeting of the Speech Communication Association, Washington, DC.

Seibold, D. R., & Meyers, R. A. (1986). Communication and influence in group decision-making. In R. Y. Hirokawa & M. S. Poole (Eds.), *Communication and group decision-making* (pp. 133-155). Beverly Hills, CA: Sage.

Seibold, D. R., Poole, M. S., McPhee, R. D., Tanita, N. E., & Canary, D. J. (1981). Argument, group influence, and decision outcomes. In C. Ziegelmueller & J. Rhodes (Eds.), *Dimensions of argument: Proceedings of the Second Speech Communication Association/American Forensics Association Conference on Argumentation* (pp. 663-692). Annandale, VA: Speech Communication Association.

Sobnosky, M. J., & Hauser, E. (1998). Initiating or avoiding activism: Red ribbons, pink triangles, and public argument about AIDS. In W. E. Elwood (Ed.), *Power in the blood: A handbook on AIDS, politics, and communication* (pp. 25-38). Mahwah, NJ: Lawrence Erlbaum.

Sotomayor, J. (1987, March 25). Homosexuals arrested at AIDS drug protest. *The New York Times,* p. B4.

Thomas, S. N. (1981). *Practical reasoning in natural language* (2nd ed.). Englewood Cliffs, NJ: Prentice Hall.

Toulmin, S. (1958). *The uses of argument.* Cambridge, UK: Cambridge University Press.

van Eemeren, F. H., Grootendorst, R., & Kruiger, T. (1987). *Handbook of argumentation theory: A critical survey of classical backgrounds and modern studies.* Providence, RI: Foris.

Vanderford, M. L. (1989). Vilification in social movements: A case study of pro-life and pro-choice rhetoric. *Quarterly Journal of Speech, 75,* 166-182.

Voss, J. F. (1991). Informal reasoning and international relations. In J. F. Voss, D. N. Perkins, & J. W. Segal (Eds.), *Informal reasoning and education* (pp. 37-58). Hillsdale, NJ: Lawrence Erlbaum.

Wachter, R. F. (1991). *The fragile coalition: Scientists, activists, and AIDS.* New York: St. Martin's Press.

Walker, G. B. (1991). Argument and conflict: Conceptual and empirical perspectives. In D. W. Parsons (Ed.), *Argument in controversy: Proceedings of the Seventh Speech Communication Association/American Forensics Association Conference on Argumentation* (pp. 182-187). Annandale, VA: Speech Communication Association.

Wallace, K. (1993). Reconstructing judgment: Emotion and moral judgment. *Hypatia, 8*(3), 61-83.

Walton, D. N. (1992). *Plausible argument in everyday conversation.* Albany: State University of New York Press.

Wenzel, J. W. (1977). Toward a rationale for value-centered argument. *Journal of the American Forensic Association, 13,* 150-158.

Willard, C. A. (1983). *Argumentation and the social grounds of knowledge.* Tuscaloosa: University of Alabama Press.

Willbrand, M. L., & Rieke, R. D. (1991). Strategies of reasoning in spontaneous discourse. In J. A. Anderson (Ed.), *Communication yearbook* (Vol. 14, pp. 414-440). Newbury Park, CA: Sage.

Woolcock, G. (1998, July). *Spreading the load: Reports of the death of AIDS activism have been greatly exaggerated.* Poster session presented at the Twelfth International Conference on AIDS, Geneva, Switzerland.

9

Enlarging the Meaning of Group Deliberation

From Discussion to Dialogue

J. KEVIN BARGE
University of Georgia

Discussion informed citizens in a democracy of basic problems and enabled them to hear all sides of a controversy. Discussion was the best way to mold public opinion and make decisions. Discussion, when contrasted with other techniques for social control such as dictatorial decree or violence and force (the thirties were the period of unrest and emerging dictatorships in Europe), was American, ethical, and noble.

Bormann (1996, p. 101)

One important reason for studying group communication is its roots in the practice of democracy in communities and societies—that is, the belief that enhancing people's abilities to engage in group discussion will make them better able to participate in democracy. The impulse of scholars to link group discussion to democratic process was evident in the scholarship and pedagogy throughout the 20th century (see Gouran, 1999). The 1920s saw Sheffield (1922) introduce the view that group discussion was a central tool in promoting democracy, a view that was expanded in Baird's (1928) book, *Public Discussion and Debate*. In the 1930s, Lewin and colleagues (Lewin, Lippitt, & White, 1939; White & Lippitt, 1960) began articulating small group leadership practices that

could promote democracy and deter authoritarianism. In the 1960s, university courses on small groups focused on teaching discussion, and one popular textbook was even titled *Discussion: Method of Democracy* (Crowell, 1963). From the 1970s through the 1990s, the conversation regarding the relationship between small groups and democracy expanded to include obstacles in group interaction that prevent democracy from occurring (see, e.g., Gastil, 1992, 1993). The lesson from this body of scholarship and pedagogy on small groups is clear: Democratic practice is enhanced by developing people's group discussion skills, such as critical thinking, problem solving, decision making, and leadership.

The focus on group discussion can be seen as representing a dominant language game within this community of scholars (Barge, 1994). A *language game* is a form of specialized discourse among members of a community that reflects their underlying view of reality and shared understandings (Wittgenstein, 1953). Astley and Zammuto (1992) observed that "these understandings are conveyed in the stylized vocabularies and protocols of communication that comprise language games" (p. 444). Research operating within the language game of group discussion has centered primarily on articulating the key functions or decision paths associated with effective group decisions (see, respectively, Gouran & Hirokawa, 1996; Poole, Seibold, & McPhee, 1996).[1] For example, learning how to advocate one's position and how to counteract flaws in another's reasoning are viewed as key processes that lead to effective group decisions (see Gouran, 1997; Meyers & Brashers, 1999, this volume; Seibold, Meyers, & Sunwolf, 1996). Consequently, a variety of discussion formats, such as devil's advocacy and dialectical inquiry, have been proposed as ways of enhancing rigorous examination of ideas and arguments through a debate-centered approach (see Jarboe, 1996; Meyers, 1997; Sunwolf & Seibold, 1999). Discussion, with its emphasis on persuasion and the debate of competing ideas as central to effective decision making, has, thus, been the dominant language game of group life constructed by communication scholars.

The notion that discussion is the primary language game that promotes democratic practice has recently been questioned. Language games grounded in dialogue that emphasize mutual understanding, collaborative inquiry into assumptions and interests informing conclusions, and the need for creativity have been proposed as central to fostering democracy (see Pearce & Littlejohn, 1997). Rather than viewing discussion as *the* primary form of communication that promotes democratic practice, discussion is viewed as one of many forms of communication within deliberative discourse that foster democracy. *Deliberation,* in the broadest sense, is a way of talking in which people recognize that they may disagree about an issue or lack an understanding of one another's position, articulate basic choices to be made, and evaluate options and strategies (Schein, 1993). Hence, discussion and dialogue both represent language games associated with democratic process; however, most researchers associate democratic deliberation with discussion and have not fully explored how dialogic forms of communication can enhance both group and democratic practices.

In this chapter, I explore alternative language games in the study of group communication that may foster strong democracy. Specifically, I focus on forms of communication that emphasize dialogue and an affirmation of what works well within a human system as a way of building community and fostering democracy (Hammond, 1998; Pearce & Littlejohn, 1997). In addition to explaining both the language games of discussion and dialogue, I present a case study that illustrates how dialogic and affirmative forms of communication can be used to facilitate group conversation. I conclude by highlighting some possible areas for future research on group communication.

THE LANGUAGE GAME OF DISCUSSION

Group communication theory and research has a long history of examining problem-solving and decision-making processes within groups (see Frey, 1996). Perhaps the best example of this discussion-centered approach to group decision making is functional theory.[2] Developed by Gouran and Hirokawa (for reviews, see Gouran, 1999; Gouran & Hirokawa, 1996; Gouran, Hirokawa, Julian, & Leatham, 1993; Hirokawa & Salazar, 1999; Poole, 1999; Waldeck, Shepard, Teitelbaum, Farrar, & Seibold, this volume), functional theory begins with the assumption that communication is instrumental to group decision making to the extent that it fulfills particular decision-making functions. The proper performance of these decision-making functions, rather than following a particular agenda per se, is said to determine the quality of the group decision made. Specifically, functional theory maintains that groups are more likely to make high-quality decisions when members do the following:

1. make clear their interest in arriving at the best possible decision;
2. identify the resources necessary to making such a decision;
3. recognize possible obstacles to be confronted;
4. specify the procedures to be followed;
5. establish ground rules for interaction;
6. attempt to satisfy fundamental task requirements by
   a. showing correct understanding of the issue to be resolved;
   b. determining the minimal characteristics any alternative, to be acceptable, must possess;
   c. identifying a relevant and realistic set of alternatives;
   d. examining carefully the alternatives in relationship to each previously agreed-upon characteristic of an acceptable choice; and
   e. selecting the alternative that analysis reveals to be most likely to have the desired characteristics;
7. employ appropriate interventions for overcoming cognitive, affiliative, and egocentric constraints that are interfering with the satisfaction of fundamental task requirements; and
8. review the process by which the group comes to a decision and, if indicated, reconsider judgments reached (even to the point of starting over). (Gouran & Hirokawa, 1996, pp. 76-77)

Functional theory has evolved over the years and elaborated the types of functions that need to be performed to make high-quality group decisions, identified the obstacles that constrain effective group decision making, and tested the theory in both laboratory and field settings. Throughout this evolution, proponents of functional theory have maintained that two forms of talk within groups are important for making effective decisions: problem talk and debate.

Problem Talk

The starting place for making any effective decision, according to functional theory, is a clear definition of the issue or problem and an identification of its causes. Because "communication is the instrument by which members of groups, with varying degrees of success, reach decisions and generate solutions to problems" (Gouran & Hirokawa, 1996, p. 55), group members need to assess "the problem situation with which they are confronted" (Hirokawa & Salazar, 1997, p. 160). As Hirokawa (1988) explained,

> Effective decision making demands that the group base its choice on an accurate (i.e., valid or reasonable) understanding of (a) the nature of the problem, (b) the extent and seriousness of the problem, (c) the possible cause(s) of the problem, and (d) the possible consequences of the not dealing effectively with the problem. (p. 489)

Talking about problems, consequently, is important because "the most consistent predictor of group performance is analysis of the problem/task" (Propp & Nelson, 1996, p. 37), and "accurate information is needed to define a problem" (Propp, 1995, p. 451; see also Propp, 1999).

A *problem situation* has traditionally been defined as the "gap" between the current and an "ideal" state (Lewin, 1951). Gaps may arise from disparities in policy issues that a group is addressing (e.g., a group needs to find a way to lower a community's teen pregnancy rate from current levels). Problem talk, therefore, uses deficit language (Gergen, 1991), which focuses attention on the shortcomings of people, processes, situations, and/or issues and moves group members toward taking action that will "fix" the deficiency. Problem talk, thus, disposes group members toward viewing situations and issues as problems to be solved and propels them along a conversational trajectory that involves identifying the problem, analyzing its causes, proposing possible solutions, and planning actions (Hammond & Royal, 1998).

Proponents of functional theory may claim that this analysis misrepresents their position because the theory is an approach to decision making, not problem solving; therefore, it is not inherently linked to problem talk. For example, some scholars use the term "issue" rather than "problem" and suggest that the foundation of good decision making involves group members showing "correct understanding of the issues to be resolved" (Gouran & Hirokawa, 1996, p. 56) and understanding "the type of answer for which the issue under consideration calls" (Gouran & Hirokawa, 1983, p. 171). The issue under consideration can be classified according to the kind of choice that a group needs to make. Gouran (1997) observed that choices can involve questions of policy (What action should be taken?), value (What is right, good, or ethical?), conjecture (What might happen?), and fact (What is true?). This distinction between problem solving and decision making, proponents suggest, gives problem talk less importance.

Drawing a distinction between problem solving and decision making, however, does not undermine the importance of problem talk within functional theory. This is particularly true when one considers that most decisions that task groups make are policy oriented in the sense that they are designed to answer the question, What action should be taken? Hence, problem assessment is crucial to developing effective group solutions. As Gouran (1997) observed,

> In a narrow sense, problem solving has to do with developing specific means for altering a condition that is creating difficulty; decision

making is the act of choosing among alternatives in a situation that requires choice. For our purposes, the distinction is not crucial. You can think of problem solving as one type of decision making. (p. 138)

Within this perspective, then, discussion involves talking about an issue/problem and generating solutions and actions on the basis of a rigorous analysis of the nature, causes, scope, and consequences of the issue/problem.

Debate

Functional theory also privileges debate as a primary form of talk that facilitates high-quality group decision making. Ellinor and Gerard (1998) defined *debate* as involving (a) breaking issues/problems into parts; (b) seeing distinctions between the parts; (c) justifying/defending assumptions; (d) persuading, selling, and telling; and (e) gaining agreement on one meaning.[3] The focus of debate on breaking apart issues/problems and offering justifications and arguments to gain agreement can be seen in both the development of functional theory and its practical prescriptions for appropriate actions by group members.

The development of functional theory has emphasized breaking apart the causes, functions, and consequences of communication in group decision making. Hirokawa's (1990) task contingency model, for example, illustrates the functionalist impulse to isolate relevant task factors that influence the role of communication in producing effective group decisions. Three task factors are identified: (a) task structure, (b) information requirements, and (c) evaluation demands. Hirokawa offers theoretical propositions that specify how each factor calls for particular communication functions, which, in turn, directly influence group performance. For example, a complex, compared with a simple, task structure is hypothesized to highlight the need for communication among group members:

Proposition 1A. When task structure is simple, group performance is dependent largely on input variables.

Proposition 1B. When task structure is complex, group performance is dependent largely on process variables. (p. 197).

Once the main effect for each factor has been demonstrated, it is then possible to explain more complex interactions between the factors. Hirokawa (1988) explained that "the next step would call for the manipulation of two dimensions simultaneously, while keeping the third constant, to identify the two-way mediating effects of those dimensions on communication/performance relationships" (p. 202). A similar logic is used to articulate how cognitive, affiliative, and egocentric factors enable and constrain group decision making (Gouran & Hirokawa, 1996).

The goal of breaking apart and identifying the individual causes of group communication and decision-making performance can also be seen in the practical prescriptions for group members' communication offered by proponents of functional theory. Two practical prescriptions are particularly illustrative. First, group members are urged to identify the nature of the choice they are to make and to be aware that their decision may be nested. *Nested decisions* occur when the principal question that needs to be addressed is contingent on answers to other types of questions; for instance, answering a question of policy may be contingent on answering a question of value (Gouran, 1997). Competent group communicators, therefore, must be able to divide the principal question into its relevant subquestions. Gouran (1997) gave the following example:

A university committee discussing whether the school should raise tuition (a question of policy), for example, would be more apt to conclude that it should . . . endorse that action if its answers to the following questions are yes:

- "Is there a shortage of operating funds?" (a question of fact)
- "Would an increase in tuition be cost-effective?" (a question of conjecture)
- "Is it fair to ask students to share most of the cost of their education?" (a question of value). (p. 141)

The ability to analyze the components of decision-making situations and identify the relevant choice points is, thus, considered by functional theory to be central to competent group decision making.

The second practical prescription is that group members need to learn how to identify obstacles present within the decision-making situation and formulate appropriate responses to those obstacles. Functional theory, therefore, emphasizes helping group members to identify obstacles that may frustrate their ability to make effective decisions. Once an obstacle is properly identified, appropriate strategies for overcoming it can be determined. Take, for example, the following prescriptions for group member behavior generated from functional theory (Gouran, 1997):

- When a decision-making group is confronting an informational obstacle, direct observations or questions about apparent inadequacies can be very helpful.
- If the members of a decision-making group are displaying analytical deficiencies, statements and questions about whether the conclusions being drawn from information are warranted can be a powerful corrective influence.
- A simple statement—"Let's be sure we understand what's wrong before we start trying to fix it"—by keeping discussion on track, can stop a group from making a premature decision.
- Key to managing the conflicts that result from differences in values is attempting to understand the other points of view. (pp. 151-153)

The assumption underlying these practical prescriptions is that the central obstacles confronting a group can be identified and subsequently linked through an "if-then" statement to appropriate responses. Typically, however, the focus is only on one obstacle and the attendant prescriptions for overcoming it and not on the interactions between multiple obstacles; the obstacles are seen as distinct rather than interrelated.

Functional theory also emphasizes forms of talk based on group members justifying and defending their positions, as well as attempting to persuade, sell, and tell others the superiority of one's views. This is not surprising given that functional theory, according to Hirokawa (1985), emphasizes rigorous analysis and evaluation of alternative choices:

> The group must assess thoroughly and accurately the positive [and negative] consequences associated with each alternative choice. Given the information available to it, the group needs to recognize all important positive [and negative] implications and outcomes likely to result from the selection of each alternative choice. (p. 205)

Rigorous analysis and evaluation of alternative choices occurs by making persuasive arguments for one's own position and refuting the positions of others (for a more detailed analysis of traditional argumentation in groups, see Meyers & Brashers, 1999, this volume).

One way in which group members challenge the thinking of fellow members is through *second-guessing*, which occurs when retrospective questioning of a previous choice is employed to challenge the assumptions and information used to make the decision (Hirokawa, 1987). By asking questions in ways that force group members to justify and defend their decisions, groups, supposedly, according to functional theory, do better at evaluating the information and reasoning they use to make their choices than groups that do not.

A second way in which group members challenge the thinking of fellow members is through *vigilant interaction*, which involves the analysis and debate of decision assumptions and alternatives. Such interaction is important because "high-quality choices [are] generally preceded by a careful, thoughtful, and systematic discussion of the pros and cons of that choice vis-à-vis other alternatives" (Hirokawa, 1987, p. 10). Hirokawa (1987) provided an example of vigilant interaction in the following snippet of conversation from a group of college students discussing what items should be salvaged to help their group survive after their plane has crashed in the Canadian wilderness:

B: I really think we should select the box of trash bags.

C: Trash bags? Why? What for?

B: 'Cause I think we really need something like that to help us keep warm, you know, protect us from the elements.

C: But how? In what way? I mean, look, we already decided on the blankets, we already have a fire—we chose the lighter for that purpose, remember? So with the blankets to cover us, and the fire to keep us warm what do we need the trash bags for? I mean I just don't see a good reason for it, you know?

B: To protect us . . .

C: From what? Protection from what?

B: To protect us from the wind, from the cold, from the snow, rain, if it rains.

C: Blankets wouldn't do that?

A: No, not really, well not as well as bags, I don't think.

B: Right, look, OK, we could use the bags like a tent, somehow string 'em together, make a lean-to shelter to keep us dry, right? OK, but also we could wear 'em too. . . . plastic sheeting is a good insulation material—people use 'em to cover their windows in the winter to keep the cold air out. . . . You ever wore one of those bags as a kid, like a costume? It got hot, right? Air couldn't get in, right? Same idea, same principle, the plastic serves as insulation which can protect us against wind chill, cold, wet grounds, rain, you name it.

A: That's right, and blankets aren't going to do that—blankets can't keep body heat in or cold air out as well as plastic, plus blankets gets wet, and if they get wet, they're useless, really.

B: So we could wear the bags over our clothes, then wrap the blankets over us, or wrap the blankets around us and then put the plastic around us. You see our point?

C: Yeah, OK, I guess . . . somehow I never thought about it that way, I was looking at it from a more limited perspective, I guess . . . yeah, you know as only for garbage and stuff.

A: OK, it's settled then, we go with the trash bags? Everyone in agreement on this?

C: Yeah, OK. (B nods also.)

A: OK, what's next? (pp. 10-11)

As this conversation demonstrates, vigilant interaction is associated with group members making arguments for their position and taking steps to counteract the perceived faulty reasoning of other members. Making counterarguments and counteracting perceived questionable inferential reasoning, according to functional theory, facilitates high-quality group decision making. As such, the ability to engage in persuasion becomes a key criterion for being an effective group member. For example, in their examination of what can be learned from the group processes that led to the space shuttle *Challenger* disaster, Hirokawa, Gouran, and Martz (1988) highlighted the importance of members' persuasive ability when they argued that "faulty decisions can be traced to the inability of decision makers to convince others to accept a high-quality alternative or reject a low-quality one" (p. 431). Persuasive ability is, thus, seen to be a key skill that enables group members to arrive

at consensus on the nature of the problem and agree on an effective solution intended to solve the problem.

AN EXPANDED CONCEPTION OF DELIBERATION

The idea that group discussion promotes and enhances democratic processes within communities has historically been part of U.S. and Western culture. This cultural predisposition has, in part, driven the emphasis on problem solving and decision making in groups. However, the dominance of the language game of discussion as the most effective form of deliberative discourse has recently been challenged. First, some critics have taken issue with the problem-centered focus of discussion. They question whether a focus on solving problems produces the kinds of transformational changes required for many communities to grow and develop. Solving problems within a community, they argue, may be different, for instance, than developing the needed resources or assets for continued sustainable growth (Benson, 1997; Kretzmann & McKnight, 1993); solving problems emphasizes identifying deficits and reducing the gap between actual and ideal states, whereas developing needed resources or assets builds the capacity of communities to work toward a constructive future. Moreover, focusing on problems has the potential to create a sense of disempowerment within people and lead them to seek out individuals and groups to blame for the problem's existence. Analyzing the causes and consequences of problems may also lead people to feel overwhelmed by the number and enormity of the problems causing them to feel paralyzed and unable to take action. Hence, critics suggest that adopting a language game that focuses on identifying and creating positive resources for change is crucial for promoting democratic deliberation.

Second, debate presupposes that the parties involved are able to understand each other. Schein (1993) said that debate is a "valid problem-solving and decision-making process only if one can assume that the group members understand each other well enough to be 'talking the same language' " (p. 47). The question, however, is whether such understanding can be assumed in societies such as the United States that are increasingly fragmented along cultural and ideological lines. The answer is "no." People often hold opposing views on controversial public issues (e.g., abortion) and are unable to comprehend or understand how others may differ from them. In such a fragmented social world, debate is not only polarized, it is polarizing (Chasin et al., 1996). By maintaining one's views at all costs with an emphasis on persuading, the act of debate often prohibits people from genuinely understanding others' positions and being able to coordinate their actions together. In contrast, the language game of dialogue is increasingly offered as an alternative means for enhancing understanding and coordination among people (see, e.g., Pearce & Littlejohn, 1997). Dialogue, therefore, becomes an important means of promoting democratic process.

The shift from discussion to dialogue suggests that democratic deliberation needs to be expanded to include alternatives to the language game that has traditionally dominated the playing field. This does not mean that discussion, problem solving/decision making, problem talk, and debate are inappropriate forms of discourse that lead to weak democracy. Discussion, with its emphasis on problem talk and debate, may be quite appropriate under particular circumstances (e.g., when people share an understanding of the problem and agree on the criteria for selecting among alternatives). My point is that the discourse of democratic deliberation needs to be augmented by including language games that represent viable alternatives to discussion, problem solving/decision making, problem talk, and debate. Such language games may be better suited for fostering democracy in particular situations, especially those that call for coordinating persons and groups that hold incommensurate worldviews. Although many

possibilities exist, two alternative language games that have begun receiving attention from scholars and practitioners are appreciative inquiry and dialogue.

From Problem Solving to Appreciative Inquiry

In the 1980s, a new approach to community and organizational development, known as appreciative inquiry (AI), was created (Cooperrider & Srivastva, 1987). Grounded in social constructionist thought (see Zemke, 1999), AI offers a unique alternative to more problem-centered forms of community and organizational development. The assumptions of AI include the following:

1. In every society, organization, or group something works.
2. What we focus on becomes our reality.
3. Reality is created in the moment, and there are multiple realities.
4. The act of asking questions of an organization or group influences the group in some way.
5. People have more confidence and comfort to journey to the future (the unknown) when they carry forward parts of the past (the known).
6. If we carry parts of the past forward, they should be what is best about the past.
7. It is important to value differences.
8. The language we use creates our reality. (Hammond, 1998, pp. 20-21)

The starting point for AI, therefore, is that which works well within a society, organization, or group, not "the problem." By focusing on what works well, a blueprint for future action can be created on the basis of the "best of what is."

Typically, some individual or group within a community or organization makes a decision to engage in an AI. For example, in a community, a group such as a city council or an individual such as a city manager may commission an AI, and within an organization, a work team or a senior-level manager may sponsor an AI. Once the AI has been commissioned, a steering committee is appointed to oversee the process. The steering committee is responsible for coordinating the four stages of an AI. First, *appreciative interviews* are conducted with members of the community. Prior to conducting these interviews, the steering committee selects a topic or issue that is the focus for the appreciative interview. The interviews then center on appreciating and valuing the best of "what is" for the selected topic. Appreciative questions focus on moments of excellence, high points, core values, proud moments, and life-giving forces related to the selected topic. For example, if appreciative interviews were conducted regarding the topic of a city's image, sample questions might include these:

- What would a newcomer to this city say is excellent about it?
- What have been your personal high points in this city? What made them so?
- What do you see as the core values that characterize this city?
- What about this city makes you the most proud of it?
- What gives life to and energizes this city?

Hence, rather than focusing on the problems the city may be having, the focus is directed to what people perceive as good and working well in the city.

Second, the focus of AI then shifts to *envisioning* "what might be." From the stories elicited during the interviews that captured the best of "what is," "provocative propositions" are developed. *Provocative propositions* are statements that remind people of what is best about their community, organization, or group for the issue that is the object of inquiry. These propositions are affirmative statements that simultaneously describe the present as well as an idealized future—"what might be." For example, provocative propositions from the preceding example might include these:

- We continually grow and develop as a city.
- People of differing racial and economic backgrounds collaborate on important civic projects.
- Our economic development is balanced with a deep respect for environmental concerns.

The provocative propositions proposed are subsequently shared with more members of the community through a series of small and large, open group meetings. These meetings provide a conversational space for members to talk about the provocative propositions and determine what additional ones, if any, are needed.

The third stage of AI is *dialoguing* over "what should be." During this stage, the steering committee schedules small and large, open group meetings where community members talk about what should occur within their community in light of the information gained from the appreciative interviews and the provocative propositions developed. In particular, people talk about possible ideas and actions that can potentially extend the provocative propositions.

Finally, the fourth stage of *innovating* concerns "what will be." Community members determine the next steps that need to be taken to create the kind of desired future articulated in the provocative propositions.

Some critics have suggested that AI is merely "happy talk" without substantive action. However, AI has demonstrated remarkable success in helping community groups, governments, businesses, colleges, and nonprofit organizations develop innovative responses to create desirable futures (see the case studies reported by Hammond & Royal, 1998). One explanation for AI's success is that it is grounded in people's lived experience. By asking what has worked well in the past, people begin to build a model for success grounded in activities that they have experienced. By focusing on how to create success, AI reaffirms those moments that have worked well and, thereby, creates an environment where affirming conversation facilitates the creation of more moments of excellence. AI, thus, creates a conversational space where members of a community are able to participate constructively in conversation about their possible futures—a space where democratic process is taken seriously.

From Debate to Dialogue

Dialogue, as mentioned at the beginning of this chapter, has been offered as a form of communication that complements discussion.[4] Whereas debate focuses on breaking problems into parts and persuading others to accept one's viewpoint, dialogue focuses on seeing things holistically and creating space for learning. As Ellinor and Gerard (1998, p. 21) observed, dialogue involves the following:

- Seeing the whole among the parts
- Seeing the connections between the parts
- Inquiring into assumptions
- Learning through inquiry and disclosure
- Creating shared meaning among many people

Creating dialogue can sometimes be difficult because people may have differing positions on key issues and may become defensive when articulating their position due to having been socialized into a debate mode. Dialogue, as a form of communication, takes care not to reinforce defensive exchanges but, instead, strives to create a field of genuine meeting and inquiry where "people gradually learn to suspend their defensive exchanges and . . . probe into the underlying reasons for why those exchanges exist" (Isaacs, 1993, p. 25).

Dialogue is, thus, a collective and collaborative communication process whereby people explore together their individual and collective assumptions and predispositions. In so doing, dialogue moves individuals and groups from engaging in single-loop to double- and triple-loop learning. *Single-loop learning* occurs when people create or learn existing norms and correct their behavior when it deviates from those established norms. For example, suppose a group has established, either explicitly or implicitly, this behavioral norm: "When another member voices an opinion on an issue you care about that is different from your opinion, strongly advocate your viewpoint and refute the other's viewpoint." The result is that group members monitor their environment, and any time another member voices an opposing opinion on a salient issue, group members will argue with that person over the validity of his or her opinion. *Double-loop learning* involves questioning whether a norm is effective and, in cases where it is not, suggesting alternatives. Using the preceding example, group members could call into question the utility of that norm and begin to explore other norms that might be more effective for guiding group discussion. *Triple-loop learning* involves exploring what influences an individual or a group to view situations as calling for the use of any particular norm. The question in this case has to do with what has led group members to view arguing against opposing viewpoints as an appropriate and preferred mode of discourse. Shifting from single-loop to double-loop and triple-loop learning, dialogue, consequently, creates a space for individuals and groups to explore and question the underlying assumptions, values, and norms that lead them toward viewing situations in particular ways and performing certain types of action.

At least three unique behavioral qualities distinguish dialogue from debate. First, dialogue shifts people from viewing the world as "either/or" to "both/and." Debate, at least in the traditional sense, is a polarized form of interaction in which participants must select between mutually exclusive positions and adopt *either* one position or the other. In contrast, dialogue adopts a position of "both/and" by recognizing that there are *both* differences *and* similarities between supposedly competing positions. The tensions between the differences and similarities provide the space for creating new possibilities for moving forward. These possibilities may reflect some of the ideas contained in either position, may reflect some combination of the positions, or may emerge from totally new ideas developed through dialogue.

Second, talk that "suspends" people's assumptions is central to dialogue (Isaacs, 1993, 1999). The notion of "suspension" has a dual meaning. One meaning involves taking individual and/or collective assumptions and suspending them in front of the interactants for examination. The suspension of assumptions in this sense means holding the assumptions up for all to see. A second meaning of suspension is for individuals or groups to suspend their most deeply held beliefs. This form of suspension is similar to Weick's (1979) admonition to doubt what you know to be true and believe what you know to be false. Suspension, in this sense, is about vulnerability—opening one's mind to consider new viewpoints and ideas and potentially letting go of one's own ideas. This latter notion of suspension differs from debate, in which parties are committed to their viewpoint and unwilling to acknowledge weaknesses in their own position and/or strengths in an opposing position.

Third, dialogue, like debate, involves balancing advocacy and inquiry (Ellinor & Gerard, 1998) but uses them in fundamentally different ways from debate. Dialogue uses advocacy as a means of sharing one's perspective in ways that enhance group members' learning. The purpose is not to force a group to accept one's view or to convince others of the superiority of that view; rather, the intent is to offer one's perspective so that the resources for building shared meanings and understanding are enhanced. Similarly, inquiry is used to explore one another's assumptions and thinking with the intent of learning about them more deeply. In contrast, inquiry in debate is typically used to collect information and learn about another's thinking so that a person can better persuade others to adopt his or her way of thinking. Hence, in dialogue, there is a commitment to both advocacy and inquiry for the purpose of fostering high-quality learning summed up in the statement, "I state my views, I inquire into your views, and I invite you to state your views and I inquire into your views" (BMR Associates, 1997, p. 3).

What are the implications for organizing group conversation if one takes AI and dialogue seriously? More specifically, what would group conversations that are more appreciative and dialogic look like? To illustrate some answers to these questions, I present in the next section a case study of group facilitation work rooted in appreciative and dialogic forms of discourse.

AMERICA'S PROMISE: THE CASE OF THE WACO YOUTH SUMMIT

From April 27-29, 1997, retired General Colin Powell hosted the Presidential Summit for America's Future in Philadelphia. Delegates included 50 governors and representatives from 140 communities. The summit focused on ways to provide children with five foundational experiences critical for their development into caring, responsible adults: (a) a healthy start, (b) an ongoing caring mentor, (c) safe places, (d) marketable skills, and (e) an opportunity to give back to their community. At the summit, four living U.S. presidents (Ford, Carter, Bush, and Clinton) and Nancy Reagan, on behalf of President Reagan, signed a document called "America's Promise," which stated that by the year 2000, 2 million children would have access to each of these five foundational experiences.

Waco, Texas, was one of the communities that sent a delegation to Philadelphia. The youth delegate, Amy Achor, returned to Waco with a commitment to bring the spirit of the Philadelphia summit to the city. During the summer of 1997, an executive committee composed of Waco youths, mentored by Rosemary Townsend (one of the adult delegates to the Philadelphia summit), planned "The Central Texas Youth Summit for America's Future." The daylong summit on September 6, 1997, brought 1,200 youths from around central Texas to the campus of Baylor University. The day was full of activities that ranged from workshops on how to work in teams to a fair emphasizing voluntarism opportunities in central Texas to live musical performances by youth rock and country and western bands.

During the day, youths attended two, 45-minute breakout sessions, titled "Dream Catcher" and "Catch the Gold Ring." These two sessions provided a group setting for young people to talk about their dreams for their community and to develop strategies for making those dreams a reality. The two sessions were designed and facilitated by members of the Public Dialogue Consortium (PDC) of which I am a member. I was responsible for coordinating the design and facilitation of the breakout sessions. The PDC is a team of teachers, practitioners, and researchers that helps individuals, groups, organizations, and communities to find new and better ways of communicating in a complex, dynamic, and diverse society (see Pearce & Pearce, 2000; Spano, 2001). These two breakout sessions were designed using the principles of AI and dialogue. Before explaining how these principles shaped the design of the breakout sessions, I provide an overview of the specific structure of the sessions.

Catching Dreams and Gold Rings

Imagine that you are 14-year-old student entering a very large room at 10:30 a.m. on a sunny Saturday. As you enter the room, you are handed a number by a facilitator wearing a bright red shirt emblazoned with a stylized Texas flag and the words "1997 Youth Summit Facilitator" directly beneath the flag. The number you have been handed directs you to sit at one of the round tables scattered around the room. You quickly see six other youths seated at your table along with another facilitator wearing a red shirt. At the front of the room, a member of the youth executive committee introduces the "lead facilitator," a member of a group called the Public Dialogue Consortium. The lead facilitator welcomes the young people gathered in the room to a session called "Dream Catcher." He high-

lights the ground rules that will guide each group's conversation:

- Asking questions is as important as making statements.
- Ask curious questions.
- Respect others' opinions, even if they are different from your own.
- Share talk time.

At that point, you notice a big pile of candy in the middle of your table. The facilitator seated at the table invites you and all the other youths sitting there to take as much candy as you would like and to count the number of pieces you have taken. The facilitator then has each person tell his or her name and as many things about himself or herself as that person has pieces of candy.

After the introductions are complete, the lead facilitator asks the members of each group to talk about their dreams for their city or town. The facilitator at your table has taken a piece of poster board, drawn a line down the middle, and written the word "Concerns" in the left-hand column and the word "Dreams" in the right-hand column. Your group takes about 10 minutes to brainstorm answers to the question, What concerns do you have about your community? The facilitator writes down all the answers in the left-hand column. The facilitator then asks, "Given these concerns, what are your dreams for your community?" In the right-hand column, the facilitator writes down all the answers given.

At the end of the 10 minutes, your table pairs up with another table and compares the two lists of dreams. The facilitators ask questions such as these:

- What dreams do you see on both lists that are similar?
- What dreams do you see on both lists that are different?
- What new dreams can you think of?
- What do you feel is the most important dream?

- What dream do you feel most excited about?

After about 15 minutes of conversation, your combined group selects what the members feel is the most important dream and writes a newspaper headline that captures that dream. The headline is written down on a piece of poster board that says "Youth Summit Gazette" at the top.

The lead facilitator then asks for everyone's attention and has each combined group report its headline to everyone in the room. The energy is high as two facilitators race around the room with cordless microphones soliciting the headline from each combined group. Once all the headlines have been reported, the facilitators at your table give you and every other member a piece of paper that looks like a blue sky with clouds. At the top of this "cloud paper" is the phrase, "I dream of a community where. . . . " You take a few minutes to write down your response to the phrase and place it in a big gold pot in the corner of the room with a sign over it that says "Dream Catcher." After everyone has done this, there is a 10-minute break.

When you return from break and sit down with your group from the first session, the first thing you notice is that all the headlines from each combined group have been posted at the front of the room. The lead facilitator welcomes you back from the break, reads through the headlines that have been posted at the front of the room, and introduces the next breakout session, which is called, "Catch the Gold Ring." For this session, each table is given five paper stars and asked as a group to decide which dreams the members want to vote for with their stars. The lead facilitator explains that if there is only one dream that your group considers to be important, all five stars may be placed on that dream; alternatively, the group may place one star on five different dreams or in any combination desired. After 10 minutes of discussion and decision making, the group elects you to go to the front of the room and place the stars on the selected

headlines as agreed on by the group. After all the stars from all the groups have been placed, the lead facilitator identifies the most popular headline on the basis of which one received the most stars.

The people at your table are then grouped with people from three other tables, and you move to a space in the room where you see on the floor a large piece of butcher paper with a big circle drawn in the center of it and lines drawn from the circle to the outer edges of the paper. It reminds you of the pictures children draw of the sun with rays of sunshine. One of the table facilitators writes in the center of the circle the most popular headline voted on by all the participants present. The facilitator then asks, "What actions can we take as a community to make this dream a reality?" and writes the responses generated in the circle. After about 15 minutes of brainstorming, the facilitator asks, "What kinds of things do you need to consider when implementing these actions?" and writes the responses offered on the lines or "rays" in the diagram. Before the session ends, the lead facilitator asks each group to report what its members talked about and how what they learned influences their ability to implement actions. At this point, the session is over and you head for lunch before the afternoon session of the summit starts.

An Emphasis on Appreciation

Several features of the event design for the facilitation described above are rooted in the principles of AI. First, the dream motif was the organizing feature for both facilitation sessions. The term, "Dream Catcher," was chosen by the PDC because it was considered important to elicit and encourage the dreams of the youths for their community. This activity is a variation of the classic AI task, "Describe three concrete wishes for the future of this organization" (Hammond, 1998, p. 56). Talking about dreams highlights the enthusiasm, hopes, and aspirations of people far more than talking about problems. As a member of the executive steering committee put it,

> I've been in several meetings within Waco where that [problems] was the definite focus . . . and the meeting—the whole make-up of it— just falls apart instantly. People have so many complaints about what's going on and so many different negative experiences that they want to bring up and make sure are heard in the community. I think that getting your voice heard in the community is great, but if you focus constantly on the negative, the communication breaks down and people get on the defensive. However, if you focus on the positive, people seem to suddenly be able to think clearer and they are able to think, "Oh, well, I can work with you and I can help build this other process," and it becomes more of a building up than tearing down.

Dreams, therefore, are viewed not as unobtainable utopian ideals but as desirable futures that can be achieved if people are willing to exert effort and energy and work together. As a member of the executive steering committee said, "If it's something that's a dream, then it's more possible."

A second feature is that time was allotted in the "Dream Catcher" breakout session for abbreviated appreciative interviews. At the beginning of the session, the members of each table were asked to generate concerns and dreams for their community. The conversation began with concerns because the PDC believed that the youths might be able to more readily identify concerns within the Waco community. The concerns, however, were used as an entry into their dreams, which then became the dominant focus for the conversation. Again, the importance of talking about dreams, as opposed to problems, cannot be underestimated. Dreams provide an opportunity to look at new possibilities for the future. As one summit facilitator said,

> I think what talking about dreams does is open up possibilities and possible futures rather than

focusing on handling the angles of the problems. And I think it's a lot harder to talk, to get the solution, when you focus on the problem. By starting on the solutions or on the dreams and visions, it just moved people into a more future-oriented place, and that's what they [the sponsors of the summit] wanted to have happen. Then, the next questions that ultimately come up are, How do I do that? and How do I get there? and that is very powerful.

The abbreviated appreciative interviews, thus, focused the group conversations on what people desired and guided the remainder of those conversations to ways in which those dreams could be accomplished.

Another summit facilitator voiced the notion that AI, rather than problem talk, made the conversations easier:

> We know that a ton of kids evidenced fears of crime, and while I believe that those are genuine concerns that those kids have—and I don't want to minimize crime in Waco . . . and this may sound like I live, you know, in a dream world— but really, Waco's crime is not that bad. To me, the emphasis on crime was way out of proportion to reality.
>
> Now, that may be those kids' perspectives, but if that's what came up when we were talking about dreams, if we had talked about problems, I think we would have spent all of our time talking about things like crime and probably not developing solutions, whereas what we did was we talked about sort of where we wanted to go and how to get there. I think that was a much healthier thing to do.

Hence, although AI does not explicitly focus on generating solutions to problems, the act of talking about possible desirable futures can lead people to articulate what they see as ways to move forward. Focusing on hopes for the future, as opposed to past problems, thus, creates a space for constructive action planning.

The third, and final, design feature is that provocative propositions were integrated into the facilitation through the use of the headlines in the *Youth Summit Gazette*. These headlines were a means of articulating the shared visions of what the larger Waco community could be in the future. The headlines/provocative propositions served as a useful bridge from envisioning the future to dialoguing about "what would/should be."

An Emphasis on Dialogue

Given that both sessions had relatively short time limits, it was not possible for the youths to engage in a sustained dialogue about community building. Nevertheless, dialogic communication was encouraged in two ways. First, the ground rules presented at the beginning of the "Dream Catcher" session emphasized the creation of a safe climate for promoting dialogue among participants. These ground rules asked the young people not only to balance their advocacy and inquiry but to inquire into the positions of others with a sense of respect for one another.

Second, the "Catch the Gold Ring" session was designed to enhance the likelihood that these youths would see connections between the different issues discussed. The choice of bringing together four tables to brainstorm using the "sunshine" diagram was strategic. One reason for this choice was to enhance the diversity present within each group, because diversity makes it possible for the participants to view situations in new ways and make new connections between possible courses of actions. One summit facilitator highlighted the value of such diversity:

I think the different viewpoints were . . . the engine that drove all the solutions and outcomes that happened. When we did the last exercises, . . . we brought all the groups together and they brainstormed and had different ideas of what could actually be done; like I said, taking their thoughts and putting them into action—different viewpoints and different ideas. I call it "the engine that drove it" because having all these different ideas—a diversity of views—coming together from different kids, you know from different socioeconomic classes, different religious backgrounds, different ethnic groups—all coming together and throwing in different ideas allowed them to see what other people thought and look at all of these views and try to determine what would be the best thing. . . . I mean, you have kids from, you know, more rural backgrounds hearing more what urban kids thought and vice versa. A lot of this is the diversity of the people there that really added to it. It's useful to see what other people experience in their lives and what are their dreams and aspirations.

Another reason for using the "sunshine" diagram was to improve the likelihood that the youths would see systemic connections between various suggested actions and implementation factors. By focusing on the dream listed in the center of the circle, the young people could see how many different possible actions might fulfill it. By focusing on the "rays," they could begin to grasp the complexity of the many different factors that could influence their ability to implement actions. As a summit facilitator put it,

In the planning session, or in the Catch the Gold Ring that followed, . . . my understanding of it and the way it seemed to work was not that you have dreamed this dream with basically no limits put on you but what it is that individuals need to do. What is it that an organization needs to do? What is it that a community needs to do to make your dreams become reality? So, they took this huge, wide, wonderful vision and didn't change it in any way but brought some pragmatic reality testing back into it and, you know, if this is a project of some kind, well, what do you need to do. How would you get those things done?

During the course of the group conversations, then, the youths had the opportunity to share their experiences with one another about important factors that they believed had to be considered when implementing action. They had the opportunity to dialogue about the challenges, contradictions, and dilemmas of working with these various factors.

CONCLUSION: ELABORATING THE LANGUAGE GAMES OF DELIBERATION

Group communication scholars, as I have explained in this chapter, have historically associated deliberative discourse with discussion, problem solving/decision making, and debate. The implicit assumption is that these ways of communicating are well suited for promoting a democratic society. However, the abilities required to participate in a democratic society today must expand to include not only the language game of discussion but also the language games of appreciative inquiry and dialogue. What, then, are the implications of these expanded language games for group communication scholarship? What new areas for research are suggested when discussion, appreciative inquiry, and dialogue are all viewed as legitimate forms of discourse that promote democracy?

First, the practices associated with appreciative inquiry and dialogue within groups warrant further elaboration. We need to understand the forms of talk and conversational practices that constitute appreciative communication and dialogue. Some research into dialogic group communication has been done in the general area of the learning organization (see Isaacs, 1999; Senge et al., 1999), as well as in the study of public participation groups (see Pearce & Littlejohn, 1997), but a good deal of work remains to be done to articulate the forms of talk that constitute appreciative and dialogic communication.

Second, the differences and similarities between discussion and dialogue need further elaboration. A basic question is, In what contexts are discussion or dialogue preferred ways of talking? Some scholars argue that discussion is best used when people have similar frames of reference, whereas dialogue is most appropriate when participants have different frames of reference and divergent thinking is required (e.g., Ellinor & Gerard, 1998). It is important, therefore, to understand how context influences the appropriateness and/or effectiveness of discussion or dialogue. This issue becomes more complex when one realizes that the question is not simply when to use discussion or dialogue but how to manage discussion and dialogic forms of talk within interactional episodes. Applying recent communication scholarship on dialectical theory (e.g., Baxter & Montgomery, 1996; see also Johnson & Long, this volume), the choice is not whether to use discussion or dialogue in group conversation but, rather, how to manage simultaneously these conversational forms.

Third, the exploration of discussion, appreciative inquiry, and dialogue as multilevel constructs merits attention. There is a tendency to view these forms of talk within an episodic framework—that is, in terms of what people say or do during the exchange of messages. The result is that the focus has been on the types and sequences of messages that are discussion, appreciative, or dialogically oriented. This foregrounding of the episodic nature of communication puts into the background other important contexts, such as the nature of the participants (see Keyton & Frey, this volume), the relationships between them, and the influence of culture (see Oetzel, this volume). It is entirely possible that the terms discussion, appreciative inquiry, and dialogue can be used not only as descriptions of specific episodes of communication but also to characterize people, their relationships, and the impact of culture on them. Doing so opens up a vast array of possibilities and questions helpful for understanding the nature of discussion, appreciative inquiry, and dialogue. For example, how should scholars make sense of dialogic communication when it occurs at an episodic level in a discussion/debate-oriented relationship? Does debate take on a different flavor when it occurs in an appreciative inquiry and dialogically oriented relationship rather than in a discussion-oriented one? These are the kinds of questions that become possible and deserve attention when discussion, appreciative inquiry, and dialogue are viewed as multilevel constructs.

Fourth, the notion of "group communication competence" needs to be reexamined in light of appreciative and dialogic communication. Group communication competence has typically been defined from a discussion-centered model that associates it with decision-making skills, such as defining the problem and generating solutions, as articulated, for instance, in functional theory (see Beebe, Barge, & McCormick, 1998). Group communication competence is also associated in the discussion-centered model with "rhetorical eloquence," which refers to people's ability to make persuasive arguments within a particular language community (Pearce & Littlejohn, 1997). Taking the ideas of appreciative inquiry and dialogue seriously, however, changes our idea of what counts as group communication competence. For example, Barrett (1995) talked about the following kinds of competence in relation to appreciative inquiry:

1. *Affirmative competence:* "The ability to draw on the human capacity to appreciate positive possibilities by electively focusing on current and past strengths, successes, and potentials"
2. *Expansive competence:* The ability to challenge "habits and conventional practices, provoking members to experiment in the margins, [make] expansive promises that challenge them to stretch in new directions, and [evoke] a set of higher values and ideals that inspire them to passionate engagement"
3. *Generative competence:* The ability to construct "integrative systems that allow members to see the consequences of their actions, to recognize that they are making a meaningful contribution, and to experience a sense of progress"
4. *Collaborative competence:* An ability to "create forums in which members engage in ongoing dialogue and exchange diverse perspectives" (p. 40)

Are these conceptions of competence germane to group communication competence?

Are there other forms of competence or eloquence that need to be considered when group communication is viewed from appreciative inquiry and dialogic perspectives? I hope that, in time, research and practice will respond to these and many other important questions.

EPILOGUE

Following the Central Texas Youth Summit, voluntarism hours by youths doubled in the Waco area. In the Axtell, Texas, high school, a new program was established in which students provided mentoring and support to other students. The city governments of Waco and Woodway (a suburb of Waco) established youth commissions. A "Facilitator's Network" composed of facilitators from that summit is in the process of being formed. This network hopes to provide ongoing training for citizens in the art of facilitation and to connect trained facilitators with local businesses and nonprofit groups. Clearly, the democratic spirit of the summit lives on.

NOTES

1. Several language games exist within group communication theory and research, including symbolic convergence theory (see Bormann's, 1996, overview) and, more recently, the bona fide group perspective (see Putnam & Stohl, 1996). However, the focus on key functions and decision paths has dominated the field (see Poole, 1999).

2. Functional theory has been chosen to illustrate the nature of the language game of discussion in group communication scholarship because of its strong ties to Dewey's (1910) work on promoting democratic process. Other theoretical perspectives, such as structuration theory (see Poole, 1999; Poole et al., 1996), that also reflect a commitment to the characteristics of group communication that are examined here—problem-centered language and debate—could also have been selected.

3. Ellinor and Gerard actually equated discussion with debate, calling it "discussion/debate."

4. There are many views of dialogue (see the essays in Cissna, 2000). For example, there is a long tradition of viewing dialogue from a Buberian perspective (see, e.g., Anderson & Cissna, 1997; Cissna & Anderson, 1994; Friedman, 1994). The perspective that I take is derived from Bohm (1996a, 1996b), whose writings have influenced the work on dialogue conducted within learning organizations (see Isaacs, 1993, 1999; Senge, 1990).

Bohm focuses on how dialogue enhances collective thinking, which mirrors, in some sense, the traditional role of debate as enhancing group deliberation.

REFERENCES

Anderson, R., & Cissna, K. N. (1997). *The Martin Buber-Carl Rogers dialogue: A new transcript with commentary.* Albany: State University of New York Press.

Astley, W. G., & Zammuto, R. F. (1992). Organization science, managers, and language games. *Organization Science, 3,* 443-460.

Baird, A. C. (1928). *Public discussion and debate.* Boston: Ginn.

Barge, J. K. (1994). On interlinking language games: New opportunities for group communication research. *Communication Studies, 45,* 52-67.

Barrett, F. J. (1995). Creating appreciative learning cultures. *Organizational Dynamics, 24,* 36-49.

Baxter, L. A., & Montgomery, B. M. (1996). *Relating: Dialogue and dialectics.* New York: Guilford Press.

Beebe, S., Barge, J. K., & McCormick, C. (1998, November). *The competent small group communicator.* Paper presented at the meeting of the National Communication Association, New York City.

Benson, P. (1997). *All kids are our kids.* San Francisco: Jossey-Bass.

BMR Associates. (1997). *Guidelines for productive conversation.* Dallas, TX: Author.

Bohm, D. (1996a). *On dialogue* (L. Nichol, Ed.). London: Routledge.

Bohm, D. (1996b). *Wholeness and the implicate order.* London: Routledge & Kegan Paul.

Bormann, E. G. (1996). Symbolic convergence theory and communication. In R. Y. Hirokawa & M. S. Poole (Eds.), *Communication and group decision making* (2nd ed., pp. 81-113). Thousand Oaks, CA: Sage.

Chasin, R., Herzig, M., Roth, S., Chasin, L., Becker, C., & Stains, R. R., Jr. (1996). From diatribe to dialogue on divisive public issues: Approaches drawn from family therapy. *Mediation Quarterly, 13,* 323-344.

Cissna, K. N. (Ed.). (2000). Studies in dialogue [special issue]. *Southern Communication Journal, 65*(2/3).

Cissna, K. N., & Anderson, R. (1994). The 1957 Martin Buber-Carl Rogers dialogue, as dialogue. *Journal of Humanistic Psychology, 34,* 11-45.

Cooperrider, D. L., & Srivastva, S. (1987). Appreciative inquiry in organizational life. In R. W. Woodman & W. A. Pasmore (Eds.), *Research in organizational change and development* (Vol. 1, pp. 129-169). Greenwich, CT: JAI Press.

Crowell, L. (1963). *Discussion: Method of democracy.* Glenview, IL: Scott-Foresman.

Dewey, J. (1910). *How we think.* Boston: D. C. Heath.

Ellinor, L., & Gerard, G. (1998). *Dialogue: Rediscover the transforming power of conversation.* New York: John Wiley.

Frey, L. R. (1996). Remembering and "re-membering": A history of theory and research on communication and group decision making. In R. Y. Hirokawa & M. S. Poole (Eds.), *Communication and group decision making* (2nd ed., pp. 19-54). Thousand Oaks: CA: Sage.

Friedman, M. (1994). Reflections on the Buber-Rogers dialogue. *Journal of Humanistic Psychology, 34,*46-65.

Gastil, J. (1992). A definition of small group democracy. *Small Group Research, 23,* 278-301.

Gastil, J. (1993). Identifying obstacles to small group democracy. *Small Group Research, 24,* 5-27.

Gergen, K. J. (1991). *The saturated self.* New York: Basic Books.

Gouran, D. S. (1997). Effective versus ineffective group decision making. In L. R. Frey & J. K. Barge (Eds.), *Managing group life: Communicating in decision-making groups* (pp. 133-155). Boston: Houghton Mifflin.

Gouran, D. S. (1999). Communication in groups: The emergence and evolution of a field of study. In L. R. Frey (Ed.), D. S. Gouran, & M. S. Poole (Assoc. Eds.), *The handbook of group communication theory & research* (pp. 3-36). Thousand Oaks, CA: Sage.

Gouran, D. S., & Hirokawa, R. Y. (1983). The role of communication in decision-making groups: A functional perspective. In M. S. Mander (Ed.), *Communications in transition: Issues and debates in current research* (pp. 165-185). New York: Praeger.

Gouran, D. S., & Hirokawa, R. Y. (1996). Functional theory and communication in decision-making and problem-solving groups: An expanded view. In R. Y. Hirokawa & M. S. Poole (Eds.), *Communication and group decision making* (2nd ed., pp. 55-80). Thousand Oaks, CA: Sage.

Gouran, D. S., Hirokawa, R. Y., Julian, K. M., & Leatham, G. B. (1993). The evolution and current status of the functional perspective on communication in decision-making and problem-solving groups. In S. A. Deetz (Ed.), *Communication yearbook* (Vol. 16, pp. 573-600). Newbury Park, CA: Sage.

Hammond, S. A. (1998). *The thin book of appreciative inquiry* (2nd ed.). Plano, TX: Thin Book.

Hammond, S. A., & Royal, C. (1998). *Lessons from the field: Applying appreciative inquiry.* Plano, TX: Practical Press.

Hirokawa, R. Y. (1985). Discussion procedures and decision-making performance: A test of a functional perspective. *Human Communication Research, 12,* 203-224.

Hirokawa, R. Y. (1987). Why informed groups make faulty decisions: An investigation of possible interaction-based explanations. *Small Group Behavior, 18,* 3-29.

Hirokawa, R. Y. (1988). Group communication and decision-making performance: A continued test of the functional perspective. *Human Communication Research, 14,* 487-515.

Hirokawa, R. Y. (1990). The role of communication in group decision-making efficacy: A task-contingency perspective. *Small Group Research, 21,* 190-204.

Hirokawa, R. Y., Gouran, D. S., & Martz, A. E. (1988). Understanding the sources of faulty group decision making: A lesson from the *Challenger* disaster. *Small Group Behavior, 19,* 411-433.

Hirokawa, R. Y., & Salazar, A. J. (1997). An integrated approach to communication and group decision making. In L. R. Frey & J. K. Barge (Eds.), *Managing group life: Communicating in decision-making groups* (pp. 156-181). Boston: Houghton Mifflin.

Hirokawa, R. Y., & Salazar, A. J. (1999). Task-group communication and decision-making performance. In L. R. Frey (Ed.), D. S. Gouran, & M. S. Poole (Assoc. Eds.), *The handbook of group communication theory & research* (pp. 167-191). Thousand Oaks, CA: Sage.

Isaacs, W. N. (1993). Taking flight: Dialogue, collective thinking, and organizational learning. *Organizational Dynamics, 22*(2), 24-39.

Isaacs, W. N. (1999). *Dialogue and the art of thinking together.* New York: Currency.

Jarboe, S. (1996). Procedures for enhancing group decision making. In R. Y. Hirokawa & M. S. Poole (Eds.), *Communication and group decision making* (2nd ed., pp. 345-383). Thousand Oaks, CA: Sage.

Kretzmann, J. P., & McKnight, J. L. (1997). *Building communities from the inside out: A path toward finding and mobilizing a community.* Chicago: Dimensions.

Lewin, K. (1951). *Field theory in social science: Selected theoretical papers* (D. Cartwright, Ed.). New York: Harper & Row.

Lewin, K., Lippitt, R., & White, R. K. (1939). Patterns of aggressive behavior in experimentally created "social climates." *Journal of Social Psychology, 10,* 271-279.

Meyers, R. A. (1997). Social influence and group argumentation. In L. R. Frey & J. K. Barge (Eds.), *Managing group life: Communicating in decision-making groups* (pp. 182-201). Boston: Houghton Mifflin.

Meyers, R. A., & Brashers, D. E. (1999). Influence processes in group interaction. In L. R. Frey (Ed.), D. S. Gouran, & M. S. Poole (Assoc. Eds.), *The handbook of group communication theory & research* (pp. 288-312). Thousand Oaks, CA: Sage.

Pearce, W. B., & Littlejohn, S. W. (1997). *Moral conflict: When social worlds collide.* Thousand Oaks, CA: Sage.

Pearce, W. B., & Pearce, K. (2000, January). *Extending the theory of the coordinated management of meaning ("CMM") through a community dialogue process.* Paper presented at the Conference on Practical Theory, Public Participation, and Community, Waco, TX.

Poole, M. S. (1999). Group communication theory. In L. R. Frey (Ed.), D. S. Gouran, & M. S. Poole (Assoc. Eds.), *The handbook of group communication theory & research* (pp. 37-70). Thousand Oaks, CA: Sage.

Poole, M. S., Seibold, D. R., & McPhee, R. D. (1996). The structuration of group decisions. In R. Y. Hirokawa & M. S. Poole (Eds.), *Communication and group decision making* (2nd ed., pp. 114-146). Thousand Oaks, CA: Sage.

Propp, K. M. (1995). An experimental examination of biological sex as a status cue in decision-making groups an its influence on information use. *Small Group Research, 26,* 451-474.

Propp, K. M. (1999). Collective information processing in groups. In L. R. Frey (Ed.), D. S. Gouran, & M. S. Poole (Assoc. Eds.), *The handbook of group communication theory & research* (pp. 225-250). Thousand Oaks, CA: Sage.

Propp, K. M., & Nelson, D. (1996). Problem-solving performance in naturalistic groups: A test of the ecological validity of the functional perspective. *Communication Studies, 47,* 35-45.

Putnam, L. L., & Stohl, C. (1996). Bona fide groups: An alternative perspective for communication and small group decision making. In R. Y. Hirokawa & M. S. Poole (Eds.), *Communication and group decision making* (2nd ed., pp. 147-178). Thousand Oaks, CA: Sage.

Schein, E. H. (1993). On dialogue, culture, and organizational learning. *Organizational Dynamics, 22*(2), 40-51.

Seibold, D. R., Meyers, R. A., & Sunwolf. (1996). Communication and influence in group decision making. In R. Y. Hirokawa & M. S. Poole (Eds.), *Communication and group decision making* (2nd ed., pp. 242-267). Thousand Oaks, CA: Sage.

Senge, P. M. (1990). *The fifth discipline: The art and practice of the learning organization.* New York: Doubleday.

Senge, P., Kleiner, A., Roberts, C., Ross, R., Roth, G., & Smith, B. (1999). *The dance of change.* New York: Currency.

Sheffield, A. D. (1922). *Joining in public discussion.* New York: George H. Doran.

Spano, S. (2001). *Public dialogue and participatory democracy: The Cupertino community project.* Cresskill, NJ: Hampton Press.

Sunwolf, & Seibold, D. R. (1999). The impact of formal procedures on group processes, members, and task outcomes. In L. R. Frey (Ed.), D. S. Gouran, & M. S. Poole (Assoc. Eds.), *The handbook of group communication theory & research* (pp. 395-431). Thousand Oaks, CA: Sage.

Weick, K. E. (1979). *The social psychology of organizing* (2nd ed.). Reading, MA: Addison-Wesley.

White, R., & Lippitt, R. (1960). *Autocracy and democracy.* New York: Harper.

Wittgenstein, L. (1953). *Philosophical investigations* (G. E. M. Ansombe, Trans.). Oxford, UK: Basil Blackwell.

Zemke, R. (1999). Don't fix that company! Maybe problem-solving is the problem. *Training, 36*(6), 26-33.

10

Self-Organizing and Complexity Perspectives of Group Creativity

Implications for Group Communication

ABRAN J. SALAZAR
University of Rhode Island

To survive, an organization has to learn from and adapt to a constantly fluctuating environment. In the marketplace, there is an increasing need for organizations in a variety of sectors to be innovative and creative. From dealing with product development and delivery of goods and services to adaptation to social, economic, and political change, the need to learn and to be creative and innovative has arguably taken on more importance now than ever before in history. This is so for at least two reasons:

Some attribute the current preoccupation with strategic innovation to attempts to come to terms with a new era of industrial organization along post-Fordist, information-intensive lines described variously as flexible specialization or mass customization. Another view is that we are experiencing a short-term adjustment to the globalization of markets and the influence of powerful new technologies. (MacIntosh & MacLean, 1999, p. 300; see also Gleick, 1999)

The recent upsurge in books and articles detailing the *social determinants* of creativity speaks to the sudden increased interest in how creativity may be enhanced by studying how individuals relate to one another. Of particular interest has been the study of social relations and systems and how they provide fertile ground for self-organizing activity that facilitates learning, adaptation, creativity, and innovation.

At the heart of creativity, learning, and innovation processes in organizations are the social systems we call groups (Stacey, 1996). According to Simonton (1997), "Much of creativity occurs in a social environment, the interplay between individual creators stimulating the emergence of ideas that might not arise by more solitary means" (p. 315). A large portion of creativity, learning, and innovation in organizations is, in essence, developed in human activities and interactions, that is, in how individuals relate to one another in a variety of social contexts, especially in groups. These group activities, interactions, and relations may be hindered or facilitated by a variety of group and organizational features (e.g., structures, such as how people make decisions, and office/departmental structuring that distances decision makers from experiencing the impact of their decisions and, consequently, has the effect of impeding learning) that are communicatively produced and reproduced (Senge, 1990). The challenges, then, are identifying salient features suitable for and conducive to group learning and adaptation in fluctuating environments, as well as identifying the initial conditions that give rise to system features that enable creative activity. These challenges have been met by scholars working in various disciplines, but unfortunately, communication scholars have not been among them.

Clearly, groups do produce novel and unique outcomes, but the processes that yield such outcomes are not clearly understood. Questions surrounding the study of group creativity abound: What conditions facilitate creativity in groups? What are the characteristics of creative groups? What role does communication play in fostering creativity in groups? These are important questions, for in comparison with what we know of creative individuals, we know relatively little about creative groups. Gaining such knowledge is important; when we are able to identify these conditions, characteristics, and roles, we can provide good advice to those wishing to enhance the creativity of their groups.

This chapter examines the literature on group creativity to identify those characteristics of groups and communication that foster creativity. In particular, I focus on the role of communication in constituting conditions that nurture and foster group creativity and adaptation to fluctuating environments. In examining the relationship between group communication and group creativity, I (a) define creativity, distinguishing it from related constructs, such as innovation and learning, and argue for a particular conceptualization of creativity when applied to groups; (b) present a brief critique of the literature that has

emphasized the role of interaction in group creativity; (c) cast communication and its relationship to group creativity against the backdrop of a framework derived from recent work in self-organization, chaos, and the sciences of complexity; and (d) provide directions that future communication-oriented group creativity research may fruitfully take when approached from the aforementioned framework.

CREATIVITY, INNOVATION, AND LEARNING: DISTINCTIONS

What constitutes creativity? Many definitions are available (see Ackoff & Vergara, 1988). Here, I propose a definition of creativity that I consider useful for the purposes of this chapter. Rather than claiming that the definition is definitive, I delineate the position from which I am approaching the definition. Such an exercise is perhaps more useful than engaging in a debate about creativity definitions (Jarboe, 1999).

In defining creativity, it becomes readily apparent that related concepts have been defined similarly. Definitions of creativity, for example, share features of closely related concepts such as learning and innovation. As related as they are, they also may be conceptually distinguished. West and Farr (1989), argued that innovation may be differentiated from creativity in that the latter meets the criterion of novelty or uniqueness that transcends a group's spatial boundaries, whereas the former does not. They defined *innovation* as "the intentional introduction and application within a role, group or organization of ideas, processes, products or procedures, new to the relevant unit of adoption, designed to significantly benefit role performance, the group, the organization or the wider society" (p. 16).

Generally, when scholars have considered innovation and creativity, definitions of the former include processes of evaluation, adoption, and implementation by a particular unit (individual, dyad, group, or organization). In contrast, definitions of creativity emphasize the emergence and novelty or uniqueness of an idea, response, process, or product. Merely because something is new to a group, such as when a new decision-making procedure is used, does not necessarily mean that it is also creative within the context of that particular group. Conversely, creativity does not necessarily entail innovation; most definitions of creativity are not likely to include evaluation, adoption, and implementation components (see definitions offered by Jarboe, 1999). The view I take in this chapter is that creativity is an emergent group phenomenon; it *emerges* from how group members communicate with one another. As such, creativity cannot be *imposed* on or applied to a group, as when decision-making methods that have been employed with success elsewhere are newly adopted by group members. Such adoption is what happens with innovation. Rather, creativity emerges from group communication, although various environmental, organizational, group, and person factors may set the stage for its emergence. Thus, innovation may be thought of as involving implementation of ideas, processes, or procedures for a particular system, whereas creativity entails unique idea and knowledge generation.

West and Farr's (1989) analysis extends the novelty/uniqueness criterion of creativity. They argued that to be labeled creative, novelty should transcend spatial and temporal boundaries; that is, what one group has uniquely created is unique for all groups across space and time. The "transcendence" criterion is perhaps an untenable one, however, if only because it can never be truly known whether an idea, response, process, or product is unique across all groups. It is perhaps more reasonable to treat the uniqueness criterion as applicable to the particular group under scrutiny; that is, an idea, response, process, or product is unique if it is novel within the localized context of that group.

A related concept to creativity and innovation is learning. Most definitions of learning highlight change as a key component (e.g., Rowland, 1999); that is, an organism (individual, dyad, group, or organization) has

learned whenever it has changed in some way. Although scholars have identified different types of learning (e.g., cognitive/knowledge and behavioral/skill), the "change" criterion remains consistent across all types. Group learning, then, occurs when a *group* has changed in some way, whether that change is in the group's knowledge base, interaction patterns, or structures. Thus, change is a precursor to creativity. That is, groups must change in some way to be creative; the greater the change the greater the potential for creativity. Although learning is necessary for creativity, not all learning leads to creativity. Group creativity, for example, enables group members to manage group-relevant problems, whereas not all group learning accomplishes this goal. One further point of import: Change enables a group to develop new ideas, responses, processes, or products necessary to adapt to a fluctuating environment.

Having distinguished creativity from innovation and learning, the following definition of group creativity, a variation of Johnson and Hackman's (1995) definition, is advanced: *Creativity is a communicatively constituted and emergent process through which a group produces novel and relevant ideas, responses, processes, or products. Creativity is concerned with the generation of unique ideas, responses, processes, or products; relatively little emphasis, except as it is necessary to fulfill the relevance criterion, is placed on their evaluation and implementation.*

The components of the definition may be described as follows. First, the definition highlights the emergent nature of that which is creative. It places an emphasis on the constitution and emergence of creativity; that is, it acknowledges that communication/interaction characteristics set the stage for the production of novel and relevant ideas, responses, products, and processes, as well as being the means though which they emerge. Second, the definition includes novel ideas, responses, products, and processes. What is meant by novel is new: Creativity requires that ideas, responses, products, or processes be new/original/unique to the group being studied. Third, ideas, responses, products, or processes must be relevant to the task at hand. Presumably, individuals and groups engage in creative activity for some purpose. To the extent that ideas, responses, products, or processes generated from the creative process pertain to that purpose, they are relevant to that purpose. Finally, creativity is concerned with the *generation* (lateral interaction—equivalent to the individual-level concept, lateral thinking) of unique ideas, responses, products, or processes. Little emphasis is placed on the *evaluation* (vertical interaction—equivalent to the individual-level concept, vertical thinking) and *application* of those ideas, responses, products, or processes (Johnson & Hackman, 1995). This is not to say that new ideas do not emerge when group members evaluate ideas; clearly they do, but such ideas are likely the result of lateral processes (idea-generation processes) that take place during evaluation rather than the result of the pure process of evaluation.

The definition of creativity advanced serves three purposes. First, it delimits the concept to new idea and knowledge development by groups. Defined within the parameters of novelty and relevance, creativity is distinguished from innovation, which involves evaluation and implementation. Second, because the concept is delimited, it serves to promote theory development and research designed to understand the processes by which groups develop new ideas and knowledge, significant processes in their own right. Finally, the definition fits well with creativity as conceptualized within the sciences of complexity, a framework for understanding group creativity that is presented in the sections of the chapter that follow.

A CRITIQUE OF GROUP CREATIVITY RESEARCH

Creativity research has been conducted at the individual, group, and organizational levels. Although research has been conducted that examines each level in isolation, to the extent that individuals are found in groups and

groups are found in many organizations, the group has been the intersection point for individual and organizational creativity research. It is this intersecting work that I critique here.

Research examining individuals in groups has emphasized group composition, with the assumption that groups composed of individuals having characteristics associated with individual creativity (e.g., spontaneity, tolerance for ambiguity, and flexibility) should produce more creative solutions than groups not composed of such individuals. Research on group creativity examines the effects of directional flow, timing, frequency, or evaluative content of communication. Such studies typically compare the effects of interactional procedures, methods, agendas, and formats on increasing group creativity by reducing the inhibitory effects of the group setting or communication. Research on groups in organizations examines how organizational environments might impinge on or facilitate group creativity. Among the organizational features that have been studied are hierarchical structure, culture, climate, reward systems, surveillance, competition, and evaluation. In addition to the studies described above, some have examined the effects of group and societal structures (such as norms and rules) on group creativity (for particular articles and reviews of these approaches, the reader is directed to Amabile, 1988; Basadur, 1997; Dunbar, 1995; Hill, 1982; Hill & Amabile, 1993; Hiltz, Johnson, & Turoff, 1986; Hollingshead & McGrath, 1995; Jarboe, 1996, 1999; Kauffman, 1995; McLeod, 1996; Osborn, 1957; Salazar, 1995, 1996b; Salazar & Witte, 1996).

To the extent that they have been applied, the approaches described above have met with varying degrees of success in spurring creativity in group settings. That success, however, has been sporadic, inconsistent, and of limited use to scholars interested in examining the role of communication in group creativity. Studies examining individuals in groups have chiefly ignored the interaction that occurs between group members, primarily because the goal of such an approach is to help *individuals* in groups become more creative or, at the very least, not have their creativity stifled by the inhibitory effects of group interaction. The utility of this research for helping scholars gain an understanding of how communication serves to build environments that set the stage for creativity emergence is minimal.

Studies of groups that have employed interactive tools for stimulating creativity have not been marked by much success. Even the much-vaunted brainstorming technique, developed especially to spur group creativity, has not stood the test of empirical scrutiny. According to Parks and Sanna (1999),

> Later tests of specific elements of brainstorming found that groups do not generate as many ideas as one would expect, and that the ideas that are proposed are usually of lesser quality than are those generated by individuals. Reviews of the brainstorming literature conducted almost twenty years apart each concluded that, in fact, brainstorming simply does not work, at least not under the conditions in which this research has been conducted. (pp. 47-48)

Despite the collective evidence against using the brainstorming technique to increase group creativity, it continues to be used by managers and other practitioners, although the reasons for its continued use may perhaps be misguided (see Brophy, 1998; Parks & Sanna, 1999). Uses of the Delphi and nominal group techniques have similarly met with conflicting results (see Salazar, 1995, 1996a, 1997), as have comparisons of technology-assisted and face-to-face groups (see Scott, 1999).

For the most part, researchers have done well in identifying group structures and features that may inhibit creativity, but relatively less well in identifying those that promote it. Furthermore, attempts to implement and develop tools that *change* inhibitory group *structures and features* have been rare to nonexistent. The same may be said of organizational approaches and studies, insofar as they examine how organizational features affect *group* creativity. Finally, work on societal and cultural features that constrain or promote creativity are practically nonexistent. What is needed, then, is an approach that emphasizes the role of communication in creativity emergence and the constitution and change of the structural features that constrain and enable creative activity. I describe such an approach in the next section.

A NEW APPROACH TO CONCEPTUALIZING THE RELATIONSHIP BETWEEN GROUP COMMUNICATION AND CREATIVITY

Although the past 30 years have seen a proliferation of theories and models regarding group decision-making performance (Campion, Medsker, & Higgs, 1993; Gladstein, 1984; Gouran & Hirokawa, 1983; Hackman, 1990; Hackman & Morris, 1975; McGrath, 1964; Salas, Dickson, Converse, & Tannenbaum, 1992; Salazar, 1996a; Sundstrom, De Meuse, & Futrell, 1990), the same cannot be said about group creativity. Furthermore, effective applications of these decision-making theories and models to group creativity is dubious for two reasons. First, these theories and models generally provide limited coverage of the processes involved in idea generation; when it is mentioned, idea generation takes a back seat to idea evaluation, use of appropriate task strategies, and the selection of criteria by which alternatives will be evaluated. Such an emphasis is not unexpected because performance theories and models attempt *primarily* to explain the processes by which groups pick the best alternative(s) out of the ones available. Performance is typically assessed according to some standards or criteria, such as workability, cost, acceptability to an external audience (that is to be affected by the alternative), and/or group viability.

Second, when idea generation is addressed, it is not in a manner consistent with the development of new, novel, or original ideas. Creativity, as I conceive of it in this chapter, of necessity entails the development of new and different ideas, responses, processes, or products. Most of the works just identified make no mention of team/group synergy and how it serves to yield something *new*. When synergy *is* mentioned (see Hackman & Morris, 1975; Salazar, 1995), the processes underlying it are not clearly specified. What is needed, then, are theories and models tailored to understanding group creativity in general and its link to communication in particular. Such an approach is afforded group communication scholars by self-organizing and complex systems perspectives.

Self-Organizing Systems and the Sciences of Complexity

The *sciences of complexity* refer to an ever-expanding body of work in dynamic nonlinear feedback systems and self-organizing systems. This work has its disciplinary roots in mathematics, physics, and biology and its philosophical underpinnings in cybernetic systems theory, general systems theory, and chaos theory (if chaos can appropriately be called a theory). Some have called the development of this work the "third wave" of theoretical interest in complex systems (Simon, 1996) and the beginning of a new scientific paradigm in the Kuhnian sense (MacIntosh & MacLean, 1999). These perspectives have served as frameworks within which to try to understand the movement of stock markets, organizational change and creativity, group psychotherapy, and group change.

Given that the sciences of complexity are still in their infancy and their application to the social sciences has been sparse and varied, inconsistency in conceptualization and specification has so far reigned. There is still a great deal of confusion over what the sciences of complexity encompass, key concepts and terms that form their corpus, and whether they can be rightfully applied to social systems at all. Consequently, what I offer in this section is a culling and interpretation of the research that has been conducted on social systems under the auspices of self-organizing

systems and complexity perspectives and that also has relevance for understanding the role of communication in group creativity. What follows is a delineation of a self-organizing and complexity framework of group creativity that emphasizes particular concepts and relationships between those concepts.

Self-organization. The self-organization systems perspective examines the order that develops in systems. Here, *system* is defined as it traditionally has been in the social sciences: a collection of interdependent parts that form a coherent whole. A group, then, is a system, for it consists of interdependent parts, which have been conceptualized in various ways (e.g., as group members, behaviors, and interactions), that form a coherent whole (for an excellent discussion of the systems metaphor in the study of group communication, see Mabry, 1999). In the discussion that follows, the term "group" may be used interchangeably with "system."

Self-organization in a system may be said to occur when a system seemingly spontaneously develops new structural features and a new order after having progressed through a disruption. The disruption, called a *perturbation*, causes a crisis in the system such that it moves away from equilibrium. This movement is characterized by a display of a greater variety of behaviors than was the case when the system was functioning at, or close to, its equilibrium point. The system's behaviors may appear to lack pattern; consequently, they are labeled *chaotic*. Over time, as a system progresses through this chaotic period, these seemingly random behaviors gradually take on a more recognizable repetitive pattern, out of which a new order and equilibrium emerge. The system, at that point, is said to have organized itself; it has *emerged* from chaos with a new order.

Self-organizing systems are dynamical systems, characterized by negative and positive feedback loops. This feedback dampens some behaviors (negative feedback) and magnifies and encourages (positive feedback) others. When a system is operating in a far-from-equilibrium condition, nonlinear, as opposed to linear, dynamics predominate. When a system is characterized by linear dynamics, an input variable has a predictable effect on an output in the system because the effect is additive. In nonlinear dynamics, the effect is unpredictable precisely because it is not additive; hence, small inputs or perturbations may have large impacts because of the interdependencies within the system and because of the system's initial state. Minute variations in the initial state of the system may yield dramatically different results or outcomes (the "butterfly effect"); this is termed "sensitive dependence on initial conditions." For example, if a group differs from another in only a minute way, the same perturbation may have dramatically different effects on the groups over time such that they may look significantly different at a later point in time from when the perturbation occurred.

The point at which a system encounters a perturbation and shifts its path (or inertia) from the one it would have followed in the event of no perturbation is called the *bifurcation point*. Multiple bifurcation points may characterize a system in crisis, one affected by multiple perturbations. Each additional bifurcation moves the system farther from its original stable state and indicates an increasingly complex state of behavior in the system. Returning to an original state of stability becomes more difficult as a system encounters increasing bifurcations. At some point, the system may become so complex that its behavior is unstable and termed "chaotic." Some scholars, however, have claimed that instead of plunging completely into chaos, a system may totter between complex stability and chaos; this state of system functioning is termed the "edge of chaos."

A key to understanding the behavior of systems—and, consequently, groups—from the viewpoint of the self-organizing systems perspective, is the "space" within which the behavior occurs. "State space" describes all possible behavioral characterizations (although a system may be characterized in other ways as well) of a system. Within this state space, a system's behavior may be said to "gravitate" toward a particular area or space. This space is defined by an *attractor*, which may be characterized as an area or basin to which behavior/interactions are "pulled"; it conceptually defines a system's "range of motion" within state space. Attractors have been characterized in various ways; here, I use Marion's (1999) delineation of three types of attractors: point, periodic, and strange.

A *point attractor* describes a system at rest. It describes lack of, or relatively little, interaction. For example, depending on the phenomenon under study, a group could be described as being at rest in a variety of ways: for instance, its role system (what particular group members are supposed to do) is not characterized by any role-specific behavior, and its ethical system (what is right and wrong or good and bad) may not exhibit any movement during the group's interaction because behaviors and interactions that make up and constitute this system are not being displayed by group members. (I will say more later about how "system" is being conceptualized and how a particular collection of individuals called a "group" may be characterized by different interrelated systems.) That a group has multiple and conceptually different systems may also help explain how a group can change in one regard and not another; how it is static in one dimension and not another.

A *periodic attractor* denotes a pattern of behavior that is regular and predictable (McClure, 1998). For example, when a group exhibits behavioral patterns indicative of a routine, a periodic attractor denotes that pattern. Repeated progression through the stages of decision making specified by a rational decision-making model is an example of group behavior being defined or gravitating toward a periodic attractor.

With a *strange attractor*, on the other hand, there is a patterning of behavior, although that pattern never quite exactly repeats itself; that is, there are always slight variations in the pattern. Furthermore, as McClure (1998) pointed out, although the pattern never repeats itself, it still occurs within some boundaries. Because the behavior reflected in a strange attractor is more varied than that associated with a point or periodic attractor, there does not appear to be a readily discernible boundary or pattern to the behavior or interaction that is emerging. The "basin" within which interaction occurs is difficult to identify. However, from the viewpoint of an outsider, or in the case of a member stepping back from the group activity, some structure may be apparent, although it is complex. This type of behavior is called chaotic; chaotic behavior, contrary to popular belief, is not random but, rather, has a very complex order. It merely appears random because the behavioral pattern is so complex that it is very difficult to discern.

According to some self-organizing systems scholars, a system is sometimes "pushed" into chaos, a state of increased dynamism of the elements making up the system. As a system is pushed into chaos and then emerges from it, a new order and, in essence, a new system emerges. The structures composing the old system have dissipated and given way to new structures and new ways of functioning. The result is that the system itself has changed (see Salazar, 1995; Smith & Gemmill, 1991).

In applying the self-organizing perspective to human groups, a group may be seen as a system that progresses from a state marked by equilibrium to one marked by a new order in the following manner. A group starts out in a state of equilibrium and then encounters a disturbance or perturbation that serves as the demarcation for a bifurcation point. If a bifurcation occurs (the group changes its path), it may be followed by others (a bifurcation cascade; see Butz, 1997) that set into motion an increased dynamism that results in complex relations between the elements making up the group. The group may now be characterized as being in a far-from-equilibrium state. The exact nature of the effect of the perturbation cannot be readily predicted, and some effects will be dampened, whereas others will be magnified (the butterfly effect). Much depends on the initial state of the group when it encounters the perturbation, including the nature of the relationships between the elements composing the group. The greater the connectedness between the elements, the greater the likelihood that the perturbation will result in an avalanche of changes that will greatly affect the entire group (Lewin, 1992).

As this complexity grows, the group moves into the realm of chaos, in which behaviors/interactions appear random but are merely indicative of a complex organization that is not readily discernible to a person who observes it. Note that a group's behavior may seem chaotic as well as orderly at the same time. This is because the group "system" may be defined and identified in different ways, depending on the observer and the observational tools available (see a discussion by Dooley & Van de Ven, 1999). For example, although a group may be experiencing chaotic behaviors/interactions in its *role* system, behaviors/interactions may appear to be quite orderly in its *task* system. These systems are examined with closer scrutiny in the sections that follow, although role and task, used here for illustrative purposes, are not the terms employed.

The sciences of complexity. The sciences of complexity, as they have been applied to social systems, have their roots in many sources, especially in the work of researchers at the Santa Fe Institute in New Mexico. Many of the concepts used in the sciences of complexity perspective are by no means new. Cohen (1999) pointed out that complexity ideas have been around for awhile but that complexity theorists have put those concepts in new frameworks for understanding system behavior.

A handful of works attempt to analogue complexity and self-organizing perspectives to the small group setting (Contractor & Seibold, 1993; Contractor & Whitbread, 1997; Guastello, 1998; McClure, 1998; Smith & Comer, 1994; Smith & Gemmill, 1991; Tschacher & Brunner, 1995; Tschacher, Brunner, & Schiepek, 1992; Wheelan, 1996). In those investigations that have examined complexity specifically, there are key similarities: "Although different in the focal points, the various applications of complexity theory demonstrate the central concepts around which the subject is organized, namely the operation of nonlinear feedback on generative rules in densely interconnected, nonequilibrium systems" (MacIntosh & MacLean, 1999, p. 301).

In general, the sciences of complexity *examine the zone between order and chaos*, the point at which a system transitions to displaying a great deal of dynamism (variety in the behaviors of the elements that make up the system). Complexity, as complex adaptive systems scholars use the term, denotes a high degree of interdependence between a system's elements, as well as a high degree of variety in the behaviors of those elements. When applied to groups, systems scholars conceptualize the elements as the individual group members (more will be said about this in the discussions that follow). Complexity may result as a reaction to some perturbation in the system. That perturbation may be, for example, a crisis in the system that results in an increased dynamism as the system attempts to cope with the crisis.

Exposure to one crisis, or perturbation, however, may not be enough to shift a system into a dynamic state; it may be that repeated exposures are necessary. Bak's (1996) notion of *criticality* states that one may never know with certainty which perturbation or crisis is likely to cause this shift. It is analogous to predicting which grain of sand, on being added to a pile of sand, will cause the pile to collapse. Sooner or later, the system reaches a critical state such that a perturbation plunges it into chaos. According to complex adaptive systems (CAS) theorists, a complex system exhibits adaptive behavior that prevents it from plunging into chaos. Such a system is able to maintain a state of functioning, as it exhibits complex adaptive behavior, between order and chaos—at the edge of chaos. As I describe in the next sections, it is at this point that the potential for group creativity is enhanced.

The preceding discussion on self-organization and complexity provides only part of the picture regarding these rich perspectives and their potential for giving communication scholars a better understanding of group processes and creativity. Many terms and concepts associated with the perspectives have not received coverage here. However, the discussion contains enough "conceptual and philosophical content rather than mathematical precision which is the key to" (Stacey, 1995, p. 485) understanding how self-organizing and complexity perspectives might inform the development of theory regarding group communication and creativity.

SETTING THE AGENDA: A COMPLEXITY VIEW OF COMMUNICATION AND CREATIVITY IN GROUPS

Dooley and Van de Ven (1999) explained the shortcomings of current applications of the complexity perspective to organizations by claiming that those applications focus on discussing the implications of such a perspective and do not seek out the generative mechanisms of chaos:

> Through the discovery of such generative mechanisms, we can begin to postulate how changes in specific organizational variables might affect the dynamics of the system. Such knowledge can help us explain the past, predict the future, and develop interventionist strategies (Glick et al. 1990; Pettigrew, 1990; Van de Ven & Poole, 1990). (Dooley & Van de Ven, 1999, p. 358)

Although Dooley and Van de Ven specify that researchers should concentrate on identifying the generative mechanisms for chaotic behavior, here, I wish to identify the generative mechanisms for complexity—that is, the increased dynamism, complex behavior, and adaptive state of a system before it plunges into chaos. *The key postulate of this chapter is that the potential for truly creative activity and adaptation is enhanced when a group (a) has emerged from chaos and established a new order (it has changed) or (b) is in a complex state (it is a complex adaptive system).* When a group has emerged from chaos with a *new order,* it has supplanted prior ways of doing things; its members have participated in the process of change and developed new mental models (Senge, 1990). When faced with tasks that necessitate creativity, group members bring to bear these new mental models. Creativity, in the sense of the emergence of new and relevant ideas, responses, processes, and products, *is* the likely result of this application. However, a group that has undergone such change may at a future time face problems with adaptation and creativity because structures and mental models that helped it cope with perturbations in a past environment may be inappropriately applied to a future, changed, environment.

Stacey (1995), explaining innovation in organizations operating in a complex state, at the *edge of chaos,* claimed that systems with well-established structural features (stability), or in chaos, are

> not inherently changeable or continuously innovative. Such organizations cannot be producing anything new because that which is truly new is by definition not in the past or the present and so is unpredictable. To be internally and spontaneously changeable and innovative, a nonlinear feedback system has to operate . . . at the edge of instability. (pp. 485-486)

Some groups operate in highly stable environments in which members' behavior is enacted according to previously established structures (norms, rules, rituals). This behavior is enacted to maintain a low level of anxiety. Lack of anxiety, however, "results in a zone of behavior that is highly stable but in which double-loop learning, the creative process, is impossible" (Stacey, 1996, p. 145). At the other extreme, a highly unstable group, characterized by dispersed power, unstructured decision making, and an atmosphere in which members freely and openly voice feelings and opinions about others, promotes "conflictual behavior in which decisions are haphazard and what is learned depends primarily on chance" (Stacey, 1996, p. 143).

In between these two extremes lies a zone in which group members are free to advance and play with ideas, analogies are commonplace, defensive behavior is kept to a minimum, and information is used and tested. In this zone, statements of ambiguity and provisionalism abound. The space between stability and instability—the edge of chaos—is where learning and creativity take place. It is this space that I examine in the sections that follow. The task of communication scholars interested in understanding group creativity lies in identifying those generative mechanisms that promote, result in, and maintain complexity. To identify those generative mechanisms, it is first necessary to understand the systemic mechanisms that inhibit change and complexity in groups.

Stable Group Systems: Communicatively Constructed Inhibitors of Change and Creativity

According to Stacey (1995), two types of group characteristics inhibit creativity: those group characteristics that promote stability and those that promote instability. Those characteristics that promote stability inhibit creativity because they allow group members to do things in the same ways they have been doing them; those that promote instability inhibit creativity because they encourage haphazard group decision making. I cast these inhibitors from a communication perspective and focus especially on those inhibitors whose locus lies in group stability.

A small group may be conceived as being composed of various interaction systems, the nature of which is defined by patterns of communicative activity (see Fisher & Hawes, 1971; Tschacher et al., 1992). From this perspective, the elements of a system are the communicative activities that take place between and among group members. These activities may be acts (an utterance on the part of one group member, such as a question) or interacts (a sequentially connected pair of acts, such as question-reply). Conceptualizing a system in this way allows the examination of a communicatively emergent system and its structural properties. These properties are named on the basis of a researcher's focus, theoretical orientation, research question, and coding system, as well as the recurring patterns of communicative activity. Among these properties are norms, roles, rules, power, decision-making procedures, and cohesion.

Here I would like to distinguish between four different systems or clusters of conceptually and functionally related activities; these activities relate to one another in particular ways that serve to denote the character of the system we call a group. The systems are inherently intertwined yet conceptually distinct. Each is also created, maintained, and re-created through group members' interacting with one another. Each system must be understood to obtain a full understanding of groups (Warriner, 1984) and group creativity (as an analogue, see Normann's, 1971, discussion of product development and how it is affected by task, cognitive, and political systems in an organization). In aggregate, these four systems form the *suprasystem*, a term that describes the totality of the group.

Each system is self-organized in the sense that organization is not imposed on the group from the outside; that is, environmental factors do not directly account for the unique pattern and character of the system, although such factors may generally shape the landscape in which the system becomes self-organized. No one, for example, directly organizes the unique pattern and character of a group's relational system (how group members relate to one another) and its associated structural property of cohesion—both emerge on the basis of how group members interact and relate with one another.

To the extent environmental factors do affect organization, it is through group members' interpretation and tacitly held knowledge of those factors and members' use of those interpretations and knowledge in interaction. Poole, Seibold, and McPhee (1985) illustrated the point in their discussion of the impact of exogenous factors on group decision making:

Thus far we have not considered conditions the group faces "from the outside"—environmental constraints or tasks—as influences on decisional structuration. It is clear, however, that exogenous factors are critical in the life of any group. The term "exogenous factors" is perhaps misleading, because it denotes influences which exist prior to and outside of interaction. Such conditions can never be simply "imposed" on a group. Rather, the group's view of factors such as the nature of the group task, the membership and size of the group, and so forth are negotiated over time within the group in light of its interpretation and outside influences. (p. 88)

From a CAS perspective, as group interaction unfolds, it provides the context for future interaction (see Contractor & Whitbred, 1997); what has come before influences what will follow. Evolving interaction patterns and, consequently, group relations, power differentials, and so forth set the context for subsequent interaction and the emergence of the unique pattern and character of the group systems.

The first system I wish to identify is the *structural system*. This system is composed of the individuals who make up the group and are connected to one another through their various interactions. Through their interactions, they become interdependent. Typically, indications of the pattern and character of the structural system include direction and frequency of talk. This system may be thought of as analogous to a communication network (Shaw, 1981), which is denoted by "who talks to whom and with what frequency." The structural system changes when directional flow and/or frequency of communication change and also may be affected by new members coming into and others leaving a group.

The second system is the *technical system*. This system provides group members a template from which to proceed in working on the task. It is grounded in members' conceptions of how work should be done—the procedures that ought to be followed and when they should be followed. These conceptions are guided by the technical system's structural properties (e.g., norms and rules). The particular structural properties embedded in the technical system may vary from task to task. Hence, for example, when confronted with a decision-making task (McGrath, 1984), group members may be guided by a structural property embedded in the technical system that generates a rational decision-making sequence. That sequence may take this form: problem analysis→criteria development→solution development→solution evaluation→choice. Variations on this sequence (indicating qualitatively different structural properties) may be enacted by a given group working on a decision-making task (see Poole & Roth, 1989), but even those variations are a part of the group's technical system in the sense that they specify how to proceed with work on the task. Structural properties embedded in the technical system, for a particular task, are probably universal for a given cultural grouping and are probably quite stable regardless of group composition.

The third system is the *relational system.* This system describes group members' ties with one another and specifies particular roles in a group as well as the interdependence of those roles. This system is *generally* not explicit in the sense that each member of a group is not *assigned* a role and a label describing each role is not explicitly identified and attached to individuals. Here, I conceptualize roles to be influenced by the expectations group members have about the behavior to be demonstrated by other group members. These expectations emerge primarily on the basis of group members' previously enacted behavior in the group setting. These expectations, in turn, are guided by structural properties (who says what, to whom, and when) embedded in the relational system. As with all the systems described here, the nature of the relational system is deduced on the basis of how group members interact with one another (Salazar, 1996b).

The fourth system is the *information system.* This system refers to interactions that reflect the assumptions the group makes or has made about what is preferred, right, correct,

and decent. The structural properties making up this system serve as guides for testing and giving weight to information to determine whether it will have relevance for further discussion. These assumptions may not always be manifest in discussion and may very well be latent in the content of group members' interactions.

The final system is what I have termed the *suprasystem.* It consists of the previously discussed systems in aggregate. When considered together, the total group may be described as having *syntality* (Cattell, 1948), or a personality. Once again, each of these four systems and, consequently, the suprasystem, is created and re-created in group members' interaction with one another. From each of these systems flow structural properties (e.g., norms and rules) that guide, constrain, and give boundary to group members' interaction. The structural properties of these four systems, because they are rules and norms that guide members' behavior and interaction, serve as attractors for the suprasystem; that is, they define the "basin" or boundaries within which interaction occurs.

For example, embedded in the relational system are structural properties that inform and guide members' interaction concerning how they are to relate to one another; embedded in the information system are structural properties that inform and guide members' behavior and interaction concerning what counts as useful information. Because structural properties are attractors, behavior and interaction made manifest in a group tends to gravitate toward, or is consistent with, the structural properties of the systems. To the extent that a group is not operating in a complex state but, rather, a stable state, these structural properties both (a) enable behavior and interaction consistent with previously established patterns and (b) constrain and bound behavior and interaction. Therefore, in the face of changing group environments and pressures for creativity, these properties inhibit group change, adaptation, and creativity. The question, then, becomes one of how to change the nature of these systems and their associated structural properties such that a group is better able to adapt to a changing environment; this, in essence, is a question of identifying the generative mechanisms for complexity. Because these systems and their structural properties are created and maintained communicatively, they may also be changed communicatively. But what might a complex group look like? I attempt to answer this question in the following section.

The Complex Group

If a group is to be conceptualized as a complex adaptive system, what might it look like? Sherman and Schultz (1998) provided insight into an answer by applying the CAS metaphor to business organizations:

> This organization would undoubtedly be less rigid, with a greatly reduced command-type hierarchic structure. The communications would be more diffuse, less top to bottom and bottom to top. There would be more people talking to one another—whether peer-to-peer or between different levels—about more things. It would also be more "scientific" in the way it goes about organizing its inquiries and evaluating alternatives, with a much greater openness to the understanding of its own vocabularies and ideologies. It would always be open to new formulations to the extent that new formulations are more adequate. Businesses have been stuck in notions of their key behaviors, which go back unchanged to much earlier periods of time. A business as a complex adaptive system would recognize that these behaviors are no longer adequate or realistic in relation to concerns that have emerged in today's world. (p. 156)

In a complex group, information flow and evaluation of ideas is promoted, political games are virtually nonexistent, and members are cognizant of systemic properties and how those properties might shape interaction, decisions, and relationships. A complex adaptive system maintains the ability to "create structures that fit the moment. . . . The system possesses the capacity for spontaneously emerging structures depending on what is required" (Wheatley, 1994, pp. 90-91). In a complex group, there is not a free-for-all flavor to member contributions; there is some structure to those contributions. Stacey (1996) described the activities that take place in a complex group as characterized by "bounded instability." A group that is not in a complex state or that fails to change its systems (as indicated by changes in the structural properties embedded in those systems) in response to a changing environment will not be creative.

In a complex group, information exchange is freer and more likely to be diverse than that exchanged in a noncomplex group. As a result, creativity is likely to be enhanced because a group will likely not suffer from the *conceptual inertia* (Ward, Smith, & Vaid, 1997), functional fixedness, and/or psychological set that are present in noncomplex systems. With complexity, a group's information base and ways of looking at the world have been *fundamentally* altered. The result is that information exchange will be substantially different or information will be treated differently than would be the case if the group was not complex. The question, then, becomes, how groups achieve and maintain states of complexity. In the next section, I identify and describe the roles of communication in generating a complex group state.

Communication and the Generative Mechanisms of Complexity in Groups

Some scholars have questioned whether a process such as creativity can be promoted by group interventions (see Kao, 1991). The view that self-organization may be induced in a group also seems self-contradictory. However, this is precisely the view taken by scholars and practitioners of the CAS perspective who have discussed its utility in achieving various group and organizational outcomes such as change and creativity. Often, group interventions employed to promote group creativity fall short of producing the types of group environments and contexts that embrace, and provide fertile ground for, creativity. What is needed, then, are new group conceptualizations and intervention tools for promoting complexity. For some new types of intervention tools, see Sunwolf, this volume) Levinthal and Warglien (1999) elucidated this point in discussing self-organizing processes:

> While processes of self-organization are powerful, they do not negate the possibility of design influences. They do, however, suggest that a new set of design tools or concepts may be useful. Self-organizing processes depend on the context in which they arise. By manipulating the context, one may indirectly influence the dynamics of the process. . . . The underlying idea is that by designing the surface on which adaptation processes take place, one may affect the quality of the adaptive process without the need to specify directly individual behavior. (p. 342)

I contend that to promote group creativity, one must first conceptualize and then employ communication strategies, tools, or interventions that build group contexts suitable for the emergence of creative activity. That is, what is needed are conceptualizations of how communication is at once used to *create* the conditions for the emergence of creativity as well as being the mechanism *through* which it emerges. Such conceptualizations are provided by self-organizing and complexity perspectives.

Schultz (1999) claimed that an intervention process consists of "facilitators, consultants, or group members with insight into effective group process . . . suggest[ing] potential remedies for altering the internal dynamics of a group" (pp. 371-372). A group intervention, then, involves the implementation of these remedies. Interventions designed to construct the group conditions for creativity emergence are likely to fail primarily because they entail change from the established, and perhaps habitual, ways of doing things (see Gersick & Hackman, 1990). Ford (1996) argued that "creative actions will be for-

saken regardless of the favorable conditions, as long as habitual actions remain attractive" (p. 1113).

The influence of systemic structural properties is instantiated in the group setting when members appropriate norms and rules as they interact with fellow group members. Sometimes group members are aware of such appropriation and instantiation, but most of the time they are not. These structural properties serve, more often than not, as tacit stocks of knowledge that guide group members' behavior and interaction. It is this general lack of awareness by group members that makes these structural properties especially difficult to tackle or alter in promoting group change and creativity (see Agazarian, 1997; Ford, 1996; MacIntosh & MacLean, 1999; Svyantek & DeShon, 1993/1994).

Another characteristic of these properties that makes them especially difficult to alter is their strength, or the degree to which they have become engrained in a group. In some groups, particular practices and, therefore, patterns of interaction, may have become so engrained that they become routine. Consequently, the systems giving rise to the structural properties guiding the production of these patterns have become a defining feature of the group; they are part of what the group is. It is not surprising, then, that these structural properties, and the systems in which they are embedded, are more difficult to change than ones that are not so engrained or central to defining a group. In the face of engrained structural properties, in instances in which group members' behavior/interaction is fairly well prescribed by structural properties, one may question how to go about achieving change if change is necessitated. Initially, an answer is to introduce perturbations into the group to potentially create instability within the group. Subsequently, communicative activities should revolve around the bifurcation-bifurcation cascade-complexity sequence proposed by Butz (1997). I now turn to possible ways in which communication may come into play in this sequence.

Ambiguity as generative mechanism: The language of learning. The role of communication in introducing perturbations into a group and, thereby, setting up the potential for bifurcation points, cannot be underestimated. Perturbations may have relevance for a particular system (e.g., structural, technical, relational, or information) or implicate more than one. A statement that challenges a leader's established authority to assign duties to group members, for example, has perhaps more relevance for the relational system than for the technical and information systems, although all three may be implicated in such a statement. Such a perturbation, then, has the potential to propel a group toward change. Whether the perturbation initiates a path toward change in the implicated system depends on whether it is amplified or dampened in group members' interaction; that is, it depends of the nature of group members' feedback. However, to introduce perturbations into one or more of a group's systems, one or more group members should, in some sense, identify, or have knowledge of, how the systems work (MacIntosh & MacLean, 1999; see also Gersick & Hackman, 1990). More will be said about introducing perturbation later in this section.

Ambiguity, then, is introduced into the group setting when members' statements, manifestly or latently, question, reinterpret, or propose alternatives to the structural properties inherent in a system. Such statements increase the options available to members; they now have different assumptions, information, and ideas with which to potentially work (Salazar, 1996a). To the extent that such assumptions, information, and ideas are not dampened but, rather, are amplified and extended, ambiguity serves to increase group learning and change. Ambiguity in the group setting helps the group to develop and establish "sufficient diversity and complexity . . . that [aid] it in meeting the diversity and complexity of an environment" (Smith & Comer, 1994, p. 558). Wheatley (1994) further explained the role of ambiguity in promoting innovation and generating knowledge:

> Innovation arises from ongoing circles of exchange where information is not just accumulated or stored, but created. Knowledge is generated anew from connections that weren't there before. When information self-organizes, innovations occur, the progeny of information-rich, ambiguous environments. (p. 113)

Group members' identification of the systems, and their associated structural properties, is neither sufficient nor necessary to introduce statements containing information that serves to perturb the systems. Perturbations, however, are introduced less haphazardly when the systems have been identified. Gaining knowledge of the systems may be facilitated by discussions about the assumptions that group members make as they conduct meetings. The goal of such interaction is to bring to light what may have been tacit assumptions; knowledge of these assumptions facilitates adaptation within the context of what the group "is" and what has come before. Change and adaptation in a group, then, is not random but generally proceeds in a manner that is consistent with the integrity of the group. Thus, a group is able to adapt while still maintaining a sense of self and history. Such adaptation is referred to as "self-referential" (Smith & Comer, 1994; Wheatley, 1994).

Bringing in trained consultants (Gersick & Hackman, 1990; MacIntosh & MacLean, 1999) or having a group member play devil's advocate are two other methods that may be used to identify the systems. Group composition may also influence identification of how the group systems work and, therefore, the likelihood that perturbations will be introduced. Groups composed of diverse members—members with knowledge and experience of *different* societies/cultures, organizations, and groups—likely will be more sensitive to how the influences of a system's structural properties are played out, and these members are in a better position to help the group in terms of introducing perturbations that have the potential to change the influence of these properties. Diversity, because of the ambiguity it introduces, is a key driver of a system to the edge of chaos. Homogeneity, on the other hand, may promote stability (Kauffman, 1993), which inhibits creativity.

An ambiguous group context, in the form of multiple perturbations to the systems, is a key to setting up the conditions under which complexity emerges. Once a perturbation has been introduced, others may follow, setting up a cascade of bifurcations. Whether the cascade occurs, however, depends on whether group members' feedback dampens or amplifies the perturbations. Understanding group members' timing and use of feedback strategies, especially those of the group's leader, is essential to understanding how perturbations are amplified and extended, and how a group's path, once filled with structural inertia, bifurcates.

Leadership as generative mechanism: Systemic thinking, sensitivity to nuance, and process amplification. All group members can and, when given the opportunity, probably should influence the amplification and extension of perturbations to each of the group's four systems. By amplification, I mean that a group is able to focus on a perturbation and ensure that it does not become lost in interaction by being dampened or dismissed entirely. Extension requires that group members, once focused on a perturbation, elaborate on it and that the structural properties and assumptions underlying it are embedded into the system(s) to which it pertains; the structural properties inherent in the perturbation replace or supplement the existing structural properties of the group system and influence, in some way, "how things are done." For example, if a group member who has consistently played the role of "tension releaser" in times of group conflict, introduces a piece of useful information (the introduction is uncharacteristic of his or her role) for accomplishing the group task, rather than dismissing

the information, members should focus on and use it in their discussion. To the extent that the information introduced by this group member is used repeatedly, the relational system is changed; the member's role in the group is also changed. In this section. I focus on processes by which members are brought to focus on perturbations—the amplification of perturbations.

Of the members in a group, the leader, when one has emerged or been assigned, is perhaps in a position of leverage when it comes to amplifying perturbations. As McClure (1998) explained,

> The group leader facilitates, supports, and at times, guides a process. His [or her] skills in building a safe environment, nurturing relationships and fostering communications create the milieu in which group members organize themselves. In a literal sense, the leader "creates the space" in which the group works. (p. 82)

A group leader is in an especially important position to influence the group context as it unfolds through interaction. A group's leader, then, has a significant role to play in shaping the emergence of group complexity.

A group leader's effectiveness in focusing the group on perturbations in an effort to shape the space within which the group works is facilitated if he or she possesses several abilities. First, a leader who is effective in shaping the space for creativity is *sensitive to nuance* (McClure, 1998). Such a leader is able to detect points of possible transition in the group, as well as sense subtle and latent meanings in interaction—to recognize a perturbation as such; that is, a leader who is sensitive to nuance is able to assess when there has occurred a "disturbance in the force." Second, it is helpful if a leader is a *systemic thinker;* that is, the group leader must be attuned to each of the group's four systems, as well as to the group as a whole (see Boscolo, Cecchin, Hoffman, & Penn, 1987). Rather than being focused on individual statements or relationships, a systemic thinker is able to place those comments and relationships in the broader group context. Such a leader is able to assess the implications of relationships and statements for each of the group's systems.

Finally, a group leader who is effectively able to shape the space for group creativity has considerable rhetorical skill. If creativity is to be nurtured by a leader with rhetorical skill, process amplification (McClure, 1998) becomes important. To the extent that the leader is able to draw connections between ideas proposed (perturbations) and their implications for the group, he or she is able to *focus* the group on a new idea (perturbation), once introduced, so that it is not lost in structural inertia, the shuffle of group work, or the mire of political games. A group leader, for example, is able to tell an interesting story that serves as a metaphor for an idea that promotes member interest in and understanding of that idea. Regardless of the rhetorical strategy used, the leader is able to ensure that an idea believed to be essential and relevant to the purpose of the group and, at the same time, potentially threatening to the established ways of doing things (structural properties), is not simply dismissed. Importantly, the leader amplifies perturbations by providing direction to a group's interaction without being directive—by giving focus without being controlling. In short, the rhetorically skilled leader is able to illumine the possibilities without imposing them on the group. As a leader illumines the possibilities, he or she opens up new paths for a group. As the group proceeds down a chosen path, other possibilities are illumined.

Metaphor as generative mechanism: Extending the perturbation. Once a leader, or other group member(s), has introduced a perturbation, its significance for promoting change in one or more of the systems has been assessed, and it has received focus so that it was not lost in interaction or dismissed after being introduced, group members must then assess its usefulness for the group; that is, group members decide whether they will accept it and use it in further discussion or discard it. If used in further discussion, the struc-

tural features (assumptions) associated with the perturbation may become part of the structural properties that make up one or more of the four group systems. The result of that process is change in one or more of the systems. In short, the group has extended the perturbation; the perturbation has opened up and helped to place the group on a new path. There are several strategies open to members in extending perturbations, but perhaps one takes on special importance in the study of groups because it has been studied in a complexity context: the use of metaphor.

Attractors, as I have described earlier, give boundaries to the patterns toward which behavior gravitates in systems. Some attractors are stable, some are periodically stable, and others seem unstable. What counts as an attractor has been conceptualized in different ways, depending on the system under study. Personality has been advanced as an attractor for individual behavior, organizational culture has been advanced as an attractor for organizational behavior, and metaphor has been advanced as an attractor for group behavior (McClure, 1998). Here, I have conceptualized the structural properties embedded in each of the four group systems as attractors for behavior.

Metaphor, as McClure (1998) used the term, represents "words, analogies, nonverbal expressions, and stories in which thoughts and feelings about an emotionally charged situation have been transferred to an analogical situation that preserves the original dynamics" (p. 148). Engaging in group metaphor is analogous to sharing fantasies or engaging in storytelling, which group members do to "communicate situational difficulties, indicate group resistance, confront group leaders, confront group members, reveal personal identities, promote insight, and provide future direction for the group" (p. 148). Members may also "share fantasies about more specific details related to problem solving, such as the nature of sound evidence, about good reasons, and about ways to make decisions" (Bormann, 1996, p. 106). Metaphor, then, serves as a vehicle for the latent manifestation of structural properties. Through metaphor, group members convey what they believe to be true and how things should be done.

Group metaphor, storytelling, or fantasy sharing are especially useful for extending perturbations. There are three reasons this is so. First, metaphor diffuses a potentially threatening situation. Because perturbations to a group system are a potential threat to the accepted way of doing things, a group using metaphor "moves to the latent level, attempting to distance itself from the affect while working to resolve issues" (McClure, 1998, p. 152). Second, metaphor is often able to convey information, ideas, and solutions in ways that promote understanding that manifest interaction is unable to. Metaphor moves ideas and information to the world of experiences. Third, the use of metaphor often results in increased likelihood of group-as-a-whole involvement in extending the perturbation. Bormann (1996), for example, described fantasy chaining as the process that unfolds as group members chime in with their own stories after hearing someone else in the group initiate one. When group members add their own stories to that of another, perturbations are extended and introduced into a group and, thereby, set up a potential cascade of bifurcations.

In essence, metaphor helps to create a climate that welcomes, if not embraces, opposing viewpoints. The establishment of such a climate is important for extending perturbations. Alderton and Frey (1983) made a similar claim in their discussion of group consideration of minority arguments, which may be considered a perturbation: "What is most important is to develop a climate within a group which encourages positive consideration of minority arguments" (p. 95).

In summary, a group that is in a stable state, at equilibrium, will likely not engage in the creative activity necessary to adapt to a fluctuating environment. To be truly creative, a system must be moved to a far-from-equilibrium condition. Such a condition is denoted by complexity. To bring about complexity, a system must be perturbed in some way. Perturba-tion, however, is not enough to set into motion a cascade of events that send a group into a complex state. The perturbation potential to move it into a complex state must be assessed by group members, and if that potential is judged to be the case, must be focused on and elaborated. To amplify and elaborate the perturbation, group members need several skills; in particular, the assigned or emergent leader is in a position of high leverage to focus the group, and making use of metaphor is a useful strategy to employ in elaborating on the perturbation so that it sets the group on a different path from the one that had been specified by its structural properties. As a group journeys down this different path, other paths become apparent as the group experiences yet more perturbations. These bifurcations (divergence into new paths) serve to bring the group to a complex state of dynamic behavior. It is this complex behavior that provides the milieu for the emergence of creativity.

CONCLUSION

A complexity approach to group creativity is a rich perspective that offers a number of implications and directions for guiding group communication and creativity research. I have attempted to provide a picture of the emergence of creativity from this perspective. Clearly, there are other ways of casting the role of communication in the emergence and maintenance of complexity, as well as casting the important research questions resulting from a complexity framework. The most pressing issues for scholars employing a complexity perspective probably concern research methods, system change, amplification and extension strategies, and effects of ambiguity and uncertainty on group members.

Issues concerning research methods revolve around refinement of conceptualizations of complexity in groups and how it differs qualitatively and quantitatively from stability and chaos. As a result, measures for assessing all three states have to be developed. Numerous measures of complexity have been proposed in a variety of contexts, but measures for assessing the level of complexity in groups are lacking. A related problem is that of assessing group change. Although change may be indicated by new patterns of group interaction, the problem comes when attempting to ascertain whether a group has undergone sufficient and relevant change to affect outcomes, such as creativity. Measures of change will have to be refined enough to capture subtle changes in behavior that may have a great impact on outcomes. Another problem concerns assessing the multisystematic nature of group interaction. Interaction, as has been discussed earlier, may implicate one or more of the four group systems. The challenge, then, is determining which system's structural properties are being changed by changing interaction patterns.

I have attempted to give suggestions regarding the use of metaphor (storytelling and fantasy sharing) as a strategy that might be employed by group members in amplifying and extending perturbations. One question that needs to be asked, however, is whether different strategies would prove more effective given that the perturbation relates more to one system (say, the technical) than to another (the relational). As well, Miller (1998) has identified some of the dangers in introducing ambiguity, uncertainty, and autonomy into a social system with the hope of instilling self-organization among its members. Members of the organization she studied, who experienced such facilitation, felt high levels of confusion, anxiety, and stress. It may very well be that a high tolerance for ambiguity among group members is necessary to implement such interventions with success. Alternatively, guidance during the process of self-organization on the part of leaders and process experts, without being directive or controlling in the unfolding of the self-organization, may help mitigate, to a certain degree, the confusion, anxiety, and stress felt by members.

These, then, are some of the important issues that need investigation when taking a complexity perspective to the study of the link between communication and creativity emer-gence in groups. Clearly, there are other issues, and they will emerge in future investigations. Ultimately, the utility of this approach will be determined by the extent to which it promotes understanding of small group processes, especially as they concern communication and creativity.

REFERENCES

Ackoff, R. L., & Vergara, E. (1988). Creativity in problem-solving and planning. In R. L. Kuhn (Ed.), *Handbook for creative and innovative managers* (pp. 77-89). New York: McGraw-Hill.

Agazarian, Y. M. (1997). *Systems-centered therapy for groups.* New York: Guilford Press.

Alderton, S. M., & Frey, L. R. (1983). Effects of reactions to arguments on group outcome: The case of group polarization. *Central States Speech Journal, 34,* 88-95.

Amabile, T. M. (1988). A model of creativity and innovation in organizations. In B. M. Straw & L. L. Cummings (Eds.), *Research in organizational behavior* (Vol. 10, pp. 123-167). Greenwich, CT: JAI Press.

Bak, P. (1996). *How nature works: The science of self-organized criticality.* New York: Copernicus.

Basadur, M. (1997). Organizational development interventions for enhancing creativity in the workplace. *Journal of Creative Behavior, 31,* 59-72.

Bormann, E. G. (1996). Symbolic convergence theory and communication in group decision making. In R. Y. Hirokawa & M. S. Poole (Eds.), *Communication and group decision making* (2nd ed., pp. 81-111). Thousand Oaks, CA: Sage.

Boscolo, L., Cecchin, G., Hoffman, L., & Penn, P. (1987). *Milan systemic family therapy: Conversations in theory and practice.* New York: Basic Books.

Brophy, D. R. (1998). Understanding, measuring and enhancing collective creative problem-solving efforts. *Creativity Research Journal, 11,* 199-229.

Butz, M. R. (1997). *Chaos and complexity: Implications for psychological theory and practice.* Washington, DC: Taylor & Francis.

Campion, M. A., Medsker, G. J., & Higgs, A. C., (1993). Relations between work group characteristics and effectiveness: Implications for designing effective work groups. *Personnel Psychology, 46,* 823-850.

Cattell, R. B. (1948). Concepts and methods in the measurement of group syntality. *Psychological Monographs, 55,* 48-63.

Cohen, M. (1999). Commentary on the *Organization Science* special issue on complexity. *Organization Science, 10,* 373-376.

Contractor, N. S., & Seibold, D. R. (1993). Theoretical frameworks for the study of structuring processes in group decision support systems: Adaptive structuration theory and self-organizing systems theory. *Human Communication Research, 19,* 528-563.

Contractor, N. S., & Whitbread, R. C. (1997). Decision development in work groups: A comparison of contingency and self-organizing systems perspectives. In G. A. Barnett & L. Thayer (Eds.), *Organization <---> communication: Emerging Perspectives V The renaissance in systems thinking* (pp. 83-104). Greenwich, CT: Ablex.

Dooley, K. J., & Van de Ven, A. H. (1999). Explaining complex organizational dynamics. *Organization Science, 10,* 358-372.

Dunbar, K. (1995). How scientists really reason: Scientific reasoning in real-world laboratories. In R. J. Sternberg & J. E. Davidson (Eds.), *The nature of insight* (pp. 365-396). Cambridge: MIT Press.

Fisher, B. A., & Hawes, L. C. (1971). An interact system model: Generating a grounded theory of small groups. *Quarterly Journal of Speech, 57,* 444-453.

Ford, C. M. (1996). A theory of individual creative action in multiple social domains. *Academy of Management Review, 21,* 1112-1142.

Gersick, C. J. G., & Hackman, J. R. (1990). Habitual routines in task-performing groups. *Organizational Behavior and Human Decision Processes, 47,* 65-97.

Gladstein, D. L. (1984). Groups in context: A model of task group effectiveness. *Administrative Science Quarterly, 29,* 499-517.

Gleick, J. (1999). *Faster: The acceleration of just about everything.* New York: Pantheon.

Gouran, D. S., & Hirokawa, R. Y. (1983). The role of communication in decision-making groups: A functional perspective. In M. S. Mander (Ed.), *Communications in transition: Issues and debates in current research* (pp. 168-185). New York: Praeger.

Guastello, S. J. (1998). Creative problem solving groups at the edge of chaos. *Journal of Creative Behavior, 32,* 38-57.

Hackman, J. R. (1990). *Groups that work (and those that don't): Creating conditions for effective teamwork.* San Francisco: Jossey-Bass.

Hackman, J. R., & Morris, C. G. (1975). Group tasks, group interaction process, and group performance effectiveness: A review and proposed integration. In L. Berkowitz (Ed.), *Advances in experimental social psychology* (Vol. 8, pp. 45-99). New York: Academic Press.

Hill, G. W. (1982). Group versus individual performance: Are $N + 1$ heads better than one? *Psychological Bulletin, 91,* 517-539.

Hill, K. G., & Amabile, T. M. (1993). A social psychological perspective on creativity: Intrinsic motivation and creativity in the classroom and workplace. In S. G. Isaksen, M. C. Murdock, R. L. Firestein, & D. J. Treffinger (Eds.), *Understanding and recognizing creativity: The emergence of a discipline* (pp. 400-453). Norwood, NJ: Ablex.

Hiltz, S. R., Johnson, K., & Turoff, M. (1986). Experiments in group decision making: Communication process and outcome in face-to-face versus computerized conferences. *Human Communication Research, 13,* 225-252.

Hollingshead, A. B., & McGrath, J. E. (1995). Computer-assisted groups: A critical review of the empirical research. In R. Guzzo & E. Salas (Eds.), *Team effectiveness and decision making in organizations* (pp. 46-78). San Francisco: Jossey-Bass.

Jarboe, S. (1996). Procedures for enhancing group decision making. In R. Y. Hirokawa & M. S. Poole (Eds.), *Communication and group decision making* (2nd ed., pp. 345-383). Thousand Oaks, CA: Sage.

Jarboe, S. (1999). Group communication and creativity processes. In L. R. Frey (Ed.), D. S. Gouran, & M. S. Poole (Assoc. Eds.), *The handbook of group communication theory & research* (pp. 335-368). Thousand Oaks, CA: Sage.

Johnson, C. E., & Hackman, M. Z. (1995). *Creative communication: Principles and applications.* Prospect Heights, IL: Waveland Press.

Kao, J. J. (1991). *Managing creativity.* Englewood Cliffs, NJ: Prentice Hall.

Kauffman, S. (1993). *Origins of order: Self-organization and selection in evolution.* Oxford, UK: Oxford University Press.

Kauffman, S. (1995). *At home in the universe: The search for the laws of self-organization and complexity.* New York: Oxford University Press.

Levinthal, D. A., & Warglien, M. (1999). Landscape design: Designing for local action in complex worlds. *Organization Science, 10,* 342-357.

Lewin, R. (1992). *Complexity: Life at the edge of chaos.* New York: Macmillan.

Mabry, E. A. (1999). The system's metaphor in group communication. In L. R. Frey (Ed.), D. S. Gouran, & M. S. Poole (Assoc. Eds.), *The handbook of group communication theory & research* (pp. 71-91). Thousand Oaks, CA: Sage.

MacIntosh, R., & MacLean, D. (1999). Conditioned emergence: A dissipative structures approach to transformation. *Strategic Management Journal, 20,* 297-316.

Marion, R. (1999). *The edge of organization: Chaos and complexity theories of formal social systems.* Thousand Oaks, CA: Sage.

McClure, B. A. (1998). *Putting a new spin on groups: The science of chaos.* Mahwah, NJ: Lawrence Erlbaum.

McGrath, J. E. (1964). *Social psychology: A brief introduction.* New York: Holt, Rinehart & Winston.

McGrath, J. E. (1984). *Groups: Interaction and performance.* Englewood Cliffs, NJ: Prentice Hall.

McLeod, P. M. (1996). New communication technologies for group decision making. In R. Y. Hirokawa & M. S. Poole (Eds.), *Communication and group decision making* (2nd ed., pp. 426-461). Thousand Oaks, CA: Sage.

Miller, K. (1998). Nurses at the edge of chaos: Application of "new science" concepts to organizational systems. *Management Communication Quarterly, 12,* 112-127.

Normann, R. (1971). Organizational innovativeness: Product variation and reorientation. *Administrative Science Quarterly, 16,* 203-215.

Osborn, A. F. (1957). *The applied imagination: Principles and procedures of creative problem-solving.* New York: Scribner.

Parks, C. D., & Sanna, L. J. (1999). *Group performance and interaction.* Boulder, CO: Westview Press.

Poole, M. S., & Roth, J. (1989). Decision development in small groups: IV. A typology of group decision paths. *Human Communication Research, 15,* 323-356.

Poole, M. S., Seibold, D. R., & McPhee, R. D. (1985). Group decision-making as a structurational process. *Quarterly Journal of Speech, 71,* 74-102.

Rowland, G. (1999). *A tripartite seed: The future creating capacity of designing, learning, and systems.* Cresskill, NJ: Hampton Press.

Salas, E., Dickson, T. L., Converse, S. A., & Tannenbaum, S. I. (1992). Toward an understanding of team performance and training. In R. W. Swezey & E. Salas (Eds.), *Teams: Their training and performance* (pp. 3-30). Norwood, NJ: Ablex.

Salazar, A. J. (1995). Understanding the synergistic effects of communication in small groups: Making the most out of group member abilities. *Small Group Research, 26,* 169-199.

Salazar, A. J. (1996a). Ambiguity and communication effects on small group decision making performance. *Human Communication Research, 23,* 155-192.

Salazar, A. J. (1996b). An analysis of the development and evolution of roles in the small group. *Small Group Research, 27,* 475-503.

Salazar, A. J. (1997). Communication effects on small group decision-making: Homogeneity and task as moderators of the communication-performance relationship. *Western Journal of Communication, 61,* 35-65.

Salazar, A. J., & Witte, K. (1996). Communication and the decision-making process. In W. Donohue & D. Cai (Eds.), *Communicating and connecting: The functions of human communication* (pp. 277-304). San Diego, CA: Harcourt-Brace.

Schultz, B. G. (1999). Improving group communication performance: An overview of diagnosis and intervention. In L. R. Frey (Ed.), D. S. Gouran, & M. S. Poole (Assoc. Eds.), *The handbook of group communication theory & research* (pp. 371-394). Thousand Oaks, CA: Sage.

Scott, C. R. (1999). Communication technology and group communication. In L. R. Frey (Ed.), D. S. Gouran, & M. S. Poole (Assoc. Eds.), *The handbook of group communication theory & research* (pp. 432-572). Thousand Oaks, CA: Sage.

Senge, P. M. (1990). *The fifth discipline: The art and practice of the learning organization.* New York: Currency-Doubleday.

Shaw, M. E. (1981). *Group dynamics: The psychology of small group behavior* (2nd ed.). New York: McGraw-Hill.

Sherman, H., & Schultz, R. (1998). *Open boundaries: Creating business innovation through complexity.* Reading, MA: Perseus.

Simon, H. A. (1996). *The sciences of the artificial* (3rd ed.). Cambridge, MA: MIT Press.

Simonton, D. K. (1997). Creativity in personality, developmental, and social psychology: Any links with cognitive psychology? In T. B. Ward, S. M. Smith, & J. Vaid (Eds.), *Creative thought: An investigation of conceptual structures and processes* (pp. 309-324). Washington, DC: American Psychological Association.

Smith, C., & Comer, D. (1994). Self-organization in small groups: A study of group effectiveness within nonequilibrium conditions. *Human Relations, 47,* 553-581.

Smith, C., & Gemmill, G. (1991). Change in the small group: A dissipative structure perspective. *Human Relations, 44,* 697-716.

Stacey, R. D. (1995). The science of complexity: An alternative perspective for strategic change processes. *Strategic Management Journal, 16,* 477-495.

Stacey, R. D. (1996). *Complexity and creativity in organizations.* San Francisco: Berrett-Koehler.

Sundstrom, E., De Meuse, K. P., & Futrell, D. (1990). Work teams: Applications and effectiveness. *American Psychologist, 45,* 120-133.

Svyantek, D. J., & DeShon, R. P. (1993/1994). Organizational attractors: A chaos theory explanation of why cultural change efforts often fail. *Public Administration Quarterly, 17,* 337-353.

Tschacher, W., & Brunner, E. J. (1995). Empirical studies of group-dynamics from the point-of-view of self-organization theory. *Zeitschrift fur Sozialpsychologie, 26*(2), 78-91.

Tschacher, W., Brunner, E. J., & Schiepek, G. (1992). Self-organization in social groups. In W. Tschacher, G. Schiepek, & E. J. Brunner (Eds.), *Self-organization and clinical psychology* (Vol. 58, pp. 341-366). Berlin: Springer-Verlag.

Ward, T. B., Smith, S. M., & Vaid, J. (1997). Conceptual structures and processes in creative thought. In T. B. Ward, S. M. Smith, & J. Vaid (Eds.), *Creative thought: An investigation of conceptual structures and processes* (pp. 1-27). Washington, DC: American Psychological Association.

Warriner, C. K. (1984). *Organizations and their environments: Essays in the sociology of organizations.* Greenwich, CT: JAI Press.

West, M. A., & Farr, J. L. (1989). Innovation at work: Psychological perspectives. *Social Behaviour, 4,* 15-30.

Wheatley, M. J. (1994). *Leadership and the new science: Learning about organizations from an orderly universe.* San Francisco: Berrett-Koehler.

Wheelan, S. A. (1996). An initial exploration of the relevance of complexity theory to group research and practice. *Systems Practice, 9,* 49-70.

PART V

Group Communication Facilitation and Educational Practices

11

Getting to "GroupAha!"

Provoking Creative Processes in Task Groups

SUNWOLF
Santa Clara University

> *But the process of creating or innovating almost always involves more than an isolated person working alone.*
>
> Scheidel (1986, p. 125)

In a global world in which change is rapid and competition pervasive, pressure increases to produce more creative ideas ever more quickly. Innovations in the world of natural task groups have been predicted to carry important consequences for the study of communication and group decision making (Frey, 1996); specifically, groups now continually confront tasks that require the devotion of at least part of the discussion time to creative problem solving. To be effective at accomplishing the demand for creativity, group members need a new set of nonlinear skills. Increasingly, task groups in communities, schools, hospitals, business organizations, and government must be able to produce a continuous supply of new ideas to adapt to the enormous changes facing them (Bookman, 1988).

Research on *creative* group problem-solving processes generally has been neglected by communication scholars in favor of a focus on problem-solving processes that help groups to structure, analyze, or agree on problems and solutions. Moreover, the study of creativity has often focused on *individual* effort and idea generation rather than examining creative products of *group* discussion. The "Aha!" creative discovery experience is too frequently connected with one individual working in isolation, in an atmosphere that is both free and unrestrained (Scheidel, 1986); in fact, Csikszentmihalyi's (1996) research on individual creativity argues that survival of the fittest has probably included *survival of the creative,* suggesting that humans are the descendants of ancestors who recognized and nurtured the importance of novelty. Contemporary communication challenges, however, require new directions in thinking about creativity for individuals in groups.

Unfortunately, the cooperative nature of *group creativity* places an added burden on problem solvers (traditionally oriented toward making decisions individually), such that they often experience frustration with group discussion processes (Johnson & Hackman, 1995). The needed shifts from critical thinking in task groups to creative thinking (and back again), consequently, may not occur at the time and in the manner that is most needed by a particular group. Getting to moments of "groupAha!" involves more than sparking creative thinking processes in individuals; members must be willing to communicate with one another in ways that provoke the generation of new ideas and novel ways of combining group members' ideas.

The 1960s and 1970s saw the emergence of research on both developmental processes of creativity and techniques designed to promote the generation of innovative ideas, such as morphological analysis (Allen, 1962), lateral thinking (de Bono, 1970), synectics (Gordon, 1961; Prince, 1970), creativity in problem-solving groups (Maier, 1970), brainstorming (Osborn, 1963), and the spiral process of idea development (Scheidel & Crowell, 1964). Subsequent research illuminated the impact of idea-generating techniques on group processes (Kramer, Kuo, & Dailey, 1997), including communication processes in small groups (Firestien, 1990). Although some models of creative group problem solving have received attention from scholars (see, e.g., Basadur & Finkbeiner, 1985; Basadur, Graen, & Green, 1982; Dennis & Valacich, 1994; Firestien, 1990), particularly brainstorming (e.g., Jablin, 1981; Kramer et al., 1997), many of the techniques developed have been largely ignored by researchers (e.g., visioning, brainwriting, morphological analysis, role storming, and semantic intuition). Even recent group communication textbooks have devoted little coverage to the processes of creativity in groups (e.g., Barker, Wahlers, & Watson, 1995; Brilhart, Galanes, & Adams, 2001; Cathcart, Samovar, & Henman, 1996; Frey & Barge, 1997; Keyton, 1999; Pavitt & Curtis, 1994), generally focusing only on brainstorming (generating ideas in groups by restricting premature judgment) or buzz groups (subdi-

viding larger groups briefly so that smaller groups can work and report back on idea-generation results on a single issue) as methods of generating ideas in groups (e.g., Beebe & Masterson, 1997; Ellis & Fisher, 1994; Schultz, 1996; Seibold & Krikorian, 1997), with two texts also referencing the Bilhart-Jochem Ideation Criteria (Cragan & Wright, 1995; Wilson & Hanna, 1993). Two group communication textbooks that have each devoted an entire chapter to the process of creative thinking in groups still describe only a few of the myriad techniques available for facilitating group idea generation (brainstorming and metaphorical thinking for generating novel ideas, Lumsden & Lumsden, 1997; and idea needlers, manipulative verbs, metaphors, and analogies, Harris & Sherblom, 1999). In a larger context, only a few scholars in the social sciences have specifically addressed the general topic of creativity in task groups (e.g., Amabile, 1996; Hare, 1982; Isaksen, 1988; Johnson & Hackman, 1995; West, 1990), and two major handbooks summarizing research on groups contain no chapters or offer only limited discussion of the creative process in groups (Hare, Blumberg, Davies, & Kent, 1994; Hirokawa & Poole, 1996). A notable exception is the handbook on group communication theory and research edited by Frey, Gouran, and Poole (1999), which devoted an entire chapter to group communication and creativity processes (Jarboe, 1999).

In addition to the lack of scholarly attention to group creativity processes, misperceptions about creativity itself have hindered attempts by many educators, group leaders and facilitators, and group members to become more creative problem solvers. Johnson and Hackman (1995) pointed out three popular but erroneous beliefs about creativity: (a) Creativity is limited to the gifted few, and others can do little to improve their creative thinking skills; (b) the creative process is a mystery in which creative ideas appear as sudden flashes of insight that defy explanation; and (c) creative thinking requires minimal effort and is, essentially, a series of exhilarating breakthroughs that require no preparation. As a result of the prevalence of these misconceptions, it is important for teachers and facilitators of group communication to expose people to methods of improving their group's creative thinking skills by helping them to develop effective, creative problem-solving strategies and, at the same time, helping them to become familiar with the time, energy, and resources needed for *creative* success in groups. As noted above, however, group communication textbooks have generally neglected most of the techniques already developed that could help groups engage in productive creativity. Consequently, students enter the real world underexposed to the rich resources available for stimulating and sustaining creativity in the many task groups in which they are destined to participate.

Considering both the applied and pedagogical importance of becoming familiar with the wide variety of creative group problem-solving strategies that currently exists, as well as the proliferation of additional prescriptive procedures currently being developed, I describe in this chapter the familiar and less widely studied techniques designed to enhance idea development in task groups and then suggest new directions for employing these techniques in applied group communication research and pedagogy. I first examine the role of communication in creative processes and what is known about whether creativity can actually be taught and then proceed to take a closer look at research findings on what may be preventing groups from engaging in successful creative problem solving. Thirty-six overlooked or neglected techniques to stimulate creativity in task groups are then described. I conclude by offering suggestions for expanding the power of collaborative creativity in groups.

WHAT IS CREATIVITY FROM A COMMUNICATION PERSPECTIVE?

Creativity has attracted the attention of scholars from many disciplines, including psychology, sociology, education, marketing, business, physics, performing arts, and literature. Indeed, there may be *no* field that has not paid attention to the creative process.

Creativity is generally viewed across disciplines as a thinking process associated with imagination, insight, invention, innovation, ingenuity, intuition, inspiration, and illumination (Henry, 1991). Although a variety of definitions of creativity have emerged (Johnson & Hackman, 1995, reported more than 100 such definitions), most scholars seem to agree that *creativity involves the generation, application, combination, and extension of new ideas.*

In viewing creativity from a *communication* perspective, attention becomes focused on *messages* rather than on mental processes or mind-sets. Although scholars from many disciplines have examined factors affecting creativity—including intelligence, gender, neurological factors, characteristics of creative people, effects of memory, cognitive processes of creativity, and perceptual organization—communication scholars point their lenses toward the sending and receiving of messages that stimulate, exchange, extend, apply, or block creative ideas. How, then, does such a conceptualization of creativity deal with the argument that creativity is a rare individual talent?

CAN CREATIVITY BE TAUGHT?

If creativity is limited to a gifted few, who themselves have little control over the sudden flashes of insight that visit their thoughts, attempts to educate individuals or groups in creative thinking processes are doomed at the outset. Studies confirm, however, that "ordinary" people can be taught to tap into and expand their creative problem-solving abilities (Baer, 1993; Isaksen, 1988).

Research during the 1960s by Torrance (1961, 1965) concluded that students could learn creative thinking skills. Later, Parnes and Noller (1972) found this to be the case in a 2-year comprehensive study of college students who completed a 4-semester sequence of creative studies courses. More recently, Baer (1993) reported a study of an elementary grade class in which the experimental group had been given training in techniques designed to enhance divergent (rather than conforming) thinking for several years prior to testing and outperformed the control group in both storytelling and collage making, two creative tasks. Firestien (1990) examined specific communication effects of training in the use of creative problem solving and found (a) that members of groups receiving training evidenced increased participation, demonstrated reduced criticism and increased support for the ideas offered by other group members, and engaged in more expressions of humor than members of groups that did not receive such training and (b) that trained groups produced more ideas than the untrained groups. Scholars examining whether creativity could be learned in the classroom have found that improving students' creative thinking and problem-solving abilities are viable educational goals. For example, Adamson (1985) demonstrated the ease with which students could learn creative processes, and Tulenko and Kryder (1990) reported the positive effect of game playing to stimulate creative processes in student groups. In field research with members of an engineering department in a large industrial organization, Basadur et al. (1982) found that participants trained in a multistage process of creative problem solving were significantly more successful at problem finding than untrained participants. What has been underinvestigated, however, are creative performances under conditions that allow sufficient time for both evaluating and revising a variety of possible solutions and the generation of possible solutions, known as multistage creativity, and that follow a set of criteria that differs from the criteria by which optimal solutions are later judged (see Baer, 1993).

WHAT DO WE KNOW ABOUT CREATIVE GROUP PROBLEM SOLVING?

Blocks to Group Creativity

Even though all groups have the potential to be creative at problem-solving tasks, group members often experience frustration when faced with the task of generating innovative ideas. Moreover, research shows that dyads sometimes produce more creative solutions than larger sized groups, such as Thornburg's (1991) finding that pairs demonstrated more frequent creativity than groups. To understand the frustration felt in being creative in group contexts and the reasons why dyads outperform groups, we must understand more about potential barriers to successful group creativity that exist at both the individual and group levels.

Groups without any special training in creative problem-solving techniques frequently make mistakes that derail the creative problem-solving process. These errors may occur when members experience perceptual, emotional, and/or cultural blocks (Johnson & Hackman, 1995; see also Comadena's, 1984, research on the effects of members' communication apprehension, ambiguity tolerance, task attraction, and productivity on brainstorming groups). Furthermore, certain physical conditions (such as group size, overcrowding, noise, distractions, or seating arrangements) and social conditions (such as criticism, distrust, power and status differentials, or lack of support) confronting task groups discourage creativity (see, e.g., Philipsen, Mulac, & Dietrich's, 1979, investigation of the diminishing effects of social interaction on group idea generation). Dislike of the group, the goal, or the task can also block creative outcomes; Amabile (1983) argued persuasively that creative thinking could only be kept alive in an atmosphere where people intrinsically enjoyed the task and the climate in which they worked.

Time constraints have also been shown to influence creativity in small groups. Time is a pervasive but often neglected variable that significantly affects the productivity of bona fide task groups. Only a few investigations, however, have examined the effects of time limits on group creativity. Kelly and Karau (1993) found that short, initial time limits led to faster rates of performance but lower creativity; surprisingly, when time pressures increased over trials, creativity increased. Kelly and McGrath (1985) found that increased creativity and originality on products were produced during longer time-limit periods in task groups. Such results suggest caution in generalizing from studies that use single-episode and short-term group tasks, and point toward the need for additional expansion of group research on creative techniques. Questions that remain to be answered include these: Would the inclusion of methodological designs that examine the relationship between time pressure and indexes of creativity in group performance more closely represent the tasks that group members face in real-world settings? Are groups with longer time limits more apt to focus on single categories for longer periods of time, or do they use the additional time in other ways? Are groups experiencing time pressures likely to jump to new categories to find more accessible ideas?

VanGundy (1984) argued that two specific but essential steps in the creative problem-solving process are most ignored by untrained discussion groups: (a) redefining and analyzing a problem, to give a group new perspectives, and (b) members allowing one another to move beyond their original perceptions. Furthermore, groups may choose the wrong problem-solving tactic for a particular problem, either out of habit or due to a lack of exposure to other available methods. For instance, groups may rely too much on words and mathematical symbols as problem-solving tools in situations for which visualization or drawing may be better suited (Johnson & Hackman, 1995).

Some groups may be handicapped in their efforts to increase creative thinking processes by a lack of diversity in their membership (see, e.g., Thornburg, 1991). One line of research has investigated the effects of ethnic diversity on creativity in small groups. McLeod, Lobel, and Cox (1996) examined the performance on a brainstorming task of groups composed of all Anglo Americans, compared with groups composed of Anglo, Asian, African, and Hispanic Americans, and found that more effective and feasible ideas were produced by the ethnically diverse groups. Because Anglo Americans often compose the majority in task groups, members from other ethnic backgrounds may, in addition, find themselves coping with the effects of majority versus minority influence in offering nontraditional ideas (for support, see Nemeth & Wachtler, 1983); specifically, when the majority is large in number, the attention of the group may focus on one point of view and disregard novel solutions offered by minority members. The practice of forming heterogeneous groups in which members have significantly different backgrounds and perspectives may encourage the emergence of minority contributions that usefully stimulate creative thinking and idea generation (see Johnson & Hackman, 1995).

Techniques to Provoke Group Genius

That is what *group genius* is all about—individuals huddling together for synergy. Fabian (1990, p. 235)

The concept of *synergy* suggests that a group may be expected to produce more creative ideas than its members will individually. "Group genius" can flourish and provide rich, innovative dividends when groups engage in team creative thinking (Fabian, 1990). The question, then, is what is needed to move a group toward group genius. Many techniques have already been developed to stimulate creativity in task groups (see Table 11.1, which is derived and expanded from Sunwolf and Seibold's, 1999, categorization of prescriptive problem-solving procedures that help groups structure, analyze, agree, or create), and these provide a partial answer to the question.

Exploring beyond the familiar exercise of brainstorming, Table 11.1 includes techniques that encourage group members to imagine the future (crystal ball and wishful thinking), use language in wide-ranging ways (analogy storm, manipulative verbs, progressive abstraction, and semantic intuition), welcome chance intrusions (lateral thinking, morphological analysis, and organized random search), activate whole-brain thinking

TABLE 11.1 Techniques That Provoke Creativity in Groups

Analogy Storm	The specific problem or the results of a previous brainstorming session are set aside to incubate while the group generates a series of analogies to the problem.
Brainstorming	Designed to generate ideas and promote creativity by reducing premature evaluation, using a facilitator to enforce four rules (no criticism, quantity is desired, the wilder the idea the better, and piggybacking on other ideas is encouraged).
Brainwriting	Group members generate ideas silently and in writing on index cards, with each member writing down one idea per card and passing it on to stimulate new ideas for the next person; members write down on a separate card any new ideas suggested.
Bug List	Group members are asked to identify things that irritate them about a situation, issue, or problem, and the generated individual lists are then consolidated to identify the bugs common to most members; the group then brainstorms solutions to each bug.
Buzz Groups	Members are divided into smaller groups for brief periods during a meeting to generate ideas on the same issue that subsequently are analyzed by the entire group.
Collective Notebook	Idea-generation method in which members do not meet face-to-face but individually generate ideas over an extended period of time. A notebook with a particular problem statement is given to each member, who writes down one idea every day for a month, with a coordinator summarizing and sharing the ideas with all members at the end of a designated period of time.
Consensus Mapping	Uses individual idea cards from group members that are sorted into various classifications to build a solution model in map form. After an extensive list of ideas has been generated, members individually write their ideas about clusters and categories that are then presented in map form as a starting point for discussion and revision. Ensures that a large number of diverse ideas are generated in a balanced fashion and, thereby, extends other idea-generating methods.
Creative Problem Solving	Contains some components of rational problem solving (data gathering, problem definition, and solution generation and evaluation) but differs by motivating members' efforts through the process of allowing for incubation phases when task work ceases, designating specific imagination phases, and focusing attention on the social dimensions of a group.
Crystal Ball	Stimulates people's imaginations and helps task groups stay on the cutting edge by putting the future in a crystal ball, leaping ahead a few months or years, and asking group members to imagine new possibilities, outcomes, targets, or conditions for a desired goal.
Excursion	Uses imaginative scenarios to stimulate ideas, encourage group members to think in contextual terms, and adopt "what if" ideation generation.
Five W's and H	The Who, What, Where, When, and Why questions from journalists are combined with the How question. Problems are redefined by asking, "In what ways might . . . ?" for each of the "W" categories. These answers are used to generate problem redefinitions, and judgment is withheld until all suggestions are recorded. The new definition that best reflects the problem is then selected.
Idea Needlers	A list of questions groups can use to gain a different perspective to view a problem (e.g., Why does it have this shape? What if this were turned inside out? Where else can this be done? What if the order were changed?)
Ideals Method	Combines solution generation with solution implementation, by having a group generate ideas about the function of the solution, then gather information, design the solution, and evaluate its effectiveness.
Idea Writing	A four-step procedure for exploring the meaning of generated ideas in writing. A group is split into subgroups; each member writes ideas to a stimulus question; forms are shared for other members' written reactions; and each member reads reactions to his or her initial response, followed by discussion.

Imaginary World	An associations/images technique that builds on people's natural inclinations to associate things. Group members are asked to select a solution to a problem, expressed in the form of a wish. The group then imagines a world remote from the world of the problem and gives associations and images that characterize the remote world. The group then relates the generated list of associations and images of that imagined remote world to the actual world of the problem, developing new associations and images and applying them in a more realistic way without diluting the innovations.
Lateral Thinking	A nonsequential method of discussion (based on divergent rather than convergent thinking) that is generative and encourages topic change for the sake of moving, does not require correctness at any stage, and welcomes chance intrusions, using variable categories, labels, or classifications.
Left-Right Brain Alternation	The objective is to use a whole-brain approach to attack a problem or examine an opportunity. Left-brain/right-brain functions are listed to remind members of the differences (i.e., left brain includes speaking, analyzing, and judging; right brain includes seeing things holistically, understanding analogies, providing insight, and synthesizing ideas). The problem is explored by alternately choosing possible solutions from the left brain and the right brain.
Lions' Den	Ongoing group members (lions) invite subgroups (lambs) in an organization to attend weekly meetings. Lambs draw a picture of their problem on a flip chart and are given 5 minutes to both explain the problem and present a challenge, and another 5 minutes to state solutions already generated. For the next 20 minutes, the lions actively brainstorm ideas (lambs listen), although the lambs ultimately choose their own solutions.
Lotus Blossom	A diagram method that functions as a visual brainstorm, in which each member is given a problem written in the center and thinks of related ideas that are written in surrounding circles, and then generates new ideas to the original problem until the diagram is complete.
Manipulative Verbs	Designed to decrease the chances of overlooking solutions, an extensive list of verbs (e.g., multiply, divide, eliminate, invert, rotate, or substitute) is generated and each verb is then applied in group discussion against certain designated aspects of the problem.
Mess Finding	A "mess" might be any selected negative or positive situation. Outcomes for the mess are generated by constructing a list of "Wouldn't it be nice if" questions. Obstacles are generated by listing "Wouldn't it be awful if" questions. New concerns and opportunities are identified for further development. Can be used as the initial stage of creative problem solving or as a stand-alone technique.
Mind Mapping	A group chooses a problem phrase and writes it in the center of a large sheet as a nucleus bubble. The "map" builds naturally as associative spin-off words are drawn with connecting lines and circles around the nucleus bubble, and ideas cluster or trigger other thoughts. A facilitator can draw the map with group input or all members can draw. Discussion and judgment are withheld until the map is complete.
Morphological Analysis	Encourages new ideas by breaking a problem into its major parts, listing all possible topics under each heading, and then randomly combining these topics to generate new solutions by forcing together elements that seem unrelated.
Object Stimulation	Designed to present a different perspective on a problem, using unrelated stimuli objects with no apparent relation to the problem. A list of objects unrelated to the problem is generated; one object is selected and described in detail; each description is used as a stimulus to generate ideas, with all ideas written down; and rounds are repeated for other objects.
Organized Random Search	Group members are encouraged to rethink a problem by breaking it into a variety of subcategories or parts, and the newly created individual subdivisions are then used as starting points for developing new ideas.
Picture Tour	A photographic journey of a problem is taken, as group members view multiple slides on a screen (of action, people, scenery, and/or objects connected with the problem). Members extract something from each picture that intrigues them or that seems to be an essential feature, and all observations are posted and used to stimulate new solution ideas.

(Continued)

TABLE 11.1 Continued

Problem Reversal	The problem is written down in a question format, and a verb is identified. The meaning of that verb is reversed, restating the problem into a second question format; answers to this reversed problem are generated and those answers are then reversed to fit the original problem-question.
Progressive Abstraction	Generates alternative problem definitions by moving through progressively higher levels of problem abstraction until a satisfactory definition is achieved. As the problem is systematically enlarged, new definitions emerge and possible solutions are then identified.
Reverse Brainstorming	Uses the same rules of brainstorming, but group members generate ideas or solutions that would make the problem worse, and after generating a list, they consider implications of doing the opposite.
Role Storming	Each group member is asked to assume the role of various people who may be affected by or who may affect the problem, and the group then brainstorms the problem from these persons' points of view.
Semantic Intuition	Reverses the normal creative procedure by first creating a name, then producing an idea on the basis of it; two sets of words related to major problem elements are generated, followed by combining two words from each set, using this new combination to generate new ideas, and repeating the process as often as desired.
Six Thinking Hats	Group members are encouraged to visualize themselves wearing various colored hats at various points during the group's discussion, which encourages novel thinking and comments by directing attention to new aspects of problems. Hat colors relate to mental function (white is concerned with facts and figures; red, emotional views; black, negative aspects; yellow, positive possibilities; green, creativity and new ideas; and blue, control of thinking and focus).
Synectics	Uses diverse-membership groups, with a leader guiding discussion through flexible stages. An explanation of the problem is given by an expert, initial suggestions are proposed, dream solutions are generated, and then the leader poses questions to stimulate new thinking, followed by an attempted force-fit of the generated creative ideas to the problem.
Visioning	Idea-generation method in which group members are guided to focus their energy on a particular desired end state, imagining specific details, their possible effects, and how such an end state might actually function.
Wildest Idea	Used when an impasse has been reached in problem solving to jog members out of their mind-set. Group members are asked to state their wildest ideas, the group is asked to build on each idea by exploring variations or extrapolations, and the facilitator then asks the group to find practical uses for every wild idea.
Wishful Thinking	Loosens analytical thinking by including a larger set of alternatives than currently imagined. Alternative solutions to the problem are stated in the form of a fantasy, such as "I wish that we could . . . " or "What would happen if we tried . . . " and then each wishful statement is converted to a more practical one, such as "Assuming that we could get around that . . . " or "It may be possible to meet our wish, but first we would have to . . . "

(left-right brain alternation and thinking hats, de Bono, 1985), consider unrelated but common objects (object stimulation), or employ fantasies and visualizations (excursion, imaginary world, picture tour, thinking hats, visioning, and wishful thinking). Some of the techniques specifically take advantage of the frustrating aspects of a task (bug list, mess finding, and thinking hats). At times, group members may be encouraged to generate innovative solutions without meeting face-to-face (collective notebook) or to first work silently and individually but later join together (brainwriting); at other times, groups may interact with outsiders (lions' den) or rely on importing members to increase diversity (synectics). Idea-incubation periods can also be created (creative problem solving). Some methods rely on changing how individuals perceive problems through perspective-changing exercises (idea needlers and role storming); others encourage mental reversing of concepts or procedures (problem reversal, reverse brainstorming, and semantic intuition). Some methods use traditional written techniques but avoid traditional linear listing (consensus mapping, lotus blossom, and mind mapping). Group members may even be encouraged to share ideas that they *know* would not be successful (wildest idea). The potential for combining various techniques, in whole or in part, offers further methods for shared creative thinking in task groups.

NEW DIRECTIONS: THE POWER OF COLLABORATIVE CREATIVITY

> Never refuse to go on an occasional wild goose chase. That's what wild geese are for. (Anonymous)

A creative perspective is necessarily future oriented. Creative perspective takers look for unusual possibilities and new ways of seeing and doing, and they are willing to engage in "upside-down" thinking. Unfortunately, group communication pedagogy and scholarship have focused on only a few idea-generating methods: (a) Management consultants, team development specialists, group facilitators, and strategic organizational planners have promulgated upside-down thinking techniques for task groups (e.g., Fabian, 1990; Miller, 1987; Ricchiuto, 1997); (b) scholars outside the communication discipline have developed innovative creativity-generating exercises (e.g., Amabile, 1996; Couger, 1995; de Bono, 1992; Kanter, 1989; VanGundy, 1987); and (c) scholars and group consultants have focused on the obvious usefulness of multiple approaches that might provoke "groupAha!" outcomes. As revealed in the previous section, dozens of techniques available for extending and expanding creative

communication in group discussion remain neglected. The next sections suggest ways group pedagogy and scholarship can be enhanced and enriched.

Enhancing Group Creativity in College Communication Courses

College students assigned to task groups in classes are rarely enthusiastic, and often horrified, at the prospect of working with fellow students to produce a group project that will be jointly evaluated. Journals written by these students often describe low energy levels, unequal participation, critical comments made about other group members, and frustration with wasting time, as their groups struggle to generate ideas. Imagine, however, a radically different group climate for students, one in which group stagnation is transformed into movement and member lethargy into energy, with members clamoring to be heard, with bizarre analogies and wild ideas zipping back and forth.

Unfortunately, the techniques for managing group communication that student groups become most familiar with come from their textbooks, which, as previously noted, focus primarily on linear procedures that help members to analyze and structure problems rather than to create innovative solutions. With 36 specific creative techniques represented in Table 11.1, it is clear that students are not being well served when they are exposed only to techniques such as brainstorming, buzz groups, and ideal-solution formats in group communication courses. Arousing the creative spirit of student task groups requires exposing them at multiple levels to the rich creative possibilities of communication in group meetings.

Group creativity processes can be effectively imported into classrooms by (a) having members practice specific techniques during class discussions; (b) providing student task groups with descriptions, training, and assignments on the use of a wide variety of creative techniques; and (c) adding more inclusive substantive materials to textbooks, as well as providing supplemental materials that address creative communication (e.g., Jarboe, 1999; Johnson & Hackman, 1995). Torrance (1961, 1965) has offered other specific suggestions for nurturing creativity in the classroom, including creating opportunities for practice or experimentation in creativity *without evaluation*. de Bono (1992), the originator of the term "lateral thinking," argued that the *creative* challenge is very different from the traditional critical challenge. This is important because the critical challenge requires people to make judgments or note faults or inadequacies during a task, whereas the creative challenge operates outside of judgment. When students are challenged with group work, the temptation is to adopt the most familiar method of problem solving; however, student groups that produce more creative solutions have been trained to ask an additional question: *No matter how excellent the critical method may be, is it the only way of proceeding?* If instructors were to move beyond assignments that are evaluated critically to include those that offer creative challenges, what changes would be required? How might student groups be further challenged if course time is scheduled such that final projects are handed back to the groups and they are requested to go beyond the thinking expressed in that project, no matter how far it had already been extended? Teaching students *creative dissatisfaction* helps propel them beyond learned reluctance to look for new ideas when something appears to be fine just the way it is. Applying creativity only to those things that seem inadequate would seriously limit its application. Students also benefit when they are taught what creative dissatisfaction of good-enough group projects might look like so that they can understand how to enhance a group project that is already "excellent" by traditional standards.

Enriching Research Agendas

As described previously, considerable research has been conducted concerning the effectiveness of group procedures in enhancing group task functions of structuring, analyzing, and agreeing (see, e.g., reviews by Jarboe, 1996; Pavitt, 1993; Sunwolf & Seibold, 1999), although insufficient attention has been paid to creative group communication processes and techniques that provoke those processes. Research is needed in three specific areas: (a) investigation of the *effectiveness* of the many untested techniques listed in Table 11.1, (b) investigation of the applicable *limits* of each technique, and (c) investigation of the *conditions* necessary for the effective use of each technique. In light of Frey's (1994, 1996) reviews of methods used to study group decision making—which found that most researchers study a single meeting of zero-history, college student groups in the laboratory or classroom solving artificial problems—the contextual variables encountered by real-world task groups using creative process techniques remain neglected. Consequently, we know little, for example, of what happens when a problem being addressed by a group is complicated by characteristics of multidimensionality (a number of underlying themes), interconnectedness (many linkages to related elements), or sequentialness (many steps, each of which may be influenced by the outcome of the previous one).

Important questions that help to set the agenda for research on group creativity and group creativity techniques include the following:

- What variables inhibit or enhance creative communication in task groups?
- Are particular types of problems more or less amenable to the use of particular creative techniques?
- Are there certain types of groups for which one technique is more applicable than others (e.g., zero-history groups, self-organized work teams, social clubs, sports teams, or juries)?
- To what degree does group size affect the effectiveness of particular techniques?
- Are there specific individual member characteristics (e.g., ethnicity, gender,

education, age, or prior group experience) that facilitate or inhibit effective participation in creative group processes?

- To what extent does training members of a group (as opposed to training a group's formal leaders or facilitators) in a creative technique influence the effectiveness of that technique?
- What are the initial and persisting effects of time limits on groups using creative process formats?

Techniques for provoking creativity may work more effectively when formal organizing structures are used to vary the application of the technique in group discussion. One of the few studies to investigate the effects of varying formal group structures on creativity was conducted by Offner, Kramer, and Winter (1996), who found that brainstorming groups with a facilitator outperformed groups with no facilitator present to suggest organization of group conversations (although flip chart recording and built-in pauses demonstrated no effect on creative group output).

The operationalization of creativity itself also needs to be reexamined. One way in which this could be done is to look at what aspects of this construct are currently unexamined, which might offer insights into the enhancement of group creativity. Dominowski (1995) argued that research tasks used to assess creative production are ordinarily ill defined, with "novelty" associated with statistical infrequency and "quality" referenced by vague or inconsistent criteria (such as measuring quantity of ideas, usefulness of ideas, or simply the cost of implementing ideas). Particular indexes may not provide adequate measures of creativity or fully tap creative processing. Prior research studies examining creativity have measured novelty of group solutions (e.g., Green, 1975; Hall & Watson, 1970; Nemeth & Wachtler, 1983) and "number of new ideas" (e.g., Anderson & Balzer, 1991; Jablin, 1981; Offner et al., 1996; Philipsen et al., 1979), but research designs that measure creativity in more than one man-

ner should be encouraged. Researchers have rarely drawn on specific definitions of creativity, such as "putting old things into new combinations and new things into old combinations" (Weick, 1979, p. 252) or reshuffling, combining, and synthesizing already existing facts and ideas (Koestler, 1964). One example of the use of multiple measurements of creativity is the research of Kelly and Karau (1993), who measured creativity using both a 7-point scale that defined creativity as originality or unusualness and an index for the number of categories generated. *Ideational fluency* (the quantity of ideas produced) needs to be supplemented with examinations of *associational fluency* (complementing relationships between factors) in groups.

Group creativity also includes a group's creative adaptability, but studies, to date, have not focused on the manner in which groups may demonstrate creative flexibility or adjustments to sudden changes in task conditions. The development of more measures that specifically test phases of creative group processes, sequencing of idea generation, or emergent structuring and restructuring processes could be used in future research to provide greater insight into creative adaptation.

New thinking is also needed concerning the communication roles that members play in creative groups. Although textbooks are replete with references to roles in decision-making groups (e.g., blocker, joker, gatekeeper, or encourager), research has not explored the roles enacted during creative phases of group communication. Miller (1987) suggested eight informal innovation roles that members adopt in helping a group to produce a *creative* output: product champions, sponsors, inventors, project managers, coaches, gatekeepers, internal monitors, and facilitators.

Furthermore, although limited research is available that specifically examines *time* variables, the research that does exist nonetheless demonstrates the importance of looking further at temporal constraints, as well as the need for longitudinal studies of group creative performance. Establishing the relationship between quantity and creativity of performance in one-shot research designs offers potentially important information but does not answer questions concerning the effects of time and time pressures on ongoing work groups. The question, therefore, is how groups cope with both an abundance and a shortage of time. Research designs that include across-trial effects, thus, are needed.

One important aspect that deserves attention is that the often-used group decision rules and consensus-building procedures familiar to group members who join new problem-solving groups may actually inhibit the emergence of creativity. Ongoing work groups that have historically adopted *cohesion* as a goal, accomplished primarily through consensus, may sacrifice their members' abilities to think both divergently and critically, because subtle coercion pressures members to conform to early trends (Johnson & Hackman, 1995). In highly creative groups, researchers have found that minority influence plays a significant and respected role, because minority members insert novel solutions but may expend more effort as they encounter conflict with majority factions. Nemeth and Wachtler (1983), for example, found that group members exposed to minority views made more novel judgments than did those exposed only to majority views, further noting that the majority in a group is often effective in obtaining agreement from other group members. Although much is known about the dangerous effects of "groupthink" (Janis, 1982) in producing ineffective group decisions, little is known about the effects of consensus building on the inhibition of group creativity. The question, therefore, is the extent to which communicative conflict is tolerated or avoided in highly creative groups.

In natural settings, as Kelly and Karau (1993) pointed out, group creativity is often judged in the context of complex and interactive tasks. Furthermore, creative group thinking has, in the past, often been directed solely at correcting known problems; neglected has been the application of creative group thinking toward actively seeking problems to solve, or *problem finding* (Johnson & Hackman,

1995). One creativity expert, Adams (1986), encouraged his engineering students to develop inventions by making a "bug" list that describes and attempts to solve the irritations in life that bother them (e.g., generating solutions for noisy clocks, vending machines that keep the money, and stamps that won't stick). The substitution of artificial research problems with tasks that encourage solutions to real-world common irritations offers added elements of saliency, motivation, and outcome satisfaction for research participants.

Group research on creativity processes may have been constrained not only by underinvestigated variables but also by inherent paradoxes. The multiple paradoxes of collaborative group creativity present both challenges and opportunities for researchers. The following paradoxes, which may themselves inhibit creative group output, have been largely ignored:

- *Nature versus nurture paradox*—whether creative thinking depends on rare individual talents or involves normal everyday processes that can be taught
- *Individual versus group paradox*—whether creative thinking is viewed as the product of gifted individual minds that can be stifled by working in groups or whether groups are synergistic and produce better ideas than individuals creating alone
- *Old knowledge versus new knowledge paradox*—whether creativity relies on the use of prior knowledge or requires that people think in new ways
- *Prepared mind versus unstructured mind paradox*—whether preparation is a necessary prerequisite to creative results or requires the setting aside of all preconceptions to avoid creative blocks
- *Practical versus imaginative paradox*—whether creative group products should be evaluated on how imaginative or on how practical they are
- *Deliberate attempts versus diverted attention paradox*—whether creative pre-

scriptive techniques should focus attention on or divert attention from the problem to generate novel solutions

- *Success versus failure paradox*—whether task groups should be rewarded for successes or failures, with the recognition that creativity processes demand a tolerance for multiple failures preceding ultimate success

Such paradoxes suggest new strategies for studying creative group communication processes and call for research designs that illuminate the conditions under which these variables may be more clearly understood. The research challenge is to investigate specific ways in which these paradoxes might be acknowledged, managed, and balanced for group members in order to enhance creative problem solving.

CONCLUSION

The 36 neglected techniques in creative group problem solving presented in Table 11.1 represent only the tip of the creativity iceberg. They offer not only multiple ways for group members to approach group task issues but also multiple perspectives from which to view group relational issues (e.g., how group roles and relationships constrain or encourage creative solutions). They are powerful tools for examining and facilitating people in their roles as group members and as individuals. There is a Native American lesson story that teaches a "Rule of Six." This rule suggests that to understand any perceivable phenomenon, at least 6 explanations should be generated; there are probably 60, but if one always creates 6, this will serve as a reminder of the complexity of the universe, while preventing a fixation on the first plausible explanation as the truth (Sunwolf, 1999).

A research and pedagogical agenda investigating creative communication processes in groups carries with it the capacity to enrich teaching and scholarship about human communication in surprising and creative ways. The search for creative solutions to problems isn't new; group idea-generation is generally experienced as pressured, anxiety provoking, and, therefore, stressful. It takes new ways of searching, however, to ignite new outcomes.

REFERENCES

Adams, J. L. (1986). *Conceptual blockbusting: A guide to better ideas* (3rd ed.). Reading, MA: Addison-Wesley.

Adamson, C. (1985). Creativity in the classroom. *Pointer, 29*(3), 11-15.

Allen, M. S. (1962). *Morphological creativity: The miracle of your hidden brain power: A practical guide to the utilization of your creative potential*. Englewood Cliffs, NJ: Prentice Hall.

Amabile, T. M. (1983). *The social psychology of creativity*. New York: Springer-Verlag.

Amabile, T. M. (1996). *Creativity in context*. Boulder, CO: Westview Press.

Anderson, L. E., & Balzer, W. K. (1991). The effects of timing of leaders' opinions on problem-solving groups: A field experiment. *Group & Organization Studies, 16*, 86-101.

Baer, J. (1993). *Creativity and divergent thinking: A task-specific approach*. Hillsdale, NJ: Lawrence Erlbaum.

Barker, L. L., Wahlers, K. J., & Watson, K. W. (1995). *Groups in process: An introduction to small group communication* (5th ed.). Boston: Allyn & Bacon.

Basadur, M., & Finkbeiner, C. T. (1985). Measuring preference for ideation in creative problem-solving training. *Journal of Applied Behavioral Science, 21*, 37-49.

Basadur, M., Graen, G. B., & Green, S. G. (1982). Training in creative problem solving: Effects on ideation and problem finding and solving in an industrial research organization. *Organizational Behavior and Human Performance, 30*, 41-70.

Beebe, S. A., & Masterson, J. T. (1997). *Communicating in small groups: Principles and practices* (5th ed.). New York: Longman.

Bookman, R. (1988). Rousing the creative spirit. *Training and Development Journal, 42*(11), 67-71.

Brilhart, J. K., Galanes, G. J., & Adams, K. (2001). *Effective group discussion: Theory and practice* (10th ed.). Dubuque, IA: William C. Brown.

Cathcart, R. S., Samovar, L. A., & Henman, L. D. (Eds.). (1996). *Small group communication: Theory and practice* (7th ed.). Dubuque, IA: Brown & Benchmark.

Comadena, M. E. (1984). Brainstorming groups: Ambiguity tolerance, communication apprehension, task attraction, and individual productivity. *Small Group Behavior, 15*, 251-264.

Cougar, J. D. (1995). *Creative problem solving and opportunity finding*. Hinsdale, IL: Boyd & Fraser.

Cragan, J. F., & Wright, D. W. (1995). *Communication in small groups: Theory, process, skills* (4th ed.). Minneapolis, MN: West.

Csikszentmihalyi, M. (1996). *Creativity: Flow and the psychology of discovery and invention*. New York: HarperCollins.

de Bono, E. (1970). *Lateral thinking: Creativity step by step*. New York: Harper & Row.

de Bono, E. (1985). *Six thinking hats*. Boston: Little, Brown.

de Bono, E. (1992). *Serious creativity: Using the power of lateral thinking to create new ideas*. New York: HarperBusiness.

Dennis, A. R., & Valacich, J. S. (1994). Group, subgroup, and nominal group in idea generation: New rules for a new media? *Journal of Management, 20,* 723-736.

Dominowski, R. L. (1995). Productive problem solving. In S. M. Smith, T. B. Ward, & R. A. Finke (Eds.), *The creative cognition approach* (pp. 73-95). Cambridge: MIT Press.

Ellis, D. G., & Fisher, B. A. (1994). *Small group decision making: Communication and the group process*. New York: McGraw-Hill.

Fabian, J. (1990). *Creative thinking and problem solving*. Chelsea, MI: Lewis.

Firestien, R. L. (1990). Effects of creative problem-solving training on communication behaviors in small groups. *Small Group Research, 21,* 507-521.

Frey, L. R. (1994). The naturalistic paradigm: Studying small groups in the postmodern era. *Small Group Research, 25,* 551-577.

Frey, L. R. (1996). Remembering and "re-membering": A history of theory and research on communication and group decision making. In R. Y. Hirokawa & M. S. Poole (Eds.), *Communication and group decision making* (2nd ed., pp. 19-51). Thousand Oaks, CA: Sage.

Frey, L. R., & Barge, J. K. (Eds.). (1997). *Managing group life: Communicating in decision-making groups*. Boston: Houghton Mifflin.

Frey, L. R. (Ed.), Gouran, D. S., & Poole, M. S. (Assoc. Eds.). (1999). *The handbook of group communication theory & research*. Thousand Oaks, CA: Sage.

Gordon, W. J. J. (1961). *Synectics: The development of creative capacity*. New York: Harper & Row.

Green, T. B. (1975). An empirical analysis of nominal and interacting groups. *Academy of Management Journal, 18,* 63-70.

Hall, J., & Watson, M. (1970). The effects of a normative intervention on group performance and member reactions. *Human Relations, 23,* 299-317.

Hare, A. P. (1982). *Creativity in small groups*. Beverly Hills, CA: Sage.

Hare, A. P., Blumberg, H. H., Davies, M. F., & Kent, M. V. (1994). *Small group research: A handbook*. Norwood, NJ: Ablex.

Harris, T. E., & Sherblom, J. C. (1999). *Small group and team communication*. Boston: Allyn & Bacon.

Henry, J. (Ed.). (1991). *Creative management*. Thousand Oaks, CA: Sage.

Hirokawa, R. Y., & Poole, M. S. (Eds.). (1996). *Communication and group decision making* (2nd ed.). Thousand Oaks, CA: Sage.

Isaksen, S. G. (1988). Innovative problem solving in groups: New methods and research opportunities. In Y. Ijiri & R. L. Kuhn (Eds.), *New directions in creative and innovative management: Bridging theory and practice* (pp. 145-168). Cambridge, MA: Ballinger.

Jablin, F. M. (1981). Cultivating imagination: Factors that enhance and inhibit creativity in brainstorming groups. *Human Communication Research, 7,* 245-258.

Janis, I. (1982). *Groupthink: Psychological studies of foreign policy decisions and fiascoes* (2nd ed.). Boston: Houghton Mifflin.

Jarboe, S. (1996). Procedures for enhancing group decision making. In R. Y. Hirokawa & M. S. Poole (Eds.), *Communication and group decision making* (2nd ed., pp. 345-383). Thousand Oaks, CA: Sage.

Jarboe, S. (1999). Group communication and creativity processes. In L. R. Frey (Ed.), D. S. Gouran, & M. S. Poole (Assoc. Eds.), *The handbook of group communication theory & research* (pp. 335-368). Thousand Oaks, CA: Sage.

Johnson, C. E., & Hackman, M. Z. (1995). *Creative communication: Principles and applications*. Prospect Heights, IL: Waveland Press.

Kanter, R. M. (1989). *When giants learn to dance: Mastering the challenge of strategy, management, and careers in the 1900s*. New York: Simon & Schuster.

Kelly, J. R., & Karau, S. J. (1993). Entrainment of creativity in small groups. *Small Group Research, 24,* 179-198.

Kelly, J. R., & McGrath, J. E. (1985). Effects of time limits and task types on task performance and interaction of four-person groups. *Journal of Personality and Social Psychology, 49,* 395-407.

Keyton, J. (1999). *Group communication: Process and analysis*. Mountain View, CA: Mayfield.

Koestler, A. (1964). *The act of creation*. New York: Macmillan.

Kramer, M. W., Kuo, C. L., & Dailey, J. C. (1997). The impact of brainstorming techniques on subsequent group processes. *Small Group Research, 28,* 218-242.

Lumsden, G., & Lumsden, D. (1997). *Communicating in groups and teams: Sharing leadership* (2nd ed.). Belmont, CA: Wadsworth.

Maier, N. R. F. (1970). *Problem solving and creativity in individuals and groups*. Belmont, CA: Brooks/Cole.

McLeod, P. L., Lobel, S. A., & Cox, T. H., Jr. (1996). Ethnic diversity and creativity in small groups. *Small Group Research, 27,* 248-264.

Miller, W. C. (1987). *The creative edge: Fostering innovation where you work*. Reading, MA: Addison-Wesley.

Nemeth, C., & Wachtler, J. (1983). Creative problem solving as a result of majority vs. minority influence. *European Journal of Social Psychology, 13,* 45-55.

Offner, A. K., Kramer, T. J., & Winter, J. P. (1996). The effects of facilitation, recording, and pauses on group brainstorming. *Small Group Research, 27,* 283-298.

Osborn, A. F. (1963). *Applied imagination: Principles and procedures of creative problem-solving* (3rd rev. ed.). New York: Scribner's.

Parnes, S. J., & Noller, R. B. (1972). Applied creativity: The creative studies project: Part II. Results of the two-year program. *Journal of Creative Behavior, 6,* 164-186.

Pavitt, C. (1993). What (little) we know about formal group discussion procedures: A review of relevant research. *Small Group Research, 24,* 217-235.

Pavitt, C., & Curtis, E. (1994). *Small group discussion: A theoretical approach* (2nd ed.). Scottsdale, AZ: Gorsuch Scarisbrick.

Philipsen, G., Mulac, A., & Dietrich, D. (1979). The effects of social interaction in group idea generation. *Communication Monographs, 46,* 119-125.

Prince, G. M. (1970). *The practice of creativity: A manual for dynamic group problem solving.* New York: Collier Books.

Ricchiuto, J. (1997). *Collaborative creativity: Unleashing the power of shared thinking.* Akron, OH: Oakhill Press.

Scheidel, T. M. (1986). Divergent and convergent thinking in group decision-making. In R. Y. Hirokawa & M. S. Poole (Eds.), *Communication and group decision-making* (pp. 113-130). Beverly Hills, CA: Sage.

Scheidel, T. M., & Crowell, L. (1964). Idea development in small discussion groups. *Quarterly Journal of Speech, 50,* 104-145.

Schultz, B. G. (1996). *Communicating in the small group: Theory and practice* (2nd ed.). New York: HarperCollins.

Seibold, D. R., & Krikorian, D. H. (1997). Planning and facilitating group meetings. In L. R. Frey & J. K. Barge (Eds.), *Managing group life: Communicating in decision-making groups* (pp. 270-305). Boston: Houghton Mifflin.

Sunwolf. (1999). The pedagogical and persuasive effects of Native American lesson stories, African dilemma tales, and Sufi wisdom tales. *Howard Journal of Communications, 10,* 47-71.

Sunwolf, & Seibold, D. R. (1999). The impact of formal procedures on group processes, members, and task outcomes. In L. R. Frey (Ed.), D. S. Gouran, & M. S. Poole (Assoc. Eds.), *The handbook of group communication theory & research* (pp. 395-431). Thousand Oaks, CA: Sage.

Thornburg, T. H. (1991). Group size and member diversity influence on creative performance. *Journal of Creative Behavior, 25,* 324-333.

Torrance, E. P. (1961). Give the "devil" his due. *Gifted Child Quarterly, 5,* 115-118.

Torrance, E. P. (1965). *Rewarding creative behavior: Experiments in classroom creativity.* Englewood Cliffs, NJ: Prentice Hall.

Tulenko, P., & Kryder, S. (1990). Game-playing as an aid to the creative process of small groups. *Journal of Creative Behavior, 24,* 99-104.

VanGundy, A. B. (1984). *Managing group creativity: A modular approach to problem solving.* New York: AMACOM.

VanGundy, A. B. (1987). *Idea power: Techniques and resources to unleash the creativity in your organization.* New York: AMACOM.

Weick, K. (1979). *The social psychology of organizing.* Reading, MA: Addison-Wesley.

West, M. A. (1990). The social psychology of innovation in groups. In M. A. West & J. L. Farr (Eds.), *Innovation and creativity at work: Psychological and organizational strategies* (pp. 309-333). Chichester, UK: Wiley.

Wilson, G. L., & Hanna, M. S. (1993). *Groups in context: Leadership and participation in small groups* (3rd ed.). New York: McGraw-Hill.

12

Exploring Consequences of Group Communication in the Classroom

Unraveling Relational Learning

TERRE H. ALLEN
TIMOTHY G. PLAX
California State University, Long Beach

Taking part in small groups is an integral part of contemporary society. Recognizing the importance of participation in groups in the educational context, in particular, researchers have studied extensively the effects of group instruction on learning outcomes (see Allen & Plax, 1999). Despite the inherent value of this research for understanding group processes, scholars interested in group processes outside the classroom have virtually ignored the wealth of empirical findings concerning the use of groups in instructional settings. Similarly, although a number of education scholars note the interpersonal implications of group performance in the classroom, no systematic effort has been made to explore the relational consequences of group instructional practices.

A number of scholars have examined the interpersonal/relational aspects of groups, but with limited attention to the classroom context. Focusing on the educational context changes the nature of the questions that one must ask about the relational consequences of group interaction. Specifically, although well-documented lines of research continue to explicate the effects of group interaction on cognitive and affective learning outcomes, little is known about what impact participation in classroom groups has on how students learn about relationships. Our purpose in writing this chapter is to draw from what is known about relational communication in groups for the purpose of ascertaining understanding about the relational aspects of group communication in the classroom. In essence, we examine what goes on in classroom groups from a vantage point that is different from what has been the traditional focus—learning outcomes. Our central concern is exploring what knowledge individuals derive about relationships from their participation in instructional groups. As such, we propose a new direction for inquiry into classroom groups by providing a metatheoretical perspective for understanding group communication processes and identifying and defining relational learning as a critical consequence of group communication in the classroom. We conclude by establishing an agenda for future research regarding communication processes and relational learning in classroom groups.

DEFINING GROUPS
IN THE CLASSROOM

A variety of terms are used to describe the structural and interactional components of contemporary educational classrooms. Two basic structural elements of classrooms are whole-class instruction and part-class instruction (Sharan, Hertz-Lazarowitz, & Ackerman, 1980). Traditionally, students receive *whole-class* instruction in terms of being taught as a single group. The teacher's role in whole-class instruction is that of leader/facilitator of communication in the classroom. *Part-class instruction,* in contrast, occurs when teachers assign students to work in small groups in the classroom. The specific structural features of the part-class instructional classroom vary according to teacher and student interactional dynamics; teachers may take the central role of leader/facilitator, or groups of students may work interdependently, without the direct supervision of the teacher.

The basic process components of contemporary classrooms can be characterized in terms of the communication roles of teachers and students and the patterns of interaction that occur in the classroom. Teachers may serve as the primary communicators, or they may recede into the background and encourage students to communicate among themselves. Contemporary research in education has focused on students communicating with other students collaboratively; the term *collaborative learning* refers to a broad range of classroom activities—including small group discussions, whole-class discussions, interactive computer sessions, and peer tutoring—in which students interact with one another (Bruffee, 1993). Collaborative learning is a type of active learning, as distinguished from the more traditional model of student as passive learner. However, collaborative learning

can take place in both whole-class and part-class instructional structures, and teachers may play either a central or peripheral role as the communication facilitator.

To underscore the importance of communication to the dynamics of small groups in the educational context, it is essential to detail the structural and interactional components that provide the bases for defining groups in this context. A review of the literature (see Table 12.1 for a summary of the group communication research in the educational context from 1970-1999) indicates that at least two elements of the structural components of groups (or part-class instruction) in the educational context have specific relevance to communication in the classroom: grouping methods and incentive structures.

Grouping Methods

Teachers use at least four methods of grouping students in achieving part-class instruction: ability, intensive instruction, cooperative learning, and collaborative learning grouping. Each of these methods constitutes a distinct group type and differs from the others in terms of group processes, including communication patterns and member and teacher roles, and learning outcomes.

Ability grouping involves teachers dividing a class on the basis of predefined academic criteria so that they can instruct a more homogeneous group of students (Cohen, 1986). *Intensive instruction grouping* involves students working in groups directly with a teacher to provide more individualized instruction in a specific academic domain (e.g., computer instruction groups). The primary difference between ability grouping and intensive instruction grouping is the criterion used to select students for group membership. In intensive instruction groups, members are not assigned on the basis of academic criteria but, rather, on some other teacher-imposed rule(s) designed to meet particular instructional needs (e.g., all students in Row 1 of the classroom or students with last names beginning with A, B, or C). *Cooperative learning grouping* occurs

TABLE 12.1 Group Communication Research in the Classroom, K-Graduate School, 1970-1999

Level 1: Educational Context	Level 2A: Type of Group	Level 2B: Teacher Roles	Level 2C: Group Outcomes	Level 3: Other Variables
Phase 1: Early childhood education (Grades K-3, ages 5-8)	Ability grouping	Teacher as group leader • Assigns turns • Delivers accounting signals	Cognitive learning outcomes Affective learning outcomes	Sex/gender Subject matter Group size
Phase 2: Upper elementary school (Grades 4-6, ages 9-11)	Intensive instruction grouping	• Patterns turn taking	Relational learning outcomes • Affinity building	Type of physical classroom
Phase 3: Middle school (Grades 7-9, ages 12-14)	Cooperative learning grouping	Teacher as facilitator • Stimulates participation • Keeps group moving	• Interpersonal attraction • Friendship formation • Cultivation of interethnic	Instructional practices Physical disorder Emotional disorder
Phase 4: High school (Grades 10-12, ages 15-18)	Collaborative learning grouping	Teacher as provider of group structure • Defines group goals • Defines individual accountability • Provides rewards	relations • Suppression of ethnocentricism & chauvinism	Intellectual disorder
Phase 5: College/university (Grades 13-17, ages 18-21)				
Phase 6: Graduate education (Grades 18-22, ages 22-26)				

when teachers assign students to work together in a group on a specific task/assignment, without direct and immediate supervision of the teacher and with learning outcomes assessed at the group level, in addition to outcome assessment at the individual level (Cohen, 1986). Cooperative learning groups operate under conditions in which there is a task-oriented exchange between classroom peers, with pupils cooperating to earn recognition, grades, and/or other rewards (Slavin, 1989, 1990). Finally, *collaborative learning grouping* is similar to cooperative learning in that teachers assign students to work together in a group without direct or immediate supervision; however, learning outcomes are assessed only at the individual level.

In general, collaborative groups are used as units for promoting peer tutoring and pupil rehearsal of learning materials planned and provided by the teacher. The primary factor that distinguishes cooperative learning grouping from collaborative learning grouping has to do with the incentive structures related to group- versus individual-level assessment and rewards, respectively.

Incentive Structures

According to Johnson, Maruyama, Johnson, Nelson, and Skon (1981), three incentive structures related to reward-based learning are employed in educational contexts: individualistic, competitive, and cooperative incentive structures. An *individualistic incentive structure* rewards students on the basis of the quality of their work, as judged by the teacher, independent of the work of other students. In a *competitive incentive structure,* the teacher provides maximum rewards to some students and minimum rewards to other students. A *cooperative incentive structure* involves teachers rewarding students in direct proportion to the quality of their group work. In the classroom context, the ways in which rewards are distributed promotes a specific type of structure that motivates students to behave individualistically, competitively, or cooperatively.

The reward structure of a classroom also affects the communicative behavior that occurs among students. Johnson and Johnson (1975) distinguished incentive structures on the basis of how each reward structure promotes different patterns of interaction between students. They identified the following 11 interpersonal behaviors that occur among students and that distinguished cooperative, competitive, and individualistic incentive structures: (a) interaction, (b) mutual liking of group members, (c) effective communication, (c) trust, (d) acceptance and support, (e) use of personal resources, (f) helping and sharing, (g) emotional involvement, (h) coordination of effort, (i) division of labor, and (j) divergent and risk-taking thinking. These researchers characterized cooperative incentive structures by a high degree of each interpersonal behavior, competitive incentive structures by a low degree of interpersonal behavior, and individualistic incentive structures by the lack of interaction between students.

Interestingly, the primary factors distinguishing the three types of incentive structures are interpersonal communication and relationship development between group members. Collaborative and cooperative groups require interpersonal and group communicative behaviors that ability and intensive instruction groups do not. In this way, incentive structures clearly influence individuals' and groups' communicative behavior. Students' and teachers' motives and behaviors required for effective cooperative incentive structures are also qualitatively and quantitatively different from those required for successful competitive and individualistic incentive structures. Cooperative and collaborative structures require that students engage in communication to build relationships that support interdependent learning environments. Student members of cooperative and collaborative learning groups maintain a certain amount of control over the amount and duration of communication between students. Competitive and individualistic structures require that teachers maintain control over the amount and duration of interaction between students. Competitive and individualistic structures also require the teacher to promote independent learning and serves as the communicator of information. The structural components and interactional dynamics of cooperative learning groups, and their impact on learning outcomes, thus, provide a great deal of information regarding group communication in the educational context. Therefore, these unique components and dynamics of cooperative learning groups require further clarification and examination.

COMMUNICATION IN CLASSROOM GROUPS

Communication patterns in classroom groups depend on group processes, members' roles, and the role of the teacher. The patterns, processes, and roles in ability and intensive instruction groups are similar to those in whole-class instruction. For instance, communication in ability and intensive learning groups requires that the teacher exercise direct supervision over students, group members communicate mainly with the teacher, and the teacher serves as the group leader or facilitator. In contrast, collaborative and cooperative learning groups involve the teacher delegating authority and supervising indirectly; consequently, communication occurs mainly between group members as they work together to engage tasks.

Apart from the interdependence of members and lack of direct teacher participation in the group, the *combination* of two elements further distinguishes cooperative learning groups from other types of classroom groups: *group incentive structure* and *individual accountability*. Only cooperative learning groups, by definition, have a cooperative incentive structure. In such groups, learning outcomes and/or rewards are directly proportional to the quality of the work done by the students as a group. Students are held individually accountable for their own work (e.g., given an individual test score or assignment grade) but are also rewarded for contributions they make to others' learning (e.g., given extra time at recess if the group performance improves). In comparison, members of collaborative learning groups are also held individually accountable for their own learning, but there is no extrinsic reward structure for making contributions to others' learning. The difference in reward structure produces some important differences in learning outcomes.

LEARNING OUTCOMES IN CLASSROOM GROUPS

Slavin (1987b) observed that groups of elementary students working together in the classroom, without individual accountability and a group reward structure, were not likely to achieve many cognitive or affective benefits. Newman and Thompson (1987) concluded that groups of secondary school students did not achieve intended cognitive learning outcomes unless they had cooperative incentive structures, individual accountability, and competition among classroom groups.

An extensive body of research has examined how each of these incentive structures affects cognitive and affective learning outcomes. However, the majority of this research focuses on cooperative, as opposed to collaborative, learning. The research regarding collaborative learning outcomes is limited to a few studies of elementary school and college students. Typically, the studies of cooperative learning compare whole-class instruction, as a control condition, with achievement outcomes of the various types of cooperative learning structures that serve as experimental conditions (e.g., Team-Games-Tournaments [TGT], Learning Together [LT], etc). Identical learning materials are given to control and experimental groups; once the teacher or the group members have discussed them thoroughly, identical tests are given to both groups. *Cognitive learning* is typically operationalized as test scores on the content of the material covered in an academic unit, with *effect size*—the proportion of a standard deviation by which an experimental group exceeds a control group (Glass, McGaw, & Smith, 1981)—used as the measure of the impact of cooperative learning on student achievement. These studies also examine the impact of cooperative grouping on *affective learning* outcomes. The following sections provide a brief review and synthesis of research on cognitive and affective learning outcomes associated with cooperative learning.

Cognitive Learning Outcomes

Education scholars have developed an extensive body of research that details the cognitive learning effects of cooperative group instruction. Research across all grade levels and a wide variety of subject areas demonstrates that cooperative learning groups can produce more significant gains in cognitive learning than whole-class instruction. The central concern of education scholars has been to determine what subjects/content areas produce the most desirable learning outcomes when taught/learned under cooperative learning conditions. As such, the literature is briefly reviewed in terms of content or subject domains across the four levels of lower elementary, upper elementary, secondary school, and college.

Studies of students in lower elementary grades (3rd, 4th, and 5th) have investigated such effects across a wide variety of subject domains, including language arts (DeVries & Mescon, 1975; DeVries, Mescon, & Shackman, 1975b; Gonzales, 1981; Slavin,

1980a); reading comprehension (Gonzales, 1981; Stevens, Slavin, Farnish, & Madden, 1988); spelling (Kagan, Zahn, Widaman, Schwarzwald, & Tyrell, 1985; Stevens, Madden, Slavin, & Farnish, 1987; Tomblin & Davis, 1985; Van Oudenhoven, Van Berkum, & Swen-Koopmans, 1987; Van Oudenhoven, Wiersma, & Van Yperen, 1987); math (Gonzales, 1981; Johnson, 1985; Madden & Slavin, 1983b; Mason & Good, 1993; Robertson, 1982; Slavin & Karweit, 1981; Slavin, Leavey, & Madden, 1984; Webb & Farivar, 1994); verbal analogies (DeVries, Mescon, & Shackman, 1975a); and computer program performance (Chernick, 1990). Studies of students in upper elementary grades (6th, 7th, and 8th) have concentrated mainly on language arts (Slavin, 1977; Slavin & Oickle, 1981), math (Edwards, DeVries, & Snyder, 1972), science (Okebukola, 1985, 1986), history (Rich, Amir, & Slavin, 1986), and literature (Sharan et al., 1984). In general, these studies indicate that, regardless of subject matter, 3rd through 8th graders in cooperative groups achieve more gains in cognitive learning than their whole-class counterparts.

Investigations of cooperative learning in Grades 9 through 12 focus mainly on science and math instruction, and a few investigations have examined cooperative learning in the humanities. For example, DeVries, Edwards, and Wells (1974) found a significant effect size for 10th, 11th, and 12th graders in cooperative learning groups compared with whole-class instruction in knowledge of U.S. history. In general, studies of high school math instruction tend to favor cooperative learning over whole-class instruction (Artzt, 1983).

Although researchers have not examined systematically the role of cooperative learning in the college classroom, what studies have been conducted indicate that college students do not achieve the same cognitive gains as elementary and secondary school students when engaging in group work. This is due, in part, to college instructors' lack of knowledge and understanding of the pedagogical issues related to assigning and structuring classroom group activities (Fraser, Diener, Beaman, & Kelem, 1977).

Affective Learning Outcomes

Education scholars have also focused on the effects of cooperative group learning compared with whole-class instruction on affective learning outcomes. Given that cooperative learning represents an active, rather than a passive, form of learning and because interdependence of group members is a key characteristic of this type of learning, education scholars hypothesize that cooperative learning should have positive effects on social, motivational, and attitudinal outcomes. In particular, they have investigated the effects of cooperative learning on students' (a) liking of the class, (b) interpersonal attraction and friendship patterns, (c) self-esteem, (d) locus of control, (e) intergroup relations, and (f) acceptance of mainstreamed students.

Liking of the class. A number of the studies reviewed previously included pretest and posttest questionnaires designed to assess the hypothesis that students in cooperative learning groups develop significantly greater liking of the class, the school, and the subject matter than do students engaged in whole-class learning. These studies indicate that this is generally the case (DeVries et al., 1974; Edwards & DeVries, 1972, 1974; Humphreys, Johnson, & Johnson, 1982; Johnson, Johnson, Johnson, & Anderson, 1976; Lazarowitz, Baird, Bowlden, & Hertz-Lazarowitz, 1982; Slavin & Karweit, 1981; Slavin et al., 1984; Wheeler & Ryan, 1973).

Interpersonal attraction and friendship patterns. Several investigators have hypothesized that cooperative learning methods will increase interpersonal attraction between classmates, operationally defined as students' reports of liking classmates and feeling liked by them (Blaney, Stephan, Rosenfield, Aronson, & Sikes, 1977; Cooper, Johnson, Johnson, & Wilderson, 1980; DeVries &

Edwards, 1973; Johnson & Johnson, 1981a; Oickle, 1980; Slavin, 1977; Slavin & Karweit, 1981; Slavin et al., 1984). This hypothesis is based on the assumption that the increased contact gained from working in cooperative learning groups should produce perceived similarity between group members. That is, because students engage in activities together that allow them to work toward common goals, interpersonal attraction between them should be increased. Representative research supports this conclusion that when students learn to cooperate, they also learn to like one another. Other investigators who have defined interpersonal attraction as mutual concern, group cohesiveness, number of friendships, or in terms of friendship patterns (e.g., Cooper et al., 1980; Johnson & Johnson, 1981b; Johnson et al., 1976; Johnson & Johnson, 1983; Slavin & Karweit, 1981; Slavin et al., 1984) have found similar results. For instance, students in cooperative learning groups named more group members as "friends" than did students in control groups.

Student self-esteem. Slavin (1990) posited that one of the most critical affective outcomes of cooperative learning groups is the degree to which participating in such groups increases students' beliefs that they are valuable and important individuals—that is, it increases their self-esteem. Several studies have found this to be the case (e.g., Allen & Van Sickle, 1984; Blaney et al., 1977; DeVries, Lucasse, & Shackman, 1980; Geffner, 1978; Johnson, Johnson, & Scott, 1978; Johnson & Johnson, 1983; Lazarowitz et al., 1982; Madden & Slavin, 1983a; Slavin & Karweit, 1981; Slavin et al., 1984).

Locus of control. According to Slavin (1990), cooperative incentive structures provide a context that allows students to attribute successful learning to their own behavior and that of their fellow group members rather than to some external source (such as luck or the teacher). He posited that because cooper-

ative learning is measured by individual gains along with group gains and because students contribute to one another's learning, they should view both themselves and their group as responsible for the gains achieved. He also argued that because internal locus of control (the attribution of responsibility to one's self) has been shown to be the personality variable related most consistently to high academic performance, researchers must explore the role of cooperative learning groups in increasing students' attributions about their responsibility for their academic success. A variety of studies indicate that internal locus of control is positively associated with experiences gained from participating in cooperative learning groups (see Allen & Plax, 1999).

Intergroup relations. A great deal of research has focused on the role of cooperative learning in promoting intergroup relations (e.g., number of friendships formed between group members of differing racial or ethnic backgrounds). Hansell and Slavin (1981), for instance, found that heterogeneous cooperative learning groups enhance interethnic relations and interracial friendship formation. On the basis of such findings, Slavin (1990) criticized traditional education (e.g., whole-class instruction) for not providing conditions conducive to promoting interaction between students of different ethnic groups. He argued that cooperative learning structures provide an ideal solution to the problem by offering opportunities for students to interact with others from different ethnic backgrounds.

Acceptance of mainstreamed students. Scholars have been interested in the role of cooperative learning in increasing students' acceptance of academically mainstreamed students. Employing the same types of procedures used to investigate intergroup relations, students are asked, "Who are your friends in the class?" and "Whom do you NOT want to work with on a class project?" In this way, investigators attempt to identify students' reported friendships between mainstreamed students and those students who are rejected by their peers. Findings from these studies have yielded somewhat mixed results regarding acceptance of mainstreamed students, in that only a few studies found that students in cooperative groups form friendships with academically mainstreamed students because of group membership (Madden & Slavin, 1983a, 1983b).

Meta-analytic studies (e.g., Johnson et al., 1981) have shown that the biggest impact of cooperative learning is in the area of affective learning. Traditionally, *affective learning* is defined as students liking to learn and/or liking the subject matter (Bloom, 1976). Education scholars examining cooperative learning have broadened this traditional operational definition to include outcomes such as interpersonal attraction between group members, improved intergroup relations, peer acceptance, and friendship formation. In broadening the definition of affective learning in this way, scholars have overlooked the wealth of information regarding relationship development and relationship learning that occurs in classroom groups. Moreover, students' communication in groups has been placed within the category of affective learning, which limits the scope of how communication is investigated as well.

In summary, although the extant literature helps define how the structural and interactional dynamics of classroom groups lead to learning outcomes, it does not provide a clear picture of the role that group interaction plays in how, and what, students learn about developing relationships with peers. In particular, conceptual and operational definitions for affective learning blur an important dimension regarding learning that, to date, does not exist in the literature: learning about relationships, or what can be called *relational learning*. Although the well-documented lines of research that continue to explicate the role of group interaction on cognitive and affective learning outcomes are important, numerous questions remain unasked and unanswered regarding relational learning outcomes. Hence, we turn to discussion of a new

direction in the study of group communication: relational issues associated with group interaction in the classroom.

A NEW DIRECTION IN CLASSROOM GROUP PROCESSES

Cultivating a new direction for research necessitates a perspective that corresponds with the issues and concerns relevant to the new approach. Since the late 1970s, social psychologists and communication scholars have used the dialectical perspective as an approach to inquiry into the seemingly contradictory relations and dynamic tensions evident in social relationships (see Georgoudi, 1983; Johnson & Long, this volume). More recently, communication scholars have applied the dialectical approach to interpersonal/relational communication (Baxter, 1988, 1990, 1993, 1994; Baxter & Montgomery, 1996; Goldsmith, 1990; Goldsmith & Baxter, 1996; Montgomery, 1993; Rawlins, 1983, 1989).

Bakhtin (1981) advanced a "dialogic" conception of relational communication by emphasizing concepts of contradiction, change, praxis, and totality (see Baxter & Montgomery, 1996). This particular dialectical approach provides a unique perspective for viewing relational communication in that it illustrates the dynamic interplay of pervasive tensions and relational exigencies that provide the vitality of human communication and relationship development. Moreover, the dialectical perspective has been used to explain how communicative responses to relational tensions influence group processes (Frey, 1994, 1999; Frey & Barge, 1997; Johnson & Long, this volume; Smith & Berg, 1987). Therefore, a dialectical perspective is appropriate for exploring the communication processes that underlie relational learning in classroom groups.

Classroom Groups: A Dialectical Perspective

In essence, group learning activities (either cooperative or collaborative) afford students opportunities for interaction that are unlike the interaction opportunities present during whole-class instruction (Slavin, 1980a, 1980b, 1980c). During whole-class instruction, the teacher serves as facilitator/leader and, thereby, controls the communication that takes place in the classroom. Participation in cooperative and collaborative learning groups, however, involves students creating and sustaining the interactional dynamics of the learning environment. Although research in education on learning groups demonstrates that relational dynamics are a relevant aspect of group member exchanges, little is known about processes that contribute to how students create and sustain meaning during group interaction.

One approach that has been applied to explain the dialectical/relational aspects of groups is the perspective detailed by Smith and Berg (1987). Their view is particularly relevant to classroom groups because it focuses on the creation of meaning and coherence within groups. The use of communication to create meaning and coherence within groups is the primary vehicle through which cognitive and affective learning occur. Education scholars have identified *constructive activities*—the use of oral communication by students to state the topic, paraphrase the learning material, refer to personal knowledge, generate questions, create analogies, and answer questions—as the central practice used in cooperative and collaborative groups to promote learning (Webb, Troper, & Fall, 1995). The degree to which students realize the benefits of learning in classroom groups, thus, depends on the nature and quality of the communicative constructive activities used by group members.

Smith and Berg (1987) contended that group members are prone toward viewing group interaction as a struggle with tensions, especially in their attempts to create meaning and coherence from the interactions that occur within the group. They posited a dialectical view of group processes in which at least three categories of paradoxes and resulting tensions exist. The first category of dialectical tensions is referred to as *paradoxes of belonging,* which include issues such as identity involvement, individuality, and boundaries between the self and the group. The second category involves *paradoxes of engaging,* which include issues such as disclosure, trust, and intimacy among group members. Third is the category referred to as *paradoxes of speaking,* which involve issues of authority, dependency, creativity, and courage. According to Smith and Berg, how members manage these tensions influences the nature of how relationships develop between members, as well as the group's movement (or the lack thereof) toward its goals or objectives.

Members of classroom groups also attempt to create meaning and coherence as they experience a set of dialectical tensions (see Figure 12.1). Unfortunately, education scholars have overlooked these dialectical tensions, and in doing so, have reduced interpersonal and group communication to "affective learning outcomes." We believe, therefore, that it is necessary to reframe, from a dialectical perspective, as a part of group life, a portion of what has typically been defined as affective learning outcomes. Finally, we contend that one outcome of attempting to manage the dialectical tensions that occur during group participation is relational learning. In the following paragraphs, we describe some of the dialectical aspects of classroom groups.

Paradoxes of belonging. Members of classroom groups certainly experience paradoxes of belonging as they attempt to manage issues related to identity involvement, individuality, and boundaries between themselves and the group. Evidence suggests, however, that participation in cooperative learning groups can lead to increased feelings of membership and involvement. In fact, for a cooperative incentive structure to occur and cooperative learning outcomes to be realized, *all* group members must experience a sense of involvement and belonging. However, individual members of these and other types of learning groups (e.g., ability or intensive instruction) do not necessarily identify with other group mem-

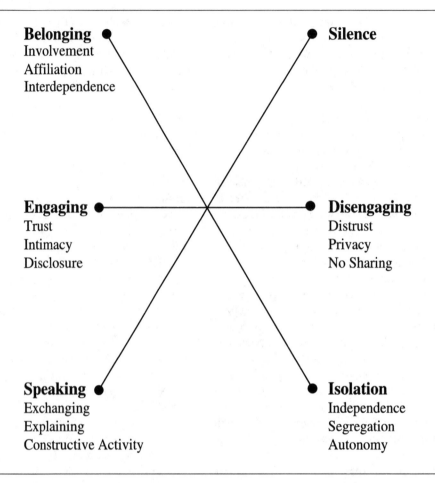

Figure 12.1. Dialectical Tensions in Classroom Groups

bers or experience a sense of involvement with the group. One important question for communication scholars to address, then, is how members of learning groups use communication to manage relational tensions associated with member participation and involvement. This is important to investigate because the benefits achieved by cooperative or collaborative learning depend on members' involvement and identification with the group and the group goal.

Paradoxes of engaging. Members of classroom groups, like member of other groups, experience paradoxes of engaging related to

development of trust, disclosure, and intimacy among members. These issues are particularly salient in cooperative and collaborative learning groups because members have the potential opportunity to interact with dissimilar others (peers of different ethnic, racial, or cultural backgrounds). The majority of research on pedagogical and instructional practices related to group work in the classroom indicates that student gains in learning are maximized when groups are heterogeneous (see Cohen, 1986), but the vast majority of cooperative and collaborative group-related instructional practices require heterogeneous group composition. Therefore, students in cooperative and collaborative groups face issues related to engaging in interaction with others whom they might not routinely select as interactional or relational partners. In fact, cooperative learning practices evolve out of a desire to increase intercultural communication in the classroom (see Slavin, 1983a, 1983b).

The ability to cooperate and collaborate depends on how students manage issues of trust, disclosure, and intimacy in heterogeneous groups. Hence, for a cooperative incentive structure to be realized by a group, group members must effectively manage the relational tensions associated with engaging one another. Research suggests that members of some heterogeneous groups demonstrate interethnic bonding as a result of working together (Slavin, 1989, 1990, 1991). Research also suggests that group work can result in students' acceptance of academically mainstreamed students (Madden & Slavin, 1983a, 1983b). However, little is known about the processes involved in managing, in classroom groups, the relational tensions associated with paradoxes of engaging.

Paradoxes of speaking. Finally, members of classroom groups experience paradoxes of speaking. One of the most central roles that classroom groups play in the instructional process is to provide students with opportunities for networking, dialoguing, and exchanging information. Cooperative and collaborative group practices are based on the premise that dialoguing and exchanging information, as promoted by the use of constructive activities, leads students to engage in cognitive elaboration of the learning materials, which increases cognitive and affective learning. However, for learning outcomes to be realized, members of classroom groups must also manage issues related to establishing authority, dealing with dependency among group members, engaging in creative thinking, and taking risks. Therefore, members of classroom groups must manage a wide variety of dialectical tensions related to speaking. Whereas establishing authority and dealing with dependency are tensions associated with structural components, creativity and the courage to take risks are tensions related to communicating about the content of the learning material. Paradoxes of speaking, thus, represent a complex cluster of tensions that appear to have a direct impact on students' learning outcomes. Paradoxes of speaking are also, perhaps, related to relational issues as well.

Participating in cooperative and collaborative groups provides students with opportunities to confront these paradoxes directly, and by doing so, potentially encourages them to manage tensions more effectively and become more involved and committed to the group. In addition, the degree to which learning outcomes are achieved during classroom group work is related to how student group members manage dialectical tensions. Moreover, a dialectical perspective emphasizes the idea that group learning is related to complex relational processes. Participation in classroom groups provides students with opportunities to engage in peer social interactions, in addition to task interaction, which require complex communication and relational skills. How effective students are in developing and using these skills during group member exchanges significantly influences both cognitive and affective learning, as well as what students learn about communication in relationships. Given the importance of relational processes to both communication and learning, scholars must seek to understand these processes more fully. The following section examines some relational issues relevant to classroom groups.

Relational Issues in Classroom Groups

As discussed earlier, an important aspect of classroom groups that has been overlooked is the relational dynamics that occur in such learning environments. In general, education scholars have conceptually and operationally defined communication in ways that reduce it to the individual or dyadic. By applying the term *interpersonal communication* to describe all the communication that occurs in classroom groups, education scholars have ignored the complexity of managing multiple relationships that is the essence of group learning. To understand classroom groups and how they contribute to relational learning, it is necessary to define in more concise terms the relational communication that characterizes classroom groups.

Keyton (1999) defined *relational communication in groups* as "verbal and nonverbal messages that create the social fabric of a group by promoting relationships between and among group members" (p. 192). She argued that relational communication constitutes both the structures and processes of a group's reality and, thereby, influences the connections and communication between group members. Through relational communication, group members produce messages that create, maintain, or alter relationships between themselves, as well as the climate within which group tasks are confronted. Keyton maintained that all groups engage in relational communication but that groups vary in terms of the quantity and quality of relational messages exchanged during interaction.

Classroom groups provide an arena for the exchange of social and intellectual messages; these exchanges, in turn, offer unique opportunities for learning about and engaging in relational development. In fact, students in lower elementary grades may experience some of their first relational learning opportunities, outside the family context, through their participation in classroom groups. For students of all age/grade levels, classroom groups provide a distinctive and important type of context for relational communication and for learning about interpersonal relations. As one example, classroom groups provide an opportunity for meeting others. Moreover, the assignment to a classroom group typically comes from the teacher, and students interact with others that they might not normally choose as interaction partners. In this way, students potentially have the opportunity for a wider variety of interaction partners than they normally would during whole-class instruction.

Classroom groups also provide an important context for formal/organized communicative exchange. Unlike the groups that exist on the playground or in other age-relevant social contexts, many classroom groups have a specified learning-outcome goal and some type of structure that leads to formalized communicative exchanges between the members. One of the most important features of cooperative and collaborative classroom groups, therefore, is that they provide a formal/organized context for both social and task communicative exchanges. As such, members have the opportunity to engage in friendship building via task accomplishment.

Classroom groups invariably take place within a context of supervised exchange, with some supervision and control exerted by the teacher. Teachers typically define group membership, tasks, and goals and provide some initial structure for classroom group interaction. Furthermore, in most traditional educational systems, the group activity takes place within the formal classroom. Because teachers generally make classroom group assignments, such groups are often viewed by members as a place for the legitimate exchange of messages (i.e., communicating with others is part of the assignment). In many instances, students who are not inclined to participate during whole-class discussions may find that a small group of students working together to complete a task provides a safe environment to practice social exchange.

Finally, classroom groups provide a place where social comparison processes are salient. Research in education has shown that the outcomes of cooperative learning groups include increased interpersonal attraction, development of friendships, improved intergroup relations, and acceptance of others. Part of the reason for these outcomes may be due to members of classroom groups being given opportunities to view others and engage in social comparisons; however, little is known about how communication between group members contributes to social comparison processes and their relevant outcomes.

Learning About Relationships

Participation in classroom groups, as explained above, can lead students to an understanding of issues related to group membership and involvement, dialoguing, networking and information exchange, nontraditional student exchanges, and management of frustrations and anxieties. Understanding and management of such issues leads to affinity building and bonding, cultivation of interethnic relationships, and the suppression of ethnocentrism and chauvinism. The process of recognizing, understanding, and managing the relational tensions of group work leads to learning about relationships.

Evidence of relational learning is inherent in the communication exchanged during group work; it should also be evidenced through students' self-understanding and self-awareness. Future research must take into account the complexities of relational communication required to achieve cooperation and collaboration in classroom groups. Furthermore, given that group work in elementary, secondary, and college education is commonplace, scholars need to explore what students learn about relationships and relational communication from their classroom group experiences. Classroom groups, thus, present a wealth of opportunities for those interested in exploring developmental issues related to relational learning and communication skill development.

CONCLUSION

In this chapter, we have presented a new direction for thinking about classroom groups. Specifically, we argued that education scholars have been unnecessarily reductionistic in their treatment of classroom groups by defining relational processes as primarily affective outcomes. We maintained that a dialectical view of classroom groups allows researchers and educators to ask questions about how

group members' communication leads to the creation, development, maintenance, and alteration of cooperative and collaborative structures, which, in turn, lead to the outcome of relational learning. Exactly how the process of relational learning unfolds remains unclear, but relational learning in classroom groups is worthy of investigation.

In this light, several compelling questions arise about the nature and consequences of group communication in the classroom: How do members of classroom groups use communication to manage the various dialectical tensions in their efforts to create a cooperative or collaborative climate? What prior knowledge about relationships do students use when engaging in group work in the classroom? Do students engage in different types of information processing in educational groups (e.g., problem solving and social information processing)? Are students more arbitrary or systematic in their information processing during exchanges in classroom groups?

From the time one begins the formal educational experience, group work is an integral part of the educational process. However, we still know relatively little about the process. Questions remain unasked and unanswered with respect to how little we know about what students learn, beyond content, from their experiences in classroom groups. We know even less about the role of communication in the educational process. In particular, we don't know how participation in classroom groups contributes to developmental learning about relational communication and its outcomes of affinity building, affiliation, interdependency, and trust. Understanding these issues and others can provide insight into the nature of issues related to relational and group communication in general and classroom group communication in particular. Systematic investigation of how students engage in learning about relationships during group participation, thus, is necessary to unravel the complicated issues involved in communication and learning in the classroom context.

The consequences of group communication in the classroom are undoubtedly related to the inevitable tensions that arise from the paradoxes associated with working alone versus working together. Frey and Barge (1997) argued that such tensions are an integral part of group life and that they are not necessarily a bad thing. They suggested that these tensions can lead to individual and group growth, but that both individuals and groups need to learn how to effectively manage these tensions. This is especially true in the classroom setting, where the management of these tensions results in learning. Our conclusion is that through the process of communicating to manage the inevitable tensions associated with classroom learning groups, students learn about relational and group communication processes. Accordingly, understanding the nature of classroom group communication is a critical step toward improving the use of groups as a method of instruction and understanding a facet of how individuals learn about relationships.

REFERENCES

Allen, T. H., & Plax, T. G. (1999). Group communication in the formal educational context. In L. R. Frey (Ed.), D. S. Gouran, & M. S. Poole (Assoc. Eds.), *The handbook of group communication theory & research* (pp. 493-515). Thousand Oaks, CA: Sage.

Allen, W. H., & Van Sickle, R. L. (1984). Learning teams and low achievers. *Social Education, 48,* 60-64.

Artzt, A. F. (1983). *The comparative effects of the student-team method of instruction and the traditional teacher-centered method of instruction upon student achievement, attitude, and social interaction in high school mathematics courses.* Unpublished doctoral dissertation, New York University.

Bakhtin, M. M. (1981). *The dialogic imagination: Four essays by M. M. Bakhtin* (M. Holquist, Ed.; C. Emerson & M. Holquist, Trans.). Austin: University of Texas Press.

Baxter, L. A. (1988). A dialectical perspective on communication strategies in relationship development. In S. Duck (Ed.), *Handbook of personal relationships: Theory, research, and interventions* (pp. 257-273). Chichester, UK: Wiley.

Baxter, L. A. (1990). Dialectical contradictions in relational development. *Journal of Social and Personal Relationships, 7,* 69-88.

Baxter, L. A. (1993). The social side of personal relationships: A dialectical perspective. In S. Duck (Ed.), *Social context and relationships: Vol. 3. Understanding relationship processes* (pp. 139-165). Newbury Park, CA: Sage.

Baxter, L. A. (1994). A dialogic approach to relationship maintenance. In D. J. Canary & L. Stafford (Eds.), *Communication and relational maintenance* (pp. 233-254). San Diego, CA: Academic Press.

Baxter, L. A., & Montgomery, B. M. (1996). *Relating: Dialogues and dialectics.* New York: Guilford Press.

Blaney, N. T., Stephan, C., Rosenfield, D., Aronson, E., & Sikes, J. (1977). Interdependence in the classroom: A field study. *Journal of Educational Psychology, 69,* 121-128.

Bloom, B. S. (1976). *Human characteristics and school learning.* New York: McGraw-Hill.

Bruffee, K. A. (1993). *Collaborative learning: Higher education, interdependence, and the authority of knowledge.* Baltimore: Johns Hopkins University Press.

Chernick, R. S. (1990). Effects of interdependent, coactive, and individualized work conditions on pupils' educational computer program performance. *Journal of Educational Psychology, 82,* 691-695.

Cohen, E. (1986). *Designing groupwork: Strategies for the heterogeneous classroom.* New York: Teachers College Press.

Cooper, L., Johnson, D. W., Johnson, R. T., & Wilderson, F. (1980). Effects of cooperative, competitive, and individualistic experiences on interpersonal attraction among heterogeneous peers. *Journal of Social Psychology, 111,* 243-252.

DeVries, D. L., & Edwards, K. J. (1973). Learning games and student teams: Their effects on classroom processes. *American Educational Research Journal, 10,* 307-318.

DeVries, D. L., Edwards, K. J., & Wells, E. H. (1974). *Teams-Games-Tournament in the social studies classroom: Effects of academic achievement, student attitudes, cognitive beliefs, and classroom climate* (Report No. 173). Baltimore: Johns Hopkins University.

DeVries, D. L., Lucasse, P. R., & Shackman, S. L. (1980). *Small group vs. individualized instruction: A field test of relative effectiveness* (Report No. 293). Baltimore: Johns Hopkins University.

DeVries, D. L., & Mescon, I. T. (1975). *Teams-Games-Tournament: An effective task and reward structure in the elementary grades* (Report No. 189). Baltimore: Johns Hopkins University.

DeVries, D. L., Mescon, I. T., & Shackman, S. L. (1975a). *Teams-Games-Tournaments' effects on reading skills in elementary grades* (Report No. 200). Baltimore: Johns Hopkins University.

DeVries, D. L., Mescon, I. T., & Shackman, S. L. (1975b). *Teams-Games-Tournaments in the elementary classroom: A replication* (Report No. 190). Baltimore: Johns Hopkins University.

Edwards, K. J., & DeVries, D. L. (1972). *Learning games and student teams: Their effects on student attitudes and achievement* (Report No. 147). Baltimore: Johns Hopkins University.

Edwards, K. J., & DeVries, D. L. (1974). *The effects of Teams-Games-Tournament and two structural varia-*

tions on classroom processes, student attitudes, and student achievement (Report No. 172). Baltimore: Johns Hopkins University.

Edwards, K. J., DeVries, D. L., & Snyder, J. P. (1972). Games and teams: A winning combination. *Simulation and Games, 3,* 247-269.

Fraser, S. C., Diener, E., Beaman, A. L., & Kelem, R. T. (1977). Two, three, or four heads are better than one: Modifications of college performance by peer monitoring. *Journal of Educational Psychology, 69,* 101-108.

Frey, L. R. (1994). The naturalistic paradigm: Studying small groups in the postmodern era. *Small Group Research, 25,* 53-66.

Frey, L. R. (1999). Teaching small group communication. In A. L. Vangelisti, J. A. Daly, & G. W. Friedrich (Eds.), *Teaching communication: Theory, research, and methods* (2nd ed., pp. 99-113). Mahwah, NJ: Lawrence Erlbaum.

Frey, L. R., & Barge, J. K. (Eds.). (1997). *Managing group life: Communicating in decision-making groups.* Boston, MA: Houghton Mifflin.

Geffner, R. (1978). *The effects of interdependent learning on self-esteem, interethnic relations, and intra-ethnic attitudes of elementary school children: A field experiment.* Unpublished doctoral dissertation, University of California, Santa Cruz.

Georgoudi, M. (1983). Modern dialectics in social psychology: A reappraisal. *European Journal of Social Psychology, 13,* 77-93.

Glass, G., McGaw, B., & Smith, M. L. (1981). *Meta-analysis in social research.* Beverly Hills, CA: Sage.

Goldsmith, D. (1990). A dialectical perspective on the expression of autonomy and connection in romantic relationships. *Western Journal of Speech, 54,* 537-556.

Goldsmith, D., & Baxter, L. A. (1996). Constituting relationships in talk: A taxonomy of speech events in social and personal relationships. *Human Communication Research, 23,* 87-114.

Gonzales, A. (1981). *An approach to interdependent/cooperative bilingual education and measures related to social motives.* Unpublished manuscript, California State University at Fresno.

Hansell, S., & Slavin, R. E. (1981). Cooperative learning and the structure of interracial friendships. *Sociology of Education, 54,* 98-106.

Humphreys, B., Johnson, R., & Johnson, D. W. (1982). Effects of cooperative, competitive, and individualistic learning on students' achievement in science class. *Journal of Research in Science Teaching, 19,* 351-356.

Johnson, D. W., & Johnson, R. T. (1975). *Learning together and alone.* Englewood Cliffs, NJ: Prentice Hall.

Johnson, D. W., & Johnson, R. T. (1981a). Effects of cooperative and individualistic learning experiences on interethnic interaction. *Journal of Educational Psychology, 73,* 444-449.

Johnson, D. W., & Johnson, R. T. (1981b). The integration of the handicapped into regular classrooms: Effects of cooperative and individualistic instruction. *Contemporary Educational Psychology, 6,* 344-355.

Johnson, D. W., Johnson, R. T., Johnson, J., & Anderson, D. (1976). The effects of cooperative vs. individualized instruction on student prosocial behavior, attitudes toward learning, and achievement. *Journal of Educational Psychology, 68,* 446-452.

Johnson, D. W., Johnson, R. T., & Scott, L. (1978). The effects of cooperative and individualized instruction on student attitudes and achievement. *Journal of Social Psychology, 104,* 207-216.

Johnson, D. W., Maruyama, G., Johnson, R. Nelson, D., & Skon, L. (1981). Effects of cooperative, competitive, and individualistic goal structures on achievement: A meta-analysis. *Psychological Bulletin, 89,* 47-62.

Johnson, J. C. (1985). *The effects of the groups of four cooperative learning models on student problem-solving achievement in mathematics.* Unpublished doctoral dissertation, University of Houston.

Johnson, R. T., & Johnson, D. W. (1983). Effects of cooperative, competitive, and individualistic learning experiences on social development. *Exceptional Children, 49,* 323-329.

Kagan, S., Zahn, G. L., Widaman, K. F., Schwarzwald, J., & Tyrell, G. (1985). Classroom structural bias: Impact of cooperative and competitive classroom structures on cooperative and competitive individuals and groups. In R. E. Slavin, S. Kagan, R. Hertz-Lazarowitz, C. Webb, & R. Schmuck (Eds.), *Learning to cooperate, cooperating to learn* (pp. 230-265). New York: Plenum Press.

Keyton, J. (1999). Relational communication in groups. In L. R. Frey (Ed.), D. S. Gouran, & M. S. Poole (Assoc. Eds.), *The handbook of group communication theory & research* (pp. 192-222). Thousand Oaks, CA: Sage.

Lazarowitz, R., Baird, H., Bowlden, V., & Hertz-Lazarowitz, R. (1982). *Academic achievements, learning environment, and self-esteem of high school students in biology taught in cooperative-investigative small groups.* Unpublished manuscript, The Technion, Haifa, Israel.

Madden, N. A., & Slavin, R. E. (1983a). The effects of cooperative learning on the social acceptance of mainstreamed academically handicapped students. *Journal of Special Education, 17,* 171-182.

Madden, N. A., & Slavin, R. E. (1983b). Mainstreaming students with mild academic handicaps: Academic and social outcomes. *Review of Educational Research, 53,* 519-569.

Mason, D. A., & Good, T. L. (1993). Effects of two-group and whole-class teaching on regrouped elementary students' mathematics achievement. *American Educational Research Journal, 30,* 328-360.

Montgomery, B. M. (1993). Relationship maintenance versus relationship change: A dialectical dilemma. *Journal of Social and Personal Relationships, 10,* 205-224.

Newman, F. M., & Thompson, J. (1987). *Effects of cooperative learning on achievement in secondary schools: A summary of research.* Madison: University of Wisconsin, National Center on Effective Secondary Schools.

Oickle, E. (1980). *A comparison of individual and team learning.* Unpublished doctoral dissertation, University of Maryland, Baltimore.

Okebukola, P. A. (1985). The relative effectiveness of cooperativness and competitive interaction techniques in strengthening students' performance in science class. *Science Education, 69,* 501-509.

Okebukola, P. A. (1986). Impact of extended cooperative and competitive relationships on the performance of students in science. *Human Relations, 39,* 673-682.

Rawlins, W. K. (1983). Negotiating close friendships: The dialectic of conjunctive freedoms. *Human Communication Research, 9,* 255-266.

Rawlins, W. K. (1989). A dialectical analysis of the tensions, functions, and strategic challenges of communication in young adult friendships. In J. A. Anderson (Ed.), *Communication yearbook* (Vol. 12, pp. 157-189). Newbury Park, CA: Sage.

Rich, Y., Amir, Y., & Slavin, R. E. (1986). *Instructional strategies for improving children's across-ethnic relations.* Ramat Gan, Israel: Institute for the Advancement of Social Integration in Schools.

Robertson, L. (1982). *Integrated goal structuring in the elementary school: Cognitive growth in mathematics.* Unpublished doctoral dissertation, Rutgers University, New Brunswick, NJ.

Sharan, S., Hertz-Lazarowitz, R., & Ackerman, Z. (1980). Academic achievement of elementary school children in small group vs. whole class instruction. *Journal of Experimental Education, 48,* 125-129.

Sharan, S., Kussell, P., Hertz-Lazarowitz, R., Bejarano, Y., Raviv, S., & Sharan, Y. (1984). *Cooperative learning in the classroom: Research in desegregated schools.* Hillsdale, NJ: Lawrence Erlbaum.

Slavin, R. E. (1977). *Student team learning techniques: Narrowing the achievement gap between the races* (Report No. 228). Baltimore: John Hopkins University.

Slavin, R. E. (1980a). Cooperative learning. *Review of Educational Research, 50,* 315-342.

Slavin, R. E. (1980b). Effects of individual learning expectations on student achievement. *Journal of Educational Psychology, 72,* 520-524.

Slavin, R. E. (1980c). Effects of student teams and peer tutoring on academic achievement and time on-task. *Journal of Experimental Education, 48,* 252-257.

Slavin, R. E. (1983a). *Cooperative learning.* New York: Longman.

Slavin, R. E. (1983b). When does cooperative learning increase student achievement? *Psychological Bulletin, 94,* 429-445.

Slavin, R. E. (1987b). Cooperative learning: Where behavioral and humanistic approaches to classroom motivation meet. *Elementary School Journal, 88,* 29-37.

Slavin, R. E. (1989). Cooperative learning and student achievement. In R. E. Slavin (Ed.), *School and class-room organization* (pp. 45-57). Hillsdale, NJ: Lawrence Erlbaum.

Slavin, R. E. (1990). *Cooperative learning: Theory, research, and practice.* Boston: Allyn & Bacon.

Slavin, R. E. (1991). Synthesis of research on cooperative learning. *Educational Leadership, 48*(5), 71-82.

Slavin, R. E., & Karweit, N. (1981). Cognitive and affective outcomes of an intensive student team learning experience. *Journal of Experimental Education, 50,* 29-35.

Slavin, R. E., Leavey, M., & Madden, N. A. (1984). Combining cooperative learning and individualized instruction: Effects on student mathematics achievement, attitudes, and behaviors. *Elementary School Journal, 84,* 409-422.

Slavin, R. E., & Oickle, E. (1981). Effects of cooperative learning teams on student achievement and race relations: Treatment by race interaction. *Sociology of Education, 54,* 174-180.

Smith, K. K., & Berg, D. N. (1987). *Paradoxes of group life: Understanding conflict, paralysis, and movement in group dynamics.* San Francisco: Jossey-Bass.

Stevens, R. J., Madden, N. A., Slavin, R. E., & Farnish, A. M. (1987). Cooperative integrated reading and composition: Two field experiments. *Reading Research Quarterly, 22,* 433-454.

Stevens, R. J., Slavin, R. E., Farnish, A. M., & Madden, N. A. (1988, April). *Effects of cooperative learning and direct instruction in reading comprehension strategies on main idea identification.* Paper presented at the meeting of the American Educational Research Association, New Orleans, LA.

Tomblin, E. A., & Davis, B. R. (1985). *Technical report of the evaluation of the race/human relations program: A study of cooperative learning environment strategies.* San Diego, CA: San Diego Public Schools.

Van Oudenhoven, J. P., Van Berkum, G., & Swen-Koopmans, T. (1987). Effects of cooperation and shared feedback on spelling achievement. *Journal of Educational Psychology, 79,* 92-124.

Van Oudenhoven, J. P., Wiersma, B., & Van Yperen, N. (1987). Effects of cooperation and feedback by fellow pupils on spelling achievement. *European Journal of Psychology of Education, 2,* 83-91.

Webb, N. M., & Farivar, S. (1994). Promoting helping behaviors in cooperative small groups in middle school mathematics. *American Education Research Journal, 31,* 369-395.

Webb, N. M., Troper, J. D., & Fall, R. (1995). Constructive activity and learning in collaborative small groups. *Journal of Educational Psychology, 87,* 406-423.

Wheeler, R., & Ryan, F. L. (1973). Effects of cooperative and competitive classroom environments on the attitudes and achievement of elementary school students engaged in social studies inquiry activities. *Journal of Educational Psychology, 65,* 402-407.

PART VI

Group Communication Contexts

13

A Bona Fide Perspective for the Future of Groups

Understanding Collaborating Groups

CYNTHIA STOHL
Purdue University

KASEY WALKER
Tulane University

In today's complex and volatile global context, companies (often competitors) are working together to solve technical problems and create high-quality products that they would otherwise be unable to produce alone. Since the late 1980s, collaborations have become common across industries and types of organizations (see Farr & Fischer, 1992; Gulati, Khanna, & Nohria, 1994; Perlmutter & Heenan, 1986). For example, the Boeing 767 aircraft was collaboratively designed by engineers from Boeing, who created the cockpit and fuel assembly; engineers of Aeritalia SAI, who conceived the rudder and fins; and a collection of Japanese firms who produced the main body frame (Hladik, 1988). Another case in point was TEAM (Technologies Enabling Agile Manufacturing), an acronym for a group of companies and university faculty members who worked together on the information needs of product realization. This collaboration represented a multi-enterprise context that relied heavily on new communication technologies to bring together distinct groups of people to work on common problems across diverse institutional types, professional training, and organizational roles (Contractor, 1995).

Collaborative arrangements provide organizations with the necessary alliances and, hence, resources to address increasing development and production costs, decreasing research-to-market times, and escalating problem and product complexity. At the center of these collaborative efforts are work groups composed of employees from different organizations, often meeting face-to-face only sporadically, and who stay together only for the duration of the special project.

In this chapter, we expand the conception of "group" to take into account the interorganizational and dynamic nature of these collaborating groups. Such groups, we argue, bring challenges for researchers, practitioners,

237

and participants that were not faced in the traditional organizational groups of the past nor in the virtual teams of a single organization that are now commonplace. Our basic argument is that previous conceptions of what is a group are insufficient to capture the nature of collaborating groups. Social scientists have traditionally conceptualized a *group* as three or more people meeting together face-to-face to address task and/or social needs. Within this conceptualization, researchers have explored a range of intragroup dynamics, including decision making, phases of group development, leadership, and conflict communication. The members of such organizational groups, however, were all employed by the same organization, worked in the same location, operated under the same organizational norms and bylaws, and were subject to the same organizational hierarchy. Furthermore, these groups were considered largely insular; the necessary skills and resources to complete assigned tasks were all within the group's defined boundaries.

In the last 10 years, however, theoretical developments (see, e.g., Poole, 1999; Putnam & Stohl, 1990), the introduction of new communication technologies (see, e.g., Scott, 1999), and the impact of globalization (see, e.g., Monge & Fulk, 1999) have radically changed the conception of a group. Researchers and practitioners have increasingly been faced with groups whose members were no longer necessarily co-located; members came from the same company but were spatially and temporally separated. Indeed, a 10-year study of consumer products manufacturing; petroleum and chemicals production; computer and electronic manufacturing; and transportation, financial, semiconductor, and retail companies found that "a) team-based structures, b) shared authority and incentive systems, c) networked coordinating mechanisms, and d) interactive, real-time information-enabled operating and management processes" (Applegate, 1999, p. 59) were part of a new but critical organizational design criterion—collaboration. Consistent with this new way of organizing, Handy (1995) has noted,

We are beginning to see more signs of these "virtual organizations," organizations that do not need to have all the people, or sometimes any of the people, in one place. . . . The organization exists, but you can't see it. It is a network, not an office. (p. 42)

Clearly, the burgeoning study of virtual groups can shed some light on the nature of collaborating groups as conceptualized here, although it is important to note that not all collaborating groups are virtual. Some consistently meet face-to-face in one specially designed environment; others come together for regular meetings but occasionally work in a virtual environment; and some most often meet via videoconference and other collaborative technologies. Nonetheless, many of the questions whose answers are of vital importance for understanding the nature of virtual groups are equally important for understanding collaborating groups. A 1998 special joint issue of *Organizational Science* and the *Journal of Computer-Mediated Communication*, for example, highlighted some of these issues; contributions examined the formation of hierarchies across space and time (Ahuja & Carley, 1998), the creation of trust in the absence of face-to-face communication (Jarvenpaa & Leidner, 1998), and the role of technology in the mediation of group member relationships (Kraut, Steinfield, Chan, Butler, & Hoag, 1998).

Although these are important steps, sole consideration of these issues is not sufficient to fully capture the nature of collaborating groups. Collaborating groups deal with relational, economic, political, structural, and cultural complexities that do not necessarily evolve in a virtual group. In this chapter, we first delineate recent changes in organizational structures and processes and resulting changes in group structure, composition, and relational boundaries. We then explore how these changes necessitate a radical shift in models for understanding group action. A bona fide group collaboration model is presented to meet that need. We conclude by identifying how this model helps us to understand and study collaborating groups through a reconceptualization of traditional group constructs.

CHANGING ORGANIZATIONAL PRACTICES CHANGE GROUP STRUCTURE AND ACTION

For some time, organizations have been situated neither in one place nor within one time; instead, they are composed of employees located in several places, temporally separated, moving in, through, and out of traditional organizational boundaries. Organizations use new technologies and loose connections between departments or business units to manage these relationship and to meet the needs of operating in the volatile and dynamic global business environment (see DeSanctis & Jackson, 1994).

Recent research has focused on these distributed organizations, variously termed *virtual, network,* and *cluster organizations* (see Ahuja & Carley, 1998; Beyerlein & Johnson, 1994; Camillus, 1993; DeSanctis & Jackson, 1994; Ghoshal & Bartlett, 1990; Goldman, Nagel, & Preiss, 1995; Miles & Snow, 1992; Mills, 1991). A virtual organization exists across time and space; its members and assets are neither co-located nor working at the same time. As such, the virtual organization generally "consist[s] of a grouping of units of different firms that have joined in an alliance to exploit the complementary skills in pursuing common strategic objectives" (Dess, Rasheed, McLaughlin, & Priem, 1995, p. 10), although in some cases the members are nominally within one organizational system. Moreover, members of virtual organizations often do not share the same first language, have differing ethnic and national identities, and have had diverse organizational experiences.

Several authors have identified key characteristics of virtual organizations (see Byrne, Brandt, & Otis, 1993; Dess et al., 1995; Miles & Snow, 1992; Monge, 1995; Nohria & Berkley, 1994). Monge's (1995) identification of a network organization captures most of these characteristics and typifies it in three important ways:

> First, they are built out of flexible, emergent internal communication networks rather than traditional hierarchies. . . . Second, highly flexible linkages connect them to a changing, dynamic network of external organizations. . . . Third, global network organizations require a highly sophisticated information technology infrastructure that supports both the flexible, emergent internal communication system [and] the extensive communication relations with external partners. (p. 135)

As organizations have changed, so too have the work groups involved. Work groups have been adapted to the virtual environment, and members now interact across distance and time, using mediated forms of communication. These teams may "see" one another only via videoconferencing or "talk" only via e-mail. Lipnack and Stamps (1997) defined a *virtual team* as "a group people who interact through interdependent tasks guided by common purpose . . . [that] works across space, time and organizational boundaries with links strengthened by webs of communication technologies" (p. 7). This definition, or some variation thereof, is typical of how virtual teams are described throughout the communication, management, information systems, and engineering literatures.

In collaborating groups, organizations use other organizations in their virtual networks. New communication technologies, advances in transportation, and the ability to share data through new knowledge management techniques make such collaborations feasible. In general, the reasons for the growing use of collaboration seem to focus on finding solutions to problems of heightened complexity with ever-increasing time constraints in the marketplace and increasing cost concerns. The expectation is that by involving multiple partners, collaboration will alleviate some of these concerns by allowing organizations to (a) complete difficult, complex projects in a timely fashion; (b) pool financial and material resources; and (c) increase innovation (especially in the area of new technologies) by leveraging the strengths, knowledge, and skills of each organizational partner involved.

Examples of collaboration are numerous. In the past, collaborative relationships were found most commonly in the motor vehicle, aerospace, telecommunication, computer, and electronic industries; in fact, by 1988, these five areas composed 87% of all collaborative agreements (Hergert & Morris, 1988). Today, newspapers around the globe are filled with stories of collaboration concerning products ranging from smart card technology to pharmaceuticals. However, although most practitioners and researchers can identify collaborations in situ, there is very little agreement on the definition of collaboration or on what are or should be the critical components of a collaboration (see, e.g., competing definitions offered by Daily, 1980; Kumar & van Dissel, 1996; Littler, Leverick, & Bruce, 1995; Roberts & Bradley, 1991; Wood & Gray, 1991). Keyton and Stallworth (in press) argued that, taken as a whole, the majority of definitions "identify collaborations as a temporarily formed group with representatives from many other primary organizations." Our definition, taken from Walker, Craig, and Stohl (1998) begins with those elements but moves on to capture the complexity and dynamism of collaboration:

> *Collaboration* [italics added] is the process of creating and sustaining a negotiated temporary system which spans organizational boundaries involving autonomous stakeholders with varying capabilities including resources, knowledge and expertise and which is directed toward individual goals and mutually accountable and innovative ends. (p. 5)

Collaboration, thus, relies on the coming together of members representing several organizations to work together in a temporary alliance as a group for a specific purpose. The relationship between the organizational members who make up the collaboration is

> somewhat distinct from the kind of relationship[s] that a large company like General Motors or Boeing has with its suppliers. In the latter case, the dominant company can dictate terms of engagement, enforce its own procedures, and make all of the critical decisions. The relationship of parties in the [collaboration] is more peer-to-peer, and therefore requires consent which is based on self-interest as each defines it. (Solberg, 1997, p. 10)

To date, researchers in this area have been most concerned with the reasons for and the effectiveness of these collaborations between organizations. In general, the effectiveness of collaboration efforts has been found to be associated with several types of structural, cognitive, and interaction-oriented variables negotiated on an ongoing basis within the dynamic and complex environment of the collaboration process. The processes associated with effective collaboration include the integration and coordination of diverse tasks across time and space (Crabtree, Fox, & Baid, 1997; Daily, 1980; Van de Ven, Delbecq, & Koenig, 1976; Wilson & Shi, 1996), appropriate allocation of scarce resources to partners (Littler et al., 1995; Tucker, 1991), capacity for transferable organizational learning about collaboration (Garvin, 1993; Hamel, Doz, & Prahalad, 1989; Inkpen, 1996), existence of a "champion" of the collaboration process itself (Inkpen, 1996; Littler et al., 1995; Lynch, 1990), creation of trust between collaborative partners (Dodgson, 1993; Lynch, 1990; Meyer & Allen, 1991), development of members' commitment to collaboration (Farr & Fischer, 1992; Lynch, 1990; Schott, 1994), and the degree and the medium of communication between the collaborating parties involved (Mintzberg, Dougherty, Jorgensen, & Westley, 1996; Olson & Teasley, 1996; Tushman, 1978).

Clearly, at the center of all inter-organizational collaborations is the collaborating group, the focus of this chapter. Collaborating groups may or may not have the components of a virtual team; although they oftentimes operate as virtual teams, at other times, some or all members meet face-to-face. In addition, collaborating group members come from different home organizations, creating a new host of issues for practitioners and researchers. To understand these groups, then, we cannot rely solely on theories and models developed from studying groups working face-to-face or virtual groups composed of members from the same organization. Instead, we propose to position these groups within a framework—the bona fide group collaboration model (Walker et al., 1998)—that allows us to understand better their complex nature.

CHANGING GROUPS NECESSITATE CHANGED MODELS

Although some variables associated with group collaboration have been examined and some models of the process have been developed (e.g., Kumar & van Dissel, 1996; Malone & Crowston, 1990; Tucker, 1991; Wilson & Shi, 1996), they do not take into account the "generative," "processual," and "embedded" nature of communication in the overall process of collaboration. Recent studies of computer-supported collaborative work (see Scott, 1999) and newly developed communication models of collaboration (see Keyton & Stallworth, in press) place communication as central to the overall cooperative/collaborative process. Scott's (1999) system-based model of computer-supported collaborative work focused primarily on the group communication technologies that make such collaborations possible. His model links a variety of inputs (e.g., proximity of group members to one another, task characteristics, and technology) with meeting processes and feedback/group learning to predict several outcomes (i.e., task/decision performance, efficiency, member satisfaction, and communication). Keyton and Stallworth's (in press)

model identifies seven components necessary for successful collaboration (e.g., shared goal, equal input, and member motivation and maturity). Their model suggests that the communication among collaboration members and the developing group culture are central to the collaboration process. Keyton and Stallworth even go so far as to argue that without a shared goal, interdependence between members, equal input by the collaboration members, and shared decision making, "collaboration cannot occur."

Although these models provide insight into how collaborative efforts might work, the very complexity of collaborations makes it impossible to delineate all the possible variables that might affect both the processes and outcomes of the collaboration. Indeed, macro-interorganizational realities, global finances, embeddedness in larger and more structured networks, and many other factors often seem to make it impossible to achieve the autonomous and egalitarian processes that Keyton and Stallworth advocate. Yet collaborations are often successful (see, e.g., the collaboration in the computing industry that created a common desktop environment and involved Hewlett-Packard, IBM, Sun Microsystems, and USL [now Novell]; Miller, 1996). Thus, in this chapter we do not develop a prescriptive model for collaborating groups; rather, our goal is to provide a framework for understanding such groups to identify relevant concerns and to begin to ask significant questions concerning the formation, performance, and eventual dissolution of collaborating groups.

Walker et al. (1998) developed a conceptual framework that links understanding of collaborating groups with their overall communication processes and allows for the generation of new theoretical explanations for their performance. Furthermore, this model frames fundamental changes that take place in the nature of collaborating groups and, thereby, allows for future investigation and increased understanding of collaborative group processes. The model is based on the precepts of the bona fide group perspective (Putnam &

Stohl, 1990, 1996; Stohl & Putnam, 1994). This perspective and the model of collaboration developed by Walker et al. (1998) recognize that groups and organizations are not only positioned within multiple contexts but are also constantly interacting with and through those environments, which results in changes for both the acting group and contexts. In short, to understand what is going on "inside" any group we must also understand what is going on "outside" it and the relation between these two spaces.

The elements of the bona fide group perspective have been discussed in great detail elsewhere (in addition to the sources cited previously, see the essays in Frey, in press; Waldeck, Shepard, Teitelbaum, Farrar, & Seibold, this volume) but, in brief, this perspective focuses on three elements of groups. First, groups have stable yet permeable boundaries that simultaneously define group membership and allow for movement in and out of the group by members. This characteristic is reflected in group members' identifications with the group, overlapping and fluctuating group membership, intergroup communication, and group member relations outside the group itself, as well as group cohesiveness. Second, groups are interdependent with the contexts (i.e., the group's multiple physical and social environments) in which they are embedded. This characteristic describes the simultaneous cause-effect relationships that exist between a group and its contexts. Third, groups have unstable and ambiguous borders that differentiate a group from its contexts. These borders are not stable in the sense that "groups continually change, redefine, and renegotiate their borders to alter their identities and embedded context" (Stohl & Putnam, 1994, p. 291). In other words, the identity of a group, as a group, changes over time.

Walker et al. (1998) extended the conceptualization of the bona fide group perspective to understand collaboration and developed a specific model—the bona fide group collaboration model (BFGCM)—that operationalizes many of the tenets embedded within the bona fide group perspective. As noted earlier, collaborative efforts involve the creation of a group or team of individuals representing all collaborating partners; this temporary, multiorganizational group is the focus of the model (see Figure 13.1).

The primary element of the BFGCM is the communicative context, which constitutes the collaboration process. Given that collaboration is "managed through its communication processes" (Blaquier & Harvey, 1995, p. 18), the model illustrates how, through communication, the various participants in a collaborative venture manage their boundaries, borders, contexts, roles, and tasks. The model identifies several other key elements (that tell the "story" of collaboration): environmental exigencies, collaborative partners, relational boundary, negotiated temporary system, innovative outcomes, mutually accountable ends, and individual goals.

Organizations participate in collaborative efforts only when there is a need, and, thus, the BFGCM begins with environmental exigencies. The impetus for a collaboration is important for all stages of the collaboration process and may include a needed response to a government directive, a sudden opportunity for expansion, and/or one organization's lack and another's surplus of needed information or skills to develop a lucrative new technology. It is important to examine these environmental exigencies because they affect both the structure and process of the collaborative effort. Obviously, the impetus for the organizations involved has direct impact on the "results" of a collaborative effort. The outcomes of a collaboration are not unitary; rather, the completion of a collaborative effort involves several components: individual goals, organizational goals, innovative outcomes, and mutually accountable ends. A primary objective drives a collaboration and is usually associated with some urgency and need for innovation—thus, the innovative outcomes and the idea that collaborative partners are mutually accountable for these ends. In addition, members have their own individual and organizational goals that are somewhat distinct from

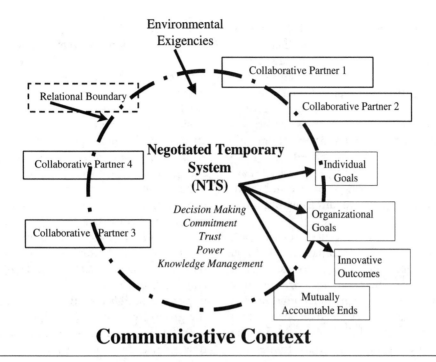

Figure 13.1. Bona Fide Group Collaboration Model

the overall objective and that can become a primary source of tension and distrust.

As a result of environmental exigencies, two or more collaborative partners (CPs) join forces to work together to achieve the various outcomes identified above. CPs vary in their level of involvement and commitment to the collaboration project, and these differences are reflected in the model by the differing degrees of overlap for each CP with the negotiated temporary system (discussed next). The "intersections" of the CPs is the relational boundary. Although this relational boundary is a "line of demarcation," it is permeable, flexible, fluid, and often invisible.

Through their interaction, CPs create a negotiated temporary system (NTS), which is at the heart of the model. An NTS is the finite system enacted by the representatives of the CPs specifically for the completion of a collaborative project and *is* the collaborating group. An NTS is negotiated over a relatively short period of time through the everyday formal and informal interactions between the group

members. As suggested earlier, an NTS, or collaborating group, is different from traditional groups in three primary ways. First, the composition of these groups is different in that they are composed of members from different organizations and backgrounds, who often have little or no status differences among themselves. Second, these groups demonstrate significant structural differences. In general, collaborative efforts are organized around a reciprocal interdependency that has very little initial structure compared with other forms of group interdependencies (Kumar & van Dissel, 1996), and this lack of initial structure is mirrored in the collaborating group. Furthermore, these groups have little or no formal hierarchy, although temporary and fluid hierarchies develop on the basis of communication between members (Ahuja & Carley, 1998). Third, the nature of the relational boundary between the collaborating group and its contexts is much more complex. Although all groups exist in multiple contexts that represent varied needs, within an NTS, members are responsible to multiple and often competing systems. The conflicting demands on group members' loyalty and actions are further confounded by structural constraints and different organizational rules and procedures not necessarily found in groups whose members come from the same organization. Awareness of relevant environmental exigencies and demands placed on group members as they carry out group tasks is magnified when there is little structure and members have allegiances to different organizations.

Traditional group concepts—such as task characteristics and coordination, decision making, cohesiveness, goals, roles, norms, power, conflict, and creativity—are certainly still important, but their conceptualizations must be adapted and reframed if collaborating groups are to be fully understood. The BFGCM provides the necessary framework for reframing conceptualizations of traditional group concepts.

CHANGING GROUP STRUCTURE CHANGES RELEVANT VARIABLES

The BFGCM makes clear ways in which collaborating groups and other types of groups are different. Given that the very nature of the composition, structure, and relationships that make up the relevant group context are different, we focus the rest of the chapter on identifying the central differences in group issues and variables. The differences address fundamental questions related to the following: *What* is relevant? *Where* do loyalties reside? *When* does trust develop? *Why* do group members do what they do? *How* do collaborative groups acquire the resources needed to accomplish their goals? For example, we need to reconsider what phenomena are relevant for understanding collaborative group processes. Particular interorganizational dynamics that may not even include NTS group members (e.g., negotiations regarding production and distribution of a different product or interactions between board members at a joint meeting) can have serious conse-

quences for collaborative group actions, such as decision making, and must now be considered relevant. As indicated earlier, we must also reconceptualize many traditional group constructs.

Overall, we suggest that the unidimensionality and temporal dimensions of constructs and the intentionality of action must be reconsidered and reconfigured from a bona fide group perspective. For example, group cohesion and group members' commitment can no longer be conceptualized as unidimensional constructs but *must take into account multiple targets* of commitment, including, but not limited to, group members' parent companies (see Craig, 1998). *When* trust develops in a collaborating group is as important as *whether* trust develops, given the group's composition and short-term nature. Furthermore, trust between collaborative partners becomes far more critical for a collaborating group when members do not have previous relationships and do not experience the same benefits and constraints on behavior that often come with the knowledge that group members will be working together long term.

Understanding why members "do what they do" in a collaborating group also becomes more intricate because status and power differences are often not clearly defined or even overtly manifested. Although a collaborating group may have a nominal leader, the fluid structure of this type of group and the relative independence of organizational hierarchies create a situation in which group members, even group leaders, must continually negotiate their positions with a collaborating group. The absence of formal positions creates additional uncertainty in the power structure of the collaborative group. Thus, the way in which power is conceptualized, operationalized, and enacted within collaborating groups becomes far more complex and less rooted in traditional behavioral and status-oriented approaches. Finally, determining how collaborating groups can acquire and then use the resources they need while simultaneously dealing with organizational firewalls is of great importance for the success of these groups. Issues of information acquisition and knowledge management take on new dimensions when collaborating groups, as they are often designed, lack the necessary knowledge and skills to complete their tasks and must depend on their relational networks to gain the knowledge and skills they require.

To adequately address these changes, we need a reframed model of group interaction. The BFGCM provides such a framework for understanding changes in group composition, structure, and relational boundaries and how these changes affect the group issues highlighted here. To illustrate how these changes might play out in investigations of collaborating groups, we highlight five group concepts: decision making, commitment, trust, power, and knowledge management.

Decision-Making Processes: What Is Relevant?

In the context of a collaborating group, the notion of a fluid relationship between the group and other individual and collective actors necessitates a redetermination of what is relevant for understanding internal group processes, such as decision making. Previous theoretical and empirical work has considered actors and events that are external to a group relevant only when a group member was directly involved. Although a collaborative group's and the group members' relations outside the group with CPs, customers, suppliers, professional organizations, and others are important, they are not the whole picture. With a collaborating group, external phenomena not involving group members per se may, and usually do, have direct impact on internal group actions. Thus, other relevant aspects of interorganizational relations are critical, such as what other (presumably those unrelated to the task of the group) decisions have been reached between the collaborating partners. Although studies of group decision making have typically investigated ingroup processes, Putnam and Stohl (1996) have convincingly argued that a bona fide group perspective

"reframes internal processes of decision making. Proposal arguments, decision premises, and even the modus operandi for making decisions hinge on external norms, cultural changes, and directives from authority" (p. 165). This conceptualization is central for collaborating groups as well. However, the decision-making process within a group is not only embedded within larger contexts but is also enmeshed with other decisions reached outside the group and must be considered within those constraining features. For example, in the situation of the collaboration between the various computer companies on the common desktop environment for UNIX, decisions reached separately between Hewlett-Packard and IBM on a completely different project or products might have directly affected the collaborating group and the decisions made.

Commitment Processes: Where Do Loyalties Reside?

Participants' commitment to a collaborative project is an essential element of the collaboration process and, as such, is especially important for a collaborating group. Traditionally, members' commitment to a group has been conceptualized and studied as *cohesion* or as the result of cohesion, generally defined as the liking or attraction group members have for one another and/or the task or the willingness of members to remain in a group (see Evans & Dion, 1991; Mudrack, 1989). Understanding group members' commitment, or cohesion, within a collaborating group, however, must be based on a consideration of external roles and relationships; group members' commitment to other targets, such as their parent organization (i.e., the CPs), must also be taken into account. This approach is consistent with the literature that has reconceptualized commitment as a dynamic and multidimensional construct in which individuals can have multiple organizational commitments (see Ashforth & Mael, 1989; Becker, 1992; Hunt & Morgan, 1994; Morrow, 1983; Perrucci & Stohl,

1997; Reichers, 1985; Scott, 1997; Scott & Fontenot, 1997).

In a recent thesis, Craig (1998) argued that within the context of a collaborative project, group members will have multiple commitments to different targets. Craig's study examined a collaboration experiment in which participants (professional engineers, undergraduate and graduate students, and faculty members) were divided into separate "companies" and asked to collaborate on a project. She found that participants had four different targets of commitment and that their level of commitment to each target changed over time. Furthermore, these changes were not uniform and the targets were differentially associated with specific patterns of communicative activity. For example, individuals' centrality in the task communication network of the collaborative system had a strong negative association with individuals' commitment to the umbrella organization for the project and a strong positive association with their commitment to the particular task. Although the implications of these findings require further study, it is clear that we can expect not only different targets of commitment but also for those various commitments to have differing impacts on a collaborating group. Within the BFGCM, then, it is essential that we understand collaborating group members' multiple commitments if we are to understand how cohesion and commitment work within the group.

Trust: When Does Trust Develop?

Trust is an equally important concept for collaboration (see Dodgson, 1993; Littler et al., 1995; Lynch, 1990; Meyer & Allen, 1991). Trust in groups has primarily been associated with creating a cooperative environment and in the successful management of conflict. Most of this research is based on theories of trust at the interpersonal or collective levels, but these theories are not sufficient for understanding trust in collaborating groups. Trust is essential for any group's success, but especially so for virtual teams and collaborat-

ing groups (Handy, 1995). When group members have different parent companies (perhaps competitors), trust is critical for promoting the sharing of information and is highly dependent on relations between members and external contact between the collaborating organizations.

In a recent essay, Jarvenpaa and Leidner (1998) explored the nature of trust in global virtual teams. They found that these groups create a form of "swift" trust (Meyerson, Weick, & Kramer, 1996) that is differentiated from the way trust has traditionally been approached in face-to-face groups. Jarvenpaa & Leidner (1998) argued that "trust might be imported, but is more likely created via a communication behavior established in the first few keystrokes [of e-mail]" (p. 32). *Swift trust* describes the type of trust that develops within collaborating groups, especially considering the short-lived nature of most of these groups. However, although the notion of swift trust addresses the virtual nature of collaborating groups, it does not address other important elements of these groups. Jarvenpaa and Leidner's sample consisted of students from various universities around the world. Consequently, issues related to comparative advantage, competitive organizational strategy, and proprietary information, among others, were not particularly salient for the participants. In NTSs in which group members come from organizations with histories of competition and exclusive rights to information, the "importation" of swift trust undoubtedly becomes even more important and complex.

Furthermore, the continuing development of trust, or lack thereof, in a collaborating group is not only a function of internal interaction but also of relations the group makes with those outside the group and the continuing interaction between the CPs. For example, in a study of collaborative groups in biotechnology, Dodgson (1993) found that interpersonal trust between the members was high but highly vulnerable to labor turnover and interpersonal conflicts. The success of these collaborations and, thus, of the collaborating groups, depended more on the development of interorganizational trust between the CPs. A collaborative effort, as Dodgson concluded, can "survive disruptive interpersonal rows and the loss of important individuals provided trust is broad-based" (p. 91). Understanding the changes "within" a collaborating group, therefore, necessitates looking "outside" the group.

Power: Why Do People Do What They Do?

Much like commitment and trust, the nature of power in groups needs to be reconceptualized when considering collaborating groups. Previous research on power in groups has focused on a range of issues, such as social influence in decision making and other group activities (e.g., Latane, 1981; Levine & Ruback, 1980; Seibold, Meyers, & Sunwolf, 1996), power resources (most based on conceptualizations by French and Raven, 1959), and leadership and status (see, e.g., Brock & Howell, 1994; Ridgeway, 1978). Consistent with a bona fide group perspective, many scholars consider group members' roles outside a group to be an important variable that influences the roles and power they exercise within the group. Furthermore, some researchers place social influence in a group within a larger context by examining how social influence processes structure the overall group process and, in turn, are structured by the larger context (see Barge & Keyton, 1994).

In collaboration projects, a key feature to their success is the balance of control among the CPs (Kumar & van Dissel, 1996; Littler et al., 1995; Tucker, 1991). This balancing of control is both reflected in and enacted through the collaborating group; it is most often where the balance of power plays out. Hence, although collaborating groups often have little formal hierarchy, they typically develop an informal hierarchy through their interactions (Ahuja & Carley, 1998) based not only on their evolving interpersonal relations but also on the relations of the CPs outside

the group. Thus, it is critical to consider group members' roles outside the group and the changing relationships between the CPs both before and during the collaborative project. Furthermore, given the lack of formal structure and high interdependence of collaborative group tasks, behavioral and status-oriented approaches are no longer sufficient for understanding power in these groups. Control in a collaborating group may be just as much about controlling the meaning of the overall goals of the project and even the meaning of the collaboration process itself as about direct social influence over the group's decisions and control of group task completion (see, e.g., Smircich & Morgan's, 1982, reconceptualization of leadership as the "management of meaning").

In a recent study of collaboration groups, for example, Stohl, Walker, and Craig (1998) found evidence that individuals who are central to the determination of what it means to collaborate are the most powerful individuals as determined by their level of involvement in the group's task. They examined the relationships between the members of five different collaborating groups to determine which group was most influential in determining the overall meaning for the term "collaboration" and which group members were the most central in the task communication network. In short, they found a strong relationship between the evolving structure of the task communication network and the structure of the semantic network (created through participants' similarities in defining the term "collaboration"). In these collaborative groups, power was derived in ways that were far more complex than what can be typically found when using only behavioral and status measures of power.

Knowledge Management: How Do Groups Acquire Needed Resources?

Effective knowledge acquisition and access are critical for the success of all task-oriented groups. A great deal of research has explored (a) the ways in which groups are formed to ensure that needed knowledge and skills are present (see, e.g., Stevens & Campion, 1994), (b) ways in which group members must communicate to create a climate conducive for sharing and processing information (see, e.g., Propp, 1999), and (c) how individuals assume particular roles within the group, such as gatekeeper, to obtain the needed information. Furthermore, experiments have been developed to identify the conditions under which necessary information is most likely brought to light during group interaction (e.g., Poole & Holmes, 1995); in these experiments, group tasks are typically designed such that all the information resides within the group (Hollingshead, 1996). In these types of studies, knowledge, information, and skill acquisition and use are considered in the traditional manner—that is, as functions of internal group processes. Within the collaborative group, however, we cannot assume that all the information is readily available; indeed, typically, the cognitive complexity of the task and the equivocal environment drive collaboration. Members of a collaborating group must often look outside the group for needed information and must continually contend with proprietary information and the firewalls constructed to control information flow. In a study of aerospace collaboration, for example, Crabtree et al. (1997) found that information acquisition and information and knowledge access concerns accounted for 60% of the problem cases. Our BFGCM highlights various relations and factors that make the overall management of knowledge and information no longer an "ingroup" issue.

Indeed, "knowledge management" is integral to the way contemporary organizations and groups operate and collaborate. The knowledge-driven and creative company is expected to be at the forefront of business (Nonaka & Takeuchi, 1995), partly because of the common realization that, in the global environment, not all relevant knowledge can be found within one known and easily accessible group of people. In general, effective knowledge management seeks to make relevant knowledge easily available to appropri-

ate individuals in a timely manner (Quintas, Lefrere, & Jones, 1997). The ease with which organizations can accomplish this goal is greatly facilitated by advances in technology, as well as the shift to information-based industries (Bassi, 1997), but a technological fix is not sufficient. Organizations and collaborating groups must devise ways of not only knowing what they need to know but also knowing who knows what, who knows whom, and who knows who knows what (Contractor, 1998).

In other words, past group research has assumed that knowledge management within a group is solely a function of internal group processes. We cannot make the same assumption when it comes to collaborating groups for three primary reasons. First, collaboration projects are multifaceted and innovative and, therefore, require knowledge and skills far beyond what any particular group may, or can, possess. Although previous research asserted that a well-formed team is one that has the necessary knowledge and skills to complete the group's tasks (e.g., Stevens & Campion, 1994), that cannot be true of a collaborating group. Second, collaboration group members will not necessarily know who outside the group has the needed information and/or skills and how to contact that person or those people. There has been little examination in the past of *how* group members actually find necessary information; in most cases, it seems to be assumed that group members who seek the information or who act as gatekeepers will know, or can easily locate, where or from whom to get the information and skills needed. This is not necessarily true of collaborating groups; existing across distance, time, and organizational boundaries and cultures, members' determination of where to find relevant information and skills is more likely an art form than an easily accomplished task. Finally, once group members do have the needed information and skills, the likelihood that they will share it with other group members is just as dependent on issues external to the group, such as organizational firewalls and interorganizational trust, as it is on the development of a supportive climate or cohesiveness within the collaborating group. Furthermore, collaborating group members' ability to access and use the needed knowledge is most likely driven more by their personal network of relations and the collaborating group's alliances with other groups and the CPs than by group openness or a supportive climate. As suggested earlier, Contractor's (1998) work on knowledge and social networks demonstrates that it is just as important to understand "who knows who knows what" as it is to determine "who knows what." The ability of various group members to determine who in their social networks can link them to the needed knowledge and skills should be a clear determinant of a collaborating group's success. Knowledge management for collaborating groups, therefore, is much more complex than for traditional face-to-face groups when considered in the context of highly innovative outcomes and interorganizational alliances.

CONCLUSION: CHANGING THE FUTURE OF GROUP RESEARCH

As group forms continue to shift and change, our understanding and studies of them must follow suit. We have shown in this chapter that changes in the composition, structure, and relational boundaries of collaborating groups in comparison with other types of task groups necessitate changes in the way we conceptualize and operationalize salient variables and theorize about the relationships between them. Researchers clearly face great challenges in creating or applying methods and theories that take into account the relevant levels of interaction and the interdependencies that characterize collaborating groups.

Although we cannot determine at this time all possible variables for understanding collaborating groups, the bona fide group collaboration model provides a framework for researchers and practitioners interested in doing so. Perhaps most important, the model enables group scholars and communication professionals involved in collaborations to approach group processes in ways that reflect the embedded and complex context in which they take place. Collaborative tasks are big, complicated questions, and previous classifications of task (e.g., McGrath, 1984) are insufficient for categorizing and explicating such activities. We suggest that it is imperative for scholars to develop a more thorough understanding of the collaborating task itself if we are to understand this type of group. In addition, investigations of collaborating groups must no longer focus solely on the internal processes of groups. Relevant actors and interactions outside a collaborative group need to become part of any investigation, for they are critical components for understanding how a collaborating group operates, makes decisions, and completes projects.

Furthermore, given the temporary and multidimensional nature of group collaboration, longitudinal and comparative case studies are necessary to understand its dynamic nature. In future studies, we believe it will be important to employ a combination of quantitative and qualitative approaches. When group members have different allegiances, are geographically dispersed, and come from diverse cultural sets, various data-gathering techniques are needed; computer and/or Web-based surveys, interviews, textual analyses, and network analyses are just some of the methods that future studies may employ. Scholars must measure group performance and change, as well as the ways groups interact with, interpret, and encode messages that permeate group boundaries and borders.

Finally, it is important to note that the unique attributes of the collaborative environment we have stressed throughout this chapter are becoming more and more commonplace. As institutions and companies respond to the increasing pressures of globalization and the correlative tumultuous economic, social, political, technological, and cultural changes, there have been fundamental alterations in organizational approaches to time, space, and identity (Stohl, 2000). New technologies bring people together in non-colocated environments; they are able to share information and data both synchronously and asynchronously across distances; relationships are fluid and diffuse; new types of coalitions and alliances emerge; groups evolve as spontaneous, structureless but managed information systems; knowledge workers become fundamental to tasks (Monge & Fulk, 1999); and organizations of all types become more decentralized, diverse, and disembedded (Waters, 1995). In other words, everyday interactions are lifted out of local contexts and restructured across time and space. Throughout the world, people are increasingly working together in formal and informal alliances regardless of location and regardless of whom they "work for" to jointly solve complex problems—the very essence of our collaboration model. Thus, we believe that as individuals and organizations no longer act as if they have walls and as organizational boundaries become ever more permeable, the insights learned from focusing on the "special case" of collaborating groups will become more and more useful for understanding all groups in the 21st century.

REFERENCES

Ahuja, M. K., & Carley, K. M. (1998). Network structure in virtual organizations. *Journal of Computer-Mediated Communication* [On-line serial; special joint issue], *3*(4). Retrieved May 1, 2001, from www.ascusc.org/jcmc/vol3/issue4/ahuja.html

Applegate, L. (1999). In search of a new organizational model: Lessons from the field. In G. DeSanctis & J. Fulk (Eds.), *Shaping organization form: Communication, connection and community* (pp. 33-70). Thousand Oaks, CA: Sage.

Ashforth, B. E., & Mael, F. (1989). Social identity theory and the organization. *Academy of Management Review, 14,* 20-39.

Barge, J. K., & Keyton, J. (1994). Contextualizing power and social influence in groups. In L. R. Frey (Ed.), *Group communication in context: Studies of natural groups* (pp. 85-105). Hillsdale, NJ: Lawrence Erlbaum.

Bassi, L. J. (1997). Harnessing the power of intellectual capital. *Training and Development, 51*(12), 25-30.

Becker, T. E. (1992). Foci and bases of commitment: Are they distinctions worth making? *Academy of Management Journal, 35,* 232-244.

Beyerlein, M., & Johnson, D. (1994). *Theories of self-managing work teams.* Greenwich, CT: JAI Press.

Blaquier, G. T., & Harvey, C. M. (1995). *A review of literature for the center for collaborative manufacturing.* Unpublished manuscript, Purdue University, Center for Collaborative Manufacturing, West Lafayette, IN.

Brock, B. L., & Howell, S. (1994). Leadership in the evolution of a community-based political action group. In L. R. Frey (Ed.), *Group communication in context: Studies of natural groups* (pp. 135-152). Hillsdale, NJ: Lawrence Erlbaum.

Byrne, J. A., Brandt, R., & Otis, O. (1993, February 8). The virtual corporation. *Business Week,* pp. 98-104.

Camillus, J. (1993). Crafting the competitive corporation: Management systems for future organizations. In P. Lorange, B. Chakravarthy, J. Roos, & A. Van de Ven (Eds.), *Implementing strategic process: Change, learning, and cooperation* (pp. 313-328). Oxford, UK: Blackwell Business.

Contractor, N. (1995, March). *Team building in engineering design teams.* Paper presented at a joint meeting of the National Electrical Engineering Department Heads Association and the Mechanical Engineering Heads Association, Nashville, TN.

Contractor, N. (1998). *Inquiring knowledge networks on the Web* [On-line presentation]. Retrieved May 10, 2001, from www.tec.spcomm.uiuc.edu/nosh/IKNOW/sld001.htm.

Crabtree, R. A., Fox, M. S., & Baid, N. K. (1997). Case studies of coordination activities and problems in collaborative design. *Research in Engineering Design, 9,* 70-84.

Craig, J. L. (1998). *Commitment, goal alignment, communication and collaboration.* Unpublished master's thesis, Purdue University, West Lafayette, IN.

Daily, R. C. (1980). A path analysis of R&D team coordination and performance. *Decision Sciences, 11,* 357-369.

DeSanctis, G., & Jackson, B. (1994). Coordination of information technology management: Team-based structures and computer-based communication systems. *Journal of Management Information Systems, 10*(4), 85-110.

Dess, G. G., Rasheed, A. M. A., McLaughlin, K. J., & Priem, R. L. (1995). The new corporate architecture. *Academy of Management Executive, 9,* 7-20.

Dodgson, M. (1993). Learning, trust, and technological collaboration. *Human Relations, 46,* 77-95.

Evans, C. R., & Dion, K. L. (1991). Group cohesion and performance: A meta-analysis. *Small Group Research, 22,* 175-186.

Farr, M. F., & Fischer, W. A. (1992). Managing international high technology cooperative projects. *R&D Management, 22,* 55-67.

French, J., & Raven, B. (1959). The bases of social power. In D. Cartwright (Ed.), *Studies in social power,* (pp. 150-167). Ann Arbor: University of Michigan, Institute for Social Research, Research Center for Group Dynamics.

Frey, L. R. (Ed.). (in press). *Group communication in context: Studies of bona fide groups* (2nd ed.). Mahwah, NJ: Lawrence Erlbaum.

Garvin, D. A. (1993, July-August). Building a learning organization. *Harvard Business Review, 71,* 78-91.

Ghoshal, S., & Bartlett, C. (1990). The multinational corporation as an interorganizational network. *Academy of Management Review, 15,* 603-625.

Goldman, S. L., Nagel, R. N., & Preiss, K. (1995). *Agile competitors and virtual organizations: Strategies for enriching the customer.* New York: Van Nostrand Reinhold.

Gulati, R., Khanna, T., & Nohria, N. (1994). Unilateral commitments and the importance of process in alliances. *Sloan Management Review, 35*(3), 61-69.

Hamel, G., Doz., Y. L., & Prahalad, C. K. (1989, January February). Collaborate with your competitors—and win. *Harvard Business Review, 67,* 133-139.

Handy, C. (1995, May-June). Trust and the virtual organization. *Harvard Business Review, 73,* 40-48.

Hergert, M., & Morris, D. (1988). Trends in international collaborative agreements. In F. J. Contractor & P. Lorange (Eds.), *Cooperative strategies in international business* (pp. 99-109). Lexington, MA: Lexington Books.

Hladik, K. F. (1988). R&D and international joint ventures. In F. J. Contractor & P. Lorange (Eds.), *Cooperative strategies in international business* (pp. 187-203). Lexington, MA: Lexington Books.

Hollingshead, A. (1996). Information suppression and status persistence in group decision making. *Human Communication Research, 23,* 193-219.

Hunt, S. D., & Morgan, R. M. (1994). Organizational commitment: One of the many commitments or key mediating construct? *Academy of Management Journal, 37,* 1568-1587.

Inkpen, A. C. (1996). Creating knowledge through collaboration. *California Management Review, 39*(1), 123-140.

Jarvenpaa, S. L., & Leidner, D. E. (1998). Communication and trust in global virtual teams. *Organizational Science/Journal of Computer-Mediated Communication* [On-line serial; special joint issue], *3*(4). Retrieved May 10, 2001, from www.ascusc.org/jcmc/vol3/issue4/jarvenpaa.html.

Keyton, J., & Stallworth, V. (in press). On the verge of collaboration: Interaction process vs. group outcomes. In L. R. Frey (Ed.), *Group communication in context: Studies of bona fide groups* (2nd ed.). Mahwah, NJ: Lawrence Erlbaum.

Kraut, R., Steinfield, C., Chan, A., Butler, B., & Hoag, A. (1998). Coordination and virtualization? The role of electronic networks and personal relationships. *Organizational Science/Journal of Computer-Mediated Communication* [On-line serial; special joint issue], *3*(4). Retrieved May 10, 2001, from www.ascusc.org/jcmc/vol3/issue4/kraut.html.

Kumar, K., & van Dissel, H. G. (1996). Sustainable collaboration: Managing conflict and cooperation in interorganizational systems. *MIS Quarterly, 20,* 279-300.

Latane, B. (1981). The psychology of social impact. *American Psychologist, 36,* 343-356.

Levine, J. M., & Ruback, R. B. (1980). Reaction to opinion deviance: Impact of a fence straddler's rationale on majority evaluation. *Social Psychology Quarterly, 43,* 73-81.

Lipnack, J., & Stamps, J. (1997). *Virtual teams: Reaching across space, time, and organizations with technology.* New York: John Wiley.

Littler, D., Leverick, F., & Bruce, M. (1995). Factors affecting the process of collaborative product development: A study of UK manufacturers of information and communications technology products. *Journal of Product Innovation Management, 12,* 16-32.

Lynch, R. P. (1990, March/April). Building alliances to penetrate European markets. *Journal of Business Strategy, 11,* 4-8.

Malone, T. W., & Crowston, K. (1990). What is coordination theory and how can it help design cooperative work systems? In D. Tatar (Ed.), *Proceedings of the Third Conference on Computer-Supported Cooperative Work* (pp. 357-370). Los Angeles: ACM Press.

McGrath (1984). *Groups: Interaction and performance.* Englewood Cliffs, NJ: Prentice Hall.

Meyer, J., & Allen, N. J. (1991). A three-component conceptualization of organizational commitment. *Human Resource Management Review, 1,* 61-89.

Meyerson, D., Weick, K. E., & Kramer, R. M. (1996). Swift trust and temporary groups. In R. M. Kramer & T. R. Tyler (Eds.), *Trust in organizations: Frontiers of theory and research* (pp. 166-195). Thousand Oaks, CA: Sage.

Miles, R. E., & Snow, C. C. (1992). Causes of failure in network organizations. *California Management Review, 34*(4), 53-72.

Miller, R. M. (1996, April). Managing a multicompany software development project. *Hewlett-Packard Journal* [on-line]. Retrieved May 10, 2001, from www.hp.com/hpj/apr96/ap96a6.pdf.

Mills, D. Q. (1991). *Rebirth of the corporation.* New York: John Wiley.

Mintzberg, H., Dougherty, D., Jorgensen, J., & Westley, F. (1996). Some surprising things about collaboration: Knowing how people connect makes it work better. *Organizational Dynamics, 25,* 60-71.

Monge, P. R. (1995). Global network organizations. In R. Cesaria & P. Schockley-Zalabak (Eds.), *Organization means communication: Making the organizational communication concept relevant to practice* (pp. 131-151). Rome, Italy: SIPI Editore.

Monge, P. R., & Fulk, J. (1999). Communication technology for global network organizations. In G. DeSanctis & J. Fulk (Eds.), *Shaping organization form: Communication, connection and community* (pp. 71-100). Thousand Oaks, CA: Sage.

Morrow, P. C. (1983). Concept redundancy in organizational research: The case of work commitment. *Academy of Management Review, 8,* 486-500.

Mudrack, P. E. (1989). Defining group cohesiveness: A legacy of confusion? *Small Group Behavior, 20,* 37-49.

Nohria, N., & Berkley, J. D. (1994). The virtual organization: Bureaucracy, technology, and the implosion of control. In C. Heckscher & A. Donnellon (Eds.), *The post-bureaucratic organization: New perspectives on organizational change* (pp. 108-128). Thousand Oaks, CA: Sage.

Nonaka, I., & Takeuchi, H. (1995). *The knowledge-creating company: How Japanese companies create the dynamics of innovation.* New York: Oxford University Press.

Olson, J. S., & Teasley, S. (1996). Groupware in the wild: Lessons learned from a year of virtual collocation. *Proceedings of the ACM Conference on Computer-Supported Cooperative Work 1996* (pp. 419-427). New York: ACM Press.

Perlmutter, H. V., & Heenan, D. A. (1986, March-April). Cooperate to compete globally. *Harvard Business Review, 64,* 136-138, 146, 150-152.

Perrucci, R., & Stohl, C. (1997). Economic restructuring and changing corporate-worker-community relations: Searching for a new social contract. In R. Hodson (Ed.), *Research in the sociology of work* (Vol. 6, pp. 178-198). Greenwich, CT: JAI Press.

Poole, M. S. (1999). Group communication theory. In L. R. Frey (Ed.), D. S. Gouran, & M. S. Poole (Assoc. Eds.), *The handbook of group communication theory & research* (pp. 37-70). Thousand Oaks, CA: Sage.

Poole, M. S., & Holmes, M. E. (1995). Decision development in computer-assisted group decision making. *Human Communication Research, 22,* 90-127.

Propp, K. J. (1999). Collective information processing in groups. In L. R. Frey (Ed.), D. S. Gouran, & M. S. Poole (Assoc. Eds.), *The handbook of group communication theory & research* (pp. 225-250). Thousand Oaks, CA: Sage.

Putnam, L. L., & Stohl, C. (1990). Bona fide groups: A reconceptualization of groups in context. *Communication Studies, 41,* 248-265.

Putnam, L. L., & Stohl, C. (1996). Bona fide groups: An alternative perspective for communication and small group decision making. In R. Y. Hirokawa & M. S. Poole (Eds.), *Communication and group decision making* (2nd ed., pp. 147-178). Thousand Oaks, CA: Sage.

Quintas, P., Lefrere, P., & Jones, G. (1997). Knowledge management: A strategic agenda. *Long Range Planning, 30,* 385-391.

Reichers, A. E. (1985). A review and reconceptualization of organizational commitment. *Academy of Management Review, 10,* 465-476.

Ridgeway, C. L. (1978). Conformity, group-oriented motivation, and status attainment in small groups. *Social Psychology, 41,* 175-188.

Roberts, N. C., & Bradley, R. T. (1991). Stakeholder collaboration and innovation: A study of public policy initiation at the state level. *Journal of Applied Behavioral Science, 27,* 209-227.

Schott, T. (1994). Collaboration in the invention of technology: Globalization, regions, and centers. *Social Science Research, 23,* 23-56.

Scott, C. R. (1997). Identification with multiple targets in a geographically dispersed organization. *Management Communication Quarterly, 10,* 491-522.

Scott, C. R. (1999). Communication technology and group communication. In L. R. Frey (Ed.), D. S.

Gouran, & M. S. Poole (Assoc. Eds.), *The handbook of group communication theory & research* (pp. 432-472). Thousand Oaks, CA: Sage.

Scott, C. R., & Fontenot, J. C. (1997, November). *Multiple identifications during team meetings: A comparison of conventional and computer-mediated interactions.* Paper presented at the meeting of the National Communication Association, Chicago.

Seibold, D. R., Meyers, R. A., & Sunwolf. (1996). Communication and influence in group decision making. In R. Y. Hirokawa & M. S. Poole (Eds.), *Communication and group decision making* (2nd ed., pp. 242-268). Thousand Oaks, CA: Sage.

Smircich, L., & Morgan, G. (1982). Leadership: The management of meaning. *Journal of Applied Behavioral Science, 18,* 257-273.

Solberg, J. J. (1997). *A briefing paper on the Purdue collaborative manufacturing testbed.* Unpublished manuscript, Purdue University, Center for Collaborative Manufacturing, West Lafayette, IN.

Stevens, M. J., & Campion, M. A. (1994). The knowledge, skill, and ability requirements for teamwork: Implications for human resource managers. *Journal of Management, 20,* 503-530.

Stohl, C. (2000). Globalizing organizational communication: Convergence and divergence. In F. Jablin & L. Putnam (Eds.), *The new handbook of organizational communication* (pp. 323-375). Thousand Oaks, CA: Sage.

Stohl, C., & Putnam, L. L. (1994). Group communication in context: Implications for the study of bona fide groups. In L. R. Frey (Ed.), *Group communication in context: Studies of natural groups* (pp. 285-304). Hillsdale, NJ: Lawrence Erlbaum.

Stohl, C., Walker, K. L., & Craig, J. L. (1998, May). *The dynamics of collaboration networks.* Paper presented at the meeting of Sunbelt XVII and the 5th European International Conference on Social Networks, Sitges, Spain.

Tucker, J. B. (1991). Partners and rivals: A model of international collaboration in advanced technology. *International Organization, 45,* 83-119.

Tushman, M. L. (1978). Technical communication in R&D laboratories: The impact of project work characteristics. *Academy of Management Journal, 21,* 624-245.

Van de Ven, A., Delbecq, A. L., & Koenig, R., Jr. (1976). Determinants of coordination modes within organizations. *American Sociological Review, 41,* 322-338.

Walker, K. L., Craig, J. L., & Stohl, C. (1998, November). *The dynamics of collaboration: Developing a communication model of the collaboration process.* Paper presented at the meeting of the National Communication Association, New York.

Waters, M. (1995). *Globalization.* London: Routledge.

Wilson, J. L., & Shi, C. (1996). Coordination mechanisms for cooperative design. *Engineering Applications of Artificial Intelligence, 9,* 453-461.

Wood, D. J., & Gray, B. (1991). Toward a comprehensive theory of collaboration. *Journal of Applied Behavioral Science, 27,* 139-162.

14

Communication in Top Management Teams

THEODORE E. ZORN, JR.
University of Waikato

GEORGE H. TOMPSON
University of Tampa

Communication in organizational groups and teams has been a concern of increasing importance to communication scholars in recent years (e.g., J. R. Barker, 1993; J. R. Barker, Melville, & Pacanowsky, 1993; Geist & Hardesty, 1992; Greenbaum & Query, 1999; Larson & LaFasto, 1989). As the structure of work organizations has evolved to emphasize teams, scholars have sought to explore the characteristics of and communication processes within organizational teams. Such research has addressed, for instance, (a) the characteristics of communication that result in team effectiveness (Larson & LaFasto, 1989), (b) changes in communication practices as a result of moving to team-based organizational structures (J. R. Barker et al., 1993; Geist & Hardesty, 1992), and (c) the control processes concomitant with team-based structures (J. R. Barker, 1993). Much of this work has focused on self-managing teams delivering products and services. However, very little research has been conducted that addresses communication within top management teams (TMTs).

Studying TMTs and their communication is important for several reasons. First, research has repeatedly shown TMTs to be the most influential groups in organizations (Child, 1972; Finkelstein, 1992; Hambrick & Mason, 1984); hence, understanding communication within TMTs will make an important contribution to our knowledge about the management of organizations. Second, organizations today, more than ever before, are typically led by TMTs rather than by individuals; strategic decisions in large organizations are rarely made by individuals acting alone (Finkelstein & Hambrick, 1996; Hambrick & Mason, 1984; Sundstrom, De Meuse, & Futrell, 1990). Third, TMTs and the strategic decisions they make are unique; they demonstrate important differences from other organizational groups and teams. Compared with other groups within organizations, TMTs are distinguished by the consequences and the complexity of the decisions that they make. For all these reasons, TMTs are an example of an important class of bona fide groups—that is, groups with stable yet permeable boundaries that are interdependent with their immediate contexts (Putnam & Stohl, 1990, 1996). Furthermore, TMTs are unexplored in the communication literature and, thus, represent an important new direction for group communication research.

In this chapter, we first discuss the nature of TMTs and communication within these groups, with a focus on the emergence of TMTs in large organizations and the unique context of the communication that characterizes these groups. Second, we discuss extant research on TMTs from the field of business policy and strategy (BPS, also known as "strategic management"), in which most prior research has been conducted. We briefly review this research for the purposes of describing (a) how TMT research fits into the domain of BPS scholarship and (b) the current status of TMT research and the trends and results in the literature. Our review shows that the research is well established but that there is much to be learned by examining and extending research at the intersection of BPS and group communication. In the third part of the chapter, we identify contributions that group researchers can make to the TMT literature, primarily by reviewing recent theory and research about group communication. Finally, we offer some tentative implications for TMT communication practice, as well as some suggestions for how research in this area can progress toward a better understanding of communication in TMTs.

THE NATURE OF TMTs AND TMT COMMUNICATION

In the 1960s, the CEO-COO model became the primary model for organizing the top management of large organizations (Nadler, 1998b). In this model, a chairperson of the board serves as chief executive officer and takes primary responsibility for strategy, external relations, and overall corporate governance; a president serves as chief operating officer and is responsible for internal operations. Nadler (1998b) suggested that three scenarios typically motivate organizations to move from this model to team-based structures at the top level. The first scenario occurs when an organization diversifies into multi-

ple businesses and subsequently finds that managing such an organization via the CEO-COO model is too difficult. In such cases, the traditional response has been to conclude that a TMT would be better able to lead the organization because the sum total of expertise brought by the team members would exceed that of a CEO-COO combination. A second scenario is when a new CEO is appointed and is hesitant to appoint a COO immediately. In lieu of hiring an individual for the role of COO, a team is assembled to perform the functional duties of a COO. The third scenario occurs when a CEO is nearing retirement and creates a TMT to assess potential successors.

Although we use the phrase top management *teams* throughout this chapter, one important issue to consider is whether TMTs really function as teams at all. Of course, that depends in part on the definition of and criteria for determining what constitutes a team. On the basis of interviews with executives, Katzenbach and Smith (1993) concluded that most top management groups actually act more like what they call "working groups" rather than teams. Katzenbach and Smith defined teams as having (among other things) shared leadership roles, mutual (in addition to individual) accountability, a specific team purpose that is distinguishable from the organizational mission, and collective work products. Working groups, in contrast, most often have a strong leader, individual accountability, a group purpose that is the same as that of the organization, and individual work products. The degree to which a TMT truly functions as a team or as a working group (or somewhere in between) depends on two factors, according to Nadler (1998a): the internal coordination requirements and the complexity or instability of external demands placed on the group. Nadler essentially suggested that teamwork becomes more important as both internal coordination requirements increase and external demands become more complex and unstable. Because these characteristics typify the environment in which most large organizations operate, most top management decision makers have adopted TMTs as an organizing form.

Unique Characteristics of TMTs

TMTs share a number of unique characteristics that need to be taken into account in understanding their communication. Past research has identified the following characteristics.

Strategic decision making. A primary responsibility of TMTs is to make "strategic" decisions. Briefly, strategic decisions are more complex, consequential, and precursive than those made by other groups in a typical organization, a distinction we will elaborate later. In today's organizations, such decisions are rarely made autonomously by individuals (Hambrick & Mason, 1984; Sundstrom et al., 1990). Even if a course of action is eventually authorized by an individual, arriving at the decision to take action is usually the product of input from several sources (Carter, 1971). This may be because groups have been shown to reach better decisions than individuals when more information is needed than any individual possesses (Maier, 1967) and when the problem is unique, ambiguous, or complex (Robbins, 1974; for a review of information processing in groups, see Propp, 1999). Of course, the superiority of group over individual decision making, even in these cases, is by no means guaranteed.

The complexity of strategic decision making is well recognized in the literature (Daft & Lengel, 1986; Mintzberg, Raisinghani, & Theoret, 1976); hence, theoretically, TMTs should be better suited for strategic decision making than any single top manager. According to Holloman and Hendrick (1972), the underlying mechanism that enables groups to reach better decisions than individuals is expressed in a *social interaction hypothesis,* whereby members' interaction provides an error-correcting function and also facilitates critical thinking and participation. Even in small organizations (fewer than 100 employees, as defined by the U.S. Small Business Ad-

ministration), strategic decisions are usually made by the owner/CEO in consultation with a few key employees (Weinzimmer, 1997).

Complexity of strategic decisions. The nature of strategic decisions makes them extremely complex and altogether different from operating or tactical decisions made elsewhere in organizations (Johnson & Scholes, 1993). Hickson, Butler, Cray, Mallory, and Wilson (1986) stated that "the problems raised by the making of strategic decisions are greater than most" (p. 26). They also suggested that the complexity of strategic decisions has three sources: rarity, consequentiality, and precursiveness.

That strategic decisions are *rare* simply means that they are not made frequently; Hickson et al. (1986) suggested that decisions about changing part of an organization's strategy are made only once per year, at most. This means not that strategic thinking can happen only annually but that major components of strategy should not be changed frequently. For instance, a TMT might make the decision to expand geographically into a new foreign market, and that decision would probably not be reviewed and evaluated until the first year's performance was completed. However, later in the same year, the TMT would probably address other aspects of strategy, such as whether to change a supplier relationship for raw materials inputs. Given that strategic decisions are made infrequently, they may constitute uncharted waters for a TMT. There is little precedent for a decision that is made only yearly, so the task must be started nearly from ground zero.

Second, the *consequences* of strategic decision making may be one (or all four) of the following: radical, serious, enduring, and quickly diffused. Because strategic decisions carry such important consequences, TMTs are under tremendous pressure to perform well. Moreover, because TMT members of many publicly traded companies earn six- and seven-figure salaries, strategic decisions are often the subject of heavy scrutiny by employees, directors, and the media. In the current age of stockholder activism, TMT members have become defendants in numerous lawsuits alleging fraud, negligence, mismanagement, and other breeches of fiduciary responsibility.

Third, the *precursiveness* of strategic decisions refers to the extent to which a decision sets parameters within which future decisions are made. Strategic decisions made in any particular year can inherently limit the options available to a TMT—not to mention other members of the organization—for many years hence. Precursiveness is demonstrated in the scores of decisions that eventually create a path dependency within organizations (Schilling, 1998). Precursive decisions lead an organization down a particular path and preclude it from following other paths in the future. Barney (1995), who attributed the success of Caterpillar to its worldwide network of distribution and support, provided a good example. The genesis of the network occurred when the U.S. government was seeking a single worldwide manufacturer and distributor of heavy equipment during World War II. Caterpillar bid for the contract, won the business, and then developed the network. Fifty years after the decision was made to bid on the contract, the network remains a fundamental component of Caterpillar's strategy. Caterpillar's TMT in the 1940s committed the organization to a course of action that is rarely scrutinized today. Abandoning the network would be too expensive and disruptive, so the current TMT persists with a strategy based on the network. Similarly, Gioia and Thomas (1996) demonstrated the precursiveness of TMT decisions in a case study of a university TMT that agreed on a vision that subsequently influenced how the group interpreted emerging issues and made later strategic decisions. By being cognizant about the precursiveness of strategic decisions, TMT members make effective use of industry foresight, but they also add layers of complexity by trying to consider multiple eventualities of their strategic decisions.

Adding to Hickson et al.'s (1986) analysis, another source of the complexity of strategic decisions may be the salience of the external environment. Nadler (1998b) suggested that the external environment is more salient and has a greater influence on TMTs than other teams because TMTs must be acutely aware of not only customers but also shareholders, boards of directors, competitors, suppliers, and financial markets. In communication terms, their social networks must be extensive and they must respond to multiple audiences.

Relative power of TMTs. The third characteristic of TMTs is that they are usually the most powerful and influential group within an organization (Child, 1972). Even in a decentralized, or "flat," organizational structure, the TMT is responsible for making strategic decisions, building a vision (Wiersema & Bantel, 1992), serving as the buffer between the organization and its external environment (Michel & Hambrick, 1992), providing external legitimacy (Hambrick & D'Aveni, 1988), building the organization's core competencies (Hamel & Prahalad, 1994), and solving "complex, ill-defined (i.e., wicked) strategic problems" (Schweiger & Sandberg, 1989, p. 31). Hence, if scholars want to understand variance in organizational performance, it makes sense to study the most powerful group within the organization.

Politicized environment. Closely related to the issue of relative power is the fact that TMTs tend to operate in a highly politicized environment compared with other teams (Nadler, 1998b). TMT members, who usually are ambitious and high achievers, tend to exhibit more intense political behavior than do other employees in an organization (Nadler 1998b). They have histories of distinguishing themselves through individual achievement, which may militate against teamwork. As Nadler (1998b) suggested, "In many U.S.-based companies the executive team ends up composed of people who have been brought up and rewarded for their success in the rugged individualism model of management" (p. 13). Since TMTs are often the stage on which executives vie for succession to the

CEO position, posturing, self-promotion, and other impression-management strategies are typical. Adding to the politicized nature of this environment is that membership in a TMT has special meanings of privilege, status, and having "made it." Because of its place at the top of the organizational pyramid, a TMT has a great deal of visibility in an organization. Finally, the team leader of a TMT is typically the CEO, which may create more social distance between members than for other teams because of the CEO's typically substantial power. As Nadler (1998b) put it, "The problem then is how this larger-than-life character [the CEO], this holder of ultimate power, this symbolic leader, can also function as the builder, facilitator, and coach of a team of individuals" (p. 14).

Thus, although TMTs certainly share some characteristics with other organizational groups—at a very basic level, members communicate to solve problems and make decisions—they exhibit a number of unique features. In the next section, we examine what is known about TMTs from existing research.

TMTS AND STRATEGIC DECISION MAKING

Broadly conceived, the field of BPS addresses organizational performance. More specifically, BPS scholars seek to predict, explain, and even enhance the means by which managers pursue organizational goals. In the private sector, these goals may be financial measures, such as profitability, market share, or sales growth. However, the fundamental concepts in the field have also been successfully applied to government agencies and nonprofit organizations. Outcomes such as job creation, efficient use of government resources, income distribution, job training, and quality of life are familiar goals that can be managed by nonprofit organizations that apply the principles of BPS. The central research question for BPS researchers is why performance differences exist across organizations, especially ones in the same industry. The simple answer to this question is that some organiza-

tions are able to create a sustained competitive advantage vis-à-vis competitors and, consequently, are able to perform better over the long run. Basically, organizations that are able to distinctively formulate and/or implement strategy demonstrate superior performance. The requirement for distinctiveness is based on the assumption that two identical organizations cannot coexist over the long run (Henderson, 1989). Identifying the source of a sustained competitive advantage has proven to be difficult, however, and with dozens of theoretical perspectives advanced to explain them (see Mintzberg, 1990), it seems safe to assume that decision-making processes of TMTs influence organizational performance. Furthermore, understanding the idiosyncratic burdens of the TMT decision-making domain should help scholars to explain the relationship between TMTs and organizational outcomes. In the following sections, we summarize the two main categories of research that address the relationship between TMT decision making and organizational performance.

Composition and Process Research

The current form of TMT research originated with the "upper echelon perspective" (Hambrick & Mason, 1984), which was concerned with whether the average characteristics of TMT members were related to decision-making outcomes. The earliest work within this perspective primarily focused on the relationship between TMT composition and organizational performance. That research examined members' demographic characteristics (Murray, 1989), experience (Wiersema & Bantel, 1992), and the size of the TMT (Eisenhardt & Schoonhoven, 1990). More recent work has de-emphasized composition and favored TMT decision-making processes instead. The process literature examines TMT behaviors and interactions by focusing on issues such as cognitive conflict (Amason, 1996), decision-making speed (Judge & Miller, 1991), environmental scanning (Tompson, 1997), information processing (Corner, Kinicki, & Keats, 1994), and procedural justice (Korsgaard, Schweiger, & Sapienza, 1995). Some recent studies have examined both TMT composition and group process (Corner & Kinicki, 1997; Smith et al., 1994). Both categories of research focus on explaining and predicting organizational outcomes as a function of TMT composition or processes, or as an interaction effect. We review both categories of TMT research but focus on process research because group communication is more germane to this category.

Content research. Researchers studying TMT composition make the assumption that demographic characteristics of people and teams reflect their underlying capabilities. Demography is not equivalent to capabilities but is an easily measurable proxy. Pfeffer (1983) argued that "demography is an important causal variable that affects a number of intervening variables and processes and, through them, a number of organizational outcomes" (p. 348). Ultimately, scholars conducting TMT composition research hope to find a "fit" between TMT composition characteristics and organizational performance. With the inclusion of moderator and/or mediating variables, the goal is to form conclusions such as, "For firms pursuing concentric diversification, TMTs characterized by ____ are best, whereas for firms in a turnaround situation, ____ TMTs are more appropriate." Such attempts at matching TMT composition to the organization's context had some early success (e.g., Gupta, 1984; Szilagyi & Schweiger, 1984) but have reached diminishing returns and have fallen out of favor.

Other scholars in this area have linked the average age of TMT members to strategic innovation (Wiersema & Bantel, 1992), TMT demography to organizational performance (Murray, 1989), and team size to performance in especially novel circumstances (Eisenhardt & Schoonhoven, 1990). More recent studies have examined characteristics of TMT members (Thomas & Moss, 1995), such as locus of control (Boone, van Olffen, & van

Witteloostuijn, 1998), and TMT tenure (V. L. Barker & Patterson, 1996).

TMT composition research has usually focused on heterogeneity—a measure of within-group variance on several criteria, including age, sex, education, functional background, industry tenure, and organizational tenure. Heterogeneity within the team is important because it means that multiple perspectives have a better chance of emerging within a TMT. Diverse perspectives help the team interpret strategic issues (Dutton & Duncan, 1987), make sense of the organization's context (Gioia & Chittipeddi, 1991), respond to environmental feedback (Sutcliffe, 1993), and minimize cognitive biases (L. Burke & Steensma, 1998). In contrast, relatively homogeneous TMT members tend to think in similar ways due to similar backgrounds, training, paradigms, and so forth. In past research, TMT heterogeneity has been found to be positively related to innovativeness in banks (Bantel & Jackson, 1989), growth rates in semiconductor firms (Eisenhardt & Schoonhoven, 1990), implementation speed in organizational restructuring (Williams, Hoffman, & Lamont, 1995), comprehensiveness in strategic planning (Bantel, 1993), and ability to enact subsequent strategic change (Boeker, 1997).

However, contradictory findings remain about the composition-performance relationship. Several studies have demonstrated that TMT heterogeneity has a detrimental influence on organizational performance. Specifically, TMT heterogeneity has been found to be negatively related to adaptive change in electronics firms (O'Reilly, Snyder, & Boothe, 1993), TMT member tenure (Jackson et al., 1991), and new product performance (Ancona & Caldwell, 1992). One reason for these findings is that heavy efficiency losses occur in teams in which members have varied vocabularies, experiences, and paradigms. These differences certainly can have benefits, but they may also create a climate of awkward communication, antagonism, and even distrust among TMT members. Thus, the gains obtained from diversity may, in some cases, be offset by the losses due to dysfunctional interaction between team members.

TMT composition research is reminiscent of the trait approach to leadership (see Stogdill, 1948), which most group communication researchers know met with limited success. Trying to establish links between individuals' traits and the performance of groups (not to mention the performance of entire organizations) simply ignores too many intervening factors. Despite "making several crude assumptions about the psychological processes of top managers" (Hambrick & Mason, 1984, p. 93), however, TMT composition research has made important contributions. Current composition research continues to study the link between TMT demographic heterogeneity and organizational performance, and usually offers a theoretical explanation for why certain demographic characteristics are thought to affect organizational outcomes.

Process research. TMT process research has focused on TMT actions rather than composition. Intragroup conflict has been the topic of several studies, and many scholars have noted the contradictory research results on the impact of conflict within TMTs. Some studies show conflict to be beneficial, whereas others have found it to be detrimental. Amason (1996) demonstrated that intragroup conflict has different effects depending on when it occurs in the decision-making process. Specifically, conflict helps TMT members to brainstorm and raise multiple alternatives to a problem and to critically evaluate ideas; it is constructive when it helps generate more thorough analysis within a TMT. However, conflict can have a dysfunctional effect for at least two reasons. First, beneficial (cognitive) conflict can be easily transformed into destructive (affective) conflict (Baron, 1988). Second, the effects of conflict can linger and make the implementation of strategy difficult, especially among TMT members whose ideas were rejected.

Another study representative of the process approach is that by Tompson (1997), who found that when TMTs became more diligent in the process of environmental scanning, two benefits accrued. First, the TMT members used more channels in subsequent communication with one another and with stakeholders, and second, they considered more alternatives when devising strategy for the organization. A final example is a study by Korsgaard et al. (1995) that examined the role of procedural justice within TMTs. They discovered that the perceived equity in TMT decision-making processes has beneficial effects on members' trust in and attachment to the team.

Content and process. A few recent studies have examined how composition influences processes in TMTs, thereby combining the two categories of TMT research. Smith et al. (1994) examined TMT size, tenure, and heterogeneity of members' experience, education, and background as composition variables; process variables included social integration (members' attraction to the group and satisfaction in working with other group members), communication formality, and communication frequency. They found that composition variables had both a direct and an indirect effect on organizational performance, whereas process variables had a direct effect. Specifically, teams that were smaller and had more homogeneous work experience among members used more informal communication channels (such as e-mail and impromptu meetings); moreover, informal communication was correlated with lower sales growth. Communication frequency was not affected by any of the composition variables but was negatively related to organizational performance. In explaining the results, Smith et al. proposed that there may be a "threshold" of communication frequency and informality such that too much of a good thing becomes counterproductive. Social integration was positively related to organizational performance. Results similar to this last finding have been found in other studies; that is, teams that demonstrate camaraderie, spirit, cohesion, and concern for the team tend to make decisions that produce good results (O'Reilly, Caldwell, & Barnett, 1989). Such findings led Hambrick (1994) to propose "behavioral integration"—the degree to which a TMT "engages in mutual and collective interaction" (p. 188)—as the critical process linking composition to organizational performance.

As is apparent in these examples, BPS scholars have devoted substantial attention to decision-making and problem-solving processes, but communication has been a peripheral, rather than a central, concern. Furthermore, as is obvious in the Smith et al. (1994) study, communication has been treated as a variable with rather simple dimensions, such as frequency and formality, rather than (as communication scholars would see it) as the central process by which TMTs are constituted and operate. Research by BPS scholars can provide insight into a number of aspects of TMTs that are clearly relevant to communication, but group communication research, although focused on contexts other than TMTs, can provide unique insights into communication processes in such teams. We now turn to this latter body of work.

GROUP COMMUNICATION THEORY AND RESEARCH: IMPLICATIONS FOR STUDYING TMTS

Group communication theory and research is likely to be informative for BPS scholars interested in TMTs, given that both group communication and BPS scholars have been greatly interested in relating characteristics of groups and group processes to performance outcomes. Among the relevant issues addressed by group communication scholars that may be used to understand TMTs, are (a) the paths groups typically take in making decisions, (b) contingency factors that affect groups' choices of discussion and decision-making procedures, and (c) characteristics of

effective versus ineffective group communication processes.

However, at least two factors limit the usefulness of this research for improved understanding of TMTs. First, although group communication research may be informative and suggestive, it is far from conclusive. Second, as discussed previously, TMTs have a number of unique qualities that make generalization from research on other groups problematic. Thus, our suggestions below are necessarily speculative, which seems warranted, given that the goal of this volume is to explore new directions in the field of group communication. Of course, we cannot hope to review all aspects of group communication scholarship that are relevant or potentially relevant to TMTs. What follows, then, is necessarily selective. We have tried to identify that which seems particularly promising for TMT research and practice.

Questions That Communication Scholars Should Ask About TMTs

A useful place to start is with questions that group communication scholars should ask about TMTs. Consistent with the primary interests of both group communication and BPS scholars, a central question is, Which aspects of communication contribute to TMT effectiveness and task performance? This sort of question has been the central focus for researchers working within the decision-outcome perspective (see Hirokawa & Salazar, 1997). This broad question could focus attention on specific issues, such as the relationship of individual and group competencies and group practices to effective TMT decision making. A second broad question to ask is, What are the processes through which TMTs interact? This type of question has guided researchers working within the decision-process perspective (see Hirokawa & Salazar, 1997) and should lead to describing both the similar and unique ways in which TMTs interact compared with other task groups.

Perhaps more fundamentally, however, we must ask the question, At what level of analysis should such research begin? Multiple levels of analysis may be useful in understanding different aspects of TMT functioning, but the choice is important. Group communication researchers might choose to investigate individual members' psychological characteristics, group interactional patterns, the functions performed by members' communicative contributions to group processes, and/or the symbols used and meanings attributed to them (for a discussion of levels of analysis in group communication methodology, see Poole, Keyton, & Frey, 1999).

Finally, pushing the boundaries of group communication research, scholars might ask how TMTs interactively construct and negotiate meanings for their individual, group, and organizational identities and for the organizational vision or strategy. They might also ask how members exert power and control within and outside TMTs and how TMT processes are controlled or influenced.

GROUP COMMUNICATION RESEARCH AND TMT EFFECTIVENESS: DECISION-OUTCOME PERSPECTIVES

Given BPS researchers' central interest in the effectiveness of TMTs, a primary overlap with the group communication research is that of predicting TMT decision-making effectiveness. The following sections consider the relevance for understanding TMTs of extant research and theory that attempts to explain characteristics that distinguish effective from ineffective groups and teams.

Characteristics of effective teams. Two sets of studies focusing on characteristics of effective teams are particularly noteworthy for understanding TMT effectiveness, although they sit somewhat uncomfortably in a review of group communication research, given that the first (Larson & LaFasto, 1989) is not focused solely on communication and the second (Alderson, 1993), although focused on

group communication, was conducted by a researcher who specializes in human resource management.

Through interviews with members of 75 teams, Larson and LaFasto (1989) identified eight dimensions of team effectiveness. They constructed a survey questionnaire that explored these dimensions and used this to assess the perceptions of 32 management teams, most of which were executive-level teams (but not TMTs). Although they argued that all eight dimensions are important, their most consistent findings were that three dimensions were most prominent in effective teams: the presence of a clear, elevating goal; competent team members; and standards of excellence. The three most prominent problems for ineffective teams were (a) the absence of unified commitment to the team and its mission (particularly members putting individual goals ahead of team goals), (b) a lack of external support and recognition, and (c) poor collaboration (particularly the absence of open and honest communication).

A second set of studies reported by Alderson (1993) focused on TMTs in the United Kingdom and other parts of Europe. Although somewhat vague about the specific research procedures, Alderson used data acquired from interviews and questionnaires with TMT members to conclude that six team competencies were essential to high-quality TMT communication and that each of these competencies was linked to organizational-level outcomes. First, interpersonal relationships between members must be good, with members understanding and respecting one another's styles and values. Second, the team must have the capacity and willingness to engage in open discussion of important and potentially contentious issues. Related to that, the third essential characteristic is a high level of trust among members. Fourth, the team must be approachable and open to feedback and criticism by others external to the team. Fifth, members must have sufficient discipline and cohesion to implement and pursue decisions on which they agree. Finally, members must have the capacity to discuss and understand both long- and short-term issues of concern to the organization. Alderson's study is noteworthy because it focuses on communication in TMTs beyond simple dimensions, such as frequency and formality. However, the research is limited by a lack of specificity about the methods employed and limited evidence provided for its conclusions.

Communication functions in effective decision-making teams. One body of group communication research likely to be informative for understanding communication in TMTs concerns the functional requisites of effective group decision making. Hirokawa and Salazar (1997) explained that functional theory, as applied to group communication, assumes that all task groups face similar task and relational obstacles to effective decision making and that certain functions, or vital activities, are necessary to overcome these obstacles. These include assessing the problem situation, specifying decision-making goals, identifying alternative solutions, and evaluating the positive and negative features of the alternatives (Hirokawa & Salazar, 1997). Gouran (1997) further explained that communication can have an inhibiting or facilitating influence on effective group decision making—first, by exacerbating or overcoming these obstacles and, second, by accomplishing the necessary functions for effective decision making.

In total, research has found partial support for the claims of functional theory. The most consistent finding is that group decision-making effectiveness is most strongly related to communication that evaluates available alternatives; fulfilling the problem analysis function has also been positively related to group decision-making effectiveness (Hirokawa & Salazar, 1999). However, results overall have been inconsistent, a problem that supporters suggest remedying with more tightly controlled studies and theoretical development that link functions with situational contingencies.

Stohl and Holmes (1993), however, argued that functional theory is simply too narrow in its current form for application to bona fide groups and made a number of suggestions to broaden and enhance the theory's application. In particular, they suggested that important functions are neglected by the theory, including a historical function, which involves members creating a shared understanding of the historical contexts of the decision within a group's ongoing life, and an institutional function—that is, helping a group to situate its decision within the larger institutional contexts in which it is embedded. These are important extensions of functional theory when applied to TMTs; a consideration of the historical and institutional contexts of decision making is likely to be vital to TMT decision-making effectiveness. For example, Gioia and Thomas (1996), in their study of university TMTs, showed how previous decisions made by those TMTs—particularly regarding the construction of an organizational vision—influenced subsequent decisions. Other studies (e.g., Zorn, 1997) have shown that top management may repeatedly ignore the vision in making decisions, and that the organization suffers dire consequences when this happens. The historical and institutional functions, therefore, may be important additions to understanding TMT decision-making effectiveness. Thus, despite the shortcomings of functional theory, it is suggestive for those who study TMTs in that it specifies functions to monitor when explaining decision-making effectiveness. The theory enables TMT researchers to move beyond simple frequency counts of communicative behavior and begin to distinguish forms of communication that differentially influence TMT decision-making performance.

The farrago phenomenon. Stohl and Schell (1991) described a dynamic within dysfunctional groups that they label the "farrago." *Farrago,* which literally means "fodder for cattle" (Stohl & Schell, p. 95), is used to describe groups exhibiting a specific set of dysfunctional characteristics that lead members to become collectively confused and ineffective. The farrago dynamic occurs when a group becomes consumed with the actions of a problem member. As Stohl and Schell explained,

> (a) Decision-making procedures are . . . compromised as a result of actions designed to avoid or accommodate one member; (b) issues are redefined against the backdrop of the member; (c) a great deal of energy is expended talking about the particular member . . . ; (d) members become so worn out in dealing with issues related to this one member that they often fail to deal with task issues and priorities become confused; and (e) members often leave such meetings angry, depressed, or frustrated with both the individual and the group. (pp. 91-92)

Stohl and Schell (1991) suggested that both habits of the problem individual and properties of the group system contribute to the emergence of the farrago dynamic. Habits of the individual include interpretive omnipotence, an individual's claim to the "one correct way" of seeing things; a heroic stance, or adopting a paternal "I know what's best for the group" posture, along with dismissing alternative views as misguided or self-serving; and undifferentiated passion, or "approaching social life with an intensity and devotion that far exceeds the emotional investment of others" (p. 100). As discussed above, TMTs are typically composed of members with strong power and achievement needs and an individualistic orientation (Nadler, 1998b) and, thus, may be more prone to the farrago phenomenon than other groups. Importantly, however, Stohl and Schell (1991) argued that the problem individual cannot create the farrago phenomenon without the group system unwittingly supporting it. Although we know of no other investigations of the farrago phenomenon, it seems a useful concept for exploration in TMTs. In particular, it would be interesting to explore the degree to which, as well as how, TMTs deal with difficult members. Practically, Stohl and Schell's suggestions may be useful for TMTs in dealing with such members; for example, they suggest that the intervention most likely to be successful

involves changing communication patterns by directly focusing "on the interactional tensions of the group and provide communication frames from within which the group can respond as a group" (pp. 106-107).

Group facilitation research. Group-meeting facilitation has received a great deal of attention for improving the effectiveness of group interaction (see Sunwolf & Seibold's, 1999, review). However, as Frey (1995b) noted, "There has not been a corresponding increase in research about the nature and effects of these techniques. . . . Research simply has lagged behind practical developments and advice giving" (p. 6; see also Hirokawa & Gouran, 1989). Two recent edited collections (Broome & Keever, 1989; Frey, 1995a) point to the promise of group facilitation methods for improving group interaction and demonstrate an emerging interest on the part of group communication scholars to investigate these methods. In particular, Frey's (1995a) volume of studies of natural groups suggests that facilitation methods are especially promising for enhancing problem solving and decision making, improving conflict management within and between groups, providing feedback for empowering groups, generating high-quality information for conducting communication campaigns, and building teams. Because two key principles of facilitation are to (a) make full use of a group's resources and (b) base decisions on complete and valid information (Schwarz, 1994), facilitation is likely to be valuable for TMTs, given that they face complex decision-making situations and operate in a highly politicized environment. That is, facilitation methods may well help TMTs to manage status differences and process complex information and, thereby, to engage in decision-making processes that are more thorough and consensus based.

Our experience suggests that facilitation methods are often used by TMTs; for example, one of us (Zorn) has served as a facilitator for several TMTs, and we know of several other organizations that have employed professional facilitators, especially for strategic planning and team-building TMT meetings. Yet we know of no research that investigates the use of facilitation in TMTs.

Team-building research. Although there is a vast practitioner literature on team building and organizational development, research on team building is mostly limited to a few case studies. In the communication field, this research is even sparser, which is somewhat surprising given that improving team effectiveness typically requires enhancing members' communication skills and developing appropriate communication processes. The few published reports do suggest interesting possibilities on this set of issues, however. Glaser's (1994) longitudinal study of a team of fire management supervisors and managers is one such example. She used an action research methodology, which involved her, as the consultant-researcher, interviewing team members multiple times over a 3-year period, feeding back her analysis to the team, and helping the team to develop new communication skills and patterns. Interviews with team members revealed consistently positive appraisals of a number of specific improvements in team functioning, which Glaser argued seemed to be due to (a) teaching concrete communication skills that addressed the specific problems the group faced and (b) the longitudinal nature of the intervention.

Alderson's (1993) research, discussed previously, includes a model for improving communication practices on intact teams that is the basis for team building at the Cranfield Business School in the United Kingdom. Although data linking the Cranfield method to team outcomes are not available, the model is promising in that it focuses on communication practices in intact teams and, thereby, seeks to improve team competencies and practices (again using an action research process) rather than just the competencies of individuals. Similarly, Larson and LaFasto (1989) also described an action research method of building team effectiveness using the instrument they created from their research on dimensions of team effectiveness. As with the Cranfield group, Larson and LaFasto worked with in-

tact teams; unfortunately, also like Alderson, they reported only anecdotal evidence of the effectiveness of their intervention method.

To move beyond functioning as a working group to truly function as a team (Katzenbach & Smith, 1993), team building may be necessary. That is, if a TMT is to take advantage of the multiple perspectives and multiple sources of expertise contained therein—the primary reason for organizing as a TMT rather than following a more traditional model—the group may need to develop and enact a team-building strategy. In addition, TMTs are an excellent context for studying the consequences of various team-building models, because, as we noted previously, their decisions are so consequential.

The theory and research reviewed in this section, focusing as it does on dimensions underlying effective outcomes of group work, suggest useful new directions for scholars and practitioners interested in understanding what differentiates effective from ineffective TMTs in terms of decision outcomes. These frameworks have the potential to move beyond a focus on simplistic conceptualizations of communication, such as frequency and formality, that have characterized TMT research thus far. They suggest that TMT decision-making effectiveness may be a result of a complex variety of communication elements, including (a) the communication functions performed; (b) the prevention of dysfunctional patterns of communication, such as the farrago phenomenon; (c) effective facilitation of decision-making processes; and (d) attention to teambuilding interventions to create the skills and interactional patterns that facilitate effective teamwork.

Group Communication Research and TMT Processes: Decision-Process Perspectives

Decision-process perspectives (see Hirokawa & Salazar, 1997) focus on the various ways that groups organize and structure their interaction in the process of making decisions. In this section, we review several lines of decision-process research that seem useful in exploring TMT interaction.

Development and structuration. Poole and his colleagues (e.g., Poole & Baldwin, 1996; Poole & Holmes, 1995; Poole & Roth, 1989; Poole, Seibold, & McPhee, 1985, 1996) have engaged in an ongoing program of theory and research focused on understanding the processes and patterns that characterize the development of decisions within groups—that is, the processes by which groups structure their decision making. This work has focused on developing two separate but related theories. In a series of studies, Poole and colleagues studied the developmental processes of decision-making groups in an attempt to go beyond traditional phase models of decision development. The result of this work—recently referred to as developmental theory (Gouran, 1999)—is a contingency theory that describes decision development in groups. Poole and Holmes (1995) summarized the intent and results of this research program as follows:

> Most theories of decision development have posited a simple, normative sequence of phases to follow, such as Bales's orientation/evaluation/control sequence. However, empirical research indicates that groups follow multiple paths. . . . The normative sequences are best thought of as ideal models that group members try to follow in organizing their activities. Generally about 30% of groups are observed to follow simple, normative sequences, whereas the remainder follow more complex decision paths, often recycling to previous phases or taking phases "out of order." Both the nature of the group task and social factors such as group size and cohesiveness are related to the complexity of group decision paths, with social factors accounting for a greater share of the variance. (p. 95)

The second theory that these scholars have developed is an adaptation of Giddens's (1979) structuration theory to explain how groups structure their decision-making interaction (Poole et al., 1985, 1996). Although this is a complex theory, the essence of it is that "groups select, adapt, and develop their own working structures" (Poole, DeSanctis, Kirsch, & Jackson, 1995, p. 305) and then reproduce (and stabilize), alter, or eliminate them. These working structures are made up of generative rules and resources that group members use in their interactions. For example, Zorn and Ruccio (1998) demonstrated how sales teams developed shared norms (i.e., structures) for communication competence and then consequently interpreted their managers' leadership practices in light of those norms.

Whereas the growth of developmental theory has been largely empirically driven, the work based on structuration theory has been largely conceptually driven. Both research programs attempt to describe the means by which groups structure their decision-making processes, which clearly could be of value when applied to TMTs. That is, the frameworks suggested by these programs could help TMT researchers conceptualize and understand the processes by which TMTs discuss and make decisions. In addition, although research on these two models has largely focused on describing decision development processes, recent work has attempted to relate particular structuring choices to group outcomes (Hirokawa & Salazar, 1997; Poole & Holmes, 1995). Specifically, Hirokawa and Salazar (1997) have developed an integrated model of group decision making that posits that when groups adopt structures (norms and rules) such as a high-achievement focus, vigilance, and a collaborative climate, they are more likely to be effective. Related to that, Poole and Holmes (1995) found that members of groups that adopted decision paths most similar to logical, normative models perceived their decisions to be of higher quality and were more satisfied and unified with decisions than members of group that used more complex paths. Thus, decision development and structuration frameworks suggest a way to get inside the "black box" of TMT decision making and begin to describe the paths along which TMTs travel in that process. As suggested by the recent work linking groups' structuring choices to outcomes, such an understanding may further elaborate our understanding of the ways in which communication processes influence TMT decision-making effectiveness. This recent work also suggests the value of facilitation procedures that may guide TMTs to create effective structures, such as ground rules (e.g., Schwarz, 1994; Sunwolf & Seibold, 1999) oriented toward encouraging vigilance and collaboration.

Symbolic convergence theory. A prominent group communication theory that has stimulated substantial research in the past two decades is Bormann's (1982, 1986, 1996) symbolic convergence theory. Although the theory was not originally developed to explain group decision-making processes, a number of scholars have demonstrated how it can be used to explain such processes (e.g., Bormann, 1986, 1996; Frey, 1996; Gouran, 1999; Poole, 1999). Of the various theories we have discussed, this theory perhaps best illustrates the possibilities for group communication researchers to explain aspects of TMT communication least likely to be addressed by BPS scholars.

Symbolic convergence theory focuses on the "symbolic bases of group culture" (Poole, 1990, p. 240). It suggests that through interaction—particularly the collective sharing of group stories or fantasies—a group consciousness emerges and members converge around a common vision. As Poole (1990) argued, one strength of this theory relative to the others is that "it applies to the whole range of group processes—task and emotional" (p. 240).

The research on symbolic convergence theory demonstrates its utility (see Waldeck, Shepard, Teitelbaum, Farrar, & Seibold, this volume). For example, Putnam, Van Hoeven, and Bullis (1991) applied the theory in a case study of a natural group—in this case, teachers' contract bargaining teams. They demonstrated how through their interactions, team members' fantasy themes produced symbolic convergence and group consciousness and, thereby, provided the teams with a common

frame of reference that facilitated their interaction. Although symbolic convergence theory has been criticized for not systematically relating group processes to group outcomes (Poole, 1990), case studies, such as Putnam et al.'s (1991), demonstrate important practical consequences of the process of symbolic convergence. In addition, Hirokawa and Salazar (1997) argued that "the successful resolution of task-related and social problems through group interaction requires symbolic convergence" (p. 172).

Along with the potential for symbolic convergence theory to explain the relation of TMT communication to performance outcomes, this theory seems promising for studying the highly political nature of TMT interaction, such as the identification of common enemies through fantasy chains and the internal struggle to promote particular stories or "frames" for interpreting the social situation. In addition, given the traditional role of top management in creating organizational visions, symbolic convergence theory could be useful for exploring the processes by which such visions emerge within TMT interaction.

TMT COMMUNICATION: TENTATIVE CONCLUSIONS, IMPLICATIONS, AND RESEARCH DIRECTIONS

A marriage of BPS and group communication literature clearly offers a firm grounding for preliminary understanding of communication in TMTs, as well as a basis for directing future inquiry in this area. In this section, we first offer several tentative conclusions and implications for practice, followed by some suggested directions for future research.

First, members of top management should carefully consider the most effective organizing structure. Teams, working groups, and individual-led organizations are the choices we have reviewed here (see Katzenbach & Smith, 1993). Although research shows that groups and teams are typically superior to individuals for making many kinds of decisions, under certain conditions, an individual-led organization may be more appropriate. In addition to investigating the relative effectiveness of these options—an issue perhaps best suited to the interests of BPS scholars—an interesting issue for communication researchers is the use of the term "team" for symbolic or rhetorical purposes. Many organizations claim to be team-based, seemingly because "teams" has become in contemporary organizational parlance what K. Burke (1969) called a "god term." An important concern, then, is studying the rhetorical purposes and means employed when top management personnel announce that they have become TMTs.

A second implication for TMT communication comes from research from the BPS literature, which suggests that TMTs should consider the frequency and formality of their communication. Initial research indicates that relatively high levels of informal communication and relatively frequent communication in TMTs lead to lower firm performance (Smith et al., 1994). However, given the counterintuitiveness of such a conclusion, and that it is based on only a single study, TMT members should probably be cautious about strategically increasing the formality of their communication and decreasing its frequency. Additional research is needed on these issues—particularly research that uses more sensitive assessments of types of communication—before confident recommendations can be made.

Third, research on communication and team effectiveness suggests that TMTs might use Larson and LaFasto's (1989) and Alderson's (1993) results as "checklists" to assess their overall health. These researchers have identified dimensions of communication related to executive team effectiveness. Further research should seek to identify the degree to which effective or successful TMTs demonstrate the usefulness of these two conceptual frameworks and the dimensions of communication they claim as essential to team effectiveness.

Fourth, research on functional theory, developmental theory, and structuration theory suggests that TMTs would do well to employ vigilant decision-making practices (Hirokawa

& Salazar, 1997) to ensure that they adopt structures (norms and rules) that encourage open discussion and critical thinking at every phase of the decision-making process. Although this research is far from conclusive, it is encouraging that several theoretical and research perspectives seem to be converging on the importance of communication functions that help to overcome the task and relational obstacles that groups face in decision-making situations (e.g., Gouran, 1997). More research from these perspectives certainly is needed on bona fide groups, in general, and on TMTs, in particular, to increase our understanding of how these processes work and how interventions may help task groups to improve them.

Fifth, TMT members should increase their awareness of processes through which they structure and symbolically converge (or don't) on particular ways of interacting and construing the group and the situations it faces. What is clear from both theory and research on structuration and symbolic convergence is that initial interactional patterns have important consequences for a group's future interaction. A group creates structures (e.g., shared understandings, visions, beliefs, and practices) that influence its subsequent processes. This is made especially clear in Stohl and Schell's (1991) farrago phenomenon, in which a group creates the conditions that either perpetuate the farrago dynamic or shut it down. What is not clear, and what research needs to discover, is how the unique context of TMTs influences the processes of structuration and symbolic convergence. Given the emphasis in extant TMT research on the precursiveness of TMT decisions, a better understanding of how TMT communication structures influence subsequent interaction is essential.

Finally, group facilitation methods may be particularly helpful for both increasing TMT members' vigilance in making decisions and creating greater group awareness (and choice) of their structuration and symbolic convergence practices. Given the complexity of TMT decision contexts, having someone monitor and guide the group process, as is the role of a facilitator, may be extremely helpful in enabling the group to adopt effective decision-making practices. Of course, group facilitation methods themselves must be researched to assess their value to TMTs.

Thus, there seem to be numerous possibilities for using group communication research to enhance TMT practice. The opportunity for collaborative research on TMTs by BPS and group communication scholars presents an equally exciting opportunity. Scholars from these two fields share many of the same interests but have rarely joined together to learn from one another. We now offer some suggestions for how the separation may be bridged in future research.

Certainly needed are qualitative, ethnographic studies of TMT communicative practices (see Frey, 1994) and more sensitive quantitative studies of those practices. To date, most of the TMT research has been based on data collected from survey instruments, even in studies of TMT process. Especially needed are longitudinal, observational studies to complement the primarily snapshot, self-report studies that have been conducted on TMT communication thus far. The contribution that group communication researchers can make will fit squarely into the BPS research on TMT process (rather than TMT composition). Compared with existing communication research on small groups, BPS research has taken a simplistic view of TMT communication, treating it as a variable with relatively few dimensions. The Smith et al. (1994) study, for example, is well regarded in the BPS field, but it measured only frequency and formality of TMT communication.

In this chapter, we have tried to offer some guidance for more sophisticated ways to characterize TMT communication processes. For TMT researchers, communication processes (when they have been considered at all) typically have served as inputs (i.e., independent variables) that help explain how organizations accomplish their goals more effectively. Quite a bit of research links TMT processes to organizational performance, but as we have discussed, very little research specifically examines TMT communication. Conversely, communication researchers have devoted significant study to understanding the nature of effective group communication processes but rarely have examined communication in the unique setting of TMTs. Research on TMT composition within the BPS field has focused primarily on the demographics of TMTs but has made little progress on examining the personal communication skills and resources within a team. This represents another area where the limited success of BPS research could be reinvigorated with the perspective of communication scholars. By considering issues such as members' communication competencies, conflict management techniques, and group communication climate within TMTs, BPS scholars could begin to overcome the use of demographics as a proxy measure for TMT decision-making processes.

We also suggest that TMT communication research broaden the range of outcomes (i.e., dependent variables) considered. Although few BPS researchers will be interested in studying communication as an end in itself, the field would benefit from learning about the antecedents to effective group communication. The link between TMT processes and organizational performance currently is tenuous, and hence, there is a need to understand how good (and bad) communication within a TMT eventually affects other parties (e.g., customers and other organizational employees). BPS researchers seem to recognize the foundational role that communication plays in the ability of TMTs to make strategic decisions but have not often included communication variables into their research designs.

Finally, more investigations of interventions for improving TMT interaction, à la the Cranfield method (Alderson, 1993) and Glaser's (1994) team-building techniques, are certainly needed. In most organizations, TMT members are the most senior employees, have substantial experience in their industry, and have risen to their positions of status because they are good at their jobs. Along with their status and executive pay come high expectations for performance, stress, and long hours. Therefore, research into improving TMT interaction is crucial.

CONCLUSION

TMTs have enormous influence on organizations and, thus, on many of our lives. Indeed, as we were writing this essay, the TMT of our university made numerous decisions that have affected us, the authors, directly. Included in these are the expansion of certain programs and contraction and amalgamation of others, redistribution of resources to work units within the university, and the collective employment contract that governs our work, just to name a few. We are not unique; many organizational members will have similar experiences. Given the significance of this influence and the understudied nature of TMT communication, it seems imperative that group communication researchers take up the challenge this new direction offers.

REFERENCES

Alderson, S. (1993). Reframing management competence: Focusing on the top management team. *Personnel Review, 22*(6), 53-62.

Amason, A. (1996). Distinguishing the effects of functional and dysfunctional conflict on strategic decision making: Resolving a paradox for top management teams. *Academy of Management Journal, 39,* 123-148.

Ancona, D., & Caldwell, D. (1992). Demography and design: Predictors of new product team performance. *Organization Science, 3,* 321-341.

Bantel, K. (1993). Comprehensiveness of strategic planning: The importance of heterogeneity of a top team. *Psychological Reports, 73,* 35-49.

Bantel, K. A., & Jackson, S. E. (1989). Top management and innovations in banking: Does the composition of the top team make a difference? *Strategic Management Journal, 10,* 107-124.

Barker, J. R. (1993). Tightening the iron cage: Concertive control in self-managing teams. *Administrative Science Quarterly, 38,* 408-437.

Barker, J. R., Melville, C. W., & Pacanowsky, M. E. (1993). Self-directed teams at XEL: Changes in communication practices during a program of cultural transformation. *Journal of Applied Communication Research, 21,* 297-312.

Barker, V. L., & Patterson, P. W., Jr. (1996). Top management team tenure and top manager causal attributions

at declining firms attempting turnarounds. *Group & Organization Management, 21,* 304-337.

Barney, J. (1995). Looking inside for competitive advantage. *Academy of Management Executive, 9,* 49-61.

Baron, R. A. (1988). Negative effects of destructive criticism: Impact on conflict, self-efficacy, and task performance. *Journal of Applied Psychology, 73,* 199-207.

Boeker, W. (1997). Strategic change: The influence of managerial characteristics and organizational growth. *Academy of Management Journal, 40,* 152-170.

Boone C., van Olffen, W., & van Witteloostuijn, A. (1998). Psychological team make-up as a determinant of economic firm performance: An experimental study. *Journal of Economic Psychology, 19,* 43-73.

Bormann, E. G. (1982). The symbolic convergence theory of communication and the creation, raising, and sustaining of public consciousness. In J. Sisco (Ed.), *The Jensen lectures: Contemporary communication studies* (pp. 71-90). Tampa: University of South Florida, Department of Communication.

Bormann, E. G. (1986). Symbolic convergence theory and communication in group decision making. In R. Y. Hirokawa & M. S. Poole (Eds.), *Communication and group decision-making* (pp. 219-236). Beverly Hills, CA: Sage.

Bormann, E. G. (1996). Symbolic convergence theory and communication in group decision making. In R. Y. Hirokawa & M. S. Poole (Eds.), *Communication and group decision making* (2nd ed., pp. 81-113). Thousand Oaks, CA: Sage.

Broome, B. J., & Keever, D. B. (Eds.). (1989). Group facilitation [Special issue]. *Management Communication Quarterly, 3*(1).

Burke, K. (1969). *A rhetoric of motives.* Berkeley: University of California Press.

Burke, L. A., & Steensma, H. K. (1998). Toward a model for relating executive career experiences and firm performance. *Journal of Managerial Issues, 10,* 86-102.

Carter, E. (1971). The behavioral theory of the firm and top level corporate decisions. *Administrative Science Quarterly, 16,* 413-428.

Child, J. (1972). Organizational structure, environment, and performance: The role of strategic choice. *Sociology, 6,* 1-22.

Corner, P., & Kinicki, A. (1997). A proposed mediator between top team demography and financial performance. *Academy of Management Best Paper Proceedings, 57,* 7-11.

Corner, P., Kinicki, A., & Keats, B. (1994). Integrating organizational and individual information processing perspectives on choice. *Organization Science, 5,* 294-308.

Daft, R., & Lengel, R. (1986). Organizational information requirements, media richness, and structural design. *Management Science, 22,* 554-571.

Dutton, J., & Duncan, R. (1987). The creation of momentum for change through the process of strategic issue diagnosis. *Strategic Management Journal, 8,* 279-295.

Eisenhardt, K. M., & Schoonhoven, C. B. (1990). Organizational growth: Linking founding team, strategy, environment, and growth among U.S. semiconductor ventures, 1978-1988. *Administrative Science Quarterly, 35*, 504-529.

Finkelstein, S. (1992). Power in top management teams: Dimensions, measurement, and validation. *Academy of Management Journal, 35*, 505-538.

Finkelstein, S., & Hambrick, D. C. (1996). *Strategic leadership: Top executives and their effects on organizations.* Minneapolis, MN: West.

Frey, L. R. (1994). The naturalistic paradigm: Studying small groups in the postmodern era. *Small Group Research, 25*, 551-577.

Frey, L. R. (Ed.). (1995a). *Innovations in group facilitation: Applications in natural settings.* Cresskill, NJ: Hampton Press.

Frey, L. R. (1995b). Introduction: Applied communication research on group facilitation in natural settings. In L. R. Frey (Ed.), *Innovations in group facilitation: Applications in natural settings* (pp. 1-23). Cresskill, NJ: Hampton Press.

Frey, L. R. (1996). Remembering and "re-membering": A history of theory and research on communication and group decision making. In R. Y. Hirokawa & M. S. Poole (Eds.), *Communication and group decision making* (2nd ed., pp. 19-51). Thousand Oaks, CA: Sage.

Geist, P., & Hardesty, M. (1992). *Negotiating the crisis: DRGs and the transformation of hospitals.* Hillsdale, NJ: Lawrence Erlbaum.

Giddens, A. (1979). *Central problems in social theory: Action, structure and contradiction in social analysis.* London: Macmillan.

Gioia, D. A., & Chittipeddi, K. (1991). Sensemaking and sensegiving in strategic change initiation. *Strategic Management Journal, 12*, 433-448.

Gioia, D. A., & Thomas, J. B. (1996). Identity, image, and issue interpretation: Sensemaking during strategic change in academia. *Administrative Science Quarterly, 41*, 370-403.

Glaser, S. R. (1994). Teamwork and communication: A three-year case study of change. *Management Communication Quarterly, 7*, 282-296.

Gouran, D. S. (1997). Effective versus ineffective group decision making. In L. R. Frey & J. K. Barge (Eds.), *Managing group life: Communicating in decision-making groups* (pp. 133-155). Boston: Houghton Mifflin.

Gouran, D. S. (1999). Communication in groups: The emergence and evolution of a field of study. In L. R. Frey (Ed.), D. S. Gouran, & M. S. Poole (Assoc. Eds.), *The handbook of group communication theory & research* (pp. 3-36). Thousand Oaks, CA: Sage.

Greenbaum, H. H., & Query, J. L. (1999). Communication in organizational work groups: A review and analysis of natural work group studies. In L. R. Frey (Ed.), D. S. Gouran. & M. S. Poole (Assoc. Eds.), *The handbook of group communication theory & research* (pp. 539-564). Thousand Oaks, CA: Sage.

Gupta, A. K. (1984). Contingency linkages between strategy and general manager characteristics: A conceptual

examination. *Academy of Management Review, 9*, 399-412.

Hambrick, D. C. (1994). Top management groups: A conceptual integration and reconsideration of the"team" label. In L. L. Cummings & B. Staw (Eds.), *Research in organizational behavior* (Vol. 16, pp. 171-213). Greenwich, CT: JAI Press.

Hambrick, D. C., & D'Aveni, R. (1988). Large corporate failures as downward spirals. *Administrative Science Quarterly, 33*, 1-23.

Hambrick, D. C., & Mason, P. (1984). Upper echelons: The organization as reflection of its top managers. *Academy of Management Review, 26*, 93-106.

Hamel, G., & Prahalad, C. K. (1994). *Competing for the future.* Boston: Harvard Business School Press.

Henderson, B. (1989, November-December). The origin of strategy. *Harvard Business Review*, pp. 139-143.

Hickson, D., Butler, R., Cray, D., Mallory, G., & Wilson, D. (1986). *Top decisions: Strategic decision making in organizations.* San Francisco: Jossey-Bass.

Hirokawa, R. Y., & Gouran, D. S. (1989). Facilitation of group communication: A critique of prior research and an agenda for future research. *Management Communication Quarterly 3*, 71-92.

Hirokawa, R. Y., & Salazar, A. J. (1997). An integrated approach to communication and group decision making. In L. R. Frey & J. K. Barge (Eds.), *Managing group life: Communicating in decision-making groups* (pp. 156-181). Boston: Houghton Mifflin.

Hirokawa, R. Y., & Salazar, A. J. (1999). Task-group communication and decision-making performance. In L. R. Frey (Ed.), D. S. Gouran, & M. S. Poole (Assoc. Eds.), *The handbook of group communication theory & research* (pp. 37-70). Thousand Oaks, CA: Sage.

Holloman, C. R., & Hendrick, H. (1972). Adequacy of group decisions as a function of the decision making process. *Academy of Management Journal, 12*, 175-184.

Jackson, S., Brett, J., Sessa, V., Cooper, D., Julin, J., & Petronnin, K. (1991). Some differences make a difference: Individual dissimilarity and group heterogeneity as correlates of recruitment, promotions, and turnover. *Journal of Applied Psychology, 76*, 675-689.

Johnson, G., & Scholes, K. (1993). *Exploring corporate strategy: Text and cases* (3rd ed.). London: Prentice Hall.

Judge, W., & Miller, A. (1991). Antecedents and outcomes of decision speeds in different environmental contexts. *Academy of Management Journal, 34*, 449-463.

Katzenbach, J. R., & Smith, D. K. (1993). *The wisdom of teams: Creating the high-performance organization.* New York: HarperCollins.

Korsgaard, A., Schweiger, D., & Sapienza, H. (1995). Building commitment, attachment, and trust in top management teams: The role of procedural justice. *Academy of Management Journal, 38*, 60-84.

Larson, C. E., & LaFasto, F. M. J. (1989). *Teamwork: What must go right/What can go wrong.* Newbury Park, CA: Sage.

Maier, N. (1967). Assets and liabilities in group problem solving: The need for an integrative function. *Psychological Review, 74,* 239-249.

Michel, J. G., & Hambrick, D. C. (1992). Diversification posture and top management team characteristics. *Academy of Management Journal, 35,* 9-37.

Mintzberg, H. (1990). Strategy formation: School of thought. In J. Frederickson (Ed.), *Perspectives on strategic management* (pp. 135-236). Boston: Ballinger.

Mintzberg, H., Raisinghani, D., & Theoret, A. (1976). The structure of unstructured decision processes. *Administrative Science Quarterly, 21,* 246-275.

Murray, A. I. (1989). Top management group heterogeneity and firm performance. *Strategic Management Journal, 10,* 125-141.

Nadler, D. A. (1998a). Executive team effectiveness: Teamwork at the top. In D. A. Nadler & J. L. Spencer (Eds.), *Executive teams* (pp. 21-39). San Francisco: Jossey-Bass.

Nadler, D. A. (1998b). Leading executive teams. In D. A. Nadler & J. L. Spencer (Eds.), *Executive teams* (pp. 3-20). San Francisco: Jossey-Bass.

O'Reilly, C. A., Caldwell, D., & Barnett, W. (1989). Work group demography, social integration, and turnover. *Administrative Science Quarterly, 34,* 21-37.

O'Reilly, C. A., Snyder, R., & Boothe, J. (1993). Executive team demography and organizational change. In G. P. Huber & W. H. Glick (Eds.), *Organizational change and redesign* (pp. 147-175). New York: Oxford University Press.

Pfeffer, J. (1983). Organizational demography. In L. L. Cummings & B. M. Staw (Eds.), *Research in organizational behavior* (Vol. 5, pp. 299-357). Greenwich, CT: JAI Press.

Poole, M. S. (1990). Do we have any theories of group communication? *Communication Studies, 41,* 237-247.

Poole, M. S. (1999). Group communication theory. In L. R. Frey (Ed.), D. S. Gouran, & M. S. Poole (Assoc. Eds.), *The handbook of group communication theory & research* (pp. 37-70). Thousand Oaks, CA: Sage.

Poole, M. S., & Baldwin, C. L. (1996). Developmental processes in group decision making. In R. Y. Hirokawa & M. S. Poole (Eds.), *Communication and group decision making* (2nd ed., pp. 215-241). Thousand Oaks, CA: Sage.

Poole, M. S., DeSanctis, G., Kirsch, L., & Jackson, M. (1995). Group decision support systems as facilitators of quality team efforts. In L. R. Frey (Ed.), *Innovations in group facilitation: Applications in natural settings* (pp. 299-321). Cresskill, NJ: Hampton Press.

Poole, M. S., & Holmes, M. E. (1995). Decision development in computer-assisted group decision making. *Human Communication Research, 22,* 90-127.

Poole, M. S., Keyton, J., & Frey, L. R. (1999). Group communication methodology: Issues and considerations. In L. R. Frey (Ed.), D. S. Gouran, & M. S. Poole (Assoc. Eds.), *The handbook of group communication theory & research* (pp. 92-112). Thousand Oaks, CA: Sage.

Poole, M. S., & Roth, J. (1989). Decision development in small groups: V. Test of a contingency model. *Human Communication Research, 15,* 549-589.

Poole, M. S., Seibold, D. R., & McPhee, R. D. (1985). Group decision making as a structurational process. *Quarterly Journal of Speech, 71,* 74-102.

Poole, M. S., Seibold, D. R., & McPhee, R. D. (1996). The structuration of group decisions. In R. Y. Hirokawa & M. S. Poole (Eds.), *Communication and group decision making* (2nd ed., pp. 114-146). Thousand Oaks, CA: Sage.

Propp, K. M. (1999). Collective information processing in groups. In L. R. Frey (Ed.), D. S. Gouran, & M. S. Poole (Assoc. Eds.), *The handbook of group communication theory & research* (pp. 225-250). Thousand Oaks, CA: Sage.

Putnam, L. L., & Stohl, C. (1990). Bona fide groups: A reconceptualization of groups in context. *Communication Studies 41,* 248-265.

Putnam, L. L., & Stohl, C. (1996). Bona fide groups: An alternative perspective for communication and small group decision making. In R. Y. Hirokawa & M. S. Poole (Eds.), *Communication and group decision making* (2nd ed., pp. 147-178). Thousand Oaks, CA: Sage.

Putnam, L. L., Van Hoeven, S. A., & Bullis, C. A. (1991). The role of rituals and fantasy themes in teachers' bargaining. *Western Journal of Speech Communication, 55,* 85-103.

Robbins, S. P. (1974). *Managing organizational conflict: A nontraditional approach.* Englewood Cliffs, NJ: Prentice Hall.

Schilling, M. (1998). Technological lockout: An integrative model of the economic and strategic factors driving technology success and failure. *Academy of Management Review, 23,* 267-292.

Schwarz, R. M. (1994). *The skilled facilitator: Practical wisdom for developing effective groups.* San Francisco: Jossey-Bass.

Schweiger, D., & Sandberg, W. (1989). The utilization of individual capabilities in group approaches to strategic decision-making. *Strategic Management Journal, 10,* 31-43.

Smith, K. G., Smith, K. A., Olian, J., Sims, H., O'Bannon, D., & Scully, J. (1994). Top management team demography and process: The role of social integration and communication. *Administrative Science Quarterly, 39,* 412-438.

Stogdill, R. M. (1948). Personal factors associated with leadership: A survey of the literature. *Journal of Applied Psychology, 25,* 35-71.

Stohl, C., & Holmes, M. E. (1993). A functional perspective for bona fide groups. In S. A. Deetz (Ed.), *Communication yearbook* (Vol. 16, pp. 601-614). Newbury Park, CA: Sage.

Stohl, C., & Schell, S. E. (1991). A communication-based model of a small-group dysfunction. *Management Communication Quarterly, 5,* 90-110.

Sundstrom, E., De Meuse, K., & Futrell, D. (1990). Work teams: Application and effectiveness. *American Psychologist, 45,* 120-133.

Sunwolf, & Seibold, D. (1999). The impact of formal procedures on group processes, members, and task outcomes. In L. R. Frey (Ed.), D. S. Gouran, & M. S. Poole (Assoc. Eds.), *The handbook of group communication theory & research* (pp. 395-431). Thousand Oaks, CA: Sage.

Sutcliffe, K. (1993, August). *What executives notice: Accurate perceptions in top management teams.* Paper presented at the meeting of the Academy of Management, Atlanta, GA.

Szilagyi, A. D., & Schweiger, D. M. (1984). Matching managers to strategies: A review and suggested framework. *Academy of Management Review, 9,* 626-637.

Thomas, A. S., & Moss, S. E. (1995). A theoretical examination of the role of personality in research on strategic process. *Psychological Reports, 76,* 403-417.

Tompson, G. H. (1997, December). A top management team approach for modelling strategic inertia. *Proceedings of the Australia & New Zealand Academy of Management, 11,* 91-101.

Weinzimmer, J. (1997). Top management team correlates of organizational growth in a small business context: A comparative study. *Journal of Small Business Management, 35*(3), 1-9.

Wiersema, M. F., & Bantel, K. A. (1992). Top management team demography and corporate strategic change. *Academy of Management Journal, 35,* 91-121.

Williams, R. J., Hoffman, J., & Lamont, B. (1995). The influence of top management team characteristics on M-form implementation time. *Journal of Managerial Issues, 7,* 466-480.

Zorn, T. E. (1997). The uncooperative cooperative: Attempting to improve employee morale at Weaver Street Market. In B. D. Sypher (Ed.), *Case studies in organizational communication: Vol. 2. Perspectives on contemporary work life* (pp. 312-336). New York: Guilford Press.

Zorn, T. E., & Ruccio, S. (1998). Motivational communication in college sales teams. *Journal of Business Communication, 35,* 468-499.

15

Cross-National Group Communication Research

Prospect and Promise

ROBERT SHUTER
Marquette University

With the globalization of the United States and the growing interdependence of world cultures and economies, there has been a significant increase in the study of culture, in general, and intercultural relations, in particular, in the field of communication (Shuter, 1990, 1998). One area, however, that has been neglected by communication researchers is cross-national research that examines small group dynamics in countries and world regions outside the United States. The overwhelming majority of cross-national group research was conducted by social psychologists between 1960 and 1969. Beginning in the early 1970s, however, social psychologists began conducting far fewer studies of small groups, and the volume of research has not increased since that period (McGrath, 1997). Interestingly, although small group research has flourished in the communication field since the 1960s, few cross-national small group investigations were conducted by communication scholars between 1960 and 1979 (Ogawa & Welden, 1972; Shuter, 1977), and communication researchers have added pre-

cious little to the literature on cross-national small groups since 1980 (Bantz, 1993; Oetzel, 1995, 1998). Because social psychologists have conducted the bulk of cross-national group studies, this research tends to focus on aspects of groups other than communication.

This chapter reviews and analyzes available cross-national research that was identified after examining more than 25,000 studies of small groups conducted since 1955. Cross-national research has essentially focused on four classical small group processes: conformity, leadership, risky shift, and social loafing. This essay examines each of these processes and its relationship to cross-national small group communication. Given that the focus here is on small group research conducted in countries outside the United States, group research on U.S. co-cultures (i.e., ethnic groups and races), commonly referred to as U.S. diversity, are not reviewed in this chapter. Finally, the chapter concludes with a research agenda for the 21st century that positions cross-national research in a central place in small group communication scholarship.

Before beginning a review of the literature, it should be noted that this chapter flows from the assumption that small groups, like individuals, are embedded in the national cultures that produce them and that these cultural forces are reflected in the behavior of groups and their members (Lewin, 1948; McGrath, 1997; Sherif, 1954). As a result, cross-national small group research can provide a window for understanding culture-specific and universal dimensions of group communication, and other important aspects of groups, and for illuminating national culture in its myriad of complexities.

GROUP CONFORMITY, COMMUNICATION, AND NATIONAL CULTURE

Although conformity in small groups is a well-documented process, there have been surprisingly few investigations across national cultures of conformity in groups. What data do exist strongly suggest that group pressure varies significantly across cultures and affects differentially individual decision making. In two replications of the classic Asch (1952) experiment in Germany (Timaeus, 1968) and Japan (Frager, 1970), significantly less group conformity was found than Asch originally discovered among U.S. students. Interestingly, Japanese research participants not only conformed less than did those from the United States but also displayed in Frager's study significant anticonformity by choosing a wrong answer purposely, even when the majority, in the Asch test, selected the right answer. Klauss and Bass (1974) also noted significant anticonformity among Japanese managers in a cross-national investigation of the impact of group discussion on individual decision making of German, Swiss, and Japanese managers. Anticonformity is rarely seen in studies of conformity, and its incidence among the Japanese is striking.

These findings are puzzling because Japan is supposed to be a highly collective society (i.e., conformity oriented), according to Hofstede's (1980, 1997) research on cultural

values, which has dominated the research agenda of most cross-national studies in the social sciences, including communication. In fact, contrary to Hofstede's research, Triandis, Bontempo, Villareal, Asai, and Lucca (1988) found Japanese and Puerto Ricans—both collective societies—to be less conforming than U.S. research participants. Curiously, these researchers found that Japanese participants conformed more than their U.S. counterparts only with members of in-groups with whom they strongly identified (i.e., family and friends). When the Japanese participants interacted with strangers, the typical design of most small group conformity studies, they exhibited significantly less conformity than the U.S. participants and also displayed anticonformity behavior.

The small group conformity studies conducted by Milgram (1961) and Kagan (1974) also raise questions about the predictive validity of cultural values such as collectivism and individualism. Replicating the Asch experiment, Milgram discovered that Norwegian research participants conformed to the group on 62% of the trials on which the group voted wrong, whereas French participants conformed on 50% of these trials. Although Norway is supposed to be a group-oriented culture and, thus, these results are expected, France has traditionally been cast as a society that values individualism, which seems incompatible with the relatively high conformity rates demonstrated by the French participants in this experiment.

Kagan's (1974) experiment of the conformity behavior of 7- and 9-year-old rural Mexican and urban Anglo American children found that although Mexicans conformed significantly more than Anglo Americans, which would be expected given Mexico's collective orientation and the individualistic orientation in the United States, 31% of the Mexican participants resisted group pressure, whereas no Anglo Americans retained their independence. This finding suggests that Mexican children may be more apt than Anglo American children to resist group pressure and deviate from group norms, which is an unexpected finding when comparing the United States, an individualistic culture, with Mexico, a collective society.

Research on conformity in small groups suggests that cultural values may not explain group behavior. As an alternative, Berry (1967, 1974) theorized that economic factors within a society—its ecoculture—influence group conformity. Berry (1967) replicated the Asch experiment among the Baffin Eskimo and Temne of Sierra Leone. He hypothesized that individuals from high food-accumulating societies (i.e., Temne) would be more responsive to conformity pressures than low food accumulators (i.e., Baffin Eskimo). This hypothesis was based on Barry, Child, and Bacon's (1959) research that high food-accumulating societies (i.e., pastoral people) rely on members' compliance and cooperation, whereas low food accumulators (i.e., hunters and gatherers) encourage members to be self-reliant and independent. Berry (1967) found that the Temne tended to conform more than the Baffin Eskimo. Barry (1974) replicated this research in additional subsistence societies of high and low food accumulators located in Australia and New Guinea and found additional confirmation of the hypothesis. However, a third study by Berry and Annis (1974) of high and low food accumulators among North American Indians did not uncover any differences in conformity between the two groups. An ecocultural explanation of group behavior does not appear to completely explain conformity either; hence, other cultural factors probably influence group dynamics.

In two more recent investigations of group conformity, Perrin and Spencer (1981) and Nicholson, Cole, and Rocklin (1986) found significantly less conformity among British and U.S. respondents than Asch reported in his 1950s experiments. Perrin and Spencer also found no conformity whatsoever among British college students when they participated in the classic Asch experiment. However, when they were placed in situations where resisting the group majority reduced personal rewards they considered important, conformity increased near the levels reported by Asch.

Clearly, Perrin and Spencer's (1981) research suggests that situational factors influence group conformity. Interestingly, Nicholson et al.'s (1985) study indicates that generational differences may also be an important factor in conformity. They found that British and U.S. research participants displayed significantly less conformity in the Asch experiment than their peers in the 1950s, which Nicholson et al. attributed to the different ethos of the times: The climate of the 1950s was a conservative period and encouraged social conformity, whereas the 1980s reflected the impact of the turbulent 1970s, when deviation was more tolerated.

The conformity studies reviewed here reveal the difficulty in identifying the etiology of cultural variations in small group conformity. Differences in cultural values do not adequately explain national cultural trends in group conformity nor do ecocultural or situational factors. Because group conformity appears to be significantly influenced by several factors, a multivariate framework would be more useful in conceptualizing future cross-national investigations of group conformity.

SOCIAL LOAFING IN GROUPS ACROSS NATIONAL CULTURES

Social loafing, first identified by Latane, Williams, and Harkin (1979), refers to the finding that when a group is responsible for completing a task, this sometimes leads to reduced individual performance on certain types of tasks. This phenomenon was observed with U.S. Americans in groups on an assortment of tasks, including idea creation, hand clapping, sound production, and typing. Latane et al. hypothesized that social loafing in groups would be more prevalent in a culture such as the United States that values individualism than in collective societies where groups are supposedly effective at motivating people. Contrary to this expectation, Gabrenya, Latane, and Wang (1983) found in their study of Taiwanese and U.S. children in groups that Taiwanese engaged in the same level of social loafing as their U.S. peers. They argued that personality traits or other values, beyond individualism and collectivism, may be responsible for social loafing, such as values regarding cooperation and tolerance of interpersonal contact. Earley (1989, 1993) also demonstrated that social loafing rarely occurred in collective societies, such as China, but was actually prevalent in U.S. groups, particularly when individual performance was not monitored.

Erez and Somech (1996) tested the effects of social identity—specifically, independent and interdependent selves—on social loafing. They discovered that Israelis from kibbutzim—a collective co-culture in Israel—possessed more interdependent selves and, hence, engaged in less social loafing on group tasks than Israelis from urban areas, who tended to have more independent selves. Their findings suggest that individual identity is a mitigating factor in explaining group behavior, and although people's identities may reflect core values of the society in which they are embedded, this is certainly not always the case. Hence, people may behave in unpredictable ways in any group investigation, regardless of their cultural affiliation with a collective or individualistic society (see Oetzel, this volume).

It is important, however, to account for the findings in Erez and Somach's (1996) research, which differ from early studies that found no significant difference in loafing behavior between collective and individualistic group members. In Erez and Somach's research, participants were placed in groups with people they already knew for at least 6 months, compared with groups composed of strangers that characterized earlier social loafing research (e.g., Gabrenya et al., 1983). The composition of the groups may be significant in explaining why Gabrenya et al. found little difference in social loafing behavior between U.S. Americans and Taiwanese. Specifically, Taiwanese may have displayed more cooperation with groups of peers than with strangers, which is consistent with Triandis et al.'s (1988) important insight that collective cultures exhibit ingroup cooperation but minimal conformity to outgroup members. Clearly, social loafing is a multidimensional group process influenced by a range of sociocultural factors, including social identity, cultural values, and contextual considerations such as composition of the group.

CROSS-NATIONAL SMALL GROUP LEADERSHIP

There are surprisingly few published studies on cross-national small group leadership. Most of the research was conducted in the 1960s and 1970s and focused on cross-national replications of the classic group leadership study conducted by Lewin, Lippitt, and White in 1939 in which groups of children were exposed to three types of leadership styles: democratic, autocratic, and laissez-faire. The thrust of these cross-national investigations was to determine the generalizability of Lewin et al.'s findings that democratic leadership produced a more positive group climate and higher productivity, at least in the long run, than autocratic or laissez-faire styles. Meade (1967) speculated that cultures more authoritarian than the United States would opt for autocratic leadership and that this would produce better morale in small groups and higher productivity than would a democratic style. He conducted the Lewin et al. experiment in India, and found that democratically led groups were less productive and less harmonious than groups led by autocrats. Meade argued that Indians respond better to autocratic controls because as children they are trained to respect and defer to authority and are not encouraged to be independent. This upbringing may prevent them from responding more positively to democratic small group leadership.

Meade's (1970) second study on group leadership involved Hong Kong Chinese and Chinese Americans. Consistent with his earlier study, the Chinese from Hong Kong thrived under autocratic leadership, which Meade argued was compatible with the authoritarian climate of Hong Kong at that time. He also found that Chinese Americans were significantly more satisfied with democratic leadership than their Hong Kong counterparts, but could also function effectively in autocratically led groups.

Japanese researchers have also replicated Lewin et al.'s (1939) studies in Japan (Misumi & Nakano, 1960a, 1960b; Misumi, Nakano, & Veno, 1958; Misumi & Okamura, 1961). Misumi and Nakano (1960b) discovered that groups led by autocratic leaders performed significantly better than democratically led groups, particularly with difficult tasks. A second study by Misumi and Nakano (1960b) varied task difficulty with the three leadership styles and found that Japanese participants performed more effectively under autocratic leadership when the task was difficult but performed better under democratic leadership for easy tasks. According to these cross-cultural studies, culture and task difficulty may have significant impact on the effectiveness of certain group leadership styles.

RISKY SHIFT IN GROUPS ACROSS NATIONAL CULTURES

Risky shift—the tendency of group members to opt for more risky decisions than their individual prediscussion positions after participating in a group discussion—has been supported in numerous studies in the United States and across the Western hemisphere (Kogan & Wallach, 1967), including studies conducted in Canada (Vidmar, 1970), France (Kogan & Doise, 1969), and New Zealand (Bell & Jamieson, 1970). Brown (1965), who proposed a cultural value hypothesis, advanced one interesting explanation of this phenomenon. He suggested that in Western societies there is an attraction to arguments that encourage risk and, hence, group members composed of individuals from Western cultures are prone to advance risky arguments and consequently engage in or make risky decisions after participating in group discussion. Brown's position also suggests

that in societies with more conservative approaches to argumentation, individuals should experience more cautious shifts after group discussion.

To test Brown's cultural value hypothesis, Carlson and Clive (1971) compared the effect of group discussion on the riskiness of decision making in the United States and Uganda, a culture that presumably values conservatism. They found that Ugandans made significantly more cautious group decisions than did U.S. participants. Gologar (1977) also conducted risky shift research in Liberia, a conservative African society, and found cautious shifts in group decisions. Saville (1971) further noted that the Japanese and Filipino cultural values of avoiding interpersonal conflict produced decisions in small groups that avoided risk.

The research on risky shift across cultures seemed to end in the late 1970s with only one published investigation uncovered since 1977, a study by Watson and Kumar (1992) of risky shift in small culturally diverse groups and homogeneous groups of a particular culture. The homogeneous groups consisted of White U.S. Americans, and the heterogeneous groups were composed of U.S. Blacks and Hispanics as well as individuals from foreign cultures not identified in the study. Watson and Kumar found that homogeneous groups produced more risky decisions than culturally diverse groups. Curiously, in interpreting the results, the investigators did not cite prior cross-national studies on risky shift nor did they mention Brown's (1965) cultural value hypothesis. Instead, they suggested that the lack of risky shifts noted in diverse cultural groups was a result of more problematic interaction that such groups experienced during the study. Hence, the specific cultures and ethnic groups represented in the small groups were not accounted for in the interpretation of the results. Although Brown's cultural value hypothesis seems to garner support in the studies reviewed here, the paucity of cross-national research on risky shift makes it difficult to draw any definitive conclusions about the relationship between culture and risk in groups.

COOPERATION AND COMPETITION IN GROUPS ACROSS NATIONAL CULTURES

Cross-national research on cooperation and competition in small groups has primarily focused on children. This research, conducted principally in the 1960s and 1970s, identified several national cultural trends of cooperative behavior. Madsen, Kagan, and Shapira have conducted a number of studies on cultural and urban/rural differences in cooperative and competitive small group behavior (Kagan & Madsen, 1971; Madsen, 1967; Shapira & Madsen, 1969, 1974). They consistently discovered that U.S. children competed more than Mexican or Mexican American children; in fact, U.S. children displayed competitive behavior even when the tasks would have been completed more efficiently if they had cooperated.

Shapira (1976) examined Israeli children and was particularly interested in rural and urban differences in cooperative and competitive group behavior. Drawing from rural kibbutzim and urban settings, he found that Israelis from kibbutzim—a communal institution—were more cooperative than their urban counterparts. In fact, urban Israeli children were as cooperative as their U.S. counterparts tested in previous studies (Shapira & Madsen, 1974). Interestingly, Arab children in Israel were less cooperative than kibbutzim children but more cooperative than Israeli urban children (Shapira & Lomranz, 1972). Clearly, small group behavior is affected by intracultural factors, such as urban/rural distinctions and other co-cultural (e.g., ethnicity and race) differences. Moreover, differences within a society can be more pronounced than differences between national cultures.

Cross-national research on cooperation and competition with adults is largely restricted to group performance in mixed-motive games such as Prisoner's Dilemma. Although it has been argued that game research may have limited applicability to actual group behavior, findings from these studies are provocative in that they suggest that U.S. Americans may not be as competitive as is generally assumed. McClintock and McNeel's (1966) study, for example, found that Belgian university students were significantly more competitive than those from the United States. Similarly, Druckman, Benton, Ali, and Bager (1976) discovered that Indians were more competitive than U.S. Americans and Argentineans in bargaining games. Alsock (1974) examined bargaining behavior under time pressure and discovered that Canadians were more competitive than U.S. Americans.

Maxwell and Schmidt (1972) found that U.S. participants cooperated more than Norwegians when the group climate was infused with interpersonal risk, such as penalties for engaging in uncooperative behavior. However, once the climate of interpersonal risk was eliminated and replaced by a cooperative milieu, Norwegians displayed significantly more cooperation than U.S. participants (Maxwell, Schmidt, & Boyeen, 1973). Hence, the social climate of a group may affect members of various cultures differently and, in the case of Norwegian groups, obviate cooperative behavior, which is supposedly a hallmark of Norwegian society.

CROSS-NATIONAL COMMUNICATION NETWORKS

Initial research on communication networks by Leavitt (1951) indicated that U.S. participants are more productive and experience greater satisfaction in decentralized rather than centralized networks. According to Leavitt's research, a decentralized network, for instance, a circle, was more effective for solving difficult tasks, although a centralized network, such as a wheel, produced faster results. Leavitt's research also found the central position in a centralized network to be more satisfying to group participants than peripheral positions.

This research, however, was conducted with U.S. participants, and quite different results have emerged when other nationalities are studied. For example, Hare's (1969) group network experiments with Nigerians, South Africans, and Filipinos found that Nigerians took much longer than the others to solve a simple problem in the wheel and circle networks. Moreover, the Nigerian in the central position of the wheel was frustrated by the amount of information received and not satisfied with the role, whereas the Nigerian peripheral members in that network were satisfied despite the length of time it took to complete tasks. Filipinos found the wheel to be more satisfying than did other cultural groups even though they performed more effectively in the circle. Hare concluded on the basis of this research that non-Europeans perform more efficiently in a circle than a wheel, take two to three times as long as Europeans to complete a similar task, maintain a higher frequency of interaction, and are more satisfied with centralized networks than their European counterparts. Hare explained these findings by referring to distinct aspects of Filipino and Nigerian cultures. For example, he argued that Filipinos send more messages than the other groups because they value "smoothing interpersonal relations." Nigerians were also said to be more satisfied despite longer periods of interaction because Nigeria is founded on "palaver," which Hare defines as extended discussion. Indigenous cultural values such as "palaver" may play a key role in understanding cross-national differences in communication networks.

AN AGENDA FOR CROSS-NATIONAL SMALL GROUP COMMUNICATION RESEARCH

Clearly, cross-national small group behavior needs to be studied with more regularity and consistency to understand the impact of national culture on the dynamics of groups. First, there are too few studies conducted on this topic. The overwhelming majority of such investigations were conducted in the 1960s and 1970s, with scholars in the late 1980s and 1990s essentially examining U.S.

ethnic groups and race rather than cross-national groups. With so few cross-national studies available, and with such significant time lapses in data collection, it is not altogether clear what is known about cross-national small group behavior.

It is also apparent that extant cross-national research has examined a limited field of small group factors—conformity, risky shift, leadership, communication networks, social loafing, and cooperation and competition. What is clearly missing from most of these studies is, for the most part, a communication focus. That is, the cross-national investigations that have been conducted have examined principally group dynamics other than verbal and nonverbal dimensions of group communication. Adding a communicative dimension to future investigations would contribute much to our understanding of cross-national small group behavior.

For example, cross-national studies should explore the verbal dimension of group leadership style, from how assigned and emergent leaders talk to the responses of group members. The arguments and communication styles that leaders use in a group in conjunction with leadership style clearly affect the reception of a message. Given that individuals are, in many ways, products of their national culture and, consequently, respond differently to argument, leadership communication should vary significantly depending on group members' national culture (Shuter, 2000b).

Western tradition, for instance, privileges logical argument and diminishes the value of emotional appeal (see Meyers & Brashers, this volume). In contrast, Eastern cultures have historically put more emphasis on intuition and affect than on reason and logic (Shuter, 2000b). These cultural differences may be revealed in the style and content of group leaders in Eastern and Western countries, and this would certainly be interesting to study within the context of cross-national group communication.

With a communication focus, studies of group conformity could provide insight into the verbal and nonverbal conformity cues that vary across cultures. In the cross-cultural conformity investigations reviewed in this essay, agreement and disagreement were expected to be communicated verbally. Relying on verbalization to communicate conformity or deviation is clearly a Western assumption and tradition. Many cultures in Africa and Asia rely on more subtle nonverbal cues to communicate agreement or deviation, including averting eye contact, rolling of eyes, producing a low whistling sound, and engaging in prolonged silence (Shuter, 2000b). These and other cues are often unnoticed or misunderstood by Westerners; yet they are key to understanding how Easterners communicate agreement and disagreement in a group.

Group cooperation and competition are also influenced by nonverbal communication, despite the absence of cross-cultural studies that focus on the nonverbal domain. Studies of cross-cultural cooperation and competition rely almost exclusively on verbal measures to assess group behavior. Not only do these investigations miss culturally significant nonverbal signals noted in the previous discussion on conformity, but they assess verbal messages with measures derived from U.S. studies of European-American participants (e.g., Dace, 1990; Deutsch, 1969; Putnam & Poole, 1987).

Typical verbal measures of cooperative behavior include sharing ideas, discussing issues without evaluating them, and offering concessions. Similarly, competitive behavior ranges from attempting to persuade others to requiring compliance. These communicative behaviors are rooted in U.S./Judeo-Christian assumptions about how individuals ought to communicate when they cooperate or compete. A Buddhist perspective on human behavior, for example, would not rely on a dichotomy that views action as either cooperative or competitive. Instead, the fundamental idea of Buddhism is to pass beyond the world of opposites in the search for truth and enlightenment. Hence, individuals rooted in a Buddhist perspective may communicate in ways that are less dichotomous and more nuanced and, thereby, produce verbal messages that are not compatible with traditional verbal measures of cooperative and competitive communication. In short, future cross-cultural research on cooperation and competition needs to develop grounded communication measures that emerge from the culture being examined rather than rely on predetermined verbal categories imposed on a group.

It is also clear that the scope of future cross-national research must expand beyond the limited field of group factors explored in previous studies. A host of group communication areas remain virtually unexplored, such as decision making and problem solving, conflict management, and creativity in groups. Extending cross-national research to additional group factors will increase our understanding of group dynamics in other national cultures as well as provide insight into the generalizability of group principles beyond specific cultures.

Future research in this area also needs to be conducted more systematically along etic and emic perspectives. In the past, this research either focused on small group behavior within a specific country—an emic approach—or it explored group behavior in relationship to selected cultural values, such as collectivism or individualism—an etic perspective. Both perspectives are useful, but there are too few studies of either type to draw any significant conclusions. For example, emic small group investigations have focused on countries in North America, Europe, Latin America, the Middle East, and Africa. Because only a couple of investigations have been conducted in any one country, little can be gleaned about how group communication operates in a particular country. An emic line of research needs to focus on small group communication *within* a particular society, which has also been called an "intracultural approach" to communication research (Shuter, 1990, 1998, 2000a, 2000b). These investigations do not compare national cultures but, rather, probe deep structures within a given society.

Future intracultural investigations should examine multiple small group factors to explain how group communication operates within a particular country. By pursuing a dedicated line of research in several neighboring countries, investigators should at some point be able to generalize about group communication in a specific world region.

Etic cross-national investigations are scant, as indicated in this essay, and have focused on specific cultural values, such as collectivism and individualism. This research seeks to link cultural values and group behavior, but it is deficient for two major reasons. First, world cultures do not fit neatly into value categories such as individualism/collectivism, power distance, masculinity/femininity, and uncertainty avoidance. Many cultures straddle more than one value category—they stress both individualism and collectivism, for example—and resist being placed in a particular category. Kluckhohn and Strodtbeck (1961) demonstrated this in their classic investigation of value orientations when they concluded that all values they identified exist in every society, but that certain values may be more prevalent in a society at a particular point in time. However, cultures are constantly changing and value orientations shift quite significantly, which makes linear categories, such as those offered by Hofstede and other scholars, of limited value.

Because value categories are problematic, researchers should avoid looking for causal links between group communication and a particular cultural value. Triandis et al. (1988) echoed this concern when they found that individualism and collectivism, among other values, are not in opposition within a society but are orthogonal constructs; for instance, Japanese can demonstrate quite independent behavior within a small group, as referenced earlier in this essay, and U.S. Americans can be conformity oriented in groups.

Culture is far too complex to be reduced to a list of value categories, no matter how dynamic they may be. Hare (1969), in his early group communication network research, offered an alternative to the value categories proposed during the 1980s and 1990s. He searched for endemic cultural factors, such as palaver in Nigeria, which may trigger specific group behaviors. Endemic cultural factors are often invisible to researchers until they discard their cultural schemes. When they do this, culture comes to life and the small group becomes a microcosm of the larger society, replete with the consistencies and contradictions that mark any culture.

CONCLUSION

In the 21st century, it is clear that global interdependence is becoming increasingly important. Contact across national borders will continue to escalate, fostered by global communication technologies and international alliances. Understanding across nations is a mandate in such a world, and small groups play a crucial role in that process (Granrose & Oskamp, 1997).

Small group communication must be returned to the research agenda of intercultural communication scholars. This will pave the way for new and exciting research on cross-national small group communication. It will also provide crucial information for professionals in education, government, and business—indeed, anyone who works with groups cross-nationally—that should help them navigate successfully through their cross-national small group encounters.

REFERENCES

Alsock, J. (1974). Cooperation, competition, and the effects of time pressure in Canada and India. *Journal of Conflict Resolution, 18,* 171-197.

Asch, S. E. (1952). Some forms of interpersonal influence. In G. Swanson (Ed.), *Readings in social psychology* (pp. 84-96). New York: Harper & Row.

Bantz, C. R. (1993). Cultural diversity and group cross-cultural team research. *Journal of Applied Communication Research, 21,* 1-20.

Barry, H., Child, I., & Bacon, M. (1959). Relations of child training to subsistence economy. *American Anthropologist, 2,* 119-129.

Bell, P., & Jamieson, B. (1970). Publicity of initial decisions and the risky shift phenomenon. *Journal of Experimental Social Psychology, 6,* 329-345.

Berry, J. (1967). Independence and conformity in subsistence level societies. *Journal of Personality and Social Psychology, 7,* 415-418.

Berry, J. (1974). Differentiation across cultures: Cognitive style and affective style. In J. M. Dawson & W. J.

Lonner (Eds.), *Readings in cross-cultural psychology* (pp. 173-193). Hong Kong: University of Hong Kong Press.

Berry, J., & Annis, R. (1974). Ecology, culture, and psychological differentiation. *International Journal of Psychology, 9,* 173-193.

Brown, R. (1965). *Social psychology.* New York: Free Press.

Carlson, J., & Clive, D. (1971). Cultural values and the risky shift: A cross-cultural test in Uganda and the United States. *Journal of Personality and Social Psychology, 20,* 393-399.

Dace, K. (1990). *The conflict-group decision-making link: An exploratory study.* Unpublished doctoral dissertation, University of Iowa, Iowa City.

Deutsch, M. (1969). Conflicts: Productive and destructive. *Journal of Social Issues, 25,* 7-41.

Druckman, D., Benton, A., Ali, F., & Bager, J. (1976). Cultural differences in bargaining behavior: India, Argentina, and the U.S. *Journal of Conflict Resolution, 20,* 413-452.

Earley, P. C. (1989). East meets West meets Mideast: Further explorations of collectivistic and individualistic work groups. *Academy of Management Journal, 36,* 319-348.

Earley, P. C. (1993). Social loafing and collectivism: A comparison of the United States and the People's Republic of China. *Administrative Science Quarterly, 34,* 565-581.

Erez, M., & Somech, A. (1996). Is group productivity loss the rule or the exception? Effects of culture and group based motivation. *Academy of Management Journal, 39,* 1513-1537.

Frager, R. (1970). Conformity and anticonformity in Japan. *Journal of Personality and Social Psychology, 15,* 203-210.

Gabrenya, W., Latane, B., & Wang, Y. (1983). Social loafing in cross-cultural perspective: Chinese on Taiwan. *Journal of Cross-Cultural Psychology, 14,* 368-384.

Gologar, E. (1977). Group polarization in non-risk-taking culture. *Journal of Cross-Cultural Psychology, 8,* 331-346.

Granrose, C. S., & Oskamp, S. (Eds.). (1997). *Cross-cultural work groups.* Thousand Oaks, CA: Sage.

Hare, P. (1969). Cultural differences in performance in communication networks in Africa, the U.S. and the Philippines. *Sociology and Social Research, 57,* 25-41.

Hofstede, G. (1980). *Culture's consequences: International differences in work-related values.* Beverly Hills, CA: Sage.

Hofstede, G. (1997). *Cultures and organizations: Software of the mind.* New York: McGraw-Hill.

Kagan, S. (1974). Field dependence and conformity of rural Mexican and urban Anglo-American children. *Child Development, 45,* 765-771.

Kagan, S., & Madsen, M. (1971). Cooperation and competition of Mexican, Mexican-American and Anglo-American children of two ages under four instructional sets. *Developmental Psychology, 5,* 32-39.

Klauss, R., & Bass, B. (1974). Influence in individual behavior across cultures. *Journal of Cross-Cultural Psychology, 5,* 236-246.

Kluckhohn, F. R., & Strodtbeck, F. L. (with Roberts, J. M.). (1961). *Variations in value orientation.* Evanston, IL: Row, Peterson.

Kogan, N., & Doise, W. (1969). Effects of anticipated delegate status on level of risk-taking in small decision-making groups. *Acta Psychologica, 29,* 228-243.

Kogan, N., & Wallach, M. (1967). Risk taking as a function of the situation, the person, and the group. In G. Mandler (Ed.), *New directions in psychology* (Vol. 3, pp. 22-27). New York: Holt, Rinehart & Winston.

Latane, B., Williams, F., & Harkin, S. (1979). Many hands make light work: Causes and consequences of social loafing. *Journal of Personality and Social Psychology, 37,* 822-832.

Leavitt, H. (1951). Some effects of certain communication patterns on group performance. *Journal of Abnormal Social Psychology, 46,* 38-50.

Lewin, K. (1948). Group decisions and social change. In T. H. Newcomb & E. Hartley (Eds.), *Readings in social psychology* (pp. 3-33). New York: Harper & Row.

Lewin, K., Lippitt, R., & White, R. K. (1939). Patterns of aggressive behavior in experimentally created "social climates." *Journal of Social Psychology, 10,* 271-299.

Madsen, M. (1967). Cooperative and competitive motivation of children in three Mexican sub-cultures. *Psychological Reports, 20,* 1307-1320.

Maxwell, G., & Schmidt, D. (1972). Cooperation and interpersonal risk: Cross-cultural and cross-procedural generalizations. *Journal of Experimental Social Psychology, 8,* 594-599.

Maxwell, G., Schmidt, D., & Boyeen, B. (1973). Pacifist strategy and cooperation under interpersonal risk. *Journal of Personality and Social Psychology, 28,* 12-20.

McClintock, C., & McNeel, C. (1966). Cross-cultural comparisons of interpersonal motives. *Sociometry, 29,* 406-427.

McGrath, J. E. (1997). Small group research, that once and future field: An interpretation of the past with an eye to the future. *Group Dynamics: Theory, Research, and Practice, 1,* 7-27.

Meade, R. (1967). An experimental study of leadership in India. *Journal of Social Psychology, 72,* 35-43.

Meade, R. (1970). Leadership studies of Chinese and Chinese Americans. *Journal of Cross-Cultural Psychology, 1,* 325-332.

Milgram, S. (1961). Nationality and conformity. *Scientific American, 205,* 45-52.

Misumi, J., & Nakano, S. (1960a). A cross-cultural study of the effect of democratic, authoritarian, and laissez-faire atmosphere in children's groups. *Japanese Journal of Educational Social Psychology, 1,* 119-135.

Misumi, J., & Nakano, S. (1960b). A cross-cultural study of the effect of democratic, authoritarian, and laissez-faire atmosphere in children's groups. *Japanese Journal of Educational Social Psychology, 2,* 65-70.

Misumi, J., Nakano, S., & Veno, Y. (1958). An experimental study of group decision. *Research Bulletin of Faculty of Education Kyushu University, 4,* 17-26.

Misumi, J., & Okamura, N. (1961). A cross-cultural study of the effect of democratic, authoritarian, and laissez-faire atmosphere in children's groups. *Research Bulletin of Faculty of Education Kyushu University 22,* 38-42.

Nicholson, N., Cole, S. G., & Rocklin, T. (1986). Conformity in the Asch situation: A comparison between contemporary British and U.S. university students. *British Journal of Social Psychology, 24,* 59-63.

Oetzel, J. G. (1995). Intercultural small groups: An effective decision-making theory. In R. L. Wiseman (Ed.), *Intercultural communication theories* (pp. 247-270). Thousand Oaks, CA: Sage.

Oetzel, J. G. (1998). Culturally homogeneous and heterogeneous groups: Explaining communication processes through individualism-collectivism and self-construal. *International Journal of Intercultural Relations, 22,* 135-161.

Ogawa, D. M., & Welden, T. A. (1972). Cross-cultural analysis of feedback behavior within Japanese American and Caucasian American small groups. *Journal of Communication, 22,* 189-195.

Perrin, S., & Spencer, C. (1981). Independence or conformity in the Asch experiment as a reflection off cultural and situational factors. *British Journal of Social Psychology, 20,* 205-209.

Putnam, L. L., & Poole, M. S. (1987). Conflict and negotiation. In F. Jablin, L. L. Putnam, K. Roberts, & L. Porter (Eds.), *Handbook of organizational communication* (pp. 549-599). Newbury Park, CA: Sage.

Saville, M. (1971). Individual and group risk taking: A cross-cultural study (Doctoral dissertation, University of Hawaii, 1971). *Dissertation Abstracts International, 31,* A1564.

Shapira, A. (1976). Developmental differences in competitive behavior of kibbutz and city children in Israel. *Journal of Social Psychology, 98,* 19-26.

Shapira, A., & Lomranz, J. (1972). Cooperative and competitive behavior of rural Arab children in Israel. *Journal of Cross-Cultural Psychology, 3,* 353-359.

Shapira, A., & Madsen, M. (1969). Cooperative and competitive behavior of kibbutz and urban children in Israel. *Child Development, 40,* 609-617.

Shapira, A., & Madsen, M. (1974). Between and within group cooperation and competition among kibbutz and non-kibbutz children. *Developmental Psychology, 10,* 140-145.

Sherif, M. (1954). Sociocultural influences in small group research. *Sociology and Social Research, 39,* 50-64.

Shuter, R. (1977). Cross-cultural small group research: A review, an analysis, and a theory. *Journal of Intercultural Relations, 1,* 90-104.

Shuter, R. (1990). The centrality of culture. *Southern Communication Journal, 55,* 237-249.

Shuter, R. (1998). The centrality of culture revisited. In J. Martin, T. Nakayama, & L. Flores (Eds.), *Readings in cultural contexts* (pp. 45-54). Belmont, CA: Mayfield Press.

Shuter, R. (2000a). The cultures of ethical communication. In L. A. Samovar & R. E. Porter (Eds.), *Intercultural communication: A reader* (9th ed., pp. 57-65). Belmont, CA: Wadsworth.

Shuter, R. (2000b). The cultures of rhetoric. In A. Gonzalez & D. V. Tanno (Eds.), *Rhetoric in intercultural contexts* (pp. 11-17). Thousand Oaks, CA: Sage.

Timaeus, E. (1968). Untersuchungen zum sogenannten konformen verhatten. *Zeitschrift für Experimentelle und Angewandte Psychologia, 15,* 176-194.

Triandis, H. C., Bontempo, R., Villareal, M. J., Asai, M., & Lucca, N. (1988). Individualism and collectivism: Cross-cultural perspectives on self-ingroup relationships. *Journal of Personality and Social Psychology, 54,* 323-338.

Vidmar, N. (1970). Group composition and the risky shift. *Journal of Experimental Social Psychology, 6,* 153-166.

Watson, W. E., & Kumar, K. (1992). Differences in decision making regarding risk taking: A comparison of culturally diverse and culturally homogeneous task groups. *International Journal of Intercultural Relations, 16,* 53-65.

16

Group Communication and Technology

Rethinking the Role of Communication Modality in Group Work and Performance

EDWARD A. MABRY
University of Wisconsin—Milwaukee

The proposition that group tasks and communication choices made by group members as they work together are interrelated is well established in group communication theory and research (see, e.g., Gouran, Hirokawa, McGee, & Miller, 1994; Hirokawa & Salazar, 1999; Jarboe, 1996; Mabry & Attridge, 1990; Mabry & Barnes, 1980; Poole, 1985; Putnam, 1979; Salazar, 1996). The recent use of technological affordances for communicating (e.g., e-mail and group decision support systems) by interacting groups raises important questions about the roles these affordances play in shaping communication and defining group task environments (see, e.g., Broome & Chen, 1992; Hollingshead, McGrath, & O'Connor, 1993; Jackson, 1996; McGrath, Arrow, Gruenfeld, Hollingshead, & O'Connor, 1993; McGrath & Hollingshead, 1994; McLeod, 1996; Nass & Mason, 1990; Poole & DeSanctis, 1992; R. E. Rice, 1992; Scott, 1999; Walther, 1994; Walther & Burgoon, 1992).

This chapter focuses on these issues by (a) assessing the social and technical dimensions of communication in groups, (b) examining interrelationships between how group tasks are defined and how group members communicate to accomplish tasks, and (c) synthesizing these issues into a perspective in which the integration of task, technology, and communication is problematized and becomes a fundamental heuristic for explication.

COMMUNICATION MODALITIES: EXPLAINING GROUP WORK THROUGH THE WAYS MEMBERS COMMUNICATE

McLuhan's (1964) casual observation that "the medium is the message" (p. 7) has served to galvanize attention on the importance of communication technologies for more than 35 years. Possibly the most compelling, but often taken-for-granted, implication of this aphorism is that communication "medium" does not inherently mean the same thing as communication "channel."

Communication *channels,* particularly those that rely on technological implementation, are links by which signals between interconnected senders and receivers travel (Shannon &

Weaver, 1949). With respect to human communication, a *medium* is a symbolic environment; it represents a symbolic context supporting the mutual presence of interpretable meanings derived from people's perceptual conjoining of social signs and symbols (Eco, 1984; Fry & Fry, 1986).

McLuhan (1964) tended to distinguish mediums, or media, according to their perceptual demands on information processing; he was less concerned with their content or the social-symbolic implications of their instrumental capabilities. There are parallels to this conceptualization in early considerations of computer communications. Sackman (1967, 1970) distinguished between *real-time,* immediately reactive, human-machine interfaces and *batch,* time-independent, processing of information. He viewed real-time computer communications as the paradigm for defining technological innovation that would have the most profound impact on society.

Modality Versus Channel

McLuhan was relatively ambivalent about the role of message content in defining media forms. Indeed, that might be why scholarly references to either channels or mediums of communication seem conceptually incomplete. Is television a channel or medium? If film is a medium, as McLuhan believed, what mediated form does film embody when it is broadcast using analog television technologies or distributed using digital audio-video delivery systems? How do we explain the mediums of computer-assisted e-mail, Internet telephony, or teleconferencing? The remainder of this first section examines these issues with respect to conceptualizing mediated communication without invoking the conventional notion of a communication channel.

What must happen if neither "channel" nor "medium" is a sufficient concept for explicating communication forms instantiated in discrete units of symbolic expressions that we call *messages?* We must then develop a concept encompassing a recognition of con-

tent defined neither by the instrumentalities implied in the concept of channel nor by the perceptual-symbolic frames implied in the concept of medium.

We can use the notion of *modality* (or mode) in the sense that Richards (1955) discussed technical language: terminology capable of providing stability of meaning across the cumulative experience of usage. A *mode* of communication is the necessary form in which meaning must be represented for it to be expressed. Thus, it is both related to and independent from what are typically referred to as "communication media" or "communication technologies" (Strate, Jacobson, & Gibson, 1996).

Types of Modalities

As a concept, "modality" does not specifically define sensory phenomena. However, communication is clearly a sensory phenomenon. Thus, conjoining these concepts can lead to a meaningful assessment of *communication modality.* Three modal types of phenomenal representation can be differentiated: textual, aural, and animatronic.

According to philosophical linguistics, *textuality* is the representation of meaning using language-like sign-symbols (Eco, 1984; Saussure, 1959). The symbol isn't indexical (or self-defining) in the symbolic system; it is the social appropriation of the sign-symbol, the assignment of meaning by symbol users, that establishes its semantic identity. The *textual* mode, then, encompasses an expectation that sign-symbolic representational meanings can be conveyed as messages. In this way, words, graphs, charts, matted pictures, speech, and mathematical expressions (among other things) can be thought of as textual.

Aural stimuli, such as lyric music, may include embedded textuality. However, not all sounds are properly understood as texts. *Symbolic sounds* are intended to evoke cathectic reactions (e.g., "mood" music and anthems). *Marker sounds* signal technological state conditions or transitions (e.g., the annoying harmonic sounds that virtually all computer software emits to denote everything from errors to end lines). Aural mode activity can be intentionally suppressed by the selective use of a technology (e.g., turning off speakers attached to a personal computer).

The *animatronic* mode distinguishes motion from visualization. Texts can be visual, but texts do not have to include motion to convey meaning (although mediums such as film and video are often studied as texts by humanist scholars). The animatronic mode can be either *graphical* or *natural*. The graphical orientation includes machine- and hand-rendered animatrons (e.g., dynamic graphs and charts, cartoons, and digital effects); natural animatrons are those images captured from lived experiences (e.g., unrehearsed film or video).

Forms of Modality Representation

Communication using technological representations of these modalities involves their behavioral integration into message activities and how these activities are perceived (Lievrouw & Finn, 1990). Modality integration requires making decisions about (a) density (or the number of modes being combined), (b) time latencies, and (c) amount of user control.

Density. The concept of modality is not intended to imply mutually exclusive sensory states. The textual mode, for example, can include sensory phenomena common to all three modalities, as is often the case with so-called multimedia messages. Density, then, is not defined by sensory complexity. Density eventuates as a function of the concurrent use of communication modes in making separate but complementary contributions to the construction of a unitary sense of meaning.

Latency. Latency involves the time-bound implications of communication modalities. Timing in technologically mediated communication is typically conceptualized in terms of its *synchrony*. *Synchronous communication* is time dependent and organized by simultaneous, overlapping, chronological event sequences. A defining example of synchronous communication is face-to-face interaction in a group. An equivalent mediated experience would be online "chat rooms" for which message senders must be online at the same time. *Asynchronous communication* does not rely on a real-time connection between message sender and receiver and, consequently, is referred to as a time-independent form of online communication. E-mail is a paradigmatic example of asynchronous communication. However, both connectivity and message responsiveness are anchored in the perceptions of message senders and receivers. Thus, asynchronous communication, such as e-mail, can emulate the continuity of synchronous communication when senders and receivers find themselves involved in sequentially contemporaneous message exchanges.

Control. An important question regarding mediated communication is message control: Is it the preserve of the message sender, receiver, or machine? Beniger (1986) advanced the proposition that technical instrumentalities exercise control over mediated messages to the extent that humans unmindfully capitulate to the functional constraints of technology. This thesis cuts both ways because technologies are also defined by what they can do. Certain technical functions, such as using cut-and-paste editing, may permit a sender to construct a message in ways not easily accomplished in either face-to-face oral interaction or real-time mediated contexts (Mabry, 1998).

Control with respect to message senders and receivers is predicated on different factors. The content of enacted messages, and thereby modality selection, is determined by the sender. However, the availability and selection of communication technology for sending and receiving messages is subject to normative and persuasive social influences, and modality selection may itself be explained by the same processes (Fulk, Schmitz, & Steinfield, 1990).

Finally, the instrumentalities of mediated communication provide the receiver with far greater control over message reception than in nonmediated communication. User control over modalities, although not complete, is dictated by the instrumental capability of technology. Receivers may, therefore, be able to control modality density or latency. In some instances, they may be able to selectively reparametize textuality. A skilled receiver of e-mail, for instance, could discern the identity of a supposedly *anonymous* sender and thereby expropriate a sender's meaningful intent as instantiated in the message text.

GROUP TASK CONTEXTUALIZATION AND COMMUNICATION AFFORDANCES

Group tasks are deceptively complex phenomena. The connection between group tasks and group communication processes is subject to varying interpretations. Mabry and Barnes (1980), embracing a *cybernetic systems theory* model of small groups, identified group tasks as *input* factors constraining the content and structure of group interaction. Propp (1999), in her examination of *collective information processing* in groups, identified groups tasks as "noncommunicative factors" affecting information-processing demands, information representations, and channel effects on information richness. Hirokawa and Salazar (1999) labeled such conceptualizations of group tasks as examples of a *mediational* perspective in which group interaction is viewed as a medium or conduit through which group inputs shape group decision-making performance.

An alternative perspective on group tasks is to view them as an *interdependent* element of group experience that exerts a constant influence on group communication. Two dimensions of task interdependence are explored in the following sections: (a) tasks as social interpretations and (b) tasks as technological representations.

The Psychosocial Interpretation of Group Tasks

Hackman (1969) posited an intersubjective model of group tasks. He argued that tasks have objective and subjective properties. Objective characteristics include things such as procedural instructions, deadlines, and productivity standards. *Subjective properties* are the inferences and construals that group members make regarding a task's objective properties. Hackman (1969) believed that both individuals and groups are constantly involved in testing subjective attributions about objective task characteristics during group interaction. These tests consist of (a) making assumptions about the meaning of objective task content, (b) acting on those assumptions, and (c) comparing actual outcomes to subjective expectations about task outcomes.

The apparent necessity for these activity cycles led Hackman and Morris (1975) to systematically investigate their effects as group process *gain* and *loss*. They found that groups benefited (gained) from these episodes to the extent that overall task performance could be improved but became less effective (lost) when episodes focused on egocentric or non-task-related activity.

Poole (1985) made similar observations about the role of a group's *task representations* in his assessment of the development of communication coherency in decision-making group interaction. Task representations are composed of (a) a *decision logic*, or theory, about how the decision should be made and (b) an *agenda* of prioritized issues that should be addressed in arriving at a specific decision.

Poole (1985) distinguished between *individual* and *collective* task representations. An individual member's task representations function as an *implicit* theory about how to make a decision and suggest strategies for action motivated by one's personal priorities regarding the substance of the decision. The group's collective task representations are co-constructed during interaction. They are the convergence of group members' task representations, embraced as part of the group's public identity and history, and the unique trajectories of activity that the group pursues as an intact entity either proactively or reactively as a consequence of members' task representations. Poole believed that collective task representations are a property of group discourse. Thus, it should be possible to trace the evolution of a group's decision through the statements that group members make as they negotiate the convergence and use of task representations.

Tasks as Forms of Technological Representation

Historically, group researchers have tended to address task technologies as experimental artifacts to be neutralized either by research participant training or statistical control over their intrusive effects on response variables of interest (McGrath & Altman, 1966). Roby's (1968) assessment of the relationship between a group's task environment and group performance redefined a task's instrumental properties, making them an active part of the overall group environment. This shift toward tasks as behavioral, procedural, technological, and social requisites of a group's sense of a workspace context is now an accepted premise in group scholarship (see, Jarboe, 1996; Mabry & Barnes, 1980; McGrath, 1984; McGrath & Hollingshead, 1994; Turoff, 1991). The nature of the task-technology relationship is less well explicated. The following sections examine the technological dimension of group tasks in greater detail.

The task-technology interface perspective. One school of thought holds that tasks and technologies are logically divisible but praxiologically interdependent. Nass and Mason (1990), for instance, distinguished "technology-as-box" versus "technology-as-task." Variables defining *technology-as-box* operationalize features of a technology irrespective of their applications (e.g., analog versus digital video signal processing, program-

mability, and reliability). Conversely, *technology-as-task* variables operationalize the functional applicability of technologies (e.g., fidelity, interactivity, and synchrony).

A variation on this perspective is the technology-to-performance model developed by Goodhue and Thompson (1995). They proposed that successful individual task performance is predicated on the extent to which technological tools, tasks (actions taken in transforming resource inputs into defined outputs), and individual skills stimulate users' appropriation of a technology in a manner that positively links technology use to desired outcomes. Their study of these linkages was supportive but not unequivocal. Task fit and use dimensions proved better predictors of individual performance separately than when combined into a more complex predictive model.

The technology-context perspective. The notion that the people performing group tasks are indispensable in understanding the nature of the work itself is a relatively recent precept in the study of human performance. In all likelihood, it traces to the post-World War II studies of European social scientists working as part of the Tavistock Institute (see A. K. Rice, 1958; see Schultz, 1999, for an overview of the institute and its research). These studies on the beneficial effects of worker participation in workplace decision making (also known as "industrial democracy") provided the initial foundation for what developed into sociotechnical systems theory (Emory & Trist, 1972; Trist, 1978).

Sociotechnical systems theory (STST) assumes that effectively organized workspaces are the product of worker-centered adaptations of the (a) technological functionality of machinery and tools, (b) cognitive schemata of task-procedural processes, and (c) sociobehavioral norms influencing performance and coworker relationships within the organizational context. Early research, such as that conducted by Sackman (1967, 1970), demonstrated that human-computer interfaces (such as a computer's switch consoles) were more effective when adaptable to the ways users preferred to use them and the types of tasks being executed.

The interpenetration of group tasks, technologies, and the sociality of a group's workspace is evident in the approaches that communication scholars are taking in attempting to explain mediated communication. Jackson (1996), noting that context and technology are conceptually independent constructs, made a compelling argument for viewing them as inseparable. She proposed that to understand any form of technological artifact, it is necessary to simultaneously represent (define) it on material and social dimensions. The *material dimension* involves the tangible properties of the technological artifact (e.g., size, shape, and programmed and/or programmable capabilities). The *social dimension* is the perceptual and behavioral construction of the material artifact-in-use. According to Jackson, the valid integration of these dimensions, or *functionality*, constitutes the interpenetration of technology and context.

The technology-as-task procedure perspective. Poole (1991) conceptually differentiated between group tasks and procedures that groups choose in organizing task processes. According to Poole, procedures for conducting group meetings appear to affect five dimensions of the group's process: (a) functional scope of application, (b) range of activities encouraged, (c) comprehensiveness of task activities covered, (d) capability to implement procedures without assistance, and (e) extent of member cooperation needed for successful implementation.

Poole (1991) noted that technologies referred to as *groupware* (e.g., computer-mediated conferencing and teleconferencing, group authoring software, project management software, and group decision support systems [GDSSs]) can provide the basis for group-based procedural management. He singled out GDSS technologies, in particular, for their relatively thorough incorporation of the five procedural dimensions.

Empirical evidence on the potential benefits of groups using technologically mediated communication procedures is mixed (see Scott, 1999, for a thorough review of GDSS research). Groups employing GDSS technologies find productive ways of adapting to the technological environment (e.g., organizing and structuring meeting activities), but other benefits of GDSSs are overlooked or confounded by ineffectual adaptations (Poole & DeSanctis, 1992; Poole, DeSanctis, Kirsch, & Jackson, 1995).

Groups in technologically mediated communication contexts appear to integrate technological functionality in their interactional processes and message constructions. Brashers, Adkins, and Meyers (1994), for example, found that GDSS groups employed the sequentiality of messages displayed to address decision issues in using valid reasoning routines, but members also engaged in what was perceived as unconstructive social argument. Mabry (1998) showed that argumentative messages exchanged in online discussion groups (groups exchanging messages via asynchronous e-mail) were less likely to be aggressive or hostile when communicators employed message copying and cut-and-paste editing to insert refutational arguments at points in the argumentative flow of previously distributed messages.

TECHNOLOGICAL INTERPENETRATION OF GROUP PROCESSES AND GOALS

Computer-mediated technologies have dominated the landscape on research into the technological facilitation of group work even though a variety of communication technologies have been applied in group contexts over the past 30 years. This section does not review that literature because recent work on the subject is available (Benbasat & Lim, 1993; Kraemer & Pinsonneault, 1990; McGrath & Hollingshead, 1994; McLeod, 1996; Scott, 1999). Instead, the thrust of this inspection into the issue focuses more broadly on the interdependence of task representations in technologically facilitated communication contexts.

Two dimensions of technological integration in group space (or the sociotechnical context formed by a group entity) are transformation efficacy and communicative utility. *Transformational efficacy* relates to the interpenetrative impact that mediated technologies interject into group space. This involves examining how mediated communication affects the group's sense of *entitativity*, the point of transition at which group members move from individualistic to collective recognition of their activities (Mabry, 1999). The *communicative utility* of technological mediation reflects the ways in which mediated communication enables a group to maintain and purposively use interactive connectivity (Mabry & Barnes, 1980).

Transformational Efficacy

Early studies of human-computer interaction noted the unique roles that flexibility and autonomy played in facilitating self-tutoring and instrumental adaptation to computer interfaces (Sackman, 1967, 1970). Technologies, even communication technologies, insinuate some measure of control over the tasks and contexts to which they are being applied as a precondition of their application (see Beniger, 1986; Beniger & Nass, 1986; McGrath & Hollingshead, 1994).

McGrath and Hollingshead (1994), in particular, advanced a variation of the task-technology-fit argument in discussing the impact of technologically mediated communication on group work. They proposed that different types of tasks require different technical functionalities. For example, an idea-generating task (such as brainstorming) might be well suited to group interaction through asynchronous e-mail or even synchronous, real-time, *chat* connections. Conversely, a complex decision-making task, involving the convergence of expert information and a range of attitudes about what constitutes the *best* group decision, might benefit from the ana-

lytic and procedural process-organizing tools in a GDSS environment.

The question remains, however, about what is to be privileged—technology or task? Ultimately, the answer might be *people*—group members or other agents of the systemic contexts in which a group is enmeshed (Fulk et al., 1990; Poole & DeSanctis, 1992). Poole and DeSanctis (1992) used a fascinating metaphor to represent human symbolic control of a computer-mediated GDSS context—*spirit*. They used this term to refer to the collective symbolic orientation to communication embodied in a communication technology.

These symbolic orientations are seen in the ways groups socially construct, or *appropriate*, their uses of a communication technology as part of their task routines. For example, their orientation may reflect felicitous uses of the technology in ways that were planned and emulated by its design (e.g., using measurement scale results to aggregate member sentiment and weight decision choices). However, groups often engage in what Poole and DeSanctis (1992) called *ironic appropriations* that emerge when members construct the technological context in ways that either contradict planned emulations or represent latent uses that were not foreseen in the technology's development (e.g., electing an anonymous message exchange option in a GDSS and then voting by a show of hands visible to all members or soliciting outside information to improve group resources through a group-supported Web site).

Communicative Utility

Mindful of the inherent instrumental control implications of communication technologies, McGrath and Hollingshead (1994) laid the groundwork for understanding the utility implications of technologically mediated communication in groups. They identified four types of technologically mediated emulations that may exist in work groups and teams: (a) group communication support systems providing intragroup communication connectivity that otherwise would be conducted in face-to-face interaction; (b) group information support systems that form the interface between a group and sources of task-relevant information (e.g., online archives and databases); (c) group external communication support systems that facilitate a group's interaction with other individuals, groups, and organizations; and (d) group performance support systems that assist groups and group members to analyze issues, give and obtain evaluative feedback, organize procedural processes, or engage in goal setting and testing routines (e.g., expert systems and GDSSs).

This approach, thus, emphasizes the features of the technologies in use. However, McLeod (1996) critiqued the approach as being too rigid in its recursive alignment of group communication technologies and task demands. She pointed out that tasks often vary in their communication demands across time and, therefore, the communication needs of a group will change, even if the technological system cannot. McLeod believed that such contingencies, in part, explain equivocal findings regarding the effects of group members' communication technology choices on task performance quality. As a corollary to this conclusion, she also pointed to evidence suggesting that a group's longitudinal accumulation of information creates an interdependent relationship with its information-processing needs.

Thus, a communication technology with a perceived functionality at one stage of group experience may become dispreferred if group perceptions of functionality change and, thereby, compel the group to seek communication technologies that better meet its functional needs (e.g., abandoning groupware limited to supporting group writing tasks for groupware that also supports "publishing" functions). Moreover, as Poole and DeSanctis (1992) implied, group appropriations are praxiological; they may change as a group's collective representations about itself are modified by its experience. An inescapable dimension of that experience comes from interacting within a context significantly influenced by a communication technology.

STUDYING GROUPS AS COMMUNICATION MODALITIES

It is hard to envision any group setting devoid of artifacts. Therefore, every group is capable of being studied as a *technological* environment, according to a definition such as Jackson's (1996). However, not all group artifacts inure communication. The artifactuality of a group's communication environment can be classified as either *communication dependent*, for which the artifact must be present for communication to ensue, or *communication independent*, for which the artifact's presence (or absence) is merely coincidental to the group's use of communication-dependent technical artifacts (e.g., a tool, an instruction, or a schematic to guide group behavior). The purpose of this concluding section is to explore some unique issues that emerge when groups are conceptualized as sociotechnical contexts proscribed by the roles that technologies play as agents of communication and task-related performance.

Conceptualizing Tasks Apart From Communication Technologies

The above distinction of communication dependencies alludes to a more complex issue in studying the technological implications of groups: When can *communication* technologies be distinguished from *task* technologies? Answering this question requires an examination of the attributional differences and communication consequences of group technologies.

Task requisite versus communication modality. Previously, the concept of *transformational efficacy* was introduced to explain the influence that mediated communication technologies have on a group's collective interpretation of itself. It seems clear that any time a group connects its use of mediated communication to its sense of task performance—in other words, demonstrates the transformational efficacy of the communication technology—it has experienced the interpenetration of communicative enactments with task behaviors.

This reflexive interpenetration may be a taken-for-granted frame of reference and not rely on the group's literal cognizance of its technological dependency. Poole and DeSanctis (1992) addressed this as part of the spirit of appropriation of a communication technology. Contractor, Seibold, and Heller (1996) found additional support for this position in their study of mutual influence in GDSSs. Individual group members' perceptions of "structures-in-use" (i.e., ease of communication, mutual stimulation of participation, and disinhibition in ideational behavior) were predicted from the levels of interactional influence and perceptions of other group members' structures-in-use.

At a more fundamental level, the taken-for-granted quality of a communication technology can be the result of felicitous *conversational coherences* designed into user interfaces (see Lansdale & Ormerod, 1994; Norman & Thomas, 1991). For example, a computer program's design can assist users in co-constructing a dialogic behavioral style of use. Computer interfaces that allow natural language instructions and questions have proved beneficial in helping users adapt to task technologies. Thus, emulating *natural* human interaction ought to make using the technology perceptibly less counterintuitive and less cognitively intrusive into the group's technological context. Nass and Steuer (1993) found that computer users' reactions to aural stimuli paralleled human receivers' impressions of human sources. Differences in the simulated vocal tone of computer-generated positive or negative feedback affected people's perceptions of feedback accuracy and friendliness.

The examples above serve to underscore how difficult it is to separate communication and task technologies. Even Jackson's (1996) cogent attempt at defining communication technology provides little assistance in making these differences unambiguously clear.

Assessing the spirit, or *ethos,* of a group's technological context is one alternative. Another approach is to *triangulate* the multiple conversations stimulated by user artifact, group artifact, and *intra*group dialogues and note patterned differences in *interlocutors* or topics (McLaughlin, 1984). Irons (1998) has demonstrated the importance of such triangulation in assessing how a collaborative writing team negotiated language use in constructing a technical document. A third alternative is to note linguistic convergence in the representation of an artifact's materiality. Group members using a GDSS, for example, can offer probative self-definition in expressions such as "overcoming anonymity," "productive balloting cycles," "vote-weighed analyses," "changing ideas without erasers," and "making virtual decisions." Such comments clearly instantiate the decision support technology—which is inherently a communication-based technology—into the group members' comprehension of the task.

Identifying communication consequences. Earlier in the chapter, the concepts of density, latency, and control were introduced to describe how technological modalities are interpretively represented. There are sound reasons to believe that these factors shape both processual and output consequences of group communication technologies.

Processually, message complexity, at the levels of both sign-symbolic (e.g., words, numbers, graphics) and modality inclusion, involves varying degrees of density, latency, and control. Density is directly related to functionality; however, the processual dimension of density might be only indirectly related to latency and control.

Increasing message density requires a larger time commitment to using the technological interface. Thus, density and latency interact with functionality. Density is a byproduct of functionality, and latency is affected by whether messages can be accomplished synchronously or asynchronously. For instance, groups that must integrate functional features of interactive multimedia as task communication technologies might find their communication processes confined to a synchronous, real-time sense of task context.

Control is similarly confounded by the interaction of density and functionality. Pre-processing and transmission demands of both task and communication technologies are additive. Hence, as functionality increases, instrumental demands of the technical artifact constrain (or disempower) users. Modality control of a communication technology is, thus, related to density and functionality. Yet the group technology researchers reviewed here have also noted the strong influence of social-relational factors in constructing the technological context of use. Therefore, a clear need exists for research that builds on these insights.

The most evident need involves establishing users' co-constructions of their social orientations toward task and communication technology artifacts. Borrowing from Poole's (1985) assessment of how decision-making task representations are revealed in group discourse, the same approach could reveal how group members discuss communication efficacy issues such as certain types of task products (e.g., graphic examples or a video clip) requiring particular forms of communicative representation (e.g., using a Web site instead of e-mail).

Group Communication Context and Group Performance

Linking communication technology and group performance is subject to the same difficulties as differentiating task and communication technologies. McLeod (1996) theorized that group decision making centers on information classification (or aggregation) and exchange influenced by constraining and enabling conditions (such as task resources or communication technologies capable of affecting collaboration) responsible for group *results*. Feedback loops between results and information exchange, and between information exchange and constraining or enabling conditions, are thought to produce changes in

relationships between those dimensions that, ultimately, affect results.

McLeod's (1996) perspective leaves unresolved the question of whether technological artifacts, and particularly their materiality, can be meaningfully integrated into an information theoretic model. The material rigidity of technological artifacts is not amenable to change through social-communicative feedback. At some point, artifactuality must define intractable constraint (e.g., e-mail will not be synchronous, and interactive media latencies will always be defined by the retrieval speeds of computer hardware).

What we need, instead, is a perspective that connects a group's technologically mediated communication with its aspirations. We must recognize the nexus of group task and communication technologies pertaining to both *internal* and *external* identities. The remainder of the chapter focuses on these issues.

Intragroup processes and mediated communication. There is a tendency to assume that technological contexts, such as those created by computer-mediated communication, have diffuse effects on group member participation outcomes (Jackson, 1996). The research on this issue is mixed. Bikson and Eveland (1990) found significantly broader and higher amounts of participation, and more positive task performance ratings, in spatially distributed work groups supported by e-mail. However, Burke, Aytes, Chidambaram, and Johnson (1999) found that, for comparisons between co-located and remote members of teams, increasing social presence and communication effectiveness did not significantly increase group performance. Research on groups in more complex mediated communication contexts (e.g., GDSSs) shows that mediated groups have less conflict and perform well on certain tasks (e.g., idea generation, information exchange, standardizable decision choices)—especially when the communication technology allows members to be anonymous (McGrath & Hollingshead, 1994; McLeod, 1996). Research also indicates, however, that these contexts can result in far less accurate information-processing outcomes (Dennis, 1996).

Less is known about the structural and semantic bases of group performance. Evidence indicates that communication-relevant task-artifact use can be integrated into collaborative interaction focusing on the application of the technology (Goodwin, 1995). Greatbatch, Luff, Heath, and Campion (1993), for example, observed physician-patient meetings in which physicians maintained ongoing use of a computerized information system. Conversational structuring of unsolicited talk turn initiations and extensions was similar to floor-taking transitions from side-sequenced talk patterns; even aural-mode information from key-striking force helped patients to correctly anticipate talk-turn floor openings.

Adkins and Brashers (1995) noted that language style affected people's perceptions of confederates working in computer-mediated decision-making groups. Using *powerful* language (e.g., direct assertions or unequivocal words) increased perceived credibility, attraction, and persuasiveness compared with *powerless* language (e.g., indirect statements, hedging, or tag questions), and groups in which confederates' language styles differed led research participants to produce more polarized perceptions of their hypothetical coworkers.

Group Embeddedness and Mediated Communication

Putnam and Stohl (1990, 1996) advanced a theory of *bona fide* groups that claims groups can best be understood by accounting for the interpenetration between systemic contexts and group entitativity. From this perspective, groups define themselves through their adaptations to internal and external changes and their management of interconnectivity with other groups or contextual agents. Thus, bona fide groups emulate Aulin's (1986) conception of sociocybernetic self-steering actors: an entity that is both enabled yet constrained either by too much dynamism in response to contextual changes or by too little flexibil-

ity created by its interactive obligations in connection with contextual roles and expectations.

Group performance that is contingent on the use of mediated communication clearly emulates the dynamics of sociocybernetic self-steering. A technology's deployment normatively compels the technology's scope of influence on a group's proximate social context (Fulk et al., 1990; R. E. Rice, 1992). In organizations for instance, the introduction of interactive mediated communication can spur transformational changes as the presence of supporting technical artifacts expands (e.g., using e-mail instead of face-to-face meeting for team collaboration). However, these technologies can also promote resistance to change when powerful norms emerge that punish using technologies in ways that are dispreferred (e.g., persisting in the use of single-copy paper files instead of electronic files).

The origin of group tasks (mentioned in passing earlier) bears revisiting. Embedded groups, like those discussed as bona fide groups, at the very most have only shared control over definition of their tasks, procedures, and requisite technologies. As previously explained, tasks have both objective and subjective dimensions. Mediated communication technologies have similar logical dimensions (i.e., the material and social dimensions of artifacts).

Not well understood is whether these technological dimensions share the same cognitive schemes, or cathectic properties, of representation when they constitute the *subject* of a message in *inter*group interaction. This leads to a series of relevant questions: Must members from different groups exert different levels of effort in, say, discussing an objective facet of a task versus a communication technology? Does convergence of subjective understandings among members take longer for tasks or communication technologies? Is members' emotional involvement higher when intergroup interaction focuses on using tools versus communication technologies? How much process loss is associated with intergroup interaction when experience with mediated communication technologies is uneven across groups?

It is important to note that speculativeness in the preceding questions is justified by a paucity of research about these issues. As McLeod (1996) noted, most research on mediated group communication has focused on a few narrowly defined, variable-analytic issues primarily concerned with establishing the efficacy of mediated contexts as equivalent to face-to-face contexts. Expanding the scope of the research agenda is clearly needed if the study of these important issues is to move forward.

REFERENCES

Adkins, M., & Brashers, D. E. (1995). The power of language in computer-mediated groups. *Management Communication Quarterly, 8,* 289-322.

Aulin, A. (1986). Notes on the concept of self-steering. In F. Geyer & J. Van Der Zouwen (Eds.), *Sociocybernetic paradoxes: Observation, control, and evolution of self-steering systems* (pp. 100-118). Beverly Hills, CA: Sage.

Benbasat, I., & Lim, L.-H. (1993). The effects of group, task, context, and technology variables on the usefulness of group support systems: A meta-analysis of experimental studies. *Small Group Research, 24,* 430-462.

Beniger, J. R. (1986). *The control revolution: Technological and economic origins of the information society.* Cambridge, MA: Harvard University Press.

Beniger, J. R., & Nass, C. (1986). Preprocessing: Neglected component of sociocybernetics. In F. Geyer & J. van der Zouwen (Eds.), *Sociocybernetic paradoxes: Observation, control and evolution of self-steering systems* (pp. 119-130). Beverly Hills, CA: Sage.

Bikson, T. K., & Eveland, J. D. (1990). The interplay of work group structures and computer support. In J. Galegher, R. E. Kraut, & C. Egido (Eds.), *Intellectual teamwork: Social and technological foundations of cooperative work* (pp. 245-290). Hillsdale, NJ: Lawrence Erlbaum.

Brashers, D. E., Adkins, M., & Meyers, R. A. (1994). Argumentation and computer-mediated group decision making. In L. R. Frey (Ed.), *Group communication in context: Studies of natural groups* (pp. 263-282). Hillsdale, NJ: Lawrence Erlbaum.

Broome, B. J., & Chen, M. (1992). Guidelines for computer-assisted group problem-solving: Meeting the challenges of complex issues. *Small Group Research, 23,* 216-236.

Burke, K., Aytes, K., Chidambaram, L., & Johnson, J. (1999). A study of partially distributed work groups: The impact of media, location, and time on percep-

tions and performance. *Small Group Research, 30,* 453-490.

Contractor, N. S., Seibold, D. R., & Heller, M. A. (1996). Interactional influence in the structuring of media use in groups: Influence in members' perceptions of group decision support system use. *Human Communication Research, 22,* 451-481.

Dennis, A. R. (1996). Information exchange and use in group decision making: You can lead a group to information, but you can't make it think. *MIS Quarterly, 20,* 433-455.

Eco, U. (1984). *Semiotics and the philosophy of language.* Bloomington: Indiana University Press.

Emery, F. E., & Trist, E. L. (1972). *Towards a social ecology.* London: Plenum Press.

Fry, D. L., & Fry, V. H. (1986). A semiotic model for the study of mass communication. In M. L. McLaughlin (Ed.), *Communication yearbook* (Vol. 9, pp. 443-462). Beverly Hills, CA: Sage.

Fulk, J., Schmitz, J., & Steinfield, C. W. (1990). A social influence model of technology use. In J. Fulk & C. Steinfield (Eds.), *Organizations and communication technology* (pp. 117-140). Newbury Park, CA: Sage.

Goodhue, D. L., & Thompson, R. L. (1995). Task-technology fit and individual performance. *MIS Quarterly, 19,* 213-236.

Goodwin, M. H. (1995). Assembling a response: Setting and collaboratively constructed work talk. In P. ten Have & G. Psathas (Eds.), *Situated order: Studies in the social organization of talk and embodied activities* (pp. 173-186). Washington, DC: International Institute for Ethnomethodology and Conversational Analysis/University Press of America.

Gouran, D. S., Hirokawa, R. Y., McGee, M. C., & Miller, L. L. (1994). Communication in groups: Research trends and theoretical perspectives. In F. L. Casmir (Ed.), *Building communication theories: A sociocultural approach* (pp. 241-268). Hillsdale, NJ: Lawrence Erlbaum.

Greatbatch, D., Luff, P., Heath, C., & Campion, P. (1993). Interpersonal communication and human-computer interaction: An examination of the use of computers in medical consultations. *Interacting With Computers, 5,* 193-216.

Hackman, J. R. (1969). Toward understanding the role of tasks in behavioral research. *Acta Psychologica, 31,* 97-128.

Hackman, J. R., & Morris, C. G. (1975). Group tasks, group interaction processes, and group performance effectiveness: A review and proposed integration. In L. Berkowitz (Ed.), *Advances in experimental social psychology* (Vol. 8, pp. 45-99). New York: Academic Press.

Hirokawa, R. Y., & Salazar, E. J. (1999). Task-group communication and decision-making performance. In L. R. Frey (Ed.), D. S. Gouran, & M. S. Poole (Assoc. Eds.), *The handbook of group communication theory & research* (pp. 167-191). Thousand Oaks, CA: Sage.

Hollingshead, A. B., McGrath, J. E., & O'Connor, K. M. (1993). Group task performance and communication technology: A longitudinal study of computer-mediated versus face-to-face work groups. *Small Group Research, 24,* 307-333.

Irons, L. R. (1998). Organizational and technical communication: Terminological ambiguity in representing work. *Management Communication Quarterly, 12,* 42-71.

Jackson, M. (1996). The meaning of "Communication Technology": The technology-context scheme. In B. Burlson (Ed.), *Communication yearbook* (Vol. 19, pp. 229-267). Thousand Oaks, CA: Sage.

Jarboe, S. (1996). Procedures for enhancing group decision making. In R. Y. Hirokawa & M. S. Poole (Eds.), *Communication and group decision making* (2nd ed., pp. 345-383). Thousand Oaks, CA: Sage.

Kraemer, K. L., & Pinsonneault, A. (1990). Technology and groups: Assessments of the empirical research. In J. Galegher, R. E. Kraut, & C. Egido (Eds.), *Intellectual teamwork: Social and technological foundations of cooperative work* (pp. 373-405). Hillsdale, NJ: Lawrence Erlbaum.

Lansdale, M. W., & Ormerod, T. C. (1994). *Understanding interfaces: A handbook of human-computer dialogue.* London, Academic Press.

Lievrouw, L. A., & Finn, T. A. (1990). Identifying the common dimensions of communication: The communication systems model. In B. Ruben & L. A. Lievrouw (Eds.), *Information and behavior: Vol. 3. Mediation, information, and communication* (pp.37-65). New Brunswick, NJ: Transaction Press.

Mabry, E. A. (1998). Frames and flames: The structure of argumentative messages on the net. In F. Sudweeks, M. McLaughlin, & S. Rafaeli (Eds.), *Network and netplay: Virtual groups on the Internet* (pp. 13-26). Menlo Park, CA: AAAI Press/MIT Press.

Mabry, E. A. (1999). The systems metaphor in group communication. In L. R. Frey (Ed.), D. S. Gouran, & M. S. Poole (Assoc. Eds.), *The handbook of group communication theory & research* (pp. 71-91). Thousand Oaks, CA: Sage.

Mabry, E. A., & Attridge, M. D. (1990). Small group interaction and outcome correlates for structured and unstructured tasks. *Small Group Research, 21,* 315-332.

Mabry, E. A., & Barnes, R. E. (1980). *The dynamics of small group communication.* Englewood Cliffs, NJ: Prentice Hall.

McGrath, J. E. (1984). *Groups: Interaction and performance.* Englewood Cliffs, NJ: Prentice Hall.

McGrath, J. E., & Altman, I. (1966). *Small group research: A synthesis and critique of the field.* New York: Holt, Rinehart & Winston.

McGrath, J. E., Arrow, H., Gruenfeld, D. H., Hollingshead, A. B., & O'Connor, K. M. (1993). Groups, tasks, and technology: The effects of experience and change. *Small Group Research, 24,* 406-420.

McGrath, J. E., & Hollingshead, A. B. (1994). *Groups interacting with technology.* Thousand Oaks, CA: Sage.

McLaughlin, M. L. (1984). *Conversation: How talk is organized.* Beverly Hills, CA: Sage.

McLeod, P. L. (1996). New communication technologies for group decision-making: Toward an integrative approach. In R. Y. Hirokawa & M. S. Poole (Eds.), *Communication and group decision making* (2nd ed., pp. 426-461). Thousand Oaks, CA: Sage.

McLuhan, M. (1964). *Understanding media: The extensions of man.* New York: McGraw-Hill.

Nass, C., & Mason, L. (1990). On the study of technology and task: A variable-based approach. In J. Fulk & C. Steinfield (Eds.), *Organizations and communication technology* (pp. 46-67). Newbury Park, CA: Sage.

Nass, C., & Steuer, J. (1993). Voices, boxes, and sources of messages: Computers and social actors. *Human Communication Research, 19,* 504-527.

Norman, M. A., & Thomas, P. J. (1991). Informing HCI design through conversation analysis. *International Journal of Man-Machine Studies, 35,* 235-250.

Poole, M. S. (1985). Tasks and interaction sequences: A theory of coherence in group decision-making interaction. In R. L. Street, Jr. & J. N. Cappella (Eds.), *Sequence and pattern in communicative behaviour* (pp. 206-224). London: Edward Arnold.

Poole, M. S. (1991). Procedures for managing meetings: Social and technological innovations. In R. A. Swanson & B. O. Knapp (Eds.), *Innovative meeting management* (pp. 53-109). Austin, TX: 3M Meeting Management Institute.

Poole, M. S., & DeSanctis, G. (1992). Microlevel structuration in computer-supported group decision-making. *Human Communication Research, 19,* 5-49.

Poole, M. S., DeSanctis, G., Kirsch, L., & Jackson, M. (1995). Group decision support systems as facilitators of quality team efforts. In L. R. Frey (Ed.), *Innovations in group facilitation: Applications in natural settings* (pp. 299-321). Cresskill, NJ: Hampton Press.

Propp, K. M. (1999). Collective information processing in groups. In L. R. Frey (Ed.), D. S. Gouran, & M. S. Poole (Assoc. Eds.), *The handbook of group communication theory & research* (pp. 225-250). Thousand Oaks, CA: Sage.

Putnam, L. L. (1979). Preference for procedure order in task-oriented small groups. *Communication Monographs, 46,* 193-218.

Putnam, L. L., & Stohl, C. (1990). Bona fide groups: A reconceptualization of groups in context. *Communication Studies, 41,* 248-265.

Putnam, L. L., & Stohl, C. (1996). Bona fide groups: An alternative perspective for communication and small group decision making. In R. Y. Hirokawa & M. S. Poole (Eds.), *Communication and group decision making* (2nd ed., pp. 147-178). Thousand Oaks, CA: Sage.

Rice, A. K. (1958). *Productivity and social organization: Technical innovation, work organization, and management: The Ahmedabad experiment.* London: Tavistock.

Rice, R. E. (1992). Contexts of research on organizational computer-mediated communication: A recursive view. In M. Lea (Ed.), *Contexts of computer-mediated communication* (pp. 113-144). London: Harvester Wheatsheaf.

Richards, I. A. (1955). *Speculative instruments.* Chicago: University of Chicago Press.

Roby, T. B. (1968). *Small group performance*. Chicago: Rand McNally.

Sackman, H. (1967). *Computers, system science, and evolving society: The challenge of man-machine digital systems*. New York: John Wiley.

Sackman, H. (1970). *Man-computer problem solving: Experimental evaluation of time-sharing batch processing*. Princeton, NJ: Auerbach.

Salazar, A. J. (1996). Ambiguity and communication effects on small group decision-making performance. *Human Communication Research, 23,* 155-192.

Saussure, F. de (1959). *Course in general linguistics.* (C. Bally & A. Reidlinger, Eds.; W. Baskin, Trans.). New York: Philosophical Library.

Schultz, B. G. (1999). Improving group communication performance: An overview of diagnosis and intervention. In L. R. Frey (Ed.), D. S. Gouran, & M. S. Poole (Assoc. Eds.), *The handbook of group communication theory & research* (pp. 371-394). Thousand Oaks, CA: Sage.

Scott, C. R. (1999). Communication technology and group communication. In L. R. Frey (Ed.), D. S. Gouran, & M. S. Poole (Assoc. Eds.), *The handbook of group communication theory & research* (pp. 432-472). Thousand Oaks, CA: Sage.

Shannon, C., & Weaver, W. (1949). *The mathematical theory of communication*. Urbana: University of Illinois Press.

Strate, L., Jacobson, R., & Gibson, S. B. (1996). Surveying the electronic landscape: An introduction to communication and cyberspace. In L. Strate, R. Jacobson, & S. B. Gibson (Eds.), *Communication and cyberspace: Social interaction in an electronic environment* (pp. 1-22). Cresskill, NJ: Hampton Press.

Trist, E. L. (1978). On socio-technical systems. In W. A. Pasmore & J. J. Sherwood (Eds.), *Sociotechnical systems: A sourcebook* (pp. 43-57). San Diego, CA: University Associates.

Turoff, M. (1991). Computer-mediated communication requirements for group support. *Journal of Organizational Computing, 1,* 85-113.

Walther, J. B. (1994). Anticipated ongoing interaction versus channel effects on relational communication in computer-mediated interaction. *Human Communication Research, 20,* 473-501.

Walther, J. B., & Burgoon, J. K. (1992). Relational communication in computer-mediated interaction. *Human Communication Research, 19,* 50-88.

Name Index

Subject Index

Action, collective, 13, 68, 69, 168
ACT UP (AIDS Coalition to Unleash Power), 141-142, 145-155
Adaptive structuration theory (AST), 15
Aggressive communication, 101, 105
Anthropological research, 53
Appreciative inquiry (AI), 166
    episodic framework and, 174
    interviews in, 166-167
    stages of, 166-168
    Waco Youth Summit, case study, 169-174
Apprehension. *See* Communication apprehension
Argument, xiv, 141-142
    aggressive communication, 101, 105
    anger/grief, expressions of, 146-147, 151-152
    argumentativeness, 101, 143
    argument-in-use model, 141, 145, 149-150, 153
    chants/slogans and, 145-146, 149-150
    convergence production, 143-144, 150-151
    conversational argument, 143
    decorum/civility in, 144, 151-152
    direct-action tactics, 145-149
    emotional, 151-152
    group discussion, social nature of, 150
    narratives, rhetorical resources of, 64
    normative/non-normative strategies for, 153-155
    opponents, vilification of, 146, 150-151
    rationality and, 142-143, 149-150
    traditional approaches, reevaluation of, 149-153
    verbal paradigm of, 144-145, 152-153
    visual elements in, 147-149, 152-153
    See also Structuration theory
Autoethnography. *See* Ethnographic practices
Behavior:
    adjustment, relational tensions and, 28, 32

    face-related, 134
    individual group members, roles of, 35
    micro-level behavioral coding, 81
    norms and, 32-34
    situated nature of, 64-65
    social, 46
    thick description of, 60, 65
Bona fide group collaboration model (BFGCM), 241-244, 243 (figure)
Bona fide group perspective:
    boundaries, permeable/fluid, 16, 17, 36, 66
    concept lattices and, 17
    decision-making and, 64
    descriptive nature of, 17
    embeddedness and, 15-16, 18
    empirical testing of, 16
    group/context, interdependence of, 16, 17
    network structures and, 17
    organizational influence in, 17-18
    See also Collaborative groups; Group Dynamics Q-Sort (GDQ)
Bonaventure House, 37, 39
Brainstorming groups, 106, 183, 291

Case study approach, 79-80, 86
Chronotope, 30, 39
Civil rights movement, 45-46
Classroom groups, xv, 219-220, 231-232
    ability grouping, 220
    affective learning outcomes, 224-226
    cognitive learning outcomes, 223-224
    collaborative learning grouping, 220, 221, 222, 223
    communication patterns in, 222-223

312

About the Editor

Lawrence R. Frey (Ph.D., University of Kansas, 1979) is Professor and Chair of the Department of Communication at The University of Memphis. He is the author or editor of 9 books, 3 special journal issues, and more than 55 published book chapters, journal articles, and book reviews. He is the recipient of nine distinguished scholarship awards, including the 2000 Gerald M. Phillips Award for Distinguished Applied Communication Scholarship from the National Communication Association (NCA); the 2000 Ernest Bormann Research Award for his coedited text (with Dennis S. Gouran and Marshall Scott Poole) *The Handbook of Group Communication Theory & Research* (Sage); a 1999 Special Recognition Award from NCA's Applied Communication Division for an edited special issue of the *Journal of Applied Communication Research* on "Communication and Social Justice Research"; the 1998 National Jesuit Book Award, Professional Studies Category, and the 1988 Distinguished Book Award from NCA's Applied Communication Division for his coauthored text (with Mara B. Adelman) *The Fragile Community: Living Together With AIDS;* and the 1995 Gerald R. Miller Award from NCA's Interpersonal and Small Group Interaction Division and the 1994 Distinguished Book Award from NCA's Applied Communication Division for his edited text *Group Communication in Context: Studies of Natural Groups.* He is Past President of the Central States Communication Association and recipient of the Outstanding Young Teacher Award from that organization.

About the Contributors

Terre H. Allen (Ph.D., Louisiana State University, 1990) is Associate Professor of Communication Studies at California State University, Long Beach, where she regularly teaches small group and interpersonal communication at the undergraduate and graduate levels. Her research interests include investigations of how individuals use knowledge structures when engaging interpersonal, group, and classroom contexts. She has contributed to journals such as *Human Communication Research, Communication Education, Communication Research Reports,* and *Communication Research.* She is currently serving as Co-Administrative Director of the Hauth Center for Communication Skills.

J. Kevin Barge (Ph.D., University of Kansas, 1985) is Associate Professor of Communication at the University of Georgia. His primary research interests are leadership within small groups and organizations, as well as public dialogue and participation within communities. He is the author of numerous articles and textbooks that explore relationships between leadership, decision making, and communication. He is currently involved with a multiyear Gear Up grant funded by the U.S. Department of Education that explores how community

dialogue processes can be used to enhance parental involvement with education.

Dale E. Brashers (Ph.D., University of Arizona, 1994) is Assistant Professor in the Department of Communication at the University of Illinois at Champaign-Urbana. His research interests include research methodology and decision making in group and health communication contexts. His work on these topics has been published in *Human Communication Research, Communication Monographs, Western Journal of Communication, Communication Studies, Southern Communication Journal, Communication Quarterly, AIDS Care,* and the *Journal of the Association of Nurses in AIDS Care.* His recent work includes a project designed to develop an intervention to assist persons living with AIDS to better manage the uncertainty associated with their illness.

Natalie J. Dollar (Ph.D., University of Washington, 1993) is an Associate Professor of Speech Communication at Oregon State University in Corvallis. Her research focuses on contributing to qualitative inquiry on cultural communication, particularly as it relates to cultural identity and intercultural communication. She teaches courses in communication theory, qualitative research methods, and cultural and intercultural communication.

W. Jeffrey Farrar (M.A., University of California, Santa Barbara) is a doctoral student in the Department of Communication Studies at the University of California, Santa Barbara. His research interests include decision making in small groups with both ethnic and opinion minorities and issues of diversity in organizations, including discrimination, intercultural situations in organizations, and multinational organizations.

Scott D. Johnson (Ph.D., Bowling Green State University, 1992) is Associate Professor and Chair of the Department of Rhetoric & Communication Studies at the University of Richmond, Virginia. His research interests include group processes, communication education, and applications of dialectic and dialogic approaches across communicative contexts.

Joann Keyton (Ph.D., The Ohio State University, 1987) is Professor of Communication at The University of Memphis. Specializing in group and organizational communication, her current research interests are in identifying the models children use in learning group communication skills, relational processes of groups, and organizational responses to sexual harassment. Her research has been published in the *Journal of Applied Communication Research, Management Communication Quarterly, Communication Studies, Small Group Research, Southern Communication Journal,* and *Communication Yearbook.* She has also authored texts on group communication and communication research methods. She is a current member of the editorial boards of *Small Group Research, Southern Communication Journal,* and the *Journal of Applied Communication Research* and previously served on the editorial boards of *Communication Monographs* and *Communication Studies.* In her community, she has developed a curriculum for facilitator training in the nonprofit sector.

Lynette M. Long (Ph.D. University of Georgia, 1997) is Assistant Professor in the School of Speech Communication at James Madison University.

Edward A. Mabry (Ph.D., Bowling Green State University, 1972) is Associate Professor in the Department of Communication at the University of Wisconsin—Milwaukee. His research and teaching focus on group and organizational communication from a social systems perspective with an emphasis on mediated communication.

Gerianne M. Merrigan (Ph.D., University of Washington, 1992) is Associate Professor of Speech and Communication Studies at San Francisco State University. Her research interests focus on empowerment as a group structuration process and on the expression of identity in communication. She teaches courses in organizational communication, training, and conflict resolution, and quantitative research methods.

Renée A. Meyers (Ph.D., University of Illinois, 1987) is Professor and Chair of the Department of Communication at the University of Wisconsin—Milwaukee. Her research interests include small group decision making and argument and the role of communication in cooperative learning groups. Her articles have appeared in *Human Communication Research, Communication Monographs, Western Journal of Communication, Communication Studies, Southern Communication Journal, Small Group Research,* and *Communication Yearbook,* among other outlets. She serves on the editorial boards of several communication journals.

John G. Oetzel (Ph.D., University of Iowa, 1995) is Assistant Professor and Director of Graduate Studies in the Department of Communication and Journalism at the University of New Mexico. He teaches courses in intercultural, group, and organizational communication as well as research methods. His research interests focus on investigating communication in culturally diverse groups and organizations, and understanding how to effectively manage conflict in these contexts. His work has appeared in journals such as *Human Communication Research, Management Communication Quarterly,* and the *International Journal of Intercultural Relations.* He is coauthor (with Stella Ting-Toomey) of *Managing Intercultural Conflict Effectively* (Sage).

Randall S. Peterson (Ph.D. University of California, Berkeley, 1995) is Associate Professor of Organizational Behavior at London Business School and Cornell University's S. C. Johnson Graduate School of Management. His research interests are in small group communication issues, especially managing conflict in organizational work teams, personality and leadership success, and top management team decision making. He has published numerous articles in journals, including the *Journal of Personality and Social Psychology, Personality and Social Psychology Bulletin, Organizational Behavior and Human Decision Processes,* and the *Journal of Applied Psychology.*

Timothy G. Plax (Ph.D., University of Southern California, 1974) is Professor of Communication Studies at California State University, Long Beach. He has done extensive research in the areas of persuasion, group communication, and organizational communication, but he is best known for his programmatic research in instructional communication. He has contributed to journals such as *Human Communication Research, Communication Monographs, Communication Education,* and *Communication Research Reports.* He has also served as an internal executive consultant for the Rockwell International Corporation. With more than 25 years as a communication researcher, he has extensive experience with groups in the corporate and instructional arenas.

Abran J. Salazar (Ph.D., University of Iowa, 1991) is Associate Professor in the Depart-

ment of Communication Studies at the University of Rhode Island. His teaching and research interests include group communication and its association with decision making, creativity, role development/change, and health.

David R. Seibold (Ph.D., Michigan State University, 1975) is Professor and Chair of the Department of Communication Studies at the University of California, Santa Barbara. His research interests include group decision making, interpersonal influence, and organizational change. He has served as Chair of the Organizational Communication Division of the International Communication Association and is former Editor of the *Journal of Applied Communication Research.*

Carolyn A. Shepard (M.A., California State University, Long Beach) is a doctoral student in the Department of Communication Studies at the University of California, Santa Barbara. In addition to small group interaction, her research interests include interpersonal communication and nonverbal communication. Her work focuses on the interpersonal dynamics of abusive relationships.

Robert Shuter (Ph.D., Northwestern University, 1973) is Professor and Chair of the Department of Communication Studies at Marquette University. His research has been published in major journals, including *Communication Monographs, Journal of Communication,* and *Journal of Social Psychology,* and he has served on numerous journal editorial boards, including *Human Communication Research* and *Management Communication Quarterly.* Interested in the influence of culture on human interaction, he has investigated cultural influences on small group, nonverbal, interpersonal, organizational, and rhetorical communication. His most recent book is *Communication in Multinational Organizations* (Sage, 1995).

Cynthia Stohl (Ph.D., Purdue University, 1982) is the Margaret Church Distinguished